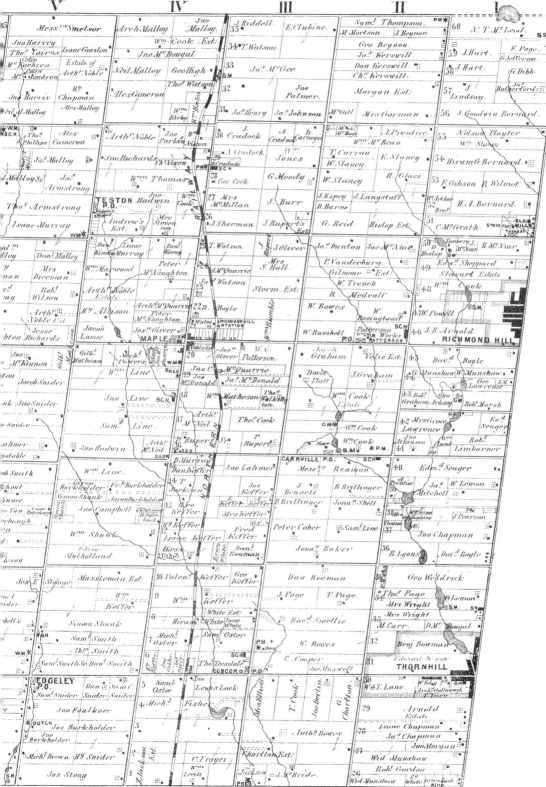

Vaughan Township in 1878. From the *Historical Atlas of the County of York* published that year.

TWO CENTURIES OF LIFE IN THE TOWNSHIP

A HISTORY OF

Vaughan Township

G. Elmore Reaman

By G. Elmore Reaman

In Education

English for New Canadians
English Grammar for New Canadians
The New Citizen
Our Canada — primer in history, geography, civics
Speak the Speech — handbook for public and radio speaking

In Psychology

Personality Rating and Character Building
The Reaman Personality Chart
Child Guidance for Parents and Teachers

In History

History of Holstein-Friesian breed in Canada
Trail of the Black Walnut
Trail of the Huguenots
Trail of the Iroquois Indians
Two Centuries of Agriculture in Ontario (two volumes)

© George C.H. Snider, 1971
Printed in Canada at the University of Toronto Press

Contents

Foreword, by George C.H. Snider   ix

Introduction   3

1.   Indian Period   7

2.   French Period   13

3.   Pioneer Periods   15

4.   Government   65

5.   Transportation   79

6.   Agriculture   85

7.   Villages   99

8.   Religion   129

9.   Education   165

10.   People   187

11.   Events   229

12.   Societies and Organizations   243

13.   Cultural Heritage   263

14.   In Retrospect, by James M. McDonald   271

     Appendices   281

     Index   293

The Years Pass By

From Irish shores, where the sea waves dip,
And English moors in a sailing ship,
From Pennsylvanie's rugged spheres
To Township Vaughan came the pioneers.
They came by foot through a wooded land,
By horse and wagon, a weary band,
To found a home in a country new,
And pitch their tents mide the maytime blue.

The sound of the ax and the oxen's bell
Were heard as the virgin pine trees fell;
The logs were placed and the roof raised high
Where a home would stand as the years rushed by;
They built a church and a small red school
There their children learned the Golden Rule;
Their hearts were stout and their course true
As they tilled the land and the young years flew.

Now cattle graze on the smooth green fields
Which once were rutted by wagon wheels,
The tractor hums and the cars speed by,
And planes fly under the midnight sky.
On the fields of yore the factories stand,
And fairways lead to a fresh green land,
But a proud salute, as our heads bend low,
To those pioneers of the long ago!

Robert D. Little

Foreword

Considering nearly two centuries have passed since the first white settlers came to Vaughan Township, it would be good to give a little information as to what took place and why.

It is of interest to recall many of the names of the first settlers — Stong, Baker, Reaman, Shunk, Smith, Snider, Keffer, Fisher, Oster, Castator, Line, Burkholder, Brown, Miller, Langstaff, Troyer, Diceman. Nearly all of these family names can still be found in Vaughan Township. They can also be found in Pennsylvania, for that was their home before coming to Vaughan Township. Before arriving in Pennsylvania many of them had been on the move since the time of the Reformation, and because of their beliefs and persecution, they were seeking a home in a new land with freedom of worship.

For example, quoting from the *Stong Genealogy,* written by Daniel Stong in 1958 (Sylvester Stong came to Vaughan in 1800 and located on Lot 12, Concession 2):

The Stongs came originally from the Palatinate in the Rhine Valley where life was made unbearable for all Protestants during the 17th century. The reformation was just then gaining its stride and in Germany, bitter prejudice and persecution was the lot of its followers.

Many left the country though flight to a foreign land was made to appear a criminal act. In the emigration of 1709, when thousands of families went to England, Switzerland; Denmark and Holland, travelling was done on foot mostly by night, with the emigrants hiding in caves during the day. Palatine Colonies were formed in different parts of the world, one of which the Stong family was part, set up in Pennsylvania.

The colonists from the German States, the Stongs, Puterbaughs, Sniders, Hoovers, Shunks, Keffers and Kaisers and many others left Germany at different times, stayed in Holland while they accumulated funds for the ocean crossing, where they remained in Bucks County for a time and finally settled in the Mohawk and Tuscorora Valleys, in Huntington County, Pennsylvania. Then in 1776 came the Declaration of Independence, and a large number of settlers began to trek north to where the Union Jack still flew.

I would like to insert another paragraph from Mr. Stong's *Genealogy,* in which he described a legacy he thought should be attributed to our ancestors, a sentiment with which I heartily agree:

They left their children and grandchildren something better than this world's goods. They left them an example of a strong and abiding faith in Jesus Christ, the world's Redeemer. They had their peculiarities (and who doesn't), and no wonder, for the people in their day and generation were all peculiar compared with the people now. The circumstances by which they were surrounded were peculiar, the way they had to live and work was peculiar compared with the way people have things now. One peculiarity they had and which all people should have was the old-fashioned way of believing and trusting in Jesus. They were plain and straightforward in their faith.

Some were Lutheran, some Mennonite, but almost all desired to worship the Lord they loved and served. Therefore, very soon after their arrival, they had a place of worship first in homes, then in a house of worship.

There were other settlers who came early to Vaughan Township whose names are still with us — McDonald, McNeil, McGillivray, Cameron, Campbell, McKinnon, Mackenzie, McClure, Beynon, Bryson. These settlers came from Scotland and Ireland, generally for a different reason — many came from large families and so some had to find new homes; therefore, many came to Canada. One of Scotland's exports has been people. We are told that over the years the population of Scotland has changed very little.

Here again these people loved their Lord and soon had a place of worship in their homes, and later built their church.

It is perhaps interesting to find that the Mennonite Church at Edgeley was built in 1824 and is still standing. The first Lutheran Church was built in 1819, and the second in 1860 is still standing, at Sherwood. The first Presbyterian Church was built in 1829 and the second, built in 1862, is still standing, at Maple.

I would not have you think these families were the only settlers but these names belong to some of the very earliest. Many more names were added in later years. Because these first settlers were satisfied and stayed in the township, the residents of Vaughan became interrelated by marriage and also in church life and this remained so for many, many years. Sorry to say, this has now almost disappeared.

In recent years, the rural character of parts of Vaughan has been radically changed. The Canadian National Railways marshalling yards opened in 1965 on 1,000 acres of good farm land. This led to the beginning of industrial development, the first centre of which was 'Vaughan Acres,' 400 acres of land to be serviced for industry. There is more such development now. The population rise has been reflected in the growth of the schools.

We should perhaps point out that over the years a history of Vaughan has not been written, although there have been local areas here and there recorded at different times by a number of interested people.

The York Chapter of the Pennsylvania German Folklore Society was formed in 1954, and because those involved felt some project was needed to merit its existence, following the suggestion of Dr. J.M.S. Careless, head of the History Department, University of Toronto, a bursary was offered for a thesis on 'The Early History of Vaughan Township.' This was in 1963. Mr. Leo Johnson accepted this challenge and wrote his thesis on that subject in 1965. For this the Pennsylvania German Folklore Society was very thankful. Efforts were made to continue and have the complete history written, but without result.

Dr. Elmore Reaman became interested and with the promise of financial support from an interested party started the history. With a great deal of information supplied by the Women's Institute from their Tweedsmuir History books in Vaughan, he had been able to complete his first draft of the manuscript when he unfortunately passed away, suddenly, on December 7, 1969.

Following this, Mrs. Jesse Bryson, Mrs. Amos Baker, and Mrs. Roy Barker, all three of whom had assisted Dr. Reaman, agreed to prepare the manuscript for printing. Dr. Reaman's daughter, Elaine, also assisted.

The Vaughan Township Historical Society was formed in 1970, and was offered the manuscript for printing at no cost, but the copyright remains with the owner. I feel this has been a Vaughan Township effort, to assemble the history of Vaughan; there has also been much assistance in the preparation from many people.

I know there has been much prayer in this venture and our Lord has marvelously guided and directed us to the final completion and printing of the History of Vaughan Township. Co-operation and unity has been very evident at all times and some of those who helped were very busy people.

A special thank you to Mr. Thoreau MacDonald, who has kindly given permission to use many of his illustrations throughout this book, to Dr. Marsh Jeanneret and Mr. Jack McBride for their valuable guidance, to Mr. Ian Montagnes for editorial supervision, to Mrs. Adelaide Allen Johnstone for preparation of the index, and to Mrs. Amy Lord. Thanks are also due to the Vaughan Township Council (1970) for their far-sighted involvement and financial support at this opportune time for a Vaughan Township history; to the members of the Vaughan Township Historical Society for their support; and to the executive of that Society for their work, the members of the executive at its organization in 1970 being James M. McDonald, George C.H. Snider, Ernest Redelmeier, William Hallawell, Fred Constable, Harold Hayhoe, Charles Miller, Mrs. Pierre Berton, and Jesse Bryson.

George C.H. Snider

George Elmore Reaman (1889-1969)

George Elmore Reaman was born on a farm, Lot 11, Concession 2, Vaughan, near Concord, on July 22, 1889. His ancestors were Yorkshire English and Swiss German. He attended Concord Public School and Richmond Hill High School, and went on to Victoria College, University of Toronto. He received a B.A. in 1911 and in 1913 became its first graduate with a Master's degree in English. He was awarded a second M.A. from McMaster University in

Hamilton, a B.Paed. from Queen's University, Kingston, and a Ph.D. from Cornell University, Ithaca, New York. He was honoured with an LL.D. by the University of Waterloo, Waterloo, Ontario, on October 24, 1969.

In 1913 he taught in Moose Jaw College and from 1914 to 1919 taught at Woodstock College. He was Educational Director for the Toronto Y.M.C.A. for four years and an editor with Macmillan of Canada Ltd., publishers, for two.

In 1925 he founded and was superintendent of the Bowmanville Boys Training School. In 1932 he returned to Toronto, where he founded Glen Lawrence Private School. He was appointed to the Ontario Agricultural College, Guelph, Ontario, in 1939, and was head of the English Department there until 1954. In that year he moved to Waterloo Lutheran College to do some teaching, become their Dean of Men, and set up their Department of Adult Education. In 1959 he moved to the new University of Waterloo and became head of the Extension Department for nearly ten years.

During his academic life he was active in community affairs. He was the first Canadian president of the International Association for Exceptional Children, and President of the Guelph Y.M.C.A. At the O.A.C. he established the first course in Canada for broadcasting in 1939, also the first course for announcers in 1942. He was the first Canadian president of the International Platform Association, and founder and Honorary President of the Guelph Foreman's Club. He set up the University of Waterloo's Department of Design and organized the University's marketing seminars for business men, the first of the kind in Canada. He was founder and President Emeritus of the Pennsylvania German Folklore Society of Ontario; founder and Honorary President of the Ontario Genealogical Society; founder and Honorary President of the Waterloo-Wellington Branch of the English Speaking Union; founder and Honorary President of the Huguenot Society of Ontario. He was awarded the Centennial Medal in 1967.

He was also the author of more than twenty publications and is best known for the *History of the Holstein-Fresian Breed in Canada* 1946; *Trail of the Black Walnut,* 1956, describing the Pennsylvania German settlement in Ontario; *Trail of the Huguenots,* 1963; *Trail of the Iroquois Indians,* 1967; and a *History of Agriculture in Ontario,* 1969. His *Teaching English for New Canadians* was his first book and was used for over thirty years.

In 1914 Dr. Reaman married Flora Josephine Green, who survives along with their daughter, Elaine Reaman. Dr. Reaman, the last surviving member of his family, was stricken at Malton Airport on Sunday, December 7, 1969, as he landed from New York, where he had addressed the National Huguenot Society. The funeral service was held in First United Church, Waterloo, of which he was an Honorary Elder. Burial was at Maple, Ontario.

Preface

History is made by people. This is a truism too often ignored by historians. Emphasis is placed on the events that took place, but little attention is given to why they happened and who brought them about. In other words, only the economic and political aspects of society are considered; the social and psychological are overlooked. That is why historical writings are so often dull: they lack human interest.

In writing my history of Vaughan Township, I have made it revolve around people. I have tried to discover who the earliest settlers were, where they originated, why they migrated, and the contributions they made to their adopted country.

To tell a full story of Vaughan Township, one must give much of the history of York County, in which it lies, as well as facts about the settlement of Upper Canada (Ontario). Furthermore, since Markham, York, and King Townships adjoined Vaughan Township, and were settled at the same time, and by members of the same families or by families related to the Vaughan settlers by marriage, reference has had to be made to them.

I have given special consideration to John Graves Simcoe, not only because he was the first Lieutenant-Governor of Upper Canada, but because he was largely responsible for the migrations into York County. Vaughan Township profited greatly from his interest in opening up Yonge Street and from his interest in the Pennsylvania Germans as settlers. Moreover, he established at Niagara in 1792 the first Agricultural Society, which played a major role in the development of agriculture in Upper Canada in succeeding years.

Because I have included several thousand names, this book will give genealogical assistance to persons working on family histories whose ancestors once lived in Vaughan Township.

It will be observed that some facts are repeated. This was inevitable as many facts belong in more than one category.

Acknowledgements

It is obvious that anyone writing the history of a township the size of Vaughan, telling the story of its founding by giving the facts about the early and late settlers, must not only do research himself but must also make extensive use of studies by others of various sections of the township.

I was most fortunate in being given access to the Tweedsmuir Histories written by the Women's Institutes of the Township of Vaughan. Therefore, I am under a deep debt of gratitude to the following Curators of these Histories: Mrs. Charles Agnew, Edgeley W.I.; Mrs. Roy Barker, Burwick W.I. at Woodbridge; Mrs. Jesse Bryson, Vellore W.I.; Miss M. Hambly, Kleinburg-Nashville W.I.; Mrs. James K. Thomson, Elder's Mills W.I.; Mrs. Frank Rumble, Richmond Hill W.I.; and Mrs. Harry Jackson, Maple W.I.

I have leaned rather heavily on published histories of two villages: Mrs. Doris M. Fitzgerald's *Thornhill 1793-1963: A History of an Ontario Village,* and Herb Sawdon's *The Woodbridge Story.* Patricia W. Hart's *Pioneering in North York* has suggested source material and an interesting pattern to follow. To them I express my keen appreciation. I also found Charles McGuirl's study of Langstaff provided much valuable information of that area. Leo Johnson's history thesis written for the York Chapter of the Pennsylvania German Folklore Society of Ontario, has been of great assistance. Family histories have been of considerable help and the Public Archives of Ontario made available what early documents pertained to Vaughan Township.

Many persons have been of great assistance in providing source material — manuscripts, old letters, newspaper clippings, photographs, and interviews. Among them I would especially mention Warren and Hazel Reaman, Amos and Edna Baker, George C.H. and Dora Snider, Mrs. James Heslop, Dr. Hardy, and Mildred Hill. To them my many thanks.

I should also like to express my thanks to Alan A. Wall, Agricultural Representative for York County, and to Russell F. Gomme, Secretary, Horticultural Society of Ontario, for information having to do with agriculture and horticulture in Vaughan Township.

James M. McDonald very generously agreed to write the section, 'In Retrospect.' For many years he has been clerk and administrator of the township and has witnessed changes taking place. I wish, therefore, to express my deep gratitude to him for his significant contribution to this work.

A HISTORY OF VAUGHAN TOWNSHIP

Introduction

It was about five o'clock in the morning; the sun was showing red over the tops of the Allegheny Mountains and the date was the first week in April in the year 1794. Four Conestoga wagons, two drawn by horses and two by oxen, were loaded to capacity with the household effects of four families about to leave their homes in Somerset County, Pennsylvania, for new homes in Canada. The preceding summer two of the men had gone to Canada to spy out the land. In the Niagara District, they had found most of the good land had been either allotted or settled upon by earlier arrivals, and so they had travelled around the head of Lake Ontario to York. Here they were told that they might get 200 acres as a grant, and that additional land would be available either for rental or for purchase at a low price.

This particular morning there was a quiet spirit of anticipation, for they were leaving good homes to live in a land of virgin forest. In the group there were grandparents as well as parents with small children, responding to an inherited drive to be pioneers in search of a new country where they could continue to live under the British flag and be free of army service and have freedom to practise their religion. The previous evening their friends had met with them to hold a religious service — they belonged to the Dunkard church — and to wish them well on their journey. Some of their well-wishers hoped to follow soon, particularly if the reports coming back were good.

The women and small children would ride in the Conestoga wagons, a means of conveyance first made in the Conestoga Valley of Lancaster County, Pennsylvania. The wagons being used on this trip were made locally out of swamp oak, white oak, hickory, locust, gum, or poplar from neighbouring woodlands, and ironed by the local blacksmith. All the work was, of course, done by hand. The wagons used on this migration were the farm type, much smaller but built along the same lines as the large transports often drawn by six horses.

This type of wagon was admirably suited to travel over poor roads, for the wagon bed was long and deep, with a considerable sag in the middle, both lengthwise and crosswise, so that, should the load shift, it would settle towards the centre and not press against the end gates. The body resembled a rowboat with square ends, and indeed was sometimes used as such after the interstices were carefully caulked with tar and the wheels removed and placed inside the wagon. Such rivers as the Susquehanna and Niagara could thus be crossed if ferries were not available.

The bows of the wagon followed the line of the ends of the body, and were slanted outwards. A white homespun tentlike cover was spread over the hoops to protect goods and persons riding in the wagon. The driver usually rode the horse on the lefthand side, or walked on that side. The drivers of the big transport wagons are given the credit for the fact that traffic in America passes on the right instead of the left, contrary to English custom.

Our calvalcade had a cow tied to the back of each wagon. Her milk was placed in a bucket under the wagon, and the rocking back and forth of the bucket turned the milk into butter. As well as the cows, there were sheep, pigs and fowl. These were to prove a considerable difficulty on the route, because of their tendency to stray far and the efforts needed to protect them from attack by wild animals. Such livestock were put in the charge of the young men and girls, particularly when streams had to be forded and the animals had to swim.

The Conestoga wagon was usually drawn by the Conestoga horse, bred, it is thought, of Flemish stallions with Virginia mares. It had a short arched neck, full mane, good clean legs, and a weight of fourteen hundred pounds or more. It was powerful and quiet but slow and thus suited for pioneer work. It was popular in Upper Canada until about 1840 when, with improved roads, faster-moving horses were sought. Other breeds such as Canadian, Clydesdale, and Shires took their place and the Conestoga disappeared.

Although most of the early settlers from Pennsylvania made the trip to Canada by Conestoga wagon, only two of the original wagons are still in existence in Ontario at the present time: one, in Waterloo County, came up in 1807; the other, and older, is in the possession of Amos Baker, Lot 11, Concession 2, Vaughan Township, whose great-great-grandfather, John Baker, drove up from Somerset County, Pennsylvania, in 1796. How well it was made was demonstrated at the centenary of Waterloo County in 1952, when it was borrowed and taken down to Lancaster County, Pennsylvania, and driven back over the same route that John Baker had taken in 1796.

There were two routes by which early settlers made their way from Pennsylvania and New York states into Upper Canada. Those who came from the central sections travelled by way of Harrisburg, Sunbury, Williamsport, Bath, Genesee, and Batavia, crossed the Niagara River at Buffalo, and then continued by St. Catharines and Hamilton as far as York. Those from the eastern sections went by way of Reading, Allentown, Wilkes-Barre, Elmira, Canandaigua, and Rochester to Lewiston. From there they followed the same route in Canada as far as Hamilton.

The settlers we are interested in came by way of Harrisburg. It was not unusual for the trip to take six weeks or more. When they arrived in the Niagara area they were almost 'home-free,' for those who had preceded them were always most hospitable and gave them the benefit of their experience. Many such migrations of families were to take place during the next twenty years.

Those who came before 1796 did not receive deeds for their property; sometimes, however, location tickets were given. Hence, those who came into Vaughan Township in the early years took up land as squatters. Normally they would put up a barn or some form of protection for the livestock before they built a house. Coming as most of them did in the early summer, the protection could be simple at first until the cold weather came. By that time adequate shelter was usually completed.

Now we must give our attention to the country where these settlers located — what kind of land it was and who had lived on it before it became a British colony in 1763. To do this we must learn something about the Indians and the French.

This Conestoga wagon — one of only two known to be preserved in Ontario — was part of the caravan that carried Jacob Baker and his wife, eight children, and sixteen grandchildren from Somerset County, Pennsylvania, to Vaughan Township. The seats rest on pieces of wood suspended from one end of the wagon to the other to serve the function of modern springs. The chain on the side was the brake: it was used to tie one wheel on steep hills. The wagon was used to take the family to church for many years.

CHAPTER I

Indian Period

The earliest inhabitants in North America were Indians whose ancestors many centuries ago came to the continent from Asia, probably by way of the Bering Strait. They were given the name Indians in 1492 by Christopher Columbus, the first white man we have any record of meeting them: because he thought he had reached India, he gave them that name from the Spanish Indios. They were often called 'Red Indians' because some of the tribes painted their bodies in such a way as to give them a red appearance.

Our special interest are the Indians of Upper Canada and New York State, who belonged to the Iroquois-speaking group of peoples. They were the Hurons who lived in the Georgian Bay area; the Petuns or Tobacco, who were located southwest of them; and the Neutrals, north of Lake Erie. The Five Nations (later Six Nations), given the name Iroquois (meaning black adders) by the French, were found in Upper New York State and consisted of five tribes — the Mohawks, Oneidas, Onondagas, Cayugas, and Senecas. Later the Tuscaroras joined them.

There has been much misrepresentation of these tribes of Indians. They were not nomadic, for they lived in villages and grew much maize, beans, squash, tobacco, and many fruits. Unfortunately, there are no written records of them and the only information we have of them — particularly the Iroquois — has come to us from their enemies, or (as with *les Relations*) was written by priests as missionary propaganda. Because Champlain about 1615 sided with the Hurons, they were the 'good boys' whereas the Iroquois, who supported the English and did not accept the Roman Catholic religion, were the 'bad boys'.

As far as we can discover the Indian wars before the whites came were insignificant, and largely for the purpose of securing young recruits for the tribe by adoption. Their only weapons were bows and arrows until the whites gave them guns. Scalping was not a factor until the whites, both French and English, offered rewards. Unfortunately, the Iroquois have been unfairly pictured by historians and the popular press as ferocious, scalp-hunting Indians, always on the warpath and completely irreligious. Actually it was the competition for the fur trade between the French and the English that got the Indian tribes involved in such war. The French could not allow the Hurons and Iroquois to be friends - which they wanted to be in order to buy and sell furs - for if this should happen, the furs which the French wanted for sale in Montreal would be deflected to the Iroquois and sold in Albany at a better price.

The burning of the mission at Midland by the French, and the dispersal of the Hurons, the Petuns, and the Neutrals by the Iroquois, were brought about by a French scheme to defeat the Iroquois; the latter learning of it, moved first. This took place in 1649.

Etienne Brulé is the first white man of whom we have any record of making his way through Vaughan. He came down the Humber Trail in 1615. (We shall have more to say about this trail later.) Brulé was an intrepid explorer, the first European to master the Algonquin and Huron languages, and the first to enter what is now known as Ontario. He was finally killed and eaten by the Hurons, probably because they wanted to possess his soul — a compliment in reverse. He has been given a very black reputation by French writers which suggests that he possibly had a Huguenot background. This was characteristic of French Catholic writers, particularly if the subject had collaborated at any time (as Brulé did) with the English.

Doubtless there were many white *coureurs de bois* besides Brulé who travelled this trail but we have no record of them. Doubtless, too, there were many Indian villages in York County, for in the township of Whitchurch many Indian relics have been discovered and also several sites which contained large deposits of ashes and other refuse such as carbonized corn cobs. One interesting remain is a circular portion of a human skull, well worn but in excellent preservation: it was perforated with seven holes and had evidently been held as a trophy, the holes being the score of enemies killed in battle by the wearer. The situation of these and other sites in adjoining townships indicates that a line of Indian villages extended from the mouth of the River Rouge to Penetanguishene. In Vaughan, to cite just one example, on the farm bought in 1816 by John Reaman and now owned by Isaac Reaman, many arrowheads, skinning stones, tomahawks and Indian pottery have been found; also a large stone used by the Indians for grinding corn.

Vaughan Township was an important area for the Indians and later for the French because of the Humber River (named after a river in Devonshire near Simcoe's estate) which was an important part of the route from Lake Ontario to Lake Simcoe and the Upper Lakes. The Humber Trail, which linked it to the Holland River, is supposed to have run north from the first rapids on the Humber, perhaps from Toronto Bay itself. It followed the east bank of the Humber fairly closely until it reached the neighbourhood of Pine Grove. There two routes became possible. One followed the main stream until it crossed the main branch near Nobleton, then turned across country to the northeast and crossed the watershed near Hackett's Lake. The trail then ran north to the Holland River, ending at a point on the West Branch above the forks. There is archaeological evidence that a more easterly route, crossing the divide ear Eversley, was in use in the seventeenth century. The Humber Trail was more important than the water routes up the Don, Rouge, or Humber, because water levels were frequently low in those rivers and the Indians preferred to make one long portage rather than many short ones. In later years the French used riding and packhorses on the trail but it is unlikely horses were much used to carry freight. It was the packhorse 'trail' that Lieutenant-Governor Simcoe followed in 1793 on his way to Lake Simcoe.

Indian villages at some distant time were located in the Woodbridge area — one was the Mackenzie Site, Lot 6, Concession 7, Vaughan, overlooking the beautiful Humber Valley. On the northern edge of the site now stands the water tower serving Woodbridge. From a vantage point can be seen the confluence of the two branches of the Humber, the surrounding valley, and what was once the Humber-Holland Trail leading northward. A great portion of this trail is the main thoroughfare through this district. There were two Indian ossuaries near this site, one to the east on the property of George Sherin, and the other to the south, a portion of which is included in the northwest corner of Hillcrest Cemetery. Remains have been unearthed from time to time, but a portion has never been under cultivation. According to archaeologists, the two ossuaries on this site would indicate occupation by two tribes at different intervals.

Another Indian village was the Barker Site, west half Lot 16, Concession 7, Vaughan. This site is situated on the east bank of the Little Humber, east branch. It is well sheltered by steep hills rising to a height of approximately fifty feet on the west and south, while to the east the rolling hills extend as far as eye can see. It is possible to obtain fresh spring water at several points near this site, which would be an ideal spot for aboriginal settlement. A short distance to the west, the Humber-Holland Trail wound northward to Lake Simcoe and Georgian Bay, the land of the Hurons. The following is quoted from the 1911 Ontario Archaeological Report which described this site and the bone awls found there:

In this collection there are some very fine specimens of bone; these awls in the Museum are probably unique. Their fine finish and beautifully rounded points mark them as having been made by some pre-Huron race.

The ash bed in which the awls were found was situated on the bank of the Little Humber, Lot 16, Concession 7, Vaughan. The peculiarity of this ash bed, situated on the second river bottom, was, in the first place, its extensive size and great elevation, some 35 feet long and 20 feet wide, with a depth of ashes from 3 to 5 feet. On making a cross-section, we found the evidence of a dual occupation — a layer of dark vegetable mould separating the ashes. That above the mould contained almost no remains except some broken pottery and remains of pipes, but in the lower deposit, the awls, forks (or whatever they may be called) were found. They vary in length from 7¾ inches to 5½ inches. Their workmanship, and the conditions under which they were found, would lead one to believe that they were pre-Huron in their origin, and the probability is that they were the work of a branch of the Iroquois family previous to the establishment of the union of the tribes, as it is a well-known fact that the Iroquois family had very little veneration for bone, and consequently they became more expert in their workmanship.

The Mackenzie Site was excavated in October 1947, and the Barker Site in November 1951, both by approximately 200 university students under the direction of Professor J.N. Emerson of the Department of Anthropology, University of Toronto. Both excavations proved that there had been permanent Indian occupation. Remains of the posts that had once supported longhouses were discovered as light discolourations in the rich loam. (These longhouses were made of a frame of poles covered with flat pieces of elm bark, which was plentiful in the area; inside, they were divided into cubicles for each family.) Working with a small trowel, each student excavated an area five feet square, sifting each trowel of earth for evidence. These small squares they carefully mapped to make a permanent record of their discoveries. Only a few inches under the black earth was rich evidence of how the Iroquois lived. Hundreds of bits of broken pottery, charred deer bones, pipe stems, flint arrow heads, bone beads, awls, etc. were found. The artifacts were carefully washed, catalogued and taken to the Royal Ontario Museum for further study. A collection of artifacts from the Barker Site has also been lent by the Roy H. Barker family to the Etobicoke Historical Museum for display.

The struggle between the French and Hurons on one side and the Iroquois on the other, which was a struggle for the fur trade, was brought to an abrupt end about 1649 for a number of years when the Iroquois dispersed the Hurons, Petuns, and Neutrals. The French moved further west and established a post at Michilimacinac; The Iroquois then controlled what was formerly a French fur trade area and all its furs were sold at Albany instead of Montreal. From then on, there was a see-saw struggle between the French and the Iroquois. Count Frontenac returned as governor of New France in 1682 and humbled the Iroquois. De Denonville, who succeeded Frontenac, made a raid on the Senecas and burned their villages, destroying some 400,000 bushels of maize. The Iroquois retaliated; they attacked Montreal Island and the massacre of Lachine took place. It is said on good authority that the Iroquois never carried out a raid on the French except in retaliation for one by the French. During the early 1700s the Iroquois were involved with the English in their war with France in America; consequently they withdrew from their private struggles with the French in Canada. However, they continued their interest in the fur trade.

Following the withdrawal of the Iroquois back to New York State after 1720, the Mississaugas, a tribe of the Ojibwas, who originally were Algonquins, took over much of the area once possessed by the Hurons and other tribes. They were a peaceful semi-nomadic people who were content to grow a little corn on the beaver meadows and depended on supplementing it with the salmon catch. The aromatic root, ginseng, which the Jesuits used to ship to China where it brought five dollars a pound, proved a sore temptation to the Mississaugas. They were faithful and well-disposed to their neighbours of Carleton Island (on the St. Lawrence), but were always clamouring for goods and rum, which they often found could be more quickly gained in ginseng trade than by going to war. Frenchmen on the Niagara portage had made a fortune from ginseng.

The Mississaugas were not much interested in controlling the fur trade and, being nomadic in nature, had little attachment for the land vacated by the Iroquois and became their allies. They were said to have sixteen villages in the Toronto region, and many of the finds in the southern part of Vaughan are probably relics of Mississauga campsites and burying grounds. An ossuary opened on Lot 25, Concession 7, in 1859, contained French-made copper kettles and other utensils (though this site may have been Huron). When the Mississaugas sold their lands to the British in 1788, that brought an end to the Indian era in Upper Canada.

CHAPTER II

French Period

The French were never interested in the colonization of what came to be Ontario, their chief interest being the obtaining of furs, with the extension of the Roman Catholic religion secondary. (This is Mason Wade's point of view in *The French Canadians*.) Consequently, forts were built which served two purposes: centres for the purchase of furs and protection against enemy attacks.

In 1720 the French reasserted their control over Lake Ontario by building *magasins royals* (government stores) at the mouths of the Niagara and Humber Rivers and at Quinte. However, the Toronto *magasin* was closed in 1729, and until 1750 the English, trading from Oswego, controlled the majority of the fur trade centered at Toronto. (Oswego had been built in 1722 by the English on the south shore of Lake Ontario and served a double purpose: it was located close to the country of the Iroquois and it was in a position to attract the Indians for the sale of their furs.) In 1749 a struggle, not only for the fur trade in Canada but for the entire Ohio territory south of Lake Erie, took place between the English and the French. It was then that, on the recommendation of Count de la Galissonière, the French decided to build a fort at Toronto in an effort to recapture the fur trade. The fort was named Fort Rouillé, after the French Minister of Marine, although it was more commonly called Fort Toronto.

Fort Rouillé was not designed to withstand attack by European forces in the Seven Years' War. When in 1758 the English attacked and burned Fort Frontenac (Kingston), the French governor-general, de Vaudreuil, gave orders that, should the enemy appear at Toronto, the fort should be burned to prevent it from falling into their hands; the occupants were to fall back to Fort Niagara which was to be defended. It didn't work out that way, however. The English laid siege to Niagara on July 6, 1759, and captured it on July 25. This meant that Fort Rouillé was defenceless and Douville, the commandant, following instructions burned it and set out for Montreal. Sir William Johnson, Colonial Indian Agent, investigated and found that the fort had been destroyed by the French.

Dr. Scadding, in his *History of an Old French Fort and its Monuments,* gave this colourful description of the event:

About this time watchers on the ramparts of Fort Niagara would see ascending from a point on the far horizon to the north-west across the lake a dark column of smoke — sure indication that the orders of de Vaudreuil were being executed, and that in a few hours all that the English or anyone else, on approaching Toronto, would discover of the once flourishing trading-post would be five heaps of charred timbers and planks, with a low chimney-stack of coarse brick and a shattered flooring at its foot, made of flag-stones from the adjoining beach, the whole surrounded on the inland side by three lines of cedar pickets more or less broken down and scathed by the fire.

Sir William Johnson, having captured Niagara, made only this brief report of Fort Rouillé's burning.

On the evening of the 27th I sent three whale-boats with a party of about thirty men to reconnoitre Fort Toronto, and on their return propose to destroy it.

And on the 30th he wrote:

At night Lieutenant Francis returned from Toronto and reported that the enemy had burned and abandoned that post and destroyed many things which they could not carry along, viz., working utensils, arms, etc.

With the signing of the Treaty of Paris in 1763, the era of French activities in what came to be known as Upper Canada ceased. Thus ends the French period of our history. France placed little value on Canada, for, given the choice of owning Canada or the sugar of Guadaloupe, she chose Guadaloupe.

CHAPTER III

Pioneer Periods

The early pioneer period is generally considered as extending from 1776 to 1812, and the late pioneer period from then to 1840, when 'Horse power took over from Hand power.' However, Vaughan Township was somewhat different from other sections of Upper Canada. In the decades from 1820 to 1840 many settlers came from Britain and many villages got their start. Often these British settlers brought money, and either bought out land and existing mills — saw and grist — and enlarged them, or built new ones. It was always the mills which created the villages. For where there was a mill there had to be a cooper to provide barrels; and staves had to be made. Next a blacksmith shop was essential, and a store to provide post office facilities and the articles and food required by the settlers. A church and school naturally followed. A village was in the process of being born, particularly if industry could be included. Many of the villages in Vaughan Tonwship came into being in the 1830s largely because many of the new settlers had been mechanics and tradesmen in the old country and farming was not to their liking.

On the following pages there are several lists of the early patentees. These have been given because each list adds bits of information. Sometimes there is disagreement because the information comes from different sources.

In the opening up of Upper Canada there was this difference from the situation in New York and other contiguous states. Following the Revolutionary War, the American settlers just moved into New York State and took over the Indian lands. In Upper Canada, the British government went through the motions of buying the lands, occupied mostly by the Mississauga Indians who were willing to sell them relatively cheaply. The Six Nations after the Revolutionary War were accommodated by being given land 'six miles on either side of the Grand River from its source to its mouth.' Here in 1784 some 2,500 settled and became friends of the early settlers.

The area including Toronto was purchased from the Mississaugas in 1788 but the boundary lines had to be agreed upon later. That same year the region that became Upper Canada was divided into four districts: Lunenburg, Mechlenburg, Nassau, and Hesse — all German names, given ostensibly out of consideration to the preponderance of Palatine and Swiss German settlers. When John Graves Simcoe was made Lieutenant-Governor of Upper Canada in 1792, being an ardent Britisher, he changed these names to Eastern (Lower Canada to Gananoque River); Midland (Gananoque River to River Trent); Home (River Trent to Long Point), and Western (Long Point to Detroit).

Simcoe's immediate problems after being appointed were to defend Upper Canada, which had been set apart from Lower Canada by the Constitutional Act of 1791, from the Americans and to attract settlers. Like William Penn in 1681, he realized that land without capable settlers was useless, and under the French, no settlement had taken place. To accomplish these two goals, Simcoe decided to lay out a network of roads which would allow both the speedy movement of troops and open up the country to the new settlers whom he hoped to attract from the lost colonies.

John Graves Simcoe was born on February 25, 1752, at Cotterstock, not far from Peterborough, Northamptonshire, in England; he was called John after his father, a brilliant naval officer, and Graves after his godfather, Admiral Graves. He was educated at Eton and spent one year at Oxford before his health forced him to leave the University and be privately tutored. He joined the army and in 1775 arrived in North America, where he obtained command of the Queen's Rangers and took part in the Revolutionary War. His approach to war in America was unconventional but successful. After being wounded several times, he went back to England in 1781 and the following year met and married Elizabeth Gwillim (the townships of East, West, and North Gwillimbury were named after her). He was thirty and she was sixteen but a very mature and talented young lady. His wife being wealthy, they bought Wolford Farm, not far from Honiton in Devon, and built Wolford Lodge. Simcoe became a Member of Parliament and helped form the Constitutional Act of Canada.

In 1791 he accepted appointment as lieutenant-governor of Upper Canada. In this office he was under Sir Guy Carleton (Lord Dorchester), the governor-general, who constantly thwarted many of Simcoe's plans for the development of the province. Dogged with ill health all the time he was in Canada, and so often frustrated by Lord Dorchester, Simcoe returned to England in 1796. The mosquitoes of Toronto were blamed for his departure. These pests were said to induce malaria and ague. (Even Mrs. Simcoe was not immune, for a bite of one of them caused such a swelling that she couldn't remove her glove.)

Simcoe returned to Wolford Lodge and organized its daily life along military lines. In 1798 he was promoted to the rank of lieutenant-general and in 1800 was in command of Plymouth. Before that he had been sent on a mission to San Domingo; however, ill health prevented him from staying. His last assignment was as commander-in-chief for India, but again his health failed and he never reached India. He died on October 26, 1806 at Exeter.

In 1800 he built Wolford Chapel and there he lies, with his

wife and six unmarried daughters. In 1966 the Ontario Government took over the upkeep of this chapel after it had been maintained for forty years by the Harmsworth family. This is the only piece of land owned by the Province of Ontario outside of Canada.

To tell the full story of Vaughan Township one must give consideration to the Toronto region, and particularly to the city of Toronto, because its establishment as the capital of the province was basic to the development of York County and Vaughan Township.

During the French occupation of the area purchased by the British from the Mississaugas, two important tasks had been accomplished. The land had been explored and mapped, and the importance of the 'Toronto' Passage had been confirmed as giving access to Lake Huron. General Simcoe was able to profit from the French achievement. However, in Vaughan Township there was nothing of importance left of either French or Indian occupations: the hoofprints of the first horses on the Humber Trail had soon disappeared; the forest took over the camp sites; remnants of French trading goods were buried and covered with soil, to be discovered by archæologists a century or two later. Thus, when the first settlers struggled up what was to become Yonge Street, they found a forest primeval.

When Simcoe took up his appointment in 1792 he learned that the parliament of Upper Canada was expected to meet at Newark (now Niagara-on-the-Lake). This site he considered too near the American border. His thought was to choose London as the provincial capital, but Lord Dorchester wanted Kingston. A compromise was reached when Toronto was selected in 1794. Simcoe apparently was no more fond of Indian names than German ones. He changed the capital's name from Toronto to York, after the King's son, the Duke of York.

There was much opposition to Simcoe's planned removal of the capital, which continued even after his return to England. For instance, in 1797 Chief Justice Elmsley, who had just arrived from England, objected to the removal of the courts from Newark on the ground that York (Toronto) was 'forty miles beyond the most remote settlements at the head of the lakes.' There was no accommodation for jurors who had to come 60 or 80 miles, or for judges, lawyers, suitors, or witnesses. Also there was no jail nearer than Montreal, nor a courthouse. However, the objections came too late and in time they were all overcome.

Elmsley's sentiments were characteristic of the English who came to Upper Canada entirely unfitted for pioneer life. They were the ones, both men and women, who wrote up their experiences and either sent them or took them back to England to be published. They were much read in Britain because a black and perhaps tragic picture always gets more attention than a bright and pleasant one.

Here is a letter written three years before that of Judge Elmsley which gives quite a different picture of York. It was dated November 20, 1794.

York formerly Toronto is situated on the best harbour round the lake, opposite Niagara; and about forty miles distant across the lake but round by land near one hundred miles, along the shore of which great quantities of fish are caught; a town is here in great forwardness, and should the seat of government be removed from Newark there, as is contemplated, it will soon become a flourishing place. From this road is cut out across to Lake Huron, a distance of forty-five miles from Lake Simcoe, thirty-six miles in length; this road affords an easy communication with Michelmachinac — From York to that Lake, a tier of lots of two hundred acres on each side of the road, called Dundas Street [Yonge Street is what he means] granted on the express condition of building and improving on them, within one year from the time they are taken up; *many of them are built upon and occupied.* [Italics mine]

On the east side and joining the rear of these lots is a settlement of near a hundred families, on an excellent tract of land, much of which is open, white oak woods; these Germans came on this summer, furnished with everything to make their situation comfortable and enable them to improve their land to advantage, and no doubt in a short time make a fine settlement; they are supported by a company who have liberally supplied them with teams, farming utensils and provisions, sent them a clergyman of their own company and are about to build their mills, a church and a schoolhouse.

Doubtless the writer was referring to the Berczy settlers, but he unfortunately was overoptimistic about their future.

Dorchester had investigated the Toronto region before Simcoe's arrival in Canada. The first exploration of the place was made by the English Government in 1788 when Deputy Collins reported to Dorchester that 'as a military post I do not see any striking features to recommend it.' In 1791 surveyors began to mark out a row of townships along Lake Ontario. Of these York Township was first and named Dublin, and Scarborough, Glasgow. In that year Dorchester ordered that grants of 700 and 1,000 acres in extent should be laid out at Toronto for three French gentlemen: de Rocheblave, La Force, and Bouchette, who had rallied to the support of the British in the struggle with the seceding colonies. However, before the order was executed the new province was duly constituted, and there was a change of regulations with the result that the three got no land near the site of the new capital.

In 1792 Simcoe divided Upper Canada into 19 counties, York being the fourteenth. Joseph Bouchette, who was in charge of the naval force located at Kingston, made an accurate survey of the Toronto harbour in 1793, the same year Simcoe visited York.

Thus permanent settlement came to a site that had long been known to white men and Indians alike. During the French era the Humber Valley had formed part of an overland route from Lake Ontario to Lake Huron. The Indians used it whenever it was safe to do so. It would appear that few Indians were permanently settled on the watershed, however, for the region was exposed to raiding by the Iroquois. As has been mentioned, Brulé crossed the Humber Trail in 1615. By 1678 the Senecas had established a village on the Humber, probably at Baby Point. LaSalle paid a visit in a sailing vessel to the river in 1678 and crossed it himself three times in 1680 and twice in 1681. The Senecas abandoned the region towards the end of the seventeenth century and it was then that the Mississaugas moved in. When in 1720 the French set up the trading post of Toronto, in all probability it was on the Humber, but Fort Rouillé was built just east of the Humber watershed. After the fort was burned in 1759, the only signs of habitation were the houses of two fur traders, until York was founded in 1793. The settlement then was moved east to the shore of the bay.

The settlement of Vaughan Township was part of the general migration to Upper Canada from the English colonies soon to be known as the United States of America. When, in the 1790s and early 1800s, settlers came to the Niagara District of Upper Canada, they found that they would have to locate in one of two other areas — York County, or farther inland in what developed into Waterloo County — because most of the good land in the peninsula had been taken up.

Migrations of groups of people never come about through one motivation. Who were these people who came with their Conestoga wagons, drawn by Conestoga horses or oxen, bringing not only a fair amount of wealth with them in animals and money but, best of all, the knowledge of how to become successful pioneers?

If we for the time being except the Six Nations Indians who, in 1784, were the largest group to come into Upper Canada at one time and settle in one place, we must give credit to the Pennsylvania Germans (popularly known as 'Pennsylvania Dutch' from the English mispronunciation of the German word Deutsch), the French Huguenots, and the Quaker and Puritan English, for being the first settlers in Upper Canada in any numbers. All three groups had been political and/or religious refugees in the English colonies.

The Germans, who were the largest group, in many instances had originated in Switzerland and had migrated around 1700 to the Rhine Palatinate, to help the Germans there rebuild their homes after the armies of Louis XIV had destroyed them while pursuing the Huguenots fleeing from France after the Revocation of the Edict of Nantes in 1685. The Swiss German is a born pioneer; he has itchy feet; and so he did not hesitate when offered free land in America by William Penn in 1682. Furthermore, he had the reputation of being the best farmer in Europe, and that was the main reason Penn invited him to settle in Pennsylvania.

The Huguenots who came to America did not come directly. When forced to leave France because they were Protestants, later called Calvinists, they fled, not as groups, but individually, into any country that would receive them. Some 80,000 of them went to the British Isles. They differed from the Germans in that they were highly skilled middle or upper class artisans, or belonged to the nobility. This accounts for the fact that, when they came to the English colonies and later to Upper Canada, they were very successful entrepreneurs. They also took an active part in the political life of the country in which they settled. Huguenot ancestry is complicated because, when they first migrated, they made every effort to conceal their origin. They married women of the country to which they migrated; they learned the language of that country; they often changed their names; and when they came to America they gave their nationality as that of the country in which they had recently lived. (There are many persons in Ontario with Huguenot ancestry who are unaware of it.)

The Quaker and Puritan English had much the same background of religious persecution. They too were very successful in trade and commerce. It is interesting to note that these three groups originally had a common religious ancestry. Furthermore, many of those who have always considered themselves to have Anglo-Saxon ancestry really are descendants of refugees from Continental Europe to the British Isles, whose names have been Anglicized. The British who came to Upper Canada before 1812 were mostly in the army or in government service in some capacity.

There were five areas in Upper Canada where settlers from the eastern states of the United States located. The Niagara district was infiltrated right after 1776; Detroit after 1778; Eastern Ontario in 1784; York County in 1792; and Waterloo in 1799.

Now let us consider the size and physical characteristics of Vaughan Township, named after Benjamin Vaughan, who, with Richard Oswald, was sent by Lord Melbourne to negotiate the Peace Treaty with the United States in 1783. The County of York was divided into halves by Yonge Street, named after Sir George Yonge, Secretary of War between 1782 and 1794. The western half then comprised the townships of York, Etobicoke, Vaughan, King, and West Gwillimbury. The Eastern half consisted of the townships of Scarborough, Markham, Whitchurch, North and East Gwillimbury, and Georgina.

The Pioneer period breaks into early and late periods in Vaughan Township. The earliest immigrants were all from the United States and there was a preponderance of settlers belonging to the Plain Folk. This migration, although it did not actually stop at the time of the War of 1812, was superseded by an influx of immigrants from the British Isles, not all of whom were agriculturists.

By the time the British arrived, most of the free land had been granted. However, the Crown Lands and the Clergy Reserves, which took up about two-sevenths of the Township property, could now be leased and after 1823 they could be purchased.

There was considerable litigation concerned with various questions of land ownership. First, some recipients of large land grants had not fulfilled the required regulations of clearing trees, building a house, and improving the road in front of the property. Second, squatters took possession of some lots, developed them, but in many cases paid no taxes; Absentee owners also provided a problem because their only interest was in making money out of their property, the value of which had been increased by the work of actual settlers in the vicinity.

Settlers with money preferred to buy property in the vicinity of York. Although the Humber River area was known much before the Yonge Street section, as soon as the latter was opened up, the Humber lots failed to attract. Consequently, settlement on the river was slow and scattered until after 1815, especially on the lower part, where many lots were reserved for the government or held by absentees. In 1818 the northwest part of the watershed was opened to settlement and filled up quickly in the next ten years. Between 1827 and 1840 most of the vacant lots on the Humber in Vaughan and King Townships were occupied.

The early settlers had to take an oath of allegiance in order to qualify for a grant of land. The Baldwin Room of the Toronto Public Library has a manuscript volume containing the oaths sworn by early settlers in Upper Canada between 1800 and 1806. These have been written out by hand with the settler's own signature or, in some cases where he was unable to write, his mark. (The oaths taken before 1800 were written out and given to each settler to present when needed.)

There were three oaths to be taken, the oath of allegiance to King George III, the oath of supremacy denying the authority of the Pope in Canada, and the oath of abjuration, which supported the claims of George II and his descendants to the throne of England against those of the Stuart line. Those of the Mennonite and Quaker faiths were allowed simply to make a 'Solemn Affirmation of Allegiance.' The oaths and affirmations were taken in the town of York before William Willcocks, who was one of the first magistrates sworn in in 1796.

Much interesting information about the pioneer settler's origin may be culled from these pages — the appearance of man, his size, his age, his place of birth, his religion, and his place of residence. The usual discrepancies may be noticed in the spelling of surnames and place names. These are left as they appear in the manuscript. The oaths of persons who did not settle in Vaughan Township have been included, because they give an interesting description of the early settlers and, in a number of cases, the person concerned had later association with Vaughan; but persons who did not settle in York County have been omitted.

J.H.I. BATTGER Farmer of the Town of York; brown Complexion five feet high thirty six Years of age, born in the City of Hamburg. Sworn before me at York on the 7th October (1800).

Will. Willcocks

I CHARLES WILLCOCKS late of Ireland, but now of the Town of York Merch't — dark complexion, five feet 9¾ inches high born in Ireland, have taken the afforesaid Oaths, and do subscribe to them at York 18th Nov'r 1800 Sworn before me the day and Year afforesaid.

Will. Willcocks   Charles Willcocks

I QUETTON DE ST GEORGE born in the South of France but now of the Town of Windham on Yonge Street Dark Complexion black Eyes five feet Eight Inches high have'g taken the Oath of Allegiance & the Other Oaths Do Subscribe the Same at York this 18th Day of Novem'r 1800
Sworn before me the day and Year aforesaid

Will. Willcocks   Quetton de St George

I GEORGE W. POST Farmer born in the State of Connecticut, Town of Hebrom, now living in Scarboro Upper Canada, fair Complexion Gray Eyes, about Six feet

high. Twenty One Years & four months Old, having taken the Oath of Allegiance &
the other Oaths prescribed by Law, do Subscribe the Same at York this 22nd day
of Decem'r 1800 Sworn before me the day & Year above written.

Will. Willcocks   George W. Post

I FRED'K ULR. E. WESTPHAL, Farmer & Secretary to the German Settlement,
born in the City of Hamburg in Germany now living in the Township of Markham,
fair Complexion, blue Eyes, about five feet nine Inches high, near Thirty Years old,
having taken the Oaths of Allegiance, and other Oaths prescribed by Law, do
Subscribe the Same at York this 17th day of March 1801
Sworn before me at York the day and Year above written

Will. Willcocks J.P.   Friech Ulrh Emyls Westphal

I JOHN PETER LINDEMAN, Blacksmith born in the City of Hamburgh in
Germany, now living in the Township of Markham, fair Complexion light Gray
Eyes, about Six feet high, Fifty two Years Old, having taken the Oaths of
Allegiance prescribed by Law, and the other Oaths — do subscribe the same at York
this 17th day of March 1801
Sworn before me at York the day & Year above written

Will. Willcocks J.P.   John Peter Lindeman His X mark

WILLIAM JONES Farmer, born in the Province of New Jersey but now living in
Scarborough Township in this Province light blue Eyes Brown hair, about five feet
5 Inches high. Fifty three Years Old, having taken the Oath of Allegiance and the
Other Oaths prescribed by Law, do subscribe the same at York this 18th Day of
May 1801
Sworn before me the Day & Year above written

Will. Willcocks   Wm. Jones

GEORGE WEIKEL Farmer, born in Germany but now living in Yonge Street in the
Township of York in this Province, dark blue Eyes, brown Hair, abouve five feet six
Inches high, Fifty nine Years Old, having taken the Oath of Allegiance and the
other Oaths prescribed by Law do Subscribe the same at York this 22'd day of June
1801
Sworn before me the day & Year above written

Will. Willcocks   Georg Weikel

I ANDREW THOMPSON Mason, born in Scotland, but now living in this town
blue Eyes, brown Hair, about five feet Eleven-Inches high, Fifty Years of Age,
having taken the Oath of Allegiance & the other Oath prescribed by Law, do
subscribe the Same at York this 30th day of June, 1801
Sworn before me the day and Year above written

Will. Willcocks   And'w Thomson

I JOHN STEGMANN born in the City of Hess-Cassall late Captain in the Hessian
Regiment of Sossberg, but now living in this Town of York, black Eyes dark brown
Hair — about five feet seven Inches high. Forty three Years Old, having taken the
Oath of Allegiance and the other oaths prescribed by Law, do Subscribe the Same,
at York this 30th Day of June 1801
Sworn before me the day and Year above written

Will. Willcocks   John Stegmann

I DAVID THOMPSON Mason born in Scotland but now residing in the Township
of Scarborough in this Province of Upper Canada, light Gray Eyes, brown Hair,
about five feet ten Inches High, Thirty Seven Years Old, having taken the Oath of
Allegiance & the other Oaths prescribed by Law, do Subscribe the same at York
this 2d day of July 1801
Sworn before me the day & Year above written —

Will. Willcocks   David Thomson

I ZACHARIAH GALLOWAY Yeoman, born in the State of New York, but now
residing at the Town of York in this Province, blue Eyes Light brown Hair, about
five feet nine Inches high and Twenty Six Years of Age, having taken the Oath of
Allegiance & the other Oaths prescribed by Law, do Subscribe the same at York in

Affidavit certifying Jacob Keffer's oath of allegiance, taken before William Jarvis, J.P., in 1799. This was before the records were filed in the Registry Office, and each applicant took his statement home to show when requested.

Overleaf: Crown deed, providing for the sale of 100 acres of Clergy Reserve land to James Bryson, June 26, 1847. This Century Farm is still owned by the Bryson family.

PROVINCE OF CANADA.

VICTORIA, by the Grace of GOD, of the United Kingdom of Great Britain and Ireland, QUEEN,
Defender of the Faith.:— To all to whom these Presents shall come—**GREETING** :

Whereas the Lands hereinafter described and granted are part of the Lands which have been from time to time, according to the provisions of Law in that behalf, allotted and appropriated, and are commonly known as *Clergy Reserves*: **And Whereas**, by an Act of the Parliament of Great Britain and Ireland, passed in the Eighth year of the late King George the Fourth, intituled, " An Act to authorize the sale of a part of the Clergy Reserves in the Provinces of Upper and Lower Canada," and by another Act of the said Parliament, passed in the Third and Fourth years of Our Reign, intituled, " An Act to provide for the sale of the Clergy Reserves in the Province of Canada, and for the distribution of the proceeds thereof;" power and authority is given to the Governor, Lieutenant-Governor, or Person Administering the Government, respectively, as well of the said Province of Upper Canada as of the said Province of Canada, with the advice of the Executive Council, to sell, grant, alienate and convey, all or any of the said Clergy Reserves: **And Whereas**, in pursuance of the power and authority given in and by the said Acts, or by any one or other of them, a contract hath been duly entered into for the sale and conveyance of the lands, tenements and hereditaments hereinafter mentioned, being part of the said Clergy Reserves, unto

James Bigum, of the Township of Vaughan, in the County of York in the Home District

Gowan, his _____ heirs and assigns, at and for the price or sum of *One hundred Pounds*

Now Know It, that in consideration of the said sum of *One hundred Pounds* _____ to Our Commissioner appointed by Us to superintend the sale of the said Clergy Reserves, to and for Our use well and truly paid, We have granted, sold, aliened and conveyed, and by these Presents do grant, sell, alien and convey, unto the said *James Bigum, his* heirs and assigns, All that Parcel or Tract of Land, situate in the Township of *Vaughan* _____ in the County of *York* _____ in the *Home District* _____ of Our said Province, containing by admeasurement *One hundred acres* _____ be the same more or less, being *the East half of* _____ the Clergy Reserve, Lot Number _____

thirty in the Sixth Concession of the said Township of Vaughan

Together with all the Woods and Waters thereon lying and being. **To have and to hold** the said Parcel or Tract of Land hereby granted to *him* the said *James Bigum, his* _____ heirs and assigns for ever: *Saving Nevertheless,* unto Us, Our Heirs and Successors, all Mines of Gold and Silver, that shall or may hereafter be found on any part of the said Parcel or Tract of Land hereby given and granted as aforesaid.

Given under the Great Seal of Our Province of Canada: **Witness**, Our Right Trusty and Right Well-beloved Cousin JAMES, EARL OF ELGIN AND KINCARDINE, Governor General of British North America, and Captain General and Governor in Chief, in and over Our Provinces of Canada, Nova Scotia, New Brunswick, and the Island of Prince Edward, and Vice Admiral of the same, &c. &c. &c.: At *Toronto* this *twentieth* _____ day of *June* _____ in the year of Our Lord, one thousand eight hundred and forty *three* _____ and in the *sixth* _____ year of Our Reign.

By Command of His Excellency in Council.

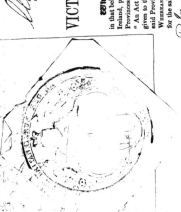

the Province of Upper Canada this 14th day of September 1801
Sworn before me the Day & Year above written

      Will. Willcocks   Zachariah Galloway

I JOHN EDGELL Farmer, born in Boston State, but now residing in the Town of York, in this Province, blue eyes dark brown hair, about Six feet high, and Thirty Years Old having taken the Oath of Allegiance and the Other Oaths prescribed by Law, Do Subscribe the same at York in the Province of Upper Canada this 23rd Day of November 1801
Sworn before me the day and Year above written

      Will. Willcocks   John Edgell

I JOHN OSTER Tanner and Farmer in Pennsylvania but now residing in the Township of Vaughan in this Province hazil Eyes brown hair about five feet nine Inches high and Twenty Two Years Old, having taken the Oath of Allegiance & the Other Oaths prescribed by Law Do Subscribe the Same at York in the Province of Upper Canada this 16th Day of February 1802
Sworn before me the Day and Year above written

      Will. Willcocks   Johannes Oster

I THOMAS HAMILTON Of the Town of York Innkeeper, born in the Province of Nova Scotia, blue Eyes, brown hair Six feet two Inches high, and Thirty Two Years Old having taken the Oaths of Allegiance & the other Oaths prescribed by Law Do Subscribe the same at York in Prov. of Upper Canada this 9th day of April 1802
Sworn before me the day and Year above written

      Will. Willcocks   Thomas Hamilton

I JAMES LOVE of Yonge Street Farmer & born in the Kingdom of Ireland, Grey Eyes light Hair Five feet eight Inches high, Twenty nine Years Old, having taken the Oath of Allegiance & the other Oaths prescribed by law, Do subscribe the same at York in the Province of Upper Canada this 18th Day of May 1802
Sworn before me the Day and Year above written

      Will. Willcocks   James Love

I DAVID LOVE of Yonge Street Farmer born in Pennsylvania, Dark Grey Eyes, brown Hair, Five feet Eleven Inches high, Twenty three Years Old, having taken the Oath of Allegiance & the Other Oaths prescribed by Law, Do subscribe the Same at York in the Province of Upper Canada this 18 day of May 1802
Sworn before me the day & year above written

      Will. Willcocks   David Love

JOHN LOVE of Yonge Street Farmer born at Sea on a voyage from Ireland, blue Eyes dark brown Hair, Five feet nine Inches high, Twenty five Years Old having taken the Oath of Allegiance & the other Oaths prescribed by Law do Subscribe the Same at York in the Province of Upper Canada this 18th Day of May 1802
Sworn before me the Day & Year above written

      Will. Willcocks   John Love

I ALEXANDER LEGG Carpenter, now of the Town of York, born in Great Britain, Hazel Eyes, Black Hair five feet Ten Inches high, and Thirty four Years Old, having taken the Oath of Allegiance and the other Oaths prescribed by Law Do Subscribe the same at York in the Province of Upper Canada this 29th Day of July 1802
Sworn before me the Day and Year above written

      Will. Willcocks   Alex. Legg

I RICE HONEYWELL Farmer of the District of Johnstown, born in the State of New York, Hazel Eyes, Dark Hair five feet Nine Inches high, Forty three Years Old, having taken the Oath of Allegiance & the other oaths prescribed by Law, Do subscribe the Same in the Province of Upper Canada this 27th Day of April 1803
Sworn before me the Day & Year above written

      Will. Willcocks   Rice Honeywell

I JONATHAN HALE Farmer of the Township of York, born in the State of Massachusetts, Grey Eyes, light Hair, about Six feet high, Twenty Three Years old have taken the Oath of Allegiance & the other oaths Prescribed by Law, Do

Subscribe the Same at York in the Province of Upper Canada the 20th day of June 1802.
Sworn before me the day & year above written
      Will. Willcocks   Jonathan Hale

JOHN COOK late of Little York Co. in Pennsylvania but now of Markham Farmer Grey Eyes, Brown hair, about five feet eight high and sixty Years old having taken the Oath of Allegiance & the other Oaths prescribed by Law Do Subscribe the same at York in the Province of Upper Canada this 21st Day of June 1803
Sworn before me the Day & Year above written   his
      Will. Willcocks   John X Cook
                                    mark

VALENTIN FISHER of Vaughan in the Home District of this Province Farmer Gray Eyes, Marked with the Small Pox, brown Hair about five feet ten Inches high, twenty four Years of Age, having taken the Oath of Allegiance & the other oath prescribed by Law Do subscribe the same at York in the Province of Upper Canada this 29th day of January 1804
Sworn before me the Day & Year above written
      Will. Willcocks   Valentine Fisher

JESSE KETCHUM Jun'r of the Township of York, in the Home District of this Province Tanner blue Eyes, light hair about five feet eight Inches high Twenty three Years Old, having taken the Oath of Allegiance and the other Oaths prescribed by Law do Subscribe the Same at York in the Province of Upper Canada this 1st Day of May 1804
Sworn before me the day & Year above written
      Will. Willcocks   Jesse Ketchum Jr.

JOHN McDOUGAL late of Schenectady, Carpenter, light blue Eyes Dark Brown hair about five feet ten Inches high, Twenty Seven Years Old, having taken the Oath of Allegiance & the other Oath prescribed by Law Do subscribe the Same at York in the Province of Upper Canada this 3d day of July 1804
Sworn before me the day & Year above written
      Will. Willcocks   John McDougall

ABRAHAM ORT of Markham Farmer, light blue Eyes foxey complexion light foxey hair about five feet seven Inches high Forty Years Old having taken the Oath of Allegiance, do subscribe the Same at York in the Province of Upper Canada this 8th day of Novem'r 1804
Sworn before me the Day & Year above written
      Will. Willcocks   Abraham Ortt

ULLRICK BORCKHOLDER late of Pennsylvania farmer light blue Eyes Gray Hair about five feet Six Inches high, born in Germany, Sixty four years Old, a Menonist having made the Solemn Affirmation of Allegiance prescribed by Law do subscribe the same at York in the Province of Upper Canada this 4th day of Decem'r 1804
affirmed before me
      Will. Willcocks, J.P.   Ullrich Bork Holder

JACOB WINN late of Vermont Blue Eyes Grey Hair about Six feet high born in Oban in Massahachusetts Bay Sixty Years Old of the People Called Quakers having made the Solemn Affirmation of Allegiance in the presence of Almighty God as prescribed by Law Do subscribe the Same at York in the Province of Upper Canada this 11th day of December 1804
affirmed before me
      Will. Willcocks J.P.   Jacon Winn

JOSHUA WINN late of Vermont, blue Eyes brown Hair about 5 feet 8 inches high born in Vermont — 21 Years Old of the People called Quakers having made the Solemn Affirmation of Allegiance prescribed by Law Do Subscribe the Same at York in the Province of Upper Canada this 11th Day of December 1804.
Affirmed before me
      Will. Willcocks J.P.   Joshua Winn

NATHAN BOSTWICK late of Virmount blue Eyes brown Hair about 5 feet 9 Inches high born in Connecticut — 26 Years Old of the People called Quakers having made the Solmn Affirmation of Allegiance prescribed by Law do Subscribe the Same at York in the Province of Upper Canada this 11th of Decem'r 1804 Affirmed before me

      Will. Willcocks J.P.   Nathan Bostwick

JAMES STARR late of Pennsylvania Farmer, blue Eyes, brown Hair about 5 feet 9 Inches high born in Pennsylv'a 42 Years old of the People Called Quakers having made the Affirmation prescribed by Law Do Subscribe the Same at York in the Province of Upper Canada this 11th Day of Dec'r 1804 Affirmed before me the Day & Year above Written

      Will. Willcocks   James Starr

HENRY WHITEMAN late of Pennsylvania, but now of Markham Farmer about 5 feet 8 Inches high — Dark Eyes 46 Years old of the People called Menonist having made the Affirmation prescribed by Law do subscribe the same, at York in the Province of Upper Canada this 22'd Day of December 1804 — Affirmed before me the day & Year above written

      Will. Willcocks J.P.   Henry Whitman

HENRY SCHANK late of Pennsylvania Farmer about 5 feet six Inches high 24 Years Old of the People called Menonist Dark hazel Eyes having made the Affirmation prescribed by Law Do subscribe the same at York in the Province of Upper Canada this 22d Day of December 1804 Affirmed before me the Day & Year above written —

      Will. Willcocks J.P.   Henry Schank

MICHAEL SCHANK late of Pennsylvania Farmer 5 feet 11 Inches high 21 Years Old of the People called Menonist light Hair & Grey Eyes having made the Affirmation prescribed by Law Do subscribe the Same at York the 22'd day of Decem'r 1804 Affirmed before me the Day & year above written —

      Will. Willcocks J.P.   Michael Schank

JACOB RAWN late of the State of New York Farmer dark Grey Eyes dark hair five feet nine Inches high born in the said State 37 Years Old, a Protestant of the Church of England, having taken the Oaths prescribed by Law & made the Declaration Do Subscribe the Same at York the 28th Day of December 1804 Sworn before me the Day & Year above written —

      Will. Willcocks J.P.   Jacob Rawn

RUSSELL HOAG late of Montgomery County near the Mohawk River Dark Eyes & Hair Six Feet two Inches high, born in York State near 40 Years Old, one of the People Called Quakers, having taken the affirmation prescribed by Law & Made the Declaration do subscribe the Same at York UC, this 28 Day of Decem'r 1804 affirmed before me the day and Year above written

      Will. Willcocks J.P.   Russell Hoag

ABRAHAM STOUFFER late of Pennsylvania Farmer, Hazel Eyes brown Hair Six feet One Inch high, born in Pennsylvania 28 Years Old a Menonist having taken the Affirmation & made the Declaration prescribed by Law Do subscribe the Same at York the 28th Day of Decem'r 1804 Affirmed before me the Day & Year above written —

      Will. Willcocks J.P.   Abraham Stouffer

LEONARD CLOUSE late of New Jersey Farmer, blue Eyes, brown Hair Six feet three Inches high, born in New Jersey 41 years Old, of the Church of England having taken the Oath of Allegiance and made the Declaration as prescribed by Law do subscribe the Same at York the first Day of January 1805 Sworn before me the Day & Year above written

      Will. Willcocks J.P.

                                  his

                        Leonard X Clouse

                                mark

PHILIP SOVERIGN late of New Jersey Farmer Hazel Eyes brown Hair Six feet high born in New Jersey 28 Years Old, of the Church of England having taken the Oaths of Allegiance & made the Declaration prescribed by Law do subscribe the Same this first day of January 1805
Sworn before me
    Will. Willcocks J.P.   Philip Sovereign

JAMES MUCKLE late of New York State Farmer 21 Years Old. of the Church of England, Hazel Eyes, black Hair, five feet nine Inches High, having taken the Oath of Allegiance & made the Declaration prescribed by Law do Subscribe the Same at York the first Day of January 1805
Sworn before me
    Will. Willcocks J.P.   James Muckle

HENRY LICHTE late of Pennsylvania but now of Markham, Farmer 55 Years Old, a Menonist, blue Eyes Grey Hair, five feet eight Inches high, having made the Affirmation and Declaration as prescribed by Law Do Subscribe the same at York the 3d day of Janua. 1805
Affirmed before me
    Will. Willcocks JP   Henry ?

PETER RISER late of Pennsylvania but now of Markham Farmer a Menonist 30 Years Old, Grey Eyes & fair Hair, five feet six Inches high having made the Affirmation and declaration prescribed by Law Do Subscribe the same at York the 3d day of January 1805
    Will Willcocks J P.   Peter Reser

JACOB STOVER late of Pennsylvania but now of Markham Farmer a Menonist 21 Year Old, Grey Eyes & fair Hair, five feet six Inches high having made the Affirmation and declaration prescribed by Law Do Subscribe the same at York the 3d day of January 1805
    Will Willcocks J P.   Jacob Stover

CHRISTIAN RESER late of Pennsylvania but now of Markham Farmer a Menonist, 56 Years old, light Hair, gray Eyes five feet ten Inches high, having made the Affirmation prescribed by law, and made also the Declaration, Do subscribe the same at York the 26th Day of January 1805
Affirmed before me at York Aforesaid
    Will. Willcocks JP   Christian Reser

JOHN McKAY late of Cornwall but now of Whitchurch Farmer, of the Church of Scotland black Hair & dark Eyes five feet seven Inches high 33 Years Old having taken the Oaths & made the Declaration prescribed by Law Do subscribe the same at York the 28th day of January 1805
Sworn before me
    Will Willcocks J P   John McKay

ELIJAH COLLARD Jun'r of Niagara Carpenter, brown hair & Grey Eyes 21 years Old about five feet seven Inches high, having taken the Oaths and made the Declaration prescribed by Law, Do Subscribe the Same at York the 29h Day of January 1805
Sworn before me
    Will. Willcocks J P   Elijah Collard Junior

ALLAN HOWARD late of Vermont but now of West Guillembury Farmer Dark Hair black Eyes 21 Years Old, five feet ten Inches high having taken the Oaths & made the Declaration prescribed by Law do subscribe the same at York the 19h Day of February 1805
Sworn before me
    Will. Willcocks J.P   Allen Howard

PHILLIP LICHTE late of Pennsylvania but now of Whitchurch Farmer Thirty three Yeard old, a Lutheran blue Eyes light hair 5 feet five Inches high having taken the Oath of Allegiance and made the Declaration prescribed by Law Do Subscribe to the same at York the 21st Day of February 1805
Sworn before me

        Will. Willcocks J P.   Phillip ?

TONIS HAGERMAN of Osewegatchea (?) Yeoman Twenty four Years Old a Protestant of the Church of England light blue Eyes brown Hair six feet high having taken the oaths & made the Declaration prescribed by law, Do Subscribe the Same at York the 3d day of March 1805
Before me —

        Will. Willcocks J P   Tunis Hagerman

JOHN WILLSON of Gwillingbury Yeoman Twenty three Years Old a Protestant, Dark brown Hair and Hazel Eyes five feet six Inches high, having taken the Oaths prescribed by Law do Subscribe the Same at York the 11h Day of March 1805
Before me

        Will. Willcocks J P   John Wilson

PHILIP BARTHOLOMAY Yeoman of Markham Twenty three Years Old a Protestant of the Church of Scotland Brown hair blue Eyes five feet three Inches high having taken the Oaths & made the Declaration prescribed by Law do Subscribe the Same at York the 12h of March 1805
Before me

        Will. Willcocks J P   Philip Bartholomay

JESSE KETCHUM of Yonge Street Tanner Sixty five Years Old a Protestant of the Church of Scotland, Grey hair blue Eyes, five feet five Inches high having taken the Oaths & made the Declaration prescribed by law do Subscribe the same at York the 12h of March 1805
Before me

        Will. Willcocks J P   Jesse Ketchum

THOMAS HAZARD of Yonge Street Farmer, Twenty three Years Old, one of the People Called Quakers, black hair & Eyes five feet seven Inches high, having taken the Affirmation of Allegiance & made the Declaration Do Subscribe the same at York the 19h day of March 1805
Before me

        Will. Willcocks   Thomas Hazard

JAMES COOK of Markham sone of Silas Cook, Farmer, Twenty two Years & Eleven Months Old of the Church of England, brown hair & blue Eyes, five feet eleven Inches high; having taken the Oaths & made the Declaration prescribed by Law Do Subscribe the Same at York the 19h day of March 1805
Before me —

        Will. Willcocks J P   James Cook

PHILIP CLINGER of York Blacksmith, A Roman Catholick, blue Eyes Brown Hair, Five feet ten Inches high Forty two Years Old, having taken the oath of Allegiance do subscribe the Same at York the 1st Day of April 1805
Sworn before me

        Will. Willcocks J P   Phillip Clinger

WILLIAM EARLL of Markham Yeoman a Protestant brown Hair, blue Eyes, Five feet three Inches high Thirty Years Old born in the State of New York having taken the Oath of Allegiance & made the Declaration prescribed by law do Subscribe the same at York the 2d day April 1805
Sworn before me

        Will. Willcocks J P   Wm. Earll

DANIEL MORGAN of Whit Church Yeoman, A Protestant, Dark hair Hazel Eyes Five feet ten inches high, Twenty four Years Old, born in Connecticot, having taken the Oath and made the Declaration prescribed by Law Do subscribe the same this 2d day of April 1805
Sworn before me
      Will. Willcocks J P   Daniel Morgan

MOSES GAMBLE of Markham Yeoman a Protestant, black hair & Eyes, five feet seven Inches high, Twenty Seven Years Old, born in Ireland, having taken the Oath and made the Declaration prescribed by Law, do Subscribe the same at York the 2d day of April 1805
Sworn before me
      Will. Willcocks J P   Moses Gamble

STEPHEN JOHNSON of Scarboro Yeoman a Protestant of the Church of Scotland light hair blue Eyes six feet two Inches hight Twenty two Years Old, born in Vermont having taken the Oath of Allegiance & made the Declaration as prescribed by Law do subscribe the Same at York UC this 2d day of March 1805
Sworn before me
      Will. Willcocks J P   Stephen Jonson

JACOB WHITEMAN late of Pennsylvania Yeoman now of Markham One of the People called Menonist, Hazel Eyes, Black hair five feet two Inches high, twenty five years old having made the Affirmation of Allegiance Do subscribe the Same at York the 10h Day of April 1805
Affirmed before me
      Will. Willcocks J.P.   Jacob Whitmann

SAMUEL JACKSON late of Pennsylvania but now of York Hatter, One of the People Called Quaker, blue eyes, brown Hair five feet ten Inches high, Forty Years Old. Having made the Affirmation of Allegiance do Subscribe the same at York the 18h day of April 1805
Affirmed before me
      Will. Willcocks   Sam Jackson

FREDERICK SPREGUE late of the State of New York in the Town of Brownsville, a Protestant Dark blue Eyes, dark Hair. Five feet nine Inches high, a Farmer, Forty two Years old having taken the oath & made the Declaration prescribed by Law do subscribe the Same at York this 22d Day of April 1805
Sworn before me
      Will. Willcocks   Frederick Sprague

HAWKINS WOODRUFF late of New York State, a Presbyterian hazel Eyes Dark, hair, five feet Seven inches high, a Jointer by Trade Fifty five Years old, having taken the Oath of Allegiance, Do Subscribe the Same at York the 23d of April 1805
Sworn before me
      Will Willcocks   Hawkins Woodruff

JOHN CLOSSON late of the State of New York, now of Scarboro, a Protestant blue Eyes, brown hair five feet four Inches high, Tanner and shoemaker by trade Twenty five Years old having taken the Oath of Allegiance & made the Declaration Do Subscribe the Same at York the 24h day of April 1805.
          John Closson

NICHOLAS KURTS late of Pensylvania Yeoman, a Mineonist, Five feet Six Inches high, Forty nine Years of Age blue Eyes & dark brown hair having made the solemn Affirmation of Allegiance Do Subscribe the same at York the 3d day of May 1805
Before   Will. Willcocks J.P.   Nicholas Kurts

ADAM BREINICH late of Pennsylvania (a Dunkard) Shoemaker five feet eight Inches high, Fifty Years Old Dark eyes, brown hair having made the Solemn Affirmation & Declaration of Allegiance Do Subscribe the Same at York the 14th Day of May 1805
before me
        Will Willcocks J.P.   Adam

CHARLES STEWARD of the Township of Barton Yeoman, Six feet two Inches high Grey Eyes dark hair Twenty three Years Old having taken the Oath of Allegiance & made the Declaration prescribed by law, do subscribe the same at York the 14 Day of May 1805
before me
        Will. Willcocks J.P.   Charles Stewart

JOHN PAUL RATTELMULLAR of Markham Yeoman, five feet ten Inches high blue Eyes & Brown hair Forty two Years Old having taken the Oath of Allegiance and made the Declaration prescribed by Law, do Subscribe the Same at York the 14th Day of May 1805
Before Me
        Will. Willcocks J.P.   J.P. Radelmuller

EZEKIEL JAMES of Whitchurch Yeoman, late from Pennsylvania One of the People called Quakers, five feet ten Inches high Grey Eyes, light hair twenty Two years Old, having made the Affirmation of Allegiance and Declaration prescribed by law. Do subscribe the same at York the 5h Day of June 1805
Before me
        Will. Willcocks J.P.   Ezekiel James

ABSOLEM SATTERLEY of York late of the State of New York, a Methodist five feet nine Inches high One Blue Eye light hair Twenty nine Years Old, having taken the Oath of Allegiance & made the Declaration prescribed by law Do subscribe the Same at York this 5th day of June 1805
before me
        Will. Willcocks J.P.   Absalom Satterly

JAMES PHILLIPSE of Yong Street late from the Mohawk River, five feet Seven Inches high black Eyes, Dark hair Forty four Years old, having taken the Oath of Allegiance & made the Declaration prescribed by Law Do subscribe the Same at York the 11h Day of June 1805
before me
        Will. Willcocks J.P.   James Philipse

TIMY MILLARD late of Pennsylvania, & one of the People called Quaker, Miller five feet ten Inches high, hazel Eyes, dark brown hair, Thirty nine years Old, having made the Affirmation of Allegiance Do subscribe the same at York the 24th Day of June 1805
before me
        Will. Willcocks J.P.   Timothy Millard

JOHN EVANS, late of Pennsylvania, One of the People called Quakers, & a Millwright Five feet Eleven Inches high, Grey Eyes, brown hair, Thirty three Years Old having made the Affirmation of Allegiance, Do subscribe the same at York the 24th Day of June 1805
before me
        Will Willcocks J.P.   John Evans

WILLIAM GARDNER late of Fort Erie, Yeoman, Five feet ten Inches high, Grey Eyes light hair, Twenty Two Years of Age, having taken the Oath of Allegiance Do subscribe the same at York the 24th Day of June 1805
before me
        Will. Willcocks J.P.   William Garnor

EVARY STILES late of the State of New York Yeoman, Five feet Eleven Inches high Blue Eyes Brown hair, Thirty four Years Old, having taken the Oath of Allegiance & made the Declaration prescribed by Law, Do subscribe the same at York the 24h June 1805

before me   his

  Will. Willcocks J.P.   Avary X Stiles

            mark

BENJAMIN TERRY, One of the People called Quakers, late of Pennsylvania waver, Five feet ten inches high, blue Eyes Dark brown hair, Fifty seven Years Old, having made the Solemn Affirmation of Allegiance and Delcaration do Subscribe the same at York the 24h Day of June 1805

before me

  Will Willcocks   Benjamin Terry

JOHN LEBAR, a protestant, late of Pensylvania Yeoman, Six feet high, blue Eyes, brown Hair, Twenty three Years Old, having taken the Oath of Allegiance & made the Declaration prescribed by Law, do subscribe the same at York the 24h Day of June 1805

before me

  Will Willcocks J.P.   John Lebar

ABRAHAM LEBAR, late of Pennsylvania Yeoman, Six feet One Inch high, blue Eyes light hair Twenty nine Years Old, having taken the Oath of Allegiance & made the Declaration prescribed by Law, do subscribe the Same at York the 24h of June 1805

before me

  Will. Willcocks J P   Abraham Lebar

ABRAHAM LANG late of Pennsylvania Yeoman, five feet four Inches high, light Grey Eyes Grey hair, Sixty years Old, having taken the Oath of Allegiance and made the Declaration prescribed by Law, do Subscribe the Same at York the 26h day of June 1805

before me

  Will. Willcocks J.P.   Abraham Lang

JOHN LUNDY late of Pennsylvania, but now of Whitchurch, one of the People Called Quakers five feet eight Inches high, blue Eyes light brown hair Twenty Eight Years Old, having made the solemn affirmation & declaration prescribed by law do subscribe the same at York this 9h day of July 1805

before me   his

  Will. Willcocks J.P.   John X Lundy

            mark

HENRY ORT late of little York in Pennsylvania, a Lutheran five feet Seven Inches high blue Eyes, Sandy hair Twenty five Years Old, having taken the Oath of Allegiance & made the declaration do subscribe the same at York the 23d of Sepr 1805

before me

  Will Willcocks   (indecipherable)

ANDREW MOORE late of Pelham Township but now of Whitechurch five feet seven Inches high, blue eyes, light hair, Twenty One Years Old last May, born in Pynsylvania having made the solemn Affirmation of Allegiance & Declaration prescribed by Law, Do subscribe the same at York this 30h Day of Decemr 1805

Before me

  Will. Willcocks   Andrew Moore

ISAAC PENROSE lately from Pensylvania but now of Whitchurch farmer, five feet seven Inches high hazel Eyes brown hair Forty nine Years Old, born in Pensylvania having made the Solemn Affirmation of Allegiance & Delcaration do Subscribe the same at York this 31h day of Decemr 1805

before me

  Will. Willcocks   Isaac Penrose

WILLIAM HORROLD late of Pennsylvania a Protestant of the Episcopal Church five feet six Inches high, dark eyes light hair Forty four Years of Age having taken the Oath of Allegiance & made the declaration prescribed by law Do subscribe the same at York the 21st Day of Janu 1806
before me

Will. Willcocks   Wm Harrold

LUKE BOWEN late of the Township of Matilda, a Lutheran about six feet high light Eyes & brown hair Twenty One Years Old, a farmer, having taken the Oath of Allegiance & made the declaration prescribed by Law, do subscribe the same at York this third day of February 1806
Before me

Will. Willcocks   Luke Bowen

ABIJAH JONES late of the State of New York, but now of Markham a Protestant of the Church of England, five feet five Inches high black Eyes brown hair Thirty One Years Old having taken the Oath of Allegiance & made the Declaration prescribed by law do subscribe the same at York this fourth Day of March 1806
before me

Will. Willcocks J.P.   Abijah Jones

CONRAD GRAM late of Pensylvania Yeoman, a Protestant, five feet six Inches high black Eyes & dark hair, Twenty One Years of Age, having taken the Oath of Allegiance & made the Declaration prescribed by law, do subscribe the same at York this 7h Day of March 1806
before me

Will. Willcocks   Conrad Gram

DAVID ALBERTSON late of New Jersey, but now of this place a Protestant of the Church of England five feet seven Inches high, brown hair & Grey Eyes Thirty three Years of Age, having taken the Oath of Allegiance & the Other Oaths prescribed by Law & made the Declaration, Do subscribe the same at York this 3d Day of June 1806
Before me

      understands sawing
Will. Willcocks   David Albertson

DAVID TAYLOR late of New Jersey but now of Barton Yeoman a protestant blue eyes, light hair, five feet five Inches high Thirty three years Old having taken the Oath of Allegiance & made the Declaration do Subscribe the same at York this 7h day of July 1806
Before me

Will. Willcocks   David Taylor

WILLIAM BARBER of the 50 Mile Creek Yeoman a protestant of the Church of England light blue Eyes brown hair five feet Eleven Inches high Thirty five Years Old having taken the Oath of Allegiance & made the Declaration do subscribe the Same at York this 7h Day of July 1806
Before me

      his
Will. Willcocks J P   Willm X Barber
      mark

JACOB FISHER of Gainsbury a protestant dark Grey Eyes & dark brown five feet Eleven Inches high Twenty five Years Old, having taken the Oath of Allegiance & made the Declaration prescribed by law do subscribe the same at York the 7th July 1806
Before me

Will. Willcocks JP   Jacob Fisher

JOHN KLEIN of Markham Yeoman, a Protestant, dark hazel Eyes & dark hair five feet Nine Inches high, Twenty three Years Old having taken the Oath of Allegiance & made the Declaration prescribed by law, Do subscribe the same at York the 8h Day of July 1806
Before me

Will Willcocks JP   John Klein

SAMUEL HAINES of the Township of King, One of the People Called Quakers, Grey Eyes, brown Hair five feet Eight Inches high, Twenty Two Years Old, having taken the Affirmation of Allegiance & made the Declaration, do subscribe the Same at York the Eighth day of July 1806
Before me
       Will Willcocks   Samuel Haines

WILLIAM ROBINSON Tanner, of Markham, a Protestant of the Church of Scotland Grey Eyes Dark brown hair five feet Eleven Inches high Thirty Years Old having taken the Oath of Allegiance & made the declaration prescribed by Law, do subscribe the Same at York the 9h July 1806
Before me
       Will. Willcocks   Wm. Robinson

PHILIP HAINES Yeoman of the Humber, a Protestant, Grey Eyes brown hair, Five feet nine Inches high. Twenty two Years Old, having taken the Oath of Allegiance and made the Declaration prescribed by Law do subscribe the same at York the 10h day of July 1806
Before me   his
       Will Willcocks JP   Philip X Haines
                                mark

MICHAEL KEFFER late of Pennsylvania a Lutheran, Grey Eyes & light hair Five feet seven Inches high Forty Years Old, having taken the Oath of Allegiance & made the Declaration prescribed by law do subscribe the same at York the 17th July 1806
Before me
       Will Wilcocks   Michael Keffer

JOSEPH YOUNG from the State of New York Grey Eyes & brown hair, five feet Eleven Inches high, Twenty four Years Old, having taken the Oath of Allegiance & made the Declaration prescribed by Law, Do Subscribe the same at York this 29h Day of July 1806
Before me
       Will Willcocks J P   Joseph Young

JOSEPH CHENEQUY late of Quebec black Eyes, black hair, five feet seven Inches high Twenty Eight Years Old, a Roman Catholic, having taken the Oath of Allegiance and made the Declaration prescribed by Law do subscribe the same at York the Seventh Day of Novemr 1806
Before me
       Will. Willcocks JP   Joseph Chenequy

JOSEPH SAWYER of Cornwall, hazell Eyes, dark hair, five feet Six Inches high Thirty five Years Old, a Protestant, having taken the Oath of Allegiance and made the Declaration prescribed by Law do subscribe the same at York the 10h Day of Novemr 1806
Before me
       Will Willcocks J P   Joseph Sawyer

The following is a partial list of the patentees in Vaughan Township and dates when grants were made:

CONCESSION 1 (Yonge Street)
Lot 26	Jacob Fisher Jr. 1798
Lot 27	Rectory of Thornhill 1830
Lot 28	Nathan Chapman 1796
Lot 29	Asa Johnson 1796
Lot 30	John Wilson Sr. 1810
Lot 31	Daniel Soules 1805
Lot 32	Robert Marsh 1802
Lot 33	William Hunter 1811

Lots 13-14	Joshua T. Cozens 1804
Lots 17-18	Capt. D. Cozens 1798
Lots 19-20	Sergt. J. Ross 1802; Lot 20, Jas. Perigo 1802
Lot 21	J. Fraser 1845
Lot 22	Thos. Metcalf 1801
Lot 23	W.B. Peters 1797
Lot 24	Alice Osburn 1802
Lot 26	W.B. Peters 1797
Lots 29-30	S.D. Kiener 1797
Lot 35	Mary Brown 1822

CONCESSION 4

Lots 1-2	Richard Lorrance 1805
Lot 3	Wm. Burkholder 1837
Lots 4-5-7-8	Capt. Lippincott 1797
Lot 9	Jas. Shinck 1837
Lots 10-11	Dan. Cozens 1801
Lot 13	J.M. Cameron 1807
Lots 14-15	Jos. Y. Cozens 1804
Lot 17	J.M. Cameron 1807
Lot 18	Capt. D. Cozens 1798
Lots 19-21	Samuel Street 1798
Lot 22	Catharine Williams 1802; T. Metcalf 1804
Lot 23	S. Street 1798
Lots 25-26	J.M. Cameron Jr. 1809
Lots 28-29-31-32	J.M. Dennis 1801
Lot 32	Garrard McNutt 1801
Lot 33	Cath. Williams 1804
Lot 34	J.M. Anderson 1800
Lot 35	Jannette Anderson 1801

CONCESSION 5

Lot 1	J. McDougall 1801 / Thos. Hill 1801
Lots 3-4	Silas Cook 1799
Lot 5	J. Smith 1839
Lot 6	Sally Miller 1802
Lot 12	Asa Johnson 1798
Lot 13	Lucy Allen 1811
Lots 14-16	Hy. Deckhout 1821
Lot 17	John Crosson 1812
Lots 18-19	George McBride 1801; Lot 19, Samuel Street 1798
Lot 20	John McDonnell 1802
Lot 22	Thos. Knight 1801
Lot 23	Sophia Dennison 1815
Lot 24	Dorothy Porter 1801
Lot 26	John Fenbroeck 1799
Lot 27	Elias Williams 1802
Lot 29	Asail Davis 1802
Lot 30	Anne Dennis 1798
Lot 32	Eliz. Davis
Lot 33	Margaret Chapman 1808
Lot 34	Isaac Puttenbough 1831
Lot 35	Alex Shaw

CONCESSION 6

| Lot 1 | John McDougall 1801 |
| Lot 2 | Priscilla Tenbreck 1799 |

Lot 34	Nicholas Cower 1798
Lot 35	Stephen Colby 1798
Lot 36	Samuel Sinckler 1805
Lot 37	Lt. Abrham Irdell 1798
Lot 38	Jonathan Willcott 1798
Lot 39	William Bowkets 1803
Lot 40	John McKarrby 1798
Lot 41	James Cram 1798
Lot 42	Michael Korts 1803
Lot 43	William Hollingshead 1803
Lot 44	John Hampsted Hudson 1806
Lot 45	James Perigo 1802
Lot 46	Abner Miles 1803
Lot 47	John C. Stokes 1808
Lot 48	Edward Stokes 1823
Lot 49	Samuel Heron 1797
Lot 50	William Flannigan 1805
Lot 51	William B. Peters 1797
Lots 52-53-54	Rowland Winborne 1834
Lot 55	Melinda Cook 1843
Lot 56	Francis Renoux 1820;
	Michael Saigen 1820
Lot 57	Julian C Bugle 1808;
	James Marchand 1820
Lot 58	Ambroise deFarcy 1806;
	Rene Augustin Comte de Chalus, 1806
Lots 58-59	Rowland Winterburne
	Queton St. George 1806
Lot 60	Rene Augustin Comte de Chalus, 1806

CONCESSION 2

Lot 1	Jacob Fisher 1798
Lot 2	James Ruggles 1801
Lots 4-5-6	Capt. James Lipincott 1797
Lot 9	Lewis Page 1838
Lots 10-11	Daniel Cozens 1801
Lots 13-14	Samuel D. Cozens 1801
Lot 15	Joshua Y. Cozens 1804
Lot 16	Thomas Cook 1842
Lot 17	John Cameron 1804
Lots 18-19	Capt. Dan. Cozens 1798
Lot 21	James Perigo 1802
Lot 22	Wm. D. Powell Jr. 1801
Lot 23-25-26	Wm. B. Peters 1797
Lots 28-29	Samuel D. Rievar 1797
Lot 31	Thomas Mercer 1841
Lot 32	Betsy Ann Holmes 1812
Lots 34-35	Bernard Carey 1798

CONCESSION 3

Lot 1	Mary Lawrence 1802
Lot 2	Benjamin Reynolds Jr. 1834
Lots 3-4-6-7	Capt. Lipincott 1807
Lot 5	Christian Troyer 1838
Lots 9-10	Dan. Cozens 1801
Lot 11	Hiram White 1844;
	Alex Wallace 1844
Lot 12	Benj. Cozens 1803

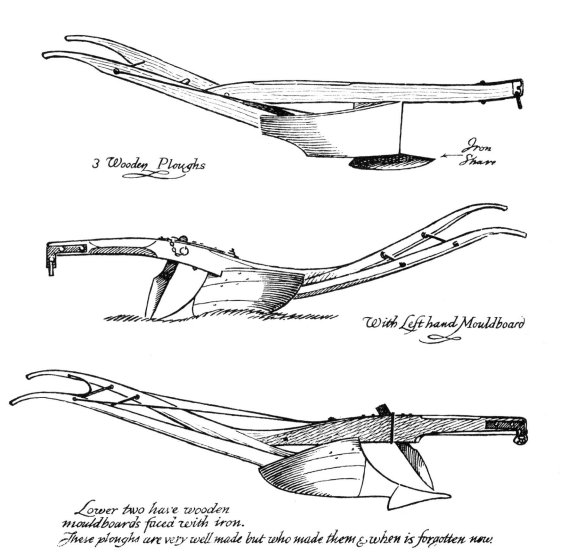

3 Wooden Ploughs

← Iron Share

With Left hand Mouldboard

Lower two have wooden
mouldboards faced with iron.
These ploughs are very well made but who made them & when is forgotten now.

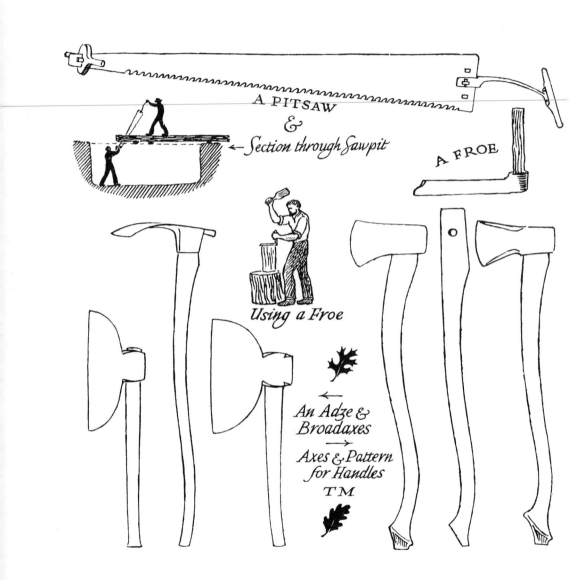

A PITSAW

&

← Section through Sawpit

A FROE

Using a Froe

An Adze &
Broadaxes

Axes & Pattern
for Handles

T M

Lot 42	in 1798 had been granted to Anthony Hollingshead.
Lot 47	In 1808 John Stootes had completed his settlement duties and was given his deed.
Lot 56	March 17, 1820, Francis Renoux, a French Royalist completed settlement duties.
	Southern part of 53 acres granted to Michael Saigson, a French Royalist.
Lot 57	Jacques Marchand, granted 300 acres, a French Royalist.
Lot 58	Tarlton St. George granted 262 acres.
Lot 60	John Hayes, an Englishman, granted 210 acres.

CONCESSION 2

Lot 3	Clergy Reserves: in 1836 purchased by Anthony Bowes.
Lot 9	Lewis Page on April 24, 1828, wrote to buy lot. In March 1838 he bought 200 acres for £200.
Lot 12	Dec. 30, 1815, Tebault Stang leased Crown Reserve.
Lot 16	1829, bought by Michael Fisher for £200; later sold to Thos. Cook. 1841, Thomas Cook paid £200 for Clergy Reserve.
Lot 20	1810, John Phillips rents Crown Land for £20; patented to King's College about 1827.
Lot 22	Dec. 26, 1800, granted to William Powell, Niagara Township.
Lot 22	and Lots 10 and 17 of Concession 10
	1835, sale of 640 acres to Stephen Jarvis.
Lot 24	1837, sold to Gilbert Milligan, Clergy Reserve; sold to Richard Vanderburgh, Dec. 3, 1849.

CONCESSION 3

Lot 2	1818, rented by Valentine Fisher and Thomas Claridge.
Lot 5	Oct. 31, 1805, Clergy Reserve rented to Nicholas Cober. April 18, 1838, Christian Troyer bought Clergy Reserve, 200 acres for £212 10s.
Lot 8	March 8, 1806, leased to Thomas Baldwin; Oct. 14, 1818, Hiram White leased the Crown Reserve when rent not paid by Baldwin.
Lot 11	April 11, 1804, Clergy Reserve leased to Peter Gramm. Requests for purchase: Jan. 27, 1827, by Peter Gramm; Dec. 25, 1828, by Benjamin Thorne; April 8, 1829, by Edward O'Brien, Feb, 16, 1830, by John Goessman; Nov. 30, 1831, by John Montgomery. June 16, 1834, Executive Council ordered that John Montgomery of the Township of York, innkeeper, be permitted to purchase this lot, a Clergy Reserve, in the usual manner. Aug. 27, 1836, Clergy Reserve sold to John Montgomery (see letters from Keffer and White).
Lot 13	property of Robert Milton.
Lot 15	Sept. 10, 1806, Peter Frank leased this Crown Reserve.
Lot 21	Feb. 19, 1811, petitioned by Michael Harman; leased by him Jan. 13, 1919; leased to Hector McQuarrie, J.P., March 19, 1833; leased to Joseph Fraser, 1833; west half sold to Jonathan Chase; east half, Feb. 23, 1837, bought by Edward O'Brien for 12s.6d. per acre. Valuation — Thomas Cook, Peter Frank, George Simpson.
Lot 22	1804, Mary Fisher, widow, sold 450 acres to Thomas Medcalf of Niagara.
Lot 30	Dec. 4, 1846, north half, 100 acres, James Lawrence sold to John Harrigan.
Lot 35	1825, John and Mary Bowen (daughter of Frederick Post, a U.E. Loyalist) sold to John Cartwright.
Lots 27	and Lots 28, 29, Concession 2: 1797, 1000 acres granted to Samuel D. Reimer (Reimer) of New York City; Lots improved 1803.

CONCESSION 4

Lot 3	1816, leased Clergy Reserve to William Burkholder. John Burkholder went surety for him.
	1816, Crown Reserve leased to Benjamin Reynolds.
Lot 6	1807, leased to John Smith.
Lot 9	1821, lot Clergy Reserve, leased to Alexander McKechanie, Schoolmaster;
	1823, ¼ rear part sold by Peter Dygert to Jacob Shunk; 1832, Part of lot sold by Jacob Fisher to James Armour for £186, 5s.;
	1837, transferred to Jacob Shunk by John Cahoun.
	1847, east half sold to James Armour.
Lot 12	1803, leased to Peter Musselman.
Lot 13	1803, leased to John Smith; Lots 13 and 17 granted 1807 to John Cameron.
Lot 16	1806, leased to Henry Lines; sold by Robert Hutcheson, now in Ireland, to Arthur McNeil, gentleman; 1832, William Mathison asks for deed of East quarter.
Lot 19	and 23
	transferred from Sergeant John Coon to Samuel Street.
Lot 22	and 32 (central part) and Lot 19 (NE half) of Concession 5
	grant to Catharine Williams, daughter of James McNabb, UE.
Lot 22	and 22 of Concession 3
	1804, grant to Thomas Medcalf.
Lot 24	leased to Aquillat Bennett;
	east half: 1846, leased by Joel Kinnee to Thomas Watts
	west half: 1839, sold to Thomas Lyon; 1841, sold again; 1848, sold to Henry Sanders, blacksmith.
Lot 30	1832 George Thompson sold one quarter to George Peterman.
Lot 34	1797, grant to John Anderson.
Lot 35	1801, grant to Jennett Anderson.

CONCESSION 5

Lot 1	1797, grant to John McDougall.
Lot 2	1807 leased to James Brown, John Shunk surety.
Lot 8	1807, Crown Reserve leased to Joseph Misler.
Lot 9	1800, grant to Nicholas Miller.
Lot 13	1811, grant to Lucy Allen, wife of Ebenezer Allen.
Lot 17	(NE half) and Lots 35 (East quarter) Concession 6 and 30 (broken) of Concession 5
	1808, grant to John Crosson.
Lot 18	(West half) and 19
	1800, grant to George McBride.
Lot 20	1797, grant to John McDonald, a discharged soldier, 84th Reg.
Lot 21	1828, Archibald Macdonald wants to purchase east half;
	1844, sold by Archibald Cameron to Michael Cranney;
	1846, Front 20 acres: Archibald Cameron leases to Joseph Mathewson;
	1848, West half sold by Michael Cranney to Rev. Peter MacNaughton.
Lot 22	1799, grant to Thomas Knight.
Lot 24	1798, grant to Dorothy Porter, wife of George Porter.
Lot 26	grant to John Tenbroeck, UE.
	1831, sold by estate of Peter Smith, Kingston, to John and Robert D. Cartwright.
Lot 27	1805, sold by Elias Williams, Haldimand Township to Joseph J. Lossee.
Lot 28	1829, bought by Charles McKinnon.
	1859, John McNair sold 50 acres to Joseph Noble.

Lot 29	and Lot 30 1797, grant to Anna Devans.
Lot 31	1820, leased to Donald McDonald.
Lot 33	1798, grant to Margaret Anderson, Spinster, daughter of John Anderson.
Lot 34	1830, sold by Isaac Gordon to Isaac Putterbaugh.
Lot 35	1799, grant to Alexander Shaw, UE, Township of Friedrichsburg.

CONCESSION 6

Lot 2	1797, grant to Priscilla Reid.
Lot 3	1798, grant to Ashsah Souls, daughter of Anthony Hollingshead. 1846, purchase by James Brown.
Lot 9	1830, purchase by James Totten.
Lot 10	1796, grant to Garret Klingerlandt, the remainder of his military lands. 1819, leased to Alexander McKay.
Lot 13	1797, grant to John Size.
Lot 14	and Lot 15, 1799, grant to Thomas Barry.
Lot 16	1849, Northwest quarter, Clergy Reserve, sold to John McArthur by John McLean.
Lot 21	1816, grant to James Richardson, Lieutenant, in Provincial Marines.
Lot 22	1801, grant to Elizabeth Thompson, widow, of Township of Niagara.
Lot 23	1850, East 50 acres, purchased by Patrick O'Connor; Daniel McDougall bought of John Murphy
Lot 24	1830, patent fee paid by Eli Stanley; 1847, 50 acres sold by Bitsy Murphy to Pat. O'Connor.
Lot 29	Grant to Mary Bowen, wife of Peter Bowen, Friedrichsburg, but claim for Lot 35, Concession 1, to be surrendered.
Lot 30	1822, **lease** to Malcolm Wilkens of east half.
Lot 31	and Lot 34 1797, grant to John Wintermute.
Lot 32	1807, grant to Joseph Williams.
Lot 35	1801, west three-quarters, grant to Gerrard McNutt; Friedrichsburg.

CONCESSION 7

Lot 5	1802, grant to Augustus Jones of Saltfleet Township.
Lot 14	1794, also east half Lot 13, to Augustus Jones.
Lot 15	1798, grant to Ann Davis.
Lot 16	1830, patent Fee paid by John Murphy; 1846, property sold to Henry Kennie on Jan. 31 and resold to Michael Burkholder Feb. 3, 1846.
Lot 17	1843, William Marsh sold to James Thomson.
Lot 18	1803, grant to Samuel Backhouse, Quebec.
Lot 22	1799, north half grant to Samuel Sinclair.
Lot 23	Grant to Peter Kuhun.
Lot 24	1833, leased to William Mitchell.
Lot 30	1836, Rev. Mayerhoffer permitted to purchase at 30 s. an acre; fell behind with payments; 1838, grant to Henry James Crassett of 192 acres.
Lot 34	1836, James MacMurchy to buy Clergy Reserve.
Lot 35	Grant to Sarah Peterson of Friedrichsburg, daughter of James McNabb, UEL.

CONCESSION 8

Lot 2	1832, purchased by John Jefferson.
Lot 3	1803, 210 acres granted to Michael Kortz. Perigo to whom several grants of land were made; he lived in York and was a speculator.
Lot 8	1796, grant of 200 acres to complete grant to Mary Fisher of her 450 acres.

Lot 9	1796, request to purchase by Thomas Smith.
Lot 34	1819, grant to David Townsend Stevenson.

CONCESSION 9

Lot 1	and Lots 3, 4, 6 and Lots 3 and 4 (Concession 10) 1798, grant of 1,000 acres to James Ruggles.
Lot 2	1797, grant to John Sullivan, now in United States.
Lot 5	1829, Clergy Reserve; east half to James Farr and Andrew Rider.
Lot 11	1830, west half given to Richard Jeffery; 1836, east half given by James Farr to Elisha Farr.
Lot 13	1830, sold to Robert Burton. Robert King. No improvements on this Crown Reserve.
Lot 16	1829, bought by Thomas Smith; 1846, sold to John Wood; 1846, sold 30 acres to Elizabeth Smith.
Lot 17	1858, east half sold by John Wood to Thomas Playter.
Lot 18	1829, west part sold in 1845 by Donald McEachern to Roger MacEachern.
Lot 19	1836, Clergy Reserve, James McLean desires to purchase; Rev. Mayerhoffer claims it for a Rectory Endowment. Rev. Mayerhoffer ceased to be rector in 1849 and succeeded by Rev. Mr. Hill. Property leased for 21 years.
Lot 21	1830, assigned to Malcolm Bealton; leased to Alexander Ross; 1846, west half bought by James Moody from Alexander Ross; 1858, Alexander Ross bought 100 acres from Peter Wardlow.
Lot 23	1797, Grant to Jane Clark of Stamford, 300 acres.
Lot 28	1830, patent fee paid by Angus Cameron.
Lot 30	1829, request for purchase by William Herd.
Lot 32	and Lot 33 1802, grant of 400 acres to Samuel Sherwood, Township of Thurlow, County of Hastings.
Lot 34	1830, Given up to Isaac Hollingshead; 1831, purchased by Thomas Hill; 1837, lease of north half to George D. Howard; 1839, lease of north half to Nicholas Overling; 1845, south half, offer of purchase by John Walker.
Lot 35	1830, deed of partition between John S. Cartwright and Robert D. Cartwright to Robert A. Cartwright. 1843, sold to David McCutcheon, King Township.

CONCESSION 10

Lot 3	and Lot 4 (broken) 1833, sold by James Ruggles to Jane Weaver, 50 acres of original grant.
Lot 5	(broken) 1822, given by Elisha Small to Joseph Atwell.
Lot 9	1830, leased to Robert Hanstock; 1832, Timothy Kelly sold to Dickinson Fletcher.
Lot 10	1796, grant to William Dummer Powell; 1802, 40 acres leased to William Dummer Powell of Niagara Township.
Lot 11	(broken) 1804, grant to John Easter (and also Lots 32 and 33)
Lot 13	and Lots 14, 15 1798, grant to William Graham.
Lot 16	1800, Clergy Reserve leased to Charles McGuire; 1855, sold to Isaac Nattress.
Lot 17	and Lots 18, 19, 21, 22 and 23: 1798, grant of 800 acres to Margaret McGregor Armstrong, mother of James Roger Armstrong and Westropp Armstrong of Kingston; there was no deed. In 1828 above divided into thirds.

Lot 24	1835, Lease to Hector MacLean; 1848, East ½, sold by Thomas Steel to Isaac Devins.
Lot 25	and 26 and small portion of broken Lots 25, 26, 27 (Concession 11) 1800, grant to Walter Roe.
Lot 28	and Lot 29 (broken) 1800, grant to Walter Roe.
Lot 28	1850, Thomas McAllister appointed pathmaster but no one could tell him where he was to operate; 1852, William Graham owned lots in Vaughan but did not live there.
Lot 30	1833, leased to John Wilkie; 1835, Alfred Jeffrey to John Beatton; 1840, leased to Malcolm Boyd; 1848, John Bealton to Afred Jeffrey; 1851 offer to purchase by John Wilkie.
Lot 31	1809, grant to Eleanor Moore of Niagara, wife of Solomon Moore and daughter of Capt. Francis Stephenson.
Lot 32	1809, grant to Louise Stephenson daughter of Capt. Francis Stephenson.
Lot 34	1815, grant to Francis Hog Stephenson, son of Capt. F. Stephenson.
Lot 35	1817, grant to John Augustus Stephenson, son of Capt. F. Stephenson.

The assessment rolls for Somerset County in Pennsylvania relate to many persons who later settled in Vaughan Township:

Brothersvalley Township, Bedford County, 1772 (This township then included what is now Somerset County lying west of the Allegheny Mountains).
      Jacob Fisher, 200 acres (12 acres cleared)
      John Miller, 300 acres (10 acres cleared)

Turkeyfoot Township, 1774
      Frederick Keever (Keffer)
      John Miller
      Michael Keever (Keffer)
      Michael Miller

Brothersvalley Township, 1775
      Jacob Fisher
      John Miller
      Joseph Miller
      Michael Miller

Brothersvalley, Turkeyfoot, 1775
      Jacob Fisher
      John Miller
      Michael Miller
      Nicholas Miller
      Jacob Winger
      Peter Winger

Taxables in Turkeyfoot Township, 1776
      Martin Kefer (Keffer)
      Michael Kefer (Keffer)
      John Lowan (Lines)

Brothersvalley Township property holders, 1779
      Adam Hoover, 30 acres
      Casper Hoover, 250 acres

Jacob Keffer, 150 acres
Michael Keffer, 100 acres
Christian Miller
John Miller, 100 acres
Michael Miller, 100 acres
Nicholas Miller, 130 — 400 acres
John Tryer (Troyer), 250 acres
Michael Tryer Jr., 50 acres
Michael Tryer Sr., 100 acres
Peter Winger, 400 acres
Adam Keffer (non-resident), 200 acres
Martin Keever (Keffer), 50 acres
Michael Keever (Keffer), 50 acres

Brothersvalley Township, tax list, 1783
Philip Baker, 200 acres
Peter Coover (Cober), 200 acres
Jacob Fisher, 300 acres
Casper Hoover, 200 acres
John Hoover, 100 acres
Nicholas Miller, 100 acres
Jacob Smith, 100 acres
Jacob Snider, 50 acres
Christian Troyer, 150 acres
John Troyer, 150 acres
Michael Troyer Jr., 80 acres
Michael Troyer Sr., 150 acres
Non-Resident Nicholas Miller, 250 acres

Turkeyfoot Township, tax list, 1783
Martin Keever (Keffer), 150 acres
Michael Keever (Keffer), 150 acres

Quemahoning Township, tax list, 1783
Jacob Kiffer (Keffer), 50 acres
Godfrey (Gottlieb) Reman, 200 acres
Jacob Smith, 100 acres

Milford Township, tax list, 1783
Adam Keffer, 400 acres
Jacob Miller, 50 acres
John Miller

Taxables with number of persons in each family, 1784
Jacob Oper (Keffer), 7 whites
Peter Coover (Cober), 7 whites
Jacob Fisher, 10 whites

Taxables in Quehamhoning with number in each family, 1784
Jacob Keffer, 7
Godfrey Reamon, 7

Following Simcoe's proclamation of free grants of 200 acres which might be increased to 1,000, a steady stream of settlers began from the Colonies and continued until 1812. The first settlers, as we have seen, were Germans from Pennsylvania who located on Yonge Street. A few of them, like Jacob and John Fisher and Nicholas Cober, arrived early enough to receive Crown Grants; but most of the later immigrants had to buy their land from the original grantees, who in most cases were ex-army men or friends of Peter Russell. Among the first to sell their lands to these Germans were Richard Lippincott and Daniel Cozens. For instance, Lots 4 and 5, Conc. 2, were sold to Jacob Cummer; Lot 7, Conc. 2 to John Reaman; Lot 8, Conc. 2 to Ulrich Burkholder; Lots 3 and 4, Conc 2 to Jacob Fisher, Jr.: Lots 6 and 7, Conc. 3 to Jacob Fisher, Sr.; Lots 4 and 5, Conc. 4 to John Snider; Lot 7, Conc. 4 to John Smith and Lot 8, Conc. 4 to Jacob Shunk; Lot 10, Conc. 2 to John Reaman; Lot 11, Conc. 2 to Jonathan Baker; Lots 9 and 10, Conc. 3 to Michael Keffer; Lot 10, Conc. 4 to Peter Musselman; Lot 18, Conc. 2 to Michael Fisher; Lot 19, Conc. 2 to Peter Franks; Lot 17, Conc. 3 to Jacob Fisher Sr.; Lot 18, Conc. 3 to Michael Fisher; Lot 18, Conc. 4 to John Feightner.

Thus the southeast corner of Vaughan soon passed into the hands of settlers who intended to make homes for themselves. Not only did they buy land but, whenever possible, rented Clergy or Crown Reserve land, which they could do for twenty-one years. It should be noted that they chose land which was highly productive. They had no interest in the sandy northern sections of the township: these were left for later immigrants, less experienced in choosing good land. Closely-knit by intermarriage, the Germans were also held together by a progressive belief in co-operation. Besides, the group included black-smiths and carpenters, and each Pennsylvania Dutchman was handy with tools, and what he lacked he made himself.

It is a mistake to consider all Pennsylvania Germans to be Plain Folk, that is, Mennonites, Dunkards or Quakers. Many of them were Lutherans and, although possessing German names, not a few had a French Huguenot background. There were also Quaker and Puritan English amongst them. Basically, however, they shared the same religious beliefs. Consequently they worked together in those early days as brothers, not only from necessity but from a common background of religious and political persecution.

There must have been communication between Upper Canada and New York State, as Nicholas Miller, a millwright, was brought by the government from New York State to build some mills in York County. He erected in 1793 the County's first flour mill — an old-fashioned coffer mill on a very small scale. The next year, on Lot 33, Conc. 1 of Markham, he built a small grist mill; and also the first flour mill on the Humber.

John Lyons, who came to Canada from New York State in 1794, after living for a while in York, settled on Lot 32, Conc. 1, Markham. He later bought Lot 36, Conc. 1, Vaughan, on which he built a sawmill. Asa Johnson and his wife Hannah had a daughter, Sally, who married Nicholas Miller. Evidently the Johnsons came to Canada about the same time as Miller, since he is credited with a patent for land in 1796, the first year patents were issued.

The question is: Was there any connection between Nicholas

Miller and John Lyons, before they were asked by Simcoe to come from New York State to Canada, and the first families on Yonge Street such as the Cobers, Fishers, and Cummers? According to the tax lists in Somerset County, Pennsylvania, Nicholas Miller is listed as a taxpayer in 1775; as the owner of 400 acres in 1779; and as non-resident in 1783. John Lowan (Lines or Lyons) is listed in 1776. Mary Cober, a daughter of Nicholas Cober, who emigrated to Canada, married Henry Lyons as her first husband. Hence persons by that name lived in that locality. Jacob Fisher was taxed in 1772 for 200 acres, 12 cleared, and in 1783 for 300 acres. In 1784 there were 10 whites in his family. Peter Cober (father of Nicholas Cober) owned 200 acres in 1783. Other families following shortly after who settled in Vaughan were the Troyers, Keffers, Reamans, Bakers and Smiths, all from Somerset County.

It would look as if Nicholas Miller and John Lyons came to New York State and in some way Simcoe got in touch with them. Doubtless it was through them that the Fisher family heard of the quality of the land in York County and emigrated, and also relations such as the Cummers, who lived in Lancaster County.

Jacob Fisher petitioned the Governor on November 20, 1798, as follows: 'That your Petitioner came into this Province in 1795 bringing with him his sons and sons-in-law with their families and his own, amounting to 22 persons. That your Petitioner served as a corporal in the 1st Btn. of the 68 Regt. in the French War of 1756-1763 — that in 1763 the Indians took part of the Company's Books whereby your Petitioner lost his pay for upwards of two years — which he never received — that your Petitioner has 400 acres of land in this Province, yet as his family is large, he humbly hopes your Honour would be pleased to indulge him with such additional grant under the New Regulations as to your Honour may seem meet and your Petitioner in duty bound shall ever pray.' This request was granted at once 'in consideration of the long services and large family of the Petr. and also of his exemplary exertions as a farmer.' He was recommended for 400 additional acres.

Elizabeth, daughter of Jacob Fisher, married Jacob Kommer (Cummer), who came to Canada in 1796, locating on 300 acres of land at Willowdale. Eva, another daughter, married Nicholas Cober, and they came in 1796, settling on Lot 34, Conc. 1, Vaughan. On their tombstone in the Cober Burying Ground, north of Concord, is the inscription: 'Of the first settlers on Yonge Street, They were the fifth family.' Doubtless they came with the same party as the Cummers, because in both cases the records state that they came with the bride's parents. That would be in 1795.

Some further proof that some of the first settlers in York County were from New York State, though originally from Pennsylvania, is found in the statement that Isaac Devins, who came with Simcoe, had married Polly Chapman of Genesee, New York, and was said to be a brother-in-law of Nicholas Miller. This may explain why Chapmans were grantees of land.

Large grants of land were given to officers. Captain Daniel Cozens from New Jersey had raised a company of soldiers to fight against the rebels. When the latter won out, he suffered the loss of a large estate by confiscation. In compensation, when he came to Canada he was made a grant of 3,000 acres in Vaughan Township, and his sons Samuel and Shivers as well received grants. Opposite Captain Cozens was Captain Richard Lippincott, another New Jersey Loyalist who had taken a prominent part in the events of the war. He also received 3,000 acres. Neither Cozens nor Lippincott was a settler; they sold their property as soon as possible.

Two men who gave their names to lakes in that area were William Bond who in 1800 established a nursery garden in York containing valuable fruits, and gave his name to Bond Lake, and Colonel William Willcocks, who in 1802 was Judge of the Home District Court. The stream flowing out of Lake Willcocks makes the beginning of the east branch of the Humber River.

And now let us see the size and physical characteristics of Vaughan Township when the first settlers took up land. Vaughan Township consists of an area of 105 square miles, about 8¾ miles wide from north to south, thirteen miles long from east to west on the north boundary, and eleven miles long on the south. This irregular shape came from its position between two of the original Upper Canada survey lines — Yonge Street on the east and the western boundary of the 'Toronto Purchase' on the west. Vaughan has an area of 67,510 acres and ranks third in size among the townships of York County, being a few acres smaller than Markham.

The eleven concession lines run north and south from the York Township line to the King Township line except Concessions 9, 10, and 11, which are cut off on the south. The side roads, like the concessions, are a mile and a quarter apart, and the lots generally consist of 200 acres each.

The lots are numbered from south to north on the concessions and range from 1 to 35 except on Concession 1, which, because it was part of the original Yonge Street survey, is numbered from 26 to 60. The survey was commenced in 1795 by Surveyor Tredell but it was not completed until 1851; ten years afterward, the side-lines were re-surveyed. Owing to mistakes in the survey of the line in the southwestern corner of the province, considerable litigation was necessary before the boundary was rectified.

In general, Vaughan can be divided into two topographical areas; the northern half consists of an interlobal moraine generally lying more than 900 feet above sea level, and the southern half consists of a glacial till plain lying between 400 and 900 feet above sea level. The northern section has an irregular pattern and consists generally of sandy and gravelly materials. Small depressions, called kettles, are common, many of them permanent ponds varying in size from a fraction of an acre to two hundred acres in extent. Because of its sandy nature, the soil dries quickly and droughty conditions result. As a result pine and oak trees abound; hence the name Oak Ridges, which has been given to part of this area. The more level southern section has undulating to rolling surfaces and consists of deep beds of glacial deposits made up of clay, clay loam, and loam, with varying proportions of shale and limestone materials. This area holds water well. Overall, the land slopes gently from northeast to southwest. There are the deeply incised stream beds of the Don and Humber systems, but, in general, geographic features of the township provided few barriers either for transportation or settlement. Rainfall, although not unusually high, is remarkably uniform, seldom varying far from an average of 32 inches per year. The growing season lasts from mid-May to mid-September and averages 140 frost-free days per year.

The foregoing soil and weather conditions have made Vaughan outstanding as a farming area. Seldom, if ever, has there been a year when there was a complete crop failure. Of course, some years are better than others but, by and large, the farmer can always expect a fair return for his labour. Furthermore, these conditions contributed to make Vaughan an ideal location for the growth of the deciduous forest which, with the exception of the sandiest northern areas, covered Vaughan Township at the beginning of the pioneer era. This is actually what attracted the first Pennsylvania German settlers, because they judged land by two particulars: they considered that the land that grew the highest trees must be good, and they preferred soil with a limestone base on which the black walnut grew. The black walnut is found in this area and in western Ontario as far north as Guelph, and it was in these areas that the 'Pennsylvania Dutch' built their homes.

In 1798 an inspection was made of all the reserved lots in Vaughan Township and this included lots on Yonge Street. It gives a good picture of the kinds of trees on Concessions 1 and 2.

Concession	Lot	Remarks	Acres	Special Remarks
First	2	Maple, elm, ash, beech	212.1	
	5	Maple, elm, ash, beech	212.1	
	8	Maple, elm, large pine	212.1	
	11	Maple, elm, basswood	212.1	A creek on this lot
	15	Maple, elm, basswood	212.1	
	21	Mixed Temper, Good Land	212.1	A creek on this lot
	25	Mixed Temper, Good Land	212.1	
	28	Mixed Temper, some swamp	212.1	
	31	Maple, elm, basswood	212.1	
	34	Maple, elm, basswood	212.1	
Second	3	Maple, elm, basswood	202	
	6	Maple, elm, basswood	202	
	9	Maple, elm, some large pine	202	A spring on this lot
	12	Maple, elm, some large pine	202	
	16	Maple, elm, basswood	202	
	20	Maple, elm, pine	202	
	24	Maple, elm, beech, basswood	202	
	27	Maple, elm, broken land	202	
	30	Maple, elm, good land	202	
	33	Maple, elm, good land	202	
TOTALS	20		4141	

Geographically, Vaughan Township was well located for its development. First, the direct route between Lake Ontario and Georgian Bay passed through it. Second, it was close to the developing metropolitan centre of York (later Toronto).

Probably for centuries before the arrival of the French fur traders and missionaries, the Humber-Holland, Don-Holland, and Rouge-Holland systems had been used as trade and transportation routes by various Indian tribes. In addition, a walking route had been established which in general followed higher ground along the east bank of the Humber River, beginning and ending below the first rapids on the Humber and Holland Rivers. The importance of these 'Passages of Toronto,' as they were called, was recognized by the French who at various times had built forts and trading posts near the mouth of the Humber. Thus it was that when John Graves Simcoe decided that one of his roads should run north from York, he first experimented with the Humber Trail of the Indians, and then finding it not to his liking, ordered Yonge Street to be surveyed. This route and the distance from York — some twelve miles, a half-day's journey over the difficult roads of the time — gave Vaughan an edge in independent social and economic development over York and Scarborough Townships and, if it hadn't been for the Berczy settlers, over Markham Township as well.

The settlement of Vaughan cannot be separated from what took place in other sections of York; particularly Markham. There are examples of members of the same family of Freundschaft settling some in York, some in Markham, and some in Vaughan, at or about the same time. For instance, the Cobers, Keffers, and Bakers settled in Vaughan, the Hoovers, Heises, and Burkholders in Markham, and the Fishers, Cummers, and Millers in York. In many cases the families were related.

The question may very well be asked: How did these and other families in Pennsylvania, related and unrelated, learn about land being available in Upper Canada? The answer is that Governor Simcoe, having made up his mind on the need for capable settlers, recalled that as head of the Queen's Rangers during the Revolutionary War he had been quartered one winter in Philadelphia, and there had had a close-up view of the eastern counties of German town as farmed by the Palatinate and Swiss Germans. The result was that he determined to invite those who farmed there to come to Canada. He was also of the opinion that there was a large number of Loyalists in the States who would welcome an opportunity once more to live under the British flag.

To this end on February 7, 1792, Simcoe issued a proclamation which, among other things, offered 200 acres to each immigrant who could show that he was in a position to cultivate and improve the land. The grantee was obliged to clear five acres of land, to build a house, and to open a road across the front of his land one-quarter mile in length. Simcoe also advertised this offer in the Philadelphia newspapers, presumably to attract the attention of the German farmers in eastern Pennsylvania. Since a number of German farmers had settled in the Niagara district during the preceding dozen years, this offer was appreciated at its full value. When Simcoe was recalled in 1796 these terms were repealed; nevertheless, many immigrants had already taken advantage of them.

From 1796 to 1812 there was what might be called the 'First Great Migration.' There were several reasons for these settlers leaving communities and farms rather well developed in the United States to come into a country of virgin forest. Basically, most of them had a racial background of pioneering: they or their forebears had left Switzerland for the Rhine Palatinate, from there had migrated to America, and then had moved from one state to another or to different parts of the same state. They had acquired wealth. They had also acquired a number of sons for whom it was necessary to provide farms, and land by this time in Pennsylvania had risen in price. Add to this the disturbed condition of the country, and the fact that the Pennsylvania German, whether he had or had not fought in the Revolutionary War, was often considered *persona non grata*. Putting all these factors together, we may see that the prospect of free or inexpensive land in Upper Canada, with guaranteed freedom of religion, was most attractive. Pioneering in the new country was never a threat but a challenge.

Much has been made by historians of the harsh treatment the Loyalists suffered in the United States. Doubtless this was true of many, particularly those who had settled in New York State. The term Loyalist, however, has by implication been applied only to those of British background. Actually, British Loyalists did not come into Upper Canada in any great numbers, and many of those who did were attached to government or army services. As a group, the British preferred to migrate to the provinces of Nova Scotia and New Brunswick which had been partially settled. The real UEL in Upper Canada included Palatine and Swiss Germans, French Huguenots, and English Quakers and Puritans. These in turn divided into two classes: combatants, such as Lutheran and Reformed Church Germans, French Huguenots, and Puritan English; and non-combatants, such as Mennonites, Dunkards, and Quaker English.

Between 1763, when the Treaty of Paris gave permanent possession of Canada to England, and 1792, when Simcoe assumed responsibility for the newly created colony of Upper Canada, few changes occurred in the Vaughan Township area although decisions were made elsewhere which shaped its future development. In the decade before Simcoe took office, the American Revolution and the immigration of the Royalists had brought the first wave of settlers to the shores of Lake Ontario. Settlements were established at either end of the lake. The government was anxious to organize these districts and to connect them by further settlements along the shore. Both it and the fur traders alike also were anxious to develop trade with the interior. As a preliminary to both goals, the various portages to Lake Simcoe were examined in order to determine the one best suited for improvement. The Toronto Carrying Place proved not only to be the most direct, but to have as well the advantage of a good anchorage nearby.

As a first step towards the establishment of a settlement, the government purchased from the Mississauga Indians a tract containing about a third of York County for £1,700 in cash and goods; the treaty was signed at the Quinté Carrying Place on September 23, 1787. (The boundaries were defined and certain defects in the original purchase corrected in a subsequent agreement signed with the Mississaugas at the Credit River in 1805.) On July 7, 1788, Alexander Aitkin at Kingston was instructed to go to Toronto and run east and west boundaries of the purchase. On September 15, Aitkin wrote a letter to the surveyor-general of Quebec, in which he stated:

Sir, agreeable to your instructions of the 7th of July last which I received the 25th of the same month, I hired a party with all possible dispatch and embarked on board the Seneca for Toronto where I landed the first of August. For two or three days after our landing we were employed in building a kind of store house to preserve the Indian presents as well as my own provisions from the rain and bad weather. I then desired Mr. Lines, the Interpreter, to signify to the Indian Chief then on the spot my intention of beginning to survey the land purchased from them last year by Sir John Johnson and pointed out to him where I was to begin. I requested him to go with me to the spot along with Mr. Lines, which he did, but instead of going to the lower end of the Beach which forms the Harbour he brought me to the River called on the plan Nechengquakekonk which is upwards of three miles nearer the Old Fort than the place you mention in your instructions. He insisted that they had sold the land no further so that to prevent disputes I had to put it off for some days longer until a few more of the Chiefs came in, when Mr. Lines settled with them that I was to begin my Survey at the west end of the high lands which I did on the 11th day of August having lost a week of the finest weather we had during my stay in Toronto.

Matters being settled with the Indians I continued my survey westward until I came to the Toronto River which the Indians looked upon to be the west boundary of the purchase until Col. Butler got them prevailed upon to give up the River Tobicoke but no further nor would they on any account suffer me to cross the River with the boundary line between them and the Government, although I had them brought twice to the spot they told us they did not look upon as a straight line as a boundary, that the creek they said was Boundary could not be altered or moved but that a line in a few years unless always cut open and frequented would soon grow up with brush and trees.

Having finished the Survey of the Front I then began the West Boundary line aforementioned which I ran perpendicular to the Front about two miles and three quarters until I fell in with the creek which I found with the course I then ran I would cross and have considerably to the Right. I then was obliged to stop rather than run the risk of having any disputes with the Indian Chief from whom the land was purchased and who was that morning along the line and had cautioned me against crossing it openly as Col. Butler and Mr. Lines were both gone and I left without anyone to settle any disputes that might arise between me and the Indians. [This Western boundary begun by Aitken is still preserved as the western boundary of York County and Vaughan Township.] ... After the land was purchased from the Indians from Toronto to Pemitescuteang (Port Hope) I thought it would be unnecessary to run the Boundary ...

A council with the Indians had been held in Toronto in 1788 for the purchase of lands between Toronto and the Bay of Quinte. In May 1793 Simcoe visited the harbour of Toronto and became enthusiastic about its possibilities, and in July of the same year he returned to the bay with a party of Queen's Rangers. The rest of that summer was spent in surveying an unnamed road which he intended to build. Having made up his mind that roads were essential as much for settlement as for defence, the Governor decided that there should be one from York to Penetanguishene and so, being a 'do-it-yourself' man, on Wednesday, September 25, 1793, accompanied by four officers and a dozen soldiers and some Indians, he set out to visit Lake Huron.

Simcoe's interests were paralleled by those of the North-West Fur Trading Company, an organization that was quite influential in the development of the Toronto area. Organized in 1787 by Montreal Scottish and French merchants and fur traders as a rival to the Hudson's Bay Company, it looked upon Toronto as a base for its operations. It used the Humber Trail as a trade route to the northwest until Yonge Street was opened up. From time to time it promised financial support for the improvement of Yonge Street, but such support did not materialize. In 1821 the North-West Company amalgamated with the Hudson's Bay Company and ceased to have any interest in this area.

Simcoe, with his handful of soldiers and Indians, found that the Humber Trail did not meet the requirements of a military road as he had anticipated. For that reason he selected a route which went across country and which, upon his return to York, he named Yonge Street. That return trip was one of considerable hardship, with food in short supply. Alex D. Bruce gives a story of the expedition told him by his grandmother, Mrs. John Dickson of Dickson's Hill, Markham Township:

When a girl in her teens, Mrs. Dickson made the acquaintance of a Mrs. Miller (wife of Nicholas Miller, the first settler on Lot 34, Yonge Street). Mrs. Miller claimed to be the first white woman on Yonge Street; and related how she and her husband began life on their land in the spring of 1793; how they commenced housekeeping in a wigwam; how they planted potatoes, this being their first venture in the cultivation of their farm. Then began the work of literally hewing a farm out of the wilderness. As the felling of trees progressed, they began to make preparations for building a house. But having no neighbors, they expected to raise the house without assistance; consequently, selected timbers that they would be able to handle. The clearing expanded; the potatoes grew; and the summer had turned to fall when one day unexpected visitors arrived.

The visitors were Governor Simcoe and his company who were on their return journey from Penetanguishene and Lake Simcoe: an exploratory journey, preparatory to making the survey of Yonge Street. Simcoe and his men were hungry, having been on short rations. Mrs. Miller had not much with which to feed so large a company, but she had an abundance of potatoes ...

The Governor made particular enquiries concerning the progress that the Millers were making. Upon learning that they had logs prepared, Simcoe ordered his men to 'raise' them; and this was completed in quick time. Mrs. Miller's one regret was that, had they known that they were to have such a strong force at their house raising, they would have selected heavier timbers and would have had a better house.

This story is substantially the same as Mrs. Simcoe relates in her diary for September 25, 1793.

Having determined where the transportation route was to be located, Simcoe's next step was to have it and the townships adjacent to it surveyed so that settlers might be encouraged to take up land.

Since Simcoe never considered himself bound by any directions from Lord Dorchester, the governor of Canada, and was sufficient of a pragmatist to disregard instructions concerning Crown and Clergy Reserves, he made his own rules regarding settlement. In a letter to Henry Dundas he stated his views:

Another exception was thought proper to make on the military communications; as it is intended that they shall be carried on, in as straight a line as possible. It was determined that such a line should divide the several Townships, and for the speedy settlement of the County, and the future maintenance of the road that no person should be allowed a Lot thereon who was not a bona fide settler, and that the Reserves which would have fallen in this line agreeable to the general plan, should be distributed among the rear concessions.

If these suggestions had been acted upon, the roads of York County and Vaughan Township would have benefited greatly. But Simcoe's successor in 1796, Peter Russell, an Irishman who had been secretary to General Clinton in the Revolutionary War, handed out grants to those who never had any intention of being real settlers or of developing the lots given to them.

Augustus Jones was the surveyor Simcoe employed. As survey-general for the government, he had made the first complete survey of the town of Niagara and its division into lots, which had been adopted on June 24, 1791. He had married the daughter of a Chippewa chief and became the father of Rev. Peter Jones, Chief of the Mississaugas. He had also laid out the townsite of York. In January 1794 he returned to York and, with the aid of the Queen's Rangers, began to survey the road to Lake Huron. When this was completed on March 8, he proceeded during the rest of 1794 to draw up plans for future townships. On December 14 he was ordered to appear before Governor Simcoe so that the latter might give names to the new townships.

In granting all lots on Yonge Street to settlers, Simcoe showed his common sense and also his initiative and courage in interpreting the Constitutional Act which set aside 'a permanent appropriation of Lands ... for the Support and Maintenance of a Protestant Clergy,' the amount to be equal in value to one seventh of lands granted in every township. In addition an equal amount of land was designated as a source of revenue for the government, making it independent of the financial control of the Provincial Assembly. The Crown and Clergy lands were to be reserved in a pattern in such a manner that with the settlement of the townships they would increase in value as the neighbouring farms were cleared. This arrangement for parcelling out the Crown and Clergy Reserves was a major cause of dissatisfaction among the settlers. Not only was the building of roads hindered; these patches of undeveloped land also harboured wild animals which were a menace to the settlers' livestock. In fact, they were one of the main causes for the Rebellion of 1837-8.

Augustus Jones may have laid out Yonge Street but it was Berczy who, with the settlers he had brought from Hamburg, Germany, to Canada by way of the Pulteney settlement in New York State, hewed out a road to the southern part of Markham. The Berczy settlers

have always loomed large in the history of York County, partly because
they came as a group and partly because they were the first persons to
locate in that county of whom we have any records. It has been
suggested that Simcoe hoped to use them originally to build his
parliament buildings, since they were mostly artisans, but was not able
to go ahead with his building when they arrived, and so they were taken
to Markham and settled on the banks of the Don River. About
Christmas 1794, Berczy was promised some 64,000 acres, and the
inducements held out to his settlers were quite generous. But he could
not sell the land, and his settlers, little interested in farming, refused to
stay and drifted back to York. Only a few, such as Eckhardt (who had
long been established in Pennsylvania), Quantz (a veteran soldier of a
Hessian Regiment), Sommerfeldt, Pingle, Stiver, Lunau, and Helmke,
remained. (There is also an Archives record which states that instead of
there being sixty-four families, actually there were only thirty-three.)

Whatever the circumstances, a settlement came into being known
as German Mills, located on Lot 4 in Concession 3, Markham Township,
where a sawmill, a flour mill, a distillery, a brewery, a malt house, a
blacksmith shop, and cooper shop were built. Unfortunately there was
not enough water on the branch of the Don River to create power for
the projected industries and after several sales the mills were finally
closed. Berczy, because of financial losses and disappointments, left and
settled in Montreal, and eventually went to New York, where he died in
1813. His son, William Bent Berczy, was later given a grant of 2,400
acres, and was postmaster of Toronto from 1840 to 1852.

Another group of settlers subsidized by the British government
has received much more attention than the results warrant. There is no
doubt that they were a colourful group but entirely unsuited as pioneer
settlers. They were known as Comte de Puisaye's Windham Emigrés,
and were refugees from the French Revolution. As early as 1792, the
personal friendship of William Pitt, the English prime minister, with
Comte de Puisaye had brought about consideration of resettling the
Comte and some forty others in Canada. The British government
proposed to furnish the émigrés with land and support them for three
years; the cost of the undertaking was to be deducted from those
moneys already being paid to support émigré noblemen in England.
When the matter was brought to Simcoe's attention, he was in favour of
it, as he thought they would support the British cause in Canada against
the United States. Included in the party there were some half dozen
who remained as settlers: Comte de Chalus, Laurent Quetton St.
George, Francois Renoult, Julian Lebugle, Jacques Marchand, and
Michel Saigon. In all, twelve of the émigrés qualified for patents,
although it was not until 1820 that some of them were granted. De
Puisaye was granted 5,000 acres, but a residence of seven years was
required before the deeds were final.

The French were located at Oak Ridges, just where the four
townships of King, Whitchurch, Vaughan, and Markham come together.
For a little while counts, viscounts, and chevaliers began roughing it in

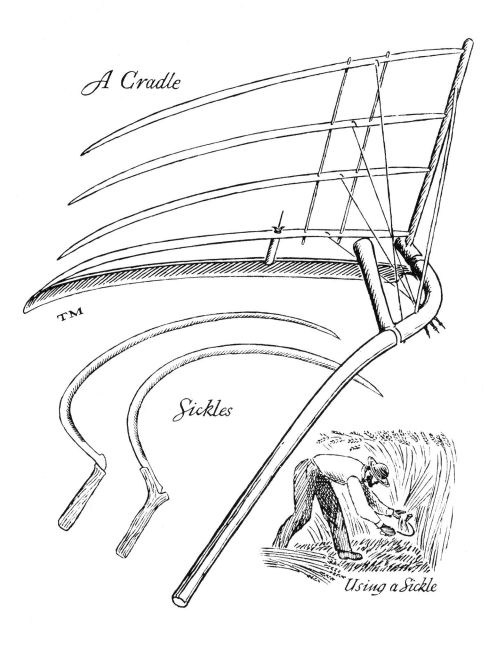

A Cradle

TM

Sickles

Using a Sickle

Using a Flail

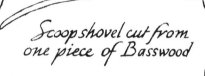

Scoop shovel cut from
one piece of Basswood

Forks **made** of Ash

A Flail

the bush. Occasionally they went down to York to add a special lustre to the balls given by the governor or other officials and it is on record that the jewels of one aristocratic lady, Madame la Comtesse de Chalus, created a great sensation. Although the Upper Canada government continued to supply them with the necessities of life, and de Puisaye sent seed, fruit trees, cattle and oxen, their inexperience counteracted this assistance and before long most of them left the farms and entered trade. De Puisaye himself made a survey of Windham in 1799 and left for Niagara, and then England, in 1803. When Louis XVIII gained the throne in 1815, most of the French settlers returned to France, where they were suitably rewarded for their loyalty. All that remained of the settlement on Yonge Street were a few dilapidated cabins.

One member of the group, Quetton St. George, was an exception. He became the first successful merchandiser in York County. From an Indian trading post at Orillia, he developed six depots on the Great Lakes. His store at the corner of King and Frederick Streets in York, built of red brick and with a tin roof, became the pride of the town. In 1805 Quetton St. George stocked everything in his 'Emporium' from thimbles and castor oil for housewives to flowered waistcoats and cognac for the gentry. In 1815 he retired to France and was made a chevalier at the French Court. His son afterwards came to York County and resided at his estate, Glen Lonely, on upper Yonge Street until his death in 1897. His three-story French chateau was a show place at Wilcocks Lake.

In 1797 the Assessors found the following persons though, in all probability they did not discover all the squatters:

In King Township: 5 men, 5 women, 20 children, a total of 30.
In Markham: 44 men, 30 women, 72 children, a total of 146.
On Yonge Street: 13 men, 9 women, 35 children, a total of 57.
In Vaughan: 19 men, 17 women, 67 children, a total of 103.
In Whitchurch: 15 men, 7 women, 22 children, a total of 44.

Two items indicate that there were settlers in the Yonge Street area earlier than we have records for. The first of these items is an advertisement in the June 8, 1793, issue of the *Upper Canada Gazette* (established that April):

For lease, a farm on Yonge Street with team, cows, hogs, geese, poultry, farming utensils — six acres and five acres, put in with wheat, timothy, and red clover; four acres of timothy and red clover one year old; one wheat stubble and potatoes; rest suitable for oats, potatoes, etc.

The other item is dated at Niagara, November 10, 1794, and occurs in a letter of Simcoe to the Duke of Portland.

The trader who lives at Matchadosh has had cattle driven to him this spring from York in six days and nearly half the road on Yonge Street is allotted to settlers. [The road was only put through on March 8, 1794.]

The first regular mail from Lower Canada reached York in January, 1808.

On April 27, 1813, 1,600 Americans under Generals Dearborn and Pike swooped down upon the little town of York and effected a landing to the west. They were pressing forward to drive out the defenders of the fort (which lay between their beachhead and the town) when the magazine suddenly exploded and a number of men on both sides were killed and wounded. Among the latter was General Pike, who died on shipboard a few hours later. The invaders pressed on to capture York and burned all the public buildings. When they were on the point of setting fire to the Parliament Buildings, it is said, they found above the Speaker's chair what they took to be a human scalp, but this startling prize, according to the legend, turned out to be only a periwig, or official peruke, left behind by its owner. The Americans had counted on those who had migrated from the United States in the preceding years to rally to their assistance in the War of 1812. The British, too, were apprehensive. However, the contrary was true and many of the early settlers rallied to the support of the Canadians during the War of 1812-15, and left the care of their farms to the women. Indeed, it is reported that Sir Isaac Brock's last words when he was struck down in battle against the Americans were addressed to these men: 'Push on, brave York Volunteers.'

In the *History of the Township of Vaughan* (County of York Book 1, 1885) we have additional information, particularly about mills:

Several patentees are French loyalist refugees who settled in the Oak Ridges region. A notable name is that of Captain Richard Lippincott, one of the United Empire Loyalists who attained considerable notoriety during the American War. He was a native of New Jersey and a Captain in the Loyalist army. Joshua Huddy, who held the same rank in the patriot forces, having been made prisoner of war, was entrusted to Lippincott's charge until an exchange of prisoners could be effected. A relative of Lippincott's named Philip White, a loyalist like himself, had fallen into the hands of the patriots and been cut down while attempting to make his escape. In retaliation Captain Lippincott, acting without any recognized authority, hanged Huddy on April 12, 1782, leaving his body suspended in the air with the following paper fastened on his breast: 'We, the Refugees, having long with grief beheld the cruel murders of our brethren, and finding nothing but such measures carrying into execution, therefore determined not to suffer without taking vengeance for the numerous cruelties, and thus begin, having made use of Captain Huddy as the first object to present to your view; and further determine to hang man for man while there is a Refugee existing. Up goes Huddy for Philip White.

This unjustifiable act — for killing of a prisoner attempting to escape was obviously no provocation for the deed — resulted in a demand by Washington for Lippincott's surrender, which was refused. Lippincott at the close of the war obtained a compensation for his dubious 'services,' three thousand acres of land, a large portion being in Vaughan. His only child, Esther Borden, married George Taylor Denison of Toronto. Lippincott died in Toronto in 1826, in his 82nd year.

Another of the early grantees, Captain Daniel Cozens, was also a New Jersey loyalist. He raised at his own cost, a company of soldiers, and at the close of the war his large estates in New Jersey were confiscated. He received from the Crown grants amounting to 3,000 acres as compensation for his losses. Captain Cozens is said to have built the first house in the Town of York. He died in 1801 near Philadelphia.

The first saw mill in Vaughan was built in 1801 for John Lyons, by Jeremiah Atkinson. John Lyons came to Canada from New York State in 1794, and after living for a while in York, settled on Lot 32, Concession 1, in Markham. The mill was built on the main branch of the Don where it crosses Yonge Street. In 1802 he constructed a small grist mill with a dam over 200' long and 10' in height. The pond was used to conceal articles taken from the Government warehouse in York at the time the Americans were in possession of the town during the War of 1812. The invaders generously presented the settlers with a quantity of agricultural implements belonging to the Canadian Government, and when they left a search was made. Many residents in this locality consigned their share of the plunder in the waters of Lyons' Mill Pond for safe-keeping. John Lyons died in 1814, and his mills and other real estate were purchased by Wm. Purdy, who added many improvements. His sons, in connection with their cousin, William Wright, built a tannery and grist mill. The Lyons Mill was afterwards used as a carding and fulling mill. A fire in 1828 consumed the new flour mill built by Purdy, and he sold the whole property to Thorne & Parsons. This firm in the year 1830, built a new flour mill on a large scale, and also a tannery, and for many years afterwards a large business was done, the locality being named 'Thornhill' in honour of the senior partner of the firm. Mr. Thorne failed in business in 1847, in consequence of heavy losses sustained on flour shipped to England, and shortly afterwards committed suicide. During the period of his prosperity he had added several other branches to his extensive business. After his failure the property fell into the hands of David Macdougall & Co. They were unfortunate; the principal buildings being destroyed by successive fires.

In 1820 Henry White built a distillery farther up the stream. On Lot 34, Concession 1, Nicholas Cober, a German, built a saw mill in 1825, which was destroyed by an incendiary fire five years later, being rebuilt the following year. In 1835 it was bought by John Barwick, who ran it for many years, and subsequently sold to George Wright. On Lot 36 in the same Concession, Barnabas Lyons, a son of John Lyons, previously mentioned, built a saw mill in the year 1830, which was worked for about thirty years. Hiram Dexter built a saw mill on Lot 37, in the year 1836, which was in operation for many years. In 1830 John Dexter put up a saw mill on the next lot, which was in use until about 1870. At this point the stream divides, the west branch passing the village of Carrville and Patterson's Agricultural Implement Factory. On Lot 16, Concession 2, now Carrville, Thomas Cook built a saw mill in 1850, which was worked for upwards of 30 years until the supply of logs failed. On Lot 16, Concession 2, Carrville, Michael Fisher built a saw mill in 1820, and the year following put up a grist mill [which was in operation until destroyed by fire November 16, 1933. The owner then was Ross Bowes, formerly run by Anthony Wilson, George Kirby and Thomas Cook respectively].

The small village of Patterson is situated on Lot 21, Concession 2, where in 1854 Messrs. Patterson commenced operations by the construction of a saw mill, afterwards establishing an extensive farm implement manufactory. On Lot 41 in the same Concession a saw mill was built by Reuben Burr in the year 1828, which was worked for about 20 years. Mr. Burr was an excellent mechanic, and constructed the first fanning mill in use north of Toronto. Rowland Burr, his son, was one of the most noted mill and factory builders in the early days. He put up a flour mill, known as the Greenfield Mill, on Lot 41, which was leased to Mr. Shephard and was destroyed by fire about the year 1840. C.E. Lawrence built a saw mill on Lot 42 in 1834, and six years afterwards built a carding and fulling mill and woollen factory, which he worked for many years, until his death, after which it changed hands frequently. On Lot 43 James Lymburner built a small log grist mill in 1811, which was afterwards owned by John Atkinson, who about 1840 put up a new grist mill at a cost of about £1,000. His property was later purchased by Edward Hawke of Toronto. A double-geared saw mill was erected on Lots 45 and 46 by James Playter in 1848. Higher up on the same branch of the stream, stood a distillery built by James McDavids in 1844. A saw mill was built by John Langstaff in 1847, which was the nucleus of various other industries dependent on the same water-power, including a foundry and edge tool factory. Mr. Langstaff also had an implement factory on another small branch of the Don in the immediate neighbourhood. This was constructed in 1850, a steel file factory being afterwards added.

On Lot 50, Concession 1, a saw mill was built in 1842 by a man named Heslop and worked for many years. Peter Frank put up a saw mill on Lot 25 in the 2nd Concession, near Patterson, which was used for about twenty years. In all, there have been first to last twelve saw mills, seven grist mills and three distilleries, built on the Don and its tributaries in Vaughan Township.

John Goesman's report of 1825 shows the following mills active at that date:

Purdy's grist mill — Lot 32, Concession 1, Thornhill
Atkinson's grist mill — Lot 43, Concession 1
Atkinson's sawmill — Lot 43, Concession 1
Reuben Burr's sawmill — Lot 41, Concession 1
Michael Fisher's sawmill — Lot 17, Concession 2
Turcotte Thesser's sawmill — Lot 12, Concession 3
David Park's sawmill — Lot 18, Concession 4
John Smith's sawmill — Lot 1, Concession 5

The first real manufacturing firm in Vaughan was probably Thorpe and Halfield's Fanning Mill Manufacturing which was operating on Yonge Street in 1828.

On the Humber, in the vicinity of Burwick (Woodbridge), a sawmill was built by John Brown in the early 1800s. Rowland Burr, the founder of the village, built a flour mill in 1837, and later a sawmill and woollen mill. Wallace Bros. erected a flour mill in 1877 near what had been John Brown's mill south of No. 7 Highway. Farther up the stream, still in the Woodbridge area, Samuel Smith built a sawmill. John Smith, his father, built a grist and sawmill at Pine Grove in 1828. Cockburn Bros. had a sawmill on the East Branch of the Humber in 1860, and at Elders' Mills on the West Branch, James Thomson built a sawmill, grist mill, and carding mill around 1850. John Klein operated a flour mill in Kleinburg about 1847 and sold it to H.S. Howland in 1852. Many more smaller mills were built along the Humber in Vaughan Township, adding a great deal to the convenience and prosperity of the settlers.

How did these pioneers go about building a mill? George Snider has the original handwritten and signed article of agreement by which John Nicholas Klein commissioned Ansel D. Melvin to build a sawmill on the big branch of the Humber on the east half of Lot 12, Concession 8 of Vaughan in 1837. It reads:

Article of agreement made and fully agreed upon the 13th day of February in the year of our Lord one thousand and eight hundred and thirty seven, between John Nicholas Kline, of the Township of Vaughan in the County of York, Home District and Province of Upper Canada, Yeoman of the one part, and Ansel D. Melvin of the Township of King, County and Province of aforesaid Yeoman of the other part, to wit:

The said Ansel D. Melvin for the consideration hereafter mentioned doth for himself, his executors and administrators covenant, promise and agree to and with the said John Nicholas Kline, his executors and administrators and assigns, that he, the said Ansel D. Melvin shall and will within the expanse of one year and six mos. next after the date here of in good and workman like manner will substantially erect, build set up and finish one sawmill on the east half of L. no 12 in the eighth Concession of Vaughan afforesaid, on the big branch of the Humber River, the spot to be pointed out by the said John Nicholas Kline or his executors, administrators or assigns, the mill to be fifty feet long and 24 twenty four feet broad, he, the said Ansel D. Melvin agrees to chop down and hew all the timber for said mill for the sum of 12 10 twelve pounds and ten shillings the one third part of which to be paid in cash when the said timber is finished and the other two thirds to be mentioned hereafter. and the said Ansel D. Melvin further agrees to frame and put up the mill and make the running gears or millright work and all the work belonging to a good and compleat sawmill for the sum of 50 fifty pounds the one third of which is also to be paid in cash so soon as the said mill shall be finished and proven to be done in a good and workmanlike manner and if any difficulty should arise between the two parties, respecting the workmanship of any part of said contract; the said difficulty to be settled by arbitration chosen by the parties, the other two-thirds of the above 50 pounds the payment of which to be accounted for here after; and the said Ansel D. Melvin also agrees to make the mill pond for to contain the water which is to drive or feed saw mill which pond is to be six rods broad and ten rods long, the embankments to be sufficiently strong to contain the water and to be about six feet or upward height the expense of this to be twenty one pounds 21 " and the said Ansel D. Melvin further agrees to make an embankment from the upper part of said pond the height of thirty rods to be high enough to correspond with the bank of the said pond and to be six feet broad at the bottom and eighteen at the top to be sufficiently strong also in the embankments to contain the water for the sum of 18 15 " " The one third of the above sums to be paid, so soon as the respective parts of the work is done which amounts to thirty four pounds one shilling and 8 pence as aforesaid (or mentioned) and the remaining two thirds which amounts to sixty pounds three shillings and four pence to be paid as follows; That is to say sixty two pounds ten shillings in Land at twelve shillings and six pence per acre, it being one half of Lot no 8 in the 12 Concession of the Township of Innisfil, County of Simcoe and the remainder of said two thirds which is five pounds thirteen shillings and four pence to be paid in cash when the work is compleated.

And he the said Ansel D. Melvin is to find his Boarding for him and his hands whilst doing the above mentioned work and the said Kline is to furnish all the necessary irons, sawed lumber, spikes, nails &c.

Sealed and delivered in
presents of

John N. Klein
Ansel D. Melvin

Census and assessment figures of the period 1801-17 demonstrate the slow but steady growth of the Vaughan settlement.

Population

Date	Men over 16	Women over 16	Male Children	Female Children	Total
1801	19	17	6	7	103
1805	52	66	39	46	203
1809	75	60	99	99	333
1817	132	107	183	149	510

Property Assessed

Date	Acres Cult.	Taxable Houses	Grist Mills	Saw Mills	Horses	Oxen	Milk Cows	Total Value
1803	450	4	0	0	20	40	63	—
1805	644	4	0	0	32	35	88	£2,280.6.0.
1812	1,990	27	2	2	79	83	215	£8,788.12.0.
1815	2,296	27	2	2	96	62	214	£9,167.8.0.
1817	2,577	33	2	2	103	51	165	£11,009.4.0.

The above figures must be accepted with reservation. Certainly there were more grist and saw mills and if their numbers cannot be relied upon, the other figures could be far from correct. However, they do give some picture of the settlement during those years. Figures in the next table do not agree with these, nor in fact do the figures in the first of these tables add up to the totals given in all cases; but in each case the figures come from the Provincial Secretary's papers in the Public Archives of Canada.

Population and property assessed, 1817–25

Year	1817	1818	1819	1820	1821	1822	1824	1825
Population	570	573	676	759	728	796	870	947
Land uncult.	20,636	20,267	21,700	17,731	17,683	17,698	21,538	21,254
Land cult.	2,577	2,909	3,094	3,171	3,253	3,354	3,824	4,090
Taxable houses	33	40	47	52	52	58	64	70
Grist Mills	2	2	2	2	2	2	2	2
Sawmills	3	3	5	5	5	5	4	6
Horses 3 yrs. up	103	105	114	124	135	137	143	149
Oxen 4 yrs. up	51	98	100	95	110	132	165	195
Milk cows	165	267	299	324	335	356	396	431
Assessed Value	£11,009	£11,648	£13,085	£11,939	£11,857	£12,440	£14,088	£15,206

The population growth of Vaughan Township was slow between the years 1817 and 1825 on the basis of these official figures. However, as in the earlier period, we know from local historians that grist and saw mills existed in far greater numbers than here listed. This casts doubt on all the figures.

There are various reasons advanced to explain a relatively slow growth of population in Vaughan Township. Absentee owners must take some of the blame. More important were the sections set aside as Crown Lands and Clergy Reserves which provided no taxes for the building of roads and were not available for purchase until the 1820s, when immigration increased from Britain. There was also the competition from neighbouring areas. On October 28, 1818, the government purchased from the Mississauga Indians an area of 648,000 acres for the sum of £8,500. Included in this area were Toronto Gore, Albion, Chinquacousy, and Caledon Townships, all of which lay just west of Vaughan Township and York County. When the first three of these townships were surveyed in 1819, settlers moved in quickly to pick up land which was cheaper than that available in Vaughan and just as accessible to York. In point of fact settlers did not take up land in Vaughan in any numbers until the Mississauga Tract was all taken up.

Beginning about 1814, land in the eastern part of the township began to increase in value. For instance, Lot 26, Conc. 1 on Yonge Street, which Jacob Fisher, Jr., had acquired as a grant in 1798, was sold the following year to Ephraim Payson when the Fishers moved farther back in Vaughan. In 1814 Payson sold the north half to Moses White for £300, and in 1819 the south half to Moses' brother, Isaac White, for £500, a total of £800 for the 210 acres. In like manner, Robert Marsh, who acquired Lot 32 on Yonge Street by grant, sold it at once to James McGill for £1,824.10.0. The price was determined by the fact the property contained a mill site which eventually became known as William Purdy's Mills.

Capital was coming into the area from Britain and the United States and the site of Thornhill (Lots 30 and 31, Conc. 1) was a favourite stopping place for travellers between York and points farther north. As a result, Lot 30, granted to Daniel Soules in 1805, was divided into lots in 1816 and sold to newcomers who put up two shops in 1817. One of the shops closed in 1818, however, and the other in 1820. It was not until about 1830 that new shops were started and this community began to enjoy a steady growth.

Lot 30, originally granted to John Wilson, Sr., in 1810, was sold in 1811 for £300 to Stilwell Wilson. It was bought in 1822 by Hon. William Allan and broken into lots in 1824. These were quickly sold and resold to such persons as John McGill and D'Arcy Boulton.

In 1820 two businessmen from Dorsetshire, Mr. Parsons and Mr. Thorne, along with persons from upper-class English families, settled along Yonge Street and by 1828 had established prosperous businesses at 'Thorne Hill', a little village. It soon increased in importance. In 1825, an irregular covered-wagon stage service from York to Georgina Township was inaugurated by Louis Bapp, and Thornhill became a stopping place.

The coming of such well-to-do British families as the Thornes, Parsons, Grappers, and O'Briens (who left diaries) and the Pagets crested an entirely new class of settler. They were friends of the ruling families such as the Strachans and built imposing houses and looked down their noses at the original settlers whom they called 'Americans.' In the O'Brien diaries there is a description of a visit to York:

Mary S and I drove to York — had a pleasant drive, did shopping, but were disappointed of our visits in lieu of which we were amused by the parties at the Inn, some with the appearance of gentlemen, others that of farmers strangely mingled together, as it seemed by politics, which they were discussing freely before us in terms too enigmatical for us to understand: — It seemed that they were all somehow connected with the *house* either as members or informants, I would not make out which, probably both ... Mr. Thorne says he never has seen so ill-qualified an assembly before.

Another remark from the same source: 'Today we had the benefit of attending regular public worship at the school house at Thornhill but I was sorry to see that the aristocracy and their dependents formed the majority of the congregation.'

Isaac Fidler in his *Observations ... on the United States and Canada* gives the situation from the standpoint of the original settlers:

Our landlady was a widow and had come originally from New York. She was one of the United States Loyalists [probably Mrs. Munshaw, N½ Lot 27, Conc. 1] and the second or third person who settled at Thornhill. This was at a time when Yonge Street, at the most a horse-path, was their only road. At that period their wheat had to be carried through forests, or by water, fifty or sixty miles [obviously an exaggeration] before it could be converted into flour; and letters might remain for six months in the Post Office at York, before they could be forwarded to the proper persons. Our landlady sometimes alluded to the changes that she had witnessed in the removal of the forests, the cultivation of lands and inconveniences of all kinds. But she deplored these changes; since people from England of some capital, who generally prefer to purchase farms partially cleared rather than seclude themselves within almost impervious forests, were hereby induced to take up their residence along the road, and to buy out the original settlers. She had witnessed the departure or death of most of her contemporary settlers and began to feel herself among a strange people of another generation, with whom she had little intercourse and less sympathy.

(The mention of selling out by the original settlers points up the fact that this was standard practice among the Pennsylvania Germans, not only in Vaughan Township but elsewhere throughout Upper Canada where they settled. When their original property was developed, they would sell for a good price and move back into undeveloped areas to repeat the performance there. Cutting down trees and opening up the land for cultivation was never any threat to the Germans for they had done it in Pennsylvania before they came to Canada. It also suggests that had they not come to York County and opened up the forests, the British might not have settled there later on. By 1840 the Germans had pretty well all moved back and Yonge Street was in the possession of the British immigrants.)

Steerage passage from England was $18 below deck. From New York it was $10 but the immigrant had to promise to provide his own food (50 pounds of oatmeal). Cabin fare to New York was $140. There must have been newcomers with money, for in 1831 they deposited £1,600,000 in banks. One man, writing back to England, described himself as being beyond the grasp of the vicar, who claimed the best bird of ten in his flock, and of the solicitor, who charged him a two-guinea fee every time he raised the rent; his wife wrote that the family was well, indeed living in plenty, and that the cats and dog were getting meat every day that would be considered a weekend treat for a family at home.

From as early as 1800, some Clergy Reserve land was leased and farmed. In 1819 the Clergy Reserve Corporation took over the management, and between 1819 and 1825 six Clergy Reserve lots were leased for the then-usual twenty-one year period. Then there was a lull until 1829 when three more lots were leased; in 1830, eleven; in 1831, seven; and in 1832, six. In 1827, part of the Crown Reserves were transferred to King's College, and the sale of the balance of them to the Canada Company followed in 1829, 1830, and 1831. The Canada Company in turn leased the lands until their sale in the 1840s and

1850s. The practice of leasing lots between 1830 and 1836 when the economy was flourishing proved a handicap to the settlers during the depression of 1836-7: prices then were low, returns were small, and the extra rental was a burden. However, among those immigrating from the British Isles between 1828 and 1835 were some who came because of the unrest at home, and brought with them enough capital to buy partially developed property. Although agriculture in Upper Canada was much different from what they had practised in Britain, they were quick to learn from the Pennsylvania Germans and soon became successful farmers.

It wasn't difficult for the new settler to get assistance and this he usually obtained by means of a 'bee.' This pioneer institution was popular for two reasons: only by getting help from one's neighbours was it possible to get a house or barn put up, and the work provided a social occasion. Women helped women to feed the men and the men were often provided with whiskey. 'Bees' were also held to burn the trees which the settler had cut down. This burning served another purpose: the ashes could be sold for cash. In 1804 a public market was established in York where beef, pork, oats, and potatoes were bought; and also potash, field and house, at $320 a ton. Black salts were the father of potash, the grandfather of pearl ash, the great-grandfather of saleratus, the great-great-grandfather of soda, and the distant relation of baking powder.

The Canada West census of 1842 listed Vaughan's population as 4,187 persons, of whom 633 were natives of England, 441 of Ireland, and 529 of Scotland, a total of 1,603 from the British Isles. There were only 130 persons who had been born in the United States. The largest single group was 1,500 'native British Canadians' who almost equalled in number the British-born immigrants. The largest immigrant group, 799 persons, was listed as 'natives of Continental Europe.' Presumably the latter were Germans, since there are no records of other nationalities locating during those years in Vaughan. It is possible that when the census taker asked those who had migrated from Pennsylvania their origin, they gave Germany, Switzerland, France, or Alsace-Lorraine, and consequently were recorded as having come from Continental Europe. The development of the township may be seen clearly in the table on page 62.

For the year 1832, the population is shown as 2,141, an increase of 417 for the year; in 1833, it was 2,472, an increase of 331 for the year; in 1834, it was 2,861 an increase of 389. In the six-year period 1828-34, Vaughan's population increased by 152 per cent. A close look at the census figures shows some anomalics, however. From 1829 to 1831 the number of oxen, milk cows, and horses apparently did not change. This is hardly likely; hence all figures for these early years should be accepted with reservation.

There were really four classes of settlers by the end of the pioneer era. There was the German who migrated with stock, money and knowhow; there was the British settler who was wealthy enough to

Population and property assessed, 1825—40

Year	1825	1827	1829	1831	1834	1836	1838	1840
Population	974	1,106	1,341	1,724	2,861	3,044	3,505	3,921
Land uncult.	4,090	4,937	5,658	6,694	10,237	12,401	15,008	16,697
Land cult.	21,254	23,795	24,645	32,773	40,494	39,099	40,054	38,214
Taxable houses	70	75	85	110	158	175	221	257
Sawmills	6	7	5	9	11	13	16	18
Grist Mills	2	2	2	4	4	4	6	6
Horses 3 yrs. up	149	154	221	221	301	391	513	632
Oxen 4 yrs. up	195	209	283	283	462	496	546	495
Milk cows	431	508	669	669	953	1,166	1,298	1,416
Merchant shops	0	0	3	3	8	10	12	11
Assessed value	£15,206	£17,021	£18,701	£24,723	£35,111	£39,648	£48,145	£51,419

buy property partially developed; there was the German who had little money but knew how to live in pioneer conditions; and finally, there was the Britisher who had little knowledge of farming, only a small amount of money, and who had to learn the ways of farming in Canada by working for those who had that knowledge.

But whatever class he belonged to, prices were high enough so that in a year or two the settler could be self-supporting. Proximity to York meant that there was always a market for what he could produce over and above what he and his family required. It cost the farmer little to provide fodder for his cattle, for they roamed at large. The one problem was that if they broke fences and ruined crops, the settler who owned the cattle had to foot the bill unless the fence-viewer determined that the fence broken through was not up to standard. The Pennsylvania German settler was, however, averse to letting his cattle roam at will. He saw to it that his fences kept them within bounds in summer and his barn protected them during winter. This explains why William Thompson could describe a farm on the 9th Concession in 1842 as follows:

He commenced operations about sixteen years ago, in the bush, without neighbors, without even enough money to pay for his hundred acres of land, the price of which was one dollar per acre. At first he built a small log hut, in which he lived for the first four years, cooking his own victuals, washing his own clothes himself, and labouring in the forest alone.

His house was situated on a green knoll, in the midst of his fields, which were all laid out and fenced in. There was a small stream of clear water running

Vaughan at one time had many small log buildings such as this, which stood in "Honeypot" on Dufferin Street, Concession 3, north of Maple sideroad. The men in the carriage were John Rumble and Richard van Loan.

This fine log house, built in 1849, was owned by James McIntyre, the central figure in the group. It stood on Lot 21, Concession 7, across the road from Purpleville Woods. The picture was probably taken about 1912 to 1914. The house was rebuilt in 1938 with great care by Duncan Ross for Mr. and Mrs. S. Saunders on Concession 7 of King.

Yoke rail fence, built about 1840, on Lot 7, Concession 4. Jacob Smith settled there in 1800, and the property remained in the Smith family until 1967.

between his large barns and outhouses and his dwelling; which was a two-story house of the best kind, built of square logs . . .

In walking up the Avenue to the house I passed a beautiful field of rich clover with more than twenty fat hogs almost hidden in it. I saw three pair of fine horses, four work oxen, and several cows and young cattle. He has two hundred acres of land, all fenced, and in beautiful order; not a stump to be seen in any of his fields except on two small enclosures of his last purchase.

Eighty dollars was all this man had when he acquired the property sixteen years before and it shows that work and determination plus 'know-how' could accomplish much in those pioneer days.

Mary Grapper, writing between 1824 and 1834 to her mother in England, was enthusiastic about opportunities in Vaughan Township.

If he (John Legg) comes out before harvest he will be able to get plenty of work in which he is quite competent; the chopping, etc. he must learn which he will soon do; labourers are much wanted and he may therefore be sure of work. Wages are 2/6 a day with keep or 3/9 without and more for many sorts of harvest work — living is about half what it is in England and clothing not much dearer. Land such as he would want may be got only a little way back for 10s to 15s per acre and be paid for in installments, possession being given within a certain part is paid tho' the prudent way is to live on labour till it is paid for. The journey to Quebec may be made for £5 or £6 a head exclusive of provisions which they must provide for themselves . . . they need not settle more than 3 or 4 miles from a church for the present if they take Mr. Sharpe's house which will be vacant in May, they would only be a mile and three-quarters.

Those who came out from England usually worked as labourers until they learned how to farm in Upper Canada. When they had saved enough money — and there wasn't much they could spend their money on — they would buy land on the installment plan. Crops were so good that often, with a good year, a man could own his own land and before long become a well-to-do farmer. William Cruikshank, who owned two farms on Yonge Street, stated that on one farm alone of 110 acres he was able to pocket £15 after paying all expenses.

By the end of the Pioneer Period, that is, 1840, Vaughan Township was pretty well opened up — one-third cleared, two-thirds bush. Of the 55,346 acres of land that had been granted, 18,026 were cleared. Yonge Street had been improved and provided a means for the farmers to market their products in Toronto. The census of 1842 reveals that the farmers were no longer interested in growing wheat only. Besides the 48,287 bushels of wheat, they produced 3,756 bushels of rye, 72,422 bushels of oats, 20,333 bushels of peas, 52,860 bushels of potatoes, and 881 bushels of Indian corn. For sweetening, Vaughan farmers kept 49 hives of bees and made 36,880 pounds of maple sugar. Some 686 horses had replaced the oxen and there were 2,725 cattle, 2,462 hogs, and 5,535 sheep.

Turning again to the history of Vaughan given in the *History of the County of York,* Book I, published in 1885, we find:

The settlement of Vaughan was completed about 35 years after the arrival of the pioneers. The general character of the land is clay and loam, which is worth from $30 to $70 per acre.

The population for Vaughan in 1842 was 4,300, increasing to 6,255 by 1850. At that time there were in the township, five grist mills and thirty-four saw mills. In the same year the number of public schools in operation was twenty.

The population, like that of several of the townships of York, shows a slight decrease during the decade 1871-81, for which the exodus to the States and to the Canadian northwest is partly responsible, but is largely accounted for in the case of Vaughan by the incorporation of Richmond Hill, a portion of which is embraced within the limits of the township. In 1871 the population was 7,657; in 1881 it was 6,828. Of the population in the latter years those of German origin numbered 993, being mostly the descendants of old settlers from Pennsylvania.

In 1881 the livestock of the township numbered as follows: Cattle 2,952; horses 2,481; sheep 4,349; and hogs 2,207. The principal breeds are Clydesdale horses, Durham cattle, long-wooled sheep, and Berkshire and Suffolk hogs. Among the owners of purebred cattle are Michael Reaman, Robert Marsh, William Agar, George Bell, Peter Frank, Jacob Lahmer and sons, and Edwin Langstaff.

In the 1920s Sir Donald Mann leased a number of farms for the right to explore for oil. After drilling over 4000 feet on West Lot 11, Con. 3, a mineral water was discovered. It is used now to keep down the dust on roads in summer and melt ice and snow in winter. An attempt to sell bottles (called Raysol) as a health tonic failed. It was too salty.

Barn Lanterns
The old pierced lanterns had no glass

CHAPTER IV

Government

The first settlers in Upper Canada lived under martial law, executed by officers of regiments stationed in the various settlements. These officers had control over the granting of land assistance, which consisted of the supplying of food and implements to new arrivals at the beginning of their pioneer life. In 1791 English law and trial by jury were introduced. A Lieutenant was nominated for each county, and he appointed the Justices of the Peace and officers of the militia. A Court of Quarter Sessions was established to look after judicial duties and various tasks now performed by the municipal council.

Modified self-government was a distinctively American institution without warrant of law until 1793. It was not welcomed by the provincial authorities in the early days, for they knew it had been used in the thirteen colonies to spread revolutionary doctrines. But the Loyalist Americans settling in Canada thought only of its convenience and insisted upon its introduction. An annual assembly of the householders of a township met and elected a town clerk, an assessor, pathmasters, fenceviewers, and a poundkeeper, and adopted such regulations as the public need demanded — for example, to govern the running at large of cattle and swine.

More serious questions of municipal management were determined by the magistrates in Quarterly Sessions. But the magistrates were appointed by the government and in many instances were not in harmony with the public spirit of the community they served. Besides, the territory under their jurisdiction, the Home District from the Bay of Quinte to Long Point on Lake Erie, was too large for them to have even a sketchy notion of public needs, and their sittings once in three months were too infrequent in view of the rapid settlement of the country.

The municipal powers of the magistrate's court were increased from time to time. Authority was given to levy taxes, to direct the road work residents were supposed to supply, to regulate the conduct of taverns, ferries, and markets, to build and maintain bridges, courthouses, and jails. Districts were divided for convenience into areas with assessors, collectors, and pathmasters.

Under the Assessment Acts an attempt was made to collect taxes not only on real estate but also on businesses, production channels, and luxuries, including lands, town lots, houses, fireplaces, stoves, horses, oxen, cows, young stock, grist mills, sawmills, shops, closed carriages, gigs, and wagons kept for pleasure. Taverns and stills were reserved for provincial taxes.

Assessments were low and the rate did not exceed ten mills on the dollar. A settler's first log cabin was free but each year he paid four cents on each acre of arable land, one cent an acre on bush land, eight cents on a farm house, thirty-two cents on a horse, sixteen cents on an ox, four cents a head on livestock, and forty-two cents on a wagon kept for pleasure. In 1811 agricultural property was distinct from other property and liable to assessment and taxations — arable land twenty shillings, uncultivated land, four shillings.

Costs of education and the care of the dependent, the aged, the infirm, the insane, the unemployable, and the unemployed became a charge on the wealth and income of society and were not an obligation on municipal taxpayers. Taxes were small. In 1830, for 200 acres of land, the annual tax was five dollars. But farmers never knew what was done with their money — and this was one reason for the Reform movement of William Lyon Mackenzie.

In 1835 an Act was passed enlarging in some measure the scope of the Town Meeting. The people assembled were charged to elect, in addition to the usual township officers, three commissioners who would meet at least three times a year, and more often if necessary, to administer the business of the township and have supervision over its officers. In 1837 the Act was amended: the commissioners became town wardens, and their powers were somewhat enlarged. In 1841 the District Councils Act entitled each township to elect one or two councillors as delegates to the District Council. The government named the warden and the treasurer of each council. Most of the administrative powers formerly possessed by the magistrates in Sessions were to be exercised in these councils, but the total assessment for local purposes was not to exceed 1½ pence per acre. In 1846 the government surrendered the right to name the wardens, and in 1849 the districts were abolished and the unit of organization became the county. Thus County Councils came into being to co-ordinate the work of the Township Councils.

Townships had no corporate existence until 1849 when the Robert Baldwin Act provided that a township should have five elected councillors, and the power to appoint officers, supervise statute labour, levy local taxes, and borrow certain moneys. Hamlets of 900 residents were incorporated as villages with additional powers. The Act also provided for the incorporations of towns; in some cases, a deputy-reeve was appointed from the members of the council.

The present municipal system came into operation in the beginning of the year 1850, and that is the year the municipal records of Vaughan began. (The County of York had previously been governed as part of the large Home District County.) A Chairman was elected annually; later a warden was elected to preside over County Council.

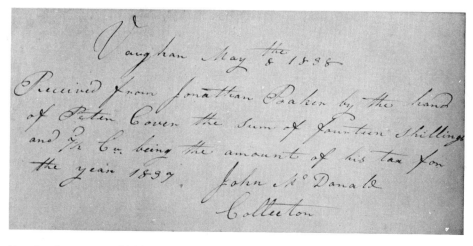

Receipt for taxes paid by Jonathan Baker in 1838.

Marriage certificate of John Diceman and Anne Line, January 23, 1833.

MARRIAGE CERTIFICATE.

I do hereby Certify, That on the *Twenty second* day of *January* in the year of our **Lord** One Thousand Eight Hundred and *thirty three* *John Diceman* — — the Township of *Vaughan* in the *Home* District, and *Anne Line* — of the Township of *Vaughan* in the *Home* District, were married by me *James Richardson* a Minister of the *Methodist Episcopal* Church, in the presence of *John Line* — and *Samuel Line* — — — which said Marriage was solemnized by *Licence*

Dated this *Twenty second* day of *January* A.D. 1833

John X Line
Saml X Line } WITNESSES.

N. B. The above Marriage was solemnized at *York* — in the *Home* District, by me, having received the necessary Certificate to solemnize Matrimony as a Minister of the *Methodist Episcopal* Church, from the Quarter Sessions of the *Midland* District.
* "Licence, or "Publication of Banns," as the case may be

Jas Richardson

The first Vaughan Township Hall, built in 1845, is in Vellore. The public school is in the background, in this 60-year-old photograph.

The building in the right foreground served as Township Offices from 1908, when it was built, until the present offices were opened in 1957. This picture was taken about 1910.

In 1850 Vaughan Township was divided into five wards. Each ward elected one councillor. The councillors in turn elected a reeve and one or more deputy reeves. At the first meeting on January 21, 1850, held in the Township Hall on Concession 6 at Vellore, John W. Gamble was elected reeve; David Smellie, deputy reeve; James Ashdown, township clerk; Nathaniel Wallace, John Stephens, and William Porter, assessors; and Neil McEachern the first treasurer. The voting was by open ballot, which meant that the voter stood before the returning officer and publicly announced his preference. His vote was recorded beside his name under the column for the candidate in question. As a result it was sometimes a lively meeting. The voting for councillors in that first election in Vaughan Township was as follows:

WARD 1
Proceedings of a Public Meeting of the inhabitants of Ward 1, Township of Vaughan, held at Smellie's School House for the election of a Councillor for said Ward on the 7th day of January, 1850. Walter Dalziel, Returning Officer.
Moved by Spencer Jupp and seconded by Anthony Bowes that David Smellie by elected Councillor for Ward 1.
Moved by Alexander C. Lawrence and seconded by William McGill that Thomas Cook, Miller, be elected for said Ward.
A show of hands having been taken on the respective motions, the majority appeared in favour of David Smellie on which a poll was demanded on the part of Thomas Cook.

For David Smellie

William Agnes
Hiram White
George Charleton
William Lane
Michael Ouster
Spencer Jupp ?
William Gerrott
Hugh Matheson
Jacob Bennett
William Jackson
Michael Burkholder
John Holland
Adam Keffer
Jonathan Keffer
John Charleton
John Morley
William Keffer
Peter Ouster
Peter Keffer
Jacob Munshaw
Peter Musselman
James Wilkie
Samuel Ouster
Isaac White
Henry White
John Pierson
Edward Seagor
John Watson
Thomas Wilkinson

Robert Ierott
Robert Fleming
John Develin
John Wilkie
David Mulholland
John Martin
Solomon Puterbaugh
Jacob Keffer
William Bowes

For Thomas Cook

Alexander C. Lawrence
William McGill
William Clark
John Atkinson
Elijah Dexter ?
Thomas Cook Farmer
Barney Lyon
John Smith
James Rutledge
Thomas Rookby
James Braithwaite
Robert Burwick
Donald Gunn
Nathaniel Burr
Peter Rupert
Robert Johnston
Michael Connor
John McPherson
Daniel Reaman
Mathew Lymburner

David Smellie duly elected.

WARD 2
        Returning Officer: John Volie.
        Running for Councillor: David Bridgeford, Daniel McDougall, and Robert
McNair. David Bridgeford elected.
        Election held on January 7, 1850.

Voters

John Granshaw	Thomas Welpton
James Hetherington	John Wood
William Nye	Joseph Fernes
Hugh McLean	Joseph Wright
John McCaffie	Thomas Banks
Joseph Erbie	James Stevenson
Albert Jonson	Martin McCloud
A. Watson	James Lawrence
Robert Metcalf	Benjamin Munshaw
Richard Homes	William Ranson
Hugh McMullen	M. Cranny
Henry Hall	Peter Vanterburg
William Brattmas	
William Hetherington	

WARD 3
        Returning Officer. Frances John Bunt.
        J. W. Gamble and A. Maitland nominated. J. W. Gamble elected.

Voters

Bernard McMahon	Robert Matthews
William Eaton	Stephen Atkinson
John Elliot	Jahy Haystead, Jr.
George Underhill	William Peacock
William Dalziel	William Gray
Adam Robinson	James Lauder
Thomas Cavena	William Burkholder
James Ashdown	Joseph Lankin
William R. Grahame	Brigham Wilkinson
John N. Kline	Charles Wallace
Thomas Haystead	Thomas Shannon
John Haystead	David Johnstone
John Armstead	Alexander Robinson
Malcolm Cormicle (Carmichael)	John Hamilton
Michael Whitmore	Francis Buttery
Thomas Danahay	Joseph Little
Martin McLean	Henry Ackim
Robert Forbus	Francis Kennedy
Samuel Makitrick	Samuel Ford
Peter Witherspoon	Samuel McGirr
James Rose	John Tanner
James Totten	John Jeffery
Joseph Brown	John Mattson
William Rujsel	Thomas Thompson
Torbit Ellis	James Hardy
Arthur McNiel	James Fowley
Thomas Underhill	Oldrin Fisher
John Brown	Robert Adams
Peter Dickout	John Maynard
John McClinchy	Stephen Burgess
John Quinn	James Matheson

John Rose
Samuel Turner
Hugh Morrison
James Lowrie
Alexander McNiel
George Cowan
Richard Brown
Samuel Smith
John F. Howel
William McCauly
Henry Philips
Richard Whitherhead
Robert Johnstone
William Rainey

John McLean
Richard Bywater
Henry Castedder
David Witherspoon
John Orr
John Strong
Henry Shaffer
William Gray
John Wright
John Crawford
Thomas NcNelly
Nicholas Shaver
Martin Branham

WARD 4

Returning Officer: William Andrew Orr
Running for Councillor: James Adams and Alexander Mitchell. James
Adams elected.
Election held on January 7, 1850.

Voters	Conc.	Lot
Jacob Snyder	5	18
John Walker	9	32
William McCutchin	9	35
Donald McKinnon	5	20
David McKutchin	9	35
Edison Miller	6	27
James Morrow	7	26
Thomas Marchel	8	25
Thomas Sharp	6	27
William McBride	7	22
John Beats	5	23
Michael Peterman	6	29
Robert Mills	7	33
Robert Henderson	6	24
Samuel Scott	6	25
Samuel Irvin	6	25
Thomas Ginn	7	32
James White	8	25
John Egan	7	27
James Orr	8	26
James McRitchey	8	27
Neil Beacon	8	28
Robert McBride	7	22
James Watson	7	32
Samuel Hughson	7	27
Robert Thomson	5	23
John Orr	6	24
James Watson	7	27
Peter Frank	5	18
William Jeffery	8	34
John Jeffery	8	34
Samuel Hughson, Jr.	8	29
Donald McKinnon	8	18
Andrew Jameson	7	27
Robert Irwin	6	28
Donald Cameron	5	30

Thomas Armstrong	5	27
Martin Smith	8	23
Archy McCaulam	7	23
Samuel Mathewson	7	23
Donald Beakon	7	25
Archy McDonnell	7	30
Lawrie McGillvary	7	30
Gibson Jarrett	7	33
John McFarlen	7	21
John Diceman	5	24
Malcolm McGlaughlin	8	24
Alexander McGlaughlin	8	24
Charles Blackston	9	27
Michael Raymon (Reaman)	8	28
Suble Nicolls	8	—
Henry Crosson	8	19
John Crosson	7	33
James Wilson	8	22
Allen Stephenson	8	20
Esau C. Matthews	6	24
William Beatty	8	26
Duncan McKinnon	8	18
John Cameron	8	24
William Wilson	9	33
Elias Robinson	9	23
Alexander Moulsey	7	21
Alex. Goff	8	24
Christopher Train	9	27
Joseph Caipner	7	21
Alexander Beaton	8	23
John Beaton	9	29
Patrick McCutchin	8	35
Charles Corrigan	8	31
John Stephenson	8	21
James Allen	8	33
James Livingston	7	28
David Kaiser	8	28
Samuel Peterman	5	30
Duncan McDugal	7	31
James McNair	5	28
John Durant	7	29
Francis East	7	27
John Egan	8	33
Duke Jarrett	6	21
Richard Egan	8	33
Henry Mosgrove	9	28
Valentine Crosson	8	19
James Farquarson	6	31
David Taylor	8	22
John Puterbaugh	6	31
John Harvey	6	34
Archy McMurchy	6	33
Joseph Hemphill	9	35
Thomas Ellis	8	31
James Craddy	8	24
Henry Craig	8	24
Joseph Snider	8	24
John Wilson	8	26

William Riching	7	23
Andrew McGinn	5	24
Andrew Scott	6	24
Malcolm Malloy	5	25
Gilbert Matthewson	6	23
George Miller	6	23
James Stephenson	8	20
James McCannus	7	23

WARD 5

Returning Officer: James Sommerville.

William Kersey, John Lawrie, Alfred Jeffrey, and John Dalziel nominated.
John Lawrie elected.

Election held January 7, 1850.

Voters	Conc.	Lot
Thomas Smith	11	29
John Hind	10	20
John Harrison	8	2
John Watson	10	27
Jacob Burkholder	9	10
Thomas Richardson	8	13
George Wallace	8	10
Henry Burton	9	13
Robert Waddell	8	16
Thomas Smith	9	16
James Thomson	8	16
Henry Burkholder	9	10
Niel McGillivray	9	18
Richard Jeffrey	9	15
Elisha Farr	9	11
Donald McGillivray	9	17
Martin McKinnon	9	9
Archibold Summerfeldt	10	13
Andrew Riddell	10	10
John Wood	9	16
George Hilson	9	12
David Blain	10	15
James Devins	10	18
Richard Agar	9	23
Donald McCockern	9	18
George Kellam	10	22
William Archer	10	11
Alder McEachern	9	19
William Kersey	10	22
Richard Burgess	10	24
Patrick Smith	10	29
William Andrew	11	28
James Paterson	9	24
John Hind	10	20
Robert Park	11	28
Benjamin Snail	11	35
James Mitchell	10	33
James Mitchell	11	33
William Mitchell	10	35
Luke Abbey	10	34
William Patterson	9	27
George Picket	11	27

Thomas Paul	10	23
James Racket	10	27
Mike Lynch	10	31
William Thomas	10	30
Neil McGillivray	9	20
Thomas Agar	10	16
Robert Voakes	10	20
Simon Shedler	9	5
Robert Agar	10	12
John Kellam	9	9
John Collitan	9	14
Joseph Akrow	10	21
Dickson Fletcher	10	9
Nathan Devens	10	18
George Middleton	9	7
J. Finnes	9	2
Charles Callaghan	9	2
William Watson	9	1
James Robison	9	1
Thomas McAlister	11	31

In 1851 the councillors were paid 6s 3d per day. The highest yearly salary recorded was to John W. Gamble of Pine Grove, the reeve, of £5 6s 3d. In 1852 he received £3 2s 6d for ten days.

In 1858 an auditor was hired to audit the accounts from January 1, 1850, to August, 1858. This was a difficult task, for many of the vouchers and cheques and even a bank book, were missing. In 1860 the township clerk was instructed to have printed in pamphlet form some 250 copies of the statement of accounts of the municipality for that year, and 50 copies were to be sent to each councillor for distribution.

A tax receipt of 1870 records that the taxes that year on seventy acres of land were $5.67. Personal property that was liable to taxation included all horses of three years and upwards, all meat cattle of three years and upwards, and all pleasure carriages of all descriptions.

In 1875 the number of deputy reeves was increased to three by reason of the growth of population.

In 1850 James Ashdown became clerk and served until 1859. G.J.F. Pearce, who followed him, served as township clerk and treasurer for nearly ten years before resigning in 1868. J.M. Lawrence was appointed to succeed him. Mr. Lawrence was of United Empire Loyalist origin. His grandfather, John Lawrence, had held the rank of captain in the Royalist forces during the American War of Independence and at its close went to New Brunswick; there he had remained until 1817, when he came to Upper Canada. Mr. Lawrence's maternal grandfather, Robert Marsh, had settled in Vaughan in 1800.

James B. McLean became the clerk-treasurer in 1898 and had his office in his home on Maple Avenue West. In 1908 he built a solid brick building on Keele Street south of the corner; he was manager of the Standard Bank which occupied the north half of the building, while the township offices were in the south half.

In 1936 James M. McDonald became the clerk-treasurer. He

The present Vaughan Township Municipal Offices. (Photo: Harry Vey)

The Vaughan Township Council, 1970, in the Council Chambers. Front row, left to right: Albert Rutherford, Deputy Reeve; Garnet Williams, Reeve; Gordon Risk. Back row: John Gilbert, Lou Wainwright, David Fraser, Dalton McArthur.

used the same offices and accomplished all the township business with the help of one secretary, Miss Marion Watson, for quite a few years. Since 1967 he has been Township Adminstrator. Frederick Jackman is Township Clerk, and Howard Burkholder is Treasurer.

Vaughan Township Councils

*denotes Warden of York County that year

1850	Reeve: John W. Gamble; Councillors: James Adam, John Lawrie, David Smellie, David Bridgeford
1851	Reeve: John W. Gamble; Councillors: David Smellie (Deputy Reeve), David Bridgeford, John Lawrie, Alexander Mitchell
1852	Reeve: John W. Gamble*; Councillors: David Bridgeford (Deputy Reeve), Thomas Cook, James Somerville, Alexander Mitchell
1853	Reeve: John W. Gamble*; Councillors: David Bridgeford (Deputy Reeve), Donald Cameron, Thomas Cook, James Thompson
1854	Reeve: John W. Gamble*; Councillors: Thomas Cook, David Bridgeford, Donald Cameron, James Thompson
1855	Reeve: John W. Gamble; Councillors: Thomas Cook, David Bridgeford, Donald Cameron, William Kersey
1856	Reeve: John W. Gamble; Councillors: Thomas Cook, David Bridgeford, Donald Cameron, Alfred Jeffery
1857	Reeve: John W. Gamble; Councillors: Geo. J.F. Pearce, David Bridgeford, Henry S. Howland, James Somerville
1858	Reeve: David Bridgeford; Councillors: Alfred Jeffery (Deputy Reeve), David Smellie, John Brown, Henry S. Howland
1859	Reeve: Henry S. Howland; Deputy Reeve: Alfred Jeffery; Councillors: David Smellie, David Bridgeford, John Brown
1860	Reeve: Henry S. Howland; Deputy Reeve: Alfred Jeffery; Councillors: Robert J. Arnold, David Bridgeford, John Brown
1861	Reeve: Robert J. Arnold; Deputy Reeve: William Cook; Councillors: John Brown, Henry S. Howland, Alfred Jeffery
1862	Reeve: Robert J. Arnold; Deputy Reeve: Alfred Jeffery; Councillors: William Cook, John Brown, Henry S. Howland
1863	Reeve: Robert J. Arnold; Deputy Reeve: William Cook; Councillors: John Brown, Henry S. Howland, Alfred Jeffery
1864	Reeve: Henry S. Howland; Deputy Reeve: Alfred Jeffery; Councillors: Dr. Jas. Langstaff, Robert J. Arnold, Thos. Grahame
1865	Reeve: Henry S. Howland*; Deputy Reeve: Thos. Grahame; Councillors: Daniel Reaman, Dr. Jas. Langstaff, Thos. Webster
1866	Reeve: Henry S. Howland*; Deputy Reeve: Thos. Grahame; Councillors: Daniel Reaman, Dr. Jas. Langstaff, Thos. Webster
1867	Reeve: Henry S. Howland*; Deputy Reeves: Thos. Grahame, Robert J. Arnold; Councillors: Daniel Reaman, Thos. Webster
1868	Reeve: Peter Patterson; Deputy Reeves: Wm. Hartman, Robert J. Arnold; Councillors: Daniel Reaman, Thos. Webster
1869	Reeve: Peter Patterson; Deputy Reeves: Wm. Hartman, Robert J. Arnold; Councillors: Daniel Reaman, Thos. Webster
1870	Reeve: Peter Patterson; Deputy Reeves: David Boyle, Robert J. Arnold; Councillors: Daniel Reaman, Thos. Webster
1871	Reeve: Peter Patterson*; Deputy Reeves: Thompson Porter, David Boyle; Councillors: Daniel Reaman, Thos. Webster
1872	Reeve: David Boyle; Deputy Reeves: Thos. Webster, Thompson Porter; Councillors: Daniel Reaman, Archibald McQuarrie
1873	Reeve: David Boyle; Deputy Reeves: Thos. Webster, Thompson Porter; Councillors: Daniel Reaman, Archibald McQuarrie

1874   **Reeve: W.C. Patterson; Deputy Reeves: N. Clarke Wallace, Thos. Webster; Councillors: Daniel Reaman, Jonathan Ellerby**

1875   Reeve: W.C. Patterson; Deputy Reeves: N. Clarke Wallace, Thos. Webster, Isaac Chapman; Councillor: Daniel Reaman

1876   Reeve: W.C. Patterson*; Deputy Reeves: N. Clarke Wallace, Thos. Webster, Isaac Chapman; Councillor: Daniel Reaman

1877   Reeve: W.C. Patterson; Deputy Reeves: N. Clarke Wallace, Thos. Webster, Daniel Kinnee; Councillor: Daniel Reaman

1878   Reeve: W.C. Patterson; Deputy Reeves: N. Clarke Wallace, John L. Card, Daniel Kinnee; Councillor: Daniel Reaman

1879   Reeve: W.C. Patterson; Deputy Reeves: N. Clarke Wallace*, Isaac Nattress, Daniel Reaman; Councillor: Jacob Lahmer

1880   Reeve: W.C. Patterson; Deputy Reeves: John L. Card, Isaac Nattress, Daniel Reaman; Councillor: Jacob Lahmer

1881   Reeve: Thompson Porter; Deputy Reeves: Wm. Cook, Isaac Nattress, Daniel Reaman; Councillor: Alexander Malloy

1882   Reeve: Thompson Porter; Deputy Reeves: Wm. Cook, Thos. Webster, Daniel Reaman; Councillor: Alexander Malloy

1883   Reeve: Thompson Porter; Deputy Reeves: Wm. Cook, Thos. Webster, Daniel Reaman; Councillor: Alexander Malloy

1884   Reeve: Thompson Porter; Deputy Reeves: Wm. Cook, Daniel Reaman, Alexander Malloy; Councillor: George Elliott

1885   Reeve: Thompson Porter; Deputy Reeves: Wm. Cook, Daniel Reaman, Alexander Malloy; Councillor: George Elliott

1886   Reeve: Thompson Porter*; Deputy Reeves: Alexander Malloy, Isaac Reaman, George Elliott; Councillor: Andrew Russell

1887   Reeve: Alexander Malloy; Deputy Reeves: Andrew Russell, Isaac Reaman, George High; Councillor: Peter Devins

1888   Reeve: Alexander Malloy; Deputy Reeves: Andrew Russell, Isaac Reaman, George High; Councillor: Peter Devins

1889   Reeve: James McNeil; Deputy Reeves: Andrew Russell, George High; Councillors: Samuel Arnold, Robert Watson

1890   Reeve: Andrew Russell; Deputy Reeves: George High, Samuel Arnold; Councillors: Robert Watson, William Watson

1891   Reeve: Andrew Russell; Deputy Reeves: George High, Samuel Arnold; Councillors: William Watson, Alexander Bryson

1892   Reeve: Andrew Russell; Deputy Reeves: George High, Samuel Arnold; Councillors: Alexander Bryson, James A. Stevenson

1893   Reeve: Andrew Russell*; Deputy Reeves: George High, Samuel Arnold; Councillors: Alexander Bryson, James A. Stevenson

1894   Reeve: George High; Deputy Reeves: Samuel Arnold, Alexander Bryson; Councillors: Jas. H. Kirby, William Watson

1895   Reeve: George High; Deputy Reeves: Samuel Arnold, Alexander Bryson; Councillors: Jas. H. Kirby, William Watson

1896   Reeve: George High; Deputy Reeves: Samuel Arnold, Alexander Bryson; Councillors: Jas. H. Kirby, William Watson

1897   Reeve: Samuel Arnold; Deputy Reeves: Alexander Bryson, Jas. H. Kirby; Councillors: William Watson, John Boyle

1898   Reeve: Alexander Bryson; Deputy Reeves: Jas. H. Kirby, William Watson; Councillors; John Boyle, Isaac Devins

1899   Reeve: Alexander Bryson; Councillors: Jas. H. Kirby, John Boyle, Donald Malloy, William Watson

1900   Reeve: Alexander Bryson; Councillors: Jas. H. Kirby, John Boyle, William Watson, Donald Malloy

1901   Reeve; Jas. H. Kirby; Councillors: Donald Malloy, Isaac Devins, John Boyle, Daniel Longhouse

1902   **Reeve: Jas. H. Kirby; Councillors: Donald Malloy, Isaac Devins, John Boyle, Daniel Longhouse**

1903   Reeve: William Watson; Councillors: Daniel Longhouse, Donald Malloy, William Thomas, Isaac Devins

1904   Reeve: William Watson; Councillors: James A. Cameron, Daniel Longhouse, Scott McNair, Isaac Devins

1905   Reeve: John Boyle; Councillors: James A. Cameron, Scott McNair, Daniel Longhouse, Isaac Devins

1906   Reeve: John Boyle; Councillors: James A. Cameron, Daniel Longhouse, Isaac Devins, Scott McNair

1907   Reeve: Isaac Devins; Depty Reeve: Daniel Longhouse; Councillors: James A. Cameron, William Thomas, Jacob Williams

1908   Reeve: Isaac Devins; Deputy Reeve: Deniel Longhouse; Councillors: James A. Cameron, William Thomas, Scott McNair

1909   Reeve: Daniel Longhouse; Deputy Reeve: James A. Cameron; Councillors: Scott McNair, William Thomas, John T. Saigeon

1910   Reeve: Daniel Longhouse; Deputy Reeve: James A. Cameron; Councillors: Henry Ellis, John T. Saigeon, Scott McNair

1911   Reeve: James A. Cameron; Deputy Reeve: Scott McNair; Councillors: John Whitmore, John T. Saigeon, Albert Witherspoon

1912   Reeve: James A. Cameron; Deputy Reeve: Scott McNair; Councillors: John Whitmore, Albert Witherspoon, Alexander Cameron

1913   Reeve: James A. Cameron; Deputy Reeve: Scott McNair; Councillors: John Whitmore, John T. Saigeon, Alexander Cameron

1914   Reeve: James A. Cameron*; Deputy Reeve: Scott McNair; Councillors: John Whitmore, John T. Saigeon, Alexander Cameron

1915   Reeve: Scott McNair; Deputy Reeve: John Whitmore; Councillors: Alexander Cameron, Walter Anderson, John T. Saigeon

1916   Reeve: Scott McNair; Deputy Reeve: John Whitmore; Councillors: Alexander Cameron, Walter Anderson, John T. Saigeon

1917   Reeve: John Whitmore; Deputy Reeve: John T. Saigeon; Councillors: Walter Anderson, Wm. O. McDonald, T.B. Weldrick

1918   Reeve: John Whitmore; Deputy Reeve: John T. Saigeon; Councillors: Walter Anderson, Wm. O. McDonald, T.B. Weldrick

1919   Reeve: John Whitmore; Deputy Reeve: Walter Anderson; Councillors: T.B. Weldrick, Geo. Kellam, Wm. O. McDonald

1920   Reeve: John Whitmore; Deputy Reeve: Walter Anderson; Councillors: T.B. Weldrick, Geo. Kellam, Wm. O. McDonald

1921   Reeve: John Whitmore; Deputy Reeves: John T. Saigeon, Wm. O. McDonald; Councillors: Geo. Kellam, James H. Robson

1922   Reeve: John T. Saigeon; Deputy Reeves: T.B. Weldrick, Geo. Kellam; Councillors: Arthur Farr, Jas. H. Robson

1923   Reeve: John T. Saigeon; Deputy Reeves: T.B. Weldrick, Geo. Kellam; Councillors: Arthur Farr, James H. Robson

1924   Reeve: John T. Saigeon; Deputy Reeves: T.B. Weldrick, Geo. Kellam; Councillors: Arthur Farr, James H. Robson

1925   Reeve: T.B. Weldrick; Deputy Reeves: Geo. Kellam, James H. Robson; Councillors: Thos. Baker, Arthur Farr

1926   Reeve: T.B. Weldrick; Deputy Reeves: Geo. Kellam, James H. Robson; Councillors: Thos. Baker, Arthur Farr

1927   Reeve: Geo. Kellam; Deputy Reeves: James H. Robson, Arthur Farr; Councillors: Thos. Baker, W.J. Johnson

1928   Reeve: Geo. Kellam; Deputy Reeves: Jas. H. Robson, Arthur Farr; Councillors: Thos. Baker, W.J. Johnson

1929   Reeve: Jas. H. Robson; Deputy Reeves: John T. Saigeon, Thos. Baker; Councillors: W.J. Johnson, Robert Dooks

1930   Reeve: James H. Robson; Deputy Reeves: John T. Saigeon, Thos. Baker; Councillors: W.J. Johnson, Robert Dooks

1931   Reeve: Geo. Kellam; Deputy Reeves: John T. Saigeon, Robert Dooks; Councillors: Duncan McMurchy, R.W. Scott

1932	Reeve: Geo. Kellam; Deputy Reeve: Robert Dooks: Councillors: Duncan McMurchy, Robert W. Scott, Boynton Weldrick
1933	Reeve: Geo. Kellam: Deputy Reeve: Robert Dooks; Councillors: Robert W. Scott, Boynton Weldrick, Duncan McMurchy
1934	Reeve: Geo. Kellam; Deputy Reeve: Robert Dooks; Councillors: Robert W. Scott, Boynton Weldrick, Duncan McMurchy
1935	Reeve: Geo. Kellam*; Deputy Reeve: Robert W. Scott; Councillors: Boynton Weldrick, Duncan McMurchy, John A. Dick
1936	Reeve: Robert W. Scott; Deputy Reeve: Boynton Weldrick; Councillors: John Hostrawser, James H. Robson, John A. Dick
1937	Reeve: Robert W. Scott; Deputy Reeve: Boynton Weldrick; Councillors: John Hostrawser, James H. Robson, John A. Dick
1938	Reeve: Robert W. Scott; Deputy Reeve: Boynton Weldrick; Councillors: John Hostrawser, James H. Robson, John A. Dick
1939	Reeve: Robert W. Scott; Deputy Reeve: Boynton Weldrick; Councillors: John Hostrawser, James H. Robson, John A. Dick
1940	Reeve: Robert W. Scott; Deputy Reeve: Boynton Weldrick; Councillors: John Hostrawser, James H. Robson, John A. Dick
1941	Reeve: Robert W. Scott; Deputy Reeve: Boynton Weldrick; Councillors: John Hostrawser, James H. Robson, John A. Dick
1942	Reeve: Robert W. Scott; Deputy Reeve: Boynton Weldrick; Councillors: John Hostrawser, James H. Robson, John A. Dick
1943	Reeve: Robert W. Scott; Deputy Reeve: Boynton Weldrick; Councillors: John Hostrawser, James H. Robson, J. Albert Dick
1944	Reeve: Boynton Weldrick; Deputy Reeve: John Hostrawser; Councillors: J. Albert Dick, Stewart Rumble, James H. Robson
1945	Reeve: Boynton Weldrick; Deputy Reeve: John Hostrawser; Councillors: J. Albert Dick, James H. Robson, Stewart Rumble
1946	Reeve: Boynton Weldrick; Deputy Reeve: John Hostrawser; Councillors: Carl Shaw, Marshall McMurchy, Herbert A. Phelps
1947	Reeve: Boynton Weldrick; Deputy Reeve: John Hostrawser; Councillors: Carl Shaw, Marshall McMurchy, Herbert A. Phelps
1948	Reeve: Boynton Weldrick; Deputy Reeve: John Hostrawser; Councillors: Carl Shaw, Marshall McMurchy, Herbert A. Phelps
1949	Reeve: John Hostrawser; Deputy Reeve: Marshall McMurchy; Councillors: Carl Shaw, James Robson, Albert Rutherford
1950	Reeve: John Hostrawser; Deputy Reeve: Marshall McMurchy; Councillors: Jas. H. Robson, Albert H. Rutherford, W.J. Agar
1951	Reeve: John Hostrawser; Deputy Reeve: Marshall McMurchy; Councillors: Jas. H. Robson, W.J. Agar, Albert H. Rutherford
1952	Reeve: Marshall McMurchy, Deputy Reeve: Albert H. Rutherford; Councillors: W.J. Agar, John W. Perry, Jas. H. Robson
1953	Reeve: Marshall McMurchy; Deputy Reeve: Albert H. Rutherford; Councillors: John W. Perry, Jas. H. Robson, W.J. Agar
1954	Reeve: Marshall McMurchy; Deputy Reeve: Albert H. Rutherford; Councillors: W.J. Agar, James Reid, Kenneth Doyle
1955	Reeve: Marshall McMurchy; Deputy Reeve: Albert H. Rutherford; Councillors: W.J. Agar, James Reid, Frank Belcher
1956	Reeve: Marshall McMurchy*; Deputy Reeve: Albert H. Rutherford; Councillors: Robert A. Kirk, W.J. Agar, James Reid
1957–58	(Two-year term) Reeve: John W. Perry; Deputy Reeve: Robert A. Kirk; Councillors: E.W. Anstey, Victor B. Ryder, Jesse Bryson
1959–60	(Two-year term) Reeve: John W. Perry; Deputy Reeve: Victor B. Ryder; Councillors: E.W. Anstey, Jesse Bryson, Bruce M. Ralph
1961–62	(Two-year term) Reeve: A.H. Rutherford; Deputy Reeve: Jesse Bryson; Councillors: Wilfred Keffer, Ruth McConkey, F.M. Windatt
1963–64	(Two-year term) Reeve: A.H. Rutherford (*1964); Deputy Reeve: Jesse Bryson; Councillors: Wilfred Keffer, Ruth McConkey, Garnet Williams

1965–66   (Two-year term) Reeve: A.H. Rutherford; Deputy Reeve: Garnet Williams; Councillors: W.R. Bryce, R.D. McArthur, S.D. Kaiser

1967-68   (Two-year term) Reeve: Brian Bailey; Deputy Reeve: Garnet Williams; Councillors: Chas. W. Birkett, M.D., R.D. McArthur, D.K. Fraser

1969-70   (Two-year term) Reeve: Garnet Williams: Deputy Reeve: Albert H. Rutherford; Councillors: Gord Risk, D.K. Fraser, Lou Wainwright, John Gilbert, R.D. McArthur

Hope Schoolhouse

CHAPTER V

Transportation

Transportation provided great problems for the settlers. There were few roads and those that did exist were often impassable until the soft places were filled in with logs to make corduroy roads. In winter, travel was easier, for sleighs could be driven over the snow. Since the settlers were handy with tools, and often there was a blacksmith in their midst, it wasn't long before wagons and sleighs were available, but even so in spring and early summer getting about was never easy. Nature had marked the face of the country with hills, gulleys, unnavigable rivers, swamps, and small water courses which made it almost impossible to construct passable wagon roads during the first thirty years of settlement. Even lower Yonge Street was not excepted. One person commenting on 'Muddy York' wrote:

It was a sight to see Captain George Playter, the Squire of Todmorden, picking his way along King Street by hopping from one stone to another, carrying a gold cane, wearing a three-cornered hat, a skirted purple jacket, knee breeches and white stockings with silver garters. His broad-toed shoes fitted with gold buckles were soon soiled.

The settlers could make their own harness from the bark of the elm and basswood trees. The bark was peeled off in the spring of the year and water-rotted, much as flax, in order to separate fibre from rind. When properly prepared, this material formed a strong, useful, and cheap rope for traces, leading lines, halters, and even bed cords. Whippletrees were originally made from the withs of twisted willow. (Withintrees became wittentrees or whippletrees.)

In the Humber Valley area the old Indian Humber-Holland Trail that wound northward to Lake Simcoe was the only path available in the 1700s until roads were gradually opened up. But in the mid-nineteenth century, improvements came, based on the plentitude of wood.

The Albion Road Company was formed in 1846 and planked the Albion Road to Claireville, continuing north along Highway 50. Later the Vaughan Plank Road Company, formed in 1860, completed the "old Vaughan Plank Road" as far as the King boundary from Thistletown, through Woodbridge, Pine Grove, and Kleinburg.

Tolls were charged, to which farmers reacted with open revolt because of the poor condition of the roads. In 1890 Andrew Russell, reeve of Vaughan, condemned the bridge at Woodbridge, thereby giving an excuse for direct action. Some sixty-three young farmers of the district from Pine Grove to Kleinburg gathered by night to cut down the toll-bar at Kleinburg. Then they went to the gate at Woodbridge, chopped off the bar, and tossed it into the Humber River with great gusto. The boys intended to go down to Thistletown and demolish the gate there, but the Woodbridge tollkeeper, Sandy McIntosh, spoiled their plans. He seized his shotgun and fired into their midst. His defence may not have been exactly legal, but it was effective. The adventure ended in a visit to the doctor for one person, a thresher from Kleinburg, who had been shot in the thigh. No more tolls were collected, and by 1896 roads were a municipal responsibility. In celebration of that memorable night some verses were written, including the following:

> Now McIntosh he was a man of chivalrous degree,
> He declared that he and Margaret could lick the 63.
> So down with the toll gates, down with them three,
> For I'm Russell the Reeve of the Township, and have set the gravel free.

Smith's *Canada: Past, Present and Future* (1851) described Yonge Street as probably the most travelled thoroughfare in the province: in certain seasons of the year more than 200 loaded teams in a day might stop at an inn north of Toronto to water their horses. Stage coaches began very early on Yonge Street, travelling between York and points as far north as Holland Landing. About 1830 Cooks began a service between Toronto and Richmond Hill. About 1870 John Thompson began his stagecoach service from Toronto to Thornhill; later he extended it to Richmond Hill. Leaving Richmond Hill, Thompson's passengers started in a light coach drawn by two horses, and transferred to a heavier coach at Thornhill. The trip to Toronto took three hours and a half and the fare was 75 cents.

It was doubtless an interesting trip, as there were numerous stops en route to pick up mail and passengers. Thompson was noted for his unfailing courtesy, and could always make room for one more passenger. In addition he always had a host of errands which he had undertaken to carry out in Toronto. Women would often be seen running out as the heavy coach rumbled by to ask John Thompson to pick up some parcel for them on the way; it was seldom that he forgot. One story is related about a mother who rushed out to catch the stage with a small child under one arm and a bundle of clothes in the other. After safely boarding the coach, she proceeded to dress the youngster.

As is always the way with progress, the slower modes of life must give way to the faster. So it was that the Metropolitan Railway, built in 1896 up Yonge Street, first to Newmarket and then to Sutton, provided formidable competition for the slower and cumbersome stagecoach, and the Thompson family ceased to operate the coach line.

Also an enterprising man named Will Carter came along with a horse-bus that took a short trip to Maple. There it was possible to get on a warm railroad car for the balance of the journey.

The tollgate house at Langstaff, operated by Henry Richards and his son, Henry.
Some of the charges were:

      Pigs, sheep, and goats of all ages   *1 halfpenny*
      Saddle or led horses, mules, and asses   *do.*
      Oxen, cows, cattle of every description   *1 penny*
      Pleasure vehicles drawn by 1 horse or other beast of draught 2 pence.

Other keepers of this tollgate were a Mr. Taylor and Leonard Klinck. Tollgates were leased to the keepers. In 1868, lessees on the York roads were James McNamara, Alex Ross, George Lee, Edward Crown, Herod Noble, and Henry Richards. Leasing prices for the gates on Yonge Street were, for Gate No. 1, $5,800 (described as an upset price); Gate No. 2, $3,250; Gate No. 3, $1,300; Gate No. 4, $780; Gate No. 5, $595; Gate No. 6, $455. Several of the tollhouses on the road were said to be in a very disgraceful condition, in some cases almost untenable.

The Metropolitan Railway Station, Richmond Hill, about 1900. The radial lines were a popular means of transportation from 1896 until 1930.

The Canadian Pacific Railway depot at Kleinburg. This station was built in 1907, replacing one built in 1870. It was a busy centre: the train from Kleinburg carried milk cans to the city, and young people to high school in Weston. This photograph was taken before or in 1926.

The Metropolitan Railway provided something altogether new in transportation for Richmond Hill and other communities along the line. Not only did the railway carry passengers, it also carried freight. Many a district farmer shipped milk and other farm products to Toronto via the Metropolitan. From Sutton there was a spur line to Schomberg. By the late 1920s, however, the financial pinch was being felt all over Canada, and the Metropolitan line began to fail. Motor cars were coming into general use and by 1930 there were through buses to the north.

The Toronto Transportation Commission entered an agreement with the municipalities of North York, Markham, and Vaughan Township and the village of Richmond Hill, to operate a street car as far as the village. For many years, during the operation of that service, the former bandstand at the corner of Lorne Avenue and Yonge Street served as a terminal. It was demolished to make way for the Bank of Nova Scotia building. In later years the street cars were removed and the tracks torn up. The whole system was replaced by T.T.C.-operated buses. This system is still in operation and under the ownership of Markham, Vaughan, and Richmond Hill. However, the North York portion was incorporated into the Toronto Transit system under the Metropolitan Toronto Act.

The Toronto Grey and Bruce, a narrow gauge railway, was completed in 1871 over a distance of 47.5 miles. The inaugural run was from Toronto Junction through Woodbridge, Elder's Mills, and Kleinburg to Orangeville. George Wyllie was the first station agent, followed by Arthur Smith and George Brownridge, until the Canadian Pacific agent, John Fraser, was appointed in 1907. He retired in 1946, and was followed by Arthur Snyder, Thomas Martin, Alex. Stewart, and Frank Hutchinson, who remained until the station was closed officially May 31, 1968. George Wyllie, the first agent, arranged an experiment whereby human voices travelled back and forth over a railway telegraph wire between Woodbridge and Mono Road.

By 1914 the Toronto Suburban Electric Railway was completed to Woodbridge, taking passengers, students attending Weston High and Vocational School, and freight, to Toronto. An express car called the 'milk-wagon car' was run for the convenience of farmers shipping milk to the city. While the express cars continued to operate for a time, the passenger cars were discontinued in 1925. Just before the decision to halt operations was made, a deputation of citizens called on an official of the railway company to protest the shutdown of the line. 'How did you gentlemen get here?' the official asked. 'By automobile,' one of the deputation replied. 'That's why we're closing down the line,' the official said. The competition of the automobile is still a hazard to public transportation.

Rowland Burr, a well-known architect and builder, and the founder of Burwick (Woodbridge), conceived the idea in 1844 of a canal following the East Branch of the Humber through Vaughan and King townships, and continuing via the Holland River, Lake Couchiching, Lake Simcoe, and the Severn River to Cook's Bay on Georgian Bay. Burr traversed twice on foot the unbroken trail through the primitive forests to lay out the course of the canal, but nothing of a practical nature was done. He tried to interest prominent citizens in his scheme, and at a convention in Toronto in 1855 a committee of three was appointed to have a thorough survey made of the route, the one described above being their final choice. In 1862, Burr petitioned the council of the United Counties of York and Peel to again petition the Legislature for a grant of land for construction of the canal, so that stock could be sold to raise funds for this purpose. Engineers engaged to make a survey made a favourable report, but the scheme lapsed in 1883. It was revived again in 1894, but interest again lagged, and few nowadays recall that such a project was seriously considered.

The Northern Railway ran the full length of Vaughan Township from Concord through Maple to King City. The first sod was turned by the Earl of Elgin on October 15, 1851, and the railway was completed to Collingwood, a distance of 95 miles, by January 1, 1855. At that time the station at Maple was called Richmond Hill, and a stage coach ran five times a week from Richmond Hill to Maple to connect with the railway. The station burned down in 1904, and when the line was bought by the Canadian National Railway, the station was rebuilt and named Maple.

Jonathan Baker in his memoirs tells of seeing the railway engineer cross Sherwood sideroad where the men of the community were doing road work in the spring of 1852. By October the railway builders had already crossed the Sherwood sideroad with cars loaded with rails. He had his first ride to Toronto on a freight car. The passengers usually stood, and when the train crew took in water, they sometimes took it with pails from roadside ditches. The conductor was John Harvie and the brakeman John Meek on the first passenger train through Vaughan.

The North-West Company had a centre in York for some of its fur trading activities and was interested in improving communications north of York. On March 9, 1799, the *Upper Canada Gazette* announced that the company had advanced twelve thousand pounds towards making Yonge Street a good road. However, nothing came of this offer and the road continued to be impassable at certain times and seasons of the year.

The maintenance of roads remained with the settlers, who were obliged to do so many days' road work each year. But this was unsatisfactory because of the absentee owners and the Clergy Reserve and Crown Lands lots. Besides, the pathmaster, whose duty it was to oversee the work, often had little knowledge himself of road building. The amount of time a settler was expected to give was determined according to the value of his property:

If his property was rated at £25 two days were required.
If his property was rated at £25 to £50 three days were required.

The J.J. Cameron carts, manufactured in Vellore, were famous throughout much of the province in the 1890s.

Amos Maynard's Carriage Shop, Woodbridge, was built about 1880 and destroyed by fire in 1919. Amos is on the balcony with an employee, and his son, Augustus, is in the buggy. The family home is still on Pine Street, Woodbridge.

Milk was delivered to Toronto from the Woodbridge area before 1920 by team and wagon. George Tayles left home at 4 a.m. in 1911 and returned by 6 p.m., having covered a milk route of 45 miles.

George W. (Chip) Bagg delivered mail on Rural Route No. 2, Woodbridge, from 1914 to 1919. His route covered 23.75 miles.

If his property was rated at £50 to £75 four days were required.
If his property was rated at £75 to £100 five days were required.
If his property was rated at £100 to £150 six days were required.
If his property was rated at £150 to £200 seven days were required.
If his property was rated at £200 to £250 eight days were required.
If his property was rated at £250 to £300 nine days were required.
If his property was rated at £300 to £350 ten days were required.
If his property was rated at £350 to £400 eleven days were required.
If his property was rated at £400 to £500 twelve days were required.

Substitutes could be hired if the property owner was unable to do his share. Statute labour was finally abolished in 1920 after having been in existence for some 125 years.

A few years before, the Toronto and York Board of Highway Commissioners was changed to the Toronto and York Road Commissions. It was about this time that hard pavements took the place of gravel roads, one of the first paved sections being on Thornhill sideroad near Woodbridge. Probably for drainage purposes it had a rounded top; in wet weather, vehicles had to travel on the crown, or might slide off to the edge of the road. This portion of the road was built between 1920 and 1923. From 1928 to 1932 Number 7 Highway was built, named, and improved from Woodbridge to Thornhill. In 1937-8, Number 27 Highway was improved and named. Maple Sideroad to Richmond Hill was paved in 1958, and Bathurst Street from Steeles Avenue to Number 7 Highway in the same year. In 1962 Bathurst Street was paved from Langstaff Road to Maple Sideroad. Dufferin Street was paved as far as Concord approximately from 1923 to 1925. Highway 400, previously the Barrie Highway, was completed in 1951. Jane Street to Maple Sideroad was paved in 1968, and Keele Street to King City by 1969.

Cutters from Thornhill

CHAPTER VI

Agriculture

Although most of the first settlers in Vaughan Township were experienced farmers, they were settling on land that was covered with trees. Their first task was to clear the land so that they could sow their seeds. Fortunately, these Germans were accustomed to cutting down trees — and they did cut them down, they did not just girdle the bark so that the tree would die. The plan adopted was to fell the trees in rows; then with oxen (for this kind of job oxen were better than horses) the trees would be piles, and some quiet evening there would be a bee and they would be burned. This burning served two purposes: it got rid of trees and it made ashes. These ashes were bought by the British Government to be used in the making of gunpowder, and were the first cash crop for the farmer.

In the early years, the sale of ashes and locally made potash was probably the largest source of local income. As early as 1799 a potashery had been established by the Kendrick Brothers, and in 1800 W. Allan advertised that 'he conceives it his duty to inform those who may have ashes to dispose of, that it will not be in his power to pay cash, but merchandise at cash price'. In 1827 David Gibson of Markham described the method of clearing land and collecting the ashes:

After harvest, but before the snow falls, the farmers cut out all the underwood and lay it into heaps, and cut the fallen dead trees into pieces from twelve to twenty feet long according to their thickness. They go over the ground in this way cutting all that will be covered with snow, then when the snow is deep in winter they have the large trees to cut down, they cut the trees so that their top will fall near a brush heap, they first cut up the body of the tree in lengths from twelve to twenty feet in proportion to their thickness, then pile up the branches on the nearest brush-heap, letting the large logs or the body of the tree be scattered on the ground until during the summer when they burn off the brush-heaps. In a very dry time the fire will run all over the patch that is cut down, burning the leaves and vegetable mould between the brush-heaps which is considered to injure the land very much. The next piece of work is to roll the large logs into piles, which they call logging. It requires three men, a yoke of oxen and a driver. The oxen is yoked with the yoke and bow and having a chain from the middle of the yoke coming between the oxen which fastens round the log, the oxen are taught to start both at once with a sudden jerk which starts the log out of its bed and draws it to the pile, the other three men during the time carrying the small logs and putting them on the pile until it is three or four logs high and about the same breadth at the bottom. Logging is very hard work having so many heavy lists, and the men are as black as chimney sweeps when at this work, the logs get burned on the outside when the brush is burning. After the log heaps are burned they collect the ashes and take them to a potash work where they can get a little whiskey, Tea, or cloth in exchange, but cash is never given on account of its scarcity here.

The German settler cleared his land of stumps as soon as he could. With them he made fences for his livestock. Probably the first seeds he sowed were potatoes and pumpkins, which could be planted around stumps by the use of a hoe. Wheat was possibly his next, because it had been a main crop with him in Pennsylvania.

Livestock consisted of animals brought from the United States. Horses were mostly of the Conestoga breed; cows were a crossbreed noted for their hardiness and sometimes used as oxen. Pigs were often allowed to run wild, to live on nuts and any other food they could discover; they were known as razorbacks. Sheep were rather tall, frequently horned, and had darkish legs and faces. Chickens likewise were of a mixed type. Ducks and geese were raised but not turkeys, for there were plenty of wild turkeys. The streams were full of fish, and there was an abundance of wild fruit.

The main early crops were potatoes, wheat, peas, and oats. The British government made every effort to encourage the Upper Canada farmer to grow hemp, but without much success: the preparation of hemp for market was not to his liking. He preferred growing wheat, but about 1800 wheat was attacked by smut and the Hessian Fly, supposed to have been brought over from Europe by the Hessian soldiers (a theory now disproved).

As early as 1792 Acts were passed by the government to protect the farmer. One, for instance, regulated 'the tolls to be taken in mills'; it forbade any mill owner from taking more than one-twelfth of any grain for grinding and belting and this Act continued in force until 1867. Acts were passed to control pernicious weeds and the straying of animals, for the appointment of fence-viewers and highway overseers, for the licensing of stills for making whiskey and the collecting of customs duty from them. In 1801 inspectors of flour, pease, and potashes were appointed.

The farm implements provided by the government to the British settlers were largely hand tools, such as an axe, a saw, a hammer, a bill-hook, and a grubbing hoe, and a cross-cut saw among several families. There was a primitive plough with one handle. About 1808 the 'hog-plough' was brought in from the United States. It had a full iron share forming the front or rising part of the mould-board, the rest of it being wood. About 1815 the farmers adopted the cast-iron share and mould-board, all cast in one piece. The blacksmith usually made the tools, although the carpenter would make the wooden forks and shovels. Often these two craftsmen worked together, as in the manufacture of a three-cornered drag. In harvesting the sickle was used first, followed by the scythe, and later the cradle. For threshing, the only tool used was the flail, which consisted of two lengths of wood coupled by a leather thong: the part designed to thresh the grain was shorter and heavier than the section held by the flailer. Another method was to have horses or cattle tread the grain. There were several methods of separating the grain from the chaff. The first was throwing the grain in the air; if there was a strong wind it would blow away the chaff. Then came the sieve, and later the fanning mill: but these cost money and the farmer often continued to use the older methods.

The housewife found much wild fruit available. Besides plums and cherries there were raspberries, strawberries, gooseberries, and currants; before long, there were flourishing apple and pear trees grown from seed. Vegetables also were soon in abundance. In most cases fruit, pound for pound of sugar, was preserved to be eaten during the winter months. (Sealed glass jars were first patented in 1855.) Most families had some hives of bees to provide honey sweetening, and maple trees were tapped in the spring for the making of maple syrup and maple sugar.

When the Pennsylvania German farmer had his land free of trees, he practised methods that he had found to be successful in Pennsylvania. He used manure, gypsum, and lime as fertilizer and rotated crops. He built large bank barns to protect his feed grain and hay, and to house his animals during the winter in the stable underneath. The barns were often more pretentious than the early houses.

There is an interesting story concerning the discovery of gypsum as a means of increasing field-crop production. We have to go for the beginning to France, where a labourer employed in mixing stucco mortar at a large building noticed that the path used or made by him threw up a luxuriant crop of clover in the following year when all other parts of the field showed the opposite. On the assumption that this extraordinary growth was due to the dust on his clothes, he tried out some gypsum on clover near his cottage, and was amazed at the results. About 1770 a Pennsylvania German went to Germany for redemptions and, learning about the value of gypsum, brought back some samples, which, after much hesitation, some farmers were persuaded to use. At first it was feared that gypsum would attract lightning, and hence it was always taken out of buildings during an electric storm. In time this fear disappeared and its wonderful effects became apparent. Gypsum was known as plaster of paris because it was first obtained from the Hill of Montmartre, near Paris. Supplies in Canada came in rock form from Nova Scotia and could be crushed in an ordinary flour mill. It came into general use in Upper Canada about 1820 among the Pennsylvania German settlers, who employed it in growing clover in preparation for a later wheat crop.

The most common variety of winter wheat was the White Flint; Red Bald wheats were spring varieties, considered at least 15 per cent less valuable than the winter varieties. There was a continuous battle with smut, rust, Hessian Fly, and finally the wheat weevil, and various kinds of grains were experimented with to avoid attack. Planting late was also often tried, but then frost might be encountered.

Barley and rye were grown and sold to the distilleries. In 1835 appeared the army worm, which was particularly destructive to rye and meadows. This creature was rather slender, dark brown with a white streak on the side, about two inches in length at full size — and could consume a blade of grass in a couple of minutes. It appeared in great numbers; hence its name of army worm.

Drainage was always a problem to the farmer. Some of his best land was of little use because of its low-lying nature. Unfortunately, tile drainage was too expensive for the average man. He therefore resorted to running surface drains.

Until the town of York achieved some size there was not much market for butter and eggs unless those commodities could find an export sale. Most farmers kept chickens, ducks, and geese, and so did many people living in towns, in all cases for domestic consumption.

Jonathan Baker of Concord, Vaughan Township, gives a picture of haying and harvesting in the late 1830s:

Peter Cober in the year 1839 had a sugar bush on shares (Lot 10), and also in 1841 had part of the farm; he in that year had about 15 acres of meadow on shares on said Lot 10, on which he let Michael Baker have three acres. John Teel, Nicholas Cober, Jr. and George Cober mowed the same. Jonathan and Peter Baker spread the grass and in the year 1842 Peter Cober also had 12 acres of fall wheat on said Lot 10, on which he one Saturday had sixteen hands cutting and putting the same on shuck. They were not all men. Thomas Sharp was the oldest hand (he was about 58), Christle Reaman was the youngest (he was about 11 years old). No reaping machine then in this part. The cradlers were: 1st, Nicholas Cober, who took the lead; 2nd, Jonathan Schell; 3rd, John Baker, who at that time lived on Lot 5 in 3rd Thornhill Station; 4th, Peter Cober. The binders were: 1st, Jacob Cober, Daniel Reaman and John Cober; 2nd, George Longhouse, Margaret Cober and Mary Reaman; 3rd, George Cober and Joseph Wageworth; 4th, Thomas Sharp, Michael Baker and Jonathan Baker Jr. Christle Reaman reaped the lodged spots and also carried water for the hands to drink.

To quote Jonathan Baker again:

As for crops we will take the fall wheat which was about 1839 and for years the crop on which the farmer most depended. We will take the farm we are most acquainted with, that is, west half of Lot 13, in 2nd Concession (Vaughan Township) with about 45 acres of clearing, then owned and occupied by Michael Baker. As for the grain in 1839 fall wheat was in this part an uncommon failure; it was badly shrunk. There was on said farm 11 acres all in one field, there was plenty of straw, but not much wheat, part of same was cut with sickle, part with cradle, the same was threshed with machine, that was the first threshing done on said farm with machine, the same was one of the old-fashioned beater machines — no cleaner yet on threshing machines. At that time, grain, chaff and straw all came out together on the barn floor, the straw was separated from the grain and chaff by hand with forks, mostly wooden forks ...

Iron scoop shovels were in 1839 yet unknown in this part. We at that time had wooden scoop shovels only, but Jonathan Baker Sr. about 1841 bought in Toronto an iron-scoop shovel, the same was at that time seemingly quite a curiousity ...

As the clearings increased in size and stumps disappeared, the demand grew for implements and machinery to take the place of the wooden plough, the V-shaped harrows, the reaping hook and scythe,

the flail, and the old-fashioned methods of threshing grain. It was not, however, until the late 1830s that some improved implements became available. Perhaps one of the early additions was the Scottish iron plough, which was imitated by Canadian blacksmiths. Harrows were made of iron, and were much more widespreading and lighter. Wagons became lighter and sleighs more comfortable. Eventually the horse-drawn wooden dump-rake replaced the wooden hand-rake. For levelling off the lumpy ground, the farmer had a roller made of a heavy log of wood, with a tongue attached, to which horses were hitched. Cultivators were used between drills of corn and potatoes, covering about five feet and working to a depth of eight inches. Mowing machines, reapers, a hay rake, a 40-tooth diamond harrow covering nine feet, a cultivator, and seed drills were soon to be available for those who could afford them.

Livestock-raising in the early years of the nineteenth century was not a commercial enterprise because there was no market. Hog-raising was probably the most remunerative, although as soon as the British came they looked for their beef and were not interested in pork products. Here we have an explanation of why the Pennsylvania Germans prepared pork in so many different forms. They sold their beef animals to the British and were left with the pork, which they cured and lived on. To people who expended much energy in their physical work, fat pork was not only desirable, but a necessity.

It took many years to persuade the farmers to use pedigreed animals. Actually there was a reason for continuing to keep crossbreeds; they were hardier than the purebreds, which was quite a consideration in those days.

The year 1840 can be considered a turning point for agriculture in Vaughan Township. About that time horsepower began to replace a good deal of the work previously done by hand. This made it possible for the farmer to increase his production many times. Agriculture was becoming an industry.

The period between 1840 and 1867 saw Vaughan Township, because of its proximity to the growing city of Toronto, exposed to any political or economic changes taking place in the province. Besides, it had received a major infiltration of British who were never satisfied with the status quo. This was the period when agriculture began to pass from a purely subsistence level to a means of making a better way of life. Basically this was brought about by education, both in common schools and in scientific agriculture. The government was about to be involved, for in 1852 there was appointed a Minister of Agriculture at the federal level. It was the agricultural societies, however, which gave the impetus to the development of scientific agriculture.

From the 1840s to the present, agriculture in Canada has been dependent for its success on export markets, either the United States or Britain. When Britain repealed the Corn Laws in 1846, for instance, Benjamin Thorne, the founder of Thornhill, lost heavily, as did many farmers in Vaughan Township. After that, only when there were poor crops in the United States or in Britain was there a ready export market for Canadians. This dependence on overseas demand even extended to whether or not Britain was building ships for war, for when she was there was a market for ships' masts, and Vaughan Township with its tall pine trees could and did provide many masts.

Life tended to be boom and bust for the farmer. Because population was small, the home market was inadequate to take care of surplus products. When there was a war in Europe or even the United States, prices were good; but when peace came, prices fell. In addition, the average farmer was inclined to put all his eggs in one basket — that is, growing wheat. If there was a surplus of wheat one year, the price was low; if it was a poor year, he had none to sell, and hence no income.

The dangers of a single crop were brought home in 1858 when the wheat midge ruined all the wheat. For the next fifteen or twenty years success in growing wheat was dependent on the activities of this insect. Fortunately a parasite must have come into active existence, for by the 1870s the wheat midge was no longer very destructive. However, it did last long enough to force the farmer at long last to go into mixed farming. This was desirable, for the Vaughan Township farmer had a growing market right at his door — Toronto!

With the building of better roads and the improvement in Yonge Street, the Conestoga horse began to lose out. He was too slow. Being a crossbreed, the Conestoga could not be successfully crossed with any other breed, and so disappeared almost entirely — so much so that even many horse breeders today have never heard tell of him. He was replaced by what came to be known as the Canadian horse, which came from Quebec and was faster moving. Also, Clydesdale and Shire horses were brought in by the agricultural societies. Even these were too slow and two breeds from the United States, known there as Black Hawks but in Canada as Clear Grits and Royal Georges, became popular.

Among cattle, Durhams or Shorthorns were the greatest favourite. In Vaughan later in the century Michael Reaman, Robert Marsh, William Agar, George Bell, Peter Frank, Jacob Lahmer and Sons and Edwin Langstaff were top breeders of Shorthorns and showed at many of the fairs. Through the efforts of the agricultural societies, the Ontario Veterinary College was established in 1862. This was the first veterinary college to function in the whole of North America.

With the average farmer for many years 'pigs is pigs.' He did not go in for the new varieties but was content to feed his grain to what pigs he could buy or raise himself. Actually, the farmer looked to his pigs to provide most of his ready cash for with them there was always a quick turnover.

As early as 1843 farmers in York County were experimenting with 'Dantzic Wheat,' and finding it quite satisfactory; but in the early 1850s, 'Fife Wheat' proved the most satisfactory of all varieties and was in use until other varieties were recommended many years later.

Butchering day at Snider's farm on Lot 2, Concession 4, in the last century. Butchering was the occasion for a small "bee." Each family had skillfully home-made equipment consisting of a wooden scalding trough, lard press, sausage stuffer, and gammon sticks, plus a sausage grinder, many sharp knives, skimmers, and scrapers. Water for the scalding was boiling by dawn, and in one day the sausages would be stuffed, the lard rendered, and the liverwurst made. The structure in the background, built between 1840 and 1850, was used as a summer house until 1875 when a new building of poured cement was erected. It was then turned into a workshop and butcher shop. It was moved to Black Creek Pioneer Village in 1967. This sketch is by Campbell Snider.

The barn on Lot 1, Concession 3, Dufferin and Steeles, is one of only 20-odd octagonal barns in Ontario, and also one of the very few barns in the province having a gambrel roof with a broken pitch. It was built for Samuel Troyer, probably in the 1870s by Isaac Hafenbrack from timbers of a former barn. There is a ramp in front of it for entrance of animals.

Interior of a Vaughan Township log barn, showing the mows interlocked at the corners. The old wooden fanning mill was bought in 1867.

Alsike or Perennial Hybrid clover made its appearance in 1857. It is thought to have originated in Sweden, where it might grow to a height of four feet. In Canada two and half feet was average. Both sheep and cattle were more fond of it than the common clover or timothy.

Farmers carried on a continuous battle with such weeds as thistle, foxtail, twitch grass, mustard, and wild oats. Pulling by hand usually kept the last two in check.

The Ontario Poultry Society was formed in 1866. Farmers, because of the demand in the United States for eggs, began to realize that poultry might become a real industry and the future proved this to be a fact. In 1852 the 'Shanghai Mania or hen fever' reached York County and fancy breeds such as Shanghai, Buff Cochin China, Chinese Geese, and Muscovy ducks made their appearance in the farmer's backyard, but most of them remained only as show poultry.

Vaughan Township never went in for cheese making. There were creameries. The farmer preferred butter making, because he could use the buttermilk for his pigs, and there was a market for butter in Toronto.

By the end of the horsepower era — which ran from 1840 to 1867 — farming had shifted in Vaughan Township from wheat growing to dairying or to mixed farming. This was to a great extent due to the introduction of horsepower over handpower. There were horsepower threshers, ploughs, harrows, stump pullers, fanning mills, gang ploughs — most of this machinery being made in Canada.

In 1850 fruits and vegetables were in abundance. Apples in use were Early August, St. Lawrence, Fall Pippin, Snow, Ribston Pippin, Greening, Baldwin, Yellow Bellflower, Russet, together with Bartlett Pears. Pests in 1859 included the bark louse, apple tree borer, apple worm, caterpillars, cherry and pear slug, the Circulio or plum weevil, birds, and field mice — all waiting for the scientist to control them.

The 1842 census showed 49 hives of bees in the township. In 1891 there were 600 hives. The honey was a valuable addition to the food supply.

There was also maple syrup — a product that can be made only in a small area of the northeastern part of North America where the sugar maple tree can grow. One of the unique features of Vaughan Township has been its fine-flavoured maple syrup, which is due in part to the fact that the roots of the trees are not in rock as in other maple-producing areas. There is no doubt the pioneers from Pennsylvania learned to make the syrup from the Indians there, for it was unknown in Europe. Early wills and lists of goods and chattels mention syrup-making equipment. Vaughan's early settlers made their own supply of maple sugar: money to buy cane sugar was scarce, and the maple variety was an important addition to their food supply. The 1842 census reported 36,880 pounds of maple sugar produced in Vaughan. In 1850 the report was 15,028 pounds. As time went on and other sugar became cheaper, fewer farmers made maple syrup. The early method was to bore a hole three inches deep into the maple tree, drive in a homemade wooden spile, and set wooden troughs to catch the drops of sap. The sap was collected with a yoke and pails and boiled in big iron kettles. Wooden buckets soon replaced the troughs. Only a few people still make syrup today. However, one family has made it continuously and now tap 7,000 trees annually where they tapped 70 trees 100 years ago. Thousands of school children come to several sugar bushes in the township to see the old and new methods of making this delicious product.

The period following Confederation saw agriculture becoming more scientific and receiving more attention from the Department of Agriculture, which had a full time commissioner and deputy minister in 1868. However, their duty was more to disseminate facts relating to agriculture than to give direction. The direction did not begin until 1888, following a report of the Agricultural Commission in 1881. In 1874 the Ontario Agricultural College was formed at Guelph.

Pests seemed to be increasing in varieties and numbers. In 1884 the clover midge appeared and caused a loss of $500,000 to farmers. The pea weevil had been destructive in York County as early as 1830. The Entomological Society came into being in 1860 with the purpose of curtailing if not eliminating pests; the potato bug was controlled, for example, by the use of Paris green. However, smut on wheat, oats, and barley continued to produce losses.

The Ontario Agricultural Commission in 1881 produced some interesting statistics about Vaughan Township:

1. Some 19,266 acres were heavy clay; 41,074 acres, clay loam; 5,670 acres, sandy loam; and 1,000 acres, sand. Of this acreage, 35,000 were first class for agricultural purposes, 20,000 second class, and 12,510 third class; prices were $70 per acre for first-class land, $50 for second class, $30 for third class. About two-thirds was clear of stumps; half of the rest had pine stumps.

2. One-third of the dwellings were brick, stone, or first-class frame; two-thirds were log or inferior frame. One-third of out-buildings were of first-class construction; two-thirds were inferior. One-third of the land was tile drained. All farmers used improved farm machinery.

3. One-half the farmers used non-organic fertilizer, with plaster on grainland.

4. 10,000 acres fall wheat, 18 bushels per acre; 2,750 acres spring wheat, 10 bushels per acre; 6,600 acres barley, 18 bushels; 6,500 acres oats, 50 bushels; no rye; 5,000 acres peas, 15 bushels per acre; no corn; no buckwheat; 700 acres potatoes, 100 bushels per acre; 700 acres turnip, 500 bushels; 500 acres other root crops, 500 bushels per acre; 6,600 acres hay, 1½ tons per acre; 8,000 acres pasture lands; 500 acres orchards; about 8,000 acres under fallow.

5. Kinds and breeds of stock: Horses: Clydesdales; Cattle: Durhams; Sheep: Long-wooled Suffolk; Hogs: Berkshire.

6. Standing timber: 11,000 acres, principally pine and hardwood.

7. Market facilities were good, with Toronto as market town; two railways ran through the front and rear of the township; two agricultural implement manufacturers.

8. Acreage: 67,510. Population: 5,635. Cleared land: 56,500 acres.

9. Numbers of horses, 2,481; cattle, 2,952; sheep, 4,349; hogs, 2,207.

About 1894 dairying and hog raising were introduced to help over the slump and trying times. Wheat and barley were the main crops. In that year prices were: wheat, 45 cents per bushel; oats, 15 cents per bushel; barley, 30 to 35 cents per bushel; potatoes, 10 cents a 90-lb. bag. Hay sold for five dollars a ton; mares were $40 in 1900 and many went to the boneyard. Milk was 42 to 43 cents per hundredweight at Maple Creamery. Wages for hired help ranged from $150 to $200 per year, $10 to $15 a month, and 50 cents a day for a labourer. In addition to the large quantity of timber and logs marketed, rougher wood was sold as firewood at Toronto at $3 and $5 a cord.

Agricultural progress in the township may be traced briefly in the following paragraphs.

Wheat and barley were the main crops, with livestock increasing in numbers.

Spring wheat was widely grown from 1890 to 1905, but since 1905 acreages have decreased considerably.

Barley equalled the acreage of wheat before 1894. Since that year barley has been largely used for feed.

Oat production in 1851 was less than half that of wheat. By 1911 oat acreage had doubled.

Rye was never extensively grown, with only 300 acres cultivated in 1900. This grain was threshed with a flail.

Buckwheat was important after 1910 as a catch crop and a smother or green manure crop.

During this period the economic prosperity of the farmer fluctuated greatly. However, many organizations to promote livestock, dairy, and fruit farming were formed. Agriculture had moved out of the pioneer stage. Vaughan Township made its contribution to the dairy herds by the introduction of Holstein cattle.

William Shunk of Sherwood, Vaughan Township, was the first farmer to introduce a Holstein cow, Annin 397, and a bull, Alexander V, into York County. This he did in 1883. His brother, Simon, Jr., at Edgeley, bought the second Holstein animals in 1884; he paid $1,800 for one bull and $1,200 for three heifers. John Line, also of Sherwood, made the third purchase of Holsteins in 1887. These men showed their animals at fairs and won prizes. William Shunk was president of the Dominion Holstein Association in 1892.

Peas produced in Vaughan Township in 1890 amounted to 100,000 bushels. Because of the weevil, pea production dropped. Some years the whole crop was destroyed. Peas were difficult to harvest.

Husking corn was not grown.

Mixed grains of oats, barley, spring wheat, peas, were not extensive until 1900. Since then large amounts have been grown.

Forage crops consisted of corn mostly and much was used for silage for winter feed for cattle.

Roots took the form of turnips and mangels, until 1900 when corn replaced them.

Potatoes were not an extensive crop, grown for the family table.

Hops were grown extensively and used for bread yeast and beverage.

Flax was a limited crop. Interest in it grew during the world wars: its fibre was required for airplane fabric.

Pasture provided grazing for livestock. Permanent pastures were developed.

Hay was much grown; loose hay was teamed to Toronto for horsefeed, the bulk of it being timothy and red clover.

Grass and clover seeds, including alfalfa, alsike, sweet clover, and red clover, were profitable crops both before and after 1900.

Soya bean, sorghum, millet, and rape were grown in small quantities.

Livestock was found on each farm. Horses, cattle, swine, sheep, and poultry were raised in sufficient numbers for domestic and market use. The horses were heavy draught, general purpose, and light driver breeds. Cattle were raised to supply milk, butter, and beef for home consumption. Fat cattle were marketed to drovers and city markets.

Hogs were killed, dressed and packed in barrels for Toronto buyers, but there was a change to lighter-weight hogs.

The beginning of the twentieth century marked a great change for the farmers in Vaughan Township, as for those in many other sections of Ontario. It was the end of the horse and buggy era, and the beginning of the gas engine period. Life on the farm had been relatively peaceful, although prices of farm products were quite low. The tempo of life was speeded up to keep pace with the motor car and the farm tractor. The first world war brought about a scarcity of farm help, which, in turn, brought into use an entirely new kind of farm machinery. During the war, prices of farm products increased, as did the wages demanded by farm help, when available. Following the close of the war, there was a slump in prices of what the farmer had to sell — but not of what he had to buy, such as fertilizer, food concentrates, and farm machinery.

It was the beginning of inflation, and of an increasing exodus from rural areas of people going to work in urban industry. Also it was the beginning of the demise of small family-owned farms in favour of the large mechanized farm owned and operated by a wealthy business tycoon.

Since Vaughan Township was so close to Toronto, real estate began to be exploited. Up Yonge Street, as far as Richmond Hill, as early as 1911 farms were bought and sold in five-acre lots to the uninitiated. New communities, such as Richvale on Yonge Street, came into existence. Villages that had remained static in population for many years, or had lost their inhabitants, suddenly found themselves increasing in size. Villages such as Thornhill, Richmond Hill, Wood-bridge, and Maple, and before long even Kleinburg, were becoming suburbia for the city of Toronto. Take Richmond Hill as an example: the author took the census in 1911 and recorded some 762 persons; fifty years later the population was over 20,000.

Time increased the demand for farm property in the southern part of the township for purposes of subdivision, and fantastic prices have been paid for land in Vaughan Township that from an agricultural

The Dick brothers, Alex and Albert, with their first threshing outfit, a J.I. Case steam engine and thresher, in 1906.

John Ireland's threshing machine at James Bell's, about 1920. The water tank behind the steam engine was filled from a nearby stream twice a day.

After threshing, the grain was taken to the barn in bags, and the straw stack was left in the field. The men in the foreground are Dan McLean, Sr., and James Bell. The Bell farm was on Lot 17, Concession 8.

point of view was worth very little. If there was a stream, a woods, or hilly ground, the property was much sought after. Furthermore, with the increase in population and the construction of new houses and other buildings, any property with sand or gravel under the top soil became exceedingly valuable, for new gravel pit machinery powered by gas engines could cope with any terrain, no matter how inaccessible or useless it had hitherto been. The Honey Pot area is an example. Once upon a time in the late nineteenth century, the front part of the Honey Pot Farm, once owned by the author's family on the maternal side, was used for a few years as a farm. Now the rear end towards Maple has become one immense gravel pit and the front portion on the third concession is a ski-run. Thus we see how the face of the township has been changed.

In like manner the farm practices have changed. Fertilizers of all kinds came on the market and were soon found to be essential for depleted soils. There were also pesticides and fungicides to control weeds, insects, and other enemies of grains and animals.

Horses were seldom found any longer on farms. The grain separator owned by the farmer (hence no more threshing bees) was driven by a tractor, and later the combine did the threshing in the fields. The old-fashioned rake drawn by one horse was supplanted by the side delivery rake. Then the baler took over and the hay or straw was compressed into small wire-bound bundles. Large barns for grain and hay were only half filled because the hay had been baled and the grain threshed in the field, with consequent saving of storage space. Buildings were lighted by electricity, and gas engines relieved the farmer of much hand work.

Proximity to communities which required fluid milk, and the development of milking machines, brought about the growth of large herds of milking cows. These herds, in turn, required special feed which could be bought ready prepared. Hybrid corn packed into silos provided succulent food for much stock.

The increase in the use of machinery meant that the farmer had to have plenty of ready cash or good credit to purchase what he considered necessary. This increase in investment in machinery brought about another change. The farmer on a small acreage could not justify putting so much money into farm equipment. Hence he had to do one of two things: sell out, or buy more land. This situation was intensified by the businessman who bought land for farm purposes. He usually had enough capital to acquire the latest farm equipment and, because he did not count on earning his living from the farm and was willing to farm as a hobby, could buy expensive machinery and pay high wages.

Vaughan Township farmers have been particularly vulnerable to all of these changes in rural-urban society. The Pennsylvania German for a long time resisted them. Having large families he, for a time, had plenty of handpower, but as time went on and higher education became more widespread, the young people left the farms for the higher wages and shorter hours of business or industry. Consequently, even these farmers were forced to use more machinery.

Real estate brokers plagued them often to sell for subdivision. Industry and business were seeking larger premises and they, too, were willing to pay for land amounts of money which could never be expected from farm products. In many cases where the farmer was either middle-aged or had sons content to farm, he sold his property and moved back into areas not so much influenced by urban development, and continued farming in the new location.

We must not forget the inflation following the Second World War because, here again, the farmer got the small end of the stick. Consumers were looking around for cheaper food substitutes and, when they discovered them, the farmer found less demand for his produce and looked to the government for subsidy. The inroads of margarine on butter is a typical example.

But the results have not been all negative. Farming now is not a matter of brawn but of brain. It has become mechanized and scientific. The farmer no longer plants just any kind of grain or keeps just any type of cattle. The Department of Agriculture is active with its agriculture representatives, Junior farmers, and 4-H Clubs, so that today's farmer can get expert advice concerning all of his activities. Furthermore, the farmers have often given leadership. Artificial insemination of cattle is a typical example — and don't forget that it really got off the ground when, in Vaughan Township, the Maple Cattle Club was started with G. Wilfred Keffer as president in 1945. This has done away with many of the scrub bulls, and there has come about a keen appreciation of the necessity for registered seed and pedigreed animals.

Farming in Vaughan Township is no longer a means of subsistence only. It is an industry which challenges and requires the best brains to carry on successfully. But let us not forget the saying of the original German Settlers, for the principles are just as true today as in the early pioneer days although the practices are vastly different: 'Kein Futter, Kein Vieh; Kein Vieh, Kein Dung; Kein Dung, Kein Erfrag' — 'Without food, no cow; without a cow, no manure; without manure, there can be no profit.'

We must also not forget the farm home, and the housewife who now lives in a house which, mechanized with electricity, is just as modern as any urban home. It now has a telephone, a radio, and a television set; in many cases the housewife has a motor car for her own use. The children are picked up by a school bus and transported to larger schools. No one, adult or child, is handicapped any longer by living on a farm.

Perhaps one of the changes most appreciated in rural domestic life has been the ease of communication that followed the introduction of the telephone. The Woodbridge and Vaughan Telephone Company Ltd. was incorporated on February 11, 1910. This name was used until December 31, 1950. For many years the company operated without a

*The first shipment of cattle to leave Canada by air was made in August 1946
from Malton airport. This trial shipment of Holstein calves, purchased by the
Cuban Minister of Agriculture, was the forerunner of a Canadian cattle export
business to South America. At the "Winged Cargo" air freighter on the tarmac
are, from left, W.H. Reid, Georgetown; Roy H. Barker, Woodbridge; Carl Weber,
Palmerston; W.H. McCaugherty, Streetsville; Ray Clarkson, Weston; W. Mort.
Wardlaw, Kleinburg. Next day The Telegram burst into poetry to comment that*
            Our Holsteins go to pastures new
            They leave their native clover
            And bills come high for bulls that fly
            As purchasers discover.

Officers of the Maple Cattle Breeders' Association were photographed during an inspection tour to the New York State Cattle Breeders' Co-operative Association facilities in June 1946. Front row, left to right: George C. Jackson, Downsview, who bred the six bulls used at the Maple unit; G.W. Keffer, Maple, president; W.P. Watson, assistant director of the livestock branch, Ontario Department of Agriculture; Maurice Johnston, Cornell University, manager of the host association. Back row: Dr. C.R. Reeds, Maple, technician; James M. McDonald, Maple, secretary-treasurer; W. Moffat Cockburn, Newmarket, Agricultural Representative for York County.

by-law controlling the erection of poles and wires, but in 1939 By-law 700 was passed by the Municipal Council of Woodbridge authorizing them to erect poles and wires on the streets for general telephone business. In 1928 the Bell Telephone Company of Canada acquired a controlling interest in the Woodbridge and Vaughan Telephone Company Ltd., and on January 1, 1940, an amalgamation took place with the Home Telephone Co. Ltd., which operated six telephone exchanges east of Yonge Street, and purchased the rural telephone connected at the Bell Telephone Port Perry Exchange. The stock of the Home Telephone Co. was chiefly owned by the Bell Company.

The first switchboard installed in Maple was around 1910 in the Henry C. Bailey general store. In Woodbridge the first switchboard was in the Medical Building, with Harold D. Mullaney, jeweller, in charge. Among the personnel of the Woodbridge and Vaughan Telephone Company Ltd. who gave long service were Dr. and Mrs. Fred W. Routley. Dr. Routley was president and Mrs. Routley secretary-treasurer. William Ingram had the responsibility of caring for the horses and vehicles when poles and wires were being constructed in the 1910-15 period. In 1926 he again became a telephone employee. Morley J. Kinnee became employed as a lineman in 1924, then became a repairman, and from 1931 to 1950 was general manager and secretary-treasurer.

One event of general interest occurred in 1924 when a general increase in rates was sought by the company from $12.00 to $15.50 per annum for a rural party telephone. At that time there was organized opposition and the company was obliged to remove almost one-third of its telephones. In due course most of these were reinstalled.

The telephone was operated on a battery system until dial was introduced. Three exchanges serve the largest portion of Vaughan Township. The Woodbridge and Kleinburg-Nashville exchanges introduced the dial system to the western part of the township on November 18, 1956, and the Maple exchange area came into being on November 1, 1959. Richmond Hill and Thornhill serve the eastern part of the township.

CHAPTER VII

Villages

Riverside hamlets followed a common growth pattern. First came the sawmill, simple and inexpensive in its construction, to make lumber out of the logs the neighboring farmers brought in. If it survived fire and flood, and the mill seat proved dependable as a source of power, a grist mill was added to supply the settlement with coarse whole wheat flour. Then came the man with the store, and the plant was converted into a commercial flour mill. The miller attracted customers who sold wheat at a dollar a bushel and took it out in store trade. Next came a cooper to make flour barrels; then the blacksmith, the cobbler, the tailor, another country store, a tavern, and in time a tannery, wagon shop, sometimes a woolen mill. A distillery was added to make use of damaged grain.

Burrlington

The story of Burrlington as a community can best be told by its mills. Although Crown deeds were issued as early as 1801, much of the property was not opened up until the late 1840s or early 1850s because parts of the township were not surveyed until about 1851, although a number of squatters had moved in.

The community was located in Concession 9. The first recorded settler was William Gaffney, a Roman Catholic from Ireland whose first child, Katherine, was born on their new location on Lot 32, in July 1848. But two other families made the community come to life.

William Graham, also from Ireland but a Presbyterian, settled on the east half of Lot 1, Concession 6, Albion Township, which he named Tormore. Later he bought property on the 10th line and built a combination grist and sawmill. In 1853 he purchased the west half of Lot 30, Concession 9, and in 1854, the east half of Lot 32, Concession 10.

In 1837 Rowland Burr came over from Yonge Street and in the same year built mills at Burwick (Woodbridge). In 1847 he bought property on the west half of Lot 35, Concession 10 but found it unsatisfactory and sold it, later buying the west half of Lot 31, Concession 9.

Here he proceeded to build a woollen mill and dammed up the water for his saw and grist mill. But he ran into difficulties because he was interfering with the supply of water that William Graham required.

There was litigation over the matter and Graham won out. Burr, although he had subdivided some of his property and sold several lots, closed his mills. This meant the end of Burrlington Village.

On the other hand, Graham's mill prospered. New houses and barns were built on the property until 1882 when Robert Dick, who had married one of the Graham daughters, was killed. Mrs. Dick carried on with the aid of her sons, Alexander, William, and Albert, until the mill burned down in 1902. With a change to steam power, the grist mill operated until 1910.

Alexander and Albert Dick bought a J.E. Case steam threshing outfit in 1906. Alexander took over in 1912 and Albert went back to the farm. In 1933 the Dick barn was burned and rebuilt. In 1939, Robert, a younger son, established a welding and general repair shop in the farm, and it was quite successful.

Burrlington no longer exists as a village and the name would be forgotten were it not for the Burrlington School and Gallows Hill. The Burrlington School is now used as a nature study school. There is much conjecture as to the origin of the name of Gallows Hill, on the 10th Concession just south of Burrlington. A man is supposed to have hanged himself at this point. And story has it that a man who worked for Rowland Burr made the remark that the hill was just like the Gallows Hill near Montgomery's Tavern on Yonge Street.

Carrville

Carrville has had mills, a store, a school, and a church. Of these only the church remains active.

The flour and sawmills were started by Michael Fisher, Sr., about 1820 on Lots 16 and 17, Concession 2, and later rebuilt. The Cooks bought the mills in 1833. In 1841 Jacob Baker put a new waterwheel in the mill, with a water pitch on a new plan for which he was able to secure a patent. In 1848–9 Thomas Cook built a new sawmill on a larger scale a few rods west of the old mill on the same dam with an overshot wheel 18 feet in diameter. The grist mills were continued by George Kirby, Anthony Wilson, and Ross Bowes and destroyed by fire on November 16, 1933.

In 1844 Thomas Cook started a small store on Lot 17, Concession 2 in a building near his grist mill, and in 1845 he erected a new building on Lot 16, Concession 2 near the road. He moved his stock of goods there and for the next seventy years or so this store served the community. Mr. Hay was the first storekeeper. In 1846 Mr. Brackenridge took over and continued until 1848. Mr. Swan was there until 1849, Thomas Scholfield and Mr. Bailey to about 1853, and Richard Love until 1858. After that came Mr. Lund, Mr. Bolitho, and Mr. Denton, and later William Mellish, Wilbert Bone, Alfred Hyde, and G.M. Mullen. Then Wilbert Bone returned and moved the post office to his farmhouse, west of the store. The store was closed and is still in use as a private home.

Carrville post office was established in 1865 and closed in 1923. Postmasters have been: Thomas Cook, William Cook, Wilbert

Carrville Mill served the community as a flour mill for over 100 years. The four-storey structure was built in 1826 by Michael Fisher, Sr., and destroyed by fire in 1933. A cider mill was connected with it. A stationary engine provided power when water supplies were low.

Claireville, looking east, in 1945.

Concord had a store at the corner of Dufferin Street and Highway No. 7 from the first one built in 1846 by Peter Oster until a successor building put up by Norman Bowes was taken down in recent years so the highway could be widened. This was one of the early stores. It was burned on May 14, 1917.

Bone, Alfred Hyde, G.M. Mullen, and Wilbert Bone.

Carrville continues to have a community spirit. Some of the old families are the Reamans who have been living there continuously since 1804, the Bones, Mitchells, Wingers, Bartons, DelBroccos, Woods, and Reads. Old families now gone are the Grahams, Pattersons, Prentices, and Middletons.

Claireville

Situated at the corners of the townships of Gore, Etobicoke, and Vaughan, this village was founded by J.P. de la Hay, who originally owned the property on which it is situated. The name was given in honour of his daughter Claire.

The first house was built in 1832 and was occupied as a public hotel by John Dark. The next building was the Congregational Church, with the Rev. Samuel Harris as minister. The first store was built by John Donaldson and occupied by Messrs. Mason and Tisdale.

This village in 1877 had about 175 inhabitants and contained besides one store a blacksmith shop, saddlers' shop, Temperance Lodge, Primitive Methodist church, and hotel. The name of the post office in 1877 was "Humber"; Robert Bowman was the first postmaster.

One of the early settlers of this district was Elisha Lawrence who was born in New Brunswick in December, 1799. He settled on Lot 2, Concession 9, Toronto Gore in 1821. He had previously made a contract to make the Gore Road as part payment for his farm. A short time after he settled he completed the contract, which proved satisfactory to all. When he first settled in the Gore he had to carry his grist fifteen miles to Richmond Hill.

As a village Claireville in time became much smaller. In 1945 there was only a store, a hotel, and a service station. The post office had disappeared with rural delivery from Woodbridge.

In 1945 the Toronto Coach Lines established a daily service running through Claireville. The same year the school had its largest attendance since its erection with Miss Small as teacher. The population remained static for many years but has gradually increased.

Coleraine

Coleraine was a little hamlet situated on the four corners of Highway 50 and Coleraine sideroad. As Highway 50 is the dividing line between York and Peel Counties, Coleraine is partly in Toronto Gore Township, Peel County, and Vaughan Township, York County.

Originally known as Frogville, this community had as an early settler before 1834 a family of Raines, along with a Mr. Cole who immigrated from Northern Ireland. The names of these two families were united to form the name Coleraine.

In the Canadian Directory of 1858 it was listed as having a post office and store, and as receiving mail daily. The property was owned and operated by Thomas St. John. The population was about 50 and along with the store there was a wagonmaker's shop run by C. Holtby, a blacksmith shop run by J. Jones, and two hotels, one with A.

Mackinnon as proprietor and the other with John Whitehead. John Mills was shoemaker for the community.

The hotel on the northeast corner was known as the Beehive Inn. One of the outstanding features of this place was a sign in the shape of a beehive hanging in the bar room. It read:

Inside this hive
We're all alive
The Whiskey keeps us funny.
If you be dry,
Step in and try
The flavour of our honey.

By 1877 Coleraine had Joseph Street as storekeeper and postmaster; D. McGahoe as blacksmith; J. Downs (nicknamed Johnny the Fiddler) and M. McFarlane as wagon manufacturers; Joseph Allan as hotelkeeper, and W. Parr, keeper of the Temperance House. At that time the population was about 100.

Thomas St. John, Jr., ran the store until 1904 when the Ward family acquired it. J. R. Scott bought it in 1906 and in 1909 Henry B. Gee took over. He in turn sold it to Mr. & Mrs. W. J. Watson who were succeeded by their son Neil and his wife Mary.

The road from Toronto was originally an Indian trail, which became a plank road, then eventually a gravel road, and was paved in 1946 as Highway 50. About the middle of the first world war the mail was delivered from Nashville by a rural mail carrier: Leonard Maggs was the first, followed by Jimmie Taylor in a Model T Ford. The store continued to be a necessity to the community until the coming of the motor car. With the widening of the road the store was demolished, having served the community for over 100 years.

The first school was established in 1853 and a brick school was built in 1868. In 1956 the "little red schoolhouse" was replaced by a modern school that was closed by Vaughan Township School Board. It is now a private home.

A Wesleyan Methodist Church began in 1861 and was closed in 1901, the congregation joining that of Shiloh.

Concord

The Fisher and Oster families were undoubtably the first settlers in the Concord area. In 1846 Peter Oster built a store on the southeast corner of Lot 6, Concession 3. Johnstone Brothers were the builders. This store was occupied by Richard Love until about 1853, and then by Henry McElroy.

The post office was named Concord and was established on January 8, 1854, with John Duncan as postmaster. He served until 1871, followed by Henry McElroy (1871—88), Mrs. Ann McElroy (1888—94), W.J. Clarke (1894—99), William Golland (1900—03), John L. McDonald (1903—08), William Carson (1908—09), Bert Heise (1909—19), Frank T. Miller (1919), Norman Bowes (1919—1947), Mrs. Evelyn Bowes (1947—50), Mrs. Evelyn Lapping (1950—63), and Mrs. Verna Madill (1963—).

The railway station was called Thornhill Station. Hiram White, who came in 1818 from Vermont, where there is a small community called Concord, may have suggested the name for Concord, Ontario.

A blacksmith shop was opened on the corner of Lot 8, Concession 3 about 1846 by Isaac White. It was continued by Thomas Keys, Aut Brillinger, Jim Fisher, Fred Minton and George Fox. The building was torn down about 1945. There was also a small two-storey building near the road 100 yards to the south, which was used as a paint shop for the buggies and wagons made at the blacksmith shop. Wilmot White was in business here about 1910.

In 1922 Fred Miller built the greenhouses in Concord. They have continued to expand and are called the Concord Floral Company. The Cooper family farmed Lot 6, Concession 2 for many years until it was subdivided, as was Tom Keffer's farm, west half Lot 5, Concession 3. This brought many new residents to the area. Lot 5, Concession 2 was owned by different families, in earlier times by the Charlton family, later by the Redman family. The west part of Lot 5, Concession 2 has been owned by William Clarke, his son George, and grandson Edward. Edward's family have built homes on the home farm. The Fisher place, the east part of Lots 3, 4 and 5, Concession 3, is now a golf course.

Edgeley

The village of Edgeley once consisted of a store, a hotel, a cider mill, a shingle and chopping mill, a church, hall, a blacksmith shop and a slaughter house. There was a woodworking shop of two storeys on the James Hoover farm, south of the townline, which supplied wagons and buggies for the people of this area.

A double house, one side a shoemaker's shop and the other side a dressmaking establishment, stood over a hundred feet west of Concession 5. On the southeast corner of Concession 5 was the store and post office. The shingle mill stood on the northwest corner. It used steam power and was operated by David Smith and his sons, Franklin, Sidney, Alfred Jos., and Carson. David Smith also manufactured caskets for the community and his wife made the casket pillows. The mill where the logs were sawed and cut up into shingles closed about 1900.

The cider mill stood a short distance south of the store on the east side of the road, behind the farm buildings and to the north of the lane. It was owned and operated by Samuel Snider on Lot 5, Concession 4. He produced only apple cider, for the machinery or press was operated by horsepower. When his son-in-law, Abraham Winger, took over, Abraham and his brother Henry put up a new building closer to the road. This mill was operated by steam power and they produced cider, apple butter, and apple jelly. In the fall the 5th, now Jane Street, saw a steady stream of horsedrawn vehicles going to the jelly mill, as it became known. This trek began early in the morning and ended late at night. Some people even stayed overnight. When Abraham moved to Carrville in 1900, they carried on for a year or two with the mill; then

Henry had it alone, then his son Jesse, then Abraham's son Asa, who later sold it to Mr. Reesor who had it until 1917. In later years it was just a chopping mill.

Garton's slaughterhouse stood south of the cider mill at one time. Carson Smith's slaughterhouse, on Lot 6, Concession 4, was moved to Pioneer Village in 1970. A beef ring was operated for a few years, then another was started in 1895. Each ring consisted of about twenty members. For a while James Garton and David Smith were the butchers; later Carson Smith killed for both rings for over forty years. Beef was as low as 5½c a pound to members. The beef ring closed in 1937. The interesting beef ring tools are preserved in the Dalziel Barn at Pioneer Village.

The blacksmith shop was occupied by Morris Gray, Jake Peterman, Joe Cousins, and William Reid, who came in 1901.

The hotel on the northeast corner was operated by Mr. MacFayden, Mr. Blackburn, Andy Lloyd and Mr. Armstrong. It was turned into a dwelling by John Jackson and in 1908 acquired by Percy Snider.

William and Daniel MacDougall owned the first threshing machine and Edgar and Arthur Kennedy owned the first tractor in Edgeley. George and Frank Bagg owned a very early chain-driven tractor. Aaron Whitmore is said to have owned the first binder in Vaughan.

The Edgeley Farmers Club was organized in 1917 and for many years the farmers in the area obtained their supplies of coal, binder twine, salt, and other necessities through this club. The oyster supper was an annual event for years. It was started in 1918 with Mr. and Mrs. Will Locke the first oyster cooks. Secretaries of the Edgeley Farmers Club have been Carson Smith, Robert Mitchell, and Paul Snider.

Each winter Jacob Hoover conducted a singing class, using a tuning fork. Each member paid from fifty cents to a dollar for a winter's course.

Edgeley post office was opened in 1872, John Barnes being postmaster until 1874. He was followed by Jesse Smith. In 1880 Jake Shunk took over the duties and he was followed by Abe Winger in 1884. From 1887 to 1905 Lafayette Whitmore was on duty. His son, L. Arthur Whitmore, held the position and served until his death in 1958. The office was closed on the death of Miss E. Whitmore in 1960. The building was demolished when Number 7 Highway was widened.

Edgeley Hall, which played a varied and important role in that community, was built in 1877 on Lot 3, Concession 4, the property of Joseph Burkholder. It had an open drive shed and an auditorium above. It was built for the use of the Independent Order of Good Templers by community contributions of money, material and labour. The first trustees were Amos Bean, Daniel Snider, and James Garton.

More than once the hall was moved to other locations, and was used by the Good Templers, as a singing school, and by a literary society. It was moved in 1902 to its last location, the west part of Lot

The Edgeley store stood on the southeast corner of Jane Street and Highway No. 7. It was torn down when Jane was widened and paved.

Highway No. 7, looking east from the 5th Concession (Jane Street) in 1910. The home is Percy Snider's, which before 1908 was a hotel.

The Kleinburg Mill, built by John N. Klein and sold to the Howlands.

The first Shaw hardware store in Kleinburg, photographed on October 21, 1890. The people are (from the left) Charles Shaw, Jr., Annie Shaw, Charles Shaw, Sr., Mrs. Gun, and Mrs. Charles Shaw, Jr. The store advertised its wares with a quantity of merchandise out front and, for the convenience of shoppers, provided a hitching post. The board sidewalk was at a considerable incline.

6, Concession 4. In 1917 the Edgeley Farmers' Club began using it, as did the Women's Institute. In 1927 it was enlarged and was used by various community organizations. When Jane Street was widened, the hall was taken down in 1965.

Elder's Mills

Elder's Mills, a farming community two and a half miles north of Highway Number 7 stretching east and west of Highway 27 and the Humber River, received its first settlers between 1830 and 1840. They were Jeffery, McClure, Lawrie, Fleming, Burton, Somerville, and King.

In 1850 a Scotsman named James Gibb Thomson built three mills on Lot 16, Concession 8 — a sawmill, a grist mill and a carding mill. The mills were sold later to Mr. McLeod, then to William Taylor. (Dan McCallum, whose grandfather came from Scotland to Quebec in 1832, bought part of the west half of Lot 16, Concession 8, from Bob Taylor, who ran the mill then. His son Donald married Constance Ross and carries on the farm with his son, John and his wife, Lynn Scarlett.) In 1854 William Taylor's nephew, David Elder, arrived from Lower Canada and, with his brother James, bought the mills in 1869. Later James sold his share to David, who was followed by his son, George, who operated the mills until 1919, thus giving the name Elder's Mills to that community.

To the carding mill farmers brought their wool to be carded so that the women could spin it into woolen thread for weaving homespun cloth or blankets, or for knitting. Every spring the farmers drove their sheep to the Humber above the mill dam to be washed before the clipping of the wool. This practice continued long after the carding mill had been dismantled.

The carding mill later served as a chopping mill until 1927. In 1900 the sawmill was moved to Nashville by Locke Card. In 1919 the grist mill ceased to exist.

In 1870 the Toronto, Grey, and Bruce Railway went through the area. In the field of education, a log school was built in 1842 and continued to be used until 1872. In 1943 the second school was remodelled and extended. Across from the school a Presbyterian church was founded in 1845.

Elgin Mills

In Smith's *Canada: Past, Present and Future,* published in 1851, Richmond Hill was said to have a steam grist mill called the Elgin Mills. The *History of York County* (1885) mentions a sawmill built in 1842 by Mr. Heslop on Lot 50, Concession 1. A large flour mill was later operated by Mr. Dixon. A small cooper shop making barrels in which to ship flour was operated by Naughton Bros. on Chip Street. North of the corner, on Yonge Street there was a large hoop and stave factory operated by Mr. Hamilton and torn down before 1883. Mr. Waterhouse started a tannery with a 15 by 20 foot store in the front corner. James Newton bought it and established the Newton Tanning Co. and enlarged the store, before 1870. The buildings went back out the sideroad to the west almost to the blacksmith shop, which was occupied successively by Thos. Coyle, William French II, and Jack and Sam Clift.

Farmers disposing of old horses either had the hides tanned or could sell them to Newton's for $1.50. Hemlock bark cut in four-foot lengths and handled like cordwood was hauled in constantly to meet the need for it in tanning the hides. As a sideline hogs were kept and fed on the trimmings of the hides. Wickets and Pickett of Toronto evenually bought the tannery, which had been rebuilt after being burnt down in 1894. They had it for about a year before closing it about 1907. Charles De Ferrari bought it and tore it down after 1914. The old wood vats, about 15 feet in diameter and 10 or 12 feet deep, are still there but are covered over with earth.

Matt. Paton bought and sold livestock about 1914 to 1916. Then he built a slaughterhouse which he used for many years.

There was a brickyard on the south side of Gamble's sideroad which was closed before 1890. The bricks for the former Catholic church in Richmond Hill came from the brickyard.

Some of the men connected with the Newton Tannery in 1898 were: J. Garness, George Sims, Sr., S. Kirkland, Bertram Newton, Mr. Garbutt, George Hopper, Tom Newton, Dave McKenzie, J. Brydon, A. Hamilton, F. Dolan, Andrew Newton, Clarence Skeele, W. Naughton, Jack Naughton, Harry Naughton, L. McLeod, and F. Granger. At one time they employed about 100 men.

The post office at Elgin Mills was established in 1900. Postmasters have been: Michael Naughton (1900–07), John Naughton (1907–21), Leonard Rainey (1921–26), William H. Espby and Mrs. Espby (1926–60), Mrs. A.F. Rogers (1960), and Leo Madden (acting) (1960–61). The post office was closed on September 23, 1961.

In 1850 the Markham, Elgin Mills Plank Road Co. was formed with M. Teefy as Secretary-Treasurer. There was a toll bar at Elgin Mills and tolls were collected until 1896. Soon after the toll gate was set up some of the young people were returning home quite late with a team and sleigh. It was too late to be let through the gate so they took the bells off their horses, lifted the gate off its hinges, and passed through, thinking it a great adventure.

Fisherville
Jacob Fisher arrived in 1795 in what came to be known as Vaughan Township from Somerset County, Pennsylvania, with sons and sons-in-law and their families amounting to twenty-two persons. He must first have had a location ticket or be known as a squatter, for he was not granted his property until 1798. His land straddled Steeles Avenue, putting it partly in Vaughan and partly in York Township. He built a mill on the West Branch of the Don River, and as usually happened a community grew up around it. His family had a saw mill before 1820, to which they added a grist mill.

The community consisted of several houses, a blacksmith shop, and an inn. The latter became a very popular stopping place and eventually became the property of the Cherry family. (It was located actually in York Township, on the southeast corner of Dufferin and Steeles Streets.)

As in similar communities, Fisherville's numbers decreased and, as Concord increased in size, it finally ceased to exist except for the Presbyterian church and the hotel. The latter was sold several times, and existed for a while as a dance hall. In 1945 the property was taken over by the University of Toronto, and the Connaught Medical Research Laboratories were expanded on it. The church has since been moved to the Black Creek Pioneer Village.

Jefferson

Jefferson was named for the Jefferson family who came to Lot 59, Concession 1 in 1837. The Jefferson store and post office were located on this lot and the building was there until about 1968.

Lots 55-60, Concession 1 were granted to the French Émigrés but they stayed only a short time. After 1830 British and Irish settlers came to the area, and familiar names have been Beynon, Dibb, Legge, Kerswill, Burnett, Neal, and Hart. Other families were Smith, Caseley, Morgan, Washington, Oster, Sliney, Glass, Wilson, Heslop, Phillips, Clubine, and Gibson.

An early church that was moved to Snowball was on the southwest corner of the King–Vaughan townline and Bathurst Street. There is a jog in the townline because of McLeod's Lake. Before 1900 the Legges had a butchering business on Yonge Street north of the school.

The post office was established in 1882. Postmasters have been: J.W. Gale (1882–90), Thos. Legge (1890–92), E. Rutherford (1892–96), W.J. Gale (1896–1902), James E. Legge (1902–04), Geo. F. Legge (1904–19), George Beynon (1919–20), Wm. McCluskey (1920–24), David Robb (1925–30), C.E. Robinson (1930–45), Mrs. M.E. Clubine (1945). The post office was closed on December 20, 1945.

Kleinburg

The story of Kleinburg began when John N. Klein built a flour mill on the West Branch of the Humber River on Lots 24 and 25, Concession 9, and a settlement sprang up around it at the foot of a hill. It was called Kleinsberg after Mr. Klein, 'berg' being the German word for hill or hilly country. The village on the top of the hill was known as Mount Vernon. By 1890 the two had grown together and were then given the name Kleinburg.

Mr. Klein built his flour mill in 1847 and operated it for five years. In 1852 he sold the mill to H.S. and W.P. Howland. Together with their brother Fred they owned four mills — at Lambton, Waterdown, St. Catharines, and Kleinburg. The Howland family came from Cape Vincent, New York, opposite Kingston. The Howlands added a sawmill and store, and thus played an important part in the development of the village. In 1860 and again in 1864 H.W. Howland was elected reeve of Vaughan Township and from 1865 to 1867 he was warden of York County. He then moved to Toronto and founded with a partner the Imperial Bank and Howland Wholesale Hardware. His son, Peleg, followed his father in the bank and hardware business. His twin sons, Thomas and William, ran the mill at Kleinburg.

The flour mill was a very successful business and remained in the Howland family as long as it was operated. It was the largest mill between Barrie and Toronto, having a grinding capacity of 200 barrels a day, and farmers came many miles to have their wheat ground into flour. Because flour was shipped in barrels and not sacks, a cooperage was needed and one sprang up next door to the mill, operated by a Mr. Gough. The cooperage needed staves, and so a stave factory came into being, and before long a planing mill was born to supply the staves. Soon after, other industries developed which included two carriage-making shops, two blacksmiths, and a tannery, and there also grew up a drugstore, several merchant shops, a school, and a couple of churches. There were three hotels, because Kleinburg was an ideal stopping place for a farmer taking a wagonload of dressed pork to Toronto. (It is interesting to note that an old Indian trail that led from Toronto to Georgian Bay passed through Kleinburg; in fact, it was the great thoroughfare of its day.) With the cutting down of the trees, however, the loss of water was so great that no waterpowered mill could properly operate.

In 1860 Kleinburg had three merchants, a tanner and currier, two hotels, a boot and shoemaker, tailor, carriage maker, doctor, saddler, and harness maker. By 1870 a few more occupations were added: chemist and druggist, cabinet maker, insurance agent, butcher, justice of the peace, tinsmith, and milliner.

In 1852 the first postmaster, H.S. Howland, was appointed and served for 18 years. Later postmasters included Mr. S. Keown (1955—65) and now George Mackenzie Watson.

The wheel has gone a complete circle. Subdivisions have been laid out for commuters who work in Toronto. The village is coming alive again. Where once there was a one-room school, now there are two schools to serve the west part of Vaughan. The old frame public library was replaced in 1966—7 by a beautiful new one.

Dr. T. H. Robinson was one of the best known persons of Kleinburg and the large area surrounding the community. It is thought that he set up his practice there when he graduated, and he remained until he died in 1929 at the age of 79. He was considered a good doctor and like many in those days he never spared himself in looking after the sick. He made many long cold drives by buggy or cutter, day and night, to see his patients. His home also was one of the more attractive dwellings in that area. He had three children, Charlotte, Dr. Howard, and Dr. Helen.

Another well-known figure in the area was Robert Hollingshead who kept store for many years. He was also an undertaker and around

1912 he kept the post office in his home. He made his own coffins and lined them with white satin.

Charles Shaw of Glasgow, Scotland, came to Canada with the 72nd Scottish Infantry and received his discharge at Kingston in 1841. Proceeding to Burwick (Woodbridge), he married Jane Colhoun, from Belfast, Ireland. He plied his trade as a tinsmith and in 1869 moved to Kleinburg where he ran a tinsmith shop, making everything he sold such as pails, boilers, dippers, tin mugs and plates, tin lamps, candle moulds, and tin toys such as horns and little wagons. His son, Charlie, learned the tinsmith trade in Newmarket, and then returned to Kleinburg and married Enes Witherspoon. Charlie and his father extended their tinsmith business until they sold all kinds of hardware. Charles Shaw, Sr., died in 1903 and Charles, Jr., went into the furniture business as well. The family is best remembered for its Binder Twine Delivery Night, which began about 1891. Farmers from far and wide came to buy their binder twine and were treated to an evening's entertainment. The Bolton Enterprise reported in 1912 that 1500 attended. This was a yearly event until 1920. During the 1920s there were several more, — the last being in 1930.

In 1921 Charlie Shaw became an Imperial Oil dealer and continued until his death in 1931. He had three sons who helped in the business, William, Carl, and Earl who carried on the hardware and furniture business. Earl's son, Frank, joined the business with his father and mother after he came home from the war. Earl Shaw died on November 30, 1956, after some years of ill health. Mrs. Earl Shaw and Mr. and Mrs. Frank Shaw carried on the business. On February 11, 1961, they held an auction sale and went out of the furniture business. They re-modelled the store and rented it to John Perry who started a variety store. On June 19, 1969, Shaw's again held an auction sale and finished selling the stock in the hardware store, the property having been sold to Norm Hall. After the sale the house and the store, two of the oldest buildings in the village, were torn down and the work began on building Norm Hall's new service station. Frank continues to do much of the work which he had done, eaves troughing, installing repairing pumps, building fences, etc. Mr. and Mrs. Frank Shaw have three sons and two daughters, and now live in their new apartment over the variety store. Carl's sons, John and Charles, live on the Shaw farm north of the village and carry on a tinsmithing and roofing business in the family tradition.

Christian Wuerster, of German background, came to Kleinburg from New York before 1860. He had his shop as a saddler and harness maker in part of his house a little south of the Shaws. His grandson, David Burgess, became secretary to the Minister of Agriculture in the R.B. Bennet government and Dominion President of the Canadian Legion.

In 1870—71 the population of Kleinburg was 350. It included: James Barbour, tanner and currier; Richard Bywater, chemist and druggist; William Cameron, farmer; A.B. Clark, teacher; Joseph Capner, farmer; John Cochrane, tinsmith; M.B. Crosby, general merchant; John

Dalziel, farmer; Charles Etchman, cabinetmaker; M. Fast, general insurance agent; Mrs. Fraser, milliner; Alexander Gough, cooper; August Groskurth, cabinetmaker; James Hayden, hotelkeeper; Howland Bros., flour mill proprietors; H.S. Howland, lumber dealer; George Hughes, shingle maker; James Livingston, general merchant; John J.P. McCallum, carriage and wagon maker; Alex. McIntosh, shingle maker; Robert McKay, Proprietor, Royal Exchange Hotel; Malcolm McKechnie, butcher; Robert Nixon, hotel proprietor; Robert Ramsay, retired; Wm. Sharpe, shoemaker; James D. Stephenson, M.D., John Train, farmer; Thomas White, general merchant; Christian Wuerster, saddler; John McCallum, justice of the peace.

Maple

Originally the main road ran eastward from Dr. Wallace's hill to Yonge Street, not going through the village because the south end was still a swamp. A few years later a road was built through the swamp, and in 1829 the Scottish people of the locality built the Presbyterian church on the east side of the road where the Presbyterian cemetery is now.

In 1837 was built Maclachlan's stone house, better known as Oliver's. In 1848 the community was called Rupertsville (sometimes Nobelville, but by 1852 the post office was Maple) and consisted of the James Woods family, the Olivers, the Ruperts, and the two Noble families. James Wood built a blacksmith shop and made and repaired wagons, buggies, and ploughs.

At one time Maple had a sawmill, a planing mill and pump works, a photo studio, and a rope factory. There were two hotels. Meals were supplied for 25 cents, and board was $4.50 a week.

Maple's first bank was the Sterling Bank. The railway station of the Northern Railway was located in the eastern section of the village in 1853, and trains stopped five times a week carrying mail for Richmond Hill. James Hood carried the mail on his back; later a stagecoach performed that service. With the opening of the railway station, Maple began to prosper.

There was a retail liquor store, two shoemakers' shops, and a funeral parlour. The latter began in 1898 when Mr. Knight moved from Teston and operated a funeral home in the Emery Mathewson house, now the home of John Wintjes. Guy Lawrie and his son Arthur carried on an undertaking business later on the southwest corner.

In 1893 a creamery was built where butter and cheese were made under the management of Bill Robinson. Leeds Richardson kept a harness shop where marriage licenses could be obtained for $2.

It is believed that the corner store on the northwest corner was built about 1852 and housed the first post office. The first postmaster was Joseph Noble, appointed in 1852. Arthur Noble was the second postmaster, and in 1871 J.P. Rupert took over. (He ran the general store and lived in the house directly north.) In 1889 William Hood took over, followed by R.S. Thomson in 1897. In 1906 Henry C. Bailey bought the corner store and ran the post office until his death in 1938. Next

MAPLE

Mr. Knight's undertaking parlours, with his home next door, in Maple. The people are Guy Lawrie, Art Lawrie, Mr. Knight (who came to Maple from Teston in 1898) and, in the buggy, Mrs. Charles Hesp and Mrs. Sam Farr. The two houses are still in use.

Maple, early in this century. The railway line was originally built by the Ontario, Simcoe and Huron Union Railroad Company, and the first steam engine in Canada West ran through here on May 16, 1853.

MAPLE.

Octagonal house near Maple was built about 1837, presumably by Adam or Jacob Rupert. All lumber used was said to have been cut on the property, the bricks burned on the site, and the scallops, frets, and brackets of interior trim cut by the Rupert daughters. The peculiar shape was said to have been easy to heat because there was less wall area for the space contained. For many years this house, on Lot 21, Concession 4, was owned by Gilbert Mathewson and later was lived in by his son, Emery. It is now part of the Shur-Gain Research Farm. (Photo: Harry Vey)

Nashville store, built around 1870 by Matthew East. To the left is a square shoemaker's shop thought to be the original one built by East. To the left of that is a brick outside cellar. The photograph was taken before 1930.

was Andrew Snider until 1946, when Eric Brice bought the store. In 1951 Mr. Brice sold the store to Dougal McCowan and moved as postmaster to the new office at Keele Street North. In 1968 the present post office was built south of the United Church.

In 1910 a telephone service was set up in the store but was moved later to Henry Bailey's house (north of the store) for greater privacy. In 1929 the switchboard was moved to a building at 4 Maple Avenue. In 1951 it was moved again to Keele Street North in the same building as the post office. When the dial system was introduced in 1952 it was moved again, this time its present location on Maple sideroad west.

Dr. Oliver Rupert built the 'Routley House' probably about 1875, and the one next door for his mother and father. They are both of poured cement construction, the cement having to be especially imported from England. After his death there were others, Dr. Rowland Orr, Dr. Sisley, and Dr. Frederick Routley, who came in 1909. The home is owned by Mr. and Mrs. J. Bodi now.

South of the corner there was a hotel; later the Noble family built the present home which was bought by Dr. W.S. Caldwell. Since 1933 Dr. R.A. Bigford has carried on his medical practice in this house, on call at all hours when needed.

William Wood was an early butcher for about thirty years. He moved to Alberta after selling to Wm. Johnson in 1906 the business which is carried on today by his son, William, as the Johnson Food Market.

In 1904, when the railway station was burned and rebuilt by the CNR, the name was changed to Maple Station. It was a busy transfer point, because Cousins and Taggart shipped cattle and hogs and farmers marketed their grain there.

In 1908 J.B. McLean built the Standard Bank. Later the Bank of Commerce and the Vaughan Township offices shared the accommodation. When the new Bank of Commerce was built in 1950, the Township offices used the whole building. In 1957 it was sold to the Humber Valet Cleaners, and was finally demolished when the corner was rebuilt. In 1908 the same builder, Tom Walker, built the Robinson store directly north, which is Adcocks' Store today.

In 1910 Bert Jackson and Dr. Routley had the first two motor cars.

Hydro came to Maple from Woodbridge, in 1914 and in 1921 a community hall was bought from the airport and rebuilt.

In 1928 Maple became a Police Village with Tom Cousins, Hiram Keffer, and Guy Lawrie the first trustees. The same year, park property was bought and the first fire reels obtained. The village has grown in population like all suburban communities, and now has some 2,000 persons living within its precincts.

In earlier days during the winter evenings, Oliver's pond was the scene of much gaiety, as both old and young tried their skill on skates (spring skates in those days, with a tongue that went into the heel of the boot and was held by a spring; the blade of the skate was slightly curved, which encouraged a fall backwards for the uninitiated or careless). The sand hill afforded a good place for sleigh riding — there were no toboggans.

In summer the young people had a raft on the pond. The old Commons was a place for fireworks and gypsy camps, but later the place was drained and a sawmill built, thus bringing to an end several kinds of amusements.

According to the *Canadian Business Directory* 1890—1, Maple had a population of 400, William Hood being Postmaster. Other businesses were J.R. Colls, tinsmith; Thomas Cousins, blacksmith; V. Denne, grain; John Dilworth, county agent; George Gardner, barber; C.T. Ham, painter; W.W. Harris, general store; Hood & Thomson, general store; William Jackson, planing mill and pump manufacturer; David Johnston, mason; Joshua Kaiser, carpenter; J. Knight, carriage builder; William McBride, wagonmaker; J.C. McQuarrie, justice of the peace; Henry Marsh, sawmill; Rowland Orr, physician; Leeds Richardson, harness, marriage licence; William Richardson, hotel; Amos Shunk, livestock; Nathaniel Shunk, carpenter; George Smith, general store; William Speight, shoemaker; William Woods, butcher and livestock.

There was a stage coach daily to Richmond Hill, with a fare of 25 cents.

August 4, 1962, is a night Maple residents will never forget. It was the night of the spectacular fire that destroyed the Superior Propane Plant beside the railway track. Many homes and buildings were damaged from the explosion of dozens of regular residential gas tanks, larger tanks, tank trucks, and several railway tank cars. Herbert Joslin, an employee, who tried to prevent the fire, was fatally burned. Fortunately the fire was brought under control because Maple is built on wells and the supply of water did not fail the firefighters: a vast amount of water was used without any lowering of the water pressure.

Dr. Frederick William Routley was a well known resident of Maple, who practised medicine there from 1909 to 1922. For 27 years he was a chief executive officer of the Canadian Red Cross Society and travelled throughout the world. Dr. Routley was one of small group of hospital workers who inaugurated the Ontario Hospital Association in 1923 and helped the develop the Blue Cross Plan for hospital care which began in 1941. He received many honours, including a Life Membership in the British Red Cross. As a young man, he 'sang his way' through university, being soloist in several Toronto churches. His wife was Gertrude Fry, a talented pianist. Dr. Routley died in 1951.

Dr. Archer Wallace moved to his home at north end of Maple in 1942. A well known United Church minister, he was editor of the United Church Sunday School paper, *Onward* for some years and the author of many books. He died in 1958.

Nashville
The small village of Nashville got its name from a man by the name of

Jonathan Scott who, with his wife, came from Nashville, Tennessee. Until their arrival the place was known as East's Corners.

This village is unusual in that it appears to have come into being because of a railway station, rather than as a result of mills. At least, it was the railway in 1870 that established a station there which was called Kleinburg and still has that name.

In 1890 there were two roads leading to the station from the east, the present road and a short road through Mr. Howland's farm. On this short road there was a hotel, and at the station Mr. Howland built a grain elevator. In 1907 the present station was built. On the corner lot just west of the railway, John R. Card kept a lumber yard, and also sold coal and wood. He also owned an elevator and bought and sold grain. There was a blacksmith's shop run by Walter Card. Nearby was a Presbyterian church. Matt East acted as magistrate and also repaired shoes. He had a high wheeled one-seater gig in which he rode all around the country selling insurance to the farmers. He and his son, Fred, and grandson, George, kept store in Nashville and Kleinburg until the early 1930s when the Kleinburg store was closed, ending a long history of East's stores in this area.

About 1930 the Canadian Grain Company built a grain elevator but later sold the business to Mr. Maw and Sons.

Nashville's post office opened in 1881 with Matthew East the first postmaster. Subsequent incumbents were Mr. Everton Lorne Bernath (1938–45), Mrs. Marion Estelle Farr (1945–52), and Mr. and Mrs. Daniel Hennessey (1952–69).

Patterson

At one time the village of Patterson had more children attending school than Richmond Hill. In these days we would call it a "company town" because it was owned by Patterson & Bros., manufacturers of agricultural implements. It began in 1851 and continued until 1891, when the firm moved the plant to Woodstock. Had they been able to obtain a spur line from the railway they would not have moved. Shortly after moving to Woodstock the firm was bought out by Massey-Harris.

There were three Patterson brothers born in New Hampshire. Peter, having invented a fanning mill, moved into western Ontario in 1840 with his brothers, Alfred and Robert, to sell it. Taking a liking to Canada, they decided to stay, locating first in London, then Dundas, and finally Richmond Hill, where they established a small plant. Two years later the Crimean War wheat market brought them so many orders for farm machinery that they were forced to find more space for their manufacturing operations.

They bought land two miles west of Richmond Hill on the Maple sideroad where now stands Don Head Farm. Here they built some 200 houses for their employees. A modern plant at that time consisted of a blacksmith shop, foundry, machine shop, storage warehouse, lumber yard, and office building. They manufactured reapers, combination mowers, scufflers, plows, and all other implements a farmer could use. There was also a grist mill. For the convenience of their employees a school, a church, and stores, were established. A post office was opened on March 1, 1865, with Peter Patterson the postmaster until 1871; W.C. Patterson was postmaster until 1883, and A.S. Patterson was the last postmaster until May 19, 1888, when the post office was closed.

When the plant moved away the village gradually disappeared. Peter Patterson, the principal owner of the firm, born in 1825, retired from business in 1891 and lived in his beautiful home in Patterson until his death in 1904. It is the home of Ernest Redelmeier today.

Peter Patterson always took a keen interest in Vaughan Township Political life. He served as reeve for three years, was warden of York County, and represented West York in the Ontario legislature for 12 years. He had four children: Elizabeth, Alfred, John, and Susan. Alfred and John joined the Massey-Harris Company, but in 1930 John came back to the old home, bought the Graham farm across the road, and proceeded to raise Aberdeen Angus cattle. Here as a gentleman farmer he lived until his death in 1940 at the age of 72. Alfred, who received none of the patrimony of his father, went to Australia. On a visit to Canada he took ill and died. Susan, one of the daughters, died in a hotel fire in New York while on a visit. Elizabeth married a man named Taylor, owner of a large brickworks firm on the Don River in Toronto. She, too, is dead.

But that property still lives on. In 1939, Willy Redelmeier came from Holland with his two sons, Francis and Ernest, and he bought the Patterson estate and eventually all the surrounding farms. The two sons, graduates of the Ontario Agricultural College, have made names for themselves in the cattle world by developing herds of Aberdeen Angus and Jerseys so that Don Head Farms is as well known as the Patterson Agricultural Works.

The name Don Head Farm was presumably arrived at because the land is part of the head of the East Branch of the Don River. The York Central Hospital was built in 1963 on part of the farm. In January 1970, Don Head Secondary School was opened. It is located east of the hospital.

Pine Grove
In 1828 John Schmidt (Smith) settled in this area on Lot 5, Concession 7, after having sold his farm on Lot 1, Concession 5 to John Dalziel, who had come from Lanarkshire, Scotland. (Dalziel's son William carried on the family farm there until 1954, when a portion of it was sold to the Metropolitan Toronto and Region Conservation Authority. John Smith had planted a field of wheat before the sale: the following spring he sold the wheat in the ground to John Dalziel for £2. The Dalziels harvested one hundred bushels, which they considered an excellent yield.) On his new land John Smith first built a grist and sawmill, and three years later a store which still stands and has been

This Gothic farm house on the Maple sideroad a couple of miles west of Richmond Hill was built about 1850 by Peter Patterson, who established the Patterson Farm Machinery Company. Its surroundings were once the community of Patterson. One of Peter's sons, John D., occupied the house until his death in 1940, when it was bought by Willy Redelmeier, who had come to Canada from the Netherlands with his family the previous year. Very few structural changes have been made in it, and those only to make the interior more comfortable. It is now occupied by Mr. and Mrs. Ernest Redelmeier. It is one of the showpieces of Vaughan.

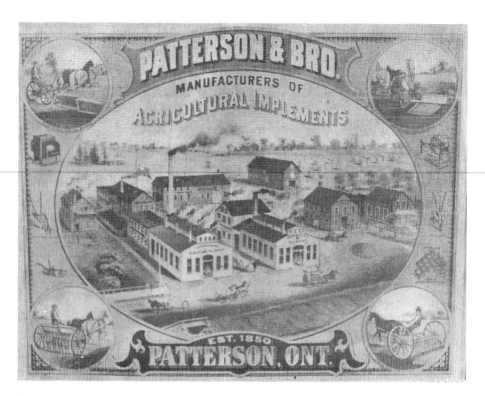

Patterson & Bro. had a sizeable factory two miles west of Richmond Hill about a century ago. There were more than 100 houses in the village of Patterson then. Now there is only one: the office building at the far right in the old advertisement.

John Maynard was proprietor of the Pine Grove Hotel, at the left, in 1870. The road through Pine Grove has had many names: the Vaughan Plank Road, the Woodbridge-Kleinburg Road, County Road No. 7, and, since 1960, Islington Avenue.

used through the years as a general store. The post office was located in that store for many years. John Smith's mill is the only one still in operation on the Humber. With the exception of one year, it has been worked continuously for well over a century.

John Gamble was the second owner of the mill, which he purchased around 1840, adding woollen mills, a distillery, etc. He was a public-minded citizen and was known as the aristocratic and unapproachable 'Pope of Pine Grove.' Tons of bran went down the river from his mill, for no use was ever made of wheat bran in early days.

Gooderham and Worts purchased the mill about 1860. They operated a distillery, sawmill, general store, and cooper shop. Farmers came from great distances with wheat and produce to the mill and general store, where they could sell all they had. Gooderham and Worts introduced goose wheat to this district, which was of great benefit to agriculture. They carried on a thriving business for over twenty years and then sold out to their head miller, William Hicks. The Willis Brothers, Richard and Robert, operated the farm portion for many years.

William Hicks operated the mill with his sons Charles, Albert, and Fred until 1906. Then he sold it to John Nichol, who only stayed two years. Fred Hicks, son of William, then purchased the mill and ran it successfully until the war broke out in 1914, when he sold it to Herb McLaughlin. But things did not go well, and the mill was idle for one year in 1918. Fred Hicks took possession again and operated it as Hicks' Flour Mill until 1935.

Two young fellows, Harold and Edwin Hayhoe, who had never seen the inside of a mill before, purchased it from Fred Hicks and set out in the milling business as Hayhoe Bros. Boyce Hayhoe joined the company in 1938. In 1946 Hayhoe Bros. exported 250 carloads of flour to Great Britain, Russia, China, Greece, Italy, Ireland, Brazil, and other parts of the world. More than 200,000 bushels of wheat purchased in this district formed part of these shipments. Harold Hayhoe in 1965 bought his brothers' shares, which he sold to his three sons, John, Donald, and Alan in 1969.

Joy Valley Greenhouses were started by Karl Lund, who had studied the growing of flowers in his native Norway and in Denmark before coming to Canada, where he was associated with a Brampton florist. He came to Pine Grove in 1938. Joy Valley specializes in violets. Their displays at the Canadian National Exhibition are outstanding, having won many top prizes through the years.

Vaughan post office, established in the Pine Grove area in 1837, was one of Vaughan Township's earliest post offices. George Stegmann was the first postmaster, followed by Richard Bywater in 1852 and Cartney James in 1853. It was closed in 1855. A post office was again established at Pine Grove in 1865, this time under the name of the village, with Alfred L. Gooderham as postmaster, followed by Chas. W. Hicks (1887–97), Fred Hicks (1897–1932), Walter E. Cornish (1932–64), and Peter Stehouwer (1964–).

Purpleville

Purpleville, like a number of communities in Vaughan, was not a village in the ordinary sense but a post office and a school. It achieved its name from a John Morrow who owned a farm close by and who was a staunch Orangeman. When the post office was opened he named it Purpleville to show the connection of the local people with this order.

The post office opened in 1866 with James Livingstone the first postmaster. Samuel Peterman was the second postmaster. Mrs. Jane Stump, the last postmaster, also kept store from 1885 until 1931, when the post office closed and the area was served by rural delivery from Woodbridge. Today the store and post office is the remodelled home of her grandaughter and her husband, Theresa and James Orser. There was a Methodist Church built in 1844 and open until 1900, and a Temperance Hall south of the store. In 1969 Vaughan Township erected a cairn in the cemetery to preserve some of the history of this tiny community.

The early settlers in this section were mostly Irish, Scottish, a few English, and some United Empire Loyalists of Pennyslvania German descent. Some of these were Edward Miller, Andrew Jameson, Robert Kerr, Peter Witherspoon, Roger and Michael Harvey, John McCubbin, a pioneer blacksmith, and John Morrow.

Richmond Hill

Richmond Hill was referred to in Smith's *Canada: Past, Present and Future* in 1851 as a 'smart little place, the population of which it is difficult to calculate, on account of the houses being so scattered but which contained a steam grist-mill [the Elgin Mills], a steam saw-mill, a tannery and two churches, Presbyterian and Methodist.' In 1885 the *History of Toronto and York County* spoke of it as 'one of the most beautiful villages to be found anywhere throughout the length and breadth of 'this Canada of ours'.'

The settlement of Richmond Hill was first named after Abner Miles and was called Miles Hill. Its next name was Mount Pleasant. Legend has it that, when the Presbyterian church was being built, the governor-general of Canada, Charles Gordon Lennox, fourth Duke of Richmond, stopped there with his retinue to rest and feed his horses. He inspected the church, talked with the workmen, and when he left, in honour of his visit, the village was renamed Richmond Hill. William Harrison, the historian of the village, in an article in *The Liberal* in 1889, stated that he could get no confirmation, however, of the visit of the governor at the time from living residents who might be expected to know or to have heard of it. Another legend is that Benjamin Bernard, the first schoolmaster and notary public, who was particularly fond of "The Lass of Richmond Hill,' suggested the name.

Richmond Hill is situated on Yonge Street about 800 feet above sea level and some 16 miles north of Toronto. Its main thoroughfare is half in Markham and half in Vaughan Townships, on Lots 46, 47, and 48 in each township. One of the first settlers was John R. Stooks (Stokes), who belonged to a family that arrived in Canada in June 1793. The patentee for Lot 46, Concession 1, was Abner Miles in 1803; for Lot 47, John C. Stokes, in 1808; for Lot 49, Samuel Heron, in 1797, all in Vaughan Township.

On the Markham side, Hugh Shaw bought Lot 46, Concession 1 for 10 cents an acre and later subdivided his land into building lots of a half-acre each. On one of these lots Barnabas Vanderburgh put up the first frame building, which became a hotel until destroyed by fire. The next lot became known as the French Block, and there David Munroe had a blacksmith shop. It is said that Mrs. Shaw would walk to Toronto, work all day, buy some groceries and return home after midnight — surely a hardy person. Hugh, her husband, died in 1813 at the age of 80 years, the second burial in the village cemetery.

Abner Miles, or Mihells as spelled in his records, had come in 1794 to Toronto, where he was both storekeeper and hotelkeeper. In 1801 he came to Richmond Hill and received the deed for Lot 45, Markham Township. On it he built a log house and again was both storekeeper and hotelkeeper. Across the road on a farm he ran an ashery until he died in 1806, and was the first white person to be buried in that area.

Lot 47 on the Markham side came to be owned by Col. S. Wilmot, a Loyalist and surveyor, who employed forty or fifty Indians who camped around the village. His house of logs was in the middle of a cedar swamp (now the Bank of Montreal location).

On the Vaughan side, Col. David Bridgeford was an early owner of Lot 47. He came to the Richmond Hill area in 1799 by ox-cart with his mother and step-father, Robert Marsh, Sr. He served in the War of 1812 and accompanied Col. Moodie in the latter's effort to warn the authorities in Toronto of the proposed attack by the Rebels.

Col. Bridgeford built a two-storey log building between Centre and Richmond Streets on Yonge Street which was the first important hotel in the village. Beverages were bought from Quetton St. George in Toronto. After a number of successful years as a hotel, the building was sold along with the front fifty acres of Lot 47 to a Mr. Gregory, who painted it red; here the first Richmond Hill Fanning Mill Co. began operations. It was taken over by Patterson Bros., who manufactured farm implements there before moving to Patterson.

The de Pusaye French émigrés were given lots north of Richmond Hill in 1807. Lot 48 became the property of Chevalier August Bointon, a Lieutenant-Colonel in the Royalist cause in the French Revolution. However, neither he nor the other French refugees did much to meet their settlement duties, and after the restoration of the monarchy in France most of them returned home. This lot is now the site of the Mills and Bedford Park Greenhouses.

The Tweedsmuir History of Richmond Hill gives the following

facts about James Miles, who can be considered a patron of the village: 'A son of Abnar Miles, first owner of Lot 46, Vaughan Township, received some 2,000 acres of land in various parts of the province from his father. He never sold an acre, dividing it among relatives and donating land for public purposes. The sites of the Presbyterian Church and Manse, the cemetery and the public school were all gifts from James Miles. Before the village was large enough to support a church, the Squire organized a Sunday School where along with religious instruction the rudiments of reading, writing and arithmetic were taught, and corporal punishment frequently administered. He frequently presented Bibles and Testaments to young people, and with each copy a pocket handkerchief also. This Sunday School was established in 1811 and it is a question whether it or one at Gananoque was the first in a Presbyterian church in Canada.

'Mr. Miles was a liberal contributor to the building of the first Presbyterian Church completed in 1821, built by all and used by all denominations in the village. In 1826 he helped to organize the Richmond Hill branch of the British and Foreign Bible Society, funds from which were to purchase Bibles and Testaments in the Indian languages. Funds for the first year were £15 5s.'

Incorporation as a village was sought in 1853 but the population did not reach the required 1,000 persons. Another attempt was made in 1857 but again failed as the boundaries had been set to include property north of Elgin Mills. Finally, in 1872, incorporation was acquired. In January 1873, the elected officers were: Abraham Law, reeve; Messrs. Warren, Powell, Hopkins, Brillinger, councillors.

Richmond Hill became a town in January 1957. William Neal was elected mayor; W.J. Taylor, reeve; Floyd R. Perkins, deputy reeve; Don Plaxton, Stanley F. Tinker, Harold Jones, and James Haggart, councillors; Russell Lynett was clerk.

In 1890—91 Richmond Hill had a population of 900. Matthew Teefy was postmaster. There were two newspapers published weekly, *The Liberal* and the *York Herald. The Liberal* is the only one which has survived to the present and is the only business that has survived those years. It is located on the same site as in the nineties but in a different building.

Names listed in the *Canada Business Directory* of 1890—1 are: Albert Anderson, barber; William Atkinson, general store; W.D. Atkinson, general store; A.J. Rupert, Bell Telephone agent; Benjamin Brillinger, hotel; O.J. Brown, grocer; Samuel Clift, blacksmith; William Cooper, blacksmith; John Coulter, tailor; Rev. J.J. Egan, Roman Catholic priest; R. Joyce, proprietor, Elgin House; C.H. Frency, physician; W.H. Glass, butcher; John Graham, confectioner; Grand Trunk Railway, G.W. Telegraph Co.; Hagerman Bros., bakers; Joseph Hall, grocer; Mrs. Christina Harrison, fancy goods; William Harrison, harness; Henry F. Hopper, butcher; Leslie Innes & Sons, saw and planing mills; Redmond Joyce, hotel; Matthias H. Keefler, books and stationery, proprietor *York Herald*; John Kennersley, boots and shoes;

J.G. Kirby, flour mill; L.G. Langstaff, physician; Lawrence and Milligan, barristers; T.P. McMahon, *The Liberal*; B. Reditt, London and Lancashire Life Assurance Co.; Francis McConaghy, boots and shoes; George McDonald, harness; Charles Mason, stoves and tinware; Alexander Moodie, general store; Naughton Bros., general store; R.W. Neville, general store; Newton Bros., tanners; John Palmer, hotel; Rev. W.W. Percival (Presbyterian); Wm. H. Pugsley, cattle dealer; A.J. Rupert, hotel and telephone agent; Rev. G.N. Rutledge (Methodist); Sanderson Bros., druggist; J.H. Sanderson, veterinary surgeon; Peter C. Savage, grocer; Robert Seivers, boots and shoes; Rev. J.M. Simpson (Methodist); Andrew L. Skeale, watchmaker; Matthew Teefy, notary and postmaster; Wm. Trench, carriage builder; Charles Trevethan, tailor; W.J. Wilson, physician; Wright Bros., undertakers.

Occupations which have disappeared during the past 75 years are blacksmiths, harness makers, wagon makers, carriage makers, cattle dealers, tanners, flour millers, saw and planing mill operators.

Abner Miles opened the first hotel in 1802 on Lot 45, Markham Township. In 1806 Col. David Bridgeford set up one on Lot 47, Markham. Another was located opposite the Presbyterian Church but this was burned in 1871. The Palmer House carried on as a hotel for three-quarters of a century. Operated by John Palmer an ardent horseman who contributed much to the village of Richmond Hill. The Dominion House across the street remained intact for many years.

The origins of several street names in Richmond Hill may be traced:

Yonge: in honour of Sir George Yonge, Secretary of War in the Imperial Cabinet
Centre: in the early days was the centre of the village
Richmond: in honour of the Duke of Richmond
Arnold: after the Arnold family who owned surrounding land
Elizabeth: named after Elizabeth Klinck, wife of Abram Law
Wright: for the Wright family
Powell: for William Powell, son-in-law of Col. Bridgeford
Mill: because it led to Innes' Mill
Lorne: for the Marquis of Lorne
Roseview: because it led to greenhouses
Reaman: after George Reaman, who owned six acres of land on Richmond Street
Rumble: after the Rumble family who owned surrounding land on Richmond Street
Crosby: after the Crosby family who owned land in that vicinity.

In 1857 a weekly newspaper with Conservative leanings was started, called the *York's Riding Gazette and Richmond Hill Advertiser*. The first issue was June 12, 1857. Its motto was, 'With or without offence to friends or foes, we sketch the world just as it goes.' The subscription price was 7s 6d a year in advance.

In 1859 it became the *York Herald* with Alec Scott as editor. On June 1, 1876, Matthias H. Keefler bought it and continued publication until some time in the 1890s.

T.F. McMahon took over *The Liberal* in 1882; it was Liberal in politics as well as name. It carried on successfully until, with advancing years, Mr. McMahon sold it to J.E. Smith. With the increase in population in Richmond Hill and the vicinity there is a large reading public, and it is now perhaps the most important news medium in that area. W.S. Cook, son-in-law of J.E. Smith, is the present publisher.

The reeves of Richmond Hill have been: Abraham Law, 1873; William Harrison, 1874; William Trench, 1875—9, 1881—2; James Langstaff, 1880; John Brown, 1883—4; William Pugsley, 1885-96, 1907-18 (warden of York County, 1891); Peter Savage, 1897—1905; Isaac Crosby, 1906; Thomas Trench, 1919—25; Jacob Lunau, 1926-32; J.A. Greene, 1933—9, 1943, 1950; Thomas Trench, 1940—2; William Neal, 1944—7, 1951; P.C. Hill, 1948—9; W.J. Taylor, 1952—8 (warden of York County, 1957); Floyd Perkins, 1959, 1961—3 (warden of York County as depty reeve, 1967); James Haggart, 1960, 1964; and Donald Plaxton, 1965—70.

Since incorporation as a town, Richmond Hill has had five mayors: William Neal, 1957, 1963; Ken Tomlin, 1958—60; James Haggart, 1961—2; Thomas Broadhurst, 1964—9; and William C. Lazenby, 1970. Two-year terms were introduced during Mr. Broadhurst's mayoralty.

There have been three clerk-treasurers of Richmond Hill: Matthew Teefy from 1873 to 1904; Alex J. Hume from 1905 to 1941; and Russell Lynett, who has held the office since 1941.

Richvale

Because many new families were moving into the area between Langstaff and Richmond Hill, a post office was opened at Richvale in 1932. George Alliston was postmaster. He was followed around 1950 by Mrs. Fenner, who was in turn succeeded by Miss G. Lever, and then by Miss Margaret Smith. The post office was closed in June 1970.

Sherwood

The village of Sherwood was located on the 4th Concession a mile and a quarter south of Maple. It was a flourishing little community before the railway came up in 1853 and the Richmond Hill Station was built in Maple. It was then that Maple began to develop.

Possibly this community came into being because of Jacob Keffer's first sawmill, built before 1812 on Lot 12 near Concession 4 on the Don River. For some time it was known as Lower Corner. A store was on one of the four corners. There were two blacksmith shops, a paint shop, and a hotel. Not far away was the Peter Rupert farm. Mr. Rupert donated land for a cemetery next to the Methodist church. The cemetery in 1966 was recognized by a cairn put up by Vaughan Township to preserve the stones and the history they tell.

The post office was kept in the store beginning in 1879, the postmasters being, in chronological order, Jacob Henry Snider, Walter J. Bull, Frank Wetchala, William Clark, Emanuel Chapman, Arthur Fry, Herbert Keffer, and in his home by Arthur Fry from 1906 to 1926, when Rural Mail Service from Maple made the post office unnecessary.

The store sold the first matches in 1839. They were bought one bunch at a time, a bunch measuring about two inches one way and five-eighths of an inch the other, about five rows one way and twenty the other, one hundred in all. These matches were carefully taken care of and it was considered extravagant to use one to light a pipe. Cooking stoves were rare and the old-fashioned fireplace was in general use, with maple wood readily available. The fire would never be allowed to go out for weeks, and only then lighted by a match, which cost 13 cents a box in 1876. Besides matches, the store sold many goods in bulk, such as brown sugar, coal oil, print material, towelling, tablecloths, and brooms.

With the development of Maple, Sherwood lost its significance. In 1885 the Disciples of Christ bought the church from Peter Rupert, the trustees being George Schell, James Higgins, and Tom Page. In 1944 Jos. Montgomery bought the land and Wm. Noble then moved the church.

Sherwood almost disappeared in the process of change when Keele Street (Concession 4) became a four-lane busy street in 1965.

Teston

Somewhere between 1847 and 1852 an Englishman by the name of Thane emigrated to Canada from the village of Heyshaw, Lancashire. He built a home for himself in the village which was then called Thanesville. Most of the first inhabitants came from Lancashire, and most of them were related. Among them were Wilsons, Garners, Jacksons, and Lunds.

At one time it was a very flourishing place and could boast two stores, a church, two halls, a blacksmith shop, a woodworking shop, undertaking business, school, hotel, and even a beer shop.

The village was given the name Teston shortly after Confederation and was named after the birthplace of an early settler, T. Chapman, who came from Teston, near Maidstone, in Kent, England. The first postmaster was George Wilson, who was later succeeded by his son, Jos. J.

The first blacksmith shop was a frame structure owned by J. Jackson. Later Jos. Lund bought the property and built a new shop. Mr. Lund was a local preacher of the Primitive Methodists and was considered everybody's friend as well as being a successful businessman. He carried on business in the Walker Store, which was built in 1870. He built the only brick house in the village and at one time was blacksmith, storekeeper, undertaker, and wheelwright. Besides building wagons, buggies, sleighs, cutters, etc., he built the first hearse that was used in this locality, and also made coffins. After his death in 1879, Wm. Knight, a son-in-law, carried on the business until his removal to Maple where he acted as undertaker for many years.

The Grange Hall stood on the west side of the road and was used by the Grangers, a farmers' co-operative similar to the UFO.

Thornhill and Langstaff

Settlement of the ten lots on either side of Yonge Street between what is now called Steeles Avenue and Langstaff began as early as 1793 as a direct result of the opening up of Yonge Street. Governor John Graves Simcoe then advertised free lots to settlers, with the conditions that those taking up land must have ten acres cleared and a house 16 by 20 feet built within two years, as well as 33 feet cleared for the road allowance.

Asa Johnson built the first log house in Vaughan Township on Lot 29, Concession 1 on property assigned to him in 1794. His step-son, Nathan Chapman, received lot 28, Concession 1 at the same time. John Lyons, Balser Munshaw, Stillwell Wilson, S.R. Frizzell, Stephen Colby, Nicholas Cober, David Soules, Elisha Dexter, and Jacob Fisher were among those who received Crown Grants in the area.

Although there were some complaints of bread being stolen from outdoor bake-ovens, the Indians became friends of the early settlers, and often brought them deer meat. Fish was plentiful in the Don River. The settlement progressed and in 1801 Jeremiah Atkinson was commissioned to build the first saw mill in Vaughan Township for John Lyons. In 1802 he added a grist mill. The area became known as Atkinson's Mills, then Lyons' Mills, then Purdy's Mills. The Methodists began having meetings and the first school was opened in Balser Munshaw's former house.

In 1799 John Lyons was one of the first pathmasters appointed to see that road duties were performed. Stillwell Wilson was overseer of highways and fence-viewer, Balser Munshaw was constable, and John Wilson, Sr., was Justice of the Peace. The War of 1812—15 was a real threat to the early settlers; Matthias Sanders was killed and Captain John Wilson and John Arnold were held as prisoners.

Benjamin Thorne came from England in 1820 and later in partnership with his brother-in-law, William Parsons, operated a grist mill, tannery, and general store and developed an extensive trade with the district for miles around and in shipments of produce to England. The mill, hotel, store, stables, sheds, tannery and other buildings were in the hollow on the west side of Yonge Street. Until 1821 the greater part of the settlement was north of the hollow, but Allan MacNab (later Sir Allan MacNab of Hamilton) was responsible for the opening up of Lot 30, Concession 1, which is the southwest corner of Yonge Street and Centre Street today. The name Thornhill was established about 1842, having been previously Atkinson's Mills, Dundurn, Thorn's Mills, Thorne's Hill, Thorne Hills, and Thorn Hill.

In 1846 the Corn Laws were repealed in England and as a result Thorne was ruined financially. There was a decline in milling, but with stage coaches operating on Yonge Street the village grew to a population of about 700 persons in 1867. The first telephone was installed in 1888. In 1898 J.H. Francis built Thornhill's first modern business block. The Metropolitan Radial Railway began service in 1896. The first banking service was in 1906. In 1921 Dr. W.J. Wesley

The Edey house, which formerly stood at Yonge and Jane Streets in Thornhill, was built about 1843 by John Edey, a skilled carpenter from London, England. It is an interesting example of Canadian Gothic design. The woodwork of every room is different. Mr. Edey chose the location because he liked to be able to fish in his own garden.

Vaughan Township Public Library at Richvale, one of three public libraries built in Vaughan as Centennial projects. The other buildings are in Maple and Kleinburg. (Photo: Harry Vey)

Vellore General Store, about 1904, with its owner, D.A. Hewgill, his family, some friends, and his fine team of horses. Standing in the foreground in this old postcard photo are Jack McNeil, Jim Elder, Alma Hewgill and her sister, Mr. Hewgill, and Archie Cummings. The driver is George Hunter. Mrs. Hewgill is on the store steps.

Another Vellore scene early in the century, looking south. To the left is the carriage shop where the Cameron carts were built before the days of the motor car. The blacksmith shop is next door.

came to the village from Mt. Albert; his son, Dr. W.R. Wesley, has followed in his footsteps and his present office is in the new Wesley Building.

In 1925 a series of incendiary fires caused much concern until the culprit was found. In 1932 a weekly newspaper, *The Leader,* was started by Walter Howell and continued for some time. One hundred and forty-seven men and five women served in the second world war and ten gave their lives. Thornhill was incorporated as a Police Village in 1931 with J.E. Francis, William Riddle, and W.C.L. Ball as the first elected trustees. In 1960 the population was 1,060. Since the second world war the area has experienced rapid growth.

The first post office was established in 1829. Postmasters have been Wm. Parsons (1829–61), Josiah Purkis (1861–81), T.A. Hewitt (1881–2), W.A. Bradley (1882–5), J.T.B. Lindsay (1885–90), J.H. Francis (1890–1905), Robert Clark (1905–36), Clayton Scott (1936–47), Ethel Wice (1947–62), and F.J. Foster (1962–   ).

In 1890/1 the *Canadian Business Directory* described Thornhill as a village on the river Don (which supplied power) twelve miles north of Toronto, the nearest bank location, and three miles east of Thornhill Station, its nearest railway point.

The famous Hawthorne Mineral Springs were located there and shipped mineral waters. The village contained Methodist, Roman Catholic, Episcopalian, and Presbyterian churches. The listings for Thornhill included: Lindsay, Francis & Co., druggists, general store, livery, insurance agents, and agents for Bell Telephone Co; Andrew H. Boniface, tailor; Wesley Chapman, butcher; James Cherry, livestock; W.M.T. Clay, millwright; Mason E. Cogswell, carriage manufacturer; Samuel S. Cooper, grain thresher; Allen Craig, agricultural implements; Dean and Barroclough, butchers; Doyle Bros., hotel; Wm. Edy, carpenter; John Ellston, crockery; Samuel Francis, livestock; Frederick J. Gallanough, veterinary surgeon; Peter Huff, shoemaker; William Hall, flour mill; Thomas Kinsella, shoemaker; G.A. Langstaff, physician; John Langstaff, manager, mineral springs; William and Robert Lellyott, masons; Thomas Lonsby, florist; Caleb Ludford, harness; James McDonald, blacksmith; John and Edward Martin, carpenters; Miller & Duncan, barristers; Arthur Muldoon, lumber, agricultural implements, and coal; Muldoon Bros., butchers; Joseph Munday, blacksmith; Benjamin Musselman, general agent; David A. Nelles, physician; Edward Parkinson, machinist, William Skardon, proprietor, Queens Hotel; H. B. Schmidt, flour mill; James Shuter, general store; John Steele, hotel; James Webster, butcher; John Wilson, undertaker and painter; Mrs. Jane Wright, sawmill.

Langstaff was named after John Langstaff, who came to the area in 1808. He was the first teacher in the Langstaff school; the Langstaffs also had a pail factory, store, and eavestrough and shingle factory on the northeast corner of Yonge Street and Langstaff sideroad. At one time there used to be an oval half-mile racetrack on the southwest corner. By 1850 Yonge Street had been stoned and toll gates were introduced; in fact, the petition for them was started in 1830. Keepers of the Langstaff gate were Leonard Klinck, John McCague, Henry Richards, and his son, Henry. Robert Thompson of Langstaff operated the stage coach from about 1870 to 1896. There was said to be a blacksmith shop about 50 yards south of the school. The Chapmans owned the property on which Garden Avenue was built.

Langstaff post office was opened in 1870 with John Langstaff the first postmaster and Henry Richards, Sr., as assistant. In 1888 the office was transferred to Henry Horne's store with Mr. Horne as postmaster until 1902. David Boyle succeeded Mr. Horne; for a time the office was held in Mrs. A. Darling's home, and later it was operated in a house opposite the school by Ben Brillinger. In 1912 David Boyle moved it to the northwest corner at Langstaff. In 1914 he built the store which was removed in 1961 when Yonge Street and Number 7 Highway were widened. Miss Hattie Brillinger was assistant postmaster until W.J. Hopper took over in 1925. In 1927 George Reynolds came; Edward Berwick was postmaster from 1932 to 1943, and F.T. Morris from 1943 to 1958. Langstaff post office was closed in 1961.

From 1829, when the Thornhill post office was set up, mail from Langstaff was brought from Thornhill. Henry Richards used to carry it on foot. When his son, Henry, took the mail over, in the winter months he used to drive a sleigh pulled by a big bulldog called 'Bull'; many stories are recalled of this powerful dog.

Vellore

Vellore is situated in the centre of Vaughan Township. In earlier days it had a public school, a township hall, a general store and post office, a blacksmith shop, a wagon maker's shop, and four dwellings, situated in the midst of a good farming community. When the village applied for a post office in 1864, various names were suggested, but the government asked for one starting with the letter 'V'. Vellore was a place in India where the Duke of Wellington had won a victory; it was chosen.

Henry Frank, a blacksmith, was the first postmaster. He was followed by John McDonald (1867–97), Charles McDonald (1897–1901), Robert Cathcart (1901–02), Richard Jarrett (1902–10), Alexander Gray (1910–13), and Mrs. Wm. Craib (1913–16). The post office was closed on July 31, 1916, and mail came from Woodbridge by rural delivery.

The Township Hall was built in 1845 and the first election was held there in 1850. In 1942 the Council meetings were moved to Maple. In 1913 the first school fair was held. An early teacher at Vellore school was Alexander Muir, who wrote 'The Maple Leaf Forever.'

John Frank, Lot 19 Concession 5, is thought to have been the first settler in the Vellore district. He was married to Elizabeth Walker on Jan. 24, 1822, by Rev. Wm. Jenkins of Richmond Hill, the two witnesses being Benjamin Robbins and John Hammond.

Woodbridge

Rowland Burr, who is credited with being the founder of Woodbridge, came of a family of English Quakers who migrated to America in 1682 and settled in Burlington County, New Jersey. Henry Burr, the original immigrant, had a son, Joseph, who spent his life at Mount Holly, New Jersey, and married Ann Abbott of Nottingham, New Jersey, by whom he had ten children. William, their ninth child, born in 1740, married Ann Edwards, and their family consisted of thirteen children. They moved into Columbia County, Pennsylvania.

William's eldest son, Reuben, when twenty-one years old, migrated to Lincoln County, Upper Canada, stayed there three years, then returned to Pennsylvania where he married Elizabeth Cleaver and remained for fourteen years. In 1805 he returned to Canada and took up land near the town of Aurora, where he was known as a 'joiner.' As there were few Quakers there, he joined the Methodists. His second son, Rowland, learned the carpenter trade with his father and in 1815 set up business for himself, very successfully. In 1819 he married Hester L'Amoureux, who was probably of Huguenot French ancestry since her parents had come from New York State and were Protestants. There is a colourful story as to how Rowland met Hester. It is said that he was riding on horseback one day, was overtaken by a rainstorm, and took shelter in her father's house on Lot 34, Concession 4, Scarborough. From this meeting developed a marriage in 1819 at St. James Cathedral, Toronto, by the Rev. John Strachan, since she was an Anglican. After the wedding she rode in her white satin dress behind her husband on horseback to their new home, which Rowland had built near Richmond Hill. After twenty years there, they moved to a log house on the Humber in a village which was named after him — Burwick — and there they lived until 1846, when they moved to Weston. Later he moved to Toronto, where he built five brick houses between Simcoe and John Streets. Rowland died in 1865 and his wife in 1886. Two great grandnieces still live in Vaughan Township, Jessie (Mrs. James Grainger) of Richmond Hill and Myrtle (Mrs. Russell Rowntree) of Woodbridge.

Washington Peck, a successful cooper, traded a hundred-acre farm with Rowland Burr, who in 1837 built a flour mill and later a sawmill and a woollen mill on the acquired property. He then proceeded to lay out the village on a definite plan. The location of the village was between Brownsville, located on the Humber at Number 7 Highway, and Smithville, named after Sam Smith who had a sawmill on Mounsey Street.

John Abell was the next industrialist to assist in the development of Woodbridge, where he settled in 1845. He first associated himself with Messrs. Wood and Etheridge in the manufacture of wagons and carriages. Abell located his plant on the west side of the Humber River at Pine Street. Here was made the first stage coach that made regular trips between Toronto and Pine Grove. More important still was the lathe he built, which was used in fabricating the first steam engine ever to be used in Vaughan Township. About this time he built his dwelling on Race Street, now 31 Clarence Street. His agricultural implement factory played a great part in the development of the village. He began by hiring twenty men, and by 1874 there were two hundred employees. Unfortunately that year his office was burglarized, and to cover up their tracks the thieves set fire to the buildings, causing a loss of some $200,000. However, the plant was rebuilt in two months.

Abell's steam engines were widely used and several awards for them came his way. In 1880 and 1881 his Triumph Traction Steam Engine was given the gold medal at tests in Toronto, and in 1886 he won the diploma and medal at the Colonial and Indian Exhibition in London, England. Had the Toronto, Grey and Bruce Railway run a switch off the main line into his factory, he would have remained in Woodbridge. But this was refused and he moved his plant to Abell Avenue in Toronto, with the result that Woodbridge lost this very important industry.

The removal of the Abell Plant to Toronto in 1885 was a severe blow to the village and the population dropped. But as newer, smaller industries came in, it increased to about 600 and remained at that size until after the first world war.

In 1847 Burwick, as it was still called, had an agricultural fair, and was large enough to support a Methodist and an Anglican church. From its very beginning it had a school, but no post office. After being known as Burwick for about eighteen years, in 1855 when they applied for a post office they could not use the name Burwick since there was another by that name; the name chosen was Woodbridge. The name Woodbridge was suggested by a son-in-law of John Gamble (then reeve of Vaughan) after his home town in England. It was particularly suitable on account of the many bridges over the Humber River.

The first postmaster in 1855 was John F. Howell. Others since then have been Frederick A. Roe, C.H. Dunning, Joel Reaman, Robert T. Wallace, Mrs. Hannah Wallace, J. Noah Stong, John J. Deane, Alfred Thompson, and Mrs. Nellie Rymill. Cecil Rowe was appointed in 1950 and in 1961 was followed by Stanley Archibald.

The old toll roads disappeared with the development of new and better roads. In the Woodbridge area there had been toll-gates at Brown's bridge and the Abell bridge on Pine Street. The County Road and succeeding developments of Highway Number 7 made great changes, and population, which usually follows good roads, rose 25 per cent between 1921 and 1931. Since that time Woodbridge has become a suburban town of Toronto.

Among the active business and professional men of Woodbridge in 1875 were S.J. Snell, Medical Hall; Wallace Bros., general dealers and direct importers; Wm. Munsie, general merchant; Amos Maynard, carriage works; Levi Elliott, blacksmith; C.H. Dunning, postmaster; James Keedwell, grocer; John Shaw, watchmaker; David Stewart, boots and shoes; Henry Keys, tinsmith; D. McCallum, bailiff; Joel Reaman, postmaster; Joseph Rowan, boots and shoes; Geo. Wallace, manufacturing; James Mann, *Woodbridge Free Press*; Brown and Muir, agricultural implements; Donald J. Grant, M.D., physician; J. Wilkinson, M.D., physician.

For the people of Woodbridge and its neighbourhood the name McLean is inseparably associated with the medical profession. More-

Before Highway No. 7 was built through Woodbridge, motorists avoided the steep hill in the foreground by following the road through the village. In front of the old iron bridge ran the tracks of the Toronto-Suburban Electric Railway, which linked Woodbridge with West Toronto from 1914 to 1925. The Elm Park Pavilion on the right opened in 1926 and was destroyed by fire in 1950. At the extreme centre right is the old Wallace Bros. mill, built around 1878, now used by the Kitchen Pride Pickle Company.

Boating on the Humber was once a pleasant pastime. Highway No. 7 is in the background.

Dr. Peter McLean
1855-1936

Dr. Garnet McLean
1883-1958

Dr. Charles McLean

The first car in Woodbridge was this McLaughlin Buick, owned by Dr. Peter D. McLean. He took Mrs. William McDougall of Edgeley for a spin on her one hundredth birthday in 1910.

over, there was only one location in the village for medical treatment in the early years, and that was opened in 1867 in the time of Dr. Devlin. He was followed by Dr. Wilkinson, who in turn was followed by the first of the McLean practitioners, Dr. Peter D. McLean, who retired after fifty years of medical practice in 1931. His son, Dr. Garnet McLean, was born in 1883 and in 1955 was honoured for another fifty years of service as a country doctor. Dr. Garnet was followed by his son, Dr. Charles, in 1945, the third generation of McLeans to practice in Woodbridge.

Dr. Peter McLean sometimes performed operations on the kitchen table. He always carried a black medical bag, box-shaped, flat and hard; when it was opened each side was seen to be lined with small bottles, containing medicine in powder or tablet form. The small children were fascinated as he filled out the prescription on the spot. He was very adept at measuring out, over a sheet of writing paper, the powder on the end of a pen knife reserved for that purpose. In 1910 he purchased the first motor car in the district.

Dr. Garnet McLean was very community-minded. He was the first president of the Woodbridge Horticultural Society, the Board of Trade, and the York Music Festival, and an elder of the United Church, choir leader, master of the Masonic Lodge, vice-president of the Liberal Association, and very active in organizing sports. His wife was Lillian E. Smith of Woodbridge. They had five children, Jean, Mary, Charles D., Anne, and Peter.

The Wallace family have played a large role in the development of Woodbridge: they have served as reeves, council members, and members of Parliament. Also notable for long municipal service have been John McClure, who was clerk for 19 years, and Ed. W. Brown, who was clerk for 50 years. Mr. Brown was also in the printing business, editing the *Leader and Recorder* as well as doing much commercial printing.

Perhaps the first hotel was the wayside tavern. With the coming of the commercial travellers, there was a demand not only for overnight accommodation but also for the rental of horses, either for pleasure or for business. The hostler at the livery stables became an important person. Hotels in Woodbridge were the Woodbridge House, the Queen's Hotel, Biddy Bell's Hotel, the Inkerman House, the Prentice Hotel, and the Dominion House. There were enough hotels to ease the thirst of townspeople as well as transients.

In 1890 there was agitation for the forming of a Village Band. It came into existence in 1898 and was going strong until 1930, when Music Association controls made it impossible to carry on.

In 1914 hydro power was first made available. It was controlled by three commissioners, who assumed office in 1915. There were 25 customers. Industry has been developed by Edwards & Edwards in the furrier and tannery business; M.M. Snider, rubber goods; W. Robinson & Son, converters, which in 1946 became the Robinson Cotton Mills Ltd. and later Monsanto Canada Ltd.

Banking services were first offered by John G. Hallett in 1892.

He came from England when eighteen and for a while worked in Wallace's store, before establishing a private bank in his own home. When the Crown Bank located a branch in Woodbridge, Mr. Hallett became the first manager. In 1908 the Crown Bank was amalgamated with the Northern Crown Bank and in 1918 was taken over by the Royal Bank.

The Woodbridge branch of the Bank of Nova Scotia was opened in 1917 in a frame building previously used as a bake shop by Henry Peters. In 1918 a brick building was erected on the same site. Ellerby Gardhouse Farr was the first manager. When this bank closed, the Royal Bank of Canada was the only one in Woodbridge for a time. In 1958, however, the Bank of Montreal opened a branch in Woodbridge with Ray Fuller as the first manager.

The Woodbridge Farmers' Company has been a successful undertaking, begun after the first world war when prices of coal and grains were high. In 1919 John G. Whitmore conceived the idea of a Farmers' Club, which became a co-op in 1921. In 1928 it was changed to the Woodbridge Farmers' Company Limited, which is still in operation. The provisional directors were T. Boyle Kellam, James Ross, William Dobson, Arthur Farr, James Elliott, Albert J. Witherspoon, Daniel C. Longhouse, John G. Whitmore, and George Farr, all of them farmers. There were five presidents — John G. Whitmore, James Ross, T. Boyle Kellam, Wm. J. Gardhouse, and Roy H. Barker — as well as two managers, John G. Whitmore and Robert N. Mitchell, who became manager in 1935. The company was purchased by Edwin Hayhoe in 1965.

At least four local newspapers have had offices on Pine Street in the past century. The earliest, Samuel E. Horne's *Woodbridge Enterprise,* operated in 1873. Two years later the *Woodbridge Free Press* was printed by James Mann. Later Edwin Brown's *Leader and Recorder* served the district for about ten years. The *Woodbridge News* — now extended to the *Woodbridge and Vaughan News* — was inaugurated in 1948 with William Kinmond as editor, and has lasted longer than any other of the community's papers. Gary Schlee is the current editor.

The reeves of Woodbridge have been: John Abell, 1882—5; Thomas F. Wallace, 1886—1901; Henry Peters, 1902—03; David Norton, 1904 and 1906—07; E.W. Lawrence, 1905; John E. Harris, 1908—12; C.L. Wallace, 1913—21 (warden of York County, 1921); Garnet D. McLean, 1922—3; W.J. Mitchell, 1924—6; A.A. Mackenzie, 1927—35; N. George Wallace, 1936—40; Abner B. Cousins, 1941—2; John Watson, 1943—5; Wilfrid R. Scott, 1946—9; R. Grant Henderson, 1950—1; Fred D. Armstrong, 1952—60 (warden of York County, 1958); Norn Garriock, 1961—6; Gordon Longhouse, 1967—8; John McLean, 1969—70.

During this period the clerks have been: Joel Reaman, C.J. Agar, 1882; C.J. Agar (with J. McClure, part-time), 1883—4; John McClure, 1885—1902; T.A. Agar, 1903 and part of 1904; Edwin W. Brown, 1904—54; W.H. Young, 1955—70.

CHAPTER VIII

Religion

From the beginning religious expression in Vaughan Township was of two kinds: Traditional (in the sense that it had government approval) — Anglican, Lutheran, Presbyterian; and Non-Conformist — Mennonites, Dunkards, Quakers. The traditional was closely linked with the political. The fact that one-seventh of all the land in Upper Canada was set aside for the support of the Anglican Church substantiates that statement; also the fact that only the Conformist clergy could perform the marriage ceremony or bury the dead.

There was another distinction between the Mennonites and Dunkards and other religious bodies. The Anglican, Presbyterian, Lutheran, and Quaker religions required their ministers in Upper Canada to be educated and ordained; they were qualified in either Britain or Pennsylvania. The Mennonites and Dunkards on the other hand selected their ministers from their own group either by election (Dunkards) or by lot (Mennonites). The Anglicans, Presbyterians, and Lutherans had only a few ministers sent to them from outside the country and these, in many cases, were little interested in persons outside their own denominations.

Into this situation came the Methodist circuit rider, who on horseback or on foot went the length and breadth of the province bringing the comfort of religion to those who were cut off from any other religious ministrations. He organized camp meetings, and his fervent and sincere emotionalism provided the spiritual sustenance that many of the settlers needed. The Methodist system of lay preachers (class leaders) fitted in admirably with pioneer requirements: as the preacher passed on to another area, his converts were looked after by these lay leaders.

The results were remarkable. Because Anglican, Lutheran, and Presbyterian ministers were so few, many adherents of these churches turned to the Methodists. S.D. Clark in *Church and Sect in Canada* states: 'Failure of the traditional institutions of religion to adapt to new social conditions accounted for the weakening of their influence within the Canadian community ... Within the new backwoods settlements the traditional attachments of the Old World — ties of folk and class — broke down in the face of powerful forces of individualization and new attachments had to be established in terms of a new social purpose. It was the failure of the traditional churches that they offered no effective support of forces of social reorganization in the Canadian backwoods society.'

Because most of the circuit riders came from the United States, they were considered by the government to be Yankees and therefore disloyal. In fact, the British put all the early settlers in that category; yet none defected to the United States in the War of 1812 or the Rebellion of 1837, proving that they stood by the oaths of loyalty they swore when they first took up land.

Thomas Radcliff, who came to Upper Canada in 1832 and settled near London, wrote in a letter to his father in Ireland:

Episcopalian, as I am, it grieves me to observe that our number of Church of England Ministers is lamentably insufficient; and that unless prompt and energetic arrangements be made, to meet the wants and desires of our rapidly increasing colonists, there will be, with the absence of sound religious principle, a proportional accession of sects, or total indifference to, and ignorance of, any religion. Many districts are in a deplorable state in this respect; and, what is the worse feature, some of the settlers themselves seem careless about it.

There are young families which have never been baptised; and, I am credibly informed, that there are father and mothers, nay, grandfathers and grandmothers, who have never been received by baptism into the Church of Christ.

When prayer-books, catechisms, and tracts have been offered to them, even without price, for the mere trouble of calling at a clergyman's house to receive them, that trouble has not been taken; the Canadians do not like to *lose time*, even for such an important object as that of spiritual instruction; and, as to wishing for clerical attendance on the sick and dying, there are many professing Episcopalians who would not spare a messenger to request their pastor's services ...

Of Roman Catholics there are comparatively very few in *our* province.

The number of Methodist Missionaries is very considerable. Wherever a settlement is formed, there they are to be found. Many of them are excellent men, and all of them are really or apparently zealous; and from all I can hear they have done infinitely more among the *Indians* in promoting a knowledge of Christianity, than our clergymen have been able, or anxious to effect. I know that there exists, at this moment, a demand, (in mercantile phraseology) for thirty, or forty Church of England clergymen.

If care be taken to select able, zealous and active men, the happiest results will follow; but if a swarm of *Drones* be sent among us, attracted merely by the temporal advantages of a settlement, without higher motives and anxieties, the degradation of *our* religion and the general contempt of inefficient ministers, must be anticipated ...

How delightful would it be, in this great and improving country, rising so rapidly into a state of civilization, which is extending every hour, through the medium of British emigration, to have this numerous body fully supplied with pastors of their own church? — and how cheering would it be to have their respective settlements anxiously superintended by a zealous, well-educated and well-informed body of clergy?

In a political point of view, also, it would be important, as here the Episcopalians are, one and all, attached to the British Constitution. In the democratic principle (wherever it appears), in the instigation to discontent, and in disaffection to the laws, may always be traced the absence of Church of England principles. In this fine province, where a single grievance does not really exist, where there are neither rents, tithes nor taxes to pay, nothing seems wanting but a resident and regular clergy, to go frequently in person among the people (who are inclined to quietness and good order) to encourage them in their moral duties, and to inform them in the spiritual doctrines of their religion.

Thousands in many parts of Canada have never seen the face of a Protestant clergyman (of the Established Church), and many thousands have been lost to our Church from the want of regular pastors and the consequent influence of itinerant teachers of innumerable creeds.

The forms of sectarian worship are very simple; they generally commence with a prayer (the congregation sometimes kneeling), then a hymn, the people standing; and a very long sermon concludes the service ... In the marriage ceremony there are (as they complain) parts that are objectionable, for instance the length of the preamble ... A woman from the STATES, in the true spirit of *independence*, left a church in this province, unmarried, from her refusal to say 'obey' ... You remember the old song:

> A maid there was who did declare,
> That if she ever married were;
> No pow'r on earth should make her say,
> Amongst the rites, the word Obey ...

I believe it is so far determined, that a clergyman appointed to a new township, is to enjoy the following benefits at the least:— Glebe, 200 acres, 50 of which are to be cleared at the expense of government; Glebe-house, at first a Log-house, to be replaced, in a year, by a Frame-house of suitable dimensions. Cash income, £100 a year. This is all that has come to my knowledge; but other advantages may be added. It is said, for instance, that surplice fees will be received, which, in a populous township, might add considerably to the clerical income, and would be a fair and fit remuneration for pastoral attention ...

An interesting sidelight is the report of the Methodists among the Mississauga Indians by Rev. James Magrath in March 1828. He and his family came out from Ireland in 1827 and settled in Erindale.

Report of the state of the Indians on the River Credit, Township of Toronto, Upper Canada, presented to the Lord Bishop of Quebec, by the Rev. James Magrath, Missionary, March, 1828. (*Authentic Letters from Upper Canada*)

Those Indians, consisting of about 200 souls, are a part of the tribe of Mississaguas; to whom a large portion of the upper part of this province formerly belonged. About four years ago, they were wandering Pagans, without any fixed habitation. In 1823, they were collected on the Grand River by Mr. Peter Jones, assisted by his brother John, who are Wesleyan Methodists. These pious men taught the Adults by rote, by frequent repetitions, the first principles of Christianity, as they were too far advanced in years to learn to read and write. They were taught the creed, and Lord's Prayer, and the commandments; as soon as they were converted, they were sensible of the evils attendant on their former ignorant and wandering state. They began to work, which they never had done before. They perceived the advantages of cultivating the soil — they totally gave up drinking, to which they had been strongly addicted; they became industrious, sober, and useful. The government, in 1826, built a handsome village for them on the River Credit, consisting of twenty houses; they have built seven more themselves; they have a Meeting-house which is also used as a School house for the boys; there is another school house for the girls, and a house for the resident Missionary. They are anxious that some trades people should be established in the village, and the boys instructed by them. They have two yoke of Oxen in common, and seven yoke private property; twelve cows, six horses, four ploughs, four sleighs and one waggon; last year they cultivated thirty-five acres of land. They have about two thousand acres round the village — thirty-five boys attend school — Mr. John Jones is Master, with a salary from the Methodist Missionary Society; at first he had but £30 per annum: this year, it has been increased to £50. He receives no remuneration from his pupils or from any other quarter. About thirty-six girls are in the female school, Miss Sillick, Mistress, without any fixed salary as yet; the children in both schools are instructed in reading, writing, and arithmetic; and in the Bible, and Church Catechism. The girls are taught sewing and knitting. They wish much to get spinning wheels; the school Mistress told me that his Excellency, the Governor, has ordered them a supply of Bible and Testaments. The pulpit and desk are open to any Clergyman of the established Church who may choose to address them. Mr. Peter Jones, (who with his brother, are half-bred Indians, and speak the Indian language fluently,) is good enough to interpret for me, as almost all the women, and about one fourth of the men, cannot speak English. I visit the village about twice a month, when my health permits.

State of Farm in 1828 —		State of Farm in 1831 —	
In tillage	35 acres	In tillage	206 acres
Oxen in common	2 yoke	Oxen in common	7 yoke
Oxen private	7 do.	Oxen in private	6 do.
Cows	12	Cows	20
Horses	6	Horses	18
Ploughs	4	Ploughs	4
Sleighs	4	Carts	2
Waggon	1	Sleighs	8

Houses lately built by the Indians:
A Work-house for all Trades
A saw-mill, a store for Merchants on the River.
NB They manufacture Gloves, Moccasins, Baskets — best gloves of Deer skin, 7s. 6d. a pair.

Mr. Peter Jones has published seven chapters of St. Matthew in the Chippewa tongue. Mr. John Jones is translating the Gospel of St. John. The moral and religious improvement of the Indians may chiefly be attributed to those *two men*. It would be highly injurious to the converts, in my opinion, were any attempt made by the clergy of the Episcopal Church to shake their confidence in the Messrs. Jones, who have a decided advantage in being able to preach to them in their native language.

> 1831 — Established by the Society of
> Methodists.
> Resident Missionary, Rev. Geo. Ryerson,
> School Master, Mr. Edwy Ryerson,
> School Mistress, Miss Eliza Rolph.

September, 1831   James Magrath.

For the Traditional congregations, the first churches in the Vaughan area were at nearby York Mills. Mennonites and Dunkards held early meetings in their barns or houses if they were large enough. Possibly, the meeting-house on Lot 34, Concession 1 was the first built in Vaughan and it was used by the Methodists, Quakers, Baptists, and others. St. John's Anglican at York Mills was built in 1816, and in 1830 Holy Trinity was built on the west side of Yonge Street, just over the hill.

Goesman in 1825 reported that there were four churches and meeting houses in Vaughan: on Lot 34, Concession 1, a school house used by Wesleyan Methodists, Quakers and Baptists; on Lot 46, Concession 1, a church, school house, and burying ground of the Church of Scotland; on Lot 12, Concession 3, a church, school house, and burying ground of the German Lutherans; and on Lot 7, Concession 4, a meeting house and burying ground of German Mennonites.

There was considerable schism among the churches that considered themselves part of Established Religion — Anglican, Presbyterian, and later the non-conformist Methodist — over the matter of State support. The Anglicans enjoyed such support. The Presbyterians desired the financial aid but not control. The Methodists were split into three major groups: Episcopal, which came into Upper Canada first, and mostly from the United States; Wesleyan, from England, which during the first few years was more closely linked with the Anglican than with the Methodist Episcopal; and Primitive, which also came from England, and had split off from the Wesleyans because they believed in camp meetings. The Wesleyans called the Episcopals 'the poor Episticles.'

The first Methodist church meeting in York County was held at Cummer's Meeting House (Willowdale) in 1803. This later became one of the appointments for the Vaughan-Yonge Street Circuit. The Wesleyans were small in numbers and finally withdrew, but in 1820 were persuaded by the Anglican Church to return and offset the 'Yankee' influence which it considered quite errroniously to be unhealthy. The Wesleyans apparently received some financial aid for this purpose and it is interesting to note that the congregations they set up were in villages like Richmond Hill, Thornhill, Kleinburg, and Woodbridge. The Primitive Methodists in Vaughan had four congregations, at Hope, Carrville, Patterson and Woodbridge. The Episcopal Methodists seem to have had only one — the Yonge Street Circuit, the Concord congregation being the important one in Vaughan Township. There were several attempts to unite the three branches of Methodism but it was not until 1883 that union took place.

Carrville United Church

Regular religious services in the Carrville neighbourhood are said to have been started by the Primitive Methodists, who about 1850 erected a church building on the northeast corner of Carrville Road and Bathurst Street. This building was later changed into a private dwelling occupied for many years by Walter Bone and since then by his grandson, Douglas Bone.

The present brick church is said to have been built in 1857. The land and the building were gifts of Thomas Cook, who also boarded the men employed in erecting the structure. There is no datestone in the building but William Cook, whose body lies in the adjoining cemetery, and who was born in 1841, used to recall how, at the age of sixteen, he helped make the brick that went into the church building.

In early years the congregation was associated with Laskay and Hope. Later, Primitive Methodist affiliation was changed to Wesleyan Methodist and the congregation became associated with Maple. Still later the circuit was again changed, and Carrville was connected with Edgeley and Concord, the minister living at Edgeley. In 1921 Carrville became associated with Headford and Richvale. In 1925, when the Methodists joined church union, this became the Carrville United

Church of Canada. In 1934 the circuit was changed to Carrville, Headford, and Victoria Square, and two years later the parsonage was built at Victoria Square. In 1942 the congregation became connected with Thornhill. Some of the ministers who have served Carrville congregation are: Rev. A. McNeil, 1921-2; Rev. J. Lavell Smith, 1921-3; Rev. Waldo Smith, 1923-4, Rev. J.C. Kell, 1924-5; Rev. Fox, 1926-8; Rev. Lunau, 1928-32; Rev. F. Maxwell, 1932-4; Rev. F. Gilbert, 1934-5; Rev. J. MacDonald, 1935-40; Rev. H.J. MacKay, 1940-42; Dr. J.S. Duncan, 1942-7; Dr. E.E. Kent, 1947-55; Dr. E.B. Eddie, 1955-9; Rev. H.R. MacDonald, 1959-62; Rev. A.I. Higgins, 1962-9; Rev. Harold Kemp 1969-70.

The Cober Dunkard Church

The Cober Church is situated on Dufferin Street about one and one-half miles north of Number 7 Highway. It is a small frame church in a beautiful setting of pine trees, almost surrounded by the well-known Vaughan woods. It was built in 1888. Adjoining the church is the old cemetery where lie some of the township's earliest settlers, including Nicholas Cober and his wife, Eve Fisher, who emigrated from Pennsylvania in 1796. Here also are buried the Reamans, Bakers, Schells, Wingers, and related families. The first known burial was in 1839.

Jonathan Baker in his 'Brief History of the Brethren In Christ Church, formerly known as River Brethren or Tunkers' names a number of families who came from Somerset and Lancaster Counties, Pennsylvania, between 1800 and 1805 and formed the nucleus of the Markham and Vaughan district of this church, which was organized in 1808 by Jacob Engle. There were fifteen members of the Baker, Heise, Steckley and Doner families. Soon members of the Quantz, Schell, Hilts, Cober, Fisher, Hoover, Miller, Reaman, Horner, Bennet, Stump, Tip, Boyington, Shank, Collins, Byer, Klinck, and Eyer families also were part of the group. It is interesting to note that Baker says, 'The Schell and Hilts families spoke a somewhat different dialect from the rest of the brethren in Canada, called "Mohawk Dutch" as they came from New York State.' He also says, 'Daniel Stump and his wife, residing in Vaughan on the west side of the River Humber were the farthest west of any in the district,' and mentions that members of one family died 'of the fever that raged in Canada between 1811 and 1813.'

John Doner, Sr., was the first bishop, Christian Steckley the first minister, and Christian Heise the first deacon. For some sixty years the meetings were rotated in sixteen different homes. Baker mentions a well attended lovefeast in the barn of Jonathan Baker, Sr. in 1846.

Peter Cober was chosen bishop in 1831. He made five trips to Pennsylvania on horseback in the interests of the church. He and Deacon Jacob Heise attended all the lovefeasts, or communions, spring and fall at Clarence Centre, Black Creek, Nottawa, and Waterloo for a period of thirty years. This entailed a trip of between five hundred and six hundred miles and was made in a one-horse buggy with wooden

Carrville United Church, still active, is said to have been built in 1857. Sunday school rooms and a kitchen were added later. The adjoining cemetery has many old graves.

The historic Cober Church on Dufferin Street was built in 1888 of local first-growth white pine, and is still in a good state of preservation. The benches show the marks of the hand-plane. This congregation was organized in 1808, and some of Vaughan's earliest settlers rest in the adjoining cemetery.

Built in 1877, Edgeley United Church was part of the Maple Circuit until it was closed in 1961. It has since been demolished.

The Mennonite Church, and cemetery, at Edgeley, about 1908. This was one of the buildings mentioned in Goesman's survey of Vaughan in 1825, and is the only one still standing of the four churches then serving the township. It was built in the previous year, and is still in good repair. The interior is of beautiful unpainted first-growth white pine timber hewn by hand. Many early settlers lie in the cemetery.

springs and a canvas top. No money was accepted for these labours. Bishop Cober spent the winter making spinning wheels, rocking chairs, and such articles. Many of his rocking chairs are still in use.

Since 1808 the bishops have been John Doner, Sr., Peter Cober, Samuel Snider, Samuel Baker, Henry Heise, Sr., Peter Steckley, and Alvin Winger, always supported by two or three other ministers and deacons.

Well preserved, so close to the border of Metropolitan Toronto, this church's quiet simplicity suggests to the passer-by a serenity, a link with the pioneer days.

Coleraine Wesleyan Methodist Church
Coleraine Wesleyan Methodist Church was situated on the north side of Coleraine sideroad a little west of Coleraine school. The land, one-eight of an acre, was given by Joseph Wilson for the sum of 5 shillings on April 26, 1861, the trustees of the church being George Kellam, James Burgess, Wm. Tedder, George Wragget, and James Suggett of Vaughan, and George Jones and John Brimsden of the Gore of Toronto. It was part of the Kleinburg circuit. The minister managed with the help of local preachers, who were granted licenses to preach on a year-by-year basis by the district meeting. In 1901 Shiloh and Coleraine amalgamated and purchased the site of the present Central United Church from John Black. It is still part of the three-point Kleinburg charge with Nobleton and Kleinburg churches.

Concord Methodist Church
The Yonge Street Circuit was quite widespread, and the various congregations came together once every three months for the Quarterly Meeting. Concord Church, until the union of the Methodist Churches in 1883, was known as Whites or Bowes. It met at a meeting house called a chapel, possibly the school house originally, and later a log structure on the corner of William Bowes' farm, west half of Lot 7, Concession 2. This congregation may have started much earlier than 1831 when William Bowes emigrated from Yorkshire, England, for it was very much alive in the early 1840s. The following are a few of the baptismal records:

July 5, 1840	Michael	Child of Michael and Sarah Vincent	Born Feb. 2, 1836
July 5, 1840	Persilla	Child of Michael and Sarah Vincent	Born Oct. 11, 1838
		by Rev. B. Brown — York Township	
Oct. 24, 1840	Elizabeth Jane	Child of Daniel and Jane Cottrell	Born Sept. 4, 1826
Oct. 24, 1840	Margaret Ann	Child of Daniel and Jane Cottrell	Born Mar. 11, 1838
		by Rev. B. Brown — York Township	

In this same record book in the possession of the author is the following information:
Stewards appointed for the Conference Year, Jan. 30, 1858 (for Yonge Street

Circuit): John McQuarry, Henry White, James Davis, Isaac Gram, John Parker, Samuel Cummer, Joshua Cummer; Class Leaders: Benjamin Parker, John Boots, Daniel Cummer, Benjamin Wincup, John McQuarry, William Bowes.

A Meeting called at Gram's Chapel to arrange for the Preacher's Claims on Yonge Street Circuit — May 18, 1858.

Br. James Richardson	—	$33.50	
Bishop Smith	—	9.	$42.50

Br. James Richardson and Bishop Smith's Claims to be paid by Collection.

By E. Lownsbury's Class	$512.	
By George Miller	150.	$662.

Grams Class	$200.	
David Cummers Class	225.	
Cook Class	32.	
Weston Class	100.	
Whites (Bowes) Class	105.	$662.

The Yonge Street Circuit was spread out, with Willowdale (Cummers) on the east in York Township, Grams in the centre, Weston on the west, and King on the north. In Vaughan Township, there were Bowes (Whites) in the centre and Rupert's Sherwood on the North. There were two ministers — a married and a single man. The salaries were $450 to $500 for the married man and half that for the single one.

In 1883 came about the union of the Wesleyan, Episcopal, Primitive, and British sections of the Methodist Church. Concord appointment became part of the Maple Circuit which included Hope, Carrville, and Edgeley churches. In 1886 the brick church was built at Concord and served until the 1930's. It was later sold and became a dwelling house.

In the very early days money was scarce and the preacher received his salary — at least part of it — in 'table expenses.' Each class leader was to supply a certain amount of food for man and beast, as well as other essentials such as wood and tallow. Here is a sample of what each Class (that is, each congregation) would supply the preacher in 1843, and its value in pounds, shillings and pence:

4 barrels Flour	4	0	0
300 lbs. pork	2	5	0
40 lbs. sugar	1	5	0
10 lbs. tallow		6	3
15 bushels potatoes		18	9
½ barrel salt		5	0
4 lbs. tea		16	0
2 tons hay	4	0	0
40 bushels oats	2	0	0
20 lbs. lard		10	0

At the time of the union of the Methodist Churches the stewards were: Bowes Appointment — Isaac Reaman, William Bowes, George Reaman; Willowdale — Joseph Shepard and George Cummer, Henry Snider, John Boynton. Recording Steward — George Reaman who remained in that position until he left the community in 1906.

Some of the ministers who served (in chronological order) from

1840 to 1885: Rev. B. Brown, Rev. H. Dockham, Rev. T. Argues, Rev. T.C. Brown, Rev. T.P. Bradshaw, Rev. C.V. Lake, Rev. B.L. Hutton, Rev. P. Elders, Rev. A.L. Thurston, Rev. T. Argue, Rev. B. Blasdell, Rev. G. Bennett, Rev. J.J. Redditt, Rev. G. Abbs, Rev. M. Fawcett, Rev. J. Barkwell, Rev. J. Pearen, Rev. P. Campbell.

The Mennonite Church, Edgeley

The Mennonite Church, Edgeley, was one of the earliest churches built in Vaughan Township. A log structure located on the north half of Lot 7, Concession 4, it was built in 1824 by the pioneers who came from Somerset County, Pennsylvania.

The first deed in the Smith name bears the date 1801 to John Smith, a bachelor, who later deeded it to his brother Jacob Smith. (John Smith is listed as a non-resident property holder owning 100 acres in the 1779 tax list of Quemahoning Township, Somerset County, Jacob Smith is listed as the owner of 50 acres in Brothersvalley Township in 1779 and 100 acres in 1783.) John gave an acre of land to be used as a cemetery. It was very much used, there being a record of 275 graves. The earliest recorded on a stone is of Henry Smith, who died October 10, 1823. As there are many flat field stones that bear no date, doubtless there were burials much earlier. One headstone bears the inscription: 'Jacob Smith. Born Nov. 2, 1751. Died Nov. 4, 1824'.

That was the same year the church was built. In 1848 it was done over with board siding at a cost of $220. As was customary with the Plain Folk, the walls, ceiling, benches, and floor, including the ministerial table used as a pulpit, were all void of any paint, exposing to view the good hand workmanship. Even the nails then used were blacksmith-made, as were the door handles and door latches. The first roof was shingled with shingles two feet long or more, split from pine blocks and shaved with a drawing knife. These shingles were hewn by experts with the broad axe, who might be paid as much as six shillings (75 cents) a day.

A wood stove was added later and stands in the centre aisle directly in front of the minister's table. On either side are benches with a single board across the back. The walls are shiny pine which appears to have just been polished. Off the main church is an anteroom, which also houses the supply of wood for the stove. Only morning services were held, but many years later two chandeliers of three oil lamps each and individual oil lamps on brackets around the walls were installed.

Early family names in the records are Shunk, Snider, Troyer, Hoover, Burkholder, Wisler, Lehman, and Schmidt. The records include measurements for digging graves and stipulate their size and location.

The church was closed from 1909 to 1915 and then monthly services were held until 1923. After being closed for forty years, it was re-opened for one Sunday, Sept. 2, 1963, to an overflow audience. Bishop Abram Smith, a great-great-grandson of Jacob Smith, Sr., conducted the service in the hand-hewn log building, and the order of service followed was that of more than a century ago except that it was in English. Services have been held more or less annually ever since.

Since 1896 the cemetery has been administered by a board of trustees. The present board members are Alan Smith, Jim Buchanan, Vern Snider, Nelson Snider, Isaac Baker.

Edgeley United Church
It is uncertain when the work began at Edgeley, but it was a flourishing community and there are records to show services were held as early as 1871. Ella Whitmore, in her *History of Edgeley,* tells of her grandfather returning one warm Sunday in May, hot, dusty, and tired from the long walk to the Lutheran Church, wearing the traditional homespun woollen shirt, and telling his widowed mother he would certainly attend the Edgeley Church when it was completed.

It was originally known as Bethel and is listed in the Wesleyan Methodist Church records as contributing to missionary funds. A brick church was built in 1877. Land for the building was granted by Andrew Mitchell. David Smith of Edgeley and Guy Hamilton of Elders' Mills were the carpenters: the latter was from England and of the old school. He used only the English metric system, never the carpenter's square. D.E. Longbottom & Son of Clairville were the masons. In 1876 the Townline Episcopal Methodist Church was closed and its congregation transferred to the Edgeley Methodist Church. With the union of the Methodist churches in 1883, Edgeley became attached to the Maple circuit. It was closed in 1961 and demolished in 1969.

Knox Presbyterian Church, Vaughan, Elder's Mills
In 1843 the old school at S.S. No. 15, Vaughan, was used as a church. The Old Kirk and the United Free Presbyterians held Sunday services alternately — until an unfortunate incident occurred. The Old Kirk people locked out the United Free Presbyterians, who then worshipped in Archie Somerville's barn until they built a church of their own. Somehow the key to the school got lost and the Old Kirk couldn't worship there either. This fact inspired someone to write a verse:

> There is a hoos upon the hill
> Where prayer is wont to be.
> It is locked up, secure and safe,
> and Satan holds the key.

In 1844 the Rev. Peter McNaughton held services in the community. Presumably the congregation had been organized some years previously but not as belonging to the United Presbyterian Church, for the first recorded Minutes of Session took place in a meeting house on March 20, 1845, and reads: 'The session of the United Congregation of Vaughan met and was constituted by the Rev. David Coutts, Moderator. Members of Session were elected and meeting closed with prayer.'

The average attendance in 1852 was 170; stipend paid was £40; and as yet no church property, preaching being done in houses and barns.

In 1854 the first frame church was opened for public worship, free of debt. Rev. Peter Glassford became pastor and a frame manse was built for him.

In 1861 there took place the union of the United Presbyterian Church and Free Church in Canada and in 1875 the union of the Canadian Presbyterian Church and Auld Kirk. At this time the congregation took the name of Knox Church, Vaughan.

In 1876 a new church was built at Bolton and it and Knox Church, Vaughan, were under one ministry. The Rev. Peter Nichol was minister from 1874 for 18 years and moved to the new manse at Bolton. In 1883 the present church was opened free of debt.

In 1925 Knox Church voted not to join with the United Church of Canada, but to continue as a Presbyterian church. Rev. J.A. Moir transferred to the United Church.

For many years George Elder led a large choir. Miss Jennie Lawrie was first organist, followed by Mary Lawrie, Mary Wood, Annie Lawrie, Florence Black, Kate McClure, Kate Cameron, Ella Gowland, Mary McClure, Gertie Burton, Verla Burton, Jean Lawrie, Jessie King, Janey Nattress, Mary McGillivray, Mrs. Wm. Lawrie, Jr., and Jean McGillivray.

Early elders in chronological order were: James Smart, James Somerville, William Archer, William McClure, Robert Somerville, John Smith, John Black, William Nattress, William Lawrie.

The board of trustees for the cemetery consisted in 1925 of Colin Cameron, William King, William Lawrie, Gordon McGillivray, Miss Hosie Elder, William Watson, and William Lawrie, Jr.

The Knox male choir was formed at the anniversary services of 1933, owing to a shortage of ladies' voices. The men's sections were augmented by former choir members, and continued to lead in the annual anniversary services of praise as the Gordon McGillivray Choir.

The Church was closed in 1961. Ministers over the years were: Rev. David Coutts, 1845-50; Rev. John Duff, 1850-1; Rev. David Coutts, 1851-2; Rev. Wm. Dickson, 1852-4; Rev. Peter Glassford, 1854-74; Rev. Peter Nicol, 1874-92; Rev. Thos. McLachlan, 1893-1901; Rev. M. MacKinnon, 1901-16; Rev. J.A. Moir, 1916-25; Rev. J.C. Davies, 1925-30; Rev. John McKenzie, 1930-4; Rev. James S. Roe, 1935-9; Rev. G.C. Lamont, 1940-2; Rev. R.G. McKay, 1942-8; Rev. John A. Ross, 1948-57; and Rev. Fred Howick, 1958-61.

Fisherville United Church
Fisherville United Church was established as a Presbyterian church in 1856. It is known that the congregation had for a number of years held services in various homes in the district, and in the school house. When the building committee met, it was in Cherry's Hotel which was across the road in the Township of York. Fisherville at that time was quite a thriving community due to the grist mill, which was second in size to that at Thornhill.

Mr. John Brack was one of the founders of the church. Another was Francis Watson, whose family had emigrated from County

Monaghan in Ireland. The exterior of the church was made of rough cast material. The interior had high backed pews with boarded ends, and when they were first built there was a door on each pew. The seats were uncomfortable enough to keep the parishioners awake.

John Wanless, Toronto jeweller, presented a bell and had a belfry constructed. There was no organ until the early 1890's when Ruth Cherry, later Mrs. Thomas Hultse, became the first organist. Hymn books did not exist; the Psalm Book was used instead.

Because the community had disappeared, the church was closed in 1910; but it was reopened in 1915 because of the location of the Connaught Laboratory, with Wm. Fenlon as a guiding spirit. In 1925 it entered the United Church of Canada and carried on until 1960, when it was again closed. With the development of the Black Creek Pioneer Village, the church was moved to a site on that property. Vaughan Township restored the cemetery in 1967 with a cairn.

Some of the early ministers, when it was connected with Fairbank Church, were Rev. Robert Monteith, Rev. Wm. Laidlaw, Rev. Robert Gray, Rev. Bennett, and Rev. J.M. Whitelaw. Rev. Rover Cochrane, once a student minister there, later became Home Mission Secretary and Moderator. In later years Revs. Ray McCleary, Thomas Laidlaw, W.S. Mack, and Clark Logan were in charge.

Hope Methodist Church
In 1832 William Craddock of Wales and Jane Heyworth of England came to Canada and were married in 1835. They settled on Lot 24, Concession 4 of Vaughan Township. There being no church in their vicinity, they gave land on the southeast corner of their property for a church and burial ground. The church became in 1858 a Primitive Methodist church.

The building was made of logs and the pews were hewn from logs, as was the pulpit. The collection box was made with a handle the length of the pews. The inside of the church was never painted, and there was no musical instrument. Wax candles, used for lighting, were made by members of the congregation. Since there was no caretaker, different families took their turns in keeping the building clean.

The congregation stood up to pray and sat to sing. A woman would lead the singing with a tuning fork. The collection was taken every other Sunday afternoon and once a month at the evening service. Sunday School was also held. Local preachers carried on the services.

The first trustees were William Baldwin, William Nixon, Joseph Lund, David White, and Thomas Burgess. Rev. Jonathan Milner of King, York County, was the first minister in charge. The church became a part of the Laskay Circuit. A three months' preacher's plan for the circuit included Laskay, Nobleton, 8th Line King, Salem, Elliotts, Glenville, Hope, Carrville, Patterson's, Thompson's, and Ebenezer Churches. Some of the superintending ministers were T.W. Jolliffe, J.E. Moore, J. Garner, T. Sims, J. Goodman, and R. Cabe. Because the circuit was so extensive, local preachers still served, some of whom were

J. Garner, J.H. Stonehouse, Wm. Nixon, T. Reynolds, J. Lund, Wm.
Lund, D. Archibald, T. Burgess, I. Welbourne, Wm. Denton, W.
Western, Wm. Kirby, H. Diceman, J. Johnson, I. Ireland, S. Sherbourn,
H. Harris, G.J. Reeves, J. Grimshaw, J. Coombs, E. Gardener, G.
Hopkins, G. Baker, W. Reed, J. Bentley, M.D., I. Jordison, C.S. Wallis,
W. Rodwell, A. Boynton, J. Thompson, W. McDonald, W. Reynolds,
and R. Fleck.

A new church was built in 1870 and located on the southeast
corner of East Lot 29, Concession 4. The log church was torn down and
the burial ground was not used after 1891, when the new cemetery at
Maple came into use. In 1963 the old gravestones were removed and the
township erected a cross to preserve the names of persons buried there.

The church was very prosperous, with annual oyster suppers
and fowl suppers. In 1883 the Primitive Episcopal and Wesleyan
Churches united, and Hope became a member of the Maple Circuit
along with Edgeley, Concord, and Carrville. The superintending
minister lived in Maple, and was given a student assistant minister. The
pioneer families in the new church were Nixons, Craddocks, Lunds,
Knights, Thomas, Cooks, Kirbys, and Crooks.

Hope Church was closed in 1966.

Humber Summit Congregational Community Church
This church is situated at the southwest corner of Vaughan Township
on Islington Avenue, north of Steeles Avenue. It originated in
Thistletown, then known as St. Andrew's. From the original minute
book we learn that in the autumn of 1849, a 'station' in connection
with the Congregational church at Pine Grove was opened at St.
Andrew's in Etobicoke by Rev. T.J. Hodgskin, who preached occasionally in the ballroom of Mr. Tibb's Tavern until 1852, when he moved to
another field. Some friends of the cause, resolving to sustain the means
of grace in the village, were successful in securing the services of the
Congregational Theology Institute in Toronto.

A public meeting was called on Sept. 6, 1852 and by July 24,
1853, a commodious chapel was opened for worship. The first services
were in the evenings. The church was officially organized on Oct. 28,
1859. People organized into the church were: Joseph T.W. Wallis, Mrs.
Joseph T.W. Wallis, George Scott, Mrs. George Scott. Some of the early
trustees were: Andrew Grubb, George Garbutt, William Ellerby, John
Watt, and Alex. Card, 1852-8; William Ellerby, John Watt, Alex. Card,
Wm. Austin Wallis, and Joseph T.W. Wallis, 1862; Joseph T.W. Wallis,
John Benjamin Riley, and Alfred Samson, Sr., 1880. Twentieth century
trustees have included Chas. Plunkett, Robert Topper, James Churchill,
and Eber McKay in 1926, and Stewart Chapman, Briton Plunkett, and
William Hamilton in 1970.

A toll gate was in operation at Islington and Steeles, and
congregation members refused to pay a toll to go a few hundred feet to
church. They therefore rented a log house near the junction of Steeles
and Plunkett Road, which they used for about eighteen months. When

the building was warm, (thanks to a large box stove) insects would come out of the logs, so the place was named 'the Bed Bug Church.'

Pine Grove and Humber Summit were sister churches with one minister until 1934, when they became independent. In February 1954, the name was changed to Congregational Community Church.

The old pine pews, made in 1854 with a swing back which enabled the congregation to face either way, were replaced with modern oak.

Ministers of Humber Summit Congregational Church have been: Rev. T.J. Hodgskin, 1849-50; students, 1850-3; Rev. Mr. Jupp, 1853 (2 months); students and others, 1853-9; Rev. Robt. Hay, 1859-69; Rev. W.W. Smith, 1869-78; Rev. E. Ireland, 1878-9; Rev. Robt. Hay (Second term), 1879-82; Rev. W. Way, 1883-5; Rev. A.W. Gerrie, 1885-7; Rev. Wilmot, 1887-91; Rev. A. Skinner, 1891-3; Rev. H. Bentley, 1893-6; Rev. W. Collins, 1896-9; Rev. Wisher, 1900-02; Rev. Halliwell, 1902-04; Rev. E. Barker and Rev. J. Findlater, 1904-06; Rev. A.B. Shirk, 1906-11; students, Sam Nielly, Chas. Ashdown, Mr. Byer, 1911-17; Rev. Geo. M. Blackett, 1917-24; Mr. C.L. Rumble, 1925-8; Mr. Ernest Root, 1929-31; J. Richie, 1931-2; John Lucas, 1932-4; Ernest Root (Second term). 1935-47; N. Holdiway, 1947-9; Mr. Gillies, 1949-53; Mr. Henderson, 1953-7; Mr. Geoffrey Still, 1957-63; supply ministers, 1963-5; Arthur Hunguski, 1965; Mr. Edward Angrove, 1966-9; Mr. Geo Thomas, 1970.

The Evangelical Lutheran Church, Kleinburg

On April 1, 1855, Jacob Burkholder and Augustus Groskurth purchased part of Lot 24, Concession 8, from Henry S. Howland and Ardelia Howland. This land contained a half acre to be used as church property. The trustees elected were Nicholas Shaver and Peter Snider.

Evidently there were difficulties in keeping this church alive. On September 23, 1869, the church and grounds were sold for $460 to James Burgess, William Tedder, George Kellam, Robert Kellam, Henry Peterman, yeomen, James Livingston, merchant and John E. Armstrong, trustees of Kleinburg Congregation of the Wesleyan Methodist Church. There was a burying ground behind the church and a clause in the deed stated that there was to be free access to the burying ground at all times by means of a road.

Kleinburg United Church

The Kleinburg Wesleyan Methodist Church, like all Methodist churches in Vaughan Township, came into being first as a congregation, then took physical shape as a log church. It was one of three churches in the Kleinburg Circuit — Central, Nobleton, and Kleinburg. In the early days there were four or five churches in the circuit. A lay minister preached in one of the churches every Sunday, taking turns with the minister in the different churches. William Irwin, of Nobleton, was one of the lay ministers who preached for a number of years. The first record we have of the existence of this church is in 1869 when the Lutheran church on Lot 24, Concession 8, was purchased. This church also owned a hall where they had worshipped, and which was sold in 1872 to the

Knox Presbyterian Church, Vaughan, was organized in 1845. A frame church was built in 1854. This brick church was opened in 1883, free of debt. It was closed in 1961.

Humber Summit Congregational Community Church, near the corner of Islington and Steeles Avenues, was built in 1853.

The Presbyterian Church at Maple, at the south end of the village on Keele Street. The church was founded in 1829, and this handsome structure was built in 1862.

Independent Order of Good Templers for $200. (It was torn down in 1925, and the lumber used to build the Kleinburg and Nashville Women's Institute Hall on Islington Avenue.)

Miss Merle Hambly gives this description in the Tweedsmuir History: 'The big white frame Wesleyan Methodist Church set on the brow of the hill overlooking the Humber Valley played a large part in the life of the community. It had frosted glass windows and no basement. It had a gallery over the entrance lobby across the front of the church and there were two aisles. It was lit with large hanging coal oil lamps with large white shades for years, and then with Coleman lamps. There was a choir loft with steps on either side to go up to it. The pulpit was on a small raised platform in front of the choir loft and there was a circular altar rail around the front of the pulpit. The church services were held in the evening and the Sunday School was held in the afternoon.'

In 1925, with Church Union, Kleinburg Methodist Church beame Kleinburg United. It was decided in 1926 that a new church was needed. John Kellam, Douglas McDonald, Mortimer Wardlaw, and James H.I. Devins and the minister, Rev. A.F. Bamford, were appointed the building committee and the new church was opened in May 1927. Services were held in the Women's Institute Hall from the time the old church was torn down until the new one was opened. Cecil and Miss Irene Mitchell gave the lot from their farm for the church to be built on. The furnace was given and installed by Shaw's Hardware. Of new red brick with a tower on the northeast corner, the new church had a full basement with kitchen and Sunday School rooms. The seats and pulpit of the old church were used in the new church.

Ministers of this church have included: Robt. Carson, 1856-7; Isaac B. Aylsworth, M.D., 1858-9; Thomas Lawson, 1860-1; Wm. Price, 1862-3; John Corbett, 1864-5; Wm. Coleman, 1866-7; John Hodgson, 1868-9; Jas. H. Locke, John C. Stevenson, 1870; Jas. H. Locke, John G. Scott, 1871; James A. McClung, Edward F. Goff, 1872; James A. McClung, Robt. G. Wellwood, 1873; James A. McClung, Jas. Waite, 1874; Wm. H. Carnduff, Geo. S. Reynolds, 1875; John Smiley, M.A., Robt. Burns, 1876; John Smiley, M.A., Geo. Hewitt, 1877; James Pearen, B.A., John H. Stewart, 1878; James Pearen, B.A., Fred W. Crowle, B.A., 1879; Shem Blanshard, Jas. Waite, 1880; Shem Blanchard, John Locke, 1881; Shem Blanchard, one to be sent, 1882; Edward Barrass, M.A., 1883-5; R. Strachan, 1886,8; T. Edwards, 1889-91; Edwin A. Pearson, B.A., 1892-3; W.P. Brown, 1894-5; C.T. Cocking, 1895-6; Reuben Toye, 1897-99; Geo. Washington, 1900-01; John Cannon, 1902-03; H.A. Fish, 1904-09; W.A. Thompson, 1909-11; T.R. White, 1911-15; W.H. Learoyd, 1915-20; J.W. Arnott, 1920-4; A.F. Bamford, 1924-9; S.J.T. Fortner, 1929-37; C.J. Bailey, 1937-45; W.A. Wescott, 1945-51; W. French, 1951-62; C.J. McLean, 1962-66; Wm. Reid, 1966- .

St. Thomas Anglican Church, Kleinburg
St. Thomas Anglican Church of Kleinburg was built in 1887 at the

south entrance to the village on the west side of the road. It was a small red brick building designed after the style of so many Anglican churches. It was entered from the churchyard through double doors at the north end. A small door allowed entry to the vestry on the east side, right from the roadside. There were two rows of seats in the centre of the church with an aisle in the middle and on each side. Plain, unpainted wooden benches were along both side walls. There was no basement and heat was provided by a stove.

Congregations were small, and services were conducted Sunday afternoons by the clergyman of Christ Anglican Church, Woodbridge. Services were discontinued at a date unknown. In 1927 the building was bought and torn down by the Kleinburg United Church; the ground became the parking lot for that church.

Langstaff Baptist Church

Langstaff Baptist Church was formed in 1925 when John B. Gillies erected a corrugated tin building on Garden Avenue and acted as minister. Later this congregation became a member of the Fellowship of Evangelical Baptist Churches in Canada and in 1936 a new brick church was built on Church Street. Pastors since its organization have been Dr. H.M. Blandin, Rev. H.H. Phinney, Rev. Albert Jones, Rev. W. Hiltz, Rev. B. McSpadden, and Rev. E.H. Mitchell.

St. Andrew's Presbyterian Church, Maple

The first record we have of St. Andrew's Presbyterian Church, Maple, is in the handwriting of Donald Cameron, in the minutes of a meeting on December 15, 1829:

This is to certify that a number of us inhabitants of the Township of Vaughan, being anxious to enjoy the means of divine grace and being destitute of a suitable house for that purpose, do hereby earnestly solicit the assistance of a generous and discerning public to erect a church on the rear of No. 19, 3rd Concession of Vaughan, aforesaid. From 90 to 100 of us, chiefly from Scotland, having lately formed ourselves into a church state, professing the doctrine, discipline and worship of the Church of Scotland and contained in the Confession of Faith, do earnestly wish to obtain a house capable of containing us and those who may afterward unite with us in the worship of God and being many of us new settlers we are thereby obliged to our generous friends and wellwishers for assistance and as duty bound shall always pray.

By authority and in behalf of above society
Neil Malloy
Donald Cameron   TRUSTEES
Hugh Earl Beggs

The next record is one which had to do with the laying out of the burying grounds which evidently had been in the possession of the community for some time, and on which ground the first church was erected, probably about 1830-1.

1. Resolved that the burying ground belonging to the said church should be laid out in squares of one rod in each square for each and every family or anyone who wishes to have a lot.

2. Resolved that a diagram of said ground should be drawn on paper and

the lots so numbered so that each member might choose whatever lot he wanted, if not taken up before, and to pay the sum of five shillings and six pence, Halifax currency, to be paid when pointed out by the person for that purpose, or to have a lot on paying the same as others.

Rev. Peter MacNaughton, who came from Scotland, was the first Presbyterian minister of Maple. He preached from 1832 to 1844 and then returned to his birthplace in Perthshire; but he stayed there only a year before returning to Canada and buying land in this country. He preached again at Maple in 1847 and 1848, and then accepted a charge at Pickering.

The charge at Maple was vacant until 1859, when Rev. D. Ross was ordained and inducted as minister. In the meantime a manse had been built. In 1862 a new church was built on Concession 4 across the road from the old church. It is still in use.

Succeeding ministers have been Rev. William Aitken, 1865-80; Rev. D. Camelon, 1881-9; Rev. C.A. Campbell, 1890-1900; Rev. W.G. Back, 1900-07; Rev. J.W. Gordon, 1908-12; Rev. S.R. Robinson, 1913-24; Rev. C.H. Bowman, 1925-58; Rev. B.F. Andrews, 1959 to the present. In 1925, St. Andrews did not join with the United Church of Canada. It still retains its connection with St. Paul's on Concession 7, with which it shares a joint session and common Communion Roll.

Lord Beaverbrook was born in Maple as Max Aitken, when his father was the minister. His mother's family, the Nobles, lived where Dr. Bigford lives now. In March 1964, Lord Beaverbrook made a gift of a carillon of bells that are played every day.

In the cemetery there is a verse on Mr. Cairns' tombstone that reads:

> Reader, reflect as you pass by
> As you are now, so once was I.
> As I am now, so you must be
> Prepare for death to follow me.

St. Stephen's Anglican Church, Maple

The Parish of St. Stephen's, Vaughan, in Upper Canada, was founded in 1836, and located on the west part of Lot 10, Concession 3. The land was granted by Michael Keffer. The present brick church in Maple was opened on December 15, 1895. The parish hall was added in 1963.

The Women's Auxiliary was organized very early in the 1870s, Mrs. Wm. Cook being the first president.

The first clergyman was Rev. V.P. Mayerhoffer, who was at Maple until 1837. He was followed by: Rev. George S.J. Hill, 1849-50; Rev. D.E. Blake, 1850-5; Rev. J. Davidson, 1863-6; Rev. C.L. Cartwright, 1867-9; Rev. T.L. Hanson, 1870; Rev. R. Harrison, 1871-2; Rev. T.J. Hodgkin, 1873-8; Rev. O.P. Ford, 1879-80; Rev. C.H. Shortt, 1881-90; Rev. W.F. Swallow, 1890-1; Rev. F.C.C. Heathcote, 1891-6; Rev. E.G. Diamond, 1898-1900; Rev. J.A.R. MacDonald, 1901-02; Rev. William Burns, 1904; Rev. F.M. Dean, 1905-07; Rev. E.J. McKittrick, 1909-14; Rev. P.W. Richardson, 1915-17; Rev. T.R. Haughton, 1918-20; Rev. P.W.A. Roberts, 1922-9; Rev. W.F. Wrixon, 1929-36; Rev. E.W.G. Worrall, 1936; Rev. D.C.H. Michell; Rev. Dr. Bruce Jennings; Rev. Dr. Ramsay Armitage, 1959- .

Organists in later years were Charles Jackson, Mary Eleanor Sheppard, Margaret Ramsay, Mrs. Rawlings, Mrs. Markham, Fred Chapman, and Dr. Charles Birkett.

St. Paul's Presbyterian Church, Vaughan
St. Paul's Presbyterian Church, Vaughan, came into being when the congregation of the Presbyterian Church of Vaughan in connection with the Church of Scotland met at Maple on January 18, 1837, with Rev. Peter McNaughton presiding. It was understood that henceforth services were to be held at Maple on two successive Sabbaths and on the third Sabbath they would be held alternately at the Upper Corner and at the Humber, commencing May 1st.

The Upper Corner was that part of the congregation north of Maple sideroad on the 6th, 7th and 8th Concessions. The Humber was the area to the south extending west to the 9th and 10th Concessions. The services in both of these localities were held in homes conveniently situated, for all had to walk, the minister coming on horseback.

In 1838 these services were all given to the Upper Corner, which left out the members and supporters on the Humber. Certain arrangements were made to meet this situation but a decision was reached on February 19, 1844, to build a church on Concession 7. An acre of land was purchased and a building committee established of Rev. Peter MacNaughton, Arthur McNeil, Hector McLean, Edward Miller, Neil McDonald, Neil McGillivary, and Donald MacNaughton.

A frame structure 38 x 30 feet was erected. The building had eight windows, a gallery, a high pulpit with a sounding board above a precentors' table, but no pews until 1847. Parishioners sat on planks laid upon blocks of wood. Services were held in Gaelic as well as English. The congregation became known as St. Paul's. A brick church was built in 1889 overlooking the Humber River valley.

Maple United Church
The first mention of Methodist services in this area was a revival meeting in 1833 in the barn of Obediah Rupert. The *Christian Guardian* reported the official opening of Rupert's Chapel on October 9, 1840, at 4 p.m.: 'A small neat and elegant Methodist Church has been erected — dimensions are 38' x 27' x 17' high and will accommodate nearly 200 persons. It has six Gothic windows and a door on the south side. There is a vestry attached to the north end. Exterior is painted a slate colour with white cornice and windows. The interior is a stone colour except the pulpit and altar railing which are painted imitation oak.' The opening service was conducted by Rev. David Wright.

The chapel was located at Sherwood on the west end of Lot 16, Concession 3.

In 1869 it was decided to build a larger church. When a difference of opinion arose as to where it should stand, it was agreed that the matter be settled at the Quarterly Meeting to be held in Thornhill. The final decision was to build in Maple on a half-acre lot given by John C. McQuarrie. The cornerstone of the present brick church was laid on Thursday, June 16, 1870 at 10.30 a.m. The building committee was Rev. C. Fish, J.P. Rupert, Henry Dickout, J.C. McQuarrie, Daniel Kinnee, Adam Rupert, Sr., Dr. O. Rupert, and Peter Frank. (Morley Kinnee, the present Clerk of Session, is a descendant of both the Kinnee and Dickout families.)

In 1871 the first land was purchased for what is now the Maple United Cemetery.

At Union in 1883, Maple circuit of the Methodist Church was formed, including Edgeley, Hope, Concord, and Carrville churches. The minister lived in Maple and was assisted by a student minister.

The same year, the Sunday School room was built.

After the United Church of Canada came into being, this became Maple United Church.

The first annual congregational meeting in 1926 had an interesting program that included vocal solos by Mrs. George Bailey and Dr. Fred Routley and violin solos by Dr. William Caldwell with Mrs. Routley at the organ.

The present Christian Education wing was opened on February 17, 1957. The sermon was preached by Rev. A.C. Forrest, a former son of the congregation. Dr. Archer Wallace cut the ribbon and Ken Jarrett sang 'Bless this House,' accompanied by the organist, Mrs. Roy Clegg.

The congregation celebrated the 100th anniversary of the church with special services during the month of June, 1970.

Ministers serving Maple United Church have been (with their years of starting): *Yonge Street North Circuit*: Rev. C. Fish, 1870; Rev. J. Hunt and Rev. E.F. Goff, 1872; Rev. J.H. Starr and Rev. A. Brown, 1875; Rev. J.W. McCallum and W.J. Jowson, 1877; Rev. J.W. McCallum & Rev. John Pickering, 1879; Rev. Peter Addison & Rev. John Pickering, 1880; Rev. John E. Starr, 1883; *Maple Circuit:* Rev. Michael Fawcett, 1884; Rev. James Pearen, 1886; Rev. Peter Campbell, 1889; Rev. George Brown, 1891; Rev. A. Bedford, 1894; Rev. J. Wallace Stewart, 1895; Rev. S.W. Dean, 1900; Rev. W.N. Chantler, 1903; Rev. J. E. Wilson, 1905; Rev. P.N. Jones, 1907; Rev. J.W. Morgan, 1909; Rev. H.S. Lovering, 1913; Rev. T.W. Leggott, 1918; Rev. Robert K. Lambert, 1922; Rev. A.S. Kerr, 1925; Rev. A.M. Partridge, 1930; Rev. J.R. MacCrimmon, 1936; Rev. C.E. Fockler, 1939; Rev. P.J. Lambert, 1949; Rev. E.H. Unstead, 1953; Rev. A.G. Donald, 1954; Rev. Harold W. Davies, 1958; Rev. Ralph C. Williams, 1962; Rev. N.H. Boogers, 1966.

Zoar Primitive Methodist Church, Nashville
Zoar Primitive Methodist Church was situated on Concession 10 on the southwest corner of the present Nashville Cemetery. In 1856 services were held at 2 p.m. on Sundays and on Thursday evenings as part of the Etobicoke circuit. Some of the family names in the Missionary Report of 1857 were Ross, Agar, Johnston, Culham, Train, Kurtz, Devins, Tedder and Atkinson.

In 1884, at the time of the Methodist union, Zoar was closed. Most of the members went to Shiloh, which was half a mile north of Central Church on the west side of Highway Number 50.

Nashville Presbyterian Church

Nashville Presbyterian Church was officially opened on Sept. 21, 1902, and became part of a two-point charge with Bolton. Land had been donated by Mr. and Mrs. Frank McCluskie. The members of the first session were Robt. Agar, James Bernath, Thos. Webster, and John Black.

It was an attractive, neat-looking red brick church with a basement finished for a Sunday School. Mr. Thos. Webster served many years as Sunday School superintendent.

In November, 1924, during a late season electrical storm, a bolt of lightning hit the building. The inside was in shambles, and no plaster remained on the ceiling. It was decided not only to repair the damage, but to enlarge the church with a twelve-foot extension to the north. The church was reopened in May 1925.

Nashville Church has always had a good choir. At the fiftieth anniversary, Norman Black had been choir leader for over thirty years, and Miss Bertha McCluskie had been organist for many years.

In 1925 Nashville voted to stay in the continuing Presbyterian Church. Its Ministers have been: Rev. Thos. L. McLachlan, 1902-06; Rev. D.M. Martin, 1907-10; Rev. W.W. Craw, Ph.D., 1910-21; Rev. Donald McKay, 1921-7; Rev. Ronald McEachern, 1927-9; Rev. D.A. Robertson, 1930-5; Rev. J.C. Ross, 1937-44; Rev. F.G. Fowler, 1944-6; Rev. J.F. Donald, 1946-8; Rev. A.L. Faris, 1949; Dr. Jos. McLellan; Rev. Marshall Jess; Rev. Warren McKinnon.

Pine Grove Congregational Church

The Pine Grove Chapel, as this church was called in the early days, was founded in 1841. A large frame church was built on a hill overlooking the village of Pine Grove, on the west of the cemetery on Gamble Street which marks its original site. It was considered a fine structure in those days. The land for the chapel, and road leading to it, was donated by George Stegmann, a brother of John Stegmann, a well-known early surveyor who assisted in laying out Vaughan Township.

The new church consisted of nine members: Rev. and Mrs. Samuel Harris (the first minister and his wife), Richard Bywater, Sarah Bywater, Sarah Taylor, James Ashdown, William Rupel, Eliza Rupel, and Sarah Lawrie. Richard Bywater and A. Wallis were the first deacons.

In 1861 the members began to talk of the advisability of building a new church, more conveniently situated on the gravel road (Islington Avenue). A building committee was appointed of Rev. R. Hay, Silas Hartman, A.W. Wallis, J. Bowman, Peter Witherspoon, W.A. Wallis, John Dalziel, and John Abell. In 1866, 25 years after the organization of the church, the cornerstone was laid by the pastor, Rev. Robert Hay.

In 1902 the church was destroyed by fire, caused by sparks from burning grass in an adjoining field. A new church was rebuilt on the same site, following the same architecture as the old. The new church was opened on July 19, 1903, by Rev. J. Findlater whose wife, Sarah Jeffery, went from the church as a missionary to India. They were at this time home on furlough.

After the opening of the new church there followed years when pastors came out from Toronto. These were not young men, and they walked many miles in visitation and to services at Pine Grove and Humber Summit.

The ministers were: Rev. Samuel Harris, 1841-4; Students of Congregational Institute, 1844-9; Rev. Hodgskin, June to December, 1849; Students of Congregational Institute, January 1850 to August 1853; Rev. Jupp, August 1853 to April 1856; Students, 1856-9; Rev. Robt. Hay, 1859-69; Rev. W.W. Smith, 1869-78; Rev. E. Ireland, 1878-9; Rev. Robt. Hay (second term), 1879-82; Rev. W. Way, 1883-5; Rev. A.W. Gerrie, 1855-7; Rev. Wilmot, 1887-91; Rev. G. Skinner, 1891-3; Rev. H. Bentley, 1893-6; Rev. W. Collins, 1896-9; Rev. Wisker, 1900-02; Rev. E. Barker, Rev. J. Findlater, Rev. A.B. Sherk, and students, 1902-17; Rev. Geo. M. Blackett, 1917-25; Mr. C.L. Rumble, 1925-28; Mr. Ernest Root, 1929-31; Mr. Ritchie, October 1931 to May 1932; Mr. J. Lucas, July 1922 to September 1934; Rev. George Kitching, January to August, 1935; Rev. W.T. Bunt, December 1935 to June 1940; Rev. J.H. Dudgeon, August 1940 to September 1949; Rev. Harold W. Kettyle, 1949-57.

In May 1957, the Pine Grove Congregational Church joined the Fellowship of Evangelical Baptist Churches in Canada, and the name was changed to Pine Grove Baptist Church. Rev. Harold W. Kettyle continued on with the ministry at the Pine Grove Baptist Church until June 1965, and was succeeded by Rev. R.A. Watson and Rev. Peter Dahnke.

The Pine Grove Congregational Cemetery was restored by Vaughan Township in 1968.

Richmond Hill Presbyterian Church
Prior to 1817 there were Presbyterian families in the district, for a call dated April 10, 1817, was sent to the Rev. William Jenkins whose ministry is recounted elsewhere. He responded and is said to have preached his first sermon in the pine grove that then covered the site of the present church and cemetery. He organized the church that year and in 1821 a frame church was built. The property was traditionally a gift to the church from James Miles, the original owner of the land, although the church bought it years later from his niece, Elizabeth Arnold, and her husband, John. Rev. Jenkins died in 1843, having done extensive missionary work over a wide area, usually on horseback.

Many of the parishioners came from Thornhill, Vaughan, and King, and when Rev. Dick became pastor in 1849 he organized congregations at Thornhill that year and at Laskay and Temperanceville in 1850. The Thornhill congregation remained affiliated with Richmond Hill for the following ninety years.

Alex Moodie became the first precentor in 1862 and some choir stalls were built around his desk. The first choir was begun in 1864 and an organ installed in 1877. The present church was built in 1880 for $6,366. A new manse had been built a few years previously; Rev. Dick lived in retirement in the old manse. A pipe organ was installed in 1915. The pewter Communion Set was given in 1839 by Robert Marsh, who with James Miles formed the first Session.

A church hall was added to the west in 1957 and in 1963 was named the George Francis Memorial Hall in memory of the late superintendent of the Sunday School. In 1961 the Sunday School of this church celebrated its 150th anniversary: when it was started in 1811 by James Miles it was one of the first Sunday Schools in Canada.

The Ministers who have served the church are: Rev. Wm. Jenkins, 1817-43; Rev. Walter Scott, 1845-7; Rev. James Dick, 1847-77; Rev. Isaac Campbell, 1877-84; Rev. J.W. Cameron, 1884-7; Rev. W.W. Percival, 1887-94; Rev. James Grant, 1894-1909; Rev. E.C. Currie, 1909-13; Rev. Robert Herbison, 1914-18; Rev. W.M. Hay, 1919-23; Rev. J.W. McIntosh, 1923-5; Rev. Malcolm Campbell, 1926-7; Rev. Chas. A. Mullin, 1928-9; Rev. David Marshall, 1929-33; Rev. J.D. Cunningham, 1934-40; Rev. S.W. Hirtle, 1941-55; Rev. J.N. Hepburn, 1955-68; Rev. Wm. Wallace, 1969- .

Richmond Hill United Church
The congregation at Richmond Hill was established, as were other Methodist congregations in Vaughan and other parts of Upper Canada, by circuit riders — in this case, Nathan Bangs and Presiding Elder Jewell, who organized congregations for the Episcopal Methodist Church. These preachers came by horseback in 1803, and in 1805 had the Yonge Street Circuit organized. It included a large territory — the townships of East and West York, Etobicoke, Markham, Vaughan, King, Whitchurch and the Gwillimburys. Before too long, because of population increase, this Yonge Street Circuit became North Yonge Street, with South Yonge Street being Bowes, Willowdale, Grams, Weston.

The North Yonge Street Wesleyan Circuit consisted of Richmond Hill, Maple, Victoria Square, Bethel, Patterson, and Headford. In 1883, at the time of the union of the Methodist Church, Maple and Bethel were transferred.

The first Methodist congregation in Richmond Hill worshipped in the public school and the Presbyterian church when available. Here they held services on Sunday afternoons.

The first Methodist church was begun in 1846 on a plot of ground where Charlton's Hardware Store used to stand. It was not completely finished and dedicated until 1860. On Sunday, December 21, 1879, it was burned to the ground. The text of the sermon that morning was, "Behold how great a matter a little fire kindleth." It must

Teston Methodist Church, photographed in 1920. Remodelled, it remains in active use in the United Church.

The first Richmond Hill Presbyterian Church, erected in 1821. The pen-and-ink drawing is based on a photograph. The present Richmond Hill Presbyterian Church was built in 1880.

Woodbridge United Church, built in 1886 as a Methodist Church.

Re-organized Church of Latter-Day Saints, Islington Avenue North, Woodbridge, built in 1970, reflects modern trends in church architecture.

have been one of the old-time "fire and brimstone" sermons. Many outstanding Methodists had preached in this church — the Ryersons (Egerton, William, and John), Jeffers, Morley Punshon, Wilkinson, Bredin, Wood, Smith, Taylor, Spence, Potts, Carrol, and Corson.

Following the disastrous fire, Abraham Law donated a half-acre of land at the corner of Yonge Street and Centre Street East, and one of the finest structures north of Toronto was built and opened in 1881 by Revs. Peter Addison and John Pickering. The Trustee Board was made up of Wm. Wright, Wm. Trench, Wm. Harrison, Wm. Glass, Wm. Atkinson, James Freak, Isaac Crosby, Henry Sanderson, John Harris, James E. Switzer, John Duncan, John Sanderson, P.G. Savage, and Charles Mason. The building cost $17,000, a large amount in those days. In 1910 electricity replaced the acetylene lamps and in 1923 a Casavant organ was installed at a cost of $5,000.

In June 1925, at the time of the Union of Churches, a number of Presbyterians joined with the Methodist congregation and the church became known as the Richmond Hill United Church.

The double house next to the church, one part of which was occupied by John Sanderson, was demolished to make room for the Christian Education wing of the church, added in 1958.

It was customary for ministers to stay in one appointment in the early years of the Methodist Church for three years. This was later extended to four, and after Church union no set length of time was stipulated. The following have been ministers at this church. (There were also assistant ministers, usually divinity students from Victoria College. The Circuit for many years included Victoria Square and Headford.)

Revs. Gatchell, Youmans, Harman, Corson, David Wright, Samuel Rose, J. Hughes, L. Warner, Wellington Jeffers, Messmore, R. Jones, Benjamin Jones, W.S. Blacklock, J.L. Sanders, H. Wilkinson, Wm. Willoughby, S.J. Hunter, E.B. Ryckman, T.A. Ferguson, John Bredin, Charles Fish, Cunningham, Garbutt, M. Fawcett, Ware, C.T. Brown, Squires, and H. Dean; John Hunt, 1873; E.F. Goff, 1873; J.H. Stan, 1875-7; B.B. Dundas, 1875; A. Brown, 1876; J.W. McCallum, 1877-80; W.G. Howson, 1877; John Pickering, 1880; Peter Addison, 1880-2; J.W. Barkwell, 1882-3; J.E. Betts, 1884; J.E. Starr, 1884; W.R. Barker, 1884; W.B. Booth, 1884-5; F. Wilson, 1886; T. Leonard, 1886; J.M. Simpson, 1888-90; G.N. Rutledge, 1887-8; J.C. Speer, 1890-3; J.T. Morris, 1890; Gardner, 1891; J.H. Oliver, 1892; John Rickery, 1893-6; S.W. Dean, 1893; Gideon Powell, 1896; Geo. McCullough, 1896-8; A.J. Paul, 1896-7; A.R. Sanderson, 1897; R.S.E. Large, 1898; N. Wellwood, 1899-1902; J.H. More, 1901; T. Campbell, 1902-06; Percy Peacock, 1902; W.G. Smith, 1903-06; A.D. Brace, 1906-10; W.S. Irwin, 1906; H.E. Toye, 1906; G. Sidney Smith, 1910-14; Wm. Trench, 1910; A. Rowe, 1911; J.R. Aikenhead, 1914-18; A. McNeil, 1918-22; H.S. Warren, 1922-5; A.A. Wall, 1925-9; J.W. McIntosh, 1926; G.E. Coulter, 1929; C.W. Follett; C.B. Brethen; Chas. G. Higginson; Norman Gibson; Robert Smith; and Alan Hallett.

Church of St. Mary Immaculate
Early members of the Roman Catholic faith in Vaughan Township and Richmond Hill were without a parish priest. They were visited occasionally by missionary priests from York (where the first Roman Catholic Church had been built in 1822) who would say mass and administer the sacrament in private homes. One of these priests who is well remembered was Rev. Father Edward Gordon.

From Richmond Hill in 1852, a request supported by Matthew Teefy, local postmaster, went forward to the Rt. Rev. Armand de Charonne, second Bishop of Toronto, for permission to build a church. The pews were made by hand and were owned and occupied by the persons who made them. The church was built in 1857 on Mill Street, between the high school and Lucas Street. It was enlarged in 1874 under Father Cassidy.

The next church was built in 1894 under the direction of the Rev. Patrick McMahon who was parish priest from 1894 until 1907 when he died. In 1894 there were only a few Roman Catholic families living within Richmond Hill. They were the Teefys, Murphys, Slineys, Cosgroves, and Naughtons.

In 1918 Father Kelly became the first resident priest at Richmond Hill. Father Reddin came in 1930, and Father E. Keene in 1931. Father F.R. McGinn was priest from 1942 to 1964. The parish has been served since 1964 by Rev. C.J. Schwalm and his associates, Rev. C.J. Dougherty and Rev. J.A. O'Donnell. In 1966 the red brick building built in 1894 was demolished and in 1968 a large new building on the same site with a parish hall, church offices, and rectory was ready to serve the expanding number of families in the parish.

St. Mary's Anglican Church, Richmond Hill
Richmond Hill Anglican parish no doubt originated from the Thornhill parish.

St. Mary's Anglican Church was built in 1872. The land was given by John Arnold, and his wife is said to have suggested the name. Earlier, Dr. Duncombe, an army doctor, had built a church which was used between 1864 and 1870, when it burned. The clergyman came from Thornhill and was paid by the Clergy Reserve Fund.

The new church was a beautiful example of the early decorative English style of architecture and followed the design of St. James Cathedral in Toronto. The first rector was the Rev. Robert Shanklin, said to be a musical genius and a very witty Irishman. He was followed by Rev. W. Bates. When Rev. John Gibson, his successor, was rector, services were at 3 p.m. except once a month, when the service was at 11 a.m. Mr. Fury was warden and also caretaker; John Brown was superintendent of the Sunday School; Mrs. J.K. Falconbridge taught the girls and was an excellent teacher.

The spire and organ were added later and a bell was given by Christopher Duncombe, nephew of the old army doctor. In 1928-9 the crypt was dug out, providing accommodation for Sunday School and social activities. Shrubs and the Boston ivy were planted in 1930. The interior was renovated and memorials added, one to H.A. Nichols, a long-time faithful member. Mrs. Mollet (the former Anna Kerswill), a faithful organist for many years, was remembered by new choir stalls. The rectory was built in 1951, and in 1953 a Hammond electric organ was installed. Wrixon Hall was built in 1956. The new St. Mary's Church was built in 1964.

Rectors of St. Mary's Anglican Church, Richmond Hill: Rev. Robert Shanklin, 1872-83; Rev. W. Bates, 1883-99; Rev. John Gibson, 1899-1912; Rev. S.A. Lawrence, 1912-15; Rev. T.R. Haughton, 1915-20; Rev. T.W. Buckly, 1921; Rev. H.F. Battersby, 1922-8; Rev. C.G. Eakins, 1928-9; Rev. Claude Secrett, 1929-36; Rev. W.F. Wrixon, 1936-52; Rev. A.A. Chote, 1952-56; Rev. James O'Neil, 1957-69; Rev. David McGuire, 1969- .

The Free Methodist Church, Richmond Hill
The Free Methodist Church in Richmond Hill was started in 1953 when a group began meeting together. The church building was built in 1956. The pastors have been; Rev. E.S. Bull, Rev. R. Holten, Rev. S.L. Slater, and Rev. D.A. Dyer.

Richvale Methodist Church, Boyletown
This church was originally held in the old Boyle barn on Lot 40, Concession 1, and was on the circuit with Carrville and Headford. Once the organist had to hurl her hymnbook at a rat that kept peeping out of a hole. Under the Rev. A. McNeil, in 1921, a local resident, Fulton Vanderburg, became the lay minister and went on to be an ordained minister in the church. The ministers who followed, Rev. J. Lavell Smith and Rev. Waldo Smith, and the congregation spent much time remodelling the barn to be more like a church. The first Richvale school was held in the basement.

During the Depression, about 1935, the church was closed. Eventually it was made into a factory, and later was torn down. Miss Edna Attwell carried on with the Sunday School for some time. The Langstaff Baptist church also had services in this area before building their church in 1936.

Richvale Gospel Chapel
Sunday School was held in the Richvale area for many years. In the fall of 1949 students from Emmaus Bible School, in conjunction with Olivet Gospel Chapel, began to hold Sunday School in the Richvale school on Spruce Avenue, with evening services also. The present building on 24 Oak Avenue was started in 1951 and opened that fall. Additions have been made to the building from time to time.

Thornhill United Church
This church dates back to 1803 when Methodist preaching was carried on regularly at the home of Benjamin Hoshel on Concession 2 of Markham, one and a quarter miles east of Langstaff. The congregation

came into being through the preaching of Circuit Rider Nathan Bangs, and under the auspices of the Methodist Episcopal Church in the United States. By 1811 the Cober School was begun and by 1815 completed and regular services were held there with Rev. John Rhodes as pastor. His congregation numbered 160 persons.

In the 1820s the Wesleyan Methodist Church was granted a lot by Elizabeth Lyons near the east end of Sinclair's or Ainsworth's. A church was erected and the remains of the old cemetery still exist. The Episcopal congregation joined with the Wesleyan Methodist Church and services were continued in that building from 1838 to 1852.

On March 1, 1846, the British Methodist Church began. This church was erected on the west side of Yonge Street on the south slope of the Thornhill hollow. Union between the two churches followed and the latter building was closed. In 1850 the Presbyterian Church bought it as a Richmond Hill appointment.

In 1852 the Methodists bought a new site and moved their church to Centre Street West. The trustees at that time were Josiah Purkiss, David Mulholland, John Hewgill, John Devlin, Wm. Segsworth, Wm. Lane, John Reid, and James Robinson.

When the Methodist Church of Canada was formed in 1883, the Thornhill congregation became a part of it, and in 1925 went with it into the United Church of Canada. The cornerstone of a new church was laid on September 9, 1957; the new brick church and education centre were completed the following year. Thus the Thornhill congregation has been in existence from 1803 to the present.

The church building erected in 1852 had a tall box pulpit in the south end and galleries on the other three sides. The organ and choir loft were in the north gallery, and during the preaching a curtain was drawn across in front of them. The organ made its appearance in 1857 and was played by Miss Maggie Reid. The Methodist Sunday School was organized in 1839 and has continued to the present day.

Camp meetings always presented opportunities for pranksters. One evening when a camp meeting was held near Langstaff, the gang were busy annoying the preacher and congregation. It was common for a horse to be unhitched and tied some distance away, or for a member to find his wheels interchanged and his lunch eaten. One event is worth mentioning because of its after-effects. Jim Rankin, one of the boldest of the gang, said, "Come on, fellows, that man has been preaching long enough. I'm going to stop him." He was as good as his word, for he marched up the aisle to the front and the unexpected happened: he was converted! Some years later he became a Methodist minister, was elected president of the Toronto Conference, and when the Anglican Church held its 50th Anniversary, he was one preacher who took part.

Some ministers of Thornhill United Church: Nathan Bangs, Rev. John Reynolds, Rev. David Peckett, Rev. Joseph Gatchell, Rev. John Rhodes, Rev. John Law, Rev. Enoch Wood, Rev. Horace Dean, Rev. T.S. Keogh, Rev. B.R. Strangways, Rev. W.E. Baker, Rev. Dr. T.T. Sparling, Rev. E.E. . Pugsley, Rev. E.B. Cook, Rev. E.A. Currie, Rev.

Dr. T.S. Duncan, Rev. Dr. E.E. Kent, Rev. Dr. E.B. Eddy, Rev. H. MacDonald, Rev. A.I. Higgins, Rev. McAlister.

Holy Trinity Anglican Church, Thornhill

Holy Trinity Anglican Church, Thornhill, was begun in 1829 and on February 29, 1830, the first service was held. The church was officially opened by John Strachan, afterwards the first Bishop of Toronto. The sermon lasted one and a half hours. Regular services had been held in the Coker schoolhouse since 1815.

The land was given by Benjamin Thorne and William Parsons. Capt. John Arnold, James Young, Col. W.G. Cruikshank, Richard, Anthony, and Southby Gapper, and Edward O'Brien were among the original supporters. Rev. George Mortimer was the first rector and William Parsons was a church warden. A letter from England to Mr. Parsons from his brother stated that he regretted not being able to send more money for the church but there was a depression in England and it was hard to collect money. This probably referred to the enlargement of the church in 1840. In 1860 the rectory was built. There was no basement in the church for Sunday School or other meetings; but in 1928 a parish hall was built. In 1950 the church was remodelled on a new site, half a mile to the south at the corner of Jane and Brooke, in Thornhill Village, this time with a basement. This is the oldest original church building in use in the Toronto Diocese. In 1960 a large red brick hall was erected beside the church. In the church proper the high pulpit and box pews have been replaced and the heating and lighting modernized.

Over the years there have been thirteen rectors: Rev. George Mortimer, Rev. Dominic Blake, Rev. Edward H. Dewar, Rev. Robert Shanklin, Rev. W. Wheatley Bates, Rev. John Gibson, Rev. Samuel Albert Lawrence, Rev. Joseph Wm. McDonald, Rev. Norman Henry Noble, Rev. John Harvey Colclough, Rev. Shirley Arthur Ralph Wood, Rev. Wm. E. Askew, Rev. H. Reginald Howden with Rev. F.C. Jackson as assistant minister.

St. Luke's Roman Catholic Church, Thornhill

There were very few Roman Catholics in the early migration to Vaughan Township; however, they came with the British influx after the Napoleonic Wars. In the beginning those in this area were ministered to by a priest from Newmarket. St. Luke's was organized in 1847 under the direction of Fathers Quinlan and Proulx. One of the founders, Edward Seager, a farmer, was the son of an Anglican clergyman, who had married Catherine Cain, a Roman Catholic.

The church was built facing the end of Colborne Street. The carpenter was John Edey. It was enlarged between 1853 and 1858, and a wing was added for a pastoral residence; but the whole building was vacated in 1879 when the present brick presbytery was built. In 1907 St. Luke's was united with Richmond Hill parish and had no resident priest until it became a separate parish in 1947. Later a parish hall was built and, in 1957, St. Luke's Separate School.

Among the rectors have been: the Rev. L. Griffa, Rev. McNulty, Rev. J. O'Donohoe, Rev. Philbert Rey, Rev. T.J. Morris, Rev. A. Finan, Rev. E. Cassidy, Rev. Beausang, Rev. W.J. McGinley, Rev. J.J. Egan, Rev. P. McMahon, Rev. J.R. Grant, Rev. E. Kelly, Father J. Reddin, Rev. E. Keans, Father F. McGinn.

A large new church, St. Paschal Baylon, was built at 92 Steeles Avenue West to serve the many new families south of Thornhill.

Thornhill Presbyterian Church

Thornhill Presbyterian Church was organized in 1849. Previously the Presbyterians in that area were ministered to from the Richmond Hill Presbyterian Church. From 1817 to 1843 Rev. Wm. Jenkins was in charge. Under Rev. James Dick they bought a frame building from the British Methodists and moved it to a new site on Lot 31 on the Vaughan side of Yonge Street. It continued to be affiliated with the Richmond Hill Presbyterian Church and was enlarged from time to time.

The congregation did not enter into union with the Methodist and Congregational churches in 1925 and has carried on, building a new church and education building on Centre Street. Rev. Calvin Chambers was the first resident pastor, and was followed by Rev. D.T. Evans. Mr. A.C. Chapman retired as choir master in 1950, having contributed a solo each Sunday for 34 years. Rev. Dillwyn Evans was elected Moderator of the Presbyterian Church in Canada for 1970-1.

Thornhill Baptist Church

The Thornhill Baptist Church, a member of the Ontario and Quebec Convention, was established in 1952 when it took over the former Yonge Street parish hall of Holy Trinity Church. The building was remodelled and modernized. The first minister was Rev. Percy Buck, who was succeeded by Rev. Minton C. Johnston.

The Canadian Reformed Church

The Canadian Reformed Church of Toronto, organized in 1955, bought the former United Church building on Centre Street in Thornhill and ministers to families from Holland who have moved into the area.

Zion Evangelical Lutheran Church, Sherwood

Jacob and Michael Keffer and Jacob Fisher came from Berlin, Pennsylvania, and founded this church in 1806. The father of the Keffer brothers, Jacob, Sr., had helped found that Berlin and had set aside some 40 acres of land, the proceeds of which were to be used for the Evangelical Lutheran Church and School and for the sake of the poor.

Jacob Keffer settled in Vaughan Township on Lot 12, Concession 3, in 1806. In 1811 he gave a plot of ground on Concession 4, near Sherwood, to the Lutheran Church. Eight years later a church was built on the property. Until that time worship was held in the schoolhouse, where Jacob acted as lay reader and taught the children until a pastor

Zion Evangelical Lutheran Church, Sherwood, was built in 1860. The church was founded in 1806.

Between 1962 and 1969, Vaughan Township Council restored eight abandoned cemeteries throughout the township, to preserve valuable history. This cairn at Sherwood was restored in 1966. (Photo: Harry Vey)

The central plaque on the cairn at Sherwood illustrated on the previous page. (Photo: Harry Vey)

was secured. The first pastors came from the German Settlement in Markham but were not very satisfactory. The oldest baptismal record for the church is January 23, 1808.

The first minister, Rev. John D. Peterson, received his call at his home in Pennsylvania. He recorded his experiences in a letter in the papers of Dr. A.E. Byerley:

There were three brothers, John, Jacob and Valentine Fisher came over here (Penn.) from Upper Canada to get us to go to Canada. At that time we lived in Allegheny Tp. Somerset Co. We left Feb. 10/1819 and arrived Mar. 1 Vaughan Tp., York County. We lived first with Valentine Fisher from 1st Mar. to 21 Sept. 1819.

We moved Sept. 21, 1819, to Markham Tp. on 50 acres of land which I bought from Wilmot for $160. Afterward I built a house to live in. After being there two years we started to build three churches. The first in Vaughan Tp., the second on Mr. George Schulz's land in Markham Tp. and the third on Mr. Phil. Eckhart's land. These three churches were the first Lutheran churches in this part of the country. The parish in Vaughan was a very troublesome one. After the church was built one of our members, Michael Kieffer made much trouble and tried to turn the members against me. The congregation got smaller and my wages decreased considerably. Only received Sept., 1827, $30 after which I handed in my resignation.

When the local Lutheran congregations were unable to get a preacher of their own persuasion, they appealed to Bishop Strachan of the Church of England for help. He sent them a German-speaking Anglican minister, Phillip Mayerhoffer.

The three Lutheran congregations agreed that, if within ten years, a Lutheran pastor could not be obtained, the churches would become Anglican permanently. Then politics came into the situation. Mayerhoffer was a strong Tory and Jacob Keffer was just as strong a Grit. Mayerhoffer was an outspoken man. Sides were taken by those who attended church and a Sunday came in December 1837 when the clergyman and those who agreed with him were locked out of the church.

There was a very real split in the congregation. Michael Keffer gave land for a church for Mr. Mayerhoffer which was consecrated on St. Stephen's Day and so named. This was on Lot 10, Concession 3, West part, and is marked by a cairn erected by Vaughan Township in 1965 to mark the old cemetery. This was the beginning of the present St. Stephens Anglican at Maple.

So critical did the situation become for the Lutherans that in 1849, and again in 1850, Adam Keffer, Jacob's son, although sixty years old, walked to Pittsburgh to plead with the synod to send them a minister. Eventually, Rev. C.F. Diehl was sent in 1850 and introduced English services in place of German. The church was reconsecrated and extensively repaired. On Jan. 11, 1854, Rev. Jeremiah Fishburn began a 25 years' pastorate, during which time the present two-storey brick building was erected in 1860.

The Canada Synod of the Lutheran Church was established in 1861, with Rev. Fishburn as president. However, this congregation maintained an independent stand until 1952, when it finally joined the synod. In 1950 fire caused heavy damage but the church was reopened in the spring of 1951.

In 1936 Zion celebrated the 130th anniversary of its founding by unveiling a memorial cairn to commemorate the extraordinary accomplishment of Adam Keffer who twice walked 500 miles to plead with the Pittsburgh Synod to send them a minister.

From the beginning one of the most important parts of the church life was the Sunday School. Children and young people walked long distances to attend Sunday School, the frequent picnics, strawberry socials, sleigh rides, and the Christmas Concert. In 1956 an addition was built. In 1962 the CBC made a TV film, "Christmas in the Country," about the history of Zion. At that time Rev. A.C. Forrest returned to the church where he had been confirmed. Rev. Fishburn's successors have been: Rev. J.P. Deck, 1881-3; Rev. A. MacLaughlin, 1884-92; Rev. J.A. Dunlop, 1892-6; Rev. J.E. Lerah, 1896-9; Rev. J.K. Hiltz, 1900-04; Rev. Wisswaesser, 1905-07; Rev. J.V. Sappenfield, 1909-12; Rev. E.N. Fry, 1913-15; Rev. Nils Willison, 1916-18; Rev. P.S. Baringer, 1921-6; Rev. E. Heimrich, 1928-31; Rev. E. Huenergard, 1932-42; Rev. Seymour Cooper, 1942-6; Rev. H.N. Lossing, 1947-9; Rev. E.J. Fisher, 1950-5; Rev. H. Lindeman, 1956-60; Rev. N. Wagner, 1961-2; Rev. Emil Lange, 1962-5; and the present pastor, Rev. John Arbuckle.

Church Of Christ (Disciples), Sherwood
In 1885, members of the Church of Christ, or Disciples as they were called, bought the Methodist church at Sherwood. The church was known as the "Bluejays." Early members were the Witty, Schell, Baker, Boston, Grainger, McKinnon, Riddell, Page, Black, McMann, Wilson, and Dale families. Some of the early ministers were: Rev. Forrester, Rev. Alex Stewart, Rev. Milligan, who used to bicycle out from Toronto, Rev. Charles Petch, Rev. S.N. Jones, and Rev. Ralph Schell. (The latter had started to preach when he was sixteen. The Schells were a pioneer family in Vaughan who came from New York State around 1805. Tragedy struck their family in 1900 when five of their children died from diphtheria in a few months.)

Others who held meetings for short periods were: Madison Wright, who composed hymns, Don Carlos James, and Daniel Summers. With the advent of the motor car, the church was closed about 1925 and the members attended church in Toronto. For years the church remained empty, with the Bible open on the pulpit. In 1944 the building was taken down and removed. In the 1950s the work was started again in Vaughan in Concord Schoolhouse. A new church was built in Concord on King High Drive and opened on September 8, 1963, with Rev. A.E. Atkinson as pastor.

Teston United Church
The first church was built on the Teston side line and was known as Hadwen Chapel. Rev. Thomas Hadwen, a Wesleyan Methodist was one of the first ministers and was ordained in England.

A new church was built on the present site in 1872. The original hall, which is disposed of now, was moved about three-quarters of a mile from the old church site. During the moving the tackle broke and the building came to a sudden stop in a creek. Finally, without further mishap, it reached its destination and for some time the Sons of Temperance met there. Many debates, spelling bees, concerts, and oyster suppers, were held there as well.

In 1934 under the leadership of Rev. D. Davis, the church was remodelled and the spire taken down. In 1957 an addition was built and the spire was replaced during the ministry of Rev. M.R. Jenkinson, the minister for 22 years.

In the beginning Teston was part of the Richmond Hill charge, and then part of Kleinburg circuit. In 1893 it became part of a three-point circuit with King and Laskay. Since 1967 Teston United continues as a one-point charge with Rev. J. Dickinson as minister.

Ministers between 1872 and 1970: Rev. Fish; Rev. Thos. Hadwen; Rev. Caldwell, D.D.; Rev. A.F. Large; Rev. R.S.E. Large; Rev. T.C. Cocking; Rev. Nurse; Rev. Moore; Rev. Webster; Rev. R.J.D. Simpson; Rev. Thos. Chapman; Rev. Geo. Robinson; Rev. Newton Hill; Rev. George Walker; Rev. F.C. Keam; Rev. D. Roy Gray; Rev. Frank Dunlop; Rev. A.E. Lunau; Rev. A. Halbert; Rev. D. Davis; Rev. H. Anderson; Rev. M.R. Jenkinson, B.A.; Rev. J. Dickinson, B.A., B.D.

The United Church, Woodbridge

As early as the 1830s, meetings were held by a few ardent Christians to study the teachings of John Wesley. The church is believed to have been built in 1836, the following being active at that time: Francis Bunt, Mary Bunt, James Burgess, Stephen Burgess, Mary Burgess, Thomas Burgess, Mary A. Burgess, Elizabeth Burgess, Washington Peck, Mercy M. Peck, James Rose, Sarah Rose, George Snider, Jane Snider, Robert Matthews, Abigal Matthews, Alfred Jeffery, Elisha Farr, James Farr, Robert Coates, Nathan Martin, John Williams, John Jeffery, David Witherspoon, Fisher Allison, Jane Allison, Richard Jeffery, Robert Hart, Ann Porter, Wm. McCauley, Thomas Playter, John Simpson, Eleanor Kline, Hannah Tedder, John Tedder, and Wm. Brown.

In 1834 an acre of land was donated by Washington Peck, a cooper, for the site of a church overlooking the valley of the Humber on Mission House Road (Church Street). The site is marked by the old Methodist cemetery. In records of the Yonge Street Circuit, we find this small mission church designated by various names: Vaughan Branch, Bunt's Chapel, and Peck's Appointment.

The old log church became too small, and a new brick church was built beside it and opened in 1856. For many years the membership of the church was divided into classes for Christian fellowship.

With the union of Methodist bodies of 1883-4, the Wesleyan and Primitive Methodists in Woodbridge united. To accommodate this union the brick church was torn down and the material was used to build a larger church on Eighth Avenue. The new church was dedicated on December 26, 1886, and built at a cost of about $6,500.

For some years the question of union between the Congregational, Methodist, and Presbyterian Churches had been uppermost in the minds of leaders of these donominations. In 1925 this forward vision became a reality. June 10, 1925, was an historic day in the life of the church in Woodbridge. All the Methodists, numbering one hundred and forty, entered Union, together with ninety-one Presbyterians from Woodbridge and Knox, Vaughan, and five members of the Congregational Church at Pine Grove. Others entered later, including some from Nashville, numbering two hundred and four members at the time of Union. The Trustee Board of the new United Church consisted of John G. Whitmore, John Darker, Joseph Watson, Arthur W. Farr, Levi Elliott, Jonathan Ellerby, John F. Kellam, N. Geo. Wallace, Edgar Watson, Herb Nattress, Alex. Cameron, and Wm. Wood.

David McKane, a member of Woodbridge United Church, was licensed as a candidate for ordination to the ministry in 1970.

The ministers of the United Church, Woodbridge, follow. *Yonge Street Circuit*: Rev. Hamilton Biggar, Rev. Thos. Fawcett, 1836; Rev. Hamilton Biggar, Rev. Adam Townley, 1837; Rev. Adam Townley, Rev. Wm. Scott, 1838; Rev. Geo. Poole, Rev. John Law, 1839-40; Rev. Thos. Bevitt, Rev. James Hutchinson, 1841; Rev. Rowley Heyland, Rev. Geo. Playter, 1842-3; Rev. Samuel Rose, Rev. Wm. Price, 1844. *Humber Circuit*: Rev. Chas. Gilbert, 1845; Rev. Chas. Gilbert, Rev. Wm. Glass, 1846; Rev. John Baxter, Rev. Wm. Blackstock, 1847; Rev. Thos. Demorest, Rev. John Baxter, 1848; Rev. John Law, Rev. James C. Slater, 1849; Rev. John Law, Rev. Wm. Ames, 1850; Rev. Samuel Philp, Rev. Wm. Richardson, 1851; Rev. Samuel Philp, Rev. Wm. McDonagh, 1852; Rev. Samuel Philp, Rev. Henry Jones, 1853; Rev. Robt. Lochead, Rev. Benjamin Jones, Rev. Edward A. Ward, 1854; Rev. Robt. Lochead, Rev. Edward A. Ward, 1855; Rev. Robt. Lochead, Rev. Ashton Fletcher, 1856. *Weston Circuit*: Rev. Richard Jones, Rev. Henry Jackson, 1857; Rev. Richard Jones, Rev. Wm. Hayhurst, 1858; Rev. Wm. Philp, Rev. Wm. Hayhurst, 1859; Rev. Wm. Philp, 1860; Rev. Joseph L. Sanders, 1861-2; Rev. Thos. Jeffers, 1863-5; Rev. Noble F. English, 1866-8; Rev. John Shaw, 1869-70; Rev. Wm. McFadden, 1871; Rev. Joseph H. Locke, 1872-4; Rev. G.F. Hewitt, Rev. R.N. Burns, 1875-8; Rev. F.A. Ferguson, Rev. T. Dunlop, 1878-80; Rev. J.W. McCallum, Rev. M.D. Conron, 1880-3; Rev. Peter Campbell, Rev. W.J. West, Rev. G.N. Rutledge, 1883-6; Rev. R. Large, Rev. R.P. Bowles, Rev. S.C. Wright, 1886-8; Rev. S.C. Philip, Rev. E.C. Laker, Rev. J.C. Wilson, Rev. E.A. Pearson, 1888-91; Rev. John Locke, Rev. Isaac Couch, Rev. F.L. Brown, 1891-4; Rev. Jos. J. Ferguson, Rev. A.G. Hudson, 1894-7. *Woodbridge and Emery Circuit*: Rev. John J. Ferguson, 1897-9; Rev. A.E. Henderson, 1899-1901; Rev. C.W. Follett, 1901-03; Rev. Gideon L. Powell, 1903-06; Rev. Geo. Kitching, 1906-09; Rev. J.G. Rogers, 1909-13; Rev. John Morgan, 1913-17; Rev. H.S. Warren, 1917-21; Rev. Dr. G.S. Smith, 1921-5; Rev. C.A. Belfry and Rev. John Moir, 1925-6; Rev. Herbert Lee, 1926-30; Rev. J.E. Anderon, 1930-7; Rev. C.W. Barrett, 1937-41; Rev. Terence V. Hart,

1941-8. *Stated Supply*: Rev. D.A. MacKeracher, 1942-5; Rev. Percy Price, 1945-6; Rev. J.A.H. Hodgson, 1948-60; Rev. Wm. D.F. Morris, 1960-3; Rev. K. Jull, 1963-7; Rev. Bailey Snow, 1968- .

Christ Church, Anglican, Woodbridge
The first services were held in 1842 in a small log building on the farm of Richard and Robert Willis of Pine Grove. Rev. Adam Townley, assistant at the Thornhill parish, frequently conducted them in 1848, Rev. Henry Bath Osler of Lloydtown added Pine Grove to his charge until 1850, when it was placed under Rev. George Dixon of Tullamore. The church became associated with St. Stephens, Maple, and Grouse Hill in 1862, and thereafter the parish changed several times.

In 1850 it was decided to build a church on the northern boundary of the Village of Burwick to accommodate the people of Pine Grove and Burwick (Woodbridge). The contract was let to Wm. Tyrrell, a well-known builder and son-in-law of Rowland Burr. The church was opened for worship in 1851, the land being the gift of John W. Gamble and William Wallis.

In 1854 a church bell was purchased. In 1856 transepts and chancel were added, and the domed tower was changed to a spire. A parsonage adjoining the church was built in 1884, and also a stable.

On Sunday morning, February 20, 1921, the white frame church with the high tower and spire burst into flames as members were preparing to attend service. It was completely destroyed. The same year, a beautiful new stone church was opened for worship on the same site.

The 100th anniversary of this congregation was celebrated in 1942.

Over the years the Wallace family has furnished several church wardens: Capt. N. Wallace and John W. Gamble were the first, in 1851-53.

Altogether the church property, including the cemetery, covers ten acres.

Following the pioneer work of Rev. Adam Townley and Rev. H.B. Osler, the rectors of Christ Church parish have been: Rev. Wm. Guise Tucker, 1850-2; Rev. J. Gilbert Armstrong, 1853-7; Rev. John Carry, 1859-62; Rev. John Davidson, 1862-6; Rev. C.E. Cartwright, 1866-9; Rev. Thomas J. Hanson, 1869-70; Rev. R.J. Harrison, 1870-3; Rev. Thomas J. Hodgkin, 1873-8; Rev. Ogden P. Ford, 1878-82; Rev. James B. Head, 1883; Rev. Henry Heaton, 1883-4; Rev. Charles H. Shortt, 1884-91; Rev. W.F. Swallow, 1891-1911; Rev. Wm. Evans, 1911-18; Rev. R.B. Patterson, 1918-25; Rev. James H. Kidd, 1928-45; Rev. B.P. Smythe, 1945-7; Rev. J. Douglas Patterson, 1947-54; Rev. A.B. Cathcart, 1954-

Woodbridge Presbyterian Church
The members of this denomination attended either Knox or St. Paul's Churches in Vaughan up to 1874, when arrangements were made to

hold services regularly in Woodbridge. The first congregational meeting was held at the home of David Todd, where the first managers were appointed, all of them men who had taken a leading part in organization: Dr. Donald Grant, Thomas Wooley, Archibald Menzies, David Wright, John McCallum, David Todd, and David Allen. For the first three years services were held in the Temperance Hall on Pine Street, under the pastoral charge of Weston.

In 1875 a portion of Lot 3, Eighth Avenue was purchased for two hundred dollars from Dr. Donald Grant for the site of a church, which was erected and dedicated in 1877 under the pastorate of Rev. R. Pettigrew. The congregation grew steadily and in 1895 a Sunday School was erected.

Woodbridge was separated from Weston in 1901 and connected with Knox (Vaughan). The Woodbridge congregation now had the advantage of a minister living in their midst. Services previously held in the afternoon were now held morning and evening, an afternoon service being held at Knox.

A very attractive manse was built on land purchased from the estate of Joseph Crosson in 1902, the building committee being: John Johnston, John Nattress, Robt. King, Wm. Watson, Lachlin Cameron, John Smith, Wm. McClure, Thomas Mounsey, Daniel Longhouse, Donald Mackenzie, and John Kaiser.

The Church Union of 1925 claimed nearly half the membership. The remainder carried on, gradually growing in numbers until in 1964 a modern Christian education centre was built.

Through the efforts of Rev. Dr. John A. Ross, Pine Ridge Presbyterian congregation was formed at Humber Summit in North York in 1951 as part of the Woodbridge Pastoral Charge, and a new church dedicated in 1955.

The ministers of Woodbridge Presbyterian Church have been: Rev. R. Pettigrew of Weston and Rev. P. Nicol of Knox Vaughan preached on alternate Sabbaths, 1874; Rev. R. Pettigrew, 1875-94; Rev. W. Reid, 1895-1900; vacancy: Woodbridge joined with Knox Vaughan Circuit, 1901; Rev. M. McKinnon, 1901-16; Rev. J.A. Moir, 1917-25; Rev. J.C. Davies, 1926-30; Rev. John MacKenzie, 1930-4; Rev. J.S. Roe, 1935-9; Rev. G.C. Lamont, 1940-2; Rev. R.G. Mackay, 1942-8; Rev. John A. Ross, 1948-57; Rev. A. Fred Howick, 1958-69; Rev. Scott Wood, 1969-70.

The Reorganized Church of Jesus Christ of Latter Day Saints, Woodbridge

The Reorganized Church of Jesus Christ of Latter Day Saints is situated on Islington Avenue North, Woodbridge. It began in the year 1882 when Charles E. Farr, of Lot 18, Concession 7, Vaughan, became converted and was baptized while visiting Independence, Missouri. On his return to Woodbridge he was greatly concerned about bringing the gospel to his locality, and meetings were held in his home.

On November 13, 1921, the branch was organized with

twenty-five charter members. A church lot was obtained and the cornerstone of the building was laid in August 1925. A long struggle followed through the depression years to pay off the mortgage, but this was accomplished and the dedication service was held on June 11, 1944. New families moved in and took an active part in the branch program. Over the years the membership grew until the little church on the hill could not accommodate those desirous of worshipping together.

The new beautiful brick church is on the site of the old one. It is built on the side of a hill, which enables the sanctuary and also the lower auditorium to be reached at ground level. The capacity of the sanctuary in the old church was ninety-five, the present one, one hundred and eighty, while the lower auditorium will now seat two hundred and fifty at banquets and other functions instead of the former ninety. The building committee consisted of Alex. Strangways (Chairman), Robert A. Withrow (Chairman of finance committee), Mrs. Ila Farr, Jim Chittenden, Lorne Goodwill, Mrs. Helen Wyer, Ben Whitworth, Ron Huntington, Les Shaw, Erik Brassen.

The following have served as pastors since the branch was organized: Floyd W. Farr, Samuel Clarke, James A. Wilson, Edward Whitworth, Fred C. Lefeuvre, William Archer (for 22 years), Robert Withrow, and Harry K. Price.

The church was opened on Sunday, June 14, 1970 with a prayer service at 9.30 a.m., services of preaching at 11 a.m. and 7 p.m, noon lunch and open house. Many members and friends participated.

St. Margaret Mary Catholic Church, Woodbridge
The Brennan family was one of the few Roman Catholic families in pioneer days in Vaughan Township. This family came from Wexford, Ireland, and farmed east of Pine Grove on Concession 7.

Roman Catholics in Vaughan were first served by priests from Toronto, who made visits until 1833 saying Mass and administering the Sacraments in private homes. Among them were Father Edward Gordon and Father Michael P. Mills, who in 1838 made a tour of this area. Following the formation of St. Luke's Parish, Thornhill, in 1847, the Woodbridge-Pine Grove district was a part of that parish until 1957, when it became a separate entity.

Father Arthur McMahon of the Thornhill Parish in 1947 made arrangements for Mass to be said in Pine Grove Memorial Hall. This continued until 1957, when Rev. Dr. E. F. Crossland brought about the beginning of St. Margaret Mary Church by purchasing a former Primitive Methodist church built in 1873 and renovating it. Roman Catholic families were few in number, but large. James Marshall had 10 children, John Pickett had 8, Dan Sullivan 3, Joseph Wiggins 11, Thomas Sullivan 9, Michael O'Rourke 7 and the McGroartys of Woodbridge 9. These all attended the Thornhill Church regularly, going in the early days in buggies or light wagons. The same year, when the mission of St. Margaret Mary became a parish, Very Rev. Monsignor John A. O'Mara, J.C.L., was named pastor. In 1960 a Separate School was opened under the direction of the Sisters of St. Joseph. Rev. Dr. Basil Courtemanche succeeded Monsignor O'Mara in 1969.

Calvary Baptist Church, Woodbridge

Calvary Baptist Church, Woodbridge, was formed in 1949 by a small group who met first in the Pine Grove Community Hall, and later in the Clarke Wallace Memorial Hall in Woodbridge. In 1950 a formal request was made for a pastor to Rev. F. D. Elliott and the church became affiliated with the Fellowship of Evangelical Baptist Churches in Canada.

By 1952 the pastor was serving full time. A church was built on Bruce Street just south of Number 7 Highway. Services began in the new church on Thanksgiving Day, 1958. The church is evangelical, conservative, and strongly missionary. Ministers have been Rev. Fred Elliott, 1950-62, and Rev. David S. Irwin, 1962-70.

Churchyard gates of wood and iron   TM '33

CHAPTER IX

Education

Education in Upper Canada, including Vaughan Township, was established from the top down. Grammar schools were thought of before common schools, and a university was suggested by Simcoe as early as the 1790s. This came about because those in charge of ruling Canada were well educated in England; consequently they thought of education as something for those who could afford it and, in their judgment, profit by it.

Education was closely linked with religion and politics. Two-sevenths of the land in twelve townships, or 740,000 acres, were set apart for the Crown and Clergy Reserves. This meant that the Church of England was state supported, and responsible for education.

In 1807 some small financial support — £100 for each teacher — was provided by the government for the establishment of one public school in each of the eight districts of Upper Canada, each district having five trustees appointed by the Governor. This public school was a grammar school and it had no effect on educating the children of the settlers. In 1816, the sum of £6,000 was appropriated among the ten districts, and the settlers were permitted to elect their trustees for each district. No allowance to any single school, however, was to exceed £25 annually.

It will be apparent that little consideration was given to elementary education among the settlers. This meant that if their children were to be given the rudiments of education, they would have to provide it themselves. As most of the settlers from the United States were accustomed to having schools for their children, they proceeded to engage teachers and eventually build their own schools.

The 1830s saw a battle for education to be made non-sectarian and for elementary education to be government-supported. This movement was directed by Egerton Ryerson, and a complete change came in 1844 with his appointment as Superintendent of Education for the province. In 1850, the real charter for the Ontario school system was set forth; it permitted a school tax on real property, and gave the school trustees full power to manage schools, with the district superintendent the liaison between government and schools. The principles of this Act were in force for over a hundred years. In 1852, the Clergy Reserve Fund in in Vaughan Township was distributed, and was invested for educational purposes.

Adult education began very early in Upper Canada with the Mechanics' Institutes. One in Toronto was established in 1830. Their activities included libraries of newspapers, and magazines, readings, reunions, concerts, lectures, exhibitions, and literary debates. In 1867-8 a five-months' course costing $3 offered the following subjects: Bookkeeping and Penmanship, Arithmetic and Mathematics, Architectural and Mechanical Drawing, Ornamental Drawing, French (elementary and advanced conversation), English Grammar and Composition, Chemistry and Natural Philosophy. Many communities had Mechanics' Institutes, including Woodbridge, Kleinburg, Edgeley, and Richmond Hill. The institutes filled a great need for many persons who had been deprived of formal education, either because it was not available or because they were taken out of school to work.

The Agricultural Societies and Farmers' Clubs offered courses in Agriculture, and annual examinations were held in that subject and in horticulture.

In the history of the County of York (1885) Vaughan Township is shown as having 18 school sections and unions with houses in them, and three unions with houses outside the municipality.

No. 1, union with Markham or Thornhill, Brick building in the Village of Thornhill. The Average attendance from Vaughan 26, Markham 29. Teachers, R.O. Harvey and Annie Hendrie.

No. 2, union with Markham. Frame building on Yonge Street, Lot 34, Concession 1, built in 1815 and probably the oldest in the county. Average attendance from Vaughan 4, Markham 15. Emma M. Ansley, teacher.

No. 3, Carrville School, on Lot 15, halfway across the 2nd concession. Had been enlarged. James Bassingthwaite, teacher. Average attendance, 38.

No. 4, union with Richmond Hill; no school of its own.

No. 5, or Hope School, west end of Lot 28, Concession 3. Brick building with a frame addition for an assistant. Average attendance 37. Teacher, Abram Carley.

No. 6, Maple School, Brick structure, somewhat awkwardly divided into two rooms. Teachers, Joseph P. McQuarrie and Jennie Walkington. Average attendance 50.

No. 7, Mudville (Concord) School, on the east end of Lot 6, Concession 3. Good brick building. Average attendance 32. Teacher, Chester Asling.

No. 8, Edgeley. Good brick building on west end of Lot 7, Concession 4. Average attendance 41, Teacher Jacob H. Hoover.

No. 9, Town Hall School, Vellore. Large frame structure on west end of Lot 17, Concession 5. Average attendance 24. Teacher Nellie Franks.

No. 10, a new brick building at northwest corner of Lot 30, Concession 5. Average attendance 24. Teacher, Robert Moore.

No. 11, Purpleville School. Good frame building, with excellent furniture. Situated on east end of Lot 27, Concession 7. Average attendance 34. Teacher William Watson.

No. 12, Pine Grove School. Good frame building at the west end of Lot 9, Concession 6. Average attendance 38. Teachers, John W. Franks and Annie Mason.

No. 13, brick building on east end of Lot 6, Concession 9. Average attendance 19, Teacher Joseph Clark.

No. 14, a union with Woodbridge. School in Woodbridge. Average attendance 9 from Vaughan.

No. 15, near the centre of Lot 15, Concession 9. New brick building. Average attendance 38. Teacher Thos. B. Hoidge. A small part of Toronto Gore in union.

No. 16, the Coleraine School, in union with 7, Toronto Gore. Brick building of unsound construction. Average attendance from Vaughan 19, from Toronto Gore 6. Teacher Miss McDonald.

No. 17, Kleinburg School, in the Village of Kleinburg. Brick building with a frame addition for an assistant. Situation fine, overlooking one branch of the Humber. Average attendance 36. Teacher Kenneth Beaton.

No. 18, near the middle of Lot 31, Concession 10. Frame structure not well furnished. Average attendance 24. Teacher, James Asher.

No. 19, Patterson School, Good brick building, on east end of Lot 21, Concession 2. Average attendance 28. Teacher, Hesse A. Nichols.

No. 20, West end of Lot 31, Concession 8. New frame building, in a good situation, and kept in fair condition. Average attendance 34. Teacher, James R. Graham.

No. 21, Jefferson, a union, with the building in Markham, about two miles north of Richmond Hill on Yonge Street. Average attendance 29.

The average salary of male teachers was $425, of female teachers, $265.

The local school boards of Vaughan were disbanded in 1960 when the Vaughan Township Public School Board was formed. The first elected school board was: Herbert A. Constable (chairman), Mrs. M.A. Robertson, Mrs. R.C. Hogg, Milton F. Savage, and S.D. Kaiser. Joseph A. Gibson was the first superintendent of schools. H.G. Kyle was maintenance supervisor, and N.C. Jackman was secretary treasurer.

The schools of Vaughan have been administered under the York County Board of Education since 1969.

The following are some of the important schools and developments in education in Vaughan Township.

Bryson School (Upper Sixth), S.S. No. 10

This school is located on the northwest corner of Lot 30, Concession 5. The first school building was of logs, and stood south of the present brick one, where Mrs. John Downing's home is now. In 1869, it is recorded in the old minute book, each pupil paid six cents a week. Teachers in the old school were Kenneth Beaton and Wm. Watson; H.A. Shier was the teacher in 1882 when the new school was built. The school board (Neil Malloy, secretary, Alex. Cameron, and Isaac Murray), paid Robt. Phillips, who owned the farm, $100 for the corner lot with the agreement that he would move the church shed on the property and take the old lot.

The school was built of red brick with white trim at a cost of $2,200. An iron fence was built the next year by J. McLaughlin. An insurance policy for $1,200 was taken out.

Neil Malloy, a bachelor, was particular, and insisted on having a good bell which was ordered from a company in Chicago at a cost of $50. A special trip with team and wagon was made to Toronto to pick it up.

Inside the building there were seats for over fifty pupils, facing the east wall. The stove was situated in the middle of the room. R.O. Harvey had the senior boys bring in one scuttle of coal and one scuttle of snow to put in the stove, to give a hot fire.

Visitors signed the guest book. An entry on March 22, 1866, read' 'Today I visited this school. Heard several classes, am pretty well pleased with the general answering of the pupils. The reading is not yet what I would like. Some of the lads are "well-up" in Arithmetic. The discipline is to me, faultless, and most of the little folks very obedient and hard working.' (signed) D. McCallum.

Another in October 1865: 'How is it that the school is so small? Is it because there is a Rate Bill? This should not be so.'

School opened on the third Monday in August. The older boys went only in the winter months, being needed at home during the busy season.

The last local trustees were Stewart Diceman, Roy Bowen, and Gordon Burbidge. The Township School Area of Vaughan took over in 1960.

The school was sold to the Rev. B.F. Andrews, a Presbyterian minister, and Mrs. Andrews, who converted it into an attractive home with an apartment upstairs, complete with bell.

Eighty years ago about one-third of the scholars were named Malloy. There is no one by that name living in the community now.

Teachers over the years have been: Miss Vina Ray, Roland Harvey, Gertrude Watson, May Milligan, Violetta Archibald, M.E. Creech, Mildred Speers, Evangeline E. Gurr, Audrey Mitchell, Barbara McCallum, Bessie Cameron, Marguerite Ezard, Gladys Harrison, Isabel Stephens, Pauline Hughes, Georgina Panke (Mrs. J. Downing), Mary Moore (Mrs. Lorne Scott), Ellen Duffield, Sylvia Foreshew, Arlene Rowat, Mrs. Stewart.

Burrlington School
Sometime between 1855 and 1860 a Roman Catholic school was built of logs on the southwest corner of the Burrlington side road and Concession 11 of Vaughan on property belonging to Thomas Smyth, Jr. Mr. Welch was the teacher. Because of the small attendance it was closed in 1862 or 1863.

Another early school serving this district was in Toronto Gore Township and was known as the Hegler School — Christian Hegler owned the farm on which it was built and was also the teacher. Each pupil paid a monthly fee. Families that supported the school were Thomases, Cravens, Clarks, Kerseys, Tibbs, and Coles. It operated from 1850 to 1865.

The Vaughan supporters felt that the school was too distant, however. In 1864 they set up S.S. No. 18 Vaughan with Benjamin Snell, William Patterson, and James Burgess as trustees. In 1865, the same year Hegler's closed, this became the Burrlington School. William Johnston was the first teacher, with twenty pupils. In winter, attendance might increase to sixty or seventy, with some pupils coming from the townships of King, Albion and Toronto Gore.

In 1899 a new foundation was put under the school and the entire building was brick-clad. In 1918, to accommodate a school garden, more land was purchased. From time to time the building was modernized. In 1960 the school became part of the Township School Area of Vaughan.

The following is a list of teachers: William Johnston, William Bealby, George Riddell, Alexander Johnston, William Nattress, Mill Heslop, Joseph Bateman, Horace Turnbull, J. Clary, James Asher, Miss Mary Dale, Miss Kate Armstrong, C.A. Boives, Miss Hosie Elder, William Jarrett, Miss Nellie Mitchell, William McClure, Miss Maude Webb, E. Ward Cornell, Miss E. Harrison, William Kersey, Miss Kate Smith, Miss Pansy Forsythe, Miss Reta Bernath, Miss Annie Smyth, Miss Barbara McCallum, Miss Blanche McCabe, Miss Florence McAllister, Miss Jean Brandon, Miss Lottie Dodd, Mrs. Hazel Weir, Mrs. Sarah Bell, Miss Kenzie Hart, Charles Conron, Miss Maxine Lemon, Miss Evelyn Thomas, Miss Greta Stanton, Mrs. C. Thomas.

Carrville Public School, S.S. No. 3
A school was built in 1846 by Nathaniel Burr. To quote Jonathan Baker:

The same was a hewed log building perhaps 30 x 30, Neil McKinnon being the teacher for the first seven years: the same started school in the fall of 1846 and taught three weeks and then quit till after New Year of 1847. The writer was among the first scholars who entered the door of the Carrville schoolhouse, which took place about the first of December, 1846. A list of scholars who attended school that winter: Sarah Ann, Elizabeth, Martha, Jesse, Hugh and John Bennett, Mary, Isaac and Phoebe Baker, Eve, Jonathan and Peter Baker, Margaret, George, Jacob and John Cober, David and Arthur Tennyson, Mary Jane, Hannah and Henry Kirby, John and Michael Kurtz, Catharine, Elizabeth Ann and Julia Ann Frank, John Velie, Julia Ann Schoolcraft, Edward Braithwaite, James and Robert Kilfedder, Luke O'Brien, Daniel Reaman, Jacob Hilts, Elizabeth Hickly, Nicholas Reaman, William Burr, William Scholfield, William Cook, William and Edmund Seager, George and Fanny Atkinson. Margaret Cober was perhaps the oldest of those who at that time attended. She was about 23 years of age and William Cook the youngest, was about five years old. Among the above number there were perhaps three or four who were studying grammar. There was only one geography in said school at that time and that belonged to the teacher. They were nevertheless in geography all in one class, from the youngest to the oldest.

It is said that the log building partially burned and was then rebuilt. This may have happened in 1858 or 1859, for there was an item for $32.00 shown in the report for repairs.

In 1860 a new frame schoolhouse was built, incorporating part of the old log building. The cost for the land and building was $550.00 and an item for collector's fees was $8.45; with the teacher's salary of $321.23, the grand total was $879.68 for 1860. The school was kept open for the twelve months of that year.

This building was enlarged before 1885 but still in use when the one hundredth anniversary was held in 1960. Soon after, the school was closed and the pupils taken by bus to other schools. The site was sold and the old building taken down.

Some of the teachers at this school were: Neil McKinnon, Alex Campbell, James Bassingthwaite (his salary was £68.8s.6d), D. McNaughton, Edmund Dyer, Thomas Ansley, Miss Etta Richeson, Miss Beatty, Miss Moran, Miss Smale, Miss Walker, Miss Gilmore, Miss Parker, Miss Younge, Miss Sleep, Miss MacMillan, Miss Haworth, Miss Weese, Mrs. V. DelBrocco, Miss Welford, Mr. Green.

Concord School District, S.S. No. 7

According to Jonathan Baker, the first school in the Concord district that he attended was a German school taught by Andrew Demerly and located on Lot 12, Concession 2, in 1835. It was kept in a dwelling house and owned by Sevald Stong, Sr. The west half of that lot was owned by Peter Cober. The children who attended that school besides Jonathan and Eve Baker were Lavina and Jacob Nafe, Jacob Spieker, Jacob and John Cober, and Mary, Daniel, and Christle Reaman.

The second school was held in 1837 by a widow, Anna Bennett, who taught in her own house. A few of the scholars were: John Velie, Solomon, Henry, and Anthony Keffer, John Snider, Jesse, Elizabeth, Mary, Eve, and Jonathan Baker, Elizabeth and Mary Ann Dexter (daughters of Hiram Dexter), Daniel Quantz, John and Katharine Kurtz, Sarah Ann, Elizabeth, Martha, Jesse, and John Bennett, Catharine McDougall, George Longhouse, and Elizabeth Jackson. This school was on the west half of Lot 14 in Concession 2, owned and occupied by Jacob Bennett, Sr., who in 1849 built on the same lot a stone house later occupied by Andrew Russell.

The third school was in 1838, and was kept by John Nelson in a carpenter shop on east half of Lot 12, which was at that time owned by Jacob Baker. Up to 1839 the teacher's salary was governed by the number of scholars who attended school; for every scholar he was paid 50 cents a month. Not long after, this was reduced to 25 cents a month, the balance being paid by taxes.

In 1839, school was held in a house on Lot 11, Concession 2. The teacher was Thomas Cummings.

The fifth school was kept in a schoolhouse in 1843 by Thomas Cummings. He was followed by Neil McKinnon and John Kennedy.

That first schoolhouse, built in 1842 was a round log building 18 x 20 feet situated about half a mile north of the Thornhill-Woodbridge sideline. In 1845 it was replaced by a hewed-log schoolhouse, 30 x 30 feet. That year bears were numerous in the vicinity: one was shot about three-quarters of a mile north of the school, close to Lot 11 which was Clergy Reserve.

In 1865 a site was chosen a quarter of a mile to the south, and in 1866 a brick schoolhouse was built on the present location. This building was used for 34 years, after which time it was felt to be unsafe and was torn down. A larger brick schoolhouse was built in 1900 with a basement and separate entrances for boys and girls. The maple trees in the schoolyard were planted about this time.

In 1931 fire destroyed the building and for some months school was held in the unused church across the road. A new school was built in 1931, and in 1949 a north room was added. Because the community was growing so rapidly school accommodation was still inadequate, however. Classes were held in the basement in 1952, and two years later two more classrooms were built. The opening night was scheduled for October 15, 1954, with the author as guest speaker. It was the night of Hurricane Hazel, and the ceremonies were postponed for a week. In 1967-8 a large gymnasium was built west of the school.

Vaughan September 30th /61

Mr David Murry

To Trustees of S. S. No 9 Dr

For 3 pupils tuition 8 months @ 25 ₵ mo. $2.00 Cents

Received payment   M. Wills Teacher

$ cts.
1.25   Mr David Murray Dr to School Section No. 9
                    Vaughan December 12th 1868.

Miss Sussannah Murray to 3 months tuition @ 15
        cents per month   cts.
                                                            .75
Miss Marry do. 3.   .75
Mr Isaac Murray do. 3.   .75
                                                          2.25

The cost of education in the 1860s was much lower than today, as these receipts for the teacher's fees paid by David Murray show. These fees were the teacher's only source of income at first.

The Cober Schoolhouse at Langstaff was started in 1811 but, owing to the war, was not completed until 1815. It was used as a school until 1892 when it was sold for $50 and moved to Edgeley, where it was destroyed by fire about 1955. Its hewn frame rafters and covering of sawn lumber were luxuries when it was built. It was also used as a church in the early years by Wesleyans, Quakers, and Baptists.

Later teachers at Concord school were: Alex. Beaton, 1856; Matthew Long, 1857 (both these teachers were paid £120); Angus McKinnon, 1858-61; Archie Campbell, 1862-3; Richard L. Munro, 1864-5; Alexander McKinnon, 1866; James Rutherford, 1866; Doyer, 1867-8; Henry Ward, 1868-74; Belamy, 1875-6; Lucia Page, 1877-9; James C. Smith, 1880-1; C. Asling, 1882-7; Mr. Walker, 1899; E.J.A. Johnson, 1900; Miss Ada Powley, 1901-02; J. McCuoig, 1903; Miss Duncan, 1904-06; Tom McCormack, 1907-10; Annie Armstrong, 1911; Mrs. A. Campbell, 1911; Miss Armstrong, 1913; Miss Malcolm; Miss Hughes; Miss Fitzgerald; Miss Westcott; Miss Smith, 1921; Miss Jardine, 1922; Miss Weatherill; Miss Ramsey; Mary Reaman; Lorne Wideman; Chas. Ratcliff; Mr. Cotterill; Audrey McNaughton; Margaret Humphreys. School Principals were: Roy McWhirter, 1951-64; Malcolm McRoberts, 1964-7; Brian Robinson, 1967-70.

Edgeley Public School, S.S. No. 8
Before 1842 the children of the community attended school on the townline in Stong's schoolhouse, which was built about 1824. The teaching at first was all in German, but gradually changed to English. The teacher at first was paid fifty cents per month and boarded by the parents, week by week from one home to another. As more pupils attended he was paid twenty-five cents per pupil per month.

In 1842 one-sixteenth of an acre, about twenty rods south of the present school grounds, was purchased from Samuel Smith (grandfather of Carson Smith) Lot 6, Concession 4, for a school site. The price was five shillings. A log building, 22 x 30 feet, was erected. One of the first teachers in this school was Mr. Irwin: the last was Michael Burkholder.

On March 6, 1869, the present school property of one-half acre was purchased from John Smith, Samuel's son. The trustees signing the deed were Walter Dalziel, Joseph Brown, and Simon Shunk. A brick building 30 x 50 feet was erected. The heating system was a large box stove using large blocks of wood as fuel. On cold mornings the pupils would sometimes find their inkwells frozen solid. For an hour or more the pupils would surround the stove, sitting on long benches until the school was warm enough to allow them to return to their desks.

Around 1880 the attendance reached 75. To accommodate them, a desk probably twelve feet long was built against the south wall at the southeast corner. The regular desks used then were built for two, but those at which the smaller children sat had place for four in each.

In 1890, when Mr. Walls taught, the enrolment was 108, with an average attendance of 88. Many of the boys, upon reaching the age of twelve, were kept home during the summer months to help on the farm, but returned in the winter to continue their schooling. Some of the pupils were young men with moustaches who were as big as the teacher. Their studies included the thre R's, some art, literature, grammar, history, geography, and occasionally sight-singing. The advanced pupils who returned in the winter months studied Latin and

Greek roots in their English studies, and also bookkeeping. At a meeting on November 8, 1873, tender was made by Jesse Snider at $4.50 to collect the school taxes for the year. They amounted to $350.00 for the school section. This was the way the school taxes were collected in those days.

Around 1900 the expenses for the school reached their lowest (which averaged about $450.00 per year). Since that time they have gradually increased. In 1950 they were about $4000 annually. In 1957 a new two-room school was built and remained for ten years before classes at this location ended.

The teachers have been: Michael S. Burkholder, 1872-6 (and probably a couple of years earlier); Jacob Hoover, 1877-85; William B. Martin, 1886-9; J. Walls, 1890; J.S. Waterford, 1891-3; Robert G. Holland, 1894-8; Robert Ingram, January-June 1899; Hugh Cunningham, 1899-1901; Miss Mabel Smith, 1902 to June 1904; J.G. McDonald, September 1904 to June 1905; Walter Mather, four months in 1905; Robert Holland, 1906-07; Duncan S. Martin, January-June 1908; Austin Ryan, September-December 1908; Mr. N. Bethune, January-June 1909; Miss Flo. E. Morgan, September 1909 to June 1911; Herb. Sawdon, September 1911 to June 1912; Miss Josie M. Beynon, September 1912 to June 1914; Miss Prentice, September 1914 to June 1915; Miss Clara Cameron, September 1915 to June 1916; Miss Florence McClure, September 1916 to June 1919; Miss S.E. Atkinson, September 1919 to June 1920; Miss Annie Stong, September 1920 to June 1928; Miss Gladys Featherston, September 1928 to June 1932; Miss Miriam Brown, September 1932 to June 1934; James McDonald, September-December 1934; Jack McCallum, January 1935 to June 1939; Miss Ann Edwards, September 1939 to March 1941; Mrs. C. Pugsley, March-June 1941; Max Fysh, September 1941 to June 1942; Miss Isabel Rumble, September 1942 to June 1946; Miss Isabel Halbert, September 1946 to June 1948; Thomas Carter, two months in 1948; Mrs. Angeline Hope, November 1948 to June 1949; Mrs. Evelyn Rattle, September 1949 to June 1950; Miss Ilene Edwards, September 1950 to June 1951; Miss Patricia Gullett (Mrs. Gordon Martin), September 1951 to November 1952; Mrs. Jean Brooks, December 1952 to June 1954; Mrs. Lena Kitchen, September 1954 to June 1955; Mrs. Katherin King, 1½ months in 1955; Albert Hood, November 1955 to June 1957; Mrs. Helen Oksanen, September 1957 to March 1958 (junior room); Mrs. Verna Bell, April-June 1958 (junior room); Miss Hulda Unger, September 1957 to June 1958 (senior room); Mrs. Miriam Wilson, September 1958 to June 1962 (junior room); Mrs. Margaret Macdonald, September 1958 to June 1961 (senior room); George Green, September 1961 to June 1962 (senior room): Miss Diana Pollock (Mrs. Brian Taylor), September 1962 to June 1964 (junior room); Allen Taylor, September 1962 to June 1964 (senior room); Mrs. Flood (September 1964 to June 1966, junior room); Glen Newis, September 1964 to June 1965 (senior room); Carl Bailey, September 1965 to June 1966 (senior room); Mrs. George Reid, September 1966 to February 1967 (Grade 7); Mr. Callahan, September 1966 to February 1967 (Grade 8); after this period of teaching only Grades 7 and 8, the school was closed on February 28, 1967 and classes were transferred to Maple.

Elder's Mills, S.S. No. 15
In 1843 Richard Jeffery sold a part of his farm, Lot 15, Concession 9, for £2 to the Commissioner of Education, Nicholas J. Klein. A log schoolhouse was built in 1843, the logs donated by parents. The bark was still left on some of the logs and the building was boarded inside to cover up the rough surface.

(The first Richard Jeffery had come out from England in 1791 as gardener to Queen Victoria's father, the Duke of Kent, who then commanded the 7th Fusiliers at Quebec. When the Duke returned to England, so did he, and there his son also became a gardener. The son, with his wife and three sons, returned to Canada with Sir Peregrine Maitland about 1818. He was a scientific horticulturist but when Maitland returned to England in 1832, Jeffery became a farmer on Lot 5, Concession 8. He bought farms in that vicinity for his sons and it was from him that the land for the school was purchased.)

There was one entrance door, on either side of which were benches and desks — one side for the boys and one side for the girls. Each side of the room the desks were built in one section, nailed to the wall; the desk tops sloped for greater ease in writing, and below it a long board, also nailed to the wall, served as a shelf. The benches used by the pupils were in front of these desks. Thus the pupils at the side had their backs to the centre of the room. There was a big wood-burning box stove in the centre of the school. Small children sat on a bench down the middle of the room so they were nearer the heat. They had no desk but placed their slates either on or under their bench. Sometimes these little ones sat on benches at the front of the school.

There was a platform at the centre of the end opposite to the entrance, a few feet wider with a rounded front. The teacher had a desk exactly the same as the pupils built to one side of the platform and fastened to the wall, but instead of a bench he had an armchair. Cupboards were built above the desk.

There was a blackboard just the width of the platform. There were three small windows on each side of the room but no window by the teacher's desk. There was one big porch at the entrance to the school, unheated. The boys hung their clothes on one side of it and the girls on the other. There was no partition.

In 1872 a new school was built of brick. Desks were now used, with two pupils sitting at each. The writing portion and the seat for the next pupil ahead comprised one unit.

Blackboards were built across the width of the school, and placed between the windows on the side walls. There were two entrances and two cloakrooms, with a bellroom between where the great bell was hung. This also served as the teacher's room. Hydro was installed in 1934.

The first teacher was Mr. Cumming, and then William Jeffery, John Nattress, and Isaac Devins. Teachers in the second school were:

James Neeley (1872), Robert Glassford, George Nattress, W.F. Moore, Irvine Kaiser, R.O. Harvey, Mr. Toole, Miss Annie Mason, James Alliston, John Simpson, Alfred Fowlie, W.E. Sibley, John Sibley, Miss Elizabeth Price, Miss Reynolds, Miss Annie Black, Miss Mande Sherman, Miss Gertrude French, Miss Francis Patton, Miss Emma North, Miss Esther McBride, Miss Muriel Vardon, Miss Ada M. Caldwell, Miss Blanche Meeker, Miss Petty, Miss Hosie Elder, Miss Jean Digby, Miss Muriel Nattress, Miss Agnes Nattress, Miss Adeline Tait, Miss Susie King, Miss Kathleen Bagg, Miss Velma Darker, Miss Marjorie Hayhoe, Allen Boake, Miss Margaret Humphreys, Miss Marion Hobson, Miss Joyce Webb, Miss Violet Curry, Bert Shore, Tom Overton, Miss Kelsey, Mrs. Huff, Mrs. Stoll, Mrs. McCabe, Mrs. Irwin, Miss Varden.

Hope School, S.S. No. 5
George Wilson, Archibald McQuarrie, and William Craddock, as trustees of S.S. No. 5, purchased three-quarters of an acre of land in 1864 from the west half of Lot 28, Concession 3. The regulations then required a high board fence surrounding the property on three sides, a good school building, and both the school and fence to be kept in good repair at all times.

When a larger school was needed another parcel of land was purchased from Norman and Doris Payne. Mrs. Payne is a granddaughter of George Cook. A new two-room school was built in 1955. With the amalgamation of schools, Hope School was closed in 1967 and later sold. It is now a nursing home.

Among the teachers at Hope were Abram Carley, for many years before 1900, with Miss Moore as his assistant when there were two rooms in operation; Thomas McCormack, for many years in the early 1900s, when only one room again was in use; Mr. Walker; Mr. Spaulding; Miss Willa Ford; Miss Miller; Marion Dixon, 1912-16; Margaret Burgess, 1920-4; Amy Brookes; Jean Curtis; Mr. Patrick; Violet Johnson; Henry McDonald, 1933-6; Del Babcock; Isabel Robertson; Beryl Le Grice; Bruce McDonald, 1939-46; Paul Mackenzie; Marnie Davis; Mr. Grigg; Mr. Ford; Charles Read; Mrs. Monahan; Sylvia Carroll; Mrs. Halverson; Mrs. Elmer Witherspoon, principal, 1959-66.

Jefferson Public School, Union of S.S. No. 21 Vaughan and S.S. No. 4, Markham
The first Jefferson school was a log building south of the present school. In 1868 a one-room brick school was built across the road in Markham. In 1881 an additional quarter acre was added to the yard.

In 1945 a room was rented from St. John's Anglican Church for a second classroom. The present large brick school was built in 1951, with the official opening on March 10, 1952. The building committee for it was Wm. Bell, Clayton Beynon, Neil Dibb, and George McNair. The trustees were Norman Burnett, Arthur Gibson, Dickson Miller, and John Passmore (chairman).

Some of the teachers have been Ethel Legge, Mr. Oliver, Harry Saigeon, Miss Fanny Brown (1911), Miss Robertson (1907), Catherine

Wood, Mary Cooper, Alfreda Haines, K.S. Rankin, B. Haggerty, Miss Corbett, Miss Downey, Jean Switzer, Mr. Green, Miss Leary, Dora Little, Margaret Mott, Elizabeth Burns, Mrs. Marie Duncan, Mrs. B. Walwyn, Penny Reid, Fred Winterton, Donna McPhail, J. Keery, Roy Robson, Mr. Hanson, Wm. Kinsley, Mrs. May Hopkins, Mrs. Janice Morgan, Mrs. G. Morrison, Mrs. V. Seel, Mr. I. Ashurst, Mrs. B. Vent, Mrs. P. Hurley, and Mrs. N. Elibrachy.

Kleinburg Public School, S.S. No. 17
The first school in Kleinburg was built of logs in 1845, on what is now the parking lot of Kleinburg United Church, but was at that time the last lot in the south end of the village. The following items come from the minutes and reports of the Home District Council: 'The Wed. 15, May, 1844. Of trustees of school district No. 17 of Vaughan praying said district to be taxed for the erection of a school house by Mr. Kline,' and 'Tues. 15, Jan. 1848. Petition of No. 17 Vaughan praying to be assessed 5 lb. to discharge a balance for building a school house by Mr. Kline.'

Ten years later a new school was needed and this time several lots were bought on Napier Street in what was known as Mount Vernon. At that time the west side of King Road, now known as Islington Avenue, was called Kleinburg and the east side of the same road was known as Mount Vernon.

This school consisted of a large one-room red brick building with (attached to the south so as to form an L) a much smaller wooden building painted red, always known as the little room. The large brick part was called the big room. The little room was opened and closed as needed. Both rooms were heated with wood burned in box stoves. Around 1916 a small cellar was dug out under the big room and a coal furnace was installed. Around the same time several more lots to the north were bought to enlarge the playground.

Mr. and Mrs. Michael Bevan bought the school in 1957, after the present Kleinburg school was built. The Mackenzie Senior Public School was built in 1967.

Among the early teachers were: Kenneth Beaton, Chas. F. Ewers, David Evans, Kate Beamish, Gertrude Aikenhead, Miss E. Johnston, Miss Hughes, J.R. Miller, Miss Annie McClure, Miss Weldon, Miss M. Semple, Ruth Woodger, Miss E. Smith, and Miss Hortense Langford. Miss Rose Rice, the junior teacher, and Mrs. Bell, the principal, were the last in the old school. Principals in the present Kleinburg School have been E.M. Wells, Peter Kurita, and John Martin, and in Mackenize Senior Public School, Malcolm McRoberts.

Langstaff School
The date given for the establishment of the Langstaff School is 1796, when at the corner of Lot 35, Concession 1, Balser Munshaw constructed a small log house with one end toward Yonge Street. When Mr. Munshaw built a new house, this structure became a school.

Like all schools in the early days, Langstaff was a private school supported by the fees of the pupils who came from as far north as Richmond Hill and from as far south as the York townline. Some of the names of the first pupils were Lawrence, Arnold, Bridgford, Dexter, Burr, Fulton, Lyons, Munshaw, Miller, and Vanderburgh.

John Langstaff was the first teacher. In 1812 he enlisted in the army and about the same time a movement was started to have a new school. Nicholas Cober gave half an acre of land for a building which could be used for church services as well as a school. Between 1811 and 1815 the new school was built. Benjamin Barnard, an Englishman, was the teacher until 1820. He was paid a "York Shilling" a quarter per pupil and was boarded for two-week periods in the homes of the children attending school. He and the children did the caretaking; the wood was provided free.

In 1846 school sections were formed. George Darling, Henry Miller, and John T. Tindall were elected trustees. The school section was known as Union School Section 2 of Vaughan-Markham. The land was purchased from P. Cober; the building became a public school.

In the early 1890s shinney continued to be a popular game among the boys. It was played with an elm stick curved at the bottom; the 'puck' was a block of wood or a ball. Not infrequently the stick missed the ball and would strike a player. One day Arthur Thompson took a husky swing at the wooden puck but missed, and hit Paddy Cronin over the eye and opened a gash. Nevertheless Paddy stayed in school. That afternoon a scuffle took place and Paddy's seat-mate shoved him out onto the floor. This time Paddy hit the other eye on a desk and opened a gash in it too.

The girls in those years spent their time skipping to the rhyme 'Andy, Bandy, sugared candy, French iron wrought.' The little tots played 'Little Sally Waters.'

The old Readers contained such pieces as 'Hannah at the Window,' 'The Face against the Pane,' 'The Gray Swan,' 'The Heroic Serf,' 'Babes in the Woods,' 'The Poor Little Match Girl,' and 'Lucy Gray.' Spelling matches were popular and work was examined in the class; that is, a line was formed at the front of the room. Pupils stood 'Toe the scratch' style in order of merit. Much of the work was done on slates, often greasy and poorly cleaned. Minor punishment consisted of writing lines or standing in a corner.

In 1892 a large one-room brick schoolhouse was built and the little old school was sold and moved to Edgeley. In 1926 a new school was built with two classrooms. The older school was also used for some time but was torn down in 1953 and four new classrooms were added to the 1926 school. The Langstaff Public School holds a record for York County, by occupying the same site since 1811. The original half-acre of land has been increased to eight acres through purchases and gifts.

The following teachers taught at the Langstaff School: John Langstaff; Elihu Pearse; Benjamin Barnard; Henry Richards, Sr.; Mr. Stiver; Mr. McLean; J.S. Waterfield, 1863-70; Reuben Milliard, 1870-2; Miss Fanny Acies, 1872-4; Mr. Reynolds, 1874-5; Mr. Wismer, 1875-7;

J.S. Waterfield 1877-84; E.R. Rutherford; E.M. Emsley, 1884; Mr. Baillie, 1885; Miss I. Morton, 1885-91; Miss J.S. Arbuthinot, 1891-2; W.G. Richardson, 1892-4; E.A. James, 1895-7; John Drury, 1897-9; Miss L. Waldron, 1900-01; Miss Harrison, 1901-09; Miss L. Walker, 1909; Miss Redpath, 1910; Mr. Sharp, 1911; Miss Elliott, 1911-17; Miss Brown, 1917-19; Miss C.G. Binnie, 191-23; John MacDonald, 1923-9; Miss Forrester, 1926-30; Miss V. Walker, 1930; L. Short, 1930-1; Miss K. Walker, 1931-5; Chas. McGuirl, 1931-45; Miss C. Wesley; Mrs. Andrew Snider. Later principals were David Smith, Robert Everist, D. Rose, Russell Urquart, E.M. Wells, Mr. Colvin.

S.S. No. 13, Vaughan (Lower Ninth)
School was first opened in S.S. 13 in 1846. The first building, a log structure later replaced by frame, was near the centre of Lot 6, east half, Concession 9 (now No. 27 Highway).

It was common practice for the parents and trustees to visit the school from time to time and to attend classes, and in some cases to test orally the pupils as to their knowledge and the quality of instruction. At regular intervals the teacher prepared the pupils for public examinations which were conducted orally. Here, before parents and trustees of the section, the children recited passages from memory, repeated various arithmetic tables, answered questions in geography, history, and grammar, and took part in spelling bees and oratoricals. The reports were very satisfactory.

In 1875, because the school building was too small, a site was purchased from Mrs. Joel Reaman and a new school erected on a corner adjacent to the old school.

In 1892 assessment on a portion of the property was transferred from S.S. 13 Vaughan and attached to Union Section 23 of Vaughan and to Section 10 of Toronto Gore.

In 1927 a basement was dug and a furnace installed. In 1938, because of the construction of a new highway, the school was moved to a site a short distance north of the old school on the east side of Highway No. 27. The new school was opened in 1939.

In 1942 a bus route was established to take the children of the section to Weston High School. The school closed in June 1965.

The teachers have been: N.C. Wallace, 1864-8; Watson, 1868; MacDonald, 1869; John Nattress, 1870-9; Hugh Ferguson, 1879-81; Julius Seager, 1881-2; Waterfield, 1882 (six months); Joseph Clark, 1882-5; Geo. Graham, 1885-7; Alex Watson, 1887-8; Miss A.F. Skene, 1888-94; Miss Clara Fortune, 1895-1900; Wm. McClure, 1900-02; Miss E. Stanley, 1902 (four months); Miss G. Burton, 1902-04; Miss C.E. Anderson, 1904-06; Miss Annie McClure, 1906-08; Miss Alice McClure, 1908-09; Miss Ethra Nattress, 1909-10; Miss Richardson, 1910-11; Miss J.B. McNaughton, 1911; Miss. A. Moran, 1911; Miss Annie Burton, 1911-13; Miss Ethel Kennedy, 1913-15; Miss Mary Morgan, 1915; Miss Gertrude Harrison, 1916-22; Miss Cora Graham, 1922-24; Miss Kate McMillan, 1924-5; Miss Annie Thompson, 1925-9; Miss Esther Bessey, 1929-36; Miss Norma Williamson, 1936-9; Miss Margaret Evans,

1939-42; Miss Barbara Ross, 1942-4; Miss Mereda Dorsey, 1944-5; Miss Verna Bryson, 1945-8; Miss Audrey Murphy, 1948-51; Miss Shirley Bowles, 1951-4; Mrs. Russell Moore, 1954-5; Mr. Elmer Henry, 1955-7; Mrs. June Matson, 1957-9; Miss Louise King, 1959-61; William Joyce, 1961-2; Miss L. Colgan, 1962-5.

Maple School, S.S. No. 6
The first school to serve this area in the first half of the nineteenth century was a log building at the corner of Keele Street and Sherwood sideroad.

Up to 1839, the teacher's salary was 50 cents per pupil per month. The teacher sometimes went around signing people up; if he got enough to make it pay, he would start a school. Soon after, the fee became 25 cents per scholar, with the rest of the teacher's salary collected by tax.

From Jonathan Baker's *History*, we have a record of a school in Sherwood as early as 1842, held in a hewed log house owned by Peter Rupert, Sr. It was the first house north of the store on the southwest corner of Lot 16, Concession 3, and has since been moved to Pioneer Village. The teacher, John Kennedy, was supposed to be so well versed in grammar that many students, including Neil McKinnon, who was studying to be a teacher, came to this school. When two men from Pine Grove offered Mr. Kennedy $300 a year to teach in Pine Grove, the school at Sherwood closed for a while. Neil McKinnon taught for a month in the spring of 1842, and then hired as a labourer for haying and harvest. In the fall he taught three months; then John Kennedy came back and Neil McKinnon became a student again. Fifty-eight pupils are listed as attending during 1842-43, some of them the ancestors of persons still living in the area.

The first school in the village that was designated as S.S. No. 6 was built in 1861 on what later was the site of the Vaughan Township Area Administration Offices. When the building became overcrowded, part of the old Presbyterian church was moved to the site and used as a second classroom. These two buildings served the needs of the area until 1896, when they were demolished and a two-room brick school, with front steps and porch, was erected.

In 1955 additional land was purchased and a four-room school named after George Bailey was opened. To it another four rooms were added in 1958.

The two-room brick school was remodelled in 1961, had the roof flattened, and became the Vaughan Township Area Administrative Offices until 1969, when the Vaughan Township School Area became part of the York County Board of Education.

In 1964 the second Maple School, the Joseph Gibson Public School, was opened on Naylon Avenue.

Among the teachers of Maple School were: Joseph McQuarrie; Miss Janet Walkington; Wm. Jewitt; John Clubine; Miss Monkhouse; Miss Annie McClure; E.H. Elliott, 1898; Miss M. Morrison, for many years after 1898; Miss Thompson; Mr. W. Thorburn, 1902; John G.

McDonald; Percy Keffer; Lorne Perkins; Mr. Rowe; Miss Gertrude Mastin; Miss Eulali Jeffs; Miss Ethel McQuarrie; Miss E.B. Carrie, in the 1920s; Miss Olivia McQuarrie; George Carter, 1929-35, principal; Ruth Reaman, 1930-7 (junior room); Henry McDonald; Dorothy Keffer; Bruce Constable; Betty McCallum; John Martin; Faith Beatty; Donald Brum; Mrs. J.L. Fletcher; Jean Morby; John Outram; Richard Colvin; Russell Urquhart; Elizabeth Jackson; Ross Kennedy; Roy Robson.

Mount Lebanon Public School, S.S. No. 20

Mount Lebanon Public School was erected in 1876. The estimated value of the lot, 148½ x 198 ft., and the schoolhouse, 40 x 26 ft., was $1106.57. The land was bought from William Ellis and was on the west end of Lot 31, Concession 8. Until the school was built, his house had been used as a school. The schoolhouse was a frame building of board and batten and was painted red. Around the year 1910 the colour was changed to white; since then the sideroad it is situated on is called the white schoolhouse sideroad. The first teacher was a Miss Duncan.

The school was damaged by fire in January 1951. When it was repaired many improvements were made. Miss Enes Shaw, a former pupil of the school, was the teacher at that time. Other residents of the area who taught there before Miss Shaw were Miss Lily Topper and Fenwick Gould followed by Miss Margaret Mainland, Miss Mary Terry, Miss Eileen Potter, Robert Russell, and Mrs. Mereda Troyer.

Sunday School was held in the school house on Sunday afternoons for many years during the 1880s and 1890s, until about 1900. Edwin Hambly, who owned and farmed the north half of Lot 34, Concession 9, was the Superintendent.

The school was closed in September 1961. A reunion was held there on June 23, 1962, before the school was sold.

The schoolhouse is now the studio of the well-known husband-and-wife team of potters, Jack and Lorraine Herman.

Patterson School, S.S. No. 19

By the year 1870 there were more children in Patterson Village than in Richmond Hill. Peter Patterson asked permission to build a school and make a section of Patterson Village. Since Patterson was not incorporated, Hugh Devlin and James McNair suggested that the land now comprising the section be included and the owners be asked to cooperate in the venture. James McNair, James Dunton, Mr. Bassingthwaite, Peter Vanderburgh, Joseph Graham, James Rumble, William Graham, Hugh Devlin, Mr. Drury, Adam Storm, and Thomas Rumble, attending the meeting, agreed, and Mr. Patterson donated the land. S.S. No. 19 was formed from parts of Jefferson, Richmond Hill, Carrville, Hope, and Maple sections.

In order to form the new section, it was necessary to get the consent of ratepayers from the sections affected. This was done, and while the school was being built, classes were held in a house in Patterson Village. The building was ready for use in 1872. Between forty and fifty pupils attended, with Mr. Boliths as the first teacher.

The old school was replaced in 1917. The last class was held in June 1964, when the school was closed. It has been now transformed into an attractive home.

The teachers were: Mr. Bolitho, 1872; Mr. Robert Coulted (later Deputy Postmaster General of Canada); Mr. Careley; Hesse A. Nichols; John Saigeon; Miss Newberry; Miss Hall; Miss Mattie Harrison; Miss Shand (Mrs. Milton Savage); Miss Jennie Walkington; Miss Elizabeth Newton; Miss Edna Anglin; Miss Laurine Wright; Miss Graham; Miss Amos; Miss King; Miss McKenzie; Miss Carrie Shunk; Miss Jessie Hart; Miss Jessie Young; Mrs. Doner; Miss Olive Boake; Miss Bessie Lennox (Mrs. Harry Charles); Miss Violet McCann; Miss Margaret Lindsay; Miss I. Haines; Miss Anne Lindsay, 1934; Lorne C. Heels; Roy L. Knox, 1938; Miss Vivian DeLong, 1940; Miss M.A. Fitz-Gibbon, 1941; Mrs. Madeleine Howarth, 1942; Miss Anne Bothwell; Miss V. Noseworthy; Miss M. Buciersfield; Mr. C. McGill; Miss I. Ritchie; Mrs. Stewart Rumble; Mrs. Mervyn McQuarrie; Mrs. W. Fishley; Miss Melodye Harrison; Miss Bonnie Robertson, 1964.

Pine Grove School, S.S. No. 12

In 1848 John Gamble had a very thriving establishment at Pine Grove, employing a considerable number of men. Cockburn Bros. had a thriving sawmill on Lot 16, Concession 7, two concessions north of Pine Grove. Several other mills in the area added to the growing population — and it was deemed necessary to build a school.

A log school was erected a short distance to the east of the mill at the top of Bywater's hill, on land donated by James and Mary Totten, once a Clergy Reserve. The old log school was later covered with siding, and in 1903 a new red brick school was built. For many years this was a one-room school, until 1941 when a second room was added.

After the formation of the Vaughan Township School Area plan, the old school was closed on June 30, 1965. All pupils were transferred to S.S. No. 25, a modern four-room public school on the north side of Gamble Street which had been opened in 1952. The first principal of the new School was George Gordon, followed by Ross Kennedy and William Hazel.

Teachers throughout the history of Pine Grove School were: Roland Harvey, Mr. Johnson, 1893; Annie Skean, Miss Thompson, Miss Bell, 1896; Robert Kerr, Miss Howlett, Mabel Burns, 1903; Ollie J. Little, Mabel Patterson, 1906; Victoria Peters, 1912; Miss Gollnitz, 1918; Mae Andrews, 1919; Robert Cowling, 1921; Lydia Carroll, 1923; Laura Neal, 1932; Gladys Agar, 1936-40; Gwen Remis, 1938-41; (after 1940 there were two teachers each year, at first both teaching in one room until the second room was added) Alice Jackson, 1940-1; Hazel Kitto, 1941-44; Nancy Witherspoon, 1941-2; Zelta Hollingshead, 1942-3; Jean A. Keffer, 1943-6; Lois B. Wray, 1944-6; Mrs. Jessie Taber, Nora Orr, 1946; Eldon R. Pipher, Joyce Halbert, 1946-9; Kathaleen Hays, Mrs. Marr, 1948-9; Wm. J. Bockmaster, 1949-50; Dennis E. Sorenson, Nora Kranstz, Margaret McGregor, 1950-4;

Jefferson Public School, opened in 1952. (Photo: Harry Vey)

Purpleville School, built in 1853, was used by classes for 109 years before being closed by the Vaughan Township School Area Board in 1962. It has since been sold. This picture was taken by one of the teachers, Miss Ida Marshall, about 1918.

Richmond Hill High School, opened in 1897 and in use until 1924, was the third high school built in that community. With additions, the structure now houses the Municipal Offices.

Florence White, Helen Way, 1952; Ellen Goggin, Miss I. McLean, Mrs. Kathleen Heffron, 1954-5; R. Chisholm, 1955-6; Mrs. Ross Miller, 1956-9; Andrew Watson, 1959-64; Ronald Baker, 1964.

Purpleville School, S.S. No. 11
The Purpleville School was built in 1853, the original trustees being Samuel Irwin, Thomas Ginn and Alexander Mounsey. It was built on the side road south of the present school, Lot 26, Concession 7. John Morrow, who owned the land on which it stood, asked too high a price when the school board sought to buy more property so as to enlarge the schoolyard. They refused to pay it. Then Mr. Jamieson offered a quarter of an acre free if they would move the school to a new site, on what is now the north half of the present yard. The other half was bought from Mr. Livingston.

The first teacher was Mr. McCarthy. The first reunion of ex-pupils and teachers of S.S. No. 11 was held in June 1936 at Musselman's Lake. The last reunion was held at the school in June 1963. In 1962 the school was closed and pupils were taken by bus to Kleinburg.

Teachers of Purpleville School from 1853 to 1962 were: Mr. McCarthy, John Morrow, Thomas Moore, Cunningham Moore, Peter McMurchy, William Watson, John Archibald Watson, J.K. Johnston, Robert J. Ross, Hugh Cunningham, G.E. Snider, Vincent Humphrey, John G. McDonald, Thos. McCormack, Miss Emily Thompson, Arthur Lindsay, Miss C.J. Adour, Miss Nellie Chambers, Frank Bradley, Henry Hyland, H.L. Ballantyne, Douglas McKenzie, Phillip Harper, Miss Ida Marshall, Miss F. Hayes, Miss Annie McMaster, Mr. Smith, Miss Alma Gallaugher, Miss Margaret McMurchy, Miss Nellie McClure, Miss Jean McClure, Miss D.E. Dovey, Miss Dora Tansley, Miss Doris L. Irwin, Miss Olga Derbyshire, J. Thompson, Miss Almeda Wilson, Miss Bertha McCallum, Ed. Hannon, Garnet Lamb, Ross Kennedy, John Arnott, Miss M. Middlebrook, Miss Helen Klassen, John Wilson.

The last local trustees were Lyman Copithorn, William Kerr, and James Donneral. A well-known student at Purpleville school, James Robson, moved in 1885 to Purpleville when he was four years old. He was active in municipal life. His family still farms in this community.

Richmond Hill Schools
In 1811 James Miles started a Sunday School where he taught the children to read and write. Later the first regular school was started in a log building, 16 x 20 feet, with seats of pine blocks and desks made of half a split log. Mr. B. Barnard was the teacher and boarded around among the pupils' homes. He was paid $12 a quarter.

Soon a new school was built, south of the present McConaghy Public School. It was a hewn log building 20 x 40 feet. In 1849 a brick school was erected, and additions were added later. In 1915 was opened a new school, which in 1957 was named the M.L. McConaghy School in honour of Mrs. McConaghy who taught there for forty years. A two-storey building, it cost $30,000 and could accommodate 300 pupils.

In 1948 an addition was built and in the same year the first Roman Catholic Separate School, Our Lady of Fatima, was built. As Richmond Hill continued to grow, the O.M. MacKillop, Walter Scott, Beverley Acres, Crosby Heights, and Pleasantville Public Schools, and Our Lady Help of Christians, St. Joseph, and St. Mary Immaculate Separate Schools, were built.

In the 1880s a Miss Campbell and a Mrs. O'Brien had private schools. The first 'Grammar School' or secondary school was started in a home in 1851, but two years later a school building was erected. The second high school followed in 1873; it was just north of the McConaghy School and was destroyed by fire in 1896. A new and quite up-to-date school was opened in 1897, which the author attended for five years. It was a two-storey building with two entrances, wide halls, and three large classrooms, one of which was a science room well equipped for those times. There was a large room for teachers, board meetings, and the Library. It was a red brick building on a stone foundation, so well built that it still stands but now houses the Municipal Offices; it also housed the Library until the new one was built.

There were two teachers at this school, Mr. Coombs being principal in 1897. About 1900 R.A. Farquarson was principal and Robert Shaw his assistant. When Mr. Farquarson left in 1902, Mr. Shaw became principal and a Mr. Andrews and a Miss Bell were engaged. In 1904 Mr. Shaw offered for the first time in that school Upper School subjects: the author and W.G. Frisby of Victoria Square took advantage of this opportunity and in two years' time secured their Senior Leaving Certificate, which was the equivalent of first year of university.

When this high school was built, M. Naughton was chairman of the board; other members were Wm. Harrison, J.A.E. Switzer, J.N. Hutchinson, M.D., A. Newton, W.T. Storey, M. McNair, J. Boyce, D. Lynett, W.H. Clubine, G. McDonald, F. McConaghy.

Because of the formation of the Richmond Hill High School District, a new and larger school had to be built. It was opened on December 5, 1924. In 1949 an extension was found necessary and was officially opened in 1952; in it was provided instruction in commercial and vocational courses. The school has since had further additions. Bayview Secondary School was built in 1961 and Don Head Secondary School in 1969.

Principals at Richmond Hill Public Schools included: M.L. McConaghy School: A.E. Lehman, Walter Scott, Grant Nighswander, Garnet McDiarmid, Duard Rose, John Hincks. O.M. McKillop School: Walter Scott, Eldon Gooding, Robert Newman, Nathan Davidson, Denis Middleton. Crosby Heights School: Eldon Gooding. Beverley Acres School: G. Nighswander, Duard Rose. Pleasantville School: Duard Rose, Denis Middleton, John Hincks, Edward Woodger.

Richvale School, S.S. No. 24
As the population increased in this area, the first school known as the Richvale School was opened in the basement of the local Methodist

church on March 19, 1923, with one teacher in charge. By 1932 three teachers were needed and a school composed of two classrooms and a basement classroom was built on a site on Spruce Avenue. A double portable was attached in 1948 and another portable added later, to make five classrooms. Mr. P. Kurita was the principal.

Rerouting of No. 7 Highway made changes necessary. The present site of six acres on Carrville Road between Yonge and Bathurst was purchased in 1962. The new school, Roselawn Public School of Vaughan Township School Area, was opened in September 1963.

The principals at Roselawn Public School have been John Martin, Mr. Kennedy and D. Painter.

Thornhill Schools
In the earliest years the community of Thornhill was closely linked with that of Langstaff, hence the first school for Thornhill was held at Langstaff.

Mrs. Fitzgerald, who has made a careful study of the Thornhill area, states in *Thornhill, an Ontario Village,* that small private schools were conducted by Mrs. Sweeney, Mr. Devine, Mrs. Lawrence, Mrs. Hughes, and Miss Notter after 1820.

In 1847, in Union S.S. No. 1, Markham and Vaughan, a school was built in Thornhill to serve children in the south end of the village, as far distant as Steeles Avenue and Bathurst Street. A brick building with a frame addition, it lasted until May 22, 1923 when it was burned, just as a new and larger school was being built. Trustees at that time were Dr. C.P. Johns, J.R. Campbell, V.S. and J.W. Breaker.

As with all public schools, new rooms had to be added, until in 1953 extensive alterations were carried out and the number of rooms increased to eleven. The first kindergarten was made available in 1959.

Other schools have been established, including the five-room Powell Road School in Vaughan Township in 1950, which closed in 1970. Miss Leary was principal. Other schools were built on the Markham side. St. Lukes, the first Separate School in the Thornhill area, opened in 1951. The Thornhaven School for Retarded Children was opened in 1954, but moved in 1960 to a modern school building in Richmond Hill; Miss Dolly Ketola was its first teacher, and was followed by Mrs. Isabella Webb and staff.

Some of the teachers in the Thornhill Public Schools have been: R.O. Hardy and Miss Annie Hendry in 1850; Mr. and Mrs. Levi Clark, 1871-4; Henry Ward, 1895-1901; Henry Bolitho, 1901; Miss Edna McGregor, 1905-07; E.T. Pherrill; Miss Effie Bird, 1922-1930; Miss M. Kirby, 1930-42 Miss Geraldine Wesley. Principals have included: Thomas McCormack, 1912-16; Douglas Dyer, 1941-6; A.F. Martindale, 1947-52; John Martin, who completed 11 years in Thornhill Public Schools; Russell Urquhart, E.M. Wells.

Other schools in the Thornhill area in Vaughan are Charles Howitt School (with the following principals: Ernest Dunning, Donald McTavish, Robert Everist, and Ralph Brown) and Ross Doan School (Roy McWhirter, principal).

In 1960 Vaughan and Markham Townships became separate school areas, Vaughan having headquarters at Maple.

Thornhill Secondary School came into being in 1955 with 410 students, who had been attending Richmond Hill High School on an afternoon shift. In 1957 a modern million dollar school building was erected on Dudley Avenue. A.S. Elson was principal and B.T. O'Brien was vice-principal. Subsequent principals were J.W. Kippen, J.H. Edwards, and W. McVicar. The school has added technical and commercial courses and the attendance is well over 1,000 students.

Langstaff has had a secondary school since 1964, with Arthur Murch as its first principal, followed by Mr. Krol.

Vellore School, S.S. No. 9

The school section was about two and a half miles square. The land for the school was bought from Jacob Snider, and the early settlers were mainly Irish, Scotch, English, and Pennsylvania German. As in other sections of the township, the teacher boarded from house to house among the people of the section.

The first school was a log structure 16 x 20 feet and was built by the people of the section. There were no desks. The pupils sat on benches, and the building was heated by a fireplace. It had one door, one small platform, a small blackboard, and no bell. The first school records date back to 1862. The board of trustees at that time consisted of Wm. Constable, Peter Franks, and J. Puterbaugh, with Mr. Dickout as secretary and Wm. Julian as auditor. The first teacher in the log school was Mr. Corrigan.

In 1868 a frame school house was built, 40 x 30 feet at a cost of $1,200. In this school heat was provided by a box stove and there were double desks. There was an adequate library with a set of new maps. Robert Kerr was the teacher at a salary of $300. Reading, writing, arithmetic, history, geography, spelling, and music were the main subjects taught.

On December 27, 1898, a meeting was held in the school to organize a Literary Society. Charles McDonald became president, Peter McNaughton, vice-president, and John McCallum, treasurer. Rules and regulations adopted were:

1. Officers to hold office for one month only.
2. Meetings to be every Friday evening.
3. Male members of the Society to pay 25 cents.
4. All members must take part.
5. The name to be 'The Vellore Literary Society.'
6. Meetings to start at 7 p.m.
7. Meetings to be held in schoolhouse.

Debates and spelling matches were held, colours were red and white, and an old organ was bought.

In 1904 much repair work was done on the school: hardwood floors, slate blackboards, single seats, a new platform in the front of the school, a drilled well, new doors. A re-shingled roof and metallic sheeting for the inside of the school made a great improvement.

Beginning in 1913, a school fair was held annually in the schoolyard for many years.

In 1918 a flag pole was erected, presented by George Julian. Andrew McNeil and Dugald McDonald raised the first flag.

In 1922 a manual training course was held one night a week for three years in the Vellore Hall; a grant of $50 was received for holding this course.

In 1925 the school was raised and bricked; a cement basement was built underneath, and a furnace installed. In 1927 Mr. Carter and Mr. Bates planted a row of maple trees in front of the school. In 1929 electric lights were installed. The school was closed in 1964.

Teachers of Vellore School: Mr. Corrigan, J. McMillan, Alexander Muir, Mr. Kerr, Mr. Waterfield, W. Cameron, Miss M. McMurchy, Miss Nellie Franks, John Ness, Miss Langstaff, Mr. Reddit, R.O. Harvey, L. McCormack, J.T. Saigeon, H. Saigeon, Mr. Carley, J.W. McDonald, Percy Keffer, Miss Annie McClure, Miss Nellie Jeffries, Miss Mabel Jeffries, Miss Gertrude Mastin, Miss Scott, Miss Doyle, Mr. Walker, Miss L. Acheson, Miss Harman, Geo. Carter, Miss Purcell, Miss Elma Farr, Mr. Argent, Miss Topper, Miss Ida Frankum, Miss Ross, Miss Doner, Mrs. Grier, Mr. Holmes, Mr. Sturgess, Mrs. B.F. Andrews.

Woodbridge Public School, S.S. No. 14

The first public school built of logs about 1830 was located on part of Lot 8, Concession 8 in Burwick, later Woodbridge. It was replaced by a brick structure, and just prior to 1875 two additions were built, one plaster-covered, the other wooden. These two additions to the old school were later moved to the Fair Grounds, where they were joined and served as a stable for many years. After being vacant for a few years the joined addition was destroyed before the 1969 fair.

In 1885 the average attendance was 112, and the teachers were George Deacon, Maggie Smithers, and Lucy Woolley.

In 1894 a new large four-room brick school was built on the same site, and in 1941 a brick addition was added for washrooms. The whole building was partly burned in 1949 and later renovated and occupied by Hydro.

A modern school was erected in 1945 on Burwick and Lansdowne Avenues. In the chimney tower the historic bell of the former school was placed. It was only a short time before further additions were required. In 1952 three classrooms, a shoproom, and stage to the auditorium were added, and again in 1957, six classrooms, a board room, and washroom facilities.

A partial list of teachers over the year includes the following names: M. Beamish, F. Bowes, Margaret R. Bell, Mary C. Bowes, Ethel M. Brown, A. Lorne Burkholder, William O. Butt, Mac A. Campbell, M.E. Follet, Barbara E. Giles, Oda Hallett, Bertha Hamilton, Pearl E. Jeffrey, Beverley Johnston, Mary Johnston, Dorothy Lynch, Agnes McClure, Sarah McClure, R.P. McBride, E.V. McEachern, Mrs. Wm.

McDowell, Edna McHugh, Cora Metcalfe, Frances Murray, Tess Norton, Martha Peters, L.A. Peterson, Beatrice Prest, Russell Reid, Mrs. Riddell, Audrey Ring, Mrs. Albert Rutherford, Thelma Shore, Miss Swanson, Mary L. Topper, Mrs. George Troyer, Ruth Wallace, Mrs. Frank Wilson, Mrs. Pearson Neal, Miss Olive Gallagher, Mrs. Bert Wright, Mrs. Della Drury, Miss Jean MacLennan, Mrs. Bertha Moore, Mrs. Redman, Mrs. Brock Barker, Mrs. J. Fisher, Mrs. Jack Boddy, Miss T.J. Artkins, J.D. McCrae, J. Clifford McGill, Frances Johnston, Mrs. Manley Clongersmith, Mrs. K. Jordan, Mrs. A. Miller, Miss Norma Weatherhead, Mrs. Dorland Houston, Mrs. Kurtz, Mrs. B. Trueman, Mrs. E. Henry.

Principals have been: Robert Cowling, 1893-6; Kenneth Langdon, Joseph L. Garvin, (Continuation School) 1896-9; John B. Hanna, 1899-1901; Wm. L. Kidd, 1901-02; W.H. Hurlburt, 1902-03; Duncan A. Carmichael, 1903-05; M. McCallum, Howard G. Kersey, 1905-07; Miss Annie McAllister, 1907-08; Robert G. Holland, 1908-10; Clara Hulse, 1910-11; Walter Scott, 1911-14; Thomas Millikin, 1914-15; Russell Reid, 1915-16; George W. Shore, 1916-39; Jack McCallum, 1939-41; Morgan Lewis, 1941-6; Herb. H. Sawdon, 1946-58; Elmer E. McFadden, 1958- .

Secondary school education in Woodbridge began in 1896 when a continuation school was established. The instructors were the principals of the public school from Jos. L. Garvin to George W. Shore.

When high school education was first offered, students went to Weston Collegiate and Vocational School. In the 1950s, when a new high school was built at Thornhill, students were transported there. In 1958 Woodbridge established its own high school with the following teachers: L.B. Morrison (principal), S. Andrews, C.J. Burgess, Mrs. N.A. Bender, P.G. Chevreau, Mrs. K.J. Feilders, J.R. Frame, J. Fortier, Miss J.E. Lee, G.D. Olds, Miss E. Hirsch, Miss C. Honnan. Registration was 193, with 287 the second year. F.W. Morrow followed Mr. Morrison as principal in 1964. From the very beginning there has been a very active student government, the first president being George Moore and Pat Heffron the first secretary.

CHAPTER X

People

The following is a brief account of the Century Farms in Vaughan Township, and of other farms which have been in the family for 100 years or more. The stories of other families of general interest are also included, but it was not possible to use all the valuable material available.

Agar Family

Thomas and Hannah Agar came from Moolson, Yorkshire, in 1830 and homesteaded in Vaughan on Lot 11, Concession 10, where they lived until their deaths. They are buried in Coleraine Cemetery.

Their son, Richard, married Elizabeth Ash in 1839 and settled on Lot 23, Concession 10. He later married Jane Frances Train. Some of his family went to Alberta, and one son went to the State of Washington, but most of his descendants are living in York and Peel Counties. One son, Gilbert, was a Methodist, and later a United Church minister.

Amos Agar married Alice Dalziel and followed his father on the family farm. Their son, Adam, married Isobella Kersey and continued the farm.

One son, Gordon, a Presbyterian minister, was a missionary in India for a number of years.

Gilbert Agar and his wife, Ruth Ezard, live on this Century Farm today, their son, Bruce, being the fifth generation of Agars on Lot 23, Concession 10.

The present Agar home was built in 1854.

Atkinson Family

John Atkinson (1764-1835) was born in Yorkshire, England. His wife, Margery, died in England in 1807. He came to Vaughan Township in 1819 accompanied by four of his children, his other three came later. The family operated the old mill on Mill Road, now called Weldrick Road.

John's family intermarried with well known families and he has many descendants in the area. Margery married James Marsh; John, Jr., married Elizabeth Kurtz; Thomas married Lenissa Holland; George married Margaret Baker; Jane married Robert Mortly. William married

Mary Graham and founded the business which later became known as Atkinson and Switzer, and which carried on 56 years of active operation in Richmond Hill.

John Atkinson, Sr., was buried with his son, George, in a plot on their farm on Lot 27, Concession 2, Markham. In 1965 the gravestone was moved to the Cober cemetery near Concord.

Baker Family: Two Century Farms
In 1800 Jacob and Mary (Breck) Baker, with eight children and sixteen grandchildren, left Somerset County, Pennsylvania, to join the migration from that county to Canada. Jacob became lost on the way and it was feared he was taken by the Indians. His widow and the family waited for two years at Black Creek, not far from Niagara Falls. Then, in 1802, the widow and six of her children and some of the grandchildren came to York County.

In 1816 one of the grandchildren, Jonathan (1792-1860), bought Lot 11, Concession 2. He married Elizabeth, the daughter of Nicholas Cober. He cleared the land, built a log barn in 1822 which is still in use, and a log house, replacing it with the present brick house in 1853. Jonathan died in 1860, having no children. The farm was carried on by his nephew, Jonathan Baker, Jr., and his son Jesse, his grandson Amos, and great-grandson Paul Baker. There is still 100 acres of hardwood bush on this Century Farm. Jesse's son, Isaac, built a leather shop on the farm which has served the community since 1930. Before that Isaac did harness and repair work in the home workshop.

The west part of Lot 13, Concession 2, has also been continuously family-owned since 1829. Another of the grandchildren from Pennsylvania, Jonathan's brother, Michael, and his wife, Mary, another daughter of Nicholas Cober, farmed there. Then it was farmed by their son, Jonathan, and then by Michael's daughter, Eve, and her husband, Ben Brillinger. It has since been owned by Jonathan's son, George, and his son, John A. Baker. The buildings were put up at the east end of the farm, because a given road used to go through this block. The house is of log, built in 1829. In 1910 the buildings were moved forward close to Dufferin Street. The City of Toronto has plans to construct a large water reservoir on this Century Farm.

There have been a number of other Baker farms, among them Lot 9, Concession 3 and Lot 14, Concession 3.

Barker Family
Aaron Barker emigrated from Yorkshire, England, in 1832 and farmed in Vaughan Township before purchasing a farm in Etobicoke. His great-grandson Roy H. Barker purchased Lots 16 and 17, west half, Concession 7 in 1928. He named the farm 'Humbercrest' and established Humbercrest pure-bred Holsteins, which were exported to many countries. He was president of the Holstein-Friesian Association of Canada in 1966. Roy married Estelle Laver of U.E.L. descent. Their only son Brock married Colleen Hodgson, the daughter of Rev. J.A.H. Hodgson, and now operates the farm.

The Agar home, built in 1854, is typical of its period with its gingerbread trim, summer cookhouse at the back, and pump over the cistern. (Photo: Harry Vey)

The Baker homestead, Lot 11, Concession 2, is often called a "living museum." The cluster of buildings is typical of early Pennsylvania-style homes. Many of the structures are pre-1860. The large log barn was built in 1822. The main brick house, built in 1853, has a "grandfather" part. There are two summer cookhouses with a bake-oven, a leach for lye for soft soap, and a log smokehouse. The past has been carefully preserved yet new methods of farming are followed. This homestead is also the subject of the drawing by Thoreau MacDonald on the jacket of this book.

Milking time on a Sunday evening at the Beamish farm, Lot 9, Concession 9, in the summer of 1916. John Beamish, Sr., and his wife Elizabeth are with their children, John, Catherine, and Archie. The photographer was another daughter, Rahno.

The Beynon farm today, with some of its fine purebred Guernseys.

Beamish Family

John Alexander Beamish was born in Etobicoke in 1856 on Lot 35, Concession 3, the first child of Henry Beamish and Susannah McCort. In 1884, he purchased Lot 9, east half, Concession 9. Two years later he married Elizabeth Cameron, daughter of Archibald Cameron of Vellore. Of their children, Henry married Mary Codlin, Archie married Olga Robinson, and John, Catherine, and Rahno never married. During the eighty years of Beamish occupation, only five children were born on this farm.

John carried on his father's farm, and lived there his entire 73 years, until his death in 1963. The Beamishes were particularly interested in purebred Shorthorns. John also raised sheep, for the hills provided excellent grazing. The farm was sold in 1964 to speculators.

A new house had been built in 1895. Some of the timbers used were from the old Presbyterian Manse at Maple. This house was burned by trespassers holding a party in 1969.

Beynon Family

John and Jane Beynon came to Vaughan Township from Ireland about 1820. They had eight children. Two were born in Canada. They lived first on Yonge Street, then moved to Lots 34 and 35, Concession 2, Vaughan. There were seven Beynon farms in the Temperanceville area. The north part of Lot 34, Concession 2 has been family-owned since 1841. The Crown deed was made out in 1798 to Bernard Carey, but in 1841 Rev. George Beynon purchased the land. His brother, John, then farmed it, and after him it was farmed by Jonathan, who was a bachelor, Jonathan's nephew, Clayton, and now Clayton's son, Robert.

The farm is a 'string hundred' extending from Bathurst to Dufferin, and has small ponds common to that area of Vaughan. A fine herd of purebred Guernseys on R.O.P. are kept. In 1940 the barn was wrecked by a cyclone and was rebuilt, with a plank truss and steel roof. From time to time modernizing has been carried out. The house is very old, consisting of two frame houses put together on thick stone walls; and it also has been remodelled.

This is the only Century Farm in this area of Vaughan.

Bowes Family

Anthony Bowes (1789-1870), his wife, Ellen, and their children came to Vaughan Township in 1831. They had landed at Quebec, and from there had travelled by steam boat to Montreal, then by Durham boat to Brockville, and then by schooner to York. They settled on Lot 3, Concession 2, Vaughan, and part of this farm was owned by the family until around 1950. It was farmed by Anthony Bowes, his son Anthony, and grandsons James and Thomas. Lot 7, Concession 2 was purchased in 1840 and was farmed by Anthony Bowes, his son William, grandsons Thomas and Henry, and great-grandsons Ross and Albert. There were a number of other Bowes farms in the Concord area. Anthony, Jr.'s son, Anthony, farmed the west part of Lot 10, Concession 3, and his son, Nelson, is on the farm now. The hill between their house and Keele

Street used to be called Gander Hill. Emmanuel Bowes, the youngest son of Anthony, Jr., was the butcher for a neighbourhood beef ring for years. He farmed the east part of Lot 11, Concession 3 and taught his son Wilfred how to clip sheep. Wilfred carried on the farm and is one of the few professional sheep shearers in Ontario.

Boyle Family

David Boyle was born in Ayrshire, Scotland, in 1820, and came to Canada in 1842. He located at York Mills where he was a blacksmith. In 1849 he bought 200 acres, Lot 45, Concession 1, on which there was a sawmill, which he operated until 1881. The mill pond was a beauty spot for many years, known as Boyle's Pond.

Mr. Boyle was a school trustee, deputy reeve, and reeve of Vaughan. He had three sons and two daughters. His son, John, carried on the farm at Richmond Hill, and his son, David, bought the east part of Lot 36, Concession 1 where David, and later his son, Morgan, farmed until it was sold for subdivision after the second world war. Morgan's sister, Marguerite, has been a greatly appreciated teacher of elocution in Thornhill for many years.

Brown Family

John Brown was the son of James Brown who came from Pennsylvania. In 1826 he married Hannah Burkholder and settled on the west half of Lot 5, Concession 7, a Clergy Reserve which he patented in 1842. They had nine children: Susannah, Michael, Elizabeth, Hannah, Catherine, Lydia, John, Mary, and James. He built his cabin on the hillside overlooking the Humber flats. The old log house has been incorporated into Lex Mackenzie's home on the property at Highway No. 7 and Islington Avenue.

A sawmill was established on the Humber flats. Here also was built a blacksmith shop and foundry, where small agricultural equipment was made, and mill irons, etc., for the Abell Agricultural Works. In 1837 John Brown had part of his property appraised at fifteen shillings per acre. He purchased 75 acres of Lot 4 to add to the water race. Another appraisement in 1839 stated that: 'He built two sawmills, the first he could make no hand of with back water, and the second is not much better.' He is listed in this appraisement as a farmer and blacksmith. In 1857 he is listed as a founder.

John Brown's great-grandson, Lex Mackenzie, said that although there was a blacksmith shop and foundry in this area and it was called 'Brownsville,' there were no dwellings except John Brown's house on the hillside.

Bryson Family

James Bryson, a watchmaker and machinist, came from Edinburgh, Scotland, and settled on Lot 30, Concession 6 in 1832. He paid £100 to a squatter, a Mr. Wilkie who had built a log cabin and cleared a few acres, and another £100 to the government before receiving the Crown Deed which is still in the family's possession. The Crown Deed was received in 1847, fifteen years after application was made.

James Bryson married Jean McCallum. They had seven daughters and one son, Alexander, who married Esther (Hettie) Snider and carried on the farm. Alexander bought two other nearby farms where his sons, William and Elmer, farmed, while the youngest son, Norman, carried on the home farm. James, the eldest son, went West on the railroad and eventually settled at Tisdale, Sask., where his family still live. Alexander's one daughter, Mabel, married Austin Robinson who kept the store and the egg grading station in Maple.

Norman married Elizabeth Ireland, who still lives on this Century Farm with her son, Ross, his wife, Marion Puterbaugh, and family.

Burton Family

Henry Burton came from Hawick, Roxburghshire, Scotland, in 1830. He was a stone mason by trade and worked on the construction of Osgoode Hall, and also built a number of stone houses in this district. In 1833 he purchased the west half of Lot 13, Concession 9 from the Crown, and married Margaret Patterson. They had eight children, of whom William married Jane McDonald; Henry and John never married; Gideon married Margaret Kersey; Nellie married Angus McKechnie; Mary married George Ezard; and Eliza married James Devins. The youngest son, Robert, born on the farm in 1852, married Margaret Lawrence of Toronto Gore in 1879 and had twelve children.

Robert Erol, son of Robert, married Mary Constable in 1936. They have five sons. Robert sold the farm in 1961 to Dr. L.W. MacPherson, after it had been in the Burton name for 128 years.

William, the eldest son of Henry, born in 1831, farmed on the west half of Lot 4, Concession 9. He married Jane McDonald in 1860, and had four children. William sold the farm to Thomas Kitchener.

Gideon, the fourth son of Henry, farmed the west half of Lot 8, Concession 8. He married Margaret Kersey, by whom he had eight children. His son, Henry, took over the farm, worked it for about five years, and sold it to Russell Ward in 1919. It was sold by Mr. Ward to Frank Medon in 1946.

Cameron Family

Donald Cameron emigrated from Baramolach, Argyleshire, Scotland, in 1819 with his wife, Christine McLeven, and settled in Caledon, where their two daughters, Agnes and Sarah, were born. Upon the death of his wife, Donald married Elizabeth Armour and soon after bought Lot 30, Concession 5 in Vaughan, where he lived until his death in 1858.

Donald also bought Lot 17, Concession 6 (200 acres) in 1842, and when his son, Archibald, married Catherine McMurchy, they settled there and raised eight children. Their son, Archibald, married Louisa Farr and remained on this farm. Archie, who was a road boss, was tragically killed when a gravel pit caved in on Lot 21, Concession 7 in 1893. His brother, Alex, and his family then came back to the home farm.

Alex was married twice, and had three sons and three daughters. His son, Archibald, married Lillian Acheson, a Vellore school teacher and remained on the home farm. Their son Archie, Jr., and grandson, Ian Archibald, are the fourth and fifth generations of Archie Cameron to live on this Century Farm.

Donald's daughter, Agnes, married Malcolm Malloy and lived in Vaughan; Sarah married James McCallum and settled at Owen Sound. Donald and Elizabeth's daughter, Jean, married Archibald McMurchy, a member of another pioneer family in the area.

Donald's son Alex married Barbara Malloy and continued to live on Lot 30, Concession 5. His son, James Cameron, was warden of York County in 1914. This farm is now the home of the Bruce Ella family.

In writing his memoirs, Donald Cameron told of many adventures in travelling to and settling in a new country, and clearing a farm in the bush. The first night he and his wife and baby arrived on their lot in Caledon, he cut some wood for firewood and then fixed some boughs of trees overhead for shelter. It was March 1, and this was their camp until he got his first log cabin built: they moved into it on March 10, 1821.

Capner and Devins Families

Joseph and Charlotte Capner left Solihull, England, for Canada in 1830. On the six-week crossing of the ocean in a sailing vessel, they provided their own food. They settled on the bank of the Little Humber about half a mile east of the site where, 32 years later, they built the present brick house of Lot 21 Concession 8.

Like all other pioneers of that day they worked hard to clear the trees to build their first long cabin, and caught fish in the Humber and gathered wild berries close at hand. Charlotte was a midwife and travelled on horseback to deliver many babies.

It is told that on one occasion, after the arrival of a baby, when the mother was settling to rest, the husband came home drunk, determined to go into his wife's room. When he persisted, Mrs. Capner grabbed the whiskey bottle from his pocket and knocked him to the floor. Later he took her before the magistrate in Woodbridge who said, 'If there were more women like Mrs. Capner in the world there would be fewer men like you.'

The Capners had ten children, including two sets of twins. Their daughter, Charlotte, married Isaac Devins, a young school teacher who turned farmer and about 1891 came to manage the farm for Mrs. Capner. Their son, James, continued on the farm until 1942 when he sold it to the Reid family. Another son Albert, married Ella Wardlaw and lived on part of the farm. Mr. and Mrs. Walter Murray now live in this Georgian home. Mr. and Mrs. James Reid built a house on the farm overlooking the Humber.

Isaac Devins was the grandson of Isaac, of Pennsylvania, and his wife Polly Chapman of Genesee Valley, New York, who came to Canada because he would not take up arms against Great Britain during the American Revolution. They came with John Graves Simcoe whose tent he assisted in putting up. Two of this Isaac's sons bought property in Vaughan at an early date.

The Donald Cameron home in 1881, on Lot 30, Concession 5. The family members are, from left, Miss Mary Cameron, Minnie Cameron (Gibson), Tena Cameron (Kurtz), Mrs. Donald Cameron, James Cameron (Warden of York County in 1914), and Elizabeth Cameron (Walkington). Jane Cameron (Ireland) was very sick in bed with measles and scarlet fever, and was being looked after by her mother, Mrs. Alex Cameron.

Joseph Capner built this fine house in 1862 with bricks made on his farm. When the Kleinburg station was built in 1870, leftover bricks were hauled from this spot for the station well. The girls in the picure are Mr. Capner's great-granddaughters, Winnifred Johnston and Eleanor Devins (Mrs. Ken Love). This is now the home of Mr. and Mrs. Walter Murray.

William Castator's farm, Lot 1, Concession 9, about 1912. The log house was built before 1840, and the hip-roofed barn (one of many barns built by Frank Smith of Edgeley) was erected in 1909. Castators lived on this farm from 1805 to 1967, when it was sold to the Ontario Food Terminal.

The first of the family on the land, Henry, bought it when he arrived from Pennsylvania in 1805. He wed Anna Maria (Mary) Keffer in 1809, and they had three daughters; after her death, he married a widow, Esther Willson, and with her had five children, three of them sons. The land was divided equally among these sons, Henry, Jr., George, and William. Henry, Jr., sold his share in 1863, but it was later bought by another member of the family. William, the youngest, sold his share to John Devins, who married William's half-sister, Johanna. The portion inherited by George remained in the family continuously for 164 years.

George married Caroline Manser in 1860, their wedding reception being held at Steele's Hotel, owned by a relative. They had 11 children and 58 grandchildren. Then in 1892 William, who had in the interval moved some miles away, returned to the family homestead with his wife, Hannah Topper. They had five daughters and three sons. William built the new barn and a new house, the latter made with bricks from the first Emery school and logs from an early log house. Harkwood, William's son, took over the farm in 1945.

Isaac and Polly's son, James, married Eleanor Christner in 1830, and located on Lot 18, Concession 10 when there were fewer than a dozen dwelling houses between Toronto and Vaughan. They had nine children. Another son, John C. Devins, bought Lot 24, Concession 10, where his son, Peter, came to live after marrying Ellen Robinson. They had a family of seven girls and three boys. In 1910 they built a new house in Nashville when he retired from farming.

Chapman Family
Nathan Chapman came from Pennsylvania on horseback. His father had died, so Nathan, Jr., received the Crown grant for Lot 28, Concession 1 in 1796, when he was only sixteen years old. He was required to clear eighteen feet of Yonge Street and build a house. His lot adjoined Lot 29, Concession 1, where his mother lived after she married Asa Johnson. The Chapman farm was the last of the local Crown grants to pass from family ownership in 1950.

The Chapmans also purchased Lot 37, Concession 1, in 1864. It was farmed by Nathan's son John, his grandson Robert, and great grandsons, Nathan and Lyman. Nathan's sister, Georgia (Murison), and her husband, Alex, moved away from the farm in 1969. Langstaff Secondary School is now located on the property.

Another member of the family, Isaac Chapman was a Justice of the Peace, a magistrate, and a deputy reeve of Vaughan Township.

Cherry Family
John Cherry came with his wife from Belfast, Ireland, and settled on 400 acres, Lots 31 and 32, Concession 9, which he purchased from the Crown in 1834.

His son, James, was born there in 1838, married Elizabeth, daughter of Samuel Sheardown, and took over the farm in 1883. They had seven daughters. In 1916, James sold his farm to Lorne McKewan and moved to Kleinburg. His descendants are still active in community affairs.

Cober Family
Peter Cober (Cover), with his wife and nineteen other families, emigrated from Germany and landed at Baltimore, Maryland, sometime after the middle of the eighteenth century. Later they moved to Somerset County, Pennsylvania.

His son, Nicholas (1763-1842), and his wife Eve Fisher (1779-1859), emigrated to Canada in 1796 along with the bride's parents. They came by horseback and it took two weeks. They made a temporary stop near Niagara Falls and then came on to Vaughan Township. Legend has it that they slept under a beech tree the first night. On their tombstone in the Cober Burying Ground are these words: 'Of the first settlers on Yonge Street they were the fifth family.' Nicholas and Eve settled on Lot 34, Concession 1 and were given a Crown Deed, still in the family's possession, dated 1798. They had eleven children and have many descendants in the township.

In 1832 the Cobers bought the west part of Lot 12, Concession 2; they sold it to a cousin, Jesse Baker, in 1923, but Peter Cober and his sister, Mary, continued to live there. The frame house is very old. Some of the walls and floors are made of wide boards. An addition for a grandfather 'part' was added over a hundred years ago. The shop where Bishop Cober made his spinning wheels and rocking chairs and other fine craftsmanship has been preserved. There were two summer kitchens, with bakeovens, and an ingenious 'dry-house' for drying quantities of apples, corn or elderberries, and the usual 'cluster' of small buildings typical of an early Pennsylvania 'Deutsch' homestead.

Cook Family
William and Thomas Cook came from England and in 1833 bought from Michael Fisher Lots 16 and 17, Concession 2, including both the flour mill and the land. The sawmill, built earlier, had deteriorated, so about 1838 they built a new one 75 rods south of the flour mill, on Lot 16.

In 1841 Thomas Cook built a mud house, which in 1856 was brick-clad and is still in good repair. In 1844 he started a small store on Lot 17, Concession 2 which remained a store and post office for many years.

Thomas Cook, Sr., had three sons. One son, George, bought the west part of Lot 28, Concession 3 in 1878. He had two sons, William and Heber, who farmed Lots 28 and 29, Concession 3. The last Cook Farm was sold by William's son-in-law, Norman Payne, in 1959.

Heber's son, Jackson Cook, is the last of the Cook family in the local area.

William Cook, Sr., had three sons. William Cook, Jr., became a Toronto lawyer and his son, Gordon, followed in his footsteps.

Constable Family
William Constable, born in Hull, Yorkshire, England, emigrated to Canada with his stepfather, William Jarott, in 1830. He was in the lumbering business in Quebec for six years, and eventually moved to Vaughan Township, Lot 16, Concession 6 in 1841. He married Mary Jackson, daughter of George Jackson, also from Hull.

William Constable's son, John George William, married Susannah Fenwick and lived at Teston, but still owned the farm. Their son, John William, and his wife, Maria Margaret Stong, came back to live on the homestead. Their son, Fred, and his wife, Elizabeth Valliere, and grandson, Kenneth, and his wife, Gail Hendry, and their families, reside on this Century Farm.

Crosby Family
Parker Crosby was a native of Cumberland, England, and came to Canada in 1844. He engaged in business in Toronto, Aurora, and Thornhill, before coming to Richmond Hill. Here he opened a store called the 'Fireproof' which he turned over to his son in 1869. The home he built on Lot 48, Concession 1, Markham was a showplace in Richmond Hill with its two cupolas.

Dalziel Family

John Dalziel brought his family from Lanarkshire, Scotland, in 1828 and settled on 200 acres on Lot 1 Concession 5 in Vaughan. They bought the land from John Schmidt, who later built mills at Pine Grove.

John's son, James, married Janet McLean in 1872 and they had a family of two boys and two girls. He is an example of a Britisher who infused enthusiasm into the working and aims of the Agricultural Society, for he imported Durham and Shorthorn cattle. He was also interested in ploughing and won several prizes. His brother, Walter, was also a successful ploughman.

In 1870 James built the storey-and-a-half solid brick house in which his son, William Dalziel and wife, Annie Mackenzie, lived and which is now the home of their daughter, Jean and her husband, Charles Agnew.

The Dalziel barn was built in 1809 by John Schmidt. The house of logs with board siding was built in 1808 and moved in the 1880s to its present location on the south half of Lot 1, where James's grandaughter, Helen Dalziel, lives now. He also built a sawmill on the south side of the farm. The evidence of the mill race still remains on the site.

In 1954 William Dalziel sold the barn and 14 acres to the Humber Valley Conservation Authority and it became a pioneer agricultural museum. That was the beginning of the Black Creek Pioneer Village.

Coming over to Canada on a sailing ship took 16 weeks. John knitted all the way over. There was much bad weather, and as they were buffeted back and forth he complained to the ship's captain: 'If we dinna get there soon the land will all be sold.'

John Schmidt had also set out a good apple orchard, which delighted John because he had left a good orchard at home. A golden pippin tree still stands.

The Dalziels still have a sample of the first crop of wheat they harvested in the field east of the barn in 1829.

Diceman (Deisman) Family

John Diceman left his home in Wellesville, Pennsylvania, on foot to visit his sister, Mrs. J. Rupert, at Maple. In 1833, he married Anne Line, daughter of John Line of Sherwood, and they came to live on the 200 acres of Lot 24 Concession 5 in Vaughan. They raised a family of six sons and two daughters. Adam and Washington farmed in Vaughan.

A letter John received in April 1846 read in part: 'Dear Brother: At our consultation concerning you selling your property for $5,000 and moving farther back in the bush. We would advise you not to go into the wild woods again, you have worked hard and got things so you can live comfortably. Of course you have boys and you want to do the best for them. If you sell, come back to your native land. Your affectionate Sisters and Brothers.' But John and Anne never sold or moved from lot 24.

On two trips back to Pennsylvania, John brought grafts of apple trees, black walnuts, black cherries, and lilac roots that were planted along the road fence. Fruits, eggs, butter, and pork were taken to Toronto and peddled in the light democrat.

Their son, William, lived all his 90 years on the home place. He married Frances Wells and they had three daughters, Bertha (Mrs. Edgar Bowen), Ethel (Mrs. David C. Murray), and Hattie.

The solid log house with its white clapboard finish, built in 1851, has been home to six generations. Ethel's son, Gordon Murray, grandson Donald Murray, and great-grandson all live on this farm now and are proud to display the Century Farm sign.

Egan Family

Johnston Egan emigrated from County Monaghan, Ireland, in 1831 and bought from the Canada Company Lot 31, Concession 7. In 1834 he bought Lot 33, Concession 8.

His son, Richard, married Jane, daughter of Joseph Hemphill of this township. They had nine children. When their son, Richard, married Christiana Peoples, they bought Lots 27 and 28, west part, Concession 7. When John and his wife, Sadie Huson, sold and moved to Kleinburg in 1969, the Egan family had farmed on the eighth concession of Vaughan for 138 years.

Elliott Family

John Edward Elliott came from Northumberland, England. He spent two years in Montreal and two years in Toronto before purchasing Lot 11, Concession 8, in 1836 from his brother, Thomas, who had bought it three years earlier from Owen Leaden. Thomas had never worked or lived on the farm, and sold it to his brother with the knowledge that a small squatters' settlement had been established as a half-way trading post. The squatters gave up possession quietly. John Edward Elliott lived in a log house believed to have been built a considerable time before 1800. He married Mary Campbell from Islay, Scotland, and had five children: George, Janet (Mrs. Wm. Tippin), Polly (Mrs. George Currie), John Edward, Jr., and Sarah (who married three times, first to John McKee). The family lived for a time in the log house, later moving to the trading-post store. Then John built for himself a beautiful stone house, which was destroyed by fire in 1967.

George, the oldest son, married Elizabeth Gowland and had seven children. It was about this time that the farm was divided, George living on the east half. George had six girls and one boy. His only son, Thomas, taught at Weston High School around 1900. George sold the farm to Charles Allan, a 'city farmer' who lived in the old trading-post store. It became vacant for years, then eventually was bought by Richard Storer of Rivalda Farms. Various divisions have been made; the Toronto Board of Trade bought part for a golf club. The old trading-post was restored by J.R. Ashbee as a residence.

After the division of the farm by John Edward, Sr., his son, John Edward, Jr., owned the west half. He married Jane Phillips. They

Dalziel Barn

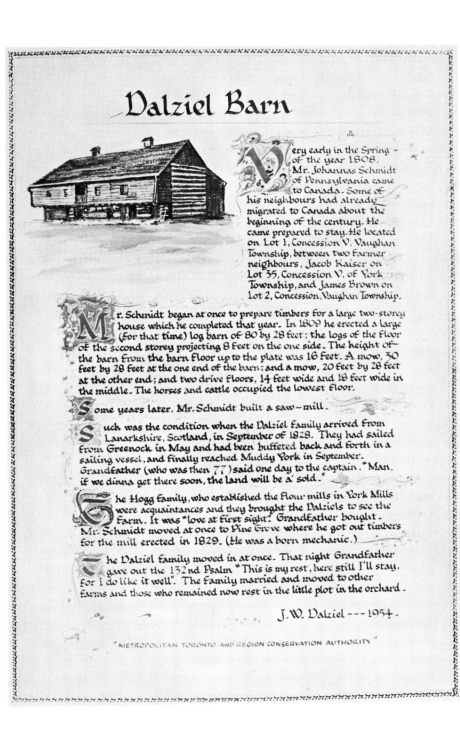

Very early in the Spring of the year 1808, Mr. Johannas Schmidt of Pennsylvania came to Canada. Some of his neighbours had already migrated to Canada about the beginning of the century. He came prepared to stay. He located on Lot 1, Concession V. Vaughan Township, between two farmer neighbours, Jacob Kaiser on Lot 35, Concession V. of York Township, and James Brown on Lot 2, Concession, Vaughan Township.

Mr. Schmidt began at once to prepare timbers for a large two-storey house which he completed that year. In 1809 he erected a large (for that time) log barn of 80 by 28 feet; the logs of the floor of the second storey projecting 8 feet on the one side. The height of the barn from the barn floor up to the plate was 16 feet. A mow, 30 feet by 28 feet at the one end of the barn; and a mow, 20 feet by 28 feet at the other end; and two drive floors, 14 feet wide and 18 feet wide in the middle. The horses and cattle occupied the lowest floor.

Some years later, Mr. Schmidt built a saw-mill.

Such was the condition when the Dalziel family arrived from Lanarkshire, Scotland, in September of 1828. They had sailed from Greenock in May and had been buffeted back and forth in a sailing vessel, and finally reached Muddy York in September. Grandfather (who was then 77) said one day to the captain, "Man, if we dinna get there soon, the land will be a' sold."

The Hogg family, who established the flour mills in York Mills were acquaintances and they brought the Dalziels to see the farm. It was "love at first sight." Grandfather bought. Mr. Schmidt moved at once to Pine Grove where he got out timbers for the mill erected in 1829. (He was a born mechanic.)

The Dalziel family moved in at once. That night Grandfather gave out the 132nd Psalm "This is my rest, here still I'll stay, for I do like it well". The family married and moved to other farms and those who remained now rest in the little plot in the orchard.

J. W. Dalziel --- 1954.

"METROPOLITAN TORONTO AND REGION CONSERVATION AUTHORITY"

The identification of Century Farms was an Ontario Junior Farmers' Centennial project in 1967. (Photo: Harry Vey)

had three boys and three girls. James, his son, married Ada Bowman, and they had six children. Weall and Cullen Nurseries Ltd. have a garden centre on a portion of the farm, and Loew's 7 and 27 Drive-in Theatre is located on the former site of the farm buildings. James' daughter, Bessie, and her husband, Dick Alford, built a home and service station on Highway 27, and are the only remaining Elliotts on this Century Farm.

Farr Family

James Farr emigrated from the neighbourhood of Weston, Hertfordshire, England, in 1829 and settled in the village of Weston, where he purchased a grist mill and 150 acres. That hamlet was then called Humber, but being a mill owner and a leading figure in the area, he renamed it Weston after his ancestral home. After selling his mill, he took up residence in Peel for a year, then located on Lot 5, Concession 9 of Vaughan. This property came into the possession of his wife (Nancy Wilcox), her family having held the Crown Deed. The farm was a forest, and their livelihood came from the sale in Toronto of wood, which had to be cut with an axe. Grain was grown in the clearings, and reaped with a sickle and later a cradle.

James passed away at fifty-seven years, leaving his sixteen-year-old son William to carry on. William married Elizabeth Fletcher in 1850, and they had one child; later he married Sarah Williams, and had four children.

Arthur, son of William, was born on the farm, where he lived for fifty years. He married Agnes Watson. Their daughter, Elta, married Joseph Snider.

The farm was sold to Frank Troyer, son of George Troyer, Sr., in 1923, and resold by Frank in 1956.

Fletcher Family

Walter Fletcher came from Lestrum, Ireland, in 1825 and settled on the west half of Lot 8, Concession 9. He had five children.

Pierce, the eldest, married Mary Nattress. They died within a few days of each other in a typhoid epidemic in 1869.

Isaac Walter bought four small parcels of land, Lots 5, 7, 8 and 9 of Concession 10, a narrow strip of land totalling 132 acres. Highway No. 7 ran through the southern part. His sons, Percy and Howard, carried on the farm. Percy remained single and Howard married Marjorie McCourt of Weston. An orchard of snow apples and northern spys marks the site today. The property is broken up in small parcels to accommodate the growing community.

Fulton Family

Captain James Fulton was the first Justice of the Peace, in 1813, in the Richmond Hill area. Born in Ireland, he had joined the army in America and, after buying his captaincy, had raised a company of dragoons, paying a guinea a head for each man. He fought at Brandywine and Bunker Hill. After the Revolutionary War was over, he came to Canada, going first to Nova Scotia, then to the Bay of Quinte and Niagara districts, and finally to Richmond Hill, where he bought land at the foot of the hill.

Captain Fulton's home soon became the place of call for the aristocracy from York, Bishop Strachan using it as a rest place when on pastoral duty. Mrs. Strachan stayed there during the American invasion, when York was in the hands of the enemy.

Captain Fulton was active during that 1812 struggle. Too old to serve as a soldier, he was seen doing his bit by running around the fort of York, encouraging the officers and distributing bread and cheese among the soldiers. He was an eyewitness to the blowing up of the fort.

In his community he was a popular figure and noted for his splendid horsemanship and soldierly bearing. He died on his farm and left considerable wealth.

His daughter, who became Mrs. Chamberlin, was also a noted figure, especially during the period when the de Puisay colonists gave their name to the section north of the village. (The south was marked on the map as the Black Ash Swamp.) Mrs. Chamberlain was born in 1811 and died in 1896. The Wellman family of Markham Township were her grandsons.

Thomas Grahame
Thomas Grahame was the son of Squire William Grahame who came from Dumfrieshire, Scotland, and acquired a block of land from the Canada Company in 1857. Tom settled on Lots 16 and 17, west half, Concession 7, cleared some of the land, and built himself a frame house. He was a member of the Vaughan Township Council, and a member of the Ontario Legislature. Land was not valued very highly in those days: in 1872, Tom paid his meat bill to Dan Mackenzie, who owned a slaughterhouse at the Toll Gate Corner, with a small piece of property from the farm.

Graham Family
William Graham was a cooper by trade and followed that trade for many years at York Mills and later in Vaughan Township. His son, Joseph, was born in 1840. William located on Lot 19, Concession 2, and Joseph farmed there and married Louise Frank in 1877. Their family consisted of Harry, Fred, Louis, Charlie, and Frank. Frank lived on this farm until it was sold to Don Head Farms.

William Harrison
About the turn of the century, William Harrison might have been called 'The Grand Old Man of Richmond Hill.' He was born in Bath, England, in 1834, and came to Canada with his parents in 1843, settling near Richmond Hill. He became a saddler by trade. In 1856 he assisted in organizing the first village fire brigade and was its first treasurer. He became a stockholder in a company established to publish a paper in Richmond Hill, *The York Riding Gazette*. To it and its successors he contributed many letters and editorials, and wrote a series of articles on

early days in Richmond Hill and the vicinity which have provided much of the information in compiling the history of the village for this volume. In 1866, Mr. Harrison formed the Richmond Hill Mechanics Institute and Literary Society with 5,000 volumes, the forerunner of the Public Library.

In 1873 he was most active in securing incorporation of Richmond Hill as a village but refused to be its first reeve. He was elected reeve the following year and was largely responsible for obtaining the monies under the Clergy Reserves and Municipal Loan Fund that belonged to the village. He was a charter member of the first Methodist Sunday School in 1848, and for fifty-one years was a teacher and superintendent. His wife was Christena Whelpten. He died in 1922.

Hemphill Family
Joseph Hemphill came from County Tyrone, Ireland, in 1841 and settled on the north 50 acres of Lot 33, Concession 9. He built a log house and log barn out of the bush. He later bought the south 50 acres from the Wilsons.

His son, William, married Jane Hamilton and carried on the farm, as did his son, Thomas, and daughter, Margaret, until they sold it in 1918 to William Hawman and moved into Kleinburg.

In 1887, William Hemphill bought the farm across the road, Lot 33, Concession 8, west half, where his son, George, farmed until 1946.

Alex J. Hume
Alex J. Hume (1858-1942) was born in Glasgow, Scotland, and came to Canada with his parents. In 1879 he came to Richmond Hill, where in 1890 he set up his own tailoring shop. When Mr. Teefy retired as clerk and treasurer of the municipality, A.J. Hume, as he was always known, took over the position and kept it until he retired in 1942.

An excellent musician, he led the choir in the Methodist Church for many years, and also the Richmond Hill band. He was librarian for the village for a number of years.

Innes Family
Leslie Innes was born in Aberdeenshire, Scotland, in 1828, and in 1857 came to Canada. His wife was Mary Ritchie of Thornhill, where they lived until 1885, when they moved to Richmond Hill. He bought Dr. Langstaff's lumber mill on the creek at the west end of Richmond Street, and formed the firm of L. Innes and Son. When the old mill burned down they built a new one which combined a saw and planing mill. It was in operation until the 1930s, and was the last of the many saw mills on the west branch of the Don River.

His granddaughter, Carol Innes Procter, is widely known for her paintings and photography, especially of wild life and flowers.

Irwin Family
William Irwin was born in Millington, Yorkshire, in 1838. He married Anne Dixon, and lived in Markham before settling on the south half, Lot 34, Concession 9 in 1882.

William was a Methodist and for about 40 years was a local preacher, preaching regularly from one to three times a Sunday both in Markham and in Vaughan on the Kleinburg Circuit of the Methodist Church.

His son, George, carried on the farm and purchased the north half, Lot 34 in 1940.

His son Douglas and grandson John continued farming the south half, where John and his wife, Dorothy Diceman, and family still live. Douglas's brother, Murray, and his family live on the north half.

William's daughter, Myretta, married Arthur Hambly, who farmed in the Kleinburg area. Their daughter, Merle, is the local historian of the Kleinburg area.

Jackson Family

John Jackson was born in England in 1821 and came to Canada as a small child with his parents, George and Ann Jackson, who lived in York Township.

He married Elizabeth Taylor in 1852 and farmed on the west half of Lot 1, Concession 3. They had a family of five sons and three daughters. He built the solid brick house in 1860 — the red bricks being made on the farm, the white bricks of blue clay being hauled from Yorkville Brick Yards.

A nephew, Frederick Jackson, took up farming on the Jackson farm after he married Priscilla Jane Snider in 1896.

Their son, Earl, married May Stephenson, who still carries on the farm with her son, Walter, and family.

Jeffery Family

Richard Jeffery, came to Canada in 1791 from Kent, England, as a gardener to Queen Victoria's father, the Duke of Kent, who then commanded the 7th Fusiliers at Quebec. He returned to England in 1799 with his young son, also named Richard.

Richard, Jr., was also a scientific horticulturalist, who returned to Canada with his wife and three sons, John, Alfred, and Richard. After following his trade of landscaping for a few years in Nova Scotia and Niagara, he became a farmer on Lot 5, Concession 8. In 1833 he bought for his son, Alfred, the land later farmed by Cameron McClure, the west half of Lot 11, Concession 9. For his son, Richard, he bought in 1835 the farm on which S.S. 15, Elder's Mills, is situated, Lot 15, Concession 9. To his eldest son, John, he gave the home place on Concession 8. In 1838 John built a beautiful stone house on the west half of the farm. Richard's son, the fourth Richard, was born in 1853. This Richard was the father of twins, Richard and John Jeffery, who were pupils of the old school, and later became chief engineers of the Hydro-Electric Power Commission of Ontario.

William Jeffery, the son of John Jeffery, married Francis Emma Standen in 1861 and built 'Summerhill' in 1872. Frances Emma Jeffery, William's third child, was born in 1867 and married Rev. Levi

Harry Coles in 1890. After Rev. Coles' retirement, he and his family permanently resided at Summerhill, Lot 5, Concession 8. In 1953 his son, Dr. Bonar Coles, and wife, Dorothy Morris, and children, Nancy and Richard, came to live at Summerhill on a few of the remaining acres, now 19 Coles Avenue, Woodbridge.

Johnston Family

David Johnston and his descendants lived a total of 120 years on their farm, the east half of Lot 3, Concession 8. David came to Canada from Scotland in 1828 with his brother, Robert, who married Margaret Anderson and settled on the adjoining Lot 2, east half.

David bought his land from Lot Hartman in 1844; it had previously been a Clergy Reserve. He proceeded to construct a small cabin and a few pieces of furniture. In 1848, it is told, he decided that a wife was very necessary to a pioneer farmer. In all probability, after this decision he took a dip in a small tributary of the Humber flowing past his cabin, trimmed his beard, and donned his high silk hat and tails (the metal hat box in which the brothers brought their formal dress across the Atlantic is still in the family's possession.) Then he set forth through the bush to the home of James Dalziel to demand the hand of his daughter, Katherine. His request was met with the indignant question, 'Is it a coo you are after? ' At this rebuff, David returned to his cabin, only to set out a year later on the same quest. On this occasion it possibly had been decided that Katherine, now thirty-seven, could do no better. Of this union five children were born: Janet, Annie (Mrs. A. Macdonald), Christina (Mrs. Silas Hartman), John, and Agnes (Mrs. William Watson).

Time passed and John inherited the farm and married Christina Lawrie. They had ten children. When his son, Robert, came back from the first world war, he married Tessie Norton and took over the farm. When his wife died, he and his young son moved to Woodbridge. The farm was rented for some years, Mary and Grace, daughters of John, living in the house. By 1964 the old homestead had been sold into small parcels.

Julian Family

William Julian and his family emigrated to Canada from Yorkshire, England, in 1851 and in 1852 settled on Lot 22, Concession 6. In 1860 they purchased the farm from William and George Wallis, Crown Deeds in two parcels. The Julians were members of the primitive Methodist Church. They had four sons, Thomas, William, George, and John; a baby died on the six-week crossing from England. William died in 1883 and his wife, Ann, in 1893.

John married Susannah Murray, and had four daughters and two sons — George, who farmed the next farm north, and David, who married Laura Watson and remained on the homestead. Their son Robert, and his wife, Clara Phillips, continue on this Century Farm.

Keffer Family

In 1806 two brothers, Jacob and Michael Keffer, brought their mother and families from Pennsylvania to Vaughan Township. Jacob settled on Lot 12, Concession 3, and Michael on Lots 9 and 10, Concession 3. We know that the brothers had visited York County several times during the 1790s but they did not come to settle until after their father, Jacob's, death.

Jacob's oath of allegiance, taken at York on July 18, 1799, before Wm. Jarvis, J.P., was among some interesting papers discovered recently. This was before official records were kept, which began in 1800.

Part of a diary kept by Jacob tells of a trip, leaving York on August 20 and arriving in Pennsylvania on September 6, 1799. On August 22 he stayed overnight with Jacob Kulb, in Vineland; on August 25, he crossed the Niagara River; and on September 3, he was nine miles from the Allegheny Mountains.

Jacob and Margaret had a family of five sons and seven daughters.

Michael and Anna Maria had four boys and one girl.

At the time of the Lutheran Church Centennial in 1906, there were 125 Keffers living in this one 1,000 acre block.

In 1946 a memorial stone was unveiled in the Lutheran Cemetery under the chairmanship of Wilbur Keffer, recording the names of the two original families.

Lot 12, Concession 3 continued to be farmed by Jacob's descendents until Wilfred Keffer sold the east half in 1959. The west half was sold in 1962 after the death of Lawrence Keffer.

Nine generations of the Keffer family have lived in Vaughan.

Kellam Family

George Kellam, who was born in 1778, came from Melton-on-the-Mowbray in Leicestershire, England, with his wife, Mary Kemp, to Vaughan Township in 1829. With them came their family, William, John, James, George, Olivia, and Sarah.

William and George bought Lot 22, east half and part of Lot 23, Concession 10 from William Kersey in 1830, paying for the farm by chopping down trees and splitting them into fence rails for Mr. Kersey. In 1850 George bought the share of his brother, William, who moved to Simcoe.

George was born in 1810 and died in 1883. He was married twice, first to Elizabeth Tyler, their family being three girls and four boys, and then to Lucy Coanet, their family being two daughters.

The first barn built in 1855 was raised in about an hour. The men then travelled up the 10th to Nashville corner and raised William Tedder's barn. They had that job completed while Mr. Tedder was driving around asking for hands to raise his barn.

The present house was built in 1860, of bricks burnt on the farm; 78,000 bricks were used, requiring the burning of 200 cords of wood.

Robert Kellam, the son of George, took over the farm and married Jane Lawrie. They had a family of two boys and eight girls. Their son, John, married Susan Cherry, and farmed on the homestead until it was sold in 1944 to Mr. Bowman, who sold it two years later to Charles Johnston. His son, Robert, married Anna Orr, a great-granddaughter of George Kellam, in 1956. They continued on the farm until they sold it in 1968 and moved to Bradford.

Everard and Lorne Kellam are great-grandsons of George's brother, John. They are farming Lot 21, Concession 10, the adjacent property.

Kerr Family

Robert Kerr was born in 1812 on the island of Guernsey. His father was a soldier in the British army and served during the Peninsular War. Robert emigrated to Canada in 1844, accompanied by his wife, Elizabeth, and two children. He located first in York Township, and came to Vaughan in 1847 to teach. His schools included Pine Grove and Vellore. In 1860 he bought Lot 23, Concession 7, where he and Elizabeth raised a family of four boys and three girls.

Their son, John, married Susan Robinson, and carried on the farm. Most of their sons farmed in the community. Son John and daughter Annie continued on the family farm. When John died, Annie sold the farm and moved to Woodbridge in 1948. Their youngest son, Nelson, lives at Vellore and was Vaughan Township Road Superintendent from April 1948 until his retirement in 1967.

The Peter Ferraro family live in this pioneer home now.

Kersey Family

William Kersey came from Norfolk, England, about 1820. His wife Margaret Beaton, was a native of the Isle of Mull. They settled on Lot 22, west half, Concession 10 and had three sons and four daughters: Thomas married Margaret McVean; Catharine married James Mitchell; William married Agnes Lawrie; Mary married Isaac Huver Lawrence; Ann married John Rezeau Lawrence; Margaret married Gideon Burton, and Jonathan married Flora Beaton.

Jonathan, the youngest son, purchased the east half of Lot 10 Concession 9 in 1884 from the estate of Jacob Burkholder, whose father had bought it from Richard Gamble. Jonathan and Flora had seven sons and two daughters. The house was of log covered with rough siding; they also had a barn made of logs. From the family records we can learn many details of agriculture at the time. The farm stock brought to this farm consisted of four horses, five head of shorthorn cattle, and a few sheep and hens. Beef cattle, hogs, butter, and eggs were sold and wheat, oats, and barley grown. A new barn on a stone foundation was erected in 1893, and a house of solid pressed brick in 1899. The bricks cost $7.00 per thousand.

In 1896, butter sold for 16 to 18 cents a pound; in 1920 the price had risen to 72 cents. Eggs were 85 cents a dozen wholesale. Oats in 1902 were 45 cents a bushel and barley 48 cents a bushel. Coal in

1895 was $5.10 per ton. A carpenter in 1895 charged $1.50 per day in the busy season and $1.25 in the off season. Taxes in 1885 were $26.42; in 1890, $34.41.

On the death of Jonathan in 1922, the farm was inherited by his four surviving sons, Edward, William, Thomas, and Joseph. In 1933 it was taken over by Edward and Thomas. Thomas died in 1950 and Edward bought his share. Joseph married Evaline Jones and moved to the west half. They have three children.

The farms were sold to speculators. Edward, Annie, and May live at Maple, and Joseph and Evaline at Kleinburg.

King Family

Robert King emigrated from Cumnock, Ayrshire, Scotland, and before settling on the east half of Lot 13, Concession 9, in 1833, he worked as a stonecutter on the construction of Osgoode Hall. He persuaded his friend, Henry Burton, to take the west half of Lot 13. Mr. King preferred the lot south and went to apply for it, but the man he met in the doorway of the registry office had just applied. His name was John Lawrie.

Robert King worked in Toronto and built a house on his farm. The original house was of mud, salt, and straw, but he found that his sheep, which were allowed to pasture around it were licking holes in the wall to get at the salt. Robert married Janet Turnbull and had a family of five daughters and two sons, Robert and John.

The second Robert farmed the land from 1867 until 1903. He married Susan Devins and had five sons and two daughters. Robert bought the adjoining Lot 14 for his son, William, who married Sarah Hanna and had one son and two daughters.

Robert's son, Charles, took over the homestead and married Florence Mathewson in 1903. Their family consisted of two sons and three daughters. Charles farmed until 1940. Then his son, Robert, who married Louise Usher, farmed the land. They had two girls and two boys.

Robert sold the farm to Pickett Nurseries in 1964 and moved to the adjoining lot 14 which he had bought in 1945 from Dan McLean, a grandson of Roderick McLean, an early settler who had helped clear Concession 7 of trees after it had been surveyed. Lot 14 was sold to speculators in 1968. The King family moved to the Bolton area, with the exception of son Bruce, who continued working the farm.

The Langstaff Family

The Langstaffs have played a major role as physicians in the eastern section of Vaughan Township. In 1808 John Langstaff came from New Jersey on horseback to visit friends in the area. He returned to make his home here and married Lucy Miles, the daughter of Abner Miles, an innkeeper. They had eight children, two of whom became doctors — Dr. George Augustus Langstaff, who located at Thornhill and had one of the first phones in the area, and Dr. James Langstaff, the youngest of the family, who was born in 1825. In April 1849 Dr. James commenced practice in Unionville but moved in September to Richmond Hill.

One of his four children, Dr. Rolph Langstaff (1869-1969), carried on the practice at 106 Yonge Street, Richmond Hill. His wife, Dr. Lillian Langstaff, practiced with him, although both had their own patients. Dr. Rolph was Medical Officer of Health for Richmond Hill for 25 years. During that time he was responsible for the introduction of pasteurization of all milk in the village and for chlorination of the water supply. Dr. Lillian's practice involved the Women's Jail Farm and she also went regularly to help at the Mercer Reformatory clinic when there was a staff shortage. A son, Dr. James Langstaff, is carrying on the tradition with offices at 50 Yonge Street in the Langstaff Building. His parents retired in 1938.

Abraham Law

Abraham Law, the first reeve of Richmond Hill, was born in Pennsylvania in 1806. He came to Canada with his parents in.1824, and in 1826 came to Richmond Hill. There were only eighteen houses in the village at that time. In 1832 he built a house of mud bricks which were nearly eighteen inches thick. It was in use until 1952, occupied during the early part of the century by his son-in-law, Amos Wright, and his son Osmond. Abraham donated the land on which the present United Church was built and was one of the original members of the first Methodist Church in Richmond Hill. For many years he was a Justice of the Peace. Elizabeth Street is named after his wife, Elizabeth Klinck. They had thirteen children.

Lawrie Family

John Lawrie was born near Glasgow, Scotland, in 1802. He married Isabella Reid and emigrated to Canada the same year. He lived in York for five years before moving to the Lot 12, Concession 9. They had five children: Gavin married Jane Bennett; Jane married Robert Kellam; Agnes married William Kersey; Mary Ann married John Nattress; Margaret was Robert Agar's second wife and later married a Nicolson and moved to Port Elgin.

There were few roads, no schools, and no churches when John came to the farm. Children were taught by their parents or a neighbour in classes held in the home. Religious services were conducted in barns and sometimes in Robert Somerville's kitchen. John Lawrie was a member of the first Council of Vaughan in 1850.

His son, Gavin, carried on the farm and had five children. William, son of Gavin, married Janet Bell and had three children. It was during his occupancy that the barn was burnt. It was burnt a second time after his son, William, Jr., took over the farm. William, Jr., married Gwen Northcott. They moved to Vancouver, selling the farm to Frank Chapman in 1952.

Longhouse Family

George Longhouse came from Pennsylvania. In 1851 he bought the east half of Lot 4, Concession 9 from Daniel Reaman. He married Mary Jane Reaman, daughter of George Reaman and Annie Heise, and they had nine children: Elizabeth (Mrs. Richard Everingham), Mary Ann (Mrs. Edward Richardson), Rachel, Dan, Annie (Mrs. Michael Burkholder), John, Susanna (Mrs. John Smith), William, and Adeline Jane (Mrs. Peter Duck). Stories are remembered by their grand-children of how they pioneered, clearing the primitive forest of trees to build a log house and barn, their only tool being an axe.

Daniel, son of George, farmed this lot after his parents retired. He married Elizabeth Nattress. They had four children, Wilbert, Gordon, Myrtle, and Mary (Mrs. Ed. Castator). A new house and barn were built in 1894, Arthur Hollingshead being the carpenter. The two sons homesteaded 300 acres at Meadow Lake, Saskatchewan, returning to Woodbridge in 1941. Gordon married Julia Bridgeman from the west; Wilbert and Myrtle never married.

The farm has since been owned by William Clarke, Archie Watts, and Russell Boynton.

Line Family

The Line family was one of the oldest in Vaughan Township, John Line having located by 1806 on Lot 15 Concession 4. They came originally from Pennsylvania, where they owned property in Somerset County.

Their youngest son, William, married in 1839 Susanna, the daughter of Jacob Snider. They had six sons, most of whom located in this immediate area. Many of their descendants still live in the area. When Gordon Line, William's great-grandson, sold his farm, the north half of Lot 19, Concession 4, a string hundred, in 1956, there had been Line families farming for 150 years in the Maple area.

Mackenzie Family

William Mackenzie, born in 1819 at Balrailan in the Parish of Ferintosh, the Black Isle, Ross-shire, Scotland, emigrated in 1842 to Vaughan. His ancestors can be traced to the year 1610 by their tomb stones in the Ferintosh cemetery.

He lived for a few years at Hart's Corners (Maple sideroad and 6th Concession), later moving his family south of Kleinburg where he became the keeper of the tollgate. The house still stands at the point where the 8th Concession meets Islington Avenue, and the gate may be seen at Black Creek Pioneer Village.

William was twice married. Three children were born of his first marriage, to Catherine McFarlane of the Isle of Iona, Argyllshire, Scotland. He died in 1904 and is buried at St. Paul's, Vaughan, where he had been the precentor for the hymns for many years when Gaelic services were held outdoors. The children were Donald, Neil, and Sarah Ann.

Donald, who was born at Hart's Corners, lived all his life in Vaughan, most of it in Woodbridge on Lot 5, Concession 7. He married Lydia Ann Addison and had five children: Annie Matilda, who married J. William Dalziel of Edgeley; William who died in infancy; Florence; Addison Alexander (Lex); and Donald Ross, who was killed in action in the first world war. Donald is buried at St. Paul's. Alexander (Lex) was

A beautiful squared stone house built by John Jeffery in 1838 on the west half of Lot 5, Concession 8 at Woodbridge.

Alexander (Lex) Mackenzie, M.C.
1885-1970
(Photo: Ashley and Crippen)

Georgian stone house on Lot 14, Concession 8, was built by Andrew McClure of
County Down, Ireland, in 1859. It is now the home of Ronald McDonald.
(Photo: Harry Vey)

born on November 1, 1885, on the old homestead, Lot 5, Concession 7, which was patented by his great-grandfather, John Brown, and has been in the family for well over a century. He went overseas in 1915 during the first world war and rose from a private to the rank of Major within two years. He enlisted with the 4th Canadian Mounted Rifles, was severely wounded in the battle of Vimy Ridge, and was confined to hospital for some time. He was awarded the Military Cross by King George V. A former councillor and reeve of Woodbridge, he was elected in 1945 to the Ontario Legislature as Member for York North, a position he held for twenty-two years. He never married and lived on the old homestead until his death in 1970.

Marwood Family
William Marwood a native of Hull, England, came to Upper Canada in 1817. Two years later he petitioned for land in the Upper Canada. The petition read:

To His Excellency Sir Peregrine Maitland K.C.
Lieutenant Governor of the Province of Upper Canada and Major General commanding His Majesty's Forces there in —

In Council
The Petition of William Marwood of the
Town of York, Taylor
Humbly Sheweth

That your Petitioner was born in the Island of Great Britain and is twenty eight years of age and has resided in this Province one year and a half and is desirous of occupying and improving a Vacant Lot of Land as an Emigrant and has taken the oath of allegiance as will appear by the Annexed Certificate and has never received any Land or order for land from the Council.

Your petitioner therefore humbly prays that your Excellency in Council may be pledged to Grant him Such a Quantity of the waste Land of the Crown as your Excellency in Council may think proper, under such regulations as your Excellency in Council may please to direct, with which he Engaged to Comply and your petitioner in duty bound will ever pray.

York. 24th, March
1819

(signed)   Wm. Marwood

He married Abigail Lyon of Thornhill and lived first in Markham Township, where two sons and one daughter were born. In 1839 he bought a lease on Clergy Land on the west half of Lot 24, Concession 4, where his son, William, and his wife, Susan Gohn, came to live. He petitioned to buy the land, the petition was granted, the land paid for, all conditions were carried out, and the land was finally his and the sale recorded in the Crown Lands Office on June 29, 1867.

William and Susan had five sons and two daughters. Their son, George, continued to farm the Crown Land farm and married Hannah Nichols. Of their family of two sons and four daughters, William followed his father on the homestead, married Florence Nightingale, and continued until this Century Farm was sold out of the family in 1967 after 128 years of possession.

McClure Family

Andrew McClure emigrated from County Down, Ireland, in 1833 and settled on Lot 14, Concession 8, as one of the first settlers in that area. He assisted in the erection of a considerable number of grist and saw mills on the Humber. He married Mary Ann Hamilton and built in 1859 the stone house of Georgian architecture now owned by Ronald McDonald. He died in 1876, aged 67.

William, his son, carried on the homestead and married Ellen Nesbitt. They had two girls and two boys. Samuel McClure was the youngest son of Andrew McClure, born in 1833. He married Nancy Cameron, eldest daughter of Archibald Cameron, in 1877. They purchased Lot 13, Concession 8, west half, in 1878, had a family of seven girls including two sets of twins and a son, Sam, who married Elizabeth Hostrawser. They raised a family of three boys and still live on the farm. A son Andrew, and his wife, Verna, a daughter of William Bryson, with their three daughters and one son, are farming the family property. Another son, Cameron, farms nearby.

The 1851 census of Canada West records that Andrew McClure was farming Lots 14 and 15, Concession 8: total acreage, 107; under cultivation, 58½; under crop, 44½; garden and orchard, 1; wheat, 20 acres, yield 400 bu.; peas, 5 acres, yield 150 bu.; oats, 6½ acres, yield 100 bu.; potatoes, 1 acre, yield 50 bu.; turnips, ½ acre; hay, 6 tons; wool, 30 lb.; tallow, 11 lb.; fulled cloth, 13 yd.; flannel, 15 yd.; bulls, oxen, steers, 5; milk cows, 4; horses all ages, 2; sheep 14; pigs 12; butter 200 lb.; cheese, 40 lb.; beef, 2 cwt.; pork, 7 cwt.

There is an interesting story connected with the west half of Lot 13, Concession 8, which Samuel bought. When the Prince of Wales, planted a tree in Queen's Park, Toronto, in 1860, the then-owner of the land is said to have uprooted the tree and transferred it to his farm home and planted it at the end of his log house. This tree is still standing; Sam McClure in 1914 registered at Ottawa the name of his farm as "Royal Locust."

Mr. M.L. McConaghy

Mrs. M.L. McConaghy (1866-1967) was a beloved teacher in Richmond Hill, where she taught for forty years. She was the daughter of Dr. James Langstaff and the sister of Dr. Rolph Langstaff. As a child she was not expected to survive but lived to be over a hundred.

She first taught at Vellore, Goderich, and Queen Victoria School in Parkdale. She married Dr. F. McConaghy in 1888. When he died in 1900 she returned to Richmond Hill with her five children, and in 1906 she began to teach in the primary room in the public school. In this school she taught until her retirement in 1940, and then again when she was called back in 1946 owing to a shortage of teachers. She was honoured in 1956 on her ninetieth birthday. The school in which she had taught so long was named the M.L. McConaghy School.

McCutcheon Family

William McCutcheon came from Ireland with his wife and family and settled near Hogg's Hollow, Toronto. Later his five sons farmed in different parts of Vaughan.

In November 1851, one of them, Patrick, purchased the west part of Lot 35, Concession 8, and set up housekeeping with his wife, Ann Parkinson, practically in the bush, with the Humber River winding through the rear limits. They had six sons and two daughters. One son, Henry, carried on the farm, then sold it to his niece, Pauline, and her husband, Stanley Cain, in 1938. After her husband's death in 1953, Pauline carried on for several years before she sold the farm to H.R. Jackman.

McDonald Family

John McDonald and his wife, Sarah MacInnes, from the highlands of Scotland adjacent to the Isle of Mull, settled on the south half of Lot 19, Concession 3 about 1805. It is believed John was a soldier who held the rank of sergeant in the British army when he came to America. He lived in New York State for several years, where some of the family were born, before coming to York County. They lived on Yonge Street for two years before coming to Vaughan. John died at the age of 46, leaving a young family of five. He is buried in the Lutheran Cemetery in Sherwood.

The oldest son, Archibald, continued on the homestead. His son, John, was a carpenter and it is believed that he is the person to whom the contract for building Maple Presbyterian Church was let in 1862.

Another son John, who settled on Concession 6, south half of Lot 19, like his father died at an early age, 33, and left his wife, Grace Muir, with a family of six and an adopted daughter all under 12 years of age.

One son, Samuel, built a home and wagon shop in Vellore. His son, Charles McDonald, now in his 90s, lives in Dixie and tells of many interesting times in Vellore. He took a great interest in the Vellore Literary Society, where debates and readings were held frequently. The following example given by Charles is typical of the readings in those days: There was always a sad emotional appeal because death was so common, particularly among the young.

> I sit afore my half oot fire
> And I am all alone.
> Nae friend hae I to daunter with
> And all my folk are gone.
> The wind blows round the owd house,
> And shucks the ane fire tree,
> And as it shucks it wakkens up
> Owd things that were dear to me,
> Wee Jamie wi' the curly head
> So burly, bing and bra',

Cut doon in the prime of youth,
The first among them a'.
If I had tears for aye all them,
Them I could greet fu' weel
To think o' Jamie, lying deed
Aneath the engine wheels
And Tom, poor Tom, so fu' o' fun,
He's worse than daid to me,
Nae' word frae him thru' the long years
Came across the sea.
If I could ken that he is weel,
As here I sit this nicht,
This world with all its faugh and care
Would look a wee thing bright.
I sit afore a half oot fire
And I am all alone.
Nae friend hae I to daunter in
For all my folk are gone.
And John, that was my ain guid man
He sleeps the moulds among,
And now a frail body like mysel'
It's time that I sould gang.

Another son, John, built the store.

Dugald, the youngest son, remained on the farm and was also a tax collector. Two daughters married Vaughan Township farmers: Annie married Ernest Carson, and Louise married James Brownlee. Dugald's youngest son, Milton, bought the store built by his uncle John, and carried on the business for the last 15 years of the Vellore General Store.

Milton's four sons all taught in Vaughan Schools — in Coleraine, Hope, Maple and Edgeley.

The only remaining descendant bearing the McDonald name still residing in the township is the third son of Milton, James McDonald, the former Township Clerk who is at present the Administrator of the Township. Jim remembers going with his father to take food to an Indian who lived in the Purpleville Woods on the north side of Maple sideroad in the sixth Concession.

McGillivray Family of Concession 7

Neil McGillivray emigrated from Argyleshire, Scotland, with his parents and located on Lot 31, Concession 7 in the early days of settlement. His son John married Nancy McGillivray in 1864. They had two sons, John and Neil, and three daughters, Sarah Catherine (who married Wesley Peterman, a member of another Vaughan pioneer family), Jessie, and Maude.

John married May Susan Cairns and continued on the farm until moving to Maple in 1941. The farm passed out of the family when John's niece, Mrs. Wilfred McGinn, and her family moved to Albion in 1947.

The five children of John and Nancy have enjoyed a remarkable record, their combined ages totalling 473 years at present. Mrs. Peterman was 101 years old when she died in 1966. The youngest and lone survivor, Maude (Mrs. Roberts) is at time of writing 94 years old.

McGillivray Family of Concession 9

Neil McGillivray came from the Isle of Mull about 1830, and bought 200 acres in King Township on Concession 10 without seeing it, for £2 sterling. He was disappointed with the location, for no one else had settled there, and traded the land for a black cow. It proved almost useless as a dairy animal.

About 1836 he bought Lot 20, Concession 9, Vaughan, which had a log house and twenty acres cleared, for £100. The property was a Clergy Reserve, and it was not until 1845 that he received a clear deed, which entitled him to the privilege of walking to Richmond Hill to vote. The house was built in 1865 at a cost of $1000, the carpenter being paid $250 for his work. Neil married Flora Beaton and had ten children: Neil, Catherine, Christena, Flora, Donald, Mary Jane, Margaret, William and two who died in infancy.

William, the youngest son, married Jane Lawrie, and carried on his father's farm. They had four children.

His second son, Gordon, and his wife, Mina Elliott, took over the farm. They had three daughters. The farm was sold in 1963 to Timothy O'Connor.

McKay Family

The east half of Lot 2, Concession 7 has been occupied by six generations of Jacob McKay's descendants since he purchased the land from the Canada Company in 1830.

A native of the United States of Scottish parentage, Jacob came to Canada about 1801, when he purchased Lot 3, Concession 3 of York Township and married Elizabeth Wilcox. All his children were born there: Margaret (Mrs. Edward Bull), Nancy, Hannah (Mrs. Peter Milne), Elizabeth (Mrs. Matthew Parsons), William, and Caroline (Mrs. Joseph Watson). Later they moved to Lot 1, Concession 7 of Vaughan, where he remained until his death in 1851.

Jacob had earlier purchased Lot 2, Concession 7, Vaughan, and his only son, William Abbot, moved there when he married Elizabeth Mattice in 1844, using both lots after his father's death. At this time the property consisted of 325 acres of bush and 75 acres cultivated. His livestock (according to the census) consisted of five oxen, four cows, two calves, seven horses, fifteen sheep and eight pigs. He had an inn on the north west corner of Steeles Avenue and Islington Avenue, which runs north and south through the centre of the property. George Topper later used the material from the inn to build the house south of Humber Summit Community Church.

William and Elizabeth had seven children. After his death at 39 years of age, his widow remarried twice. In 1870 the Toronto Grey and Bruce Railway was built diagonally through the western end of the farm, dividing the pasture from the barns. This then became a park-like area, with the cattle keeping the grass and weeds under control. Many people enjoyed picnics and swimming over the years. The view from the top of the cliff was beautiful.

William, Jr., and Jacob, Jr., next took over the homestead. Jacob's family was born in a log house northwest of the brick one, which he built in 1892 at a cost of $1941.56. The logs and materials were used to build and repair the barns.

A third Jacob and Eber next managed the farm. That Jacob's son, Albert, was born on the farm, but the family moved to Whitby in 1911. Eber married Elsie Castator in 1910; one son and three daughters were born on the farm.

There have been a total of twenty people born on this property; Jacob, Jr., being the first, and Eleanor, daughter of Eber, the last. Eber spent almost 85 years on the property until his death in 1969.

McKinnon Family

Donald McKinnon emigrated from the Isle of Mull, Scotland, in 1820 and settled on Lot 20, Concession 5, in 1842.

His son, John, married Ann Drummond in 1860 and had two sons and one daughter. He remembered in the early days helping his father clear the farm, then all bush; he also remembered when the school teacher boarded among the different families. Big John McKinnon, so called because there were five John McKinnons, was a Justice of the Peace.

His son, John, married Martha Keffer and continued on the farm. Of their three sons, Norman lives in Teston, and Elmer and Arthur continued on this pioneer farm until they sold it to Findlay Dairy Farm in 1962 and moved to Richmond Hill.

Donald's brother, Martin McKinnon, kept store in Maple in the early 1800s. One of his eleven children, Hugh, was an athlete of note; for some years he distinguished himself against all comers as the champion all-round athlete of America, retiring when he became police chief of Belleville in 1877.

T.F. McMahon

Thomas Franklin McMahon was born in Whitchurch Township, near Aurora, in 1852. He taught school for thirteen years and for four years was principal of Richmond Hill Public School. In 1882 he purchased "The Liberal", the weekly newspaper of Richmond Hill, and continued to publish it until a year before his death in 1926. He also maintained a book and stationery store. He was secretary of the Library Board for twenty years.

He had three children, of whom a son, Starr, was killed in the first world war.

McNair Family

Robert McNair came from Kelso, Scotland, to Vaughan Township in 1829. He had been a land surveyor and soil tester in the old country and was pleased with the land he purchased, Lot 25, Concession 2. The front was "slashed", but Robert cleared the rest of the farm. It grew prize crops of Delhi wheat and he also had prize-winning sheep. The barn was built in 1830 with hand-hewn plates sixty feet long and is still

The McKay homestead, Lot 2, Concession 7. The house was built by Jacob McKay in 1892. Mrs. Eber McKay and her daughter, Eleanor, still live there.

The "old swimming hole" on the McKay farm as it appeared about 1935. The stately elms that once graced Vaughan's countryside now stand stark and bare, victims of the Dutch Elm disease.

The McNeils' frame house was built in 1837 like a barn, with four bents over two stumps. The flour bin in the upstairs storeroom took a good-sized load. A stone building nearby, beside the well, kept milk cold in summer and meat and fowl frozen in winter. When Margaret McNeil was married in 1862 the cooking for the wedding was done in the fireplace and the outdoor bake oven.

The author's birthplace. The hip-roof barn was built by Frank Smith of Edgeley for Emmanuel Bowes in 1921, after the author's parents retired.

standing. The house was built in 1834, with five fireplaces. A kitchen part was added in 1869.

This Century Farm is still in the family, having been farmed by Robert, his son James, his grandson Scott, and great-grandson Leslie. Leslie and his sister, Edna, have many visitors to see Edna's interesting collection of old glass.

McNeil Family

Arthur McNeil came from County Caven, Ireland, to York County in 1819 and worked in Toronto. In 1829, he and his brother, Alex, a weaver, bought Lot 14, Concession 6 in Vaughan. Arthur married Margaret Jamieson in 1831. Nine children, sons and daughters, were born. Arthur was active in agricultural matters, being the first to introduce the Galloway breed of cattle into his district.

When his father died in 1881, Charles, a bachelor, farmed until 1902. Then his nephew, Livingston McNeil, and his wife, Elizabeth McClure, came to farm with him.

In 1940, on his return from the Navy, a nephew, Alex, with his wife Nan, moved onto this old homestead. Livingston died in 1951. Alex's four sons and one daughter are the fifth generation of McNeils on this Century farm.

McQuarrie Family

Lachlan McQuarrie brought his family from New York State in 1827, located south of Maple on Concession 3 in 1829, and died in the fall of the same year. His wife then purchased 25 acres of Lot 23, Concession 4, but two years later she too died. The young family of three girls and five boys managed to support themselves very well.

One son, John C. McQuarrie, at the age of 14 went to work with a carpenter, from whom he received $5.00 per month in the summer and no money at all in the winter, when he was able to receive a little schooling. He became a Justice of the Peace.

Another son, Archibald, married Emma Pickering and continued on the family land. They had ten children. He bought 300 acres of Lots 32 and 33, Concession 3, where his descendants farmed for some years. Lot 23, Concession 4 continued in the McQuarrie family until it was sold in 1956 to settle the estate of Matthew McQuarrie, a son of Archibald.

Mitchell Family

James Mitchell was born in Polmont, Stirlingshire, Scotland, and married Grisell Calder. They had eleven children — Andrew, David, James, William, John, Elizabeth, Jean, Agnes, Alexander, Robert, and Peter.

In 1835 the two oldest sons sailed for Canada, landed at York, and took up land in Vaughan. Two years later the parents followed with the remaining nine, the baby, Peter, then being 2 years old. There was considerable excitement when, just as they were about to land, son John, a teenager, fell into the water; fortunately he was rescued and all landed safely. James was a joiner and builder by trade and built at least four comfortable log homes for his family, including the furniture, which was mostly of cherry and maple.

Andrew, a bachelor, farmed the 200 acres at Edgeley, including Lot 7, East part of Concession 5.

Another son, Robert, married Helen Bryson. Their son, Peter, a bachelor, and later another son, James, lived on this farm at Edgeley. James married Lavina Devins. Their son, Robert married Dorothy Cousins, and continued on the farm until Robert became manager of Woodbridge Farmers and sold the farm and moved to Woodbridge in 1938.

Miller Family

Nicholas Miller came from Somerset County, Pennsylvania, in 1794 and married Sara Devins of Vaughan Township. They settled on Lot 34, Concession 1, Markham. He built a grist mill, using a very ingenious method of making flour: in the stump of an oak tree, he hollowed out a space in which the grain could be placed; then a high post was erected, with a crotched top which held a long cross-piece; from one end of the cross-piece a heavy block of wood was hung directly over the stump; this block was pulled up with a rope, then let go crashing down on the grain to reduce it to flour.

His son, Henry, was a carpenter by trade but farmed the old homestead as well. Henry, Jr., became a well-known beekeeper and fruitgrower, residing in Richmond Hill, where he moved in 1853. Before that he was a teacher and farmer in Scarborough. After moving, he travelled for Patterson Brothers, selling farm implements. When they ceased operation at Patterson he manufactured pumps for fifteen years in Richmond Hill.

Murray Family

Christopher Murray brought his family from Turkeyfoot Township, Somerset County, Pennsylvania, to Canada in 1818. The journey of 450 miles was made on horseback. The boys, David and Isaac, were carried in a canvas pouch thrown across the back of their father's horse, one on each side, while their sister (Mrs. S. Lines of Maple) was carried on another horse with her mother.

After some years in York Township at Emery, Christopher moved to Vaughan in 1833 and purchased Lot 26, Concession 5.

His son, Isaac, remained on the homestead. He was very much interested in bees; in one season he took out 2,400 lbs. of honey.

David located on Lot 26, Concession 6 and married Jacob Lahmer's sister in 1846. They had two sons, George, who farmed nearby, and Isaac, who took over the family farm in 1876, and daughters, Susannah (Mrs. John Julian) and Mary (Mrs. George Keffer).

David and his wife were members of the Lutheran Church. He founded the Murray Lutheran Chapel located on Lot 29, Concession 6 in 1886, and was its principal supporter. It became part of the Sherwood Lutheran charge. Services were held Sunday afternoons by

Rev. Alex McLaughlin. Officers elected were David Murray and Nicholas Donneral, elders, and David Murray and George Keffer, trustees. Services were held until 1900. Eventually the property was sold back to the owner of the farm, Mr. Diceman.

In 1890 the family moved to the farm on which the Mennonite cemetery is located in Edgeley, where they are buried.

David's son, Isaac, married Elizabeth Richards and had a family of two girls and three boys. The farm was carried on by a son, John, who married Jean Ireland, and two grandsons, Bruce and Leonard, until it was sold in 1963. Bruce and his wife, Glenna Seed, still farm the adjoining property, Lot 27, Concession 6.

Newton Family

James Newton migrated from Scotland in 1834 and died in 1892. He established the Newton Tanning Company at Elgin Mills, with two of his sons in charge, James, Jr., and Andrew. Andrew's son, J. Earle Newton, was one of Richmond Hill's most eminent musicians. He became a concert pianist, music supervisor, instructor, and examiner, but died at an early age. His wife was Georgia Boyle.

Oliver Family

Joshua Oliver came from Kent County in England with his wife, Anne Wade, and bought Lot 20, Concession 3 in 1845 from the Porter brothers. They had built the stone house during the years 1837. When the railway company came in 1852, it swung around the house, just taking part of the orchard.

When their son, Thomas, took over the farm, Joshua and Anne built a home nearby in Maple. Thomas married Eliza Pickering. Their family consisted of Laura, Forrest (who still lives in Maple with his wife, the former Nellie Thomas), and William (who married Lydia Keffer). William carried on the home farm until he sold it to Mr. Hamilton in 1945, and the stone house and one acre to Wills Maclachlan in 1946.

Oster Family

John Oster was born in 1780 and was a farmer and tanner in Pennsylvania. His oath of allegiance is dated February 16, 1802, at which time he was residing in Vaughan. He married Rachael Fisher and in 1826 they bought Lot 7, Concession 3 from her father, Jacob Fisher. (The family still have the old deed for the property dated 1805, when Jacob Fisher bought it from Jacob Keffer of Somerset County, Pennsylvania. This rare old document has a linen-like texture with the indented top common to the indentures of the day.)

John Oster's sons, Michael and Samuel, carried on the farm, followed by Michael's sons, Thomas and Aaron, followed by Thomas's sons, Alan and Lorne, and then by Alan's son, William. Lot 7, Concession 3 was owned by the Oster family from 1826 to 1960, and William Oster continued to live there and farm after the property was sold, until 1968.

Lot 6, Concession 3 was owned by Peter Oster, who also came early to the area. He built the first store in Concord in 1846. The east part of Lot 6, Concession 3 was sold to Thomas Teasdale in 1874 and part is still owned by his son, Frank. The Teasdales built a fine red brick house, a large barn, and other buildings. They were well-known for their dual purpose shorthorns, as well as their love of gardening and flowers.

Page Family

Lewis Page came to Vaughan Township from the United States. His wife was Rebecca Rupert. In 1822 he purchased Lot 9, Concession 2, a Clergy Reserve, for which he received the Crown Deed in 1838. He died in 1858 and his sons, Thomas and John, carried on the farm. Later the west half was sold to Arthur Evans and farmed also by his son, Ernest Evans, a champion plowman, until it was sold to Pasquale Brothers.

John Page, Thomas's son, farmed the east half. It was sold in 1959 after 137 years of family ownership. The large brick house was built about 1875. The bricks were made on the farm from clay from a knoll near the spring. This freshet is the beginning of one of the tributaries of the Don River. The area where the little creek crosses Bathurst Street has always been called locally 'Beartrap.'

Lewis Page, Jr., farmed the west half of Lots 33 and 34, Concession 1 for many years. His son, Stewart, recently retired after serving for forty-two years as Agricultural Representative in Simcoe County.

Pearson Family

The Pearson family came early to the Thornhill area. They lived on Lot 27, Concession 1 for some time, later moving to the east part of Lot 38, Concession 1 where they farmed, until in recent years the farm was sold and has become the site of many homes. James Pearson (1816-88) had seven children. His son, James, used to tell often of holding a faggot from the fireplace to provide light for his grandmother to see to knit.

William Powell

William Powell was born at Beverley, Yorkshire, 1814, and came to Canada in 1830. He worked for a few years for James Langstaff; then he rented Colonel Moodie's farm, Lot 49, Concession 1, Markham. In 1835 he married Margaret, daughter of Colonel Bridgeford. His second wife was Elizabeth Chamberlain. He moved to Lot 47, Concession 1 in Vaughan in 1835. He was a member of the first Council in Richmond Hill, and during the Rebellion of 1837 he was a member of Captain Gapper's Troop of Horse. He had twelve sons and three daughters.

Holy Ann Preston

Ann Preston was born in an Irish shanty in 1810 and became the house servant for Dr. and Mrs. J. Reid of Armagh. When they came to Canada and located in Thornhill in the 1830s they brought Ann with them.

While still in Ireland, Ann had become an ardent Methodist.

Although without any formal education, she had become proficient in knowledge of the Bible and quoted frequently from it. She acquired her sorbiquet when some jokers chalked on her door, 'Holy Ann lives here. Go in and have a word.' Naturally she was hurt by this act because the name stuck, but she overcame her feelings by praying that it might be a true statement.

Many persons came to her with their problems and she would say confidently 'I'll speak to the Father about it.' As might be expected, legends grew up about her, the best known being the 'miracle' of Reid's well which often went dry in the summer. Because the Reid boys had then to go some distance for water, they asked Ann one day, 'Ann, why don't you pray for water in the well?' This she did and when the bucket was lowered the next morning it was full of water. After the death of the Doctor and his wife, she lived for a time in one half of a little double house on Yonge Street. She spent the later years of her life with other members of the Reid family or with friends in Toronto. She lived until June 21, 1906, to 96 years of age. She was buried in Mount Pleasant Cemetery. Ministers of six denominations paid tribute to her and the mayor of Toronto was one of the pall bearers.

Puterbaugh Family

John Puterbaugh came from Pennsylvania to Vaughan Township in 1813. He purchased Lot 13, Concession 5 and received a Crown Deed which is still preserved by the family. John had a family of thirteen children. The property he purchased was farmed by his son Isaac, grandson Isaac, great-grandson Edgar, and great-great-grandson Percy, who sold the farm in 1962. Percy's daughters were the sixth generation of the family to live on the farm, which they owned for 149 years. In 1813 John built a log house, and soon after a log barn similar to the Dalziel barn at Pioneer Village. Still in good condition, it was removed in 1963 and the timbers were used at the McMichael Conservation of Art building at Kleinburg.

Reaman Family

The Reaman family have two century farms in Vaughan Township.

Their ancestry has been traced to the Canton of Argau in Switzerland, where the name is still found. Jacob Reaman came to America in 1753 and settled in Somerset County, Pennsylvania, in 1768. Members of the family still own the farm there.

John Reaman came to Vaughan Township and bought Lot 15, Concession 2 in February 1804. Part of this lot is still held by the family, probably a record for the township of continuous family ownership. It has been farmed by John Reaman, his son Josiah, grandson Daniel S., and great-grandson, Walter.

Part of Lot 10, Concession 2, purchased by John Reaman in 1815, also has been continuously family-owned. It has been owned by John Reaman, his son George, his grandson Daniel, great-grandson Isaac, great-great-grandson Daniel J., and great-great-great-grandson

Isaac J., whose children are the seventh generation on the farm.

John Reaman built log barns like the Dalziel Barn at Pioneer Village on both these farms. One was taken down and used to build two new barns in 1905, and the other was struck by lightning and burned down in 1931. He also bought other farms for his six sons, and Lots 6 and 7, Concession 9, were in the family for some years.

This is the author's family.

Rumble Family

William Rumble and his wife Mary came from Norfolk, England. The transatlantic trip by sailing vessel took so long that food supplies ran out and the situation became very critical. They reached Vaughan Township in 1843, and their first home was a log house on Lot 21, Concession 3, the northwest corner of Maple sideroad and Dufferin Street. They had one daughter, Mary, who died young, and seven sons, John, Thomas, Robert, Henry, James, William, and David. All the sons were farmers, and Robert later became the proprietor of the Maple Hotel.

Many Rumbles have farmed in Vaughan, especially between Maple and Richmond Hill. Rumble's pond, at the corner of Bathurst and Mill Street, is a secluded beauty spot.

East Lot 23, Concession 2 has been farmed since 1861 by Rumbles — William, his son David, and his son and grandsons. The large, well-preserved log house has large first-growth pine beams. Following a barn fire in 1914, the family erected the first steel barn in York County. A son of this farm, Stewart Rumble, was warden of York County in 1969.

Sanderson Family

The Sanderson family came early to Richmond Hill, for on June 10, 1806, John Sanderson was given the right to use his house 'for religious worship by his Majesty's Protestant dissenting subjects commonly called Methodists.' John Sanderson, Jr., was born in Richmond Hill in 1846. He was one of eight students in the first graduating class of the Ontario Veterinary College, and carried on an active professional life for sixty-two years. The Sanderson name is still well-known in the town today.

Seager Family

Edmund and Edward Seager, twenty-one-year-old sons of the Rev. John Seager, Vicar of Welsh Becknor, England, came to the Thornhill area in August 1832. For a time they operated a sawmill on Yonge Street. Edmund lived on Lot 40, Concession 1 for many years. Edward purchased Lot 31, Concession 1 in 1847.

The west part of this lot was farmed by Edward, his son Albert, and grandson Edward for a hundred years. The interesting set of buildings on this farm were designed and built by John Edey about 1840. There is a cluster of buildings typical of the era, including a barn, driving shed, hay barn, pig pen, cattle shed, dwelling house, and a number of other small buildings, about thirteen in all. Originally the house had a beautiful skylight.

Thornhill pond, an attractive area in Thornhill today, is not far east of the Seager buildings. It was just a small pond in a low spot with fields and trees around until a spring on the west bank was uncapped some time ago.

Smellie Family

David Smellie (always pronounced Smiley) emigrated from Lanarkshire, Scotland, in 1830, and purchased Lot 8, Concession 2 from Ulrich Burkholder. The farm became known as one of the showplaces of the township. The Smellies took prizes for their Leicestershire Cotswold sheep and Ayrshire cattle.

The farm was carried on by David, Jr., and later by his son, Nelson, who sold it to the City of Toronto. It was used as the Women's Municipal Jail Farm. During the second world war it was used as a mental hospital, and since then part of the west part is used by the Salvation Army for their 'House of Concord.'

Smith Family

John Smith came to Vaughan Township from Somerset County, Pennsylvania, in 1799. In 1801 he purchased Lot 7, Concession 4, and was joined by his brother Jacob.

Jacob had eight children. He farmed the family property and was followed by his son, Jacob, Jr., and grandsons, Abraham and Samuel. The north part was sold; Samuel's son, Menno, and grandson, Allan, farmed the south 100 acres. In 1966, after 165 years of family ownership, the property was taken over by the Canadian National Railway as part of their large marshalling yard.

Allan has a grandfather clock which was brought up from Pennsylvania. It is unusual — in that if one wished to know the time during the night, all he had to do was pull a string and the clock would strike the last hour. Menno, who was something of a poet, wrote this about the clock:

> That clock has kept on running
> From that day unto this.
> Excepting only for repairs
> A few days it would miss.
> Grandfather style it surely is
> And a thirty hour kind:
> A dial to tell the date as well
> Within each month you'll find.
> Make no mistake when days of month
> Have thirty-one in each,
> In other months just turn the dial
> So number one is reached.

Samuel's other son, Jerry, became internationally known as an expert watch and clock-maker. His business in Richmond Hill was well known for over half a century. He made a reflex time-keeper that varied only a few seconds in a year. He showed outstanding ability even when he was young, making a steam engine that would run from parts of an old sewing machine and odds and ends around the barn. In later years the chime clock that he designed and made was an exceptionally accurate timepiece. One of the finest parts he made was a tiny gear, almost invisible to the naked eye, for a wristwatch less than a quarter of an inch across.

There were many Smith farms in the area. Lot 6, Concession 4 was owned by the family for over a hundred years. It was farmed by Samuel, son of Jacob Smith, Sr., his son, John, and then by John's nephew, Carson Smith. Carson was the butcher for the beef rings, and active in the Edgeley Farmers Club.

David Smith (1823-1905) had a shingle mill at Edgeley and was a builder by trade. His son, Frank (1865-1940), also built many barns. A few built by David and many built by Frank are still standing. Some of the barns they built were for Louis Locke, Samuel Stong, George Robinson, Carson Smith (one in 1914 and another in 1918), Ken Stephenson, Anthony Bowes; Emmanuel Bowes, Alfred Stong, John Riley, Will Riley, Miss Chem (Weston), Robert Brownlee, Heise (Victoria Square), Daniel J. Reaman, and Henry Winger. The last barn Frank and his helper, Jos MacLaughin, built was Warren Reaman's in 1931, which replaced one they had built in 1905. Daniel, another son of Jacob Smith, Sr., had the east part of Lot 6, Concession 4. Later it was farmed by the Bagg family for years. Mr. Alf Bagg was one of the best known Jersey breeders in the world, due largely to the breeding of 'Sunbeam of Edgeley,' an outstanding Jersey cow.

Jacob Snider Family

In 1800 a family named Snider emigrated from near the Susquehanna River in York County, Pennsylvania. Jacob Snider was born during the journey and eventually lived near Maple in 1821. In 1830 he settled on Lot 18, Concession 5. It is said that Jacob Snider had considerable skill in surgery and was much sought after by the settlers, as there was a scarcity of doctors. He was also tax collector and assessor of the township for many years.

His son John settled on Lot 17, Concession 5. It was he who gave the land at Vellore for a Township Hall. The date on the hall is 1845.

John married Mary Stump. Their children were Susannah (Mrs. Richard Jarrett), Jacob, and David. John purchased Lot 19, Concession 5. Now there were three adjoining Snider farms. John also helped Abel Machinery, manufacturers of Woodbridge, to create one of the first threshing machines in the area.

Elmo Snider sold the north farm in 1956 and moved to Richmond Hill. After 126 years of occupation there are not any Sniders or descendants living on the three farms formerly owned by the family.

Samuel Snider Family

Samuel Snider came from Washington Township, York County,

Pennsylvania to York Township with his wife, Ann Nell, in 1806. He was a farmer, a blacksmith, and a sawmill operator.

Lot 2, Concession 4 in Vaughan was bought by Jacob Shunk in 1828, and in 1836 his daughter, Mary, and son-in-law, Henry Snider (a son of Samuel) settled on this farm.

Their son, Henry, married Catherine Campbell and in 1875 built a new house of poured cement. They had five children. One son, Eli, farmed across the road on Lot 2, Concession 3, west part; Charles Henry continued on the home farm and married Anna Keffer. When the first world war ended in 1918, communications took time. At 4.30 a.m. on November 11, Charles heard a terrific noise from Toronto — church bells and horns. He called the telephone operator to ask what the racket was about. The operator, who manned the switchboard from home at night, was short-tempered at that hour — but, before Charles had laced his boots, called back to say, 'The war is over!'

The sons of Charles and Anna, George C.H., Campbell, and Bruce, farmed Lots 2 and 3, Concession 4, until the property was sold in 1966. Continental Can now stands where the Sniders lived for 138 years.

Thomas Steele
Thomas Steele came to the township before 1837 from Yorkshire, England. Steeles Avenue is named after his family.

John Morley from Newtonbrook had built a tavern on the northwest corner of Steeles Avenue and Yonge Street in 1847. Thomas Steele, who had been farming and later had a hotel at Bond Lake, bought Morley's hotel in 1856. It was called Steele's Hotel, Poplar House, and The Green Bush Inn. (The first Green Bush Inn had been opened in 1830 on the northeast corner of Steeles and Yonge but the owner had moved away.)

John C. Steele, Thomas's son, carried on the hotel. In 1938 it was moved around the corner on to Steeles Avenue by Thomas Collins. In 1961 the owner, Miss Ruth Collins, gave two benches to the Black Creek Pioneer Village. The hotel's future is uncertain. There has been some discussion of restoring it.

Matthew Teefy
Matthew Teefy, born in Tipperary, Ireland, on April 18, 1822, came to York with his parents when two years of age. He became an apprentice in the printing trade in 1836, working for Thomas Dalton, publisher and editor of a *The Patriot,* who also printed the 'Appendix' to Lord Durham's Report.

As late as 1850, all appointments as postmaster were officially made in England. Mr. Teefy received his commission as Postmaster at Richmond Hill from the Marquess of Chanricarde, then Postmaster of England, although the post office in Canada was under the control of T.A. Stayner, Deputy Postmaster-General. A year later, in 1851, the Canadian government took over all control of the postal system, with Hon. James Morris as the first Postmaster-General in Canada. Mr. Teefy held the position for 61 years, and when he retired he was the oldest and had the longest years of service of any postmaster in Canada. Twenty-two Postmasters-General had held positions during those years.

When the village was incorporated in 1873, he was made the first clerk of the municipality, a position he held until his retirement in 1905. He was also treasurer and magistrate. A keen archaeologist and antiquarian, he possessed many papers and documents of historical importance. These, with his diaries, are now in the Provincial Archives in Toronto.

Thomas Family

Originally of Welsh ancestry, Richard Thomas came from Yorkshire, England, at an early age with his family, who settled in Etobicoke about 1820.

His son, William, with his second wife, Elizabeth Bailey, came to Lot 28 Concession 4, Vaughan in 1876. In 1893 he sold this farm to his brother Henry, who brought his wife, Lucy Hannah Kellam, and family of three boys and three girls to the farm, and bought the adjoining Lot 28, Concession 4, south half from the Nixons.

Henry's son, George, moved onto this farm in 1922 and his son Henry is now the only family farmer on Keele Street, the 4th Concession of Vaughan, between Maple and King City.

Thomson Family

James Gibb Thomson was born in Wishawaton, near Glasgow in Scotland, and came to Canada about 1830. He was a carpenter and millwright by trade.

A story is told that James and a William Nicol both courted Ann Thomson (no relation), but Nicol won her hand in marriage. Not to be outdone, James stated he would wait and marry their first daughter. This he did. But three months after their marriage, James lost his right arm in a threshing accident, in January 1864.

James built the mills on lot 15, Concession 8 that he later sold to Mr. McLeod, and in 1869 moved to Lots 12 and 13 on Concession 8, better known as the "Hollow," where he built a new mill, a large brick house, and a frame barn. As a successful business man he helped his five sons acquire farms within a few miles' range. One son, Christopher, remained on the "Hollow" for some years. It is owned by Karl Haas now. Son John married Jane Lawrie and settled on Lots 16 and 17 west half Concession 7.

Another son, William, married Sarah Jane Bolton in 1890 and bought the 200 acres of Lot 18, Concession 8 from Duncan and Donald McKinnon. Upon William's death in 1937, his farm was divided between his sons, James receiving the east half and William John the west half. James married the former Dorothy Aitchison and raised four children; their son, Gordon, carries on the farm in the Thomson name since his father's death in 1964. William John married Luena Robinson and had two sons, Boyle and Bruce. Their property was sold in 1967 and they retired in Kleinburg, where William John died in 1968.

An unfortunate tragedy occurred in the Thomson family following William's death in 1937. About two weeks after his burial, his body was removed from the grave, and no clue as to its whereabouts has ever been found.

Train Family

The Train family originated in France and crossed to Scotland. In 1831 Christopher and Ann Train sailed from England, their son John being born on the boat coming over. Christopher got a job in York sawing lumber. Then he bought Lot 20, Concession 10 to go farming.

Their son, John, married Ann Gimmerson and in 1865 bought Lot 27, Concession 8 for £1,400. They had nine sons and two daughters.

John, Jr., took over this pioneer farm, married Alice Ann Goodfellow, and had two sons and two daughters.

His son, Arthur, inherited the farm and married Irene Devins. They have a family of two boys and two girls. One of the sons, Robert, is following in the family footsteps and is the fifth generation to farm on this Century Farm.

Trench Family

William Trench left Dunbar, on the east coast of Scotland, about 1837. By 1842 all the family had migrated to Canada. William Trench, Jr., brought his wife and six children to Canada in 1842. His son, the third William, had fourteen children.

The Trench Carriage works in Richmond Hill became well known. They were started in partnership with Archibald Wright, but William later carried on alone until his son, Thomas, was taken into partnership. A factory was built at the corner of Lorne and Yonge Streets in 1874, and later equipped with a steam plant.

Wyck Trench became public school inspector for York County. The fourth William Trench became a Methodist minister. Frances married William Atkinson, of the firm of Atkinson & Switzer; Mary Agnes married A.J. Hume, long-time clerk of Richmond Hill; and Susan married A.G. Savage, for many years postmaster.

Topper Family

Lot 1, Concession 7 was bought in 1837 by Jacob McKay, who willed it to his son, William, who kept a hotel on the premises. After passing through several ownerships, it was purchased by George Topper in 1869.

Mr. Topper came from Barton-on-the-Humber, in Yorkshire, at fourteen years of age. He married Elizabeth Middleton, from Ebenezer, Ontario in 1861. They moved to Malvern, and in 1871 came to Vaughan and settled on the former McKay property. Since that time his descendants have lived on the old homestead. George built a large brick house of eleven rooms with six bedrooms about 1881 for his family, which consisted of six girls and four boys: Mary Ann and Sarah Jane, who were twins, Christopher, George, Martha, Lucinda, Robert, Emily, Myra, and John, who died at three years. George gave property for the local Congregational Church at Islington and Steeles Avenues on a lease for 99 years. The Toronto Grey and Bruce Railway was built through the farm in 1870.

Robert Topper, a son of George, carried on the farm and married Jennie Hendry. They had eleven children.

Alvin Topper, Robert's son, continued on the farm. He married Florence Peelar and has two children, Fred and Mary. In 1947 the house was destroyed by fire of unknown origin and rebuilt. The land is sandy loam. Gardening has been carried on for many years, and Alvin and his son-in-law, D. Grantham, now carry on a garden centre.

Troyer Family
Christian Troyer (1756-1839) Somerset County, Pennsylvania, settled on Lot 5, Concession 3 in 1804. His first wife was Barbara Yoder, and his second Elizabeth Becker.

Christian, Jr., born in 1798, married Magdalena Cober, and had a family of ten children. Their fifth son, Samuel, married Mary Ann Baldwin, by whom he had six children. He built an eight-sided barn on their farm at Fisherville (at Steeles and Dufferin) which is still standing.

Jacob, the oldest son of Christian, Jr., purchased 100 acres, the west half of Lot 4, Concession 8 near Woodbridge, in 1881 from John Williams. Jacob was married twice, first to Ann Haking and then to Annie Gram. His second wife met a tragic death, leaving a large family of little ones. On a drive to Toronto with the youngest twins, Martha and Emma, the horse shied at one of the horse-drawn street cars which had recently been introduced in the city, and she was thrown out of the vehicle.

The farm was later carried on by Jacob's son, George, who had six children. In 1945 it was sold to the Toronto General Burying Grounds.

Frank, son of George, purchased Lot 5, east half, Concession 9. George, Jr., bought Lot 5, west half, Concession 8, part of the Jeffery homestead. Both are now retired from farming.

This is a very limited sketch, as scores of Troyers have been born and raised in Vaughan.

Wallace Family
The west half of Lot 10, Concession 8 was patented by John Leaden in 1801 and sold to his brother, Owen, in 1833. Owen sold it to Nathaniel Wallace, son of Thomas and Martha Wallace of Carney, County Sligo, Ireland in 1833. Nathaniel married Ann Wallace and in 1842 sold it to his wife's brother, George Frazier Wallace, who was born in Ireland in 1800.

George Frazier Wallace married Catherine Weir and had six children: Hannah (Mrs. Levi Elliott), John, George Frazier, Catherine, Margaret (Mrs. Ebenezer Barber), and Charles. George Frazier, Sr., told many interesting stories of how he cut his way through the bush with an axe, built his buildings of logs, and cleared the land to grow grain, which he cut with a sickle and threshed with a flail. Bears were troublesome, stealing pigs, so he kept his gun handy.

George Frazier, Jr., born in 1849, was the next occupant of the farm. He married Elizabeth Harper from Markham, and they had twelve children.

John Walter Wallace, his son, carried on the farm until his decease in 1963. He married Muriel Chapman and had three children: George, Eleanor, and Doris. His eldest daughter, Eleanor, married Raymond Maltby and worked the farm until it was sold to speculators in 1967. From this farm, which had been in the Wallace family for 133 years, they moved to a farm at Thornton.

Wardlaw Family
Lot 21 Concession 9 was Crown land acquired by the Wardlaw family at an early date. Peter Wardlaw, grandson of Peter Wardlaw who emigrated with his family to Canada in 1835, came to live on the family property when he married Elizabeth Parsons in 1875. Later he bought parts of Lot 22 and 23. He had six children, William, Ella, Effie, Mortimer, Herbert, and Laura. The three boys stayed in the community and farmed for many years.

Watson Family
William Watson was born in Lanarkshire, Scotland, in 1831 and married before coming to Canada in 1856. After living first in Scarborough, he and his wife came to Vaughan and settled on the east half of Lot 7, Concession 6. They had seven children.

Their sons, James and then Robert, farmed the homestead. The west half of the same lot was acquired for a son, William. At one time there were three adjacent Watson farms.

The pioneer Watson farm was sold in 1962 for a Dominion Government weather station. A great-grandson of William, Bruce Watson, is still farming on the west half of Lot 7, Concession 6 in 1970.

William took pride in his horses and had a fine pair of groomed horses. He was an elder of Woodbridge Presbyterian Church and had a great deal to do with building the new church. On the morning of the opening, everyone was ready for the special services but the Watson family were late. Word finally came that William had been kicked by a horse and killed.

Weldrick Family
George Weldrick was born in Hull, Yorkshire, in 1828 and came to Canada in 1849. He first located in Scarborough, then moved to Markham, and finally located in Vaughan on Lot 35, Concession 1. He married Hannah Boynton in 1852. He became well known for the excellence of his breeds of cattle, sheep, and horses, his Leicester sheep and Durham cattle being much admired.

George had one daughter, Annie, and four sons, George, Jr., John, William, and Burwick (born on Burwick [Woodbridge] Fair Day and so named). Burwick and his family farmed on Lot 29 Concession 4, west part for 50 years, leaving in 1963 when they sold to Lorne Goodwill.

White Family

Hiram White (1788-1859), who came to Canada from Vermont, was descended from an English family who had settled there before the Revolutionary War. His wife was Magdalena Stong (1795-1869) and they had nine children. He leased the Crown Reserve, Lot 8, Concession 3 on October 14, 1818. His son, Hiram, Jr., carried on the farm, followed by his grandson, William, who died in 1922. The farm was then sold and has since been owned by John Bone, William Baker, and W.J. Lawson.

Miss Sarah White continued to live on part of the farm. She died in 1939. Her sister, Ida (Mrs. John Ash), born in 1873, lived to the age of 97, dying in September 1970.

John Williams Family

John Williams, known as 'Welsh' Williams, was the second settler west of the Humber. He purchased 200 acres in 1825 for £75, the west halves of Lots 3 and 4, Concession 8.

John and his brother David had come from North Wales in 1821, unable to speak a word of English. He boasted that he would not marry until he could properly support a wife. He very soon replaced his first log cabin with one of large dimensions, with eight-inch beams and fourteen to eighteen inches wide, all free of knots. Four fireplaces built of beautiful field stone testify to the solidity of the home. A kitchen with a huge brick and stone bake oven was erected about 1850.

John married Sarah Shunk, who was born in 1811 on the Fifth line of Vaughan. They had five children: Elizabeth and David, who died in their youth, Mary (Mrs. Jonathan Ellerby), Sarah (Mrs. Wm. Farr), and Ellen (Mrs. George Wallace).

Upon John's death in 1881, Jacob Troyer settled on the land, and his descendants occupied it until 1954. There have been but two families living there in 160 years since the granting of the Crown Deed.

Williams Family

Lot 14, Concession 10, where Garnet Williams now lives, originally was purchased in 1837 by Archibald Somerville, a native of Lanarkshire, Scotland. His son, Robert, took over the farm after Archibald passed away in 1873. The Somervilles played an active part in church affairs, holding services in their home before Knox Church was built at Elder's Mills.

John and Archie Somerville, nephews of the former owners, worked this farm of 150 acres until Richard Williams purchased it in 1929. He in turn farmed it until 1939, when his son, Garnet, and his wife, Jean Dale, took over. They have three daughters, Betty Lou, Margaret, and Dianne. In 1961, 140 acres of the property were bought by the Huntingdon Golf and Country Club, but the Williams family reserved the house and ten acres, where they still reside. Mr. Williams was elected reeve of Vaughan Township in 1969, and the first mayor of the Town of Vaughan.

George Witherspoon Family

The west half of Lot 5, Concession 9 is a Century Farm, having been in the Witherspoon family since 1869.

George Witherspoon and his wife, Eliza Shuttleworth, helped clear the land and built a log house and barn. They had two sons and three daughters: George, who never married, Albert James, Eliza (Mrs. William Appleton), Jessie (Mrs. Donald McPherson), and Jane.

Albert James, who married Edith Foster in 1891, continued to work the family farm. They built a large modern house and barn in the early 1900s. The barn was only up a few years when it was struck by lightning and burned to the ground. They rebuilt immediately and have since had very attractive farm buildings. They had one son and two daughters. When their son, William, was married to Annie Copeland about 1919, Albert and his wife retired. William farmed for about twelve years, and then bought a farm and dairy at Harriston, Ontario.

Albert's daughter, Viola, and her husband, Roy Livingston, took over the farm a few years later. They had four sons and one daughter. Their son, Gerald, and his wife, Lois Williams, now work the farm.

Peter Witherspoon Family

Peter Witherspoon settled in Vaughan Township on Lot 12, Concession 7, but moved to Lot 25, Concession 7 in 1863 when David, the youngest of three sons, was seven years old.

David's wife was Mary Elizabeth Blough, also born in Vaughan, near Teston. They had three sons, Frank, Wilbert, and Elmer, and two daughters, Florence, (Mrs. Garnet Hoover) and Annie (Mrs. Herbert Farr).

Elmer married Hortense Langford, a school teacher, and carried on the home farm. Today they still live on this Century Farm, as do their sons, Keith and Ross, who have built new homes for their families.

Witty Family

The Witty family came from Osprey Township to the Pine Grove area in Vaughan. They farmed Lots 10 and 11, Concession 6, and were in the area until Charlie Witty and his sisters passed away around 1950. John Witty's son, Michael, and later his son, Bert, farmed on the east part of Lot 10, Concession 3 for many years. There have been six generations of Wittys in the township.

Wray Family

John Wray came from England as early as 1829, and bought the east half of Lot 1, Concession 9 from James Armstrong. He cleared the land of virgin forest. John died in 1856 and his wife, Rebecca Marr, in 1863. They were buried in a family plot on the farm.

The farm was taken over in 1854 by their son, John, Jr., who was twice married, first to Grace Harland, then to Mary Pumfrey. He had two children by his first wife — Mary (Mrs. William Smith) and John — and ten by his second wife — Grace (Mrs. Jonathan Ellerby), William, Harriet, George, Elizabeth (Mrs. Charles Gardhouse), Martin, Rebecca, Sarah (Mrs. Neil McCallum), Annie, and Vina (Mrs. Elmer McCallum)

George, son of John, Jr., took over the farm and married Mary Robinson. They had five children. George sold milk, and each morning at 7 a.m. he met the milk wagon for Toronto at Albion Road. He was concerned that his daughters might lose the art of butter-making, so to solve the problem he bought a Jersey cow, and the girls not only supplied the family with butter, but had a surplus to sell.

George bought the Oliver Burton farm, Lot 2, Concession 9, and there he moved in 1920, his son William and his wife, Thelma Cowan, taking over the old homestead. On George's death, the family moved to Thistletown in 1946. Harold Barker took over Lot 2 in 1953, and Ross Barker Lot 1 in 1955.

Wright Families of Richmond Hill

There were several Wright families in Richmond Hill. One had as an ancestor Abraham Wright, who was born in New Haven, Vermont, in 1786. In 1815 that family came to Richmond Hill, farming on Yonge Street. A son, Amos, was elected to the Canadian Parliament, where he represented East, and later West, York for twenty years. In 1875 he became Dominion Auditor with the Department of Finance. His son, William, lived all his life in this district. William's son, Amos, had a son, Osmond, whose son is Dr. Laverne Wright.

Another Wright family came to Richmond Hill in 1871 when Archibald Wright, of a Loyalist family of Scottish descent, established a carriage building firm. His son, Ashford, was associated with his father in the business, which won awards at the Canadian Industrial Exhibition. Ashford became head of the firm of Wright Bros. Funeral Home, and later a senior partner in the firm of Wright and Taylor. He was a member of the choir for sixty-four years in the Methodist, later United, Church. His wife was Margaret McCague and they had two daughters, Margery (Mrs. Stewart L. Page) and Mildred (Mrs. A.S. Hardy Hill).

CHAPTER XI

Events

The Rebellion of 1837

Although the Rebellion of 1837 was something of a tempest in a tea pot, it had far-reaching effects. Like all events of this nature there were several causes, but basically the chief reason was the poor economic situation. Matters were further aggravated by two classes of Britishers: the well-to-do and domineering, such as the Gappers, the O'Briens, the Parsons, and the Family Compact, who looked down their noses at the 'Americans,' not realizing that if it hadn't been for them there would have been no sections of the province opened for them to exploit; and others — mostly Scottish labourers — who had emigrated after 1825 in the hope of becoming landowners but because of economic conditions were forced to continue as labourers.

Vaughan Township, as we have observed, had a large percentage of Germans who were either pacifists or had their fill of fighting. This possibly explains why William Lyon Mackenzie received little active support from that township, and those who did respond were located near Yonge Street. Of the 422 men who were imprisoned after the Rebellion in the Home District, only 12 belonged to Vaughan and these were not representative of the township's settlers. This doesn't mean that there weren't many sympathizers in Vaughan, but they took little active part. Those who were arrested were:

John Brown, Yeoman, Lot 1, Concession 2. As this lot was owned by the Canada Company in 1837, it was probably leased. Brown purchased it from the Canada Company in 1845.

Dougal Campbell, Yeoman, Lot 9, Concession 2, A Clergy Reserve lot leased by Campbell.

John Cherry, teacher, Lot 32, Concession 9. In 1837 this lot was owned by William Blakely, from whom Cherry bought it in 1851.

John N. Kline, labourer, Lot 12, Concession 4. This was a King's College lot purchased by Mr. Kline with a £600 mortgage in 1836.

John McCormack, physician, Lot 25, Concession 5. This lot had been a Crown Reserve lot which had been sold to the Canada Company in 1829. In 1836 the lot was purchased by Joel Kinnee. Probably McCormack was an absentee landlord.

John McDougall, labourer, Lot 15, Concession 3. In 1837 this lot belonged to King's College.

Peter Musselman, Yeoman, Lot 10, Concession 4. Peter Musselman had purchased this lot from his father, one of the original settlers, in 1836 for £100.

Joseph Noble, labourer, Lot 22, Concession 5. Noble purchased this lot from William B. Jarvis on March 30, 1836, for £25 in down payment and a mortgage for £180.

Adam Rupert, labourer, Lot 21, Concession 4. Rupert was a younger son of one of the original German settlers.

Peter Storey, labourer, Lot 23, Concession 3. Storey resided on the farm of Adam Sturm.

Thomas Thompson, labourer, Lot 37, Concession 1. Nothing is known.

Thomas Watts, Yeoman, Lot 24, Concession 4. Watts leased a King's College lot.

It will be noted that only two of the above list are professional men — John Cherry, teacher, and John McCormack, physician, both absentee owners. Most of the balance were either labourers or men with mortgages. With the exception of Adam Rupert and Peter Musselman, none had any connection with the original German settlers.

Nevertheless, there was considerable bitterness over the Rebellion. 'You are a rebel, or 'You are the son of a rebel,' were epithets when used at a mill or tavern which brought on many a fist fight.

While it lasted, the Rebellion provided much drama on Yonge Street. It failed in its immediate objective, which was to seize the government in Toronto in a surprise coup. Unfortunately, the date was moved forward from December 7 to December 4 without Mackenzie's knowledge; consequently, there was much confusion. Neither the full complement of men, nor Col. Von Egmont, who was to lead them, were available when needed. Food supplies also were lacking. Mackenzie might have been a good newspaperman and promoter, but he was far too fussy and uncertain in his plans to be a leader. Besides, the authorities in Toronto were warned ahead of time.

This warning came about through Richard Frizzell, 'a young Loyalist of convivial habits' who lived at the corner of John and Yonge Streets, Thornhill. He got wind of the proposed march on Toronto, evaded his mother who hid his clothes, tried to hire a horse unsuccessfully, and finally ended up by walking to Toronto. Although Mr. Thorne did not give him any assistance, he had given him his encouragement. Sir Francis Bond Head, the Lieutenant-Governor, impervious as usual to a strange idea, refused to believe Frizzell's story but others did, and a scouting party was sent out which discovered the rebel party.

In the meantime, Col. Moodie of Richmond Hill, Col. Bridgeford, and one other attempted to warn the Lieutenant-Governor. There were no mishaps until they reached the rebel headquarters at Montgomery's Tavern on Yonge Street, where they were challenged by a sentry. Col. Moodie shouted indignantly, 'Who are you to stop me on the Queen's highway? ' and rashly fired a shot, which was returned by the sentry. Moodie toppled from his horse, crying, 'I am shot, I am a dead man.' And so he was in two hours. He was buried in Trinity Anglican Church cemetery, Thornhill, a man who had gone safely through the Peninsula War and the Battle of Queenston Heights.

A bridge over the Humber on John Brown's property was

associated with William Lyon Mackenzie's escape to the United States. He described his flight in the following words:

Finding myself closely pursued and repeatedly fired at, I left the high road with one friend and made for Shepard's Mills. The fleetest horseman of the official party was so close upon us that I had only time to jump off my horse and ask the miller (he a Tory) whether a large body of men, then on the heights were friends or foes, before our pursuers were climbing up the steep ascent almost beside us. When I overtook Colonel Lount, he had, I think, about ninety men with him, who were partly armed. We had some refreshments at a friendly farmer's near by. Lount was for dispersing — I proposed that we should keep in a body, and make for the United States, but only sixteen persons went with us. I had no other arms but a single-barrel pistol, taken from Capt. Duggan during our Tuesday's scuffle, and we were all on foot.

We made for the Humber bridge through Vaughan, but found it was strongly guarded; then we went up the river some distance, got supper at the house of a farmer, crossed the stream on a foot bridge [this was on the John Elliot, Sr., farm] and by next morning reached the hospitable mansion of a worthy settler on Dundas Street, utterly exhausted and cold with fatigue.

The troops of Mackenzie were so poorly equipped and led that the Rebellion soon petered out, although many were arrested for their supposed support of it. Many spent some time in jail, where they were fed by their friends and relatives. In order to put in time they made trinkets of one kind or another. Col. Von Egmont became ill and died the day before his pardon was issued. Lount and Matthews, two of the leaders, were hanged, but Mackenzie escaped through the help of friends in the province to the United States. In 1849 he was pardoned and returned to Toronto; eventually he became a member of the Legislature for Haldimand, but later resigned because of impaired health. He died in 1861.

The Rebellion of 1837 threw a scare into the British Parliament and Sir Francis Bond Head was withdrawn. Lord Durham was sent out from England to make a study of the situation and a new era began for Upper Canada, not just politically, but also agriculturally. Vaughan Township farmers were quick to take advantage of their proximity to a growing city like Toronto and have never looked back.

Simon Miller of Unionville, in an interview with *The Sun* in July 1898, gave a first-hand picture of the early days and the Rebellion:

There was a black ash swamp a little way from Unionville here that was then full of wolves. One winter the Indians came and, camping in the woods, made war on the wolves and the animals were never so plentiful afterwards. The forest all about was full of the red men, and many a time a saddle of venison appeared on our table at home which was a gift from them.

At that time all the Indians from the north came down to Toronto every fall to receive the money and goods which the government gave them in return for the surrender of their lands. I have seen them marching past in twos and threes, magnificent specimens of manhood, their heads decorated with eagle plumes and carrying their war spears in their hands.

Too often, they came back in very different condition. The white man knew the Indian's fondness for whisky, and bad whites waylaid these children of the forest and offered them, when returning, fire-water in return for the supplies just received from the government. Frequently, by the time the Indians reached

Thornhill on the way home they had neither guns, blankets nor money, and had to beg their way back. Notwithstanding the manner in which the Indians were robbed, and despite the fact that they were armed, I never heard of a white man being killed during the orgies following the filling of the natives with whisky. Eventually, however, the scandal became so great that the government adopted the plan of paying the Indians at their reservation further north.

Simon Miller was a hale old gentleman who enjoyed life's evening in a beautiful home out at Unionville. He had as one of his most precious possessions a document signed by J.G. Simcoe and directed 'to the officer commanding at Fort Niagara.' The document is dated at Navy Hall, 29th day of April, 1793 — a time when Niagara was the seat of government for Upper Canada, and a British garrison still held the fort on the side of the Niagara River over which the Stars and Stripes float today. The document, made in accordance with an ordinance of the Governor and Council at Quebec, passed in the twenty-eighth year of the reign of George III, was 'to command and authorize you (the officer at Niagara) to permit Nicholas Miller, Asa Johnson, Jacob Phillips, Abraham and Isaac Devins and Jacob Schooner' to bring in free of duty from the United States, 'such goods and effects as household furniture, chairs, tables, chests of clothing,' etc.

Simon Miller himself was born in 1826, and his first clear recollections were of the Rebellion of 1837.

'They have been going down the road all night,' he heard the hired man tell his father one morning at breakfast. The 'they' were the followers of Mackenzie, who were then assembling at Montgomery's Tavern for the skirmish which ended so disastrously for them a little later.

Next day Mr. Miller was at the old Langstaff schoolhouse which had been started in 1811, held in check by the war, and finished in 1815. While puzzling over the 'three R's' a hoarse boom was heard coming over the hills in the direction of Hoggs Hollow. It was the opening gun fired by the forces of Sir Allan McNab. The teacher thought that when war was at the door it was time to dismiss school, and he told the pupils to go home. As young Miller was on his way he met a company of Highlanders headed by skirling bagpipes, coming out of Vaughan to join Mackenzie. But they were too late for the affair; the rebel leader was then in retreat, and the Highlanders returned home without even seeing the enemy.

'For weeks and weeks afterwards,' said Mr. Miller, 'loads of prisoners used to pass our door on the way to Toronto to stand their trial on the charge of treason. Many of these had been taken by men who had actually been implicated in the uprising and took this method to divert suspicion from themselves. But the tearing of the prisoners from their families was not the worst effect of the rebellion. The feuds it gave rise to lasted for generations, and for years afterwards the first taunt hurled during a quarrel was, 'you are a rebel' or, 'the son of a rebel.'

There are not many accounts of the time of the Rebellion from the original settlers. Jonathan Baker described the era in his quaint way:

A.D. 1837.

PROCLAMATION.

BY His Excellency SIR FRANCIS BOND HEAD, Baronet, Lieutenant Governor of Upper Canada, &c. &c.

To the Queen's Faithful Subjects in Upper Canada.

In a time of profound peace, while every one was quietly following his occupations, feeling secure under the protection of our Laws, a band of Rebels, instigated by a few malignant and disloyal men, has had the wickedness and audacity to assemble with Arms, and to attack and Murder the Queen's Subjects on the Highway—to Burn and Destroy their Property—to Rob the Public Mails—and to threaten to Plunder the Banks—and to Fire the City of Toronto.

Brave and Loyal People of Upper Canada, we have been long suffering from the acts and endeavours of concealed Traitors, but this is the first time that Rebellion has dared to shew itself openly in the land, in the absence of invasion by any Foreign Enemy.

Let every man do his duty now, and it will be the last time that we or our children shall see our lives or properties endangered, or the Authority of our Gracious Queen insulted by such treacherous and ungrateful men. MILITIA-MEN OF UPPER CANADA, no Country has ever shewn a finer example of Loyalty and Spirit than YOU have given upon this sudden call of Duty. Young and old of all ranks, are flocking to the Standard of their Country. What has taken place will enable our Queen to know Her Friends from Her Enemies—a public enemy is never so dangerous as a concealed Traitor—and now my friends let us complete well what is begun—let us not return to our rest till Treason and Traitors are revealed to the light of day, and rendered harmless throughout the land.

Be vigilant, patient and active—leave punishment to the Laws—our first object is, to arrest and secure all those who have been guilty of Rebellion, Murder and Robbery.—And to aid us in this, a Reward is hereby offered of

One Thousand Pounds,

to any one who will apprehend, and deliver up to Justice, WILLIAM LYON MACKENZE; and FIVE HUNDRED POUNDS to any one who will apprehend, and deliver up to Justice, DAVID GIBSON—or SAMUEL LOUNT—or JESSE LLOYD—or SILAS FLETCHER—and the same reward and a free pardon will be given to any of their accomplices who will render this public service, except he or they shall have committed, in his own person, the crime of Murder or Arson.

And all, but the Leaders above-named, who have been seduced to join in this unnatural Rebellion, are hereby called to return to their duty to their Sovereign—to obey the Laws—and to live henceforward as good and faithful Subjects—and they will find the Government of their Queen as indulgent as it is jus

GOD SAVE THE QUEEN.

Thursday, 3 o'clock, P. M.
7th Dec. 1837

☞ The Party of Rebels, under their Chief Leaders, is wholly dispersed, and flying before the Loyal Militia. The only thing that remains to be done, is to find them, and arrest them.

R. STANTON, Printer to the QUEEN'S Most Excellent Majesty.

EXECUTORS' SALE

of

FARM STOCK & IMPLEMENTS.

The Undersigned has received instructions from the Executors of the

LATE DANIEL REAMAN,

To sell by Public Auction, on Lot 10, Rear 2nd Con. Vaughan,

ON WEDNESDAY, MARCH 25TH, 1885,

The following valuable Farm Stock, Implements, &c.,

HORSES.
1 Span Horses, G. P.
1 Black Mare, 6 years old.
1 Driving Horse, 6 years old.
2 Colts, rising 2 years.

CATTLE.
3 Fresh Milch Cows.
3 Cows, in calf.
1 Heifer, 2 years old, in calf.
2 Heifers, 2 years old, in calf.

3 Heifers, 1 year old.   1 Bull.
1 Bull Calf, Thorough-Bred.
1 Fat Cow.   3 Fat Steers.

SHEEP.
7 Southdown Ewes.
9 Southdown Rams.
10 Cotswold Ewes.
2 Cotswold Rams.

PIGS.
6 Fat Pigs.   4 Store Pigs.

1 Brood Sow in Pig.
1 Berkshire Boar.

IMPLEMENTS.
1 Box Waggon.
1 Lumber Waggon.
1 Spring Waggon.
1 Cart & Harness.   1 Gig.
1 Bob-Sleigh.   1 Light Sleigh.
2 Cutters.   1 Cultivator.
1 Land Roller.   1 Clod Crusher.

1 One-Horse Land Roller.
1 Set Iron Harrows.
1 Set Grub Harrows.   1 Iron Plow.
1 Gang Plow.   1 Potato Harrow.
4 Other Plows.   1 Root Cutter.
1 Broadcast Seeder.   1 Cutting Box
2 Horse Rakes.   2 Fanning Mills.
2 Sets Team Harness.
1 Set Single Harness.
1 Steel Collar,and other articles.

SALE WITHOUT RESERVE !

Sale to Commence at 11 O'Clock.

LUNCH PROVIDED.

TERMS OF SALE :

For Fat Pigs, Fat Cattle and all sums of $10 and under, Cash;   over that amount Seven Months' Credit on approved joint notes.

SALEM ECKARDT, Auctioneer.

George Reaman, Isaac Reaman, John D. Reaman, Executors.

Concord, March 16th, 1885.   (LIBERAL PRINT, Richmond Hill.

Concerning the Rebellion, as for the excitement there was seemingly a threefold cause, whereas at that time there was yet fear among the white settlers of the Indians breaking out which in this part has now seemingly died out, there was the Indian scare and the rebel scare and lastly the scare caused by those who went out to arrest the rebels, and little doubt but that where the nerves were weakest the excitement would be greatest and in such case they, in general flock around those who seem strong in nerve. There was an old man who with his wife and five children came to Michael Bakers place Lot 13, in 2nd of Vaughan one night begging admittance with the seemingly rumour of hearing their next door neighbours north of them crying murder but as we never heard the slightest corroborating witness, it was without doubt imagination, only in some places those in a neighborhood would go together at one house for the night, only all this seemingly on account of the Indians which in the end proved to be a panic only; both the Indian trouble and Rebellion were in same year. As for the political trouble . . . those around us who we were best acquainted took no part . . . yet there were many somewhat panic-stricken through those who went out to arrest the rebels fearing they might be arrested as rebels. There were some who begged admittance again at Michael Bakers Lot 13 in 2nd of Vaughan but this time borrowed blankets and took to the barn for concealment, others took to the bush and whereas there were more than one company in the bush unknown to each other . . . the noise of leaves would sometimes . . . cause a panic . . . a farmer near where King Station now is said he and his hired man worked themselves in middle of straw mow for concealment. The chief cause of a rebellion in my opinion is because there are so few . . . who do unto others as they would have others do unto them . . . The first step in that line in our opinion is to guard against self . . .

Auction Sales

An auction sale in 1843 was held on Lot 22, Concession 7 to close the estate of John McBride and his wife Jane McNeil. The following is a record of it:

Livestock: 3 horses, 1 yoke of oxen, 5 cows, 4 heifers, 2 heifer calves, 2 steers, 5 sheep, 1 sow, 11 pigs, 16 geese (sold for £1)

Implements: 3 sickles, 1 scythe, 1 cradle, 1 double sleigh, 1 ox sleigh, 1 cutter, 1 plough, 1 drag, 1 shovel plough, 1 fanning mill, 1 wagon and rack, 1 saddle, 1 bridle, 1 bit, 1 string of bells, 2 sets of harness, 1 turnpike shovel, 1 cow bell, hoes, forks, rakes, spades and flails.

Other Goods: 1 grindstone, 1 lantern, 1 maul and wedge, 1 square, 1 logging chain, 2 wheel barrows, 2 bake kettles, 2 sugar kettles, 1 butt, 1 tea kettle, 2 barrels, 2 kegs, 2 jugs, 4 tables, 4 bedsteads, 1 churn, 2 flat irons, 1 clock and case (grandfather), 47 lbs. wool in rolls, 48 yds. fulled cloth, china and crockery, 1 military coat, 1 military cap, 1 military sash (Mr. McBride was a captain in the York Militia), 2 sets bed curtains, 1 decanter & glasses, 2 candle sticks, 2 steel yaws, 1 tea tray, 1 bread basket, 1 sword, 1 musket, 1 pistol.

Prices: large spinning wheel 10s, small spinning wheel £1, cow bells 10s, lumber £30, military coat £2 10s, military cap 5s, sword £2, musket £1, sash 15s, pistol 10s, 1 bed £3, 2 sets bed curtains £1 5s.

Purchasers: Mr. Ritchie, Mr. McCormack, Mr. Puterbaugh, Wm. Orr, Robert Irwin, Jas. White, Mr. Bigham, John McLean, Mr. Miller, Neil McDonald, Jr., Daniel Orr, Neil McDonald, Sr., James Orr, George Addy, Mr. Hemphill, Thos. Armstrong, Robert Johnson, Archie Cameron, Mr. Blackburn, Dougald Boyd, Duncan Beaton, Archie McDonald, Archie McDonald, Jr., Archie McDonald (7th Concession), John McDonald, Martin McLean, Arthur Cowan, Anthony McKinnon, Andrew Jamieson, Joseph Capner, Wm. McBride, Michael Piterman, James Adams, James Watson, William Beaton, Arthur McNeil.

Hogs and fat cow must have been slaughtered and sold for there is a record of beef, pork, tallow, lard and hide.

Total value of the sale was £225 5s 4½d. The fees of the auctioneer, clerk, and advertising amounted to £ 15s 3d. (Sales were often announced after church services.) The last item on the statement consisted of whiskey for the vendors, the wages for the man-servant, and the taxes on the farm. These amounted to 17s 6d. The crop of wheat, oats, and potatoes was also sold.

Barn Raisings

One of the most spectacular types of 'bee' in rural Ontario until very recently was the barn raising. Large barns no longer being essential because of the combine, such events no longer occur except in a county like Waterloo, where the Conservative Mennonites and Amish have not modernized their farm machinery.

However, as late as 1929 a barn raising was held on the farm of Charles Rutherford on Concession 6, just south of Vellore, which can be considered typical of the barn raisings of earlier times. The story of the event as reported in the Tweedsmuir History of the Vellore Women's Institute is as follows:

Hundreds were there from all parts of Vaughan, Albion, King, North York and Markham Townships as well as several visitors from Toronto and surrounding towns and villages. The barn, when completed, will be one of the largest in the district and in fact one of the largest in Ontario, is 130 long by 60 feet wide with an additional 74 feet by 24 feet. The stone wall is 204 feet around and the new barn will cover 9,588 sq. ft. It is about three times the size of the average barn which is 40 by 80 feet.

The new barn is on the farm which for years was in the MacNaughton family. Mr. Rutherford, formerly of Albion, purchased it some seven years ago from Mr. Alex MacNaughton. It is a fine 200 acre farm and is known as 'one of the best.'

The new barn was built under the direction of A.J. Saint of Bradford, and it reflects credit on his workmanship that the whole structure went together on Friday without a hitch. This is the 65th barn which Mr. Saint has built.

About 300 men took part in the actual raising operation and the floor was a mass of swarming men responding to the call of the leaders who encouraged and directed the work with the language peculiar to barn raisings and notable for the 'Yo Heave' so familiar to all those who have taken part in such events. A.L. McNeil and George Brownlee were the captains and they chose their sides in the time honoured fashion. In the final race George Brownlee's side won by a small margin.

After the work of the afternoon, the huge army of workers and spectators were fed on tables spread on the lawn. Hundreds of pies, cakes and tarts, hundreds of loaves of bread and pounds and pounds of meat were necessary to satisfy the hunger of the crowd. A glance at the cellar literally packed with eatables of all kinds was convincing evidence that all the work of the barn was not done by the men. The women folk surely had a herculean task as well, but it was done to the king's taste and there was plenty for all and some to spare.

The old barn which the new structure replaces was built 42 years ago. Some who were present on Friday were also present at the raising of the old barn. Among those who could recall being at the event were Deputy-Reeve J.T. Saigeon and Mr. Dugald McIntyre, Vaughan Township tax collector.

Four movie camera men from the Ontario Government Moving Picture Bureau were on hand and took movies of the operations throughout the afternoon.

In the evening a real old-time dance was held and it attracted young people from all parts of York County. Henderson's Orchestra of Bolton supplied the music.

The early Pennsylvania settlers built large log barns designed in a distinctive style, which they introduced into Upper Canada because they kept more cattle than was usual on the frontier. Such barns are virtually all gone today, but there are still at least two in Vaughan Township. This type of barn cost four times as much to build as an ordinary log barn and could be built only where good stands of pine were handy. They were built of logs hand-dressed with an adze, carefully notched, and dovetailed at the ends. Large supporting timbers across the stable top projected nearly eight feet beyond one wall to provide a characteristic cantilever overhang. The full diameter of the trees used must have been 20 to 26 inches.

The barn raisings in that period were different from later raisings. The log barn's main structures were two square mows interlocked at the corners 'dove-tail' fashion from ground to roof. The timbers were perfectly hewn and the ends rough dovetailed, and all timbers were made ready for the big event. The neighbours came from surrounding townships, for it required a lot of help to handle the quantity of heavy freshly-cut timber. Four expert carpenters stood at their places to put the finishing touches on the technical corners. The helpers would put the log in place on its edge while these experts decided if and where more trimming was needed. Then the log would be turned back on the skid and held there until the carpenters were satisfied it was now ready to put it in place. Always there were two opposite logs being put up together. When one pair of east and west logs was in place, next would be a north and south pair. Each carpenter stayed at his corner and attended to the logs as they were rolled up. One wonders what food the ladies served. Most of these log barns were built before 1830 and some, we know, as early as 1808.

Soap Making
In the days when the farm was self-sufficient, the making of soap was part of the work of the housewife. Soap-boiling involved an important basic rule in rural economy — never throw away anything that can be used or re-used on the farm. In this case fat scraps and drippings were saved and transformed, through chemical action with lye, into homemade soap. Even the lye was homemade, from the wood-ash residue from kitchen fires.

The ash leach was usually a permanent fixture in some out-of-the-way corner of the back yard. It was frequently built in the form of a hopper about four feet square at the top. In the leach was placed first a layer of straw, then a quantity of lime, and on that the hardwood ashes. Soft water was then poured on, which, as it soaked through, dissolved the alkaline salt. Rain water was particularly good for this purpose. The lye was caught at the bottom of the hopper in an iron kettle. When soap was being made, the kettle was hung on a pole supported at each end. A brisk fire was built under the kettle and kept going all day. When fat was put in the lye, it made soft soap. To get hard soap, longer boiling was necessary and the addition of a little salt. Soft soap was used for cleaning cooking utensils. With hot water in a pail and an old broom, it whitened the board walks. Hard soap was used for washing the hands and, before other soaps were available, for bathing purposes.

To make soap successfully, the pioneer woman always made it in the right time of the moon. For these Germans the almanac was most important, for it gave them the changes of the moon. Of course scientists pooh-poohed such beliefs, but probably there is a kernel of truth in all such legends. No one disputes the effect of a beautiful moonlit night on a man and a maid.

The Tragedy of Thomas Kinnear and Nancy Montgomery
In the summer of 1843 and for some time previously, Thomas Kinnear resided about a mile north of Richmond Hill. He was well off and had Nancy Montgomery as housekeeper. James McDermott, an Irish lad of twenty, and Grace Marks, also Irish, a girl of sixteen, were the servants. They became envious and very dissatisfied.

The two servants believed that Mr. Kinnear intended to bring a considerable amount of money with him on his return from a trip to Toronto, and plotted together. Nancy was their first victim. Later they shot Mr. Kinnear. After rifling the body for keys and money, McDermott and Grace Marks harnessed the horse and set out for the United States, planning to be married. About 5 a.m., however, Mr. Kingswell, the high bailiff, came and arrested them at Lewiston.

McDermott was sentenced to be hanged. The girl was also found guilty, but because of her youth and good looks, she was sentenced to be imprisoned for life in Kingston Penitentiary. Years later, after many petitions for her release, she was given a pardon. She then went to New York, where she changed her name and soon afterwards married.

Singing Schools
Throughout the latter part of the nineteenth century singing schools were quite popular. The singing school at Vellore was organized on February 27, 1868. The following are the minutes and the names of class:

At a meeting held at Vellore, Mr. Cameron, being in the chair, stated the object of the meeting, was to make arrangements to form a singing class to be held in the schoolhouse. It was moved, seconded and carried that we employ Mr. Peter Lawrence to teach the class. The names of those present being subscribed it was proposed that Arthur McNeil and Charles McLean be appointed to see parties not present at the meeting. Salary of teacher $26 for 13 lessons. Number of nights each week — 3. Mode of teaching — by note. Place — log schoolhouse.
Members of the Class: Donald McKechnie, Duncan McArthur, Donald Cameron, John Frank, Jr., John McLean, Arch'd Cameron, Charles McLean,Jr., Alex McNeil, Alex McNeil, Jr., James McNeil, Charles McLean, Wm. Kyle, Peter McNaughton, George Peterman, James O'Connor, Wm. J.G. Constable, Donald McDonald, Samuel McDonald, Wm. Watson, Nancy Cameron, Flora Malloy, Louisa Frank, Margaret McArthur, Nancy McArthur, Catherine McLean, Barbara Smith, Ann Jane Kyle, Mandy Frank, Eliza Jane Frank, Christina McNaughton, Flora McDonald, Agnes Bell, Mary McDonald, Ellen Watson.

At Edgeley, Jacob Hoover conducted a singing school in the homes of the various members. Michael Burkholder followed him, with William Locke the third conductor. Concerts were given in neighboring towns and villages for a number of years. Mrs. William Locke was accompanist. Some of the members of the Edgeley group were Robert Holland, William Locke (Bass), George Boynton, Lloyd Watson (first tenor), George Watson (2nd tenor). Among their popular songs was 'A Little Farm well Tilled' and a round 'When You Go A-Courtin' '.

Hallowe'en Pranks

Hallowe'en in the early days was a time for serious pranks, as can be seen from the following examples.

At the Langstaff corner, Mr. John Langstaff had a pail factory. Part of his equipment was a pair of wheels more than six feet tall, and an axle and chain, used to haul large logs into the factory by means of a team of oxen. The pranksters seized the wheels and hoisted them to the roof of Cook's Hotel. How they ever managed to do this is hard to imagine, for the wheels were very heavy and awkward to handle. The men of the village had great difficulty in getting them down the next day.

Another practical joke played at Langstaff was to frighten people with a make-believe ghost. The 'spirit' was a sheet stuffed with straw and strung with wire so that it might be lowered in front of an unsuspecting villager. This went on until one man was so frightened that he went into hysterics. That put an end to the ghost at Langstaff.

Two young lads in the 1870s had a mania for stealing ducks and chickens. Again and again raids were made on chicken coops and the stolen fowl were stored in an out-of-the-way shed. After a while some of the boys of the village located this hideout and set the fowl free. Mrs. Biddy Greaves of Thornhill was one of those who had had her hens stolen and she went down to claim them. The neighbors wondered how she would pick them out but it was a simple matter for her. All her birds had been named and when she called them they gathered around her. It must have been an amusing sight to see her coming home followed by a line of hens.

The Water Witch and his Craft

'Water witching' is still practised in many areas today. It can be done by a man or a woman, but only certain persons, depending on the sign of the moon when you were born, can successfully discover where water can be located. No explanation has ever been found for it but the fact is that a water smeller can often discover where the well should be dug when drilling has failed.

A water smeller's equipment consists of a divining rod. A green apple, peach, willow, or hazel forked twig serves best. In more recent years a pair of pliers or an aluminum rod have been used. With the twig firmly grasped in his two thumbs and forefingers in front of him, and the butt end pointing upward or outward, the water smeller strolls across the area in which the well is to be located. After ranging back and forth over the area, he will have narrowed down the location to several sites by the degree of pull of the underground stream. The stronger the flow, the harder the pull. Sometimes the force or pull is so great that the divining rod jerks from his hands, rotates at such rapid speed as to cause blisters on his hands, or (if it is a twig) twists off completely from the force. The twig may twist in such a fashion as to loosen the bark in the holder's hands.

Sometimes water finders use a straight green twig about three feet in length and the thickness of a thumb and finger at the heavy end. By holding the thin end of the twig with both hands several inches from the ground, they can feel a sensation or pull on the rod when they come upon a vein. The butt end will move vertically back and forth. By counting the number of dips, the water smeller can determine the depth of the stream and suggest how far down the water is from the surface.

Samuel Winger, Lot 15, Concession 3, was a noted water diviner in Vaughan Township. He discovered wells for the Water Resources Commission in the Township.

Floods and Ice Storms

From time to time floods washed out dams and ruined mills. In April 1850, the Don River was in flood and washed out a section of Yonge Street 100 feet in length. This flood destroyed or wrecked McDougall's Mill dam, tannery, and mill and John Brunskill's mills on John Street. In March 1857, another freshet flooded homes and ravines on Yonge Street, doing considerable damage.

In September 1878, following a three-day rainfall, five inches of rain fell. The bridge at Thornhill was the first washed out. North of Concord, a washout stopped the southbound Northern Railway train. Altogether some 30 dams and 20 bridges were destroyed. Road repairs were extensive, and many mills never were rebuilt.

In 1893 an ice storm destroyed pine trees all through Vaughan, many of them 300 years old. In one bush alone, 93 first-growth pines were blown down and in the following year 39 more died from effects of the storm. Only four were left, and by 1917 only one. When the pines were destroyed the hardwoods took over and black raspberry bushes grew in quantity. People from surrounding villages came and picked them.

The most recent major flood followed 'Hurricane Hazel' on October 15, 1954. Vaughan Township suffered a terrific loss, both on the Don River side and the Humber River side. Heavy rains began early in the morning and winds of high velocity toppled trees, broke down wires, and flooded the Thornhill area as far south as Morgan's Hill. Bridges were swept away. At Concord the underpass on Number 7 Highway was filled. Commuters were unable to reach their homes and had to be put up by friendly citizens, but there was no loss of life.

In the Woodbridge area the dams on the Humber at Pine Grove and Woodbridge were swept away, and the buildings on the low lands were destroyed or carried down the river. Ten lost their lives in the

A barn raising on Charles Rutherford's farm, just south of Vellore, on July 26, 1929. About 300 men took part in the actual raising under the direction of A.J. Saint of Bradford. A.L. McNeil and George Brownlee were captains and chose sides in the time-honoured fashion.

Later the same day. The workers ate at long tables on the lawn and in the evening enjoyed an old-tyme barn dance.

The Woodbridge and District Memorial Arena in Woodbridge was opened in 1951 as a tribute to the men and women who served in the second world war.

Woodbridge area, and hundreds had to be sheltered, fed and clothed. Destruction was such that it became a provincial government matter. The Red Cross directed emergency activities, and portable houses were set up in the Fair Grounds. Compensation was given to those who had lost their homes. Future building in certain areas was prohibited.

In Memory: Two World Wars

In the spring of 1919 a celebration was held in the fair grounds at Woodbridge for the returned men of Woodbridge and Vaughan Township. The master of ceremonies was Ellerby Farr, manager of the Bank of Nova Scotia in Woodbridge. The crowd that gathered was like a Fair Day, and the weather was bright and sunny. Each mother who had a son killed while serving in the war overseas received a gold medal. Each man serving in the forces was presented with a Waltham gold watch.

At another ceremony nearly four decades later, on Remembrance Day, November 11, 1947, Vaughan Township Council remembered those who had lost their lives in the second world war. On behalf of the ratepayers, a Bible with a suitable inscription was presented to the next of kin. Beige travelling bags were presented to fourteen girls, and the boys received brown leather bags with the inscription 'Township of Vaughan for service rendered, 1939-45.' The Township Hall at Vellore was decorated with Union Jacks and the Canadian Ensign, and filled to capacity. Reeve Boynton Weldrick was chairman. Jack Smith, M.P., and Major Lex Mackenzie, M.P.P., spoke briefly. The guest speaker, Rev. W.F. Wrixon of Richmond Hill, Rural Dean of West York and Chaplain to the Forces of Richmond Hill and Vaughan Township, was introduced by Rev. Bowman. The service opened with 'O Canada' and closed with 'God Save the King.' Refreshments were served by Vellore Women's Institute.

The men of Vaughan Township who lost their lives in two world wars are listed on a memorial plaque in Vaughan Municipal Office.

1914-1918

Agar, M.J.	Keen, Irwin
Bowes, Edgar	Lendrum, Harry
Burgess, Frank	Little, Reginald
Cooper, Arthur	McDonald, John
Cordery, Albert E.	McGillivray, Wm. B.
Coward, Wm.	Nash, Charles
Evans, Fred	Phillips, Roscoe
Fleming, Norman	Raeside, Robert
Gardiner, Mons W.	Robb, Stanley D.
Grady, John J.	Scott, Alfred
Green, T.A.	Scott, John
Houghton, G.R.	Ward, John W.
Howard, Geo.	Warrell, Stanley
Jackes, F.P.	Witherspoon, David

1939-1945

Adams, George C.	
Bales, George E.	Brownlee, John B.
Bales, Thomas I.	Dix, Walter
	Eberle, Raymond F.

Ezard, Howard R.
Findlay, Wm. J.
Good, Ernest A.
Gourlie, D. James
Hill, Charles
Kerswill, James G.
Maxey, Wilfred R.
McNeil, Cameron L.

Norton, John E.
Norton, Joseph E.
Sanford, Norman
Smith, James
Sparkes, Raymond R.
Stapley, John
Thompson, Louis
Wice, Russell

Maple Artificial Breeding Association

Vaughan Township has the credit for setting up the first well-organized artificial breeding plant. Actually the first attempt was made at Hespeler, then Waterloo, but there was too little known about it to be successful. The pattern set up in Vaughan had the support of the Ontario Livestock Branch of the Department of Agriculture, and it became the model for other stations to follow.

On January 12, 1945, a meeting was held at the home of Roland Keffer, at Maple, with fifteen persons present, to discuss the question of artificial insemination. At this meeting G. Wilfred Keffer was elected president, with Jim Darlington as secretary. It was decided to hold an organization meeting on January 29, 1945, in the Vellore Hall, and to invite W.P. Watson, assistant director of the Ontario Livestock Branch, to speak.

At that meeting, the following directors were appointed: G.W. Keffer, Maple; Norman Porter, Richmond Hill; R.J. Darlington, Maple; Fraser Gee, Gormley; Russell Rowntree, Woodbridge; secretary-treasurer, J.M. Macdonald, Maple, the clerk of Vaughan, who offered his services free for one year.

The directors were to canvass the area; if the farmers showed sufficient interest, they were to go ahead with the project. The objective was 100 members owning 1,200 cows.

The club purchased an old barn and an acre of land at Maple from Mrs. George Bailey and remodelled it to have two box stalls, two single stalls with safety aisles at each of them, and a breeding pen.

Four bulls were purchased, including a four-year-old double grandson of Montvic Rag Apple Netherland, from Lloyd Turner of Stouffville. The other bulls, sired by Lonelm Texal Fayne, were bought from Stanley B. Watson, Agincourt, W.J. McEvoy, Glanford Station, and a yearling from the partnership of Alex Forrest and Gordon Watson, Maple.

On June 5, 1945, the barn was officially opened with some 150 in attendance. G. Wilfred Keffer asked W.M. (Moff) Cockburn, agricultural representative for York County, to act as chairman. He in turn introduced Mr. Watson; Professor R.G. Knox, head of the Department of Animal Husbandry, O.A.C.; L.E. O'Neill, director of the Live Stock Branch; Dr. C.R. Reeds, technician; Dr. A. Moynihan of the Health of Animals Branch; C.D. Graham, supervisor of agriculture representatives; and George C. Jackson, president of the Holstein-Friesian Association of Canada.

Membership was open to owners of grade, accredited, and listed herds within a ten-mile radius of Maple. This was later changed to include York County, and in 1946 Simcoe County. With the discovery of frozen semen, it was extended to anywhere in the world.

Today the organization is known as the United Breeders, Inc. of Guelph. The new headquarters building was officially opened June 20, 1970, by the Right Honorable Pierre Elliott Trudeau, Prime Minister of Canada.

Southern Ontario Research Station
This experimental station, situated on Lots 23-25, west half of Concession 2, one and a quarter miles east of Maple, was started in 1945. It was built there because it was felt that many problems could be worked out only in a rural or semi-rural setting. Many activities in connection with the Department of Forestry were moved out from Queens' Park. Research has included testing of fire-fighting equipment, highways materials, aerial photography, and studies in wildlife. A main radio station was set up here in 1950 which is in constant contact with forest rangers and other government workers in isolated parts of the province.

Official Opening of the Municipal Building, Maple
At the official opening of the new Municipal Building of Vaughan Township at Maple on September 19, 1957, Scott McNair was chosen to represent all the public-spirited citizens who had served the township in former years. Mr. McNair, 95, a former reeve, at that time residing with his daughter at Brampton, cut the ribbon to officially open the building. Mr. McNair had served on the Council from 1904 to 1916 continuously with the exception of 1907, and was reeve in 1915 and 1916. He was assisted in the ceremony by Master Ross McMurchy, two-and-a-half-year-old son of Marshall McMurchy, another former reeve. In 1957 the reeve was J.W. Perry, and J.M. McDonald was clerk.

J.W. Perry acted as chairman at this ceremony. Many dignitaries were present, including Reeve W.J. Taylor of Richmond Hill, the warden of York County. Members of the Vaughan Township Council present were Deputy-Reeve Robert Kirk and Councillors W. Anstey, and J. Bryson, besides three members of the preceding Council, M. McMurchy, W.J. Agar, and J. Reid.

Groups of army, navy, and air force men as well as members of the Canadian Legion were present. A wreath was placed and the Last Post played at the War Memorial in the rotunda of the building.

Kleinburg Binder Twine Festival
In 1967, when Canada was celebrating its one hundredth birthday and every city, town, and little hamlet throughout the land was commemorating the event, the Kleinburg Rotary Society, under its president, Vic Ryder, an old Kleinburg boy, decided to hold a Shaw's Binder Twine Festival as Kleinburg's celebration and try to enjoy again the pleasures of that big event. The idea met with the approval of every one. All organizations and citizens, old families and new families,

including Pierre Berton, a well-known Canadian author and his family, co-operated and made it an outstanding success.

The Shaw's Binder Twine Festival was held on Saturday September 9, 1967, from 1 p.m. until midnight. It took place in the same old place, with a platform built in front of Shaw's house, and the main street closed off with the same detour as in earlier days. Booths for selling food were set up on the Shaw property. In MacEachern's field, behind Shaw's, were all kinds of games of chance and pony rides. During the festival, a full program provided a variety of pleasure including bands, a pet parade, a parade of decorated bicycles and doll carriages, the newly-formed fire brigade display, an antique car rally, a homemade apple pie contest, a Centennial Costume parade with prizes, a magician, and a street dance until midnight with both young and old style bands. The apple pie contest was won by a life time resident and one of the oldest residents, Mrs. Albert Devins. (The prize was a vacuum cleaner, donated by Gordon A. MacEachern.)

Many former residents were among the large crowd attending and they enjoyed a visit to the old hardware store, now run by Mr. and Mrs. Frank Shaw, a grandson of the late Charles Shaw, Jr. The Shaw family co-operated in every way with the celebration. Many of them wore old-fashioned costumes and the prize for the girl's costume was won by little Kathaleen Shaw, daughter of Frank Shaw, while the boy's prize was won by Wayne Kitchen of Schomberg, a grandson of Mrs. Earl Shaw. Frank also had some old-time merchandise on display in the store.

The Binder Twine Festival was such a success that it was decided to hold it every year.

Well framed doors

CHAPTER XII

Societies and Organizations

Women's Institutes

The Women's Institute, now a worldwide organization, was founded by Mrs. Adelaide Hoodless. Her maiden name was Adelaide Hunter and she was born in a house just off Number 5 Highway between Brantford and St. George's in Brant County, Ontario.

Adelaide's only formal education was at St. George Public School. She married a well-to-do Hamilton businessman, John Hoodless. In those days one child in five died and every family had its small graves in the churchyard. Her family was no exception, for she lost a baby and learned that its death had been caused by contaminated milk. She was shocked that she herself could be so negligent. She was also aware that farmers trusted their prize animals only to qualified men, but for their children's care anyone would do.

With all this in mind she set out to educate girls and women about sanitation, economics, hygiene, value of food and fuel, and more scientific care of children. Her first step toward her goal was when, as president of the Hamilton Y.W.C.A., she attended the World Conference of Representative Women in Chicago in 1893. In 1895 she started a household science class in the Hamilton Y.W.C.A. and, using her own words, 'I started my class alone and in a small way, but in strong faith.' There was criticism. People asked if mothers hadn't time to teach their daughters household duties at home and why Mrs. Hoodless wouldn't stay at home and look after her own family.

As she believed that the management of the home had more to do with the moulding of character than any other influence, she, on one occasion, stated that there was justification for any effort to secure a place for home economics and domestic science in educational institutions. She frequently used such sayings as, 'You purify society when you purify the home,' 'A nation cannot rise higher than the level of its homes,' and, 'The welfare of the family underlies the welfare of society.'

In 1907, in Nova Scotia, a Teachers' Training School and a domestic course were introduced with success. Ontario centres began to ask for teachers. Public opinion was strongly in favour or Mrs. Hoodless's ideas and support grew. Sir William Macdonald was persuaded to donate $125,000 for a domestic science building at the Ontario Agricultural College, Guelph, and in 1904 the Macdonald

Institute was opened, with Mrs. Hoodless as one of the teachers.

In the winter of 1896 a young farmer from Stoney Creek, Erland Lee, had heard Mrs. Hoodless argue that if men could benefit by banding together to work and study, women could do likewise. He asked her to speak at a meeting in Stoney Creek and she agreed. The outcome was that on February 19, 1897, one hundred and one women responded to her call to form an association dedicated to building a better nation by building better homes. Thus was formed the first Women's Institute, which is now so wide and favourably known an organization throughout twenty-seven countries. Mrs. Hoodless passed away in the midst of her work, for she was stricken with a heart attack in 1910 while addressing the Women's Canadian Club of Toronto about the need for larger and more advanced teachers' training colleges in domestic sciences. She faltered, took a sip of water, collapsed, and died in a few minutes.

Her original home now belongs to the Women's Institute of Ontario and has become a historic site. In 1959 a Canadian postage stamp was issued commemorating the World-Wide Organization of Women's Institutes.

Maple Women's Institute was one of the earliest in the province, perhaps the second. In April 1898 it was organized by Miss Maddock, with Miss Jennie Rumble as president and Miss F. Thomas (Mrs. Wm. Cook) as secretary. The first meeting was held in an old shed at the hotel known as Richardson's, where dances were also held. Early members as recorded in district books were: Mrs. H.C. Bailey, Mrs. T. Cousins, Mrs. C. Crooks, Mrs. M. Craddock, Miss E. Campbell, Mrs. N.L. Cook, Mrs. C. Crooks, Mrs. W.A. Coneil, Mrs. G.J. Cook, Miss A. Gordon, Mrs. Geo. Garrow, Miss M. Hezzelwood, Miss H. High, Mrs. J. Kirby, Mrs. T. Keys, Mrs. J. Manning, Mrs. D. McMillan, Miss B. McNaughton, Mrs. M. Nixon, Miss Gertie Nixon, Mrs. James Oliver, Miss J. Oliver, Miss Jennie Rumble, Miss Ida Rumble, Miss Lizzie Rumble, Mrs. W. Sisley, Mrs. N. Shunk, Miss F. Thomas, Miss Flo. Traviss, Mrs. H. Thomas, and Mrs. Wm. Thomas.

The meeting on May 31, 1904, was held in Maple Public Library with 23 present. Mrs. Torrance of Quebec spoke on 'The Apple and its Relation to Domestic Comfort.' Miss Shuttleworth spoke on 'Cold Dishes for Summer Use.' The 50th, 60th and 65th anniversaries of the founding of this Institute were attended by many members of neighboring institutes. At the 50th anniversary there were two women who had been members for all fifty years, Mrs. H.C. Bailey and Mrs. Joshua Manning.

The Kleinburg and Nashville Women's Institute was organized in February 1900, by Miss Laura Rose at a meeting held in the Gobeil Hotel, Kleinburg. There are no records of the beginning of the branch since the first minute book to 1906 was lost. The first known officers were for the 1904-05, when the president was Mrs. Ed. Bray and the secretary Miss Ella Wardlaw (now Mrs. Albert Devins). Three charter members are known to have been Mrs. Peter Wardlaw, Mrs. Douglas

McDonald, and Mrs. Robert Watson. Nashville was added to the name in 1908 when a number of ladies from that community joined. Meetings were held monthly and membership varied from five or seven in 1900 to ten in 1906, 43 in 1910-11, and 44 in 1914-16. The branch is unusual in that it owned a hall where its meetings were held, and which was also rented to other organizations. The hall was sold in November 1960.

Thornhill Women's Institute was organized on February 21, 1902, and has been very active in service work in the village. In 1963 the branch gave $1,300 to furnish a room in York Central Hospital in Richmond Hill. Presidents have been: Mrs. David James (1902-1915), Mrs. S.W. Moyle, Mrs. Andrew Hall, Mrs. Robert Thompson, Mrs. O. James, Mrs. James Pearson, Mrs. Wm. Riddell, Mrs. R. Holmes, Mrs. P. Bone, Mrs. H. Swabey, Mrs. Evan McKeen, Mrs. S.S. Findlay, Mrs. C. Sinclair, Mrs. A.W. Crowhurst, Mrs. C. Clifford, Mrs. C. Thompson, Mrs. C.J. Sinclair, Mrs. Mizen, Mrs. R. Holmes, Mrs. Ann Jackson.

The Women's Institute of Woodbridge was organized in 1904 with Mrs. W.O. Duncan as president, Mrs. George Sutton, secretary, and Miss Mabel Wise, treasurer. At the first meeting there were only six ladies present; Mrs. N. Clarke Wallace, Mrs. William Watson, Mrs. William Farr, Mrs. Duncan, Mrs. Sutton, and Miss Irene Wallace. By the end of the first year the membership was fifty-seven. Presidents through the years were: Mrs. W.O. Duncan, Mrs. W. Jackson Farrand, Mrs. Arthur Harris, Miss Minnie Elliot, Miss Lillian McNeil, Mrs. Fred Hicks, Mrs. William Mitchell, Mrs. Arthur Hollingshead, Mrs. George Bagg, Mrs. Russell Ward, Mrs. Henry N. Smith, Mrs. John Robb, Mrs. James Elliot, Mrs. Charles Rutherford, Mrs. William Bryant, Mrs. Douglas McDonald, and Mrs. Mary Chapman. This branch of the Institute disbanded in 1964 on its Sixtieth Anniversary.

Edgeley Women's Institute was organized on January 23, 1913, at the home of Mrs. J.W. Dalziel, by Mrs. W.O. Duncan, West York district president and Mrs. Lambie, the district secretary. Officers elected were: Mrs. Edgar Kennedy, president; Mrs. Fred Bagg, first vice-president; Mrs. J.W. Dalziel, second vice-president; Miss V. Aitcheson, secretary-treasurer, Mrs. Jas. Mitchell, Mrs. James Robb, and Mrs. Bagg, directors; Mrs. Alfred Bagg and Miss Gertrude Locke, music committee. The 50th Anniversary was celebrated in the same home and with the same hostess. Many former members attended, including three charter members, Mrs. Dalziel, Mrs. Alfred Bagg, and Mrs. Leslie Robb (Gertie Locke). Presidents through the years have been: Mrs. J.W. Dalziel, Mrs. Jesse Keffer, Mrs. Welsey Stong, Mrs. George Brintnell, Mrs. Ed. Phillips, Mrs. J.G. Snider, Mrs. Robert Mitchell, Mrs. Clarence Stong, Mrs. Paul Snider, Mrs. Eldon Fierheller, Mrs. Charles Agnew, Mrs. James Spencer, Mrs. A.W. Cook, Mrs. R.J. Darlington, Mrs. Fred Bodker, Mrs. C.H. Boake, Mrs. Frank Locke, and Mrs. Bruce Snider.

Richmond Hill Women's Institute was formed on January 27, 1913, at a meeting in the Masonic Hall. Miss Lulu Reynolds, district secretary for East York, was the organizer and conducted the first election of officers: Miss A. Trench, president; Mrs. J. Switzer, vice-president; Miss Bertha Palmer, secretary-treasurer; Miss H. Pentland, district representative. Monthly meetings were held first on the second Wednesday of each month, and later on the second Thursday. The office of president was held by: Miss A. Trench, Miss A. Moyle, Mrs. A.L. Phipps, Mrs. J. Smith, Mrs. G. Yerex, Mrs. T. Moore, Mrs. G. Irwin, Mrs. W. Sayers, Mrs. H. Mackay, Mrs. L. Zuefelt, and Mrs. James Pollard. The Tweedsmuir history was begun in 1949 by Mrs. L. Zuefelt who carried on until 1955 when Mrs. F.S. Rumble took over. Mrs. C.E. Little and Miss Mary Dawson were members of the committee in 1949. This Institute took a lively interest in agriculture and Canadian industries, citizenship and education, community activities, and public relations, particularly during the world wars. It ceased to exist in 1964.

The Vellore Women's Institute was formed on July 10, 1915, when seventeen ladies met in the Township Hall. They were: Mrs. Andrew McNeil, Mrs. Alex Cameron, Mrs. Richard Jarrett, Mrs. Milton McDonald, Mrs. Duncan McKinnon, Mrs. George Bishop, Mrs. David Blain, Mrs. William Bates, Mrs. A.L. McNeil, Miss K. McNaughton, Miss Mary Cameron, Miss Lizzie Fenwick, Miss Susie Fenwick, Miss Gertie Wilson, Miss Gladys Hesp, Miss Louise McDonald, and Mrs. W.O. Duncan, the district president. The following officers were elected: Mrs. D. McKinnon, president; Mrs. R. Jarrett, first vice-president; Mrs. M. McDonald, second vice-president; Mrs. A.L. McNeil, secretary-treasurer; Mrs. Bishop, Mrs. Blain, Mrs. Bates, and Miss S. Fenwick, directors. It was decided to meet the fourth Thursday of each month. Among members who joined the first year were Mrs. Ernest Carson, Mrs. Jack McNeil, Miss Annie Kerr, and Mrs. David Julian. The last three and four charter members, Mrs. A.L. McNeil, Mrs. Elmer Bryson (Mary Cameron), Mrs. William Snider (Lizzie Fenwick), and Mrs. James Brownlee (Louise McDonald) are still members today.

The Burwick Women's Institute of Woodbridge was organized as a Junior Institute, at the close of a short course in 1925, with forty-three members. The first officers were: Annie McCallum, president; Margaret Watson, secretary; Alma Weatherill, treasurer. In 1938 the name was changed to Burwick Women's Institute, after the former name of the Village of Woodbridge. Presidents through the years: Miss Annie McCallum, Miss Annie Kersey, Miss Estelle Standen, Mrs. Harry Fieldhouse, Miss Agnes McCallum, Miss Margaret Wallace, Miss Evelyn Brown, Mrs. Leo Watson, Mrs. George Stewart, Mrs. Alvin Wood, Mrs. Goldwin Vanderburgh, Mrs. Roy Barker, Mrs. Gordon Miller, Mrs. Arthur Howl, Mrs. Harry Wood, Mrs. Robert Mitchell, Mrs. Clarence Graham, Mrs. Everard Kellam, Mrs. Joseph Weatherill, Mrs. Herb Farr, Mrs. Lorne Barker, and Mrs. Gordon Miller.

The Elders' Mills Women's Institute was organized on May 2, 1949, at the home of Mrs. Garnet Williams with the following officers elected: Mrs. Roy Arlow, president; Mrs. Robert Burton, vice-president; Mrs. John Boddy, second vice-president; Mrs. Edward Roden, secretary; Mrs. Don McCallum, treasurer. Mrs. William Lawrie, Mrs. Chas. Johnston, and Mrs. Edward Whitworth, directors; Mrs. Garnet Williams, district director. The other charter members were: Mrs. Bert Douglas, Mrs. Earl Risebrough, Mrs. Lawrence Dicks, Mrs. Arthur Dalziel, Mrs. Pearson Neal, Mrs. Joseph Kersey, Mrs. Gordon Miller, Mrs. Allan Craggs, Mrs. Frances Murray, Mrs. Roscoe Peacock, Mrs. Norman Wiley, Mrs. John Hostrawser, Mrs. Gordon McGillivray, Mrs. John Hostrawser, Sr., Mrs. Reginald Robinson, Mae Kersey, Mrs. Gordon Williams, Mrs. Audrey Brass and Mrs. Roy Barker.

The Mark-Vaun Women's Institute really began on August 17, 1950, when a group of ladies met and formed a homemakers' club. In 1951 they became a Women's Institute with Mrs. A.T. Matthews as the first president. Other presidents have been Mrs. H. Morrison, Mrs. H. Glassey, Mrs. M. Roy, Mrs. R. Hamblyn, Mrs. Glassey, and Mrs. Drew. This active group of about ten ladies donated $500 to York Central Hospital to purchase equipment for the baby's ward, and their Centennial project was a rug for the new library. For years they have given a Valentine Party for the pupils of Thornhaven School for the Retarded.

There is also a Langstaff Women's Institute which started as a junior girls' institute sometime before the Mark-Vaun Institute.

Tweedsmuir Histories are compiled by each Women's Institute. This activity began when Lord Tweedsmuir was Governor-General of Canada from 1935 to 1940. He and Lady Tweedsmuir were concerned that Canadians knew so little of their country and so little of historical value was being preserved. Lady Tweedsmuir suggesting compiling Village Books similar to ones in England, and the work was started as part of the Women's Institute program. Much would have been lost in local history if this had not been done. Most of the Vaughan Township histories were begun in 1945. Lady Tweedsmuir wrote a foreward for the volumes:

I am so glad to hear that the Women's Institutes of Ontario are going to compile village history books. Events move very fast nowadays; houses are pulled down, new roads are made, and the aspect of the countryside changes completely sometimes in a short time.

It is a most useful and satisfying task for Women's Institute members to see that nothing valuable is lost or forgotten and women should be on the alert always to guard the traditions of their homes, and to see that water colour sketches and prints, poems and prose legends should find their way into these books. The oldest people in the village will tell fascinating stories of what they remember, which the younger member can write down, thus making a bridge between them and events which happened before they were born. After all, it is the history of humanity which is continually interesting to us, and your village histories will be the basis of accurate facts much valued by historians of the future. I am proud to think that you have called them 'The Tweedsmuir Village Histories.'

Farm Organizations

Farmers' organizations have had to contend over the years with two factors: the ebb and flow of the farm economy and the highly individualistic character of the average farmer. Agreement on policy is hard to achieve and maintain. Early farmers' clubs came into existence, bloomed, and expired in a short space of time.

Then came the Grange in 1874 from the United States, and it lasted until 1913. The 'Patrons of Industry' was next, also originating in the United States about 1889. Both these organizations had Lodges and attempted to keep the farmer in purchasing and distribution. The latter for a time figured in politics. In 1914, the United Farmers of Ontario established a new group and the United Farmers Co-operative was incorporated. To its surprise and that of everyone else, the U.F.O. was swept into power in 1919, but was defeated in 1923 largely because of internal disagreement regarding policy.

In 1936 the Ontario Federation of Agriculture was formed and in 1941 opened up a provincial office. This has been reasonably successful, particularly in the Co-operative Company. But again dissension arose, and the Ontario Farmers' Union became a rival. It was felt that the Ontario Federation of Agriculture no longer represented the 'grass roots' farmer but was too closely allied with the large operator and the government. This rivalry has persisted unfortunately up to the present day in spite of governmental efforts to bring about one farm organization.

Government encouragement of agriculture began with the fortunate personal interest of Upper Canada's first Lieutenant-Governor, John Graves Simcoe. Immediately after the first session of the Legislature at Niagara, in the autumn of 1792, he organized The Agricultural Society of Upper Canada and offered an annual premium of £10 together with a set of Arthur Young's *Annals of Agriculture*. Dinner meetings of the society were held once a month at which problems common to farmers were discussed, such as the treating of wheat for smut or Hessian Fly, the use of plaster of paris as fertilizer, and the breeding of animals.

There were two types of farmers during the period up to 1840, Pennsylvania German and British. The former had had experience in America and the latter had not. However, the British were strong on organization and contributed much to the farming economy through the Agricultural Societies; in fact, they acted in the capacity of a Department of Agriculture until such a department was set up in 1888. They promoted fairs and ploughing matches and did much to improve the quality of animals and grains, first, by importing them, and second, by giving worthwhile prizes at the Fairs.

The first Agricultural Society in the County of York that we have any record of was the York Society, established in 1806 with Mr. Justice Thorpe as president. It had a membership of fifty, all in political life. This Society lasted for at least two years, but the disturbed political situation probably interfered with it.

The next Society was formed in 1818 and again it was made up of politicians who were in many cases interested in farming because, at that time, it was the only industry.

Not all fairs came into existence through the Agricultural Societies, although the purposes were much the same regardless of origins. Fairs were really set up for market purposes, but as such made their contributions to the improvement of livestock, and better strains of grains.

There are no records as to when the Vaughan Agricultural Society was formed, but it must have been after 1830, when grants were given for fairs. We know that the present Richmond Hill Society resulted in the amalgamation in April 1849 of several Agricultural Societies of Vaughan and Markham, and that they had been in operation for some time. It was first called the Yonge Street Society, but the name was changed in 1900. The first fair in 1833 was held in fields near hotels on Yonge Street, then on the present location of the M.L. McConaghy Public School, and finally in the Richmond Hill town park, one block off Yonge Street. Since 1880 the fair has been held at its present location. This Society marked its centennial in 1949. A large arena and curling rink and fair board office are among the buildings.

The first prize list showed classes for horses, cattle, swine, dairy produce (10 pounds of butter), and ploughs made in the province. Prizes of iron or iron-headed ploughs and a wooden plough were offered in the ploughing matches, and cash prizes for boys' ploughing.

Presidents of the Richmond Hill Agricultural Society: Captain McLeod (Chairman of 1st meeting), 1849; G.P. Dickson, 1849-54; David Bridgeford, 1855; G.P. Dickson, 1856-9; Robert Marsh, 1860-2; Ed Sanderson, 1863; G.P. Dickson, 1864-74; Wm. C. Patterson, 1875-81; Peter Patterson, 1882-7; Thomas Lloyd, 1888; Wm. Trench, 1889-97; W.H. Clubine, 1898; Thomas Lloyd, 1899-1900; H.W. Pugsley, 1901-02; D. Lynett, 1903-04; J. Slater, 1905-06; Geo. Leek, 1907-08; George Gormley, 1909-10; George Padget, 1911-12; J.S. McNair, 1913-14; J.N. Breakley, 1915-16; J.J. Lunau, 1917-18; W.J. Wells, 1919-20; Jas. McLean, 1921-2; J.E. Francis, 1923-4; R.S. Thompson, 1925-6; W.H. Legge, 1927-8; Fred A. Clark, 1929; T.H. Trench, 1930-2; John Green, 1933-5; R.W. Scott, 1936-7; Harry Charles, 1938-40; F.S. Tyndall, 1941-2; R.L. Stiver, 1943-4; D.G. McAllister, 1945-6; O.D. Robinson, 1947-8; Wesley Middleton, 1949-50; Dalton Rumney, 1951-2; Stewart Rumble, 1953-4; Boynton Weldrick, 1955-6; Gordon Atkinson, 1957-8; Norman Tyndall, 1959-60; Milton Savage, 1961-2; Lloyd Beatty, 1963-4; Graeme Bales, 1965-6; Arnold Mortson, 1967-8; Fred Bovaird, 1969-70.

The Woodbridge Agricultural Society was organized in 1847 under the name of West York Agricultural Society and Vaughan Agricultural Society, but took its present name in 1908. Its first fair in 1847 was held on the property known as the Stegmann Estate in Pine Grove, on the corner of Gamble Street and Islington Avenue. The next year the fair was moved to Burwick, as Woodbridge was known until 1871, and until 1885 it was held alternately at Weston and Woodbridge. At Woodbridge it was held on the Humber flats, the property of John Abell, between the Humber River and Wallace Street. Around 1885 the Ontario government passed an Act that agricultural fairs must be permanently located, and since that time it has been held at Woodbridge. That year the present fair property was purchased from

William Farr. Since 1939 the fair has been held continuously on Thanksgiving Day and the Saturday previous. Woodbridge became a Class 'B' Fair in 1957.

The prize lists of the 1870s include what would be considered today to be unusual classes. Women were making butter on the farm at this time so there were classes for the best crock or firkin of butter. Many items were home-manufactured, and classes were provided accordingly for home-made wines, home-made blankets, soap, boots and shoes, bunches of shingles, fine rag carpets, flower wreaths, seed wreaths, sets of harness, best-made hammer-finished horseshoes, etc.

After Hurricane Hazel in 1954, the fair grounds were used for temporary housing for a few months.

Until the West York Agricultural Society and the Vaughan Agricultural Society amalgamated in 1908, the president of the former body served both societies. Presidents have been: John Gamble, 1847-59; John Abell, 1860-86; W.J. Smithson, 1887-8; William Farr, 1889-90; Andrew Barker, 1891; A.J. Griffith, 1892; N. Clarke Wallace, MP, 1893-4; John Reaman, 1895; Sam McClure, Sr., 1896-7; Geo. F. Wallace, 1898-9; Richard Willis, 1900; J. Mark Gardhouse, 1901; Ebenezer Smith, 1902; Tom F. Wallace, 1903; W. Ellerby, 1904; Wm. R. Rowntree, 1905; John Bayliss, 1906; James A. Cameron, 1907; Wm. McClure, 1908; John W. Smithson, 1909; Dan C. Longhouse, 1910; John Gardhouse, 1911; Albert J. Witherspoon, 1912; Chas. A. McNeil, 1913; Arthur W. Farr, 1914; Fred. H. Miller, 1915; R.K. Johnston, 1916; John T. Saigeon, 1917; Sam McClure, Jr., 1918; A. Livingston McNeil, 1919; Will O. Duncan, 1920; Henry N. Smith, 1921; Thos. Cousins, 1922; Fred Cousins, 1923; Andrew Stewart, 1924; Chas. Len Wallace, 1925; Edwin W. Brown, 1926; George W. Bagg, 1927; Alex Cameron, 1928; George Brownlee, 1929; Dan C. Longhouse, 1930; T. Berwick Weldrick, 1931; Bert Wright, 1932; Wm. J. Gardhouse, 1933; Robert Wilson, 1934; Geo. Kellam, 1935; Chas. H. Wallace, 1936-7; Wm. Clarkson, 1938; Wilbert Cousins, 1939; Alfred Thompson, 1940; Wm. J. Rowntree, 1941; Eb. Smith, 1942; Boynton Weldrick, 1943; Robt. Dooks, 1944; John H. Kellam, 1945; John Hostrawser, Sr., 1946; James Cameron, 1947; James MacDonald, 1948; Robt. Mitchell, 1949; Bruce Watson, 1950; Clarence Graham, 1951; Chas. Smith, 1952; Lawrence Keffer, 1953-4; Albert Rutherford, 1955; Goldwin Vanderburgh, 1956; George Troyer, 1957; Dr. Thos. Darlington, 1958; Britten Plunkett, 1959; James Robson, 1960; Pearson Neal, 1961; Norman Bagg, 1962; Clark Torrance, 1963; Robt. King, 1964; James Darlington, 1965; Donald McCallum, 1966; Gordon Miller, 1967; Percy Puterbaugh, 1968; John Hostrawser, 1969; Gilbert Agar, 1970.

Secretaries of the Woodbridge Society have been: W. Harvey, John McNeil, Thornhill Agar, Duncan McCallum, Joel Reaman, Jr., Thos. F. Wallace, C.L. Wallace, N. Geo. Wallace (for nineteen years), Stanley McNeil, Wm. Myers, Wm. Gibbons, and Kenneth Maynard. Until 1908 the secretaries also held the position of Treasurer. Since then the Treasurers have been: Eb. Smith, Edwin Brown (for thirty five years), Ray McAfee, and Roy H. Barker.

Timber smokehouse near Maple

Barn & Rack
Thornhill

Field crop competitions were started as early as 1829 and were carried on much the same as today. But with the development of horsepower machinery about 1840, the whole picture changed. Farmers were more willing to take the advice of the Agricultural Societies, particularly when it came to be realized that they were instrumental in the creation of a Minister of Agriculture (federal in our day) in 1852 and a Board of Agriculture. In 1862 the Upper Canada Veterinary School (later known as the Ontario Veterinary College) was organized, John H. Sanderson of Richmond Hill being one of its first eight graduates.

Doubtless through the activities of the Societies, the government was encouraged to appoint in 1864 the first Deputy-Minister of Agriculture, and in 1868 a Commissioner of Agriculture who in 1888 became a full-time Minister of Agriculture. From then on, the Agricultural Societies gave over the direction of agriculture to this minister and devoted themselves to holding fairs and promoting plowing matches.

The following report shows the state of the Agricultural Societies in Vaughan Township in 1867:

Number of members   187

To balance on hand	$402.52	
To subscriptions	274.40	
To municipal grants	75.00	
To government grant	130.67	
To admissions to show	299.50	$1,182.09
By prizes paid	$568.50	
By working expenses	128.87	$ 697.37
Balance in hand		$ 484.72

Co-op Returns for 1868, York, West Riding

Fall Weat — 26 bushels per acre. Better than 1867, 5,000 acres
Spring Wheat — 20 bushels per acre, Quality good, 2,000 acres
Oats — 30 bushels per acre, 5,000 acres
Rye — 20 bushels per acre, quality good — 1,000 acres.
Barley — 30 bushels per acre, sample light, colour bright, 6,000 acres
Peas — 16½ bushels per acre, 4,500 acres, Bean — none grown
Hay — 1½ tons per acre, better than 1867, 3,000 acres
Turnips — medium, 1,000 acres
Corn — a poor crop, 400 acres
Potatoes — about a half crop, 3,000 acres
Carrots — medium, 400 acres
Parsnips — not grown
Mangels — half a crop — 300 acres

Fall wheat good. Spring wheat good. Hay good. Not over 5% damage by wheat midge.

Vaughan Township has produced some champion plowmen over the years. James Mclean, who had a farm on the northwest corner of Yonge Street and Carrville sideroad, won many medals for his plowing and later was a judge. Stanley Tyndall was also noted for his success in plowmen's contests and he, too became a judge in many parts of the province. His farm is now part of Richmond Hill.

His son, Norman Tyndall, kept up the tradition when at Woodstock, Ontario, in October 1951, he won the gold medal at the International Plowing Match and an all-expense trip to Britain. There he won the Overseas Class, open to non-residents of the United Kingdom (and against plowmen from Holland, Switzerland, and Norway) at the International Plowing Match at the north of Ireland.

The following report from *The Liberal* of 1887 gives us the flavour of old-time plowing matches. It has been preserved by Elmer McKinnon, on whose family farm the match was held.

VAUGHAN PLOWING MATCH, A GREAT SUCCESS! All was favorable for the Vaughan Township Plowing Match which was held on the farm of John McKinnon, a mile and a half west of Maple last Tuesday, Nov. 1st., 1887.

The roads were in first-class condition, the weather was delightful in the extreme, the committee of management had completed their arrangements satisfactorily, consequently the crowd which gathered to witness the skill of the plowmen was very large. The plowing was east and west, and every class was well filled. No better sod field could have been secured, considering the dryness of the weather; although in some parts of the field it was difficult to make smooth plowing. Except in the boys' class the competition was open to the Dominion. In all there were 28 competitors and the Townships of Vaughan, Markham, King, Scarboro and York were well represented.

The stubble plowing was executed on the opposite side of the road on the farm of Jesse Richards. The special for sulky plows was well contested and many old and experienced farmers were surprised to see what excellent work could be done by these plows. From one end of a sixty rod field to the other, the furrows were straight, and the draught was apparently easy on the horses. The following is the prize list in full:-

FIRST CLASS OPEN TO ALL PLOWMEN:-

1st.	John Morgan, Willowdale, Masson Horserack	$28.00
2nd.	James McLean, Vaughan, Fleury Plow	18.00
3rd.	Spencer Crowley, Vaughan, Cash, S.C.	12.00
4th.	Thomas McLean, Vaughan, Cash S.C.	7.00

SECOND CLASS — OPEN TO ALL PLOWMEN WHO HAD NOT TAKEN TWO FIRST PRIZES IN ANY CLASS OR ANY IN 1ST CLASS.

1st.	Benjamin McKay, Vaughan, Wilkinson Plow	18.00
2nd.	J.A. Drury, Markham	13.00
3rd.	Frederick Keffer, Vaughan C & C.	10.00
4th.	William Gilham, Vaughan, Cash	6.00

THIRD CLASS — open to all plowmen who had not taken two first prizes in any class or any prize in first or second class. Plow to be used, wrought beam, cast head and share.

1st.	Frank Stiver, Markham, plow	18.00
2nd.	John H. Prentice, Vaughan, Cash & C.	12.00
3rd.	J.B. Ross, King, Cash & C.	10.00
4th.	Forbes Lloyd, King, Cash & C.	6.00

FOURTH CLASS — stubble plowing open to boys under 18, resident in the Township of Vaughan.

1st.	Neil Malloy, Vaughan, Patterson plow	18.00

| 2nd. | Robert Walkington, Vaughan, Cash & C. | | 13.00 |
| 3rd. | William Smith | Cash & C. | 9.00 |

FIFTH CLASS:- stubble plowing, open to all plowmen who had not taken two first prizes at any Society's match in stubble class.

1st.	Robert Smith, Vaughan — pair of iron harrows	18.00
2nd.	John R. Wilson, Vaughan, Cash & C.	12.00
3rd.	John Enwright, Vaughan, Cash & C.	8.00
4th.	Duncan McLean, Vaughan, Cash & C.	5.00

SIXTH CLASS — special for sulky plows:-

| 1st. | Wm. Hood, Scarboro, Cash by Society | | 15.00 |
| 2nd. | R. Ross, King | Cash by Society | 10.00 |

The two last named plowmen did their work with a Cockshutt plow.

Mr. J. Morgan was awarded the prize for the best plowed land in the field and also for making the best finish. The silver cup valued at $25.00 presented by John Holderness, Proprietor of the Albion Hotel, Toronto was awarded to Neil Malloy for the best work in the boy's class.

Mr. Ephriam Line, Vaughan, received the pair of horse blankets presented by R. Cheyne, Toronto for the best team at work in the match.

Mr. John Duncan's prize of $2.00 for the plowman who handled his team the best in the match was taken by James McLean.

Robert Walkington was the smallest plowman in the boy's class and consequently carried home the special prize given by E.B. Harris of Woodbridge.

In the class open to professional gentlemen only the excitement ran high, but when time was called to start, no entries had been made. One gentleman said his forte lay in cutting cordwood, another was prepared to stake a wager on cradling around a ten-acre field, whilst others declared that if the prize had been the future 'Empire' instead of 'The World' they would willingly enter the contest. And thus it ended.

After the decision of the judges in the various classes had been made known by the secretary, W.T. Robinson, the lucky competitors were asked to go to Maple, where the treasurer awarded the prizes. After this the officers, directors, judges and plowmen dined at Richardson's Hotel. The directors are to be congratulated on the success of their undertaking, as everything seemed to pass off with the greatest harmony.

The King and Vaughan Branch of the Ontario Plowmen's Association still holds an annual plowing match, one year in Vaughan and the next year in King township.

Horticultural Societies

Horticultural societies in Vaughan Township came into existence very early in the history of York County. Furthermore, Richmond Hill is one of the outstanding rose centres in Ontario.

As early as 1834, the York Horticultural Society (Toronto), the first in Upper Canada, was formed. In 1830 the first financial aid was given to promote the growing of flowers, fruits and vegetables. Of course, all who profited by grants were amateurs, but with the guidance of the Agricultural Societies (of which they were a part), they gradually took on more technical characteristics, particularly when greenhouses became more common.

In November 1904, the Ontario Horticultural Association was organized and in 1906 the province was divided into seven districts, with a director for each district. In 1924 the number was increased to ten districts and in 1952 to sixteen. On March 14, 1924, the Ontario Horticultural Association became a corporate body.

At the present time Vaughan has three Horticultural Societies: Richmond Hill, formed in 1914, with 195 members; Thornhill, formed in 1914, with 124 members; Woodbridge, formed in 1923, with 107 members.

Vaughan Township has had some outstanding nurseries: H.J. Mills Ltd., Richmond Hill, rose specialists; Frank Reeves & Son, Woodbridge, originally asparagus growers, and greenhouse plants: Concord Floral Co. Ltd., Concord; Bedford Park Floral, Richmond Hill (now Horticultural Products), also rose specialists; Endean Nurseries, Richmond Hill; and Joy Valley Greenhouses, Pine Grove, violet specialists.

Rose growing moved to Richmond Hill in 1912, and was important because it was the first new industry there in some years. W.J. Lawrence, the founder of the Lawrence Park section of North Toronto, built extensive greenhouses at the village. He was soon followed by H.J. Mills, who bought out J.H. Dunlop, who had come from Toronto in 1913. A disastrous hurricane destroyed many of the greenhouses and Mr. Lawrence sold to Ofield and Cotton in 1919 and Richmond Roses in 1931. In 1916, Mr. Arnold founded a rose business and later sold to Bedford Park Floral Company. The rose industry has meant much to the village, not only in advertising its name but in employing over one hundred men with an annual payroll of $250,000.

Doubtless the location of the rose growers was largely responsible for the formation of the Richmond Hill Horticultural Society on April 15, 1914, by John H. Sanderson. The first officers were: John H. Sanderson, president; J.H. Dunlop, first vice-president; W.J. Lawrence, second vice-president; G.F. Allen, secretary-treasurer. Later a committee to arrange a flower show was formed consisting of Mrs. T.F. McMahon, Mrs. G.F. Allen, Dr. Lillian Langstaff, L.E. Hand, H.E. Stirling and A.J. Campbell.

The Richmond Hill Society has been active over the years in encouraging children to grow flowers and vegetables and in planting trees. In 1921, when Scott McNair was president, apple seedlings were distributed to boys and girls, and later seedlings of native trees. Many trees have been added throughout the village. The Horticultural Society has more than once won the Mulock Cup for the best basket of flowers, and in 1934 won first prize at the Toronto Horticultural Society. In 1937 the Men of the Trees gave acorns and seedlings to commemorate the coronation of King George VI. Service medals for long-time support have been won by Mrs. Phipps, Mrs. Hume, Mrs. Angle, and R.D. Little.

The Thornhill & District Horticultural Society was organized in April 1914 with R.H. Nesbitt as the first president. The charter from the Ontario Horticultural Society was received in January 1915. One of the members, Percy Bone, has been president of the Thornhill Society, president of the Ontario Horticultural Society, a director of the Canadian National Exhibition, and chairman of the Horticultural

Building at the C.N.E. Other members who are well known authorities on gardening, nature study, and flower arrangement have been Phil Delf, Joe Wain, Jack Watson, Ernie Kohler and A.W. Galbraith.

The Woodbridge Horticultural Society was organized in 1923, with a membership of 107 the first year. Previously many had been members of the Weston Society. The first officers were: Dr. Garnet D. McLean, President; Miss Lillian McNeil, first vice-president; Miss Bessie Wallace, second vice-president; John G. Rolph, secretary-treasurer. The directors were Mrs. W.O. Duncan, Mrs. Henry N. Smith, Miss Grace Johnston, Miss Mary Burton, George Shore, Rev. John A. Moir, C.L. Wallace, Rev. R.B. Patterson, Rev. G.S. Smith. The membership grew to 475 in 1930, which was a peak year for the Society.

There have been many excellent flower shows, which became one of the main social events of the season. Junior activities have been arranged; members have exhibited at various Garden Clubs, the O'Keefe Centre, Canadian National Exhibition, and International Gladioli Show; and a flower arranging course was a popular event. Many projects have been undertaken such as planting trees, shrubs, and flowers in public areas. A year book has been issued since 1951, which in 1966 won first prize at the convention.

Agriculture Representatives, Junior Farmers and 4-H Clubs
Probably no organization of the twentieth century has had more influence amongst the rural youth in Ontario than the Junior Farmers. Actually this movement began with Junior Farmer Clubs organized by the agricultural representatives. There were two purposes: the dissemination of the value of experimental agriculture among farmers, and the providing of social outlets.

The agricultural representatives came into being in 1907 when six men were appointed to demonstrate the importance of scientific agriculture to the farmer. They soon came to the conclusion that the quickest and most successful way of accomplishing their purpose was to work with the young people. This they did at two levels: school fairs (1909) for the younger ones, and farm clubs for the older. The office of the Ontario Department of Agriculture, York County, was opened in Newmarket in June, 1911, and has operated continuously since that time. Its present address is the Ontario Department of Agriculture and Food, Newmarket Plaza in Newmarket. The representatives have been: W.E.J. Edwards, June to November, 1911; J.C. Steckley, 1911-22; R.J. Rogers, 1922-8; M.C. McPhail, 1928-9; R.E. White, 1929-36; W.M. Cockburn, 1936-60; Allan A. Wall, 1960- .

Out of the Farm Clubs developed the Junior Farmers as a provincial organization in 1944. They, in turn, became influential in the Ontario Federation of Agriculture. The Junior Farmers took as their motto 'Self-Help and Community Betterment'. Girls were put on an equal footing with boys. Vaughan Township had the honour of providing the first president in the person of Gordon Orr of Maple, with a brother-in-law, Carl Boynton, president in 1954. Eleanor Syracuse was the first girl president in 1951. This organization has carried on many community activities, one of the most recent being the recognition of Century Farms.

Among the boys' and girls' clubs, the earliest in Vaughan Township was the Woodbridge Boys' and Girls' Calf Club, organized in 1932 by Ralph White, the agricultural representative. The membership has included Albert Rutherford, Norman Bagg, Alex McNeil, Bill Hodgson (present M.P.P. for York North), Cameron Boake, Everard Kellam, Cliff Rumble, Grant Barker, Ernest Thurston, Charles Robson, Walter Dalziel, and Roy Phillips.

Up to 1932, a lot of the club work was done on a county basis, with grain and potatoes being the most popular projects. There are records of Albert Rutherford and Cliff Rumble, for example, being in county clubs in 1929 and following years.

The Woodbridge Foal Club was organized in 1935 by Ralph White. The members were Norman Bagg, Gilbert Agar, Howard Turton, Kenneth Devins, Harvey Turton, Kenneth Hodgson, Robert Kersey, Harford Robertson, Allen Boake, Aubrey Ella, Ross Cameron, Roy Usher, and Harry Price.

Through the thirties, many boys from Vaughan were members of the County Grain Clubs. In 1939, the Grain Club was organized at Woodbridge by Moff Cockburn. The members were Carman Livingston, Bert Livingston, Keith Barker, Raymond Glass, Wilbert Hadwen, Bruce McClure, Gordon Orr, Edward White, Robert Grogan, Donald Bagg, Cameron McNeil, and Clair Stevens.

From the 1930s up to the present time, junior projects have centered mainly around the Woodbridge Calf Club in the boys clubs. As a rule, it has been the largest in York County, with membership ranging from 25 to 40. The Achievement Days have always been held at Woodbridge Fair and a good percentage of the active farmers in the township were members at one time. The Girls' Homemaking Clubs have been just as active, taking projects in the homemaking subjects, cooking and sewing.

The Canadian Council on 4-H Clubs was formally incorporated in 1933. It is now an international society as well as interprovincial. In 1963 David McCallum of Woodbridge was one of Ontario's delegates to the National Conference of 4-H Clubs. The 4-H stands for 'Head, Heart, Hands and Health.' This organization, besides arranging exchanges of young people, carries on a broad scope of educational activities to develop rural leadership and makes its members more knowledgeable in agriculture and home economics through 'Learn to do by doing.' In Vaughan Township both Boys and Girls' 4-H Clubs have been quite successful.

The following are some of the important dates in history for the Junior Farmers' movement in Vaughan:

1913   First school fair in Vaughan Township, sponsored by the Department of Agriculture. School fairs were continued each year at the Township Hall and grounds at Vellore.

1915   First agricultural short course for Vaughan Township, one month long, held at Woodbridge, sponsored by the Department of Agriculture.

1920   Junior Farmer Associations in York County were reorganized into three groups. One of the groups, called West York, centred in the Woodbridge-Thistletown area.

1922   Another short course (one month long) under the sponsorship of the Department of Agriculture was organized at Maple, with 48 boys and 48 girls enrolled.

1923   A Junior Farmer Club at Maple was mentioned, with enrolment of 60, and another at Thistletown with an enrolment of 50.

1924   First Junior Farmers organized in Vaughan. Presidents were Fred Gordon, Concord; Clarence Graham, Richmond Hill; Robert Mitchell, Edgeley; Roy Barker, Thistletown.

1925   Month-long short course held at Woodbridge with an enrolment of 51 boys and 50 girls. First Junior Institute organized at Woodbridge.

1930   Vellore Junior Farmers organized. First three-month short course, sponsored by the Department of Agriculture, held at Maple, beginning in November.

1937   All school fairs cancelled because of polio epidemic. Resumed again in 1938 until 1940. Following the 1940 school fair, many activities were cancelled because of war, and school fairs were not continued again.

Vellore Junior Farmers and Junior Institute, 1930-1970
A week's short course was held at Vellore in February 1930. The girls met in the hall and boys in the basement of the school. Archie Cameron, Jack McNeil, and Pass Keffer, along with R.E. White, the agricultural representative, helped organize this course, which was a preview for a three-month course from November 25, 1930, to February 27, 1931, at Maple.

There were 43 boys and 30 girls on the roll and ages ranged from 15 to 40 years. This was the first three months' course in York County, and it was a decided success. Special features included a trip to Toronto with visits to the Parliament Buildings, the Laura Secord factory, Eaton's store, and the U.F.O. The girls made visits to farm homes in the district to study house plans, decorating, etc. The boys had numerous stock judging trips.

The Vellore Junior Farmers' Club was organized in March 1930 at the home of Mr. & Mrs. C.H. Rutherford; Stewart Rutherford was the first president and Mary Constable the first secretary. Soon there was a paid up membership of 125.

The girls organized as a Junior Women's Institute in January 1937 with Gladys Harrison as president and Clara Phillips as secretary. After 28 years the Junior Institute disbanded in March 1965 and the girls became members of the Junior Farmers' Club.

Presidents through the years of the Vellore JuniorFarmers' Club have been: Stewart Rutherford, Woodbridge, R.R. 2, 1931; Newton Watson, Kleinburg, 1932; Alex McNeil, Woodbridge, R.R. 2, 1933; Albert Rutherford, Woodbridge, R.R. 2, 1934-6; Murray Irwin, Kleinburg, 1937; Austin Rumble, King, R.R. 1, 1938; Howard Heacock, Maple, 1939; Bruce Watson, Woodbridge, R.R. 3, 1940; Jesse Bryson, Woodbridge, R.R. 3, 1941; Gordon Orr, Maple, R.R. 1, 1942-3; Mason Fletcher, Maple, 1944; Charles Grubbe, Weston, 1945; Bruce Snider, Maple, 1946; Archie Fletcher, York Mills, 1947; Allan Orr, Maple, R.R. 1, 1948; Bruce Hoiles, Nobleton, 1949; Archie Cameron, Woodbridge,

R.R. 2, 1950; Carl Boynton, Woodbridge, R.R. 2, 1951; Howard Plunkett, Woodbridge, R.R. 2, 1952; Duncan Watson, Woodbridge, R.R. 2, 1953; Bruce King, Woodbridge, R.R. 3, 1954; Ross Taylor, Kleinburg, 1955; Robert Beynon, Maple, R.R. 2, 1956; Gary Herrema, King City, R.R. 3, 1957; Bruce Fieldhouse, Woodbridge, R.R. 1, 1958; Bruce King, Woodbridge, R.R. 3, 1959; Henry VanderPost, King City, R.R. 3, 1960; John Naylor, Maple, R.R. 1, 1961; Walter Jackson, Downsview, R.R. 1, 1962; Spencer Finch, King, R.R. 1, 1963; David McCallum, Woodbridge, 1964-5; John McCallum, Woodbridge, 1967; David Darlington, Kleinburg, 1968; Stanley Irwin, Kleinburg, 1969; Richard Agar, Woodbridge, 1970.

Presidents of the Vellore Junior Women's Institute have been Gladys Harrison, 1937; Marion Phillips, 1938; Doris Cook, Maple, 1939; Catherine Brownlee, 1940; Agnes Watson, 1941-2; Margaret Humphreys, 1943; Orphie Orr, 1944-5; Jean Keffer, 1946; Mary McGillivray, 1947; Mary Keffer, 1948; Evelyn Hare, 1949; Marion Puterbaugh, 1950; Anna Orr, 1951-2; Jean McGillivray, 1953; Evelyn Whitehead, 1954; Ruth Beynon, 1955; Helen Thomas, 1956; Alwyn Neal, 1957; June Bowman, 1958; Lois Livingston, 1959; Evelyn Mactaggart, 1960; Ruth Miller, 1961; Joan Constable, 1962; Mary Naylor, 1964-5.

Masonic Lodges

The history of Freemasonry in Ontario starts very early. It was imported from the British Isles and the United States. In the latter country it had received recognition from George Washington, Benjamin Franklin, and Sir William Johnson. Governor Simcoe was doubtless a member of an English Lodge, and probably knew of Freemasonry in the Colonies: it was not out of character that, in 1792, he organized the Grand Lodge in Upper Canada.

William Jarvis was Grand Master until his death in 1817. In 1822, Simon McGillivray took over and acted in that capacity until 1840. In 1845 Sir Allan McNab (who first settled in Vaughan Township) became Grand Master. In 1824, the Richmond Lodge No. 23 was formed in Richmond Hill.

Grand Lodges operating in Upper Canada were under the jurisdiction of the Grand Lodge of England. However, little or no attention was given by the English, and a movement began to break away and form an Independent Grand Lodge in Upper Canada. This movement was encouraged by the fact that the Grand Lodge of Ireland was far more sympathetic and granted charities throughout the province. King Solomon's Lodge in Toronto was best known among the so-called Irish Lodges; as we shall see, the Vaughan Lodges were involved in this situation.

Richmond Lodge A.F. & A.M. No. 23, G.R.C. originated in 1824 and carried on under V.W. David Bridgeford as Master until 1831. From 1832 to 1845 records are missing, doubtless due to the troubled state of affairs. Commencing in 1846 the history is continuous, with the present charter dating from 1858. Since Colonel Bridgeford's regime, seventy men have held the office of Worshipful Master up to 1957. Colonel Bridgeford was born in 1785 and came to Canada when seven years of age. He eventually became a farmer in the Richmond Hill area and became an active Mason and a colonel in the Sedentary Militia. He took part in the War of 1812-15 and the Rebellion of 1837. In the latter, when Col. Moodie was killed, he was arrested and sentenced to be hanged by the rebels at noon. He asked William Lyon Mackenzie if the hanging could be postponed until 2 p.m. His request was granted, and by that hour reinforcements arrived from Toronto, the prisoners were liberated, and the tavern burned. He lived on Lot 47, on the south side of Richmond Street, and died there in October 1868.

The Masonic Hall in Richmond Hill was built in 1870 and for many years the Public Library was located at the rear of the hall. A new one was built in 1959.

The following Past Masters of Richmond Lodge have received Grand Lodge Honours: V.W. Bro. David Bridgeford, V.W. Bro. John C. Burr, V.W. Bro. Andrew McBeth, V.W. Bro. A.L. Skeele, V.W. Bro. Thos. Newton, R.W. Bro. H.A. Nicholls, V.W. Bro. T.F. McMahon, V.W. Bro. T. Trench, R.W. Bro. E.A. Coombs, V.W. Bro. David Hill, V.W. Bro. T.A. Lamon, R.W. Bro. W.H. Legge, V.W. Bro. Fred J. Graham, R.W. Bro. J.R. Herrington, V.W. Bro. A.A. Eden, V.W. Bro. D.M. Chamney, V.W. Bro. Peter G. Savage, V.W. Bro. Cecil C. Mabley, V.W. Bro. Harry W.R. Sayers, V.W. Bro. Jas. Hamilton.

Vaughan Lodge was organized in 1854 by a group of men in the vicinity of Nobleville (as Maple was then called) who had Irish connections. James Woods, the first Master of the Lodge, was born in Ireland in 1818 and joined Lodge No. 798. He moved to Canada and became a blacksmith in Nobleville, where he with others determined to establish a local Lodge. Their efforts were negated by the Grand Lodge of England and so they applied to the Grand Lodge of Ireland, which granted them a charter.

On September 21, 1854, members of King Solomon's Lodge, Toronto, came to Nobleville and installed the first officers of Vaughan Lodge, as it came to be called. The first officers were: W. Bro. James Woods, (then 36 years of age), W.M.; Bro. John Noble, S.W.; Bro. James Dick, J.W.; Bro. G. Bernard, S.D.; Bro. Uriel Chamberlane, J.D.; Bro. Robert Moore, I.G.; Bro. I. Caprouse, Tyler. The Charter number, 236 came from Ireland. When the Grand Lodge in Upper Canada was formed in 1856, Vaughan Lodge was given the number 54.

The first meetings are said to have been held in a room in Noble's Hotel but in 1866 a two-storey building was erected. In 1923 this building was greatly enlarged under the committee of Bro. George Brownlee, V.W. Bro. Thomas Cousins, and R.W. Bro. J.B. McLean. Again in 1949 the building was extended under a committee of R.W. Bro. M. Kinnee, W. Bro. A. Cameron, and V.W. Bro. G. Brownlee.

The following Past Masters have received Grand Lodge Honours: R.W. Bro. J.B. McLean, 1912; V.W. Bro. T. Cousins, G.S., 1913; V.W. Bro. G. Brownlee, G.S., 1936; R.W. Bro. I.B. Musselman D.D.G.M., 1937; V.W. Bro. J. Routley G.S., 1938; R.W. Bro. M.J.

Kinnee, G.S.W., 1940; V.W. Bro. A. Cameron, D.D.G.M., 1953; V.W. Bro. E.A. Carson, G.S., 1953; V.W. Bro. J. McDonald G.S., 1954; V.W. Bro. C. McCloskey G.S., 1957; V.W. Bro. R. Rumble G.S.B., 1960.

Blackwood Masonic Lodge, Woodbridge, was founded in 1874, when a few Masons residing in Woodbridge — members of Masonic Lodges at Bolton, Maple, and Toronto — decided to form a Lodge. Through the support of Thomas F. Blackwood of Ashlar Lodge, Toronto, assistance was given and a charter was obtained. The Lodge was named after its founder, who became the first Master. Charter members and officers were Thomas F. Blackwood, Joel Reaman, Michael S. Burkholder, Jonathan Wilkinson, C.H. Dunning, Chas. Medforth, Stewart Blair, Gideon Burton, R. Roberts, J. Nash, J. Zeilinskie, Gilbert Gilmore, F.A. Moore, H. Seymour, and Albert Wilson. Lodge meetings were held on the second floor of Joel Reaman's hardware store on Pine Street; later, they were held in 'Orphans Home,' property of the Abell Foundry.

After a few years, membership and interest lessened in the Lodge work until Dr. Peter D. McLean became Past Master of the Lodge. The situation changed and interest was revived to such an extent that in 1900 a Masonic Temple was erected on Eighth Avenue. For this building Albert Harris donated the land, Frank Smith was Building Contractor, and David Norton provided the bricks; all these men were Lodge officers.

The following Past Masters have received Grand Lodge Honours: R.W. Bro. T.F. Blackwood, V.W. Bro. Amos Maynard, V.W. Bro. Frank Smith, V.W. Bro, J.J. Watson, V.W. Bro. Geo. W. Bagg, R.W. Bro. Geo. W. Shore, V.W. Bro. Sidney W. Mayhew, V.W. Bro. Sam McClure, V.W. Bro. Gordon L. McGillivray, V.W. Bro. Alex. E. Kearney, V.W. Bro. Samuel D. Kaiser, V.W. Bro. Roy H. Barker.

Woodbridge now has two Masonic Lodges, Bridgewood Lodge No. 713 being instituted on October 30, 1965, with V.W. Bro. Samuel D. Kaiser as Master.

Patterson Masonic Lodge received its charter on July 11, 1872. It was named for Peter Patterson, Vaughan Township implement dealer and Member of Parliament. At first the meetings were held at Butterie's Hall, near Concord Station. Mr. Butterie was a charter member. Others were John Kirby, Dr. John N. Reid, A. Gallanough, James Bowman, C.H. Keffer, E. Martin, John Brumwell, and D. Snider. The first Senior Warden was John Lane. After 1875, meetings were held in Victoria Hall in Thornhill. A modern brick temple was built on Elgin Street, Thornhill, in 1960. William Keiller was Worshipful Master in 1970.

The following Past Masters have received Grand Lodge Honours: R.W. Bro. J. Edward Francis, R.W. Bro. Edgar A. James, R.W. Bro. Neil G. MacDonald. V.W. Bro. James Cherry (1887), V.W. Bro. Robert Thompson, V.W. Bro. J. Arthur Thompson, V.W. Bro. S. Alsop, V.W. Bro. Earl Brown, V.W. Bro. Alan L. Francis, V.W. Bro. J.J. Madill, V.W. Bro. George Russell, V.W. Bro. Robert Aston, V.W. Bro. George Loxton.

Temperance Societies

It has already been stated that in the early pioneer days wheat was made into whiskey, which in turn became legal tender. It was cheap and it was plentiful, which encouraged much drunkenness.

To combat this situation, Temperance Societies were organized as early as 1828. Members were pledged not to drink liquor. Actually these societies were more than for the promotion of temperance; they were semi-literary in character, placing much emphasis on public speaking and debating. Furthermore, there was no age limit. George Reaman joined when he was sixteen and Martha Ann White, who afterwards became his wife, was fourteen. Male members paid twenty cents a month and female members ten cents. Rules were quite strict. One member in 1865 was expelled for violation of rules. Others were expelled for non-payment of dues. Each case was considered carefully.

The Order of Good Templars, a society of abstainers from liquor, was formed at Utica, New York. It soon became an international organization. It came in 1842 into Upper Canada, where there were 147 distilleries and 96 breweries serving a population of fewer than 500,000 people. Here it became known as the Independent Order of Good Templars, and established lodges. In 1850 the Grand Lodge was organized to direct no less than 56 local lodges in Upper Canada. Within five years there were 350 lodges with a total membership of almost 20,000.

In 1868 the Sons of Temperance, organized in 1847 in New Brunswick, Nova Scotia, and Lower Canada, and the Good Templars merged to form the Ontario Temperance and Prohibitory League. Organized and promoted as a social organization where debates were held and social activities encouraged, it lost its appeal when it existed largely to promote temperance. As a result its younger members joined other societies.

Garibaldi Lodge, No. 486, Independent Order of Good Templers, located in Vaughan Township in the vicinity of Concord, held a meeting on October 18, 1864; the following are the minutes:

The Templer going into the committee of the whole to try the Benet (sic) case. Bro. Flemming being appointed Chairman. Bro. Mathew King appointed Secret(ary) of the Committee. Bro. Benet being called upon to state the nature of the case said not enjoying good health he was ordered to drink Beer and Porter by Doctor Lodder and consequently absented himself from the lodge. Bro. Munro after speaking a little of the nature of the case moved that the charge be sustained second by Bro. Watson, the motion carried. Moved and second that Bro. Benet find some money and see by way of the amount that he be reformed ... [Last sentence indecipherable].

Conservation Authorities

The Humber and Don Valley Conservation Authorities were formed in 1948 to manage the 337 square mile Humber watershed and the Don watershed of 141 square miles.

In 1954 the Humber Valley Conservation Authroity acquired the 1809 Dalziel barn and 14 acres at Jane Street and Steeles Avenue.

This was the beginning of Black Creek Pioneer Village.

On October 15 and 16, 1954, Hurricane Hazel dropped almost nine inches of rainfall after a week of rains. The flood on the Humber destroyed homes and bridges; 36 people died, five in the Woodbridge area.

In 1956 land was purchased near Pine Grove that has become the Boyd Conservation Area.

When the Metropolitan Toronto and Region Conservation Authority was established in 1957 to amalgamate the nine watersheds around Toronto, covering 1,000 square miles, the Humber and Don, both partly in Vaughan, became part of this larger unit. Vaughan Township is now one of the 23 municipalities included in the M.T.R.C.A. Representatives from Vaughan Township to the Authority are Jesse Bryson and Francis Redelmeier, and from Woodbridge Grant Henderson.

In 1966 Robert and Signe McMichael of Kleinburg gave their property, including their home 'Tapawingo' and their collection of Canadian art, much of it paintings by the Group of Seven (the McMichael Conservation Collection of Art), to the Province of Ontario. The 40-acre property overlooks the east branch of the Humber River and is administered for the Province by the Authority.

In 1968, J. Grant Glassco, a leading Canadian business executive, left his Cold Creek Farm overlooking the Humber, Lots 21 and 22 on Concession 7, to the Province of Ontario when he died. It will be administered by the M.T.R.C.A. as green belt.

Sugar Camp

CHAPTER XIII

Cultural Heritage

Mary Gapper O'Brien's diary, written to be sent back to England to tell relatives and friends about life in Vaughan Township around 1830, is now in the Ontario Archives. She lived for a time on Lot 38, Concession 1 and Lot 19, Concession 2. She describes visits to the neighbours, the Reaman family on Lot 15, Concession 2. On August 11, 1829, she wrote of walking to the Reaman farm 'for the sake of getting some meat and seeing the cleanest house in the district. The fine estate which these good folks now possess they settled on twenty-seven years ago . . . without a neighbour within two miles and a half. She told us that she got so wild that she would run and hide herself if she saw anyone coming.' Of a return visit she wrote: 'Old Mrs. Reaman [Mrs. Reaman was then only 43] came to make me a visit and to tell me the right time of the moon for gathering apples and destroying bugs. She brought me an offering of a winter radish as large as a mangel-wurzel.'

On February 19, 1830, she wrote: 'We left home to pay a visit to old Mrs. Reaman for the purpose of tasting her sauerkraut. So that I might better judge of its merits she prepared for us fried pork and applesauce with a due complement of pickles, bread, butter and tea . . . Edward then took me to poor old Mrs. Munshaw whom I found deeply involved in the painful task of nursing her husband who is now past all help. I consulted with her upon my symptoms to gratify her for the mortification she might feel for not being employed for me as a midwife.'

On February 12, 1829, she wrote of a drive on what is now Langstaff Road from Yonge Street to the 4th Concession (Keele Street).

It was snowing a little but nevertheless a beautiful drive through woods of various growth, then down a steep hill thickly clothed with hemlock pines. A winding road, just wide enough for our passage, led to the bottom of a narrow glen through which a stream found its way in spite of the ice and snow with which it was concealed except where the cattle had made openings for drinking. We crossed the stream [the Don River] on a log bridge . . . After we had ascended the other bank of the ravine and traversed a thick forest of pine, we came to a wider road. [This is her description of what is now the corner where Bathurst Street, Number 7 Highway and Langstaff Road meet, which no doubt will be the site of a large cloverleaf interchange if the proposed highway 407 is built.] Here we came to clearings and neat farmhouses along the roadside at different intervals. [These would be the

Reaman, Baker, and Keffer homes. The Baker barn built in 1822 would be the only building that she saw that is still standing in 1970.] A group of these on the bank of a small ravine was now before us. The largest of the group, a log house [the Musselman home, Lot 11, Concession 4], was the object of our search.

We entered a small passage and proceeded from thence into the family apartment — a low and rather dark room with walls of their natural brown colors — two beds covered with dark blue counterpaines at the farther end and two massive tables at that from which we entered and along the sides various chests and a few chairs — in the centre a large stove close to which sat the mistress of the mansion, Mrs. Musselman, in a close cap and gown of homespun — variously scattered and grouped about were two infants, the mother, the widowed daughter-in-law, two or three girls of different ages and a boy clad in the accustomed orange-tawny homespun and scarlet cap. The women had all a strong national character both in their countenance which was shrewd and lively emanating from rather square faces with pale complexions and dark eyes — the squareness of their faces was rendered most conspicuous by their little close flat topped caps and they wore petticoats of blue homespun with jackets of the same — the whole party and especially the infants told me that I was in the interior of a Flemish or German cottage. Accordingly that I had mistaken only so far I was let to do by the vagueness of my information on the costumes and manners of the Germanic tribes — the family had emigrated from Switzerland to Penn. in the time of the old lady's daddy and mamy and from thence she had come thither in her youth; but through all their wanderings they had still preserved to a certain extent habits, costume and language, which though she called it High Dutch was to me wholly unintelligible as they spoke it amongst each other. The old lady saw us enter as if it did not much concern her who came in and went out of her mansion; but on addressing her received us with great civility and entertained us with perfect ease and good breeding. I was much pleased with my visit and shall repeat it at the first convenient opportunity.

Vaughan Township was the recipient in pioneer days of four cultures: Pennsylvania German, English, Scottish, and Irish. Each of these had a background of many centuries in Europe and although there might be similarities, there were many strong psychological differences. For instance, there was a difference in religion. The Pennsylvania Germans were Plain Folk, interested primarily in agriculture and in maintaining their religion, customs, language, and family relationships. They, by and large, were averse to holding public office. Conversely, the English were anxious to duplicate in Upper Canada governmental procedures which, they thought, proclaimed them as belonging to a superior way of life. The Scottish brought with them their love of learning, a frugality, and a capacity to win their way to the top. The Irish, on the contrary, brought their love of life and people and the ability to adjust to new situations.

Of these four groups three were Protestant. One — the Irish — included many Roman Catholics, and its members were late comers to the province. The English, belonging to the State Church in England, tended to look down on other religions. The Scots were Presbyterians with a tenacity to establish their beliefs in Canada. The Pennsylvania Germans were content to worship in each other's homes and shut themselves away from the world in general. The Irish for many years, because of their scattered numbers, were without much help and guidance from their church, yet, in most cases, remained loyal to it.

Pioneers
near Maple

The Garden

But it was not only in the field of religion that these four groups differed and consequently made their individual contributions to Vaughan Township. There were differences in language, food, building, farm practices, and folk arts generally.

As the Pennsylvania Germans were the earliest settlers, let us consider them first. Their typical home was a log building which was soon extended into a house — perhaps frame or brick — which had one section for the parents when they gave over the farm. This was known as the 'Doddy' house. Across a stoop from the main house there was a separate building, called the summer kitchen, used to keep the heat out of the main part of the house in summer, and used often as storage space in the winter. There was a brick bake oven, also by itself, and probably a shop where articles were made and repaired. Most of the furniture was homemade. The barn was usually a bank barn with a basement for cattle, always with a hangover. Amos Baker at Concord has perhaps the only example of a Pennsylvania German set of buildings in Vaughan Tonwship.

The English, when they came in any numbers, that is after 1815, brought their own ideas of houses and barns. In England, barns like those built in Vaughan were unknown, because in most parts of England animals were not housed indoors during the winter months. Barns there were more like sheds. The English houses in Vaughan were soon built of brick and their furniture in many cases was brought with them from England. Because many were persons with ready cash, and land was cheap and labour plentiful, a number of the English landscaped their properties until they resembled what they were accustomed to in England.

The Scots, because many of them were stone masons by trade, built large stone houses, some of which still exist today. In many Scottish homes there were large families, and they were more interested in acquiring more land than in making elaborate homes. Not that their homes were not comfortable, but Scottish frugality forbade unnecessary expenditure in such matters. They were quick to learn from the Germans the techniques of farming in Vaughan Township.

The Irish seldom brought any wealth with them. They frequently worked as labourers for the British who had preceded them, until such time as they could acquire property of their own. On account of their adaptability and good nature, they were always acceptable in any community, and it wasn't long until many of them went into business of some kind where they were usually successful.

Now let us consider foods. The Pennsylvania Germans have always had the reputation of being excellent providers of rich and appetizing foods. Being keen on hard physical work, they could enjoy rich food without damage to their stomachs. Take pork for example — they were interested in pig raising for two reasons: pigs grew into money more quickly than any other animal, and the food pigs consumed might otherwise have been wasted.

A typical Pennsylvania Dutch dish was potpie. It was dough cut into squares and cooked in some form of meat broth. Chicken potpie was the most popular, though turkey might be substituted. Seven sweets and seven sours were usually found at most meals. The sweets might be spiced apples or peaches, apple butter, apple sauce, cottage cheese, or jelly; the sours, chow-chow, corn relish, assorted pickles, red beet eggs, or watermelon pickles.

There was always a ready market for beef among the British. The English people have always been great meat eaters; that is, when they could get it. Writers on foods in England during the eighteenth century have pictured a very gloomy picture. Only the very well-to-do had meat or poultry. The working classes lived on cheese, bread and tea. 'By the end of that century cheeses had a brand name — Cheshire, Gloucester, Wiltshire, Stilton and so on — and cheese making, traditionally the duty of the farmer's wife, became a profitable sideline of farming,' wrote Elizabeth Burton in *The Georgians at Home*.

The situation in Scotland was almost worse. Milk was not plentiful. Porridge was the main dish, and mutton the meat when they could afford it. The Irish were in a similar situation. Potatoes were their staple diet and when in the 1840s there was a potato famine, many left the homeland for America.

This information concerning the food situation in the British Isles is given to suggest the good fortune of the Pennsylvania Germans who came up to Vaughan Township around 1800 and had never suffered lack of food. The natural resources to be found in Pennsylvania and Vaughan Township were such that no one need ever go hungry. There were wild fruits, wild animals and fish in abundance, and the soil was so fertile that as soon as space could be found to plant seeds such as potatoes, corn, or pumpkin, the yield was always large. Furthermore, these Germans had been accustomed to living in pioneer conditions and had learned how to make use of what nature provided. Let us now enumerate some of the dishes the Pennsylvania German housewife, with her initiative, created.

As wild fruits were so plentiful she preserved them with sugar, pound for pound, for use in the two-crust pie which she invented (in Europe they made a deep pie with a top crust only). As soon as she had sealed jars (about 1855), she canned her fruit, a process that took less sugar. When apples were available she dried them for winter use or made them into apple butter. Pumpkins might be used with apple cider to make 'Punkin' Sauce.' About the only fruits she bought were prunes and raisins, both of which were used at the time of funerals, doubtless because of their sombre colour.

Sauerkraut and coleslaw were made from cabbage. Cheese was more often soft cheese or smearkase, that is, soft curds mixed with sweet cream. 'Koch Kase' was another form of soft cheese.

In the spring, the soft shoots of dandelion, horsedock, burdock, and lambs' quarters were sought for the medicinal value of early greens. The Pennsylvania Germans preferred their lettuce and greens trimmed with a dressing of cream and vinegar (sweetened).

Not only did the housewife make delicious bread in the outside bake oven, but she also made cinnamon buns, fat cakes (doughnuts), and animal cookies. 'Dunking' doughnuts or tea cakes was quite the thing to do.

Any mention of the food prepared by these people would be incomplete without calling attention to their curing of pork, making sausage, head cheese, and liverwurst. This has been taken over by the packing industry but it all began when the pioneer farmer killed his four or eight hogs at a butchering 'bee' which was one of the early social events.

The foods provided by the Pennsylvania Germans have been discussed at some length because practically all those mentioned were soon adopted by the British immigrant and are now basic in the menus of all Ontario people at the present time.

The Scottish people never departed from their love of oatmeal porridge and oat cakes. For this reason they always grew a fair amount of oats. As many of them had been shepherds or crofters in Scotland, they enjoyed their mutton. Fish was just as palatable and available too, and it wasn't long before the Scotsman's table rivalled that of any other race in variety as well as quantity.

Although the Irishman was brought up on potatoes, he too, soon adopted the food which nature provided, such as fish, wild animals, and fruits, and before long was growing plenty of vegetables.

But if the Pennsylvania Germans excelled in the food line, the English, Scots, and Irish made their contributions in other ways. It was in the field of economics that they excelled, and in their interest in life outside their immediate community. Since the population was small, it was inevitable that there would be intermarriage among the groups. This was particularly noticeable among the Scots and the Pennsylvania Germans. These two groups had much in common. Each was exceedingly frugal, honest, and religious. Even the Scottish dialect had a great resemblance to the German. What was more, each had a farm background. The English, on the other hand, in many cases became more interested in commerce than farming, and they belonged to a church which considered itself more distinguished than others. Besides, there was a fair number of Army personnel among them, and they lumped together the early pioneers who had taken up land in the eastern part of the township and called them 'Yankees.'

Differences in religion made for a division among the various groups which continued for many years. For instance, the Methodists in the eastern part were opposed to dancing, cards, theatres, and smoking, whereas the Scottish Presbyterians in the western sections enjoyed their square dances and their card parties. Of course, there were Presbyterians who were stricter than the Methodists. For instance, organs in churches were anathema to many Scots. Sunday for the Pennsylvania Germans was a day when every member of the family attended church. But it was also a highlight in their week, for 'wisiting' was the order of the day. Several families would have a meal together at one of their homes, and quantities of food would be consumed and arrangements made for 'bees' and other events. Perhaps in the evening the young people would gather for a singsong, which was a preliminary for 'sparking' and was part of the pattern of courtship.

Among folk arts and crafts, let us first consider Fraktur. This is an art practised in Upper Canada by only a few persons, and those in a very amateurish way. The term 'Fraktur' means broken Gothic letters done in pen or paint. It originated in Europe and was practised by the monks in the monasteries; it involved the use of symbols such as *The Tree of Life, The Tulips, The Distelfink* (Goldfinch), and *The Dove*, and geometric designs and religious motives such as *The Cross* and *Angels*. These were usually done in bright primary colours — red, green, yellow, orange, blue, and violet. The designs were brought over from Europe to Pennsylvania and used by local artists in patterns for birth and marriage certificates. Many families have German Bibles, in the centre of which are the records of births, marriages, and deaths. All around the names will be found in coloured ink fruit and flowers, birds and animals depicted according to the wishes of the painter.

Not only are these symbols found drawn on paper; they also appear as designs on quilts, towels, and hope chests, always in bright colours. Although the people might dress themselves in drab colours, they compensated by having their kitchen floors bright yellow and their windows full of bright flowering plants. Fraktur art is very much alive in Pennsylvania at the present time, and it is hoped that it will be developed in Ontario because it is indigenous with the province's earliest settlers.

The mention of quilts — and we can associate rugs with them — suggests an art which is very much alive today. In the early days quilting and rug frames were set up in the parlour where, from time to time, 'bees' would be held at which the best quilters and ruggers would gather to demonstrate their skills. The patterns, particularly with the quilts, were often symbolic, like those used in Fraktur painting. Various kinds of quilts were made. They included patchwork quilts, made of pieces of material of several sizes sewn together in geometric patterns, and appliqué quilts of designs created by sewing pieces of cloth on a basic background. Samplers were also popular, many of them so elaborate and decorative that they were placed in frames under glass. The name of the maker and even the date were often worked into the pattern or put at the bottom of the sampler.

Rugs had more sophisticated patterns such as a dog, a flower, or even a house. Sometimes the cloth from used clothing was cut into strips that were sewn end to end, plaited or braided. The braids were then sewn together to make one kind of rug.

The British were much more expert in the use of the needle than the Germans. Many of the British had come from textile areas or had learned how to make fine lace from the French Huguenot refugees. They were soon expert in piecing and quilting bedspreads in which the pieces adorning pillow cases and the like were made by these people. Knitting yarn for clothing was another art for all four groups. In the early days it was a necessity; the wool was provided by the farmer's sheep and processed by the housewife until carding and fuller mills were in operation.

The furniture found in the homes of English immigrants in many instances had come from England. It was beautifully made of oak and beautifully finished. It might consist of a sideboard, a chest of drawers, tables, beds, and even a grandfather clock. The Scots and Irish brought little furniture and so made much of what they needed themselves. This was also true of the Pennsylvania Germans: their group always included a cabinet maker who made chairs, chests, tables, beds — and always a corner cupboard, for which he would select the best pine wood. Anything made was fastened with dowels; nails were either unavailable or undesirable. That is why many kitchen chairs and cupboards are just as sound today as when they were made a century or more ago.

Turning to language, we find that English superseded the Pennsylvania German dialect. The Scots and Irish softened or lost certain consonants and vowels but never altogether. Each group brought its special ways of expressing themselves. The Germans frequently used proverbs and sayings which have now been accepted as an integral part of English speech, among them are: where there's life there's hope; it makes my mouth water; silence gives consent; flat as a pancake; wet as a dishrag; to work like a dog. Doubtless a number of these sayings had been used in Europe before they came to America; however, by their frequent use they have added colour to our speech. The author has a list of over two thousand proverbs and sayings of the Pennsylvania Germans.

Beliefs and superstitions existed among all the four groups but with considerable differences. The Pennsylvania Germans had a touch of the mystic in them. In Pennsylvania the barns were usually painted red and 'hex signs' — wheels or stars — were outlined on them. Actually it was for decorative purposes rather than for superstitious reasons that they were used. This never happened in Vaughan Township, for barns were seldom painted. But the Germans did believe that pow-wow doctors could 'charm' certain diseases at a specified time of day or change of the moon; that beans and potatoes should always be planted at full moon and before 11 a.m.; that hogs should never be killed during the new moon for the meat would shrivel away when cooked in a pan. They had many 'good luck' charms, such as finding a four-leaved clover or a horseshoe. It was bad luck to open an umbrella in a house, spill salt, or start on a journey on Friday.

The English believed in ghosts, and tortured witches; fortunately, in Vaughan Township there is no record of the latter, although several instances of the former are remembered. Most of the Scots who came were lowlanders and were pretty hard-headed and down-to-earth people who did not indulge their fancies except to be inordinately proud of Robert Burns. At the other extreme were the Irish, who loved to conjur up banshees and leprechauns. Wakes were an integral part of their lives.

For over a century the people of Vaughan consisted mainly of descendants of these four cultures and all contributed something. Since the second world war, many new families have come to live in Vaughan, bringing new cultural heritages with them.

CHAPTER XIV

In Retrospect

J.M. McDonald, Township Administrator

The history of the Township of Vaughan has been moulded by the events which transpired within its boundaries from the time of its settlement. The details assembled by Dr. E. Reaman speak for themselves, but complex and conflicting ideas underlay the township's evolution during recent years. To link all these events into a pattern, or to relate them to a common theme, would distort the facts. Many things in recent history have influenced the direction of the township's development.

Meanwhile, there is existence today, when the events are not deemed suitable for either news or history — on the one hand too old and on the other still unripe — but await that nice blend of new knowledge and new ignorance that gives perspective and clears away the untidiness of too close a view.

Dr. E. Reaman requested me, because of my close association with the township over the past thirty-five years, to contribute to the history. But one's own direct awareness of contemporary events does not make those events history, because everyone is subject to bias and is likely to form opinions based on incomplete information and to arrive at premature conclusions.

As the pendulum of time swings from one extreme to the other, so the form of local government swings — from part of a larger unit to an individual unit and back again to part of a larger unit. Initially, Vaughan was a part of the Home District in the early nineteenth century; it became a compact unit at the beginning of the twentieth century, and now is part of the new 'York Region'. A few short decades ago, a town or village, with its rural atmosphere, was a self-contained entity, and the standard of services was established from the resources of the people within the community.

Today, we no longer live in a community that can be independent of the larger area. The constant improvement in transportation, communication and technology has greatly changed our towns and villages. In keeping with this evolution, it was necessary that local government should change to provide uniform services over a larger area. The forthcoming change is understandable, but this event cannot yet be blended into township history.

As we enter a new era — no longer the Township of Vaughan

but the Town of Vaughan — with modified boundaries on the north and east and an adjustment of the southern boundary pending, we try to envisage the role of the Town of Vaughan in the new 'York Region.' It is in this environment, with the approaching re-establishment of local government on a regional basis, that one reflects on the local government of years gone by — when the Quarter Sessions of the Peace were held by the Justices of our Lord the King, assigned to keep the peace in the Home District.

The minutes of the early Quarterly Sessions of the Peace and the minutes of the early council meetings reveal many interesting events — events old enough to be history but not of a nature to be linked together into a pattern or a common theme other than 'local government' providing for the health, safety, and welfare of the residents. In retrospect, there are interesting comparisons to be made with the past generations' local governing policies.

Taxes and Tax Collecting

For the year 1969, the Council of the Township of Vaughan levied for municipal and school purposes an amount exceeding five million dollars. The current collection during 1969 was slightly less than 90% of the levy. The collection of the remaining tax levy continues during the ensuing months, with registration of the title of the land with the township in default as a final endeavour to secure collection of unpaid taxes.

At the turn of the last century, while the tax roll was not of the same proportion, a return of the collector's roll shows an amount of $1.38 as uncollected, and written opposite this entry is the comment 'Nothing to Distrain.'

Problems must have also prevailed in the early part of the nineteenth century, as may be noted from the records of the Quarter Sessions of the Peace on August 6th, 1801, where it is recorded:

Abnar Miles, the Collector for Taxes for last year for the Townships of Vaughan, Markham and Whitchurch, appeared before the Court and upon oath, declared that he had not received any assessment roll from the Assessor for the above mentioned Townships for the year commencing in March 1800, therefore, he had collected no part of the said assessments.

ORDERED — that Nicholas Miller and Robert Marsh, the Assessors for the aforementioned Townships for the said year 1800, be directed to show cause why they had not made return of the assessments to the collector, Abnar Miles; that the Clerk of the Peace do furnish the said Collector with a copy of the said assessment and the said Collector do upon receipt thereof, forthwith make the collection required and pay the same into the hands of the Treasurer of the District at the General Quarter Sessions of the Peace in October next. It having been represented that Peter Vanderburg, Tax Collector for the aforementioned Townships for the current year, had left the settlement without having collected his assessment roll.

ORDERED — that the Clerk of the Peace do write a letter to John Wilson and Wilson Graham Esquire, Justices residing in the above mentioned circle, requesting that they make enquiry whether the said Peter Vanderburg had paid any money as Collector, into their hands or to any other person and how much or whether any one had been nominated to execute his office.

Township Hall and Office

In the year 1956, a new municipal building was constructed in Maple to provide facilities for meetings and the administration of current local government affairs. The involvement of the local government today in many aspects of health, welfare, and safety differs extensively from the functions of local government when the previous township municipal hall was built in 1845 through the enactment of a by-law passed by the Home District Council. This by-law, numbered 70, was passed on May 15, 1845, when Nicholas J. Kline and Joseph Milburn were representatives on the District Council from the Township of Vaughan. The by-law provided as follows:

To assess the inhabitants of the Township of Vaughan in the sum of One Hundred and Forty Eight Pounds to be applied for the purpose of erecting a Town Hall in the said Township. The Collector of the Township is authorized to levy and collect One Hundred and Forty Eight Pounds to be paid to Neil McDonald, Chairman of the Building Committee appointed for the erection of the aforesaid Town Hall upon the order of the Township Councillors.

Welfare

Welfare is a service to the local residents that has gradually been transferred to authorities having jurisdiction over larger areas. During the depression and the ensuing years, the local authorities were responsible for participating in providing welfare and assistance to the residents. In 1936, the welfare allowance was $6.50 per month for a single person. As other forms of welfare under the provincial authorities were established, the local municipality has been participating in a diminishing role.

In the year 1868, the township expended a sum of $638.65 for welfare. The items expended were nominal in the amounts, and the purpose designated for each expenditure indicated the purpose for which the funds were provided.

A record in the Quarter Session minute book for October 11, 1803, reveals how welfare was administered during that period of time:

Abnar Miles
John H. Hudson
John Lines
All of the grand inquest of the previous session (but now discharged) appeared and represented to the Court that a certain Moses Martin of the Township of Markham in the said District, Yeoman; this family consisting of a wife and four children, were in very great distress; that Moses Martin himself was in a very ill state of health — that his head and face were almost destroyed by cancer; that his wife neglected both him and his family and that his children were naked and without food.

IT IS ORDERED:
John H. Hudson   Town Warden of said Township of Markham
Abnar Miles
John Lines
or any two to be a committee, to take into their custody and possession, all of the moveable property and chattels belonging to the said Moses Martin consisting of two oxen, four cows, two young cattle and several hogs and to sell and dispose of the whole or such part of the said cattle and hogs as to them may seem expedient

and the proceeds to be used and employed in the providing of food and clothing and other necessities for the said Moses Martin and his family.

And it is also ordered that the said committee do render a true and just account of their proceedings, in trust aforesaid, at the next meeting or other subsequent general Quarter Sessions of the Peace or whenever called upon by the Magistrate of the said district.

Administration of Justice

Currently, the administration of justice in the Township of Vaughan is included in the provincial jurisdiction. Justice is administered in these courts by a presiding judge with Legal Aid for the accused where necessary.

In the year 1867, the Township Treasurer received $74.20 as fines levied by the following Justices of the Peace who resided in the Township of Vaughan: John W. Gamble, Robert J. Arnold, Wm. Devlin, A. Law, J.P. McQuarrie, and Thos. Page. There is no indication that these Justices of the Peace made any other account of their court proceedings than to pay to the treasurer the amount of the fine imposed.

On October 17, 1801, there is a record in the Quarter Session of the Peace minutes that comments on the provision of food for prisoners:

After Court took into consideration, a report of the Special Session of the Peace of the 6th day of August 1801, to the expenditure of a claim upon the district and having duly examined the same,

ORDERED — that four pennies worth of wheaten bread per day and *no more* be allowed and given to each prisoner committed to the district gaol.

There are many, many references in the minutes of the Quarter Session of the Peace to persons who appeared before the court and were tried for numerous petty offences including assault, larceny, and trespass. There are numerous convictions wherein the accused was committed to jail for a period of time or required to pay a fine in a stipulated amount. If the fine was not paid forthwith, the accused was confined in jail until the fine was paid. The condition of the jail would leave much to be desired, as may be noted in the records of the Quarter Sessions of the Peace on December 7, 1811. The Sheriff submitted to the court, the following:

I beg leave to state to you that the prisoners in the cell of the gaol of the Home District suffer much from cold and damp, there being no method of communicating heat from the chimneys nor any bedsteads to raise the straw from the floor which lies nearly, if not altogether on the ground, therefore I have to request that you will represent these matters to the Town Brothers Magistrates and suggest that a small stove in the lobby of each range of cells, a rough bedstead for each cell together with some rugs or blankets will add much to the comfort of the unhappy persons and it is to be hoped, will remove the grievance complained of.

Following the foregoing, there was ordered on reading the above requisition of the Sherrif that 'The Treasurer do procure two small metal stoves and pipes and direct them to be put up in the lobby of each range of cells; to furnish such bedsteads, blankets or rugs as may be found necessary for the prisoners.'

On the February 18 following, at the Special Sessions of the Peace held at the Clerk of the Peace office at the Town of York, the chairman signified to the court, 'That the Keeper of the Home District gaol, prayed that the Court would grant him firewood for the two stoves lately erected for the use of the prisoners in the lobby of the cells. ORDERED — that the treasurer be requested to purchase a cord of firewood for the use of the said stoves this Winter.'

Allowances (Salary)

Current labour negotiations provide a contract between management and the employees for numerous conditions. Suffice it to say that employees today enjoy many benefits unheard of by our forefathers. In the Quarter Sessions of the Peace minutes for the meeting held on Wednesday, October 11, 1809, there appears the following item:

William Bond petitioned for an allowance for acting as Town Clerk for the Township of York since the year 1800 to which Their Honours were pleased to answer that the funds of the district were not sufficient to discharge the same.

The District Municipal Council in the year 1843 enacted a by-law to designate salaries for various township officials. A clerk in a township where two hundred or under freeholders resided, was entitled to £4 per annum. If there were over four hundred freeholders, the remuneration was increased to £6 per annum. The assessor was entitled to six and one half per cent of the assessment if it were under £50 for the township. If the assessment exceeded £400, the assessor was entitled to only two per cent of the assessed value. The remuneration elsewhere varied between two percent and the six and one half percent according to the amount of the assessment. Specific rates were fixed for pound keepers according to the age and the weight of the animals. The tax collector was granted as a remuneration a percentage of the amount of the tax roll he was to collect.

Liquor Regulations

In 1906, the Council of the Township of Vaughan passed a by-law prohibiting the sale of liquor in the township.

Throughout the minutes of the various local governments during the nineteenth century, continuous reference had been made to the issuance of licenses to innkeepers, storekeepers, and shopkeepers. In the early years of the nineteenth century, the Quarter Session minutes reveal that the number of tavern licences was limited to ten or so. This number changed within a year or so, and after the war of 1812 the list of tavern licenses issued increased astronomically. During the years 1842 to 1849, the issuance of tavern licenses was in the jurisdiction of the District Municipal Council of the Home District, and with the inception of the local Council for the Township of Vaughan, in the year 1850, the issuance of tavern licenses came within the jurisdiction of the Vaughan Town Council. In the year 1862, twenty-eight licenses were issued by the township at a cost of $40 each, yielding to the township treasury the sum of $1,120. By-law Number 54, passed by the Council of the Township on December 5, 1853, provided, among other items, regulation and control. It is interesting to note some of these provisions:

That it be enacted that it shall not be lawful for any storekeeper, shopkeeper or other person to vend by retail in quantities less than five gallons, any wine, brandy or other spirituous liquor, ale or beer without first having obtained a license for that purpose from the Treasurer of the Township and such license shall not extend to authorize such shopkeeper, storekeeper or other person to vend such liquor as aforesaid in a *smaller* quantity than one quart.

The By-law further provides that it shall be encumbent on the person applying to prove the satisfaction of the majority of the inspectors assembled for any meeting for that purpose that he or she is a person of unblemished character and sober habits; that she or he holds at the place where he or she intends to keep an inn or a house of public entertainment, personal property to the amount of Fifty Pounds; that the house for which the license is desired contains at least three furnished bedrooms with six comfortable beds and a furnished sitting room over and above the bar room or tap room and the rooms required for the use of the family of such innkeeper, together with a good shed or driving house having stabling for at least three pair of horses with a sufficient supply of food for that number always on hand.

It would appear that the Township Council appointed inspectors of taverns, and the inspectors met separately from the Council to deal with the issuance of licenses for the tavern. The clerk of the township was designated as a secretary to the innkeepers. It would be interesting to find the minute book relating to the meetings of the tavern inspectors.

Council Representation

Since 1800, there have been three distinct local governing councils: from 1800 to 1841, the Quarter Session of the Peace; from 1842 to 1849, the Home District Council; from 1850 to 1970, the Vaughan Township Council.

The Quarter Sessions of the Peace for the Home District was composed entirely of Justices of the Peace who were appointed to that office. The Justices of the Peace for the district met and elected one of their number to act as chairman. Normally, the court was composed of four to eight justices but there are occasions when many more did attend.

In 1801 and each succeeding year, the Quarter Session of the Peace appointed one or more constables for the Township of Vaughan. This is of particular significance because the appointed constable was to hold a town or township meeting of the residents at which local officers were elected: the assessor, the tax collector, the pound keepers, the fence viewers and clerk. There does not appear to have been any remuneration for any of the officials and it was common to find a person relieved of an appointment if he had served in that capacity in the preceeding year or two.

The District Municipal Council Act (1841) provided for the election of one or two councillors (according to the number of freeholders) from each township in the Home (or other) District to levy and collect taxes and administer the local affairs in the individual townships and the district as a whole. Vaughan Township's representatives to this Home District Municipal Council were: Nicholas J. Kline and Alexander McKechanie, 1842; Nicholas J. Kline and Joseph Milburn, 1843-5; Nicholas J. Kline and John W. Gamble, 1846-9. The authorization of the construction of the Township Hall and of collection from the township freeholders are examples of this council's function.

Recorded in the minutes for the Home District Council on January 26, 1847, a by-law was enacted appropriating the surplus revenue for the year 1847 for the improvements of roads and bridges as follows:

That John Delie, Arthur McNeil and Elisha Farr be Commissioners to lay out and expend the sum of One Hundred and Seventy Pounds granted to the Township of Vaughan on such roads and bridges as they may think advisable.

The Council known to us as the local Council (since 1850) is elected by the ratepayers to administer a broad range of measures for the benefit of the residents. The reeve and deputy-reeve have represented the local municipality on a County Council dealing with area-wide policy and participation. The Township Clerk and Treasurer since 1850 are as follows:

Year	Clerk
1850	James Ashdown, Clerk; Neil McEachern, Treasurer
1851-1858	James Ashdown, Clerk-Treasurer
1858-1868	George Pearce, Clerk-Treasurer
1868-1899	James Lawrence, Clerk-Treasurer
1899-1936	James McLean, Clerk-Treasurer
1936-1968	James McDonald, Clerk-Treasurer
1968-	James McDonald, Administrator; Fred Jackman, Clerk; Howard Burkholder, Treasurer

Fire Protection

The Township of Vaughan provides a service to the residents of the township through fire fighting equipment, with 24 permanent fire-fighters and 62 volunteer firefighters. The complement of the township equipment currently consists of six pumpers, two aerial ladder trucks, and two tank trucks, with other sundry equipment.

Earlier means of providing against fire is noted in the minutes of the Quarter Sessions of the Peace meeting held on March 13, 1800, when there was enacted a regulation to guard against fire:

On or before the 1st day of October next, every housekeeper shall provide and keep two buckets for carrying water, covered with canvas — or painted on the outside and covered with pitch on the inside. Each bucket shall be marked with the Christian and Surname of the housekeeper who shall also provide two ladders.

Assessment

Taxes have been levied and collected since the inception of local government — prior to 1800. The amount of tax has always been computed by applying a mill rate on assessed values.

The basis of determining assessed value has varied during the past centuries. Currently, it is contended that assessed value is established by an analysis of sales which determines market or assessed value. Assessed value in preceeding years was determined by unit replacement costs. The cost of constructing a specific type of house or building with basic building materials was determined and when the unit value was applied to the measured area of the building, the replacement cost of the building was established. The value of the land was added and the assessment was determined by applying numerous other influencing factors, such as age, location, obsolescence, etc. which would usually lower the value for assessment purposes.

Effective January 1, 1820, an Act of Parliament to provide a more equal and general assessment of lands and other rateable property throughout the province was enacted. The assessment in the year 1820 and for an interval of years thereafter was determined as follows:

every acre of arable land (pasture or meadow)	20 shillings
every acre of uncultivated land	4 shillings
every town lot in York, Kingston, Niagara, or Queenston	50 pounds
every town lot in Cornwall, Johnstown or Belleville	25 pounds
every town lot in sundry other built up areas	20 pounds
every one storey house, timber squared or hewed on two sides — not more than 2 fireplaces	20 pounds
each additional fireplace	4 pounds
every two storey house timber square or hewed on two sides — not more than 2 fireplaces	30 pounds
each additional fireplace	8 pounds
every two storey house framed — not more than 2 fireplaces	35 pounds
each additional fireplace	5 pounds
every one storey brick or stone house not more than 2 fireplaces	40 pounds
each additional fireplace	10 pounds
every two storey brick or stone house not more than 2 fireplaces	60 pounds
each additional fireplace	10 pounds
every grist mill: wrought with water 1 pair of stones	150 pounds
every additional pair of stones	100 pounds
every merchant shop, store house, operated for receiving and forwarding goods for hire or gain	190 pounds
each horse — 3 years and upward	8 pounds per head
each oxen — 4 years and upward	4 pounds per head
milch cow	3 pounds per head
horned cattle — 2 to 4 years	20 shillings per head
every closed carriage — 4 wheels for pleasure	100 pounds
every phaeton or open carriage, 4 wheels for pleasure	25 pounds
every curricle or gig (with 2 wheels) for pleasure	20 pounds
every wagon — for pleasure	15 pounds

By-Law No. 902.

WHEREAS it is expedient in Conformity with the provisions of the Consolidated Municipal Act of 1903, and Amendments thereto, to pass a By-Law appointing Overseers of Highways, for the Township of Vaughan for the year 1911.

Therefore the Corporation of the Township of Vaughan by the Council thereof enacts as follows:-

That the following named persons be and are hereby appointed Overseers of Highways in and for the Township of Vaughan for the year 1911, and until their successors are appointed and receive their List.

No of Beat.	Names.	No of Beat.	Names.
No 1.	James Bowes.	No. 20.	John Slivey
" 2.	Edward Seager	" 21.	Isaac Bales.
" 3.	Berwick Meldrick	" 22.	Alex Gordon.
" 4.	Matthew Boyle.	" 23.	Thomas Keffer.
" 5.	Wm Browning	" 24.	Arthur Rumble.
" 6.	Wesley Wellman.	" 25.	Harvey Swallow
" 7.	James Murphy.	" 26.	John H Watson
" 8.	Thomas Bowes.	" 27.	Perry Watson
" 9.	Alex Prentice.	" 28.	Ernest Kirby
" 10.	George Bone.	" 29.	George Stevenson
" 11.	Alfred Rumble.	" 30.	Elmer Atkinson
" 12.	Wm S Rumble.	" 31.	James Mullock
" 13.	Henry Wilson.	" 32.	David Wright
" 14.	J H Baynon.	" 33.	Michael Powers.
15.	P La Rose	" 34.	Wm Kyle
" 16.	T ~~Frank~~ Teasdale	" 35.	Chas A Malloy
" 17.	A S Russell.	" 36.	Ralph Sutton Jr
" 18.	John Wilson	" 37.	John Evans
" 19.	Wm Graham	" 38.	Garrett Blough

No. of Beat.	Names.	No. of Beat.	Names.
No. 39.	John A McNeil	No. 63.	Arthur Farr
" 40.	Andrew Carson	" 64.	Wm King
" 41.	Isaac Murray	" 65.	John Jeffrey
" 42.	Robert Phillips	" 66.	Wm Gilliway
" 43.	Henry Sutton	" 68.	John Train
" 44.	James Huston	" 69.	Allan Moody
" 45.	Walter Stevenson	" 70.	Thomas Towland
" 46.	Wm Bell	" 71.	Wm Mainprize
" 47.	Pass Keffer	" 72.	James Wood
" 48.	John Kerr	" 73.	Wm Tomilson
" 49.	Wesly Peterman	" 74.	Richard Agar
" 50.	Daniel Doneral	" 75.	John E Parr
" 51.	Jesse Phillips	" 76.	James Hutchinson
" 52.	Wm Hendry	" 77.	James Smith
" 53.	Robt Willis	" 78.	Robert Allan
" 54.	J T Peacock	" 79.	Wm J McAllister
" 54A.	Jas Bell.	" 80.	Herman Casely.
" 55.	L A McCallum.	" 81.	J T Nattress
" 56.	R J Train.	" 82.	Nathan Chapman
" 57.	Arthur Hambly.	" 83.	John A McCutcheon
" 58.	John J Cowan	" 84.	Frank McCluskey
" 58A.	Samuel Hillard	" 85.	Isaac Fletcher
" 59.	James Sloan	Maple.	H A McDonald
" 60.	Thomas Sloan	Kleinburg.	Wm Mullen
" 61.	Edward Button	Thornhill.	Herbert Hooper
" 62.	James N Kellam		

Passed in open Council this 11th day of April, A.D. 1911.

J B McLean
Clerk.

James A Cameron
Reeve.

Provided always that every stove erected and used in a room where there is no fireplace shall be deemed to be a fireplace.
Taxes shall never exceed one penny in the pound on the assessed sum.

Statute Labour

Statute labour was abolished in Vaughan Township in 1926, at which time a road superintendent was appointed and subsidy was paid on township road expenditures. Prior to 1926, labour was performed by all male freeholders according to the assessed value of their lands as follows:

Effective statute labour performance in 1820:

Assessed value	25 pounds	2 days statute labour
25 —	50 pounds	3 days statute labour
50 —	75 pounds	4 days statute labour
75 —	100 pounds	5 days statute labour
100 —	150 pounds	6 days statute labour
150 —	200 pounds	7 days statute labour
200 —	250 pounds	8 days statute labour
250 —	300 pounds	9 days statute labour
300 —	350 pounds	10 days statute labour
350 —	400 pounds	11 days statute labour
400 —	500 pounds	12 days statute labour

for every additional 100 pounds up to 1000 pounds	1 additional day
for every additional 200 pounds	1 additional day

Provided always that every person possessed of a wagon, cart or team of horses or oxen or beasts of burden or draft used to draw the same shall be liable to work on the highway or road not less than three days: notwithstanding anything herein contained to the contrary. Unoccupied lands shall be assessed at the rate of 1/8 of a penny per pound.

By-law Number 902 appointed the pathmasters for a designated portion of a road and it was the duty of the pathmaster to certify at the year end that all statute labour had been performed.

Sundry Items of Interest

On February 13th, 1816, the Quarter Sessions of the Peace meeting enacted a regulation that provided:

That every person or persons travelling with sleighs on any road, highway or beaten plank in this Province, shall have affixed two or more bells to the harness thereof, and any person neglecting to do so, shall upon conviction thereof by Commission or by the Oath of one creditable witness before any one of His Majesty's Justices of the Peace for the district in which such offence may be committed shall forfeit and pay the sum of Five Shillings to be levied by distress and sale of the offenders goods and chattels.

From numerous items that appear in the minute book of the Quarter Sessions of the Peace meetings, it is obvious that the Justices of the Peace had varying authority that is distinctively different from the jurisdiction of present local councils. Recorded on Tuesday, January 10, 1804, was the following: 'Personally appeared, Ida Dexter, wife of Gency Dexter and released to Jacob Shunk, her dower in the lot numbered 8 in the Fourth Concession of Vaughan.'

On April 8, 1817, a Grand Jury was selected. The following is noted from the minutes: 'The Commission was opened and read. The Grand Jury called and sworn as follows: Daniel Soules (Foreman), Nicholas Johnson, Charles Grams, Jacob Fisher, Nicholas Cover, Henry

Kersey, Jacob Munshaw, Henry White, Abraham Walker, John Oster, Samuel Arnold, John McDonald, John Smith, John Arnold, William Garner, Michael Kiffer, Abraham Wright, John Ramen.'

It would appear that the Grand Jury called to duty on this occasion was taken from the assessment roll for the Township of Vaughan. Daniel Soules was formerly a constable for the township and the other names appear quite consistent with the early settlers in the township.

John W. Gamble from Pine Grove was active in early local government for a lengthy continuous period. His name first appears in the minute book of the Quarter Sessions of the Peace in 1837 as a Justice of the Peace in and for the Home District. He was elected chairman of the Quarter Session of the Peace and resigned from that office at the third session in 1841 so he could qualify to be elected to the Home District Council in 1842 from the Township of Etobicoke. Moving to Pine Grove, he was elected to the Home District Council in 1846 from Vaughan Township, continuing as a councillor without interruption. He was elected reeve of the Township of Vaughan Council for its first eight years of existence and his name again appears as a Justice of the Peace acting in the Township of Vaughan in the year 1867. Among many community interests, he was especially active in sponsoring and supporting schools and education.

These few highlights are culled from a mass of other interesting events that could be enumerated. All have a place in the history of the township, but in many instances their pattern is irregular, with a limited general theme.

Meanwhile, history is still being made — frequently by the blending of current events with events that occurred years ago. Today's history is noteworthy when related retrospectively to the happenings of the past. As we endeavour to change the things we dislike or that no longer are applicable in today's society, let us not uphold and nurture the undesirable features of the past that our forefathers fought to change as they struggled to improve their lot in life. Let us cherish those qualities which inspired the pioneers of Vaughan, and their successors, to build this community, which we have inherited.

Appendices

VAUGHAN — 1837

NAME	CON.	NO.			
Ackrow, Joseph	10	20	Betham, Geo.	7	21
Ackrow, Samuel	10	19	Black, Hugh	3	28
Adams, James	7	26	Black, Alex	2	22
Adams, Robert	6	11	Blake, Geo.	6	7
Aikam, Adam	6	6	Bowers, Anthony	2	3
Allis, Tobit	8	6	Boyd, Dougal	7	28
Allison, Joseph	8	2	Boyd, John	7	28
Aliby, Jonathan	9	9	Boyd, Francis	1	53
Allan, James	8	33	Brand, James	10	12
Archibald, Samuel	4	25	Branham, Martin	6	10
Archibald, Jno.	4	25	Brathwaite, Wm.	2	19
Armour, James	4	9	Brawlie, Samuel	8	6
Armstrong, Thomas	4	32	Brieson, Jas.	6	30
Armstrong, Widow	7	25	Bridgford, D. Richmond Hill	1	47
Arnold, Samuel	1	37	Brown, Wm.	8	22
Arnold, Robert	2	4	Brown, Jas. Sr.	5	2
Arnold, John	9	22	Brown, Jas. Jr.	5	6
Arnold, John	1	29	Brown, John	2	1
Atkinson, John	1	41	Brown, John	7	5
Atkinson, John	1	43	Brown, Jacob	7	12
Atkinson, Jeremiah	1	36	Burkholder, Henry	8	7
			Burkholder, Wm.	4	3
Baker, Jonathan	2	11	Burkholder, Michael	4	14
Baker, Michael	2	13	Burchard, Wm.	1	38
Baker, Jacob	2	12	Burgess, Stephen	7	8
Barkay, Isaac	6	9	Burgess, Richard	10	24
Barker, Aaron	1	37	Burgess, Thos.	8	12
Barwick, John	1	34	Burr, Rowland	1	41
Baynon, John	2	35	Burton, Robert	9	2
Baxter, Wm.	3	1	Burton, Henry	10	13
Beaton, Duncan	7	25	Bunt, Francis J.	16	13
Beaton, Alexander	5	27			
Beaton, John	10	30	Cain, James	7	21
Beaton, Neil	9	28	Cairns, John	6	33
Beaton, Malcolm	9	21	Cairns, Donald	6	32
Beaton, John	9	20	Cake, John	16	12
Bell, John	4	20	Calhoun, Jno.	4	9
Bell, Hugh	6	32	Cameron, Angus	9	17
Bennett, Jacob	2	14	Cameron, Donald	5	30
Bennett, Stephen	3	2	Cameron, Archibald	5	17

Cameron, Malcolm	2	23	Eaton, William	—	—
Cameron, Arch	7	34	Eagan, Johnston	8	33
Cameron, Archibald	5	21	Edgar, Robert	2	25
Cameron, Wm.	—	—	Elliott, John	8	11
Camm, John	1	30	Endicott, John	1	56
Campbell, Aaron	4	20			
Campbell, Niel	9	28	Farr, Elisha	9	11
Campbell, Dougall	2	9	Farr, James	9	5
Capner, Joseph	7	21	Feightnor, John	3	18
Castator, Henry	6	1	Fisher, Thomas	1	37
Cedar, Anthony	—	—	Fisher, Michael	3	3
Chadwick, Thos.	4	30	Fisher, Jacob	3	3
Chadwick, Jno.	4	32	Fleming, Donald	3	8
Chamberlain, Ariel	1	54	Fletcher, Walter	9	9
Chapman, Nath'l	1	28	Forbes, Donald	1	59
Charleton, Geo.	2	3	Frank, John	5	18
Chase, Jonathan	3	21	Fraser, Joseph	3	21
Cherry, John	9	32	Fuller, Jonathan	1	56
Clark, John	1	46			
Clarkson, Thos.	1	31	Gallanough, Jas.	1	30
Clarkson, Thos.	1	36	Gamble, James	1	59
Clearing, Thos.	1	50	Gapper, Mary	1	38
Clifford, Wm.	1	46	Garrett, Wm.	3	12
Cochrane, Cornelius	5	3	Gennin, Mathew	4	33
Connor, Michael	1	38	Gibson, Wm.	2	25
Cooie, Samuel	1	30	Gilmore —	—	—
Cook, Wm.	1	36	Goodwill, John	3	13
Cook, Thos. & Wm.	2	17	Gordon, Isaac	5	34
Cover, Peter (Cober)	3	12	Graham, Jas.	6	28
Coulter, Hugh	—	—	Graham, David	1	31
Countryman, Conrad	1	50	Graham, Wm.	7	15
Couter, Henry	9	31	Grain, Mayman	10	20
Cradock, Wm.	4	28	Grumm, Peter	3	11
Cradock, Anthony	4	13	Guthrie, John	3	1
Crandon, Chris'r	5	17			
Crannie, Michael	4	22	Hair, Wm.	5	31
Crew, Wm. B.	1	49	Hamilton, Andrew	8	9
Croft, Robert	3	28	Harrison, John	1	51
Crosson, Abraham	6	35	Harrison, Edward	8	2
Crozier, James	—	—	Hart, Robert	9	7
Cunningham, Thos.	10	33	Hartfield, Justice	1	32
Currie, Donald	—	—	Healing, John	1	30
			Henry, John	3	31
			Hetherington, Wm.	3	30
Dales, Isaac	1	27	Hetherington, James	3	26
Dallas, Alex	3	20	Hewson, John	1	32
Dalziel, John	10	26	Hind, John	10	19
Dalziel, John Sr.	5	1	Hind, Thomas	10	24
Dalziel, Walter	5	8	Hilson, George	10	12
Darling, John	5	35	Hilts, L.	2	35
Devins, James	10	18	Hislop, James	2	26
Devins, Nathan	10	18	Hodgson, Richard	4	25
Develin, John	2	4	Holland, John	2	4
Dexter, Hiram	1	37	Howard, Geo. S.	9	34
Dexter, Mrs.	1	34	Hoyles, Robert	3	21
Dial, Timothy	5	21	Hunter, Robert	8	22
Diceman, John	5	24	Huttner, Jacob	3	12
Dickhout, Peter	5	14	Hutchinson, Richard	4	10

Irwin, Robert	7	31	Line, Henry	4	18
			Line, Peter	6	23
Jackson, Samuel	1	26	Lodman, James	1	34
Jackson, Peter	1	35	Long, Joshua	0	00
Jackson, Edward	1	36	Lymbunner, Matt	1	41
Jackson, Geo.	3	1			
Jacob, Henry	1	30	Madill, John	6	27
Jeffery, Richard	8	4	Malloy, Malcolm	5	25
Jeffery, John	8	5	Malloy, Archibald	4	35
Jeffery, John	9	11	Mathison, Hugh	5	11
Jeffery, David	8	34	Mathison, Alexander	4	16
Johnston, David	8	3	Mathews, Robert	0	00
Johnston, Joseph	8	9	Maxwell, Wm.	2	6
			Melville, A.	4	19
Kay, George	0	00	Mercer, William	0	00
Keefer, Jonathan (Keffer)	3	12	Miles, James	1	45
Keffer, Jacob "	3	12	Miller, Edward	6	27
Keefer, Adam "	3	13	Miller, Samuel, Jr.	6	7
Keefer, William "	3	9	Mills, Joseph	6	7
Keefer, Peter "	3	12	Milligan, Gilbert	2	24
Keefer, Daniel "	3	10	Mitchell, Wm.	8	24
Keefer, Henry "	3	13	Mitchell, Cunningham	5	22
Keefer, Valentine "	3	9	Mishlar, Isaac	6	8
Keefer, Michael "	3	14	Morrow, James	7	26
Kellam, John	9	9	Morrison, Neil	9	20
Kelly, T.	10	9	Mortimer, George	1	27
Kellam, George	10	22	Mullin, Barnabas	—	—
Kellam, Wm.	10	22	Mulloy, Neil	5	31
Kellam, John	7	12	Mulloy, James	5	29
Kerr, Angus	4	22	Munshaw, Aaron	1	51
Kersey, Wm.	10	22	Munshaw, Charles	1	44
Kersey, Edward	10	23	Munshaw, Jacob	1	27
Keworth, Wm. Sr.	3	29	Murphy, John	6	24
Keworth, Wm.	3	22	Murray, Christopher	5	26
Kinnee, Abel	4	28	Murray, William	1	2
Kinnee, Joel	5	25	Musselman, Peter	4	10
King, Robert	9	13	Musselman, Abraham	4	11
Kisor, Benjamin	4	2	Musselman, Henry	4	26
Kisor, Daniel	5	9	McArthur, Charles	5	21
Kline, John N.	4	12	McArthur, Angus	5	28
Kline, Adam	8	12	McAulay, Wm.	8	6
Kurtz, Abraham	1	34	McBride, Wm.	7	22
Kurtz, John	1	38	McBride, John	7	22
			McCallum, Donald	4	19
Lane, William	1	30	McCallum, Duncan	5	34
Langstaff, Miles	1	48	McCallum, Dougall	4	12
Lanstadt, Wm.	5	14	McCallum, Donald	9	21
Laundees, Wm.	9	15	McCarter, Angus	5	28
Laurie, Widow	5	8	McCarter, Collin	5	28
Lawrence, Alex. C.	1	42	McCarty, Owen	1	30
Lawrence, Mary	1	42	McCormack, John	5	23
Lawrence, Charles	1	42	McCormack, John	9	1
Law, Abraham	1	47	McCue, Patrick	4	31
Laymer, Widow	5	16	McCoune, James	1	37
Levitt, Thomas	3	1	McDonald, Archibald	7	29
Levistone, James	7	27	McDonald, Alexander	7	29
Line, John	4	15	McDonald, Andrew	5	21

McDonald, Archibald	5	23	Newton, James	1	50
McDonald, Ar'd, Sr.	6	21	Neuby, Thomas	6	5
McDonald, Donald	6	19	Nichols, James	9	8
McDonald, Neil	3	19	Noble, Joseph	5	22
McDonald, John	6	19	Noble, Thomas	5	22
McDonald, Neil B.	6	20			
McDonald, Arch. Jr.	3	19	O'Brian, Lucius	1	38
McDougall, John	3	15	O'Brian, Daniel	1	38
McDougall, Archibald	8	19	Ocklie, John	2	19
McFudgeon, Donald	9	28	Orr, John F.	8	27
McGill, Peter	4	24	Oster, Peter	3	6
McGilvray, Archibald	8	19	Oster, John	3	7
McGilvray, John	7	26	Oster, Jacob	3	6
McGilvray, John	8	19			
McGilvray, Neil	4	33	Paterson, Arch	9	15
McGilvray, Lauch	5	27	Peck, Washington	7	8
McGilvray, John	3	32	Peterman, George	5	30
McGilvray, Donald	9	17	Peterman, John	6	29
McGilvray, Neil	9	18	Peterson, Richard	6	6
McGilvray, Neil	9	17	Phoff, Anthony	3	15
McGuire, Charles	10	16	Pickering, Mathew	2	28
McGuire, Alex	6	8	Plough, John	6	18
McKay, Jacob	7	1	Porter, William	9	8
McKechnie, A.	1	46	Porter, John	9	9
McKechnie, Colin	5	33	Porter, David	4	19
McKechnie, Donald	9	18	Powers, Michael	4	20
McKechnie, Donald	10	23	Prentice, Pascal	5	34
McKellop, Duncan	—	—	Putherbough, Wm.	7	23
McKinnon, Anthony	6	24	Putherbough, John	5	13
McKinnon, Charles, Jr.	5	28	Putherbough, Isaac	6	34
McKinnon, Allan	5	27	Putherbough, Sol'm	5	13
McKinnon, John	4	27	Putherbough, Henry	7	35
McKinnon, Charles, Sr.	4	27	Ray, John	9	1
McKinnon, John	9	28	Raymond, John (Reaman)	2	7
McKinnon, Archibald	4	16	Raymond, George "	2	10
McKenzie, David	1	58	Raymond, John "	2	15
McKetchum, David	9	35	Raymond, Michael "	9	7
McLean, Hector	5	15	Record, John	4	29
McLean, John	4	21	Rider, Andrew	10	5
McLean, Alexander	3	21	Riddle, Isaac	3	35
McLean, Mrs.	19	18	Riddle, Andrew	10	12
McLean, John	6	16	Robins, Benjamin	4	32
McMullen, Archibald	4	22	Robins, Caleb	4	32
McMullen, Donald	4	21	Robinson, Martin	5	8
McMullen, Hugh	3	27	Robinson, David	9	22
McMurroshy, James	6	33	Rogers, John	—	—
McMurroshy, James	7	34	Roney, George	4	2
McNair, Robert	2	9	Rose, James	6	12
McNaughton, Peter	6	15	Royal, Peter	1	58
McNaughton, Donald	5	19	Rupert, Jacob	4	21
McNeil, John	7	27	Rupert, Peter	3	16
McNeil, Arthur	6	13	Rupert, Adam	4	21
McPhee, Peter	6	34			
McPherson, John	1	1	Sawyers, Richard	—	—
McQuarrie, Hector	3	21	Scott, Wainman	3	20
McQuarrie, Archibald	4	23	Seager, Edward	5	12
McVicar, John	5	33	Sergeant, William	1	47
			Shaver, Nicholas	7	9

Sharp, Thomas	6	27		Stump, Jacob	7	24
Shell, Henry F.	2	3		Sutton, Ralph	4	29
Shepherd, Edward	1	5		Swander, S. Neigh	7	10
Shell, Andrew	2	33				
Shooter, Mary Ann	1	30		Taylor, Benjamin	10	6
Shore, Anthony	—	—		Teder, John	8	5
Shunk, John	5	7		Temple, John	3	33
Shunk, Jacob	4	8		Thompson, Thomas	1	37
Shunk, Simpson	4	8		Thompson, Archibald	10	25
Shuttleworth, Benjamin	10	21		Thompson, George	4	30
Simpson, Wm.	1	1		Thompson, Joseph	3	24
Smith, John	1	37		Thorne, Benjamin	1	32
Smith, John Jr.	8	21		Totten, James	4	6
Smith, John Sr.	7	9		Train, Christopher	10	20
Smith, Thomas, Jr.	9	16		Trench, Robert	1	31
Smith, Thomas, Sr.	9	16		Troyer, Christian	3	1
Smith, Samuel	7	9				
Smith, Peter	4	19		Velie, John	—	—
Smith, Daniel	4	12				
Smith, Daniel	4	6		Wallace, Nathaniel	8	10
Smith, Jacob	4	7		Ward, Joseph	9	25
Smith, Samuel	4	6		Watts, Thomas	4	24
Smith, John	5	5		Watson, John	10	27
Smith, Larratt	1	52		Watson, James	9	1
Smithers, John	1	31		Watson, John	3	8
Smellie, David	2	8		Watson, John	6	12
Snider, George	8	9		Webster, John	10	19
Snider, Jacob	5	17		Weir, John	2	23
Snider, Samuel	—	—		Weir, Lachlan	7	35
Snider, John	4	4		Weir, John	8	17
Snowden, William	1	30		Welsh, Henry	3	14
Somerville, James	10	13		Whelpton, Thomas	4	23
Soules, Daniel	1	34		White, Henry	1	33
Soules, George	1	32		White, Ira	3	8
Soules, Peter	1	32		White, Eber	1	1
Spiker, Moses	3	11		Wilkie, James	1	33
Spiker, John	3	9		Wilkie, Thomas	1	45
Spiker, Jacob	8	22		Wilkinson, John	1	26
Stafford, John	1	4		Willson, Geo.	1	32
Stanley —	5	19		Williams, James	1	31
Steel, Thomas	1	43		Williams, John	8	3
Stegman, George	6	8		Williams, John	1	43
Stephenson, John	3	17		Williamson, John	6	7
Stevenson, Allan	8	20		Wood, John	9	16
Stewart, Captain	2	28		Wrickett, James	10	27
Stickney, John	3	25		Wright, Archibald	2	25
Stokes, Christopher	2	17		Wright, Abraham	1	47
Stone, Joseph	4	31		Wright, Joseph	2	20
Stonehouse, John	8	16		Wylie, Edward	1	30
Storey, Wm.	1	30		Wyse, Jacob	—	—
Storey, Peter	3	23				
Storm, Adam	3	23		*POPULATION* —		
Stong, John	6	2				
Stump, John	7	11		Males above 16 —		831
Stump, Joseph	7	7		Males under 16 —		789
Stump, Daniel	8	8		Females above 16 —		669
Stump, Solomon	4	13		Females under 16 —		750
				Total —		3,039

Appendix B
Vaughan Township Marriages by Rev. Wm. Jenkins, Richmond Hill

Rev. Wm. Jenkins, a native of Scotland, after completing a divinity course at Edinburgh, came first to New York as a missionary to the Oneida Indians. There he spent twelve years, but feeling that his real work lay among the struggling pioneers of Upper Canada, he set out for his new and chosen field on his own resources. It has generally been claimed that he came to Canada via Kingston in 1817, but from family tradition it seems certain that he arrived a year earlier and the intervening twelve months were spent in itinerant preaching which took him through much of the Bay of Quinte region and westward as far as the Caledon Mountains.

Calls came in 1817 from little groups of settlers at Scarborough and Richmond Hill. He responded by organizing churches at these points, and later at many others. He was active in the organization in 1834 of what was known as 'The Missionary Presbytery of the Canadas in connection with the United Associate Synod of Scotland.' He and Bishop Strachan, although chums in Scotland, often crossed swords, for the Bishop (originally a Presbyterian) had gone over to the Anglican Church. Meeting him on one occasion, the Bishop remarked, 'Your coat's getting pretty threadbare, William.' Mr. Jenkins gave the cutting reply: 'Yes, Jock, but I hae nae turned it.'

Mr. Jenkins was an activist at times. A parishioner who not only went to sleep but snored loudly was rudely awakened when the preacher hurled a Bible at his head with the remark, 'If you will not hear the Word of God, then feel it.'

He was the only non-conformist minister in several townships who could perform the marriage ceremony. Because the money was scarce, often the marriage fees were paid in loads of pumpkins or coils of home-made sausages. Once, when the married couple came from farther north from one of the Highland Scottish settlements, they brought a piper along and everyone joined in a dance after the snow had been cleared from the yard.

Since ministers' salaries were quite small, he augmented it by operating a 200-acre farm near Cashel in Markham Township. His wife was Mary H. Stockton, daughter of Dr. Stockton of New Jersey, and they had 11 children, nine of whom survived infancy. He died in 1843 aged 64 years, and his wife died in 1866. Both are buried in Richmond Hill Cemetery.

Mr. Jenkins' private marriage register from 1819 to 1843 was preserved by the family. Entries were recorded in a leatherbound volume 8¼ by 12¾ inches. Some of the writing is indistinct and the ink pale. Names are often spelled phonetically. Sometimes it appears the record was brought up to date by memory, for likely some marriages were performed at great distance from the manse. His parish was very large, from York (Toronto) to Lake Simcoe, from the Township of Pickering to the Township of Esquesing (in Halton County).

The record contains a total of 857 ceremonies, and with the

names of the two witnesses for each, there are over 3,400 names. The following were from Vaughan Township:

(P) Published by reciting Banns.
(L) Licensed.

	DATE	MARRIED	WITNESSES
	June 14, 1819	John Adams — Sylva Allen	John Allen James Lawrence
	Jan. 2, 1819	Samuel Stonely — Hannah Mullroy	Jonas Snyder Thos. Musselman
	Apr. 12, 1820	John Puterburk — Catherine McDonald	Peter Puterburk Samuel McQuerie
	March 27, 1820	Alexander Matteson — Annie McKennin	John Payne Peter McNaughton
	No date	Isaac Cample — Betsey McQuerie	John McDonald John McQuerie
(P)	Jan. 21, 1822	James Wilkey — Mary Keyles	Thomas Morgan James Goodfellow
(P)	Jan. 24, 1822	John Frank — Eliz. Walker	Benjamin Robbins John Hammond
(L)	April 2, 1822	Joseph Matteson — Margaret Sprawl	John Matteson John Snyder
(L)	June 5, 1822	Christian Troyer — Sarey (Magdalene) Cover	David Leek Nickles Cover
(P)	Aug. 13, 1822	Alexander McKay — Sally McQuiree	Daniel Sutherland Hector McQuerrie
	Sept. 17, 1822	George Stong — Polly Sherer	John Frank Daniel Stong
	April 17, 1823	Robert Turnbull — Cathrine McKinnon	Alexander Mateson John Kerr
(P)	April 8, 1824	John Velie — Anne Frank	Abram Corts Leonard Clink
(P)	April 13, 1824	Robert Cample — Kathrine Pratts	Charles Keiler David Porter
(P)	Nov. 22, 1824	Amos Dextor — Phebe Spiker	Francis Jonston John Thomson
(P)	Feb. 13, 1825	Thomas Nattress — Mary Dexter	Hierum Dexter James Harvey Cutler
(P)	April 12, 1825	Jacob Baker — Kathrine Bennet	Jonathan Baker Peter Cober
(P)	April 28, 1825	William Cassels — Isabella Park	Timothy Terry Eliza Terry
(P)	July 17, 1825	Washington Peck — Sophia Wilcoks	Steven H. Sands Agnist McKeay
(P)	Aug. 2, 1825	Jacob Brown — Lydia Smith	Samuel Smith Eliz. Brown
(P)	Aug. 16, 1825	Samuel Smith — Eliz. Brown	John Brown Hannah Burkholder
(P)	Aug. 9, 1825	Richard Peterson — Lundy Millar	Samuel Cassler Joseph Mishler
(P)	Feb. 13, 1826	Peter Curts — Mary Anne Leavan	John Mortmon Michael Curts
(P)	Feb. 14, 1826	John Brown — Hannah Burkholder	Joseph Stump Joanne Foweler
(P)	March 7, 1826	Barney Lions — Martha Atkinson	Jesse Purdy Isaac Miller

(P)	March 20, 1826	Joseph Stump — Joanna Fowler	Elias Meshler Susannah Stump
(P)	Sept. 26, 1826	John McVane — Sarah Mattice	William Mattice Hugh McCall
(L)	Oct. 6, 1826	John Williamson — Cathrine Millar	George Millar Henry Frebold
(L)	Oct. 31, 1826	Jesse Purdy — Sarah Winoms	Henry Wimoms John Sanders
(P)	Dec. 5, 1826	John Gamble — Jane Banyon	Thomas Banyon Elizabeth Gamble
(P)	Jan. 30, 1827	John Cairns — Margaret Meloy	John Armour Mary McColm
(P)	Jan. 30, 1827	Donald McCarther — Cathrine McDonald	Frederick Frank Andrew Henderson
(P)	Nov. 18, 1827	John Kennedy — Hannah Chapman	John Chapman Henry Miller
(P)	Feb. 14, 1828	Michael Baker — Mary Cover	Jacob Bennot Cathrine Cover
(P)	Feb. 19, 1828	John Riccard — Betesy Bennet	Michael Baker Mary Cover
(P)	Feb. 19, 1828	Allen Smith — Sarah Barb	Wm. Rogers Mary Baker
(P)	Apr. 10, 1828	Henrey Valeire — Sary MacQuere	Jesse Berd Elizabeth Monshaw
(P)	May 28, 1828	Archibald McDonald — Mary White	Hugh Beggs Laury McKinnon
(P)	June 4, 1828	Jacob Bennet — Mary Dudgeon	Joseph Fraser Elizabeth Burkholder
(P)	Oct. 15, 1828	Hugh Carl Beggs — Flora McKinnon	John McDonald Anne McKinnon
(P)	Nov. 25, 1828	Solomon Prentice — Mary Cyser	Hirem Prentice Eve Prentice
	Nov. 25, 1828	Newton Godell — Mary Smith	Robert Smith David Leek
(P)	Mar. 27, 1829	Amos Dexter — Mary Beaty	Patty Anderson Katren Dexter
(P)	Mar. 27, 1829	Lewis Frederick Jahn — Elizabeth Garland	Peter Butterhaulder Mary Garland
(P)	Oct. 12, 1829	Elisha Dexter — Mary Kane	George Bowles Hirem Dexter
(P)	Oct. 22, 1829	John McDonald — Grace Moore	Arcbald McDonald Mary McKinnon
(P)	Nov. 15, 1829	Hirem Macy — Eliza Anne Lawrence	David Bridford Nathan Troop
(P)	Nov. 18, 1829	Jesse Bennet — Anne Durgeon	Nathan Troop Margaret McQuere
(P)	Dec. 9, 1829	Henery Sanders — Elizabeth Hawman	David Porter Joseph Walker
(P)	Jan. 5, 1830	Isaac Meshler — Marg. Stump	Peter Dehout Peter Bunt
(P)	Jan. 5, 1830	Joseph Coon — Anne Maynard	Able Kenny William Burkholder
(P)	Jan. 5, 1830	Elezur Sanley — Rachel White	John Marman Frances Bunt
(P)	Jan. 21, 1830	John Williams — Sarah Shunk	John Hendery John Shunk
(P)	Mar. 2, 1830	Henry Line — Elizabeth Feighner	Wm. Beggs Elizabeth Burkholder

(P)	Mar. 9, 1830	Thomas Perry — Martha Wilson	John Perry Elizabeth Gilmore
(P)	April 19, 1830	Tobias Spiker — Susan Shunk	John Spiker Mary Shunk
(P)	Oct. 19, 1830	Henry Snyder — Mary Shunk	Jacob Shunk Jean Shunk
(P)	Oct. 26, 1830	Gabriel Howman — Elizabeth Burkholder	David Frank Dory McKinnon
(P)	Dec. 1, 1830	Charles McKinning — Christy Black	Neil McDonald Janet Moor
(P)	Jan. 18, 1831	Jacob Burkey — Susan Blough	Joseph Mishler John Mishler
(P)	Jan. 25, 1831	Neil McLamont — Cathrine Black	Neil McKinnon John Matteson
(P)	Feb. 8, 1831	Neil Meloy — Christy McCathrine	John Meloy Sr. James McCathrine
(P)	Mar. 24, 1831	Gilbert Milligan — Sarah Ralston	James Quagly Peter Grant
(P)	May 17, 1831	Abram Law — Elizabeth Clink	John Grant Amos Wright
(P)	May 21, 1831	David Smellie — Anne Dalziel	James Hogg Wm. Dalziel
(P)	Nov. 1, 1831	Walter Dalziel — Jane Moor	John Armour Archibald McDonald
(P)	Nov. 15, 1831	James McMurchy — Agnist McDougal	Archibald Campble Archibald McDougal
(P)	Dec. 16, 1831	James Hutcheson — Jane Sampson	George Bowells Mary Anne Hunt
(P)	Jan. 5, 1832	James Gamble — Elizabeth Gilmore	Elijah Miller Mary Gamble
(P)	Feb. 28, 1832	Peter Stover (Pickering) — Margaret Coover (Vaughan)	Nickles Holms Samuel Snyder
(P)	Mar. 8, 1832	Thomas Moor (Markham) — Margaret Shooter (Vaughan)	Camble Querey Hellen Purcell
(L)	June 7, 1832	Duncan Weir (Scarboro) — Mary Wright (York)	John Weir Hugh Wright
(P)	Sept. 25, 1832	George Lilley — Mary Anne Castator	James Brown Elizabeth Wilson
(P)	Nov. 13, 1832	Robert Adams — Anne Ritche	Andrew Hamilton John Millar
(P)	Nov. 13, 1832	Neils Holms — Susan Coover	Daniel Crider Samuel Snyder
(P)	Nov. 12, 1832	James B. Flanagan — Mary Knitchler	Leonard Countryman Susannah Countryman
(P)	Feb. 18, 1833	Christopher Crouder — Rosina Keefer	George Lemore Sally Keefer
(L)	Feb. 22, 1833	James Walson — Mary McVicar	Neil Meloy Donald Camble
(P)	Mar. 6, 1833	David Gailly (Markham) — Jane Jamison (Vaughan)	John Jamison James Shenold
(P)	April 4, 1833	James Meloy — Jane Armour	Donald Cameron James Murphy
(P)	May 22, 1833	Joseph Fraser — Barbara Raymond	John Raymond David Porter
(P)	June 11, 1833	George Blake — Betsy Miller Tecomptsu	John Williamson Joseph Miller
(P)	Sept. 3, 1833	John Spiker — Hulda Thorn	Tobias Spiker Moses Spiker

(P)	Dec. 23, 1833	John Harlan — Jane Little	John Peterman John Richard
(L)	Oct. 2, 1834	James Pringle — Joan Wanlesse	John Pringle John Brake
(L)	Dec. 19, 1834	John McKay — Flora McKinnon	James Wilkey James Breyson
(P)	Dec. 24, 1834	William T. Wolfe — Mary Parkison	Barkley Doyle — John Wilson
(L)	Dec. 26, 1834	James Brayson — Margaret McKay	Robert Miller John McKay
(P)	Jan. 6, 1835	Moses Spiker — Eliza Cysie	Jacob Keysie Cathrine Lighty
(P)	Apr. 28, 1835	Henrey Musselman — Sarah Butterbaugh	Solomon Butterbaugh Esther Musselman
(P)	June 11, 1835	Thomas Banks — Jannet Geffery	Joseph Wright James Heslip
(P)	Oct. 27, 1835	Michael Fisher Sarah White	Mark Burkholder Cornelius Dunkam
(P)	Nov. 17, 1835	Nathan Burns — Janet Wilkey	David McDugal James Newton
(L)	Mar. 10, 1836	George Ross — Euphemia Sutherland	Alexander McKechney Alexander Ross
(P)	Nov. 8, 1836	John Hislop — Helen McGowen	John Hislop Wm. Giffery
(L)	Dec. 6, 1836	Michael Dey Whitmore — Cathrine McLellan	Samuel Lyon Sarah Fisher
(P)	Jan. 29, 1837	Alfred Bagshaw — Fanny Millar	Benjamin Lee Mary Ann Bassentway
(P)	Mar. 14, 1837	Abram Stump — Mattey Leno	Joseph Stump Amelia Burkholder
(P)	April 11, 1837	Anthony Pfaff — Solomina Millar	Nickke Overling Jacob Histner
(P)	Dec. 25, 1837	John Baker — Barbra Cover	Jacob Cover Susan Baker
(P)	Mar. 12, 1838	John Oster — Jane Antony	Michael Oster Rebeca Matteson
(P)	Apr. 10, 1838	Michael Burkholder — Rebeca Lion	Samuel Leon Cathrine Lehman
(P)	May 1, 1838	Joseph Stump — Cathrine Lehman	Samuel Lehman Cathrine Stump
(P)	Jan. 24, 1839	Silas Fuller — Rachel Phillips	William Jenkins Jr. Sarah White
(P)	July 16, 1839	James McLoud — Sarah Fisher	Jacob Stone Mary Keefer
(P)	Nov. 13, 1839	Charles McKinnon — Jane McGown	Angus McKinnon Neil Cample
(L)	Feb. 16, 1840	Thomas Banks — Alice Merreth	William Smith Cathrine M. Higgins
(P)	May 4, 1840	Robert Travis — Sarah Grahm	Neilson Grahm Susan Moor
(P)	May 27, 1840	William Evans — Mary Reid	A.P. Lawrence Matilda Evans
(L)	June 17, 1840	Thomas Wilson — Sarah Leymburn	George Shepherd Charlot Leymburn
(L)	April 2, 1842	Thomas Morgan — Susan Clark	Alex. Meohony James Wilkey

(P)	April 30, 1842	William Paterson — Mary McMawn	John Maloy Margaret Munshaw
(P)	July 9, 1842	David Coalman — Sarah Gilmore	Thomas Lauder Jane Anne Coalman
(P)	Mar. 26, 1843	William Walton — Hannah Hamilton	Jesse Toten Luissa Hamilton
(P)	July 30, 1843	John Carter — Esther Cresler	John Cresler Eliza Phillips

Appendix C
Nineteenth Century Buildings in Vaughan Township

The pattern of early buildings in Vaughan Township is the same as in the rest of Ontario and, therefore, a more detailed study of early buildings applicable to this region can be found in *'The Ancestral Roof'* (Macrae and Adamson) and *'Building with Wood'* (Rempel). As elsewhere, the first structures were of log but here it seems that the material was found to be logical and so many of the finer and larger structures in Vaughan were so constructed. Elsewhere it was usual that the log building was only used for the first temporary structures. The Stong Farm, for all that is is not located in Vaughan Township, nonetheless is very representative. Immediately across the road in Vaughan is another splendid log house on the Dalziel property. There are many more such log houses in the Edgely district and these buildings are examples of the finest of log work done anywhere in the province of Ontario.

These buildings were built by people of Pennsylvania German stock who by their very nature were conservative and preferred simplicity in taste. The result is that many of these buildings appear much older than they actually are. The meeting house — Cober Church — on Dufferin Street above the Langstaff crossroad, while built in 1888, would appear to be a structure of considerably greater age. The farm complexes of the Allan Smith farm on Jane Street at Edgeley and of Amos Baker on the Langstaff Road show this reserved, orderly taste with a very traditional feeling.

The Edey House in Thornhill and the Burwick House in Woodbridge, both dating to the 1840s, are perhaps architecturally the finest two residences in Vaughan. Both these houses are of such exceptional quality that they have been preserved for all time, the Edey House being relocated in Markham Township and restored privately, and the Burwick House being relocated in Black Creek Village as a museum house in that Conservation Authority area. The Edey House, built by a local contractor, is in the Regency Cottage style, while the Burwick House is in the Ontario Classic style with much emphasis on the Greek Revival. This style was designed to impress from the outside, which the Burwick House does admirably. It is always a surprise to visitors to find how small and almost mean the house is within.

There are many handsome landmarks surviving today in Vaughan, including an octagonal house at Maple, and many variations of red patterned brick structures. Even Mary Gapper O'Brien's house on Bathurst Street is worthy of note.

Vaughan does have a distinctive type of building construction, only occasionally found outside the township in neighbouring municipalities. It is the vertical plank construction, an unusual manner of building whereby the walls are three-inch vertical planks set in grooves on heavy timber sills and roof plates. The attached diagram by A.H. Sabean shows this in more detail, based on several houses and particularly a house which stood next to the school in Sherwood built in 1844. Buildings of this type turn up with amazing regularity in Vaughan and many of them appear to tie in to the history of the Keffer family. The construction is not unique, for it turns up in the State of Vermont in considerable buildings, but here in Ontario, outside of Vaughan, they are rarely found. The Laskay Emporium, now at Black Creek Village, is of this construction. Like it, all of them originally appeared as a board and batten structure, but over the years they have been sided in clapboard or brick veneer.

Napier Simpson

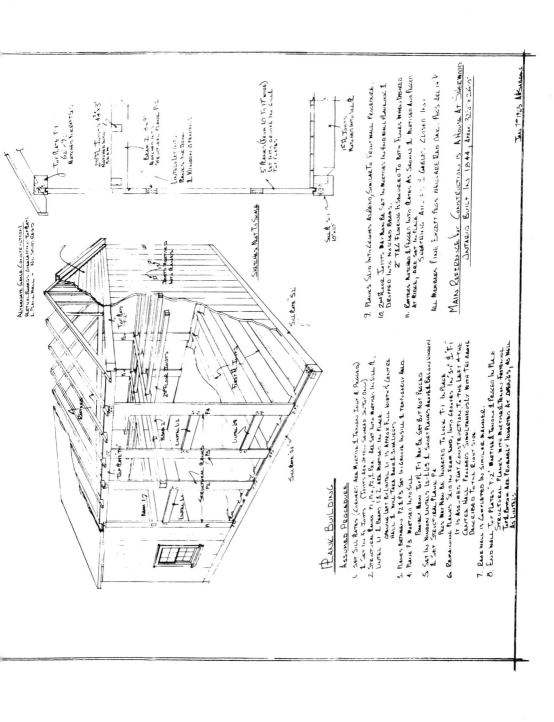

Plank Building

Assumed Procedure

1. Set Sill Plates (corners are mortise & tenon joint & pegged)
1. Cast in F. Joists (corners are mortise sawdust dovetail dog)
2. Structural Beams P1, P2, & B2a are set into mortise in sill it, Install L1 & Beam 1 & 2 are mortise in place. Groove left by lintel L1 is approx full width (center hall & will take brace shoulders)
3. Planks between P2 & P3 set in groove in sill & temporarily held
4. Plank P3 mortise into sill. Probably beam top P1, T1 may be set but not pegged
5. Set in window lintels L1, L1.1 & short planks above & below window & set structural plank P4. Pegs may now be inserted to lock T1 in place
6. Remaining planks slid in from end, into grooves in "sil" & T1. It is assumed that construction to the left & the center hall proceeded simultaneously with the attic proceeded to the right side.
7. Rear wall is completed in similar manner.
8. End wall top plates "T2" mortise & tenon & pegged in place. Structural planks with mortise/tenon fastening top & bottom are probably inserted as desired, as well as lintels.
9. Planks slid into grooves as before, similar to front wall procedure.
10. 2nd floor joists bay have be set in mortise in end wall plank & 1 dropped into notched beam. 2" T&G flooring is secured to both planks when desired
11. Rafters notched & pegged into plates as shown & mortise and pegged at ridge, are set in place. Sheathing ... & gable, closed in.

All members pine except pegs which are dead oak. Pegs are 1" x 1"

Main Reference for Construction is a House at Sherwood, Ontario built in 1844, Approx. 32'0 x 26'0

Alternate gable construction. Vertical planks overlapping top plate. End walls - no noted beam

Top Plate T1 62+/-. Mortise & tenon etc.

2"x4" joists 4"x3" notched into beam

Beam 2 2"x9" notched into structural plank P2

Installed into planks for doors & windows are identical

3" planks (from 10 to 17" wide) let into groove in sill top plates.

F&L joists, notched into sill it.

Sill Sill 10x10

Sketches Not To Scale

Jan 7 1925 AK Sherrett

Index

A

Abbs, Rev. G., 137

Abell, John, 125, 128, 148, 249, 250

Abell Agricultural Works, 125, 126, 190, 220, 260

Acheson, Lillian, see Cameron, Mrs. Archibald

Acies, Fanny, 176

Adams, George C., 239

Adams, James, 69, 73, 233, 281

Adams, Thos., 35

Addison, Lydia Ann, see Mackenzie, Mrs. Donald

Addison, Rev. Peter, 147, 151

Addy, George, 233

Administration of justice, 274-75

Adour, Miss C.J., 181

Agar, Adam and Mrs. Isobella (née Kersey), 187

Agar, Amos and Mrs. Alice (née Dalziel), 187

Agar, Bruce, 187

Agar, C.J., 128

Agar, Gilbert, and Mrs. Ruth (née Ezard), 250, 256, illus. opp. 188

Agar, Gladys, 180

Agar, Rev. Gordon, 187

Agar, M.J., 239

Agar, Richard and Mrs. Elizabeth (née Ash), and Mrs. Jane Frances (née Train), 71, 187, 258

Agar, Robert and Mrs. Margaret (née Lawrie), 72, 148, 205

Agar, Thornhill A., 128, 250

Agar, Thomas and Mrs. Hannah, 72, 187

Agar, W.J., 76, 241

Agar, William, 64, 90

Agar family, 147, 187

Agnew, Mrs. Charles (née Dalziel, Jean), xiv, 245

Agricultural Representatives, 255

Agricultural Societies xiii, 248-251

Aikenhead, Gertrude, 175

Aikenhead, Rev. J.R., 151

Aitcheson, Miss V., 245

Aitchison, Dorothy, see Thomson, Mrs. James

Aitken, Rev. William, and Mrs., 145

Aitkin, Alexander, 49

Albertson, David, 31

Alford, Dick and Mrs. Bessie (née Elliott), 197

Allan, Charles, 196

Allan, Joseph, 102

Allan, Hon. William, 59, 85

Allegheny Mountains, 41, 202

Allen, David, 162

Allen, Ebenezer and Mrs. Lucy, 34, 38

Allen, G.F., 254

Allen, James, 70

Allison, Fisher, 159

Allison, Jane, 159

Alliston, George, 120

Alliston, James, 174

Alsop, S., 260

Ames, Rev. Wm., 160

Amos, Miss, 180

Anderson, Albert, 118

Anderson, Miss, C.E., 177

Anderson, Rev. H., 159

Anderson, Rev. J.E., 160

Anderson, Jannette, 34, 38

Anderson, John M., 34, 38, 39

Anderson, Margaret, see Johnston, Mrs. Robert

Anderson, Walter, 75

Andrews, Mr., 182

Andrews, Rev. and Mrs. B.F., 145, 168, 185

Andrews, Mae, 180

Andrews, S., 186

Angle, Mrs., 254

Anglin, Edna, 180

Angrove, Edward, 142

Ansley, Emma M., 166

Ansley, Thomas, 169

Anstey, E.W., 76, 241
Anthony, Richard, 155
Appleton, William and Mrs. Eliza (née Witherspoon), 227
Arbuckle, Rev. John, 158
Arbuthinot, Miss J.S., 177
Archer, William, 71, 139, 163
Archibald, D., 141
Archibald, Stanley, 126
Archibald, Violetta, 168
Argent, Mr., 185
Argue, Rev. T., 137
Arlow, Mrs. Roy, 246
Armitage, Rev. Dr. Ramsay, 145
Armour, Elizabeth, see Cameron, Mrs. Donald
Armour, James, 38, 281
Armstrong, Miss, 171
Armstrong, Mr., 104
Armstrong, Annie, 171
Armstrong, Edward W., 36
Armstrong, Fred D., 128
Armstrong, Rev. J. Gibert, 161
Armstrong, James Roger, 40
Armstrong, Jas. B., 36
Armstrong, John E., 142
Armstrong, Kate, 169
Armstrong, Margaret McGregor, 40
Armstrong, Thomas, 70, 233, 281
Armstrong, Westropp, 40
Arnold, John and Mrs. Elizabeth, 122, 149, 152, 155, 280, 281
Arnold, Robert J., 73, 274, 281
Arnold, Samuel, 74, 280, 281
Arnold family, 119, 176
Arnott, J.W., 143
Arnott, John, 181
Artkins, Miss T.J., 186
Arts & Crafts, 268-9
Ash, Elizabeth, see Agar, Mrs. Richard
Ash, John and Mrs. Ida (née White), 226
Ashbee, J.R., 196
Ashdown, Chas., 142
Ashdown, James, 67, 68, 72, 148, 277
Asher, James, 167, 169
Ashurst, Mrs. I., 175
Askew, Rev. Wm. E., 155
Asling, Chester, 166, 171
Assessment, 65, 66, 278; see also Census; Population
Assessment Roll (1837), 281-85
Aston, Robert, 260
Atkinson, Rev. A.E., 158
Atkinson, Fanny, 169
Atkinson, George and Mrs. Margaret (née Baker), 169, 187, 188

Atkinson, Gordon, 249
Atkinson, Jane, see Mrs. Robt. Mortly
Atkinson, Jeremiah, 54, 122, 281
Atkinson, John, 55, 67, 281
Atkinson, John Jr. and Mrs. Elizabeth (née Kurtz), 187
Atkinson, John Sr. and Mrs. Margery, 187, 189
Atkinson, Margery, see Marsh, Mrs. James
Atkinson, Miss S.E., 172
Atkinson, Thomas and Mrs. Lenissa (née Holland), 187
Atkinson, W.D., 118
Atkinson, William Jr. and Mrs. Frances (née Trench), 223
Atkinson, William Sr. and Mrs. Mary (née Graham), 118, 151, 187-88
Atkinson family, 68, 147, 187-88
Atkinson & Switzer, 188, 223
Attwell, Edna, 153
Atwell, Joseph, 40
Auction Sales, 233-34
Aylsworth, Dr. Isaac B., 143

B
Babcock, Del, 174
Back, Rev. W.G., 145
Backhouse, Samuel, 36, 39
Bagg, Alfred, and Mrs., 220, 245
Bagg, Donald, 256
Bagg, Frank, 104
Bagg, Mrs. Fred, 245
Bagg, George and Mrs., 104, 245
Bagg, Geo. W., 250, 260, illus. opp. 82
Bagg, Kathleen, 174
Bagg, Norman and Mrs. Mary (née Bowes, 185, 250, 256
Bailey, Mr., 100
Bailey, Brian, 77
Bailey, C.J., 143
Bailey, Carl, 172
Bailey, Elizabeth, see Thomas, Mrs. Wm.
Bailey, George and Mrs., 147, 178, 240
Bailey, Henry C., and Mrs., 97, 110, 111, 244
Baillie, Mr., 177
Baker, Amos and Mrs. Edna, xi, xiv, 14, 188, 265, 291
Baker, Eve, see Brillinger, Mrs. Ben
Baker, G., 141
Baker, George, 188
Baker, Isaac, 138, 169, 188
Baker, Jacob and Mrs. Kathrine (née Bennet), 100, 170, 281, 287

Baker, Jacob and Mrs. Mary (née Breck), 188, illus. opp. 85
Baker, Jesse, 170, 188, 194
Baker, John, 4, 88
Baker, John A., 188
Baker, Jonathan, and Mrs. Elizabeth (née Cober), 43, 88, 188, 281, 287
Baker, Jonathan Jr., 82, 88, 134, 169, 170, 178, 188, 232, illus. opp. 66
Baker, Margaret, see Atkinson, Mrs. George
Baker, Mary, 169, 170, 288
Baker, Michael and Mrs. Mary (née Cober), 88, 188, 233, 281, 288
Baker, Paul, 188
Baker, Peter, 88, 169
Baker, Philip, 42
Baker, Ronald, 181
Baker, Bishop Samuel, 135
Baker, Thos., 75
Baker, Rev. W.E., 154
Baker, William, 226
Baker family, ix, 44, 47, 134, 158, 169-70, 188, 238
Baker homestead, illus. opp. 188
Baldwin, Mary Ann, see Troyer, Mrs. Samuel
Baldwin, Thomas, 37
Baldwin, William, 140
Bales, George E., 239
Bales, Graeme, 249
Bales, Thomas I., 239
Ball, W.C.L., 123
Ballantyne, H.L., 181
Bamford, Rev. A.F., 143
Bangs, Nathan, 150, 154
Banks: 73, 81, 108, 110, 111, 117, 128
Bapp, Louis, 59
Barber Ebenezer and Mrs. Margaret (née Wallace), 224, 246
Barber, William, 31
Barbour, James, 109
Baringer, Rev. P.S., 158
Barker, Aaron, 188, 281
Barker, Andrew, 250
Barker, Brock and Mrs. Colleen (née Hodgson), 186, 188
Barker, Rev. E., 142, 149
Barker, Grant, 256
Barker, Harold, 228
Barker, Keith, 256
Barker, Mrs. Lorne, 246
Barker, Ross, 228
Barker, Roy H. and Mrs. Estelle (née Laver), xi, xiv, 10, 128, 188, 246, 247, 250, 260

Barker, Rev. W.R., 151
Barker family, 188
Barkwell, Rev. J., 137, 151
Barn raisings, 234-35, illus. opp. 238
Barnard, Benjamin, 116, 176, 181
Barnes, John, 104
Barrass, Edward (M.A.), 143
Barrett, Rev. C.W., 160
Barry, Thos., 35, 39
Bartholomay, Philip, 27
Barton family, 101
Barwick, John, 55, 281
Bassingthwaite family, 166, 169, 179, 290
Bateman, Joseph, 169
Bates, Mr., 185
Bates, Rev. W., 152, 153, 155
Bates, Mrs. William, 246
Battersby, Rev. H.F., 153
Battger, J.H.I., 21
Baxter, Rev. John, 160
Bayliss, John, 250
Bealby, William, 169
Bealton, John, 41
Bealton, Malcolm, 40
Beamish, Archie and Mrs. Olga (née Robinson), 189, illus. opp. 189
Beamish, Catherine, 175, 189, illus. opp. 189
Beamish, Henry and Mrs. Susannah (née McCort), 189
Beamish, Henry and Mrs. Mary (née Codlin), 189
Beamish, John, 189, illus. opp. 189
Beamish, John Alexander and Mrs. Elizabeth (née Cameron), 189
Beamish, M., 185
Beamish, Rahno, 189, illus. opp. 189
Bean, Amos, 104
'Beartrap,' 216
Beaton, Alex, 171
Beaton, Alexander, 70, 281
Beaton, Duncan, 233, 281
Beaton, John, 70, 71, 281
Beaton, Kenneth, 167, 175
Beaton, Margaret, see Kersey, Sr., Mrs. William
Beaton, William, 233
Beatty, Miss, 169
Beatty, Faith, 179
Beatty, Lloyd, 249
Beausang, Rev., 156
Beaverbrook, Lord (Max Aitken), 145
Becker, Elizabeth, see Troyer, Mrs. Christian
Bedford, Rev. A., 147
'Bees', 61
    Barn raising, 234-35, illus. opp. 238

Butchering, illus. opp. 90
Beggs, Hugh Earl, 144
Belamy, Mr. 171
Belcher, Frank, 76
Belfry, Rev. C.A., 160
Bell, Miss, 180, 182
Bell, Mrs., 175
Bell, Agnes, 236
Bell, George, 64, 90
Bell, James, illus. opp. 95
Bell, Janet, see Lawrie, Sr., Mrs. William

Bell, Margaret R., 185
Bell, Mrs. Sarah, 169
Bell, Mrs. Verna, 172
Bell, Wm., 174
Bender, Mrs. N.A., 186
Bennet, Jacob and Mrs. Mary (née Dudgeon), 67, 170, 281, 288
Bennet, Jesse and Mrs. Anne (née Durgeon), 169, 170, 288
Bennet, Kathrine, see Baker, Mrs. Jacob
Bennet family, 134, 261
Bennett, Mrs. Anna, 170
Bennett, Aquillat, 38
Bennett, Elizabeth, 169, 170
Bennett, Rev. G., 137, 140
Bennett, Hugh, 169
Bennett, Jane, see Lawrie, Mrs. Gavin
Bennett, John, 169, 170
Bennett, Martha, 169, 170
Bennett, Sarah Ann, 169, 170
Bentley, Rev. H., 149
Bentley, J. (M.D.), 141
Berczy settlement, 52
Bernard, G., 259
Bernath, Everton Lorne, 113
Bernath, James, 148
Bernath, Reta, 169
Berton, Pierre and Mrs., xi, 242
Berwick, Edward, 124
Bessey, Abigail, 36
Bessey, Esther, 177
Bethune, N., 172
Betts, Rev. J.E., 151
Bevan, Michael and Mrs., 175
Bevitt, Rev. Thos., 160
Beynon, Clayton, 174, 189
Beynon, Geo., 107
Beynon, Rev. George, 189
Beynon, John and Mrs. Jane, 189, 281
Beynon, Jonathan, 189
Beynon, Josie M., 172
Beynon, Robert, 189, 258
Beynon, Ruth, 258
Beynon family, x, 107, 189, 288, illus. opp. 189

Bigford, Dr. R.A., 111, 145
Biggar, Rev. Hamilton, 160
Bigham, Mr., 233
Binnie, Miss C.J., 177
Bird, Effie, 183
Birkett Dr. Chas. W., 77, 146
Bishop, Mrs. George, 246
Black, Annie, 174
Black, Florence, 139
Black, John, 135, 139, 148
Black, Norman, 148
Black family, 158, 281
Black Creek Pioneer Village, 134, 195, 217, 218, 221, 262, 291, 292, illus. opp. 90
Blackburn, Mr., 164, 233
Blackett, Rev. Geo. M., 142, 149
Blacklock, Rev. W.S., 151
Blackstock, Rev. Wm., 160
Blackwood, Thomas F., 260
Blain, David and Mrs., 71, 246
Blair, Stewart, 260
Blake, Rev. D.E., 145, 155
Blakely, William, 229
Blandin, Dr. H.M., 144
Blanshard, Shem, 143
Blasdell, Rev. B., 137
Blough, Mary Elizabeth, see Witherspoon, Mrs. David
Boake, Allen, 172, 256
Boake, Cameron, and Mrs., 245, 256
Boake, Olive, 180
Board of Trade, Woodbridge, 127
Bockmaster, Wm. J., 180
Boddy, Mrs. John (née Norma Williamson), 177, 186, 246
Bodi, J. and Mrs., 111
Bodker, Mrs. Fred., 245
Bointon, Lt. Col. Chevalier August, 117
Boives, C.A., 169
Bolitho, Henry, 100, 179, 180, 183
Bolton, Sarah Jane, see Thomson, Mrs. William
Bond, William, 45, 275
Bone, Douglas, 133
Bone, John, 226
Bone, Percy, and Mrs., 245, 254
Bone, Walter, 133
Bone, Wilbert, 100
Bone family, 101
Boniface, Andrew H., 123
Boogers, Rev., N.H., 147
Booth, Rev. W.B., 151
Boots, John, 136
Boston family, 158
Bostwick, Nathan, 24
Bothwell, Anne, 180
Bouchette, Jos., 18

Boulton, D'Arcy, 59
Bovaird, Fred, 249
Bowen, Mrs. Edgar (née Diceman,
    Bertha), 196
Bowen, John and Mrs. Mary (née
    Post), 37
Bowen, Luke, 31
Bowen, Peter and Mrs. Mary, 35, 39
Bowen, Roy, 168
Bowes, Albert, 189
Bowes, Anthony Sr. and Mrs. Ellen,
    37, 67, 189, 281
Bowes, Anthony Jr., 189
Bowes, Anthony (III), 189, 220
Bowes, Edgar, 239
Bowes, Emmanuel, 189-90, 220
Bowes, Mrs. Evelyn, 102
Bowes, F., 185
Bowes, Henry, 189
Bowes, James, 189
Bowes, Mary C., see Bagg, Mrs. Norman
Bowes, Nelson, 189
Bowes, Norman, 102, illus. opp. 101
Bowes, Ross, 55, 100, 189
Bowes, Thomas, 189
Bowes, Wilfred, 190
Bowes, William, 67, 135, 136, 189
Bowes family, 189-90
Bowles, Rev. R.P., 60
Bowles, Miss Shirley, 178
Bowman, Ada, see Elliott, Mrs. James
Bowman, Rev. C.H., and Mrs. (née
    Olivia McQuarrie), 145, 179, 203,
    239
Bowman, James, 148, 260
Bowman, June, 258
Bowman, Robt., 101
Boyce, J., 182
Boyd, Dougal, 233, 281
Boyd, Malcolm, 41
Boyd Conservation Area, 262
Boyington family, 134
Boyle, David, 73, 124, 190
Boyle, Georgia, see Newton, Mrs. J.
    Earle
Boyle, John, 74, 75, 190
Boyle, Marguerite, 190
Boyle, Morgan, 190
Boyle family, 153, 190
Boyletown, 153
Boynton, A., 141
Boynton, Carl, 255, 258
Boynton, George, 237
Boynton, Hannah, see Weldrick, Mrs.
    George
Boynton, John, 136
Boynton, Russell, 206
Brace, Rev. A.D., 151

Brack, John, 139
Brackenridge, Mr., 100
Bradley, Frank, 181
Bradley, W.A., 123
Bradshaw, Rev. T.P., 137
Braithwaite, Edward, 169
Braithwaite, James, 67
Brand, James, 281
Brandon, Jean, 169
Brass, Mrs. Audrey, 247
Brassen, Erik, 163
Bray, Mrs. Ed., 244
Breakey, J.W., 183
Breakley, J.N., 249
Breck, Mary, see Baker, Mrs. Jacob
Bredlin, 151
Breinich, Adam, 29
Brennan family, 163
Brentnell, Mrs. George, 245
Brethen, Rev. C.B., 151
Brice, Eric, III
Bridgeford, Col. David, 68, 73, 117,
    119, 216, 230, 249, 258-59, 281,
    288
Bridgeford, Margaret, see Powell, Mrs.
    William I.
Bridgeman, Julia, see Longhouse, Mrs.
    Gordon
Brillinger, Aut, 103
Brillinger, Ben and Mrs. Eve (née
    Baker), 118, 124, 169, 170, 188
Brillinger, Hattie, 124
Brimsden, John, 135
Broadhurst, Thomas, 120
Brookes, Amy, 174
Brooks, Mrs. Jean, 172
Brown, Miss, 177
Brown, Rev. A., 147, 151
Brown, Rev. B., 135, 137
Brown, Earl, 260
Brown, Edwin W., 127, 128, 250
Brown, Eliz., see Smith, Mrs. Samuel
Brown, Ethel M., 185
Brown, Evelyn, 246
Brown, Rev. F.L., 160
Brown, Fanny, 174
Brown, Rev. George, 147
Brown, Jas. (II), 39, 190, 281
Brown, Rev. John, 151
Brown, John Sr. and Mrs. Hannah (née
    Burkholder), 35, 38, 56, 68, 73,
    120, 152, 190, 207, 229, 230, 281,
    287, 289
Brown, Joseph, 68, 171
Brown, Mary, 34, 190
Brown, Miriam, 172
Brown, O.J., 118
Brown, Ralph, 183

Brown, Rev. T.C., 137
Brown, W.P., 143
Brown, Wm., 159, 281
Brown and Muir, 126
Brown family, ix, 69, 190
Brownlee, Catherine, 258
Brownlee, George, 234, 250, 259, illus. opp. 232
Brownlee, James and Mrs. Louise (née McDonald), 210, 246
Brownlee, John B., 239
Brownlee, Robert, 220
Brownridge, George, 81
Brownsville, 125, 190
Bruce, Alex D.. 50
Brule, Etienne, 8, 18
Brum, Donald, 179
Brumwell, John, 260
Brunskill's Mills, 238
Bryant, Mrs. William, 245
Bryce, W.R., 77
Brydon, J., 106
Bryson, Alexander and Mrs. Esther (Hettie) (née Snider), 74, 191
Bryson, Elmer and Mrs. Mary (née Cameron), 191, 246
Bryson, Helen, see Mitchell, Mrs. Robert
Bryson, James and Mrs. Jean (née McCallum), 190, 191, 281, illus. opp. 23
Bryson, Jesse and Mrs. Jean (née Keffer) xi, xiv, 76, 180, 241, 257-8, 262
Bryson, Mabel, see Robinson, Mrs. Austin
Bryson, Norman and Mrs. Elizabeth (née Ireland), 191
Bryson, Ross and Mrs. Marion (née Puterbaugh), 191, 258
Bryson, Verna, see McClure, Mrs. Andrew
Bryson, William, 191, 208
Bryson family, 190-1
Buchanan, Jim, 138
Buciersfield, Miss M., 180
Buck, Rev. Percy, 156
Buckly, Rev. T.W., 153
Bugle, Julian C., 33
Bull, Rev. E.S., 153
Bull, Walter J., 120
Bunt, Francis J., 68, 159, 281, 288
Bunt, Mary, 159
Bunt, W.T., 149
Burbidge, Gordon, 168
Burgess, C.J., 186
Burgess, David, 109
Burgess, Elizabeth, 159
Burgess, Frank, 239

Burgess, James, 135, 142, 159, 168
Burgess, Margaret, 174
Burgess, Mary, 159
Burgess, Mary A., 159
Burgess, Richard, 71, 281
Burgess, Stephen, 68, 159, 281
Burgess, Thomas, 140, 141, 159, 281
Burkholder, A. Lorne, 185
Burkholder, Hannah, see Brown, Mrs. John
Burkholder, Henry, 71, 281
Burkholder, Howard, 73, 277
Burkholder, Jacob, 71, 142, 203
Burkholder, John, 38
Burkholder, Joseph, 104
Burkholder, Michael and Mrs. Rebeca (née Lion), 35, 39, 67, 237, 281, 290
Burkholder, Michael and Mrs. Annie (née Longhouse), 171-2, 206, 237, 260
Burkholder, Ulrich, 24, 43, 219
Burkholder, William, 34, 38, 68, 281, 288
Burkholder family, ix, 47, 137
Burnett, Norman, 174
Burnett family, 107
Burns, Elizabeth, 175
Burns, Mabel, 180
Burns, Rev. R.N., 160
Burns, Robt., 143, 270
Burns, Rev. Wm., 145
Burr, Henry, 125
Burr, Joseph, 125
Burr, Nathaniel, 67, 169
Burr, Reuben and Mrs. Elizabeth (née Cleaver), 55, 56, 125
Burr, Rowland and Mrs. Hester (née L'Amoureux), 55, 56, 81, 82, 99, 100, 124, 125, 161, 281
Burr, William and Mrs. Ann (née Edwards), 125, 169, 172
Burr family, 176
Burrlington, 99
Burton, Annie, 177
Burton, Eliza, see Devins, Mrs. James
Burton, Elizabeth, 266
Burton, G., 177
Burton, Gertie, 139
Burton, Gideon and Mrs. Margaret (née Kersey), 191, 203, 260
Burton, Henry and Mrs. Margaret (née Patterson), 36, 71, 190, 191, 204
Burton, John, 190
Burton, Mary, see Ezard, Mrs. Geo.
Burton, Nellie, see McKechnie, Mrs. Angus
Burton, Oliver, 228
Burton, Robert and Mrs. Margaret (née Lawrence), 40, 191

Burton, Robert Erol and Mrs. Mary
(née Constable), 191, 246, 257
Burton, Verla, 139
Burton, William and Mrs. Jane (née
McDonald), 191
Burton family, 105, 191
Burwick, 56, 81, 99, 109, 125, 126,
161, 185, 249
Burwick, Robt., 67
Burwick House, 291
Burying Grounds:
    Carrville United Church, 133, illus.
    opp. 134
    Christ Church Anglican, Wood-
    bridge, 161
    Church of Scotland, Vaughan, 132
    Cober Dunkard Church, 44, 134,
    188, 193, illus. opp. 134
    Coleraine, 187
    Fisherville United Church Cairn,
    140
    Hillcrest, Woodbridge, 9
    Lutheran, Sherwood, 202, 209
    Maple Cairn, Langstaff Rd., 157
    Maple United, 141, 147
    Mennonite, Edgeley, 132, 137-38, 215
    Methodist Church Cairn, Sherwood,
    120, illus. opp. 156
    Nashville, 147
    Pine Grove Congregational, 149
    Presbyterian, Maple, 110
    Purpleville Cairn, 116
    Richmond Hill Presbyterian, 118,
    149, 281
    St. Andrew's Presbyterian, Maple,
    144-45
    St. Paul's, Vaughan, 206
    Trinity Anglican, Thornhill, 230
    Wesleyan Methodist Church, Klein-
    burg, 142
    Wesleyan Methodist Church, Thorn-
    hill, 154
    Wesleyan Methodist Church, Wood-
    bridge, 159
Butler, Col., 49
Butler, Thos. Sr., 35
Butt, William O., 185
Butterie, Mr., 260
Byer, Mr., 142
Byer family, 134
Byerley, Dr. A.E., 157
Bywater, Richard, 69, 109, 115, 148
Bywater, Sarah, 148
Bywater's hill, 180

C

Cabe, R., 140
Cain, Catherine, See Seager, Mrs.
Edward

Cain, James, 281
Cain, Stanley and Mrs. Pauline, 209
Cairns, see Burying Grounds
Cairns, Mr., 145
Cairns, May Susan, see McGillivray,
Mrs. John, Jr.
Caldwell, Rev., 159
Calder, Grisell, see Mitchell, Mrs.
James
Caldwell, Ada M., 174
Caldwell, Dr. W.S., 111, 147
Calhoun, Jane, see Shaw, Mrs. Charles
Calhoun, John, 281
Callaghan, Charles, 72
Callahan, Mr. 172
Camelon, Rev. D., 145
Cameron, Agnes, see Malloy,
Mrs. Malcolm
Cameron, Alex and Mrs. Barbara (née
Malloy), 160, 167, 191, 192, 246,
250, illus. opp. 192
Cameron, Alexander, 75
Cameron, Angus, 40, 281
Cameron, Archibald and Mrs.
Catherine (née McMurchy), 38, 189,
191, 208, 233, 236, 281, 282
Cameron, Archibald and Mrs. Louisa
(née Farr), 191
Cameron, Archibald and Mrs. Lillian
(née Acheson), 185, 191, 259,
260
Cameron, Archie, 192, 257
Cameron, Bessie, 168
Cameron, Clara, 172
Cameron, Colin, 139
Cameron, Donald and Mrs. Christine
(née McLeven), and Mrs. Elizabeth
(née Armour), 69, 73, 191, 192,
236, 281, 289, illus. opp. 192
Cameron, Elizabeth, see Beamish, Mrs.
John Alexander
Cameron, Hugh, 35
Cameron, Ian Archibald, 192
Cameron, J.M., 34
Cameron, J.M. Jr., 34
Cameron, Rev. J.W., 150
Cameron, James, 75, 192, 250, illus.
opp. 192
Cameron, Jean, see McMurchy, Mrs.
Archibald
Cameron, John, 33, 38, 70
Cameron, Kate, 139
Cameron, Lachlin, 162
Cameron, Mary, see Bryson, Mrs. Elmer
Cameron, Nancy, see McClure, Mrs.
Samuel
Cameron, Ross, 256
Cameron, Sarah, see McCallum, Mrs.
James

Cameron, W., 185
Cameron, William, 109
Cameron family, x, 191-92
Cameron Carriage Shop, Vellore, illus. opp. 83 and 123
Campbell, Miss, 182
Campbell, Mrs. A., 171
Campbell, A.J., 254
Campbell, Alex, 169
Campbell, Archie, 171
Campbell, Rev. C.A., 145
Campbell, Catherine, see Snider, Mrs. Henry
Campbell, Dougal, 229, 282
Campbell, Miss E., 244
Campbell, Rev. Isaac, 150
Campbell, J.R., 183
Campbell, Mac. A., 185
Campbell, Rev. Malcolm, 150
Campbell, Mary, see Elliott, Mrs. John Edward
Campbell, Rev. Peter, 137, 147, 160
Campbell, Rev. T., 151
Canada Company, 60, 196, 198, 211, 229
Canadian Grain Company, 113
Canadian Legion, 109, 241
Cannon, John, 143
Capner, Albert and Mrs. Ella (née Wardlaw), 192
Capner, Charlotte, see Devins, Mrs. Isaac
Capner, Joseph and Mrs. Charlotte, 70, 109, 192, 233, 282, illus. opp. 192
Capner, Louise, illus. opp. 192
Capner family, 192-93
Caprouse, I., 259
Card, Alex, 141, 191
Card, John L., 74
Card, John R., 113
Card, Locke, 105
Card, Walter, 113
Careless, Dr. J.M.S., x
Careley, Mr., 180
Carey, Bernard, 33, 189
Carley, Abram, 166, 174, 185
Carmichael, Duncan A., 186
Carnduff, Wm. H., 143
Carrie, Miss E.B., 179
Carrol, 151
Carroll, Lydia, 180
Carroll, Sylvia, 174
Carrville, 55, 100, 133, 153, 179, illus. opp. 100
Carry, Rev. John, 161
Carson, Ernest and Mrs. (née McDonald, Annie), 210, 246
Carson, Robt. 143
Carson, William, 102

Carter, George, 179, 185
Carter, Thomas, 172
Carter, Will, 80
Cartwright, Rev. C.E., 145, 161
Cartwright family, 37-8, 40
Case, J.E., 100
Caseley family, 107
Cassidy, Father, 152, 156
Casson, John, 35
Castator, Mrs. Ed. (née Longhouse, Mary), 206
Castator, Elsie, see McKay, Mrs. Eber
Castator, George and Mrs. Caroline (née Mansor), illus. opp. 193
Castator, Harkwood, illus. opp. 193
Castator, Henry and Mrs. Anna Maria (Mary) (née Keffer); and Mrs. Esther (née Willson), 69, illus. opp. 193
Castator, Henry Jr., illus. opp. 193
Castator, William and Mrs. Hannah (née Topper), illus. opp. 193
Cattle and Livestock, 94
   Introduction of prizestock, 93; air shipment, illus. opp. 96; Ayreshire, 219; Berkshire hogs, 64; Durham, 90, 195, 225; Gallway, 213; Guernsey, 189, illus. opp. 189; Holstein, 188, illus. opp. 96; horses, 3, 4, 9, 19, 86, 89, 90; Jersey, 220, 228; Leicester sheep, 225; Leicestshire Cotswold sheep, 219; Lonelm Texal Fayne, 240; Montvic Rag Apple Netherland, 240; Shorthorn, 90, 189, 195, 216; Suffolk hogs, 64; 'Sunbeam of Edgeley,' Jersey, 220
Cathcart, Rev. A.B., 161
Cathcart, Robert, 124
Cemeteries: see Burying Grounds
Census, 64; (1801-17) 57-8 (1842) 61, 63; (1851) 208
Century Farms, 187, 228; illus. opp. 197
Chamberlain, Uriel, and Mrs., 198, 259, 282
Chamberlain, Elizabeth, see Powell, Mrs. William
Chambers, Rev. Calvin, 156
Chambers, Nellie, 181
Chamney, D.M., 259
Chantler, Rev. W.N., 147
Chapman, A.C., 156
Chapman, Emanuel, 120
Chapman, Frank, 205
Chapman, Fred, 146
Chapman, Georgia, see Murison, Mrs. Alex
Chapman, Hannah, see Kennedy, Mrs. John

Chapman, Isaac (J.P.), 74, 193
Chapman, John, 193, 288
Chapman, Lyman, 193
Chapman, Margaret, 34
Chapman, Mrs. Mary, 245
Chapman, Muriel, see Wallace, Mrs.
   John Walter
Chapman, Nathan Jr., 32, 122, 193, 282
Chapman, Nathan Sr. and Mrs., 193
Chapman, Polly, see Devins, Mrs.
   Isaac
Chapman, Robert, 193
Chapman, Stewart, 141
Chapman, T., 121
Chapman, Rev. Thos., 159
Chapman family, 123, 124, 193, 288
Charles, Harry and Mrs. Bessie (née
   Lennon), 180, 249
Charlton family, 67, 103, 282
Chase, Jonathan, 37, 282
Chem, Miss, 220
Cherry, James and Mrs. Elizabeth (née
   Sheardown), 123, 193, 260
Cherry, John and Mrs., 193, 229, 230,
   282
Cherry, Ruth, see Hultse, Mrs. Thomas
Cherry, Susan, see Kellam, Mrs. John
Cherry family, 107, 193
Chevreau, P.G., 186
Cheyne, R., 253
Chisholm, R., 181
Chettenden, Jim, 163
Chote, Rev. A.A., 153
Christner, Eleanor, see Devins, Mrs.
   James
Churches: see also Burying Grounds,
   129-164
   Anglican:
      Christ Church, Woodbridge, 126,
         144, 161
      Holy Trinity, Thornhill, 132,
         155-6
      St. James Cathedral, Toronto,
         152, 185
      St. John's, York Mills, 132, 174
      St. Mary's, Richmond Hill, 152-3
      St. Stephen's, Maple, 145-6, 157,
         161
      St. Thomas, Kleinburg, 143-4
   Baptist:
      Langstaff, 144, 153
      Pine Grove, 149
      Thornhill, 156
   'Bed Bug', Humber Summit, 142
   Canadian Reformed Church of
      Toronto, Thornhill, 156
   Church of Christ (Disciples),
      Sherwood, 121, 158

Cober Dunkard, Concord, 134-5, 291,
   illus. opp. 134
Congregational:
   Humber Summit Community 141-
      42, 211, illus. opp. 142
   Pine Grove, 142, 148, 160
   Episcopalian, Thornhill, 123
   Gram's Chapel, North York, 186
Lutheran:
   Evangelical, Kleinburg, 142
   Murray Lutheran Chapel, 214
   Zion, Sherwood, x, 138, 156-
      58, 214, illus. opp. 156
Mennonite, Edgeley, x, 137-38,
   illus. opp. 135
Methodist:
   British, Thornhill, 154, 156
   Bowes, Concord, 135
   Burwick, 126
   Carrville, 101
   Central, Nashville, 148
   Concord, 135-37
   Cummers Meeting House,
      Willowdale, 133
   Edgeley, 138
   Free, Richmond Hill, 153
   Hadwen's Chapel, Teston, 158
   Hope, 140-41
   Kleinburg, 143, 200
   Laskay, 140
   Purpleville, 116
   Richmond Hill, 116, 119, 199,
      205
   Richvale (Boylestown), 153
   Sherwood, 120
   Thornhill, 123
   Teston, illus. opp. 150
   Wesleyan, Coleraine, 102
   Wesleyan, Kleinburg, 142-43
   Wesleyan, Thornhill, 154
   Wesleyan, Woodbridge, 159
   Whites, Concord, 135
   Woodbridge, 159
   Zoar, Nashville, 147-48
Nobleton, 140
Olivet Gospel Chapel, 153
Patterson, 140
Presbyterian:
   Auld Kirk, 139
   Knox, Elder's Mills, 105, 138-9, 160,
      162, 226, illus. opp. 142
   Maple, x, 110, 144, 209, 288, illus.
      opp. 143
   Nashville, 113, 148
   Pine Ridge, Humber Summit, 162
   Richmond Hill, 116, 118, 119, 149-
      50, 156, illus. opp. 150
   St. Paul's, Vaughan, 146, 161, 206

Thornhill, 123, 156
Woodbridge, 161-2, 225
Re-Organized Church of Jesus Christ
of Latter Day Saints, Woodbridge,
162-63, illus. opp. 151
Richvale Gospel Chapel, 153
Roman Catholic:
St. Luke's, Thornhill, 123, 155-56
St. Margaret Mary, Woodbridge,
163-64
St. Mary Immaculate, Richmond
Hill, 106, 152
St. Paschal Baylon, Thornhill, 156
United Church:
Carrville, 133-4, illus. opp. 140
Coleraine, 135
Edgeley, 138, illus. opp. 135
Fisherville, 107, 139-40
Kleinburg, 142-3, 175
Maple, 146
Richmond Hill, 150-51
Teston, 158-9
Thornhill, 153-5
Woodbridge, 159-61, illus.
opp. 151
Churchill, James, 141
Claireville, 99, illus. opp. 101
Claridge, Thomas, 37
Clark, A.B., 109
Clark, Fred A., 249
Clark, Jane, 40
Clark, Levi and Mrs., 183
Clark, Joseph, 166, 177
Clark, Robert, 123
Clark, S.D., 129
Clark, William, 67, 120
Clark family, 168
Clarke, Edward, 103
Clarke, George, 103
Clarke, Samuel, 163
Clarke, William, J., 102, 103, 206
Clarkson, Wm., 250
Clary, J., 169
Clay, W.M.T., 123
Cleaver, Elizabeth, see Burr, Mrs.
Reuben
Clegg, Mrs. Roy, 147
Clergy Reserves, 20, 43, 51, 58, 60, 82,
152, 165, 170, 180, 190, 199, 201,
207, 211, 216, 229
Clifford, Mrs. C., 245
Clift, Jack, 106
Clift, Sam, 106, 118
Clinger, Philip, 27
Clingersmith, Mrs. Manley, 186
Closson, John, 28
Clouse, Leonard, 25
Clubine, John, 178

Clubine, Mrs. M.E., 107
Clubine, W.H., 182, 249
Clubine family, 107
Coanet, Lucy, see Kellam, Mrs. George
Coates, Robert, 159
Cober, see also Coover, Cover
Cober, Elizabeth, see Baker, Mrs.
Jonathan
Cober, George, 88, 169
Cober, Jacob, 88, 169, 170
Cober, John, 88, 169, 170
Cober, Magdalena, see Troyer, Mrs.
Christian, Jr.
Cober, Margaret, 88, 169
Cober, Mary, 194
Cober, Mary, see Baker, Mrs. Michael
Cober, Mary, see Lyons, Mrs. Henry
Cober, Nicholas, Jr., 88
Cober, Nicholas, Sr. and Mrs. Eve (née
Fisher), 33, 37, 42, 44, 55, 122,
134, 176, 188, 193, 279, 287
Cober, Bishop Peter and Mrs., 42, 88,
134, 135, 170, 176, 193, 194, 282,
287
Cober family, 44, 47, 134, 193-94
Cochrane, John, 109
Cochrane, Rev. Rover, 140
Cockburn, W.M. (Moff), 240, 255,
256, illus. opp. 97
Cockburn Bros., 56, 180
Cocking, Rev. C.T., 143, 159
Codlin, Mary, see Beamish, Mrs.
Henry
Coffin, Nathaniel, 35
Cogswell, Mason, E., 123
Colby, Stephen, 33, 122
Colclough, Rev. John Harvey, 155
Cole, Mr., 101
Cole family, 168
Coleman, Wm., 143
Coleraine, 101
Coles, Dr. Bonar and Mrs. Dorothy
(née Morris), 201
Coles, Rev. Levi Harry and Mrs.
Frances Emma (née Jeffery),
200-201
Coles, Nancy, 201
Coles, Richard, 201
Colgan, Miss L., 178
Collard, Elijah, Jr., 26
Collins, Deputy, 18
Collins, Ruth, 221
Collins, Thomas, 221
Collins, Rev. W., 142, 149
Collins family, 134
Colls, J.R., 112
Colvin, Richard, 177, 179
Communications: 43

Bell Telephone Co. of Canada, 97;
Bell Telephone Co., Richmond Hill,
118; Bell Telephone Co., Thornhill,
123; G.W. Telegraph Co., 118;
Home Telephone Co., 97; Postal
services, 15, 53, 60, 80, 101, 102,
221, illus. opp. 82; railway telegraph,
81; telephone exchanges, 97; Wood-
bridge and Vaughan Telephone Co.,
96, 97
Concord, xi, 44, 70-1, 82, 83, 88, 102,
107, 133, 166, 188, 189, 216, 238,
257, 261, 265, illus. opp. 101
Concord Floral Company, 103, 254
Coneil, Mrs. W.A., 244
Connaught Medical Research
Laboratories, 107, 140
Conron, Charles, 169
Conron, Rev. M.D., 160
Conservation Authorities, 261-2
Humber and Don Valley, 261
Humber Valley, 195
Metropolitan Toronto and Region,
262, 291
Constable, Bruce, 179
Constable, Fred and Mrs. Elizabeth
(née Valliere), xi, 194
Constable, Herbert A., 167
Constable, John George William and
Mrs. Susannah (née Fenwick), 194
Constable, John William (II) and Mrs.
Maria Margaret (née Stong), 194
Constable, Kenneth and Mrs. Gail (née
Hendry), 194
Constable, Mary, see Burton, Mrs.
Robert Erol
Constable, Joan, 258
Constable, William, 184, 194, 236
Constable family, 194
Continental Can Company, 221
Cook, Mrs. A.W., 245
Cook, Doris, see Payne, Mrs. Norman
Cook, Rev. E.B., 154
Cook, George, and Mrs., 141, 174,
194, 244
Cook, Gordon, 194
Cook, Heber, 194
Cook, Jackson, 194
Cook, James, 27
Cook, John, 24
Cook, Melinda, 33
Cook, Mrs. N.L., 244
Cook, Silas, 27, 34
Cook, Thomas, 33, 37, 55, 67, 73, 100,
133, 194, 282
Cook, W.S., 120
Cook, William, Jr., 74, 100, 133, 169,
194

Cook, Wm. Sr., and Mrs., 73, 194, 282
Cook family, 41, 145, 194
Coombs, Mr., 182
Coombs, E.A., 259
Coombs, J., 141
Coon, Sergeant John, 38
Cooper, Arthur, 239
Cooper, Mary, 175
Cooper, Samuel S., 123
Cooper, Rev. Seymour, 158
Cooper, William, 118
Cooper family, 103
Copeland, Annie, see Witherspoon (II),
Mrs. William
Copithorn, Lyman, 181
Corbett, Miss, 175
Corbett, John, 143
Cordery, Albert E., 239
Cornish, Walter E., 116
Corrigan, Mr., 184, 185
Corson, Rev. 151
Cosgrove family, 152
Cotterill, Mr., 171
Cottrell, Daniel and Mrs. Jane, 135
Couch, Rev. Isaac, 160
Coulter, Robert, 180
Coulter, Rev. G.E., 151
Coulter, John, 118
Council Representation, 276-7
Counties and Districts
Home District, Upper Canada,
16, 24, 65, 229, 271, 272, 274,
280
Niagara District, 3, 20, 47, 198, 200
Simcoe Cy., 57, 216, 241
Somerset Cy., Pa., 3, 4, 41, 44, 106,
134, 137, 157, 188, 193, 206,
214, 215, 217, 219, 224, illus.
opp. 5
York Cy., xiii, 8, 17, 19, 20, 21, 82,
90, 101, 120, 128, 157, 166,
176, 187, 188, 202, 209, 213,
218, 223, 234, 240, 241, 248,
253, 256, 257, illus. opp. 97, 192
York Cy., Pa., 220
Countries: including places of origin
Canada, 10, 116, 157, 191, 194,
205, 206, 252, 286
England, ix, 8, 16, 59, 121, 122,
126, 128, 187-8, 192, 194, 197-
203, 215-6, 218, 221, 223, 225,
227, 231, 263, 265
France, 87, 119, 207, 268
Germany, ix, 21, 22, 51, 193, 268
Great Britain, 15, 23, 115, 192,
203, 207, 226, 252, 256, 258
Holland, ix, 114, 156, 252, illus.
opp. 114

India, 7, 16, 124, 187
Ireland, x, 21, 23, 109, 115, 163,
    189, 193, 196, 197, 209, 212,
    213, 216, 221, 224, 252, 259,
    illus. opp. 207
Norway, 115, 252
Russia, 115
Scotland, x, 22, 109, 190, 195-6,
    198-204, 206, 209, 211-13,
    215, 219, 222-3, 225-6, 266,
    286
Switzerland, ix, 19, 48, 217, 252,
    264
United States of America, i, ix,
    4, 8, 10, 13, 20-1, 24, 28, 40-1,
    47, 54, 79, 103, 107, 113-4,
    125, 156-7, 161-2, 193, 195,
    208, 211, 216, 218, 228, 231-2,
    236, 243, 248, 258, 261
Wales, 140, 226
County Councils, 66
Court of Quaker Sessions, 65
Courtemanche, Rev. Dr. Basil, 163
Cousins, Abner, B., 128
Cousins, Dorothy, see Mitchell, Mrs.
    Robert
Cousins, Fred, 250
Cousins, Joe, 104
Cousins, T. and Mrs., 111, 112, 244,
    259
Cousins, Wilbert, 250
Coutts, Rev. David, 138, 139
Cover, Sarey (Magdalene), see Troyer,
    Mrs. Christian
Cowan, Arthur, 233
Cowan, George, 69
Cowan, Thelma, see Wray, Mrs.
    William
Coward, Wm., 239
Cowleng, Robt., 180, 186
Coyle, Thomas, 106
Cozens, Benj., 33
Cozens, Dan, 33, 34, 45, 143, 154
Cozens, Joshua T., 34
Cozens, Joshua Y., 33
Cozens, Samuel D., 33, 45
Craddock, Mrs. M., 244
Craddock, William and Mrs. Jane (née
    Heyworth), 140, 174
Craddock family, 141, 282
Craggs, Mrs. Allan (Dorothy), 247
Craib, Mrs. Wm., 124
Craig, Allen, 123
Cram, James, 33
Crane, James, 35
Crannie, Michael, 38, 68, 282
Crassett, Henry James, 39
Craven family, 168

Craw, Rev. W.W., 148
Crawford, John, 69
Creech, M.E., 168
Crooks, Mrs. C., 244
Crooks family, 141
Cronin, Paddy, 176
Crosby, Isaac, 120, 151
Crosby, M.B., 109
Crosby, Parker, 194
Crosby family, 119, 194
Crossland, Rev. Dr. E.F., 163
Crosson, Henry, 70
Crosson, John, 34, 36, 38, 70
Crosson, Joseph, 162
Crossan, Valentine, 70
Crowhurst, Mrs. A.W., 245
Crowle, Fred W., 143
Crowley, Spencer, 252
Crown, Edward, illus. opp. 80
Crown deeds, 99, 190, 193, 197, 201,
    216, 217, 226
Crown and Clergy lands, 20, 51, 58,
    82, 213, 225
Crown Grant, illus. opp. 23, 122, 193
Crown Reserve Land, 43, 51, 60, 165,
    226, 229
Cruikshank, Col. William G., 63, 155
Culham family, 147
Cummer, Daniel, 136
Cummer, David, 136
Cummer, George, 136
Cummer, Jacob, (Kommer), and Mrs.
    Elizabeth (née Fisher), 43, 44
Cummer, Joshua, 136
Cummer, Samuel, 136
Cummer family, 44, 147
Cummings, Archie, illus. opp. 123
Cummings, Thomas, 170, 173
Cunningham, Hugh, 172, 181
Cunningham, Rev. J.D., 150
Currie, Rev. E.A., 154
Currie, Rev. E.C., 150
Currie, Mrs. George (née Elliott, Polly),
    196
Curry, Violet, 174
Curtis, Jean, 174

D

Dahnke, Rev. Peter, 149
Dale, Jean, see Williams, Mrs. Garnet
Dale, Mary, 169
Dale family, 158
Dally, Annie, 35
Dalton, Thomas, 221
Dalziel, Alice, see Agar, Mrs. Amos.
Dalziel, Anne, see Smellie, Mrs. David
Dalziel, Mrs. Arthur (Mary), 247
Dalziel, Helen, 195

Dalziel, Mr. and Mrs. J. William Dalziel, (née Mackenzie Annie Matilda),114, 195, 206, 245
Dalziel, James and Mrs. Janet (née McLean), 195, 200
Dalziel, Jean, see Agnew, Mrs. Charles
Dalziel, John, 71, 109, 110, 114, 148
Dalziel, John Sr., 195, 282
Dalziel, John and Mrs. Christina (née Lawrie), 201
Dalziel, Katherine, see Johnston, Mrs. David
Dalziel, Walter and Mrs. Jane (née Moor), 67, 171, 195, 256, 282, 289
Dalziel family, 195
Dark, John, 101
Darker, John, 160
Darker, Velma, 174
Darling, Mrs. A., 124
Darling, George, 176
Darlington, David, 258
Darlington, James and Mrs., 240, 245, 250
Darlington, Dr. Thos., 250
Davidson, Rev. John, 145, 161
Davidson, Nathan, 182
Davies, Rev. Harold W., 147
Davies, Rev. J.C., 139, 162
Davis, Ann, 36, 39
Davis, Rev. D., 159
Davis, Eliz., 34
Davis, James, 136
Davis, Marnie, 174
Davis, Sarah, 36
Dawson, Mary, 246
Deacon, George, 185
Dean, Rev. F.M., 145
Dean, Rev. Horace, 151, 154
Dean, Rev. S.W., 147, 151
Deane, John J., 126
Dearborn, Gen., 54
de Chalus, Comte René Augustin, 33, 52, 53
de Charbonne, Rt. Rev. Armand, 152
Deck, Rev. J.P., 158
Deckhout, Hy, 34
De Denonville, 10
De Ferrari, Charles, 106
Defoe, Richard, 36
Deisman, see Diceman
de la Galissonière, Count, 13
de la Hay, Claire, 101
de la Hay, J.P., 101
DelBrocco, Mrs. V., 169
DelBrocco family, 101
Delf, Phil, 255
Delie, John, 277
De Long, Vivian, 180
Demerley, Andrew, 169

Demorest, Rev. Thos., 160
Denison, George Taylor and Mrs. Esther (née Borden), 45, 54
Denne, V., 112
Dennis, Annie, 34
Dennis, J.M., 34
Dennison, Sophia, 34
Denton, Mr., 100
Denton, Wm., 141
de Puisaye, Comte, 52, 53, 117
Derbyshire, Olga, 181
de Rocheblave, 18
de Vaudreuil, xiv, 13, 14
Devaus, Anna, 39
Devine, Mr., 183
Devins, Abraham, 232
Devins, Albert and Mrs. Ella (née Wardlaw), 241, 244
Devins, Eleanor, see Love, Mrs. Ken
Devins, Irene, see Train, Mrs. Arthur
Devins, Isaac Sr. and Mrs. Charlotte (née Capner), 192, 232
Devins, Isaac and Mrs. Polly (née Chapman), 41, 44, 74, 75, 173, 192
Devins, James and Mrs. Eliza (née Burton), 191, 192
Devins, James and Mrs. Eleanor (née Christner), 143, 193
Devins, John C., 192
Devins, Kenneth, 256
Devins, Lavina, see Mitchell, Mrs. James (II)
Devins, Peter and Mrs. Ellen (née Robinson), 74, 193
Devins, Sara, see Miller, Mrs. Nicholas
Devins, Susan, see King, Mrs. Robert Jr.
Devins family, 72, 147, 192-93, 282
Devlin, Dr., 127
Devlin, Hugh, 179
Devlin, John, 154
Devlin, Wm., 274
Dewar, Rev. Edward H., 155
Dexter, Elisha and Mrs. Mary (née Kane), 122, 288
Dexter, Elizabeth, 170
Dexter, Hiram, 55, 170, 282, 288
Dexter, John, 55
Dexter, Mary Ann, 170
Dexter family, 67, 176, 279, 282, 287-8
Diamond, Rev. E.G., 145
Dibb, Neil, 174
Dibb family, 107
Diceman, Mr., 215
Diceman, Adam, 195
Diceman, Bertha, see Bowen, Mrs. Edgar
Diceman, Dorothy, see Irwin, Mrs. John

Diceman, Ethel, see Murray, Mrs. David C.
Diceman, H., 141
Diceman, Hattie, 196
Diceman, John and Mrs. Anne (née Line), 70, 195, 282, illus. opp. 66
Diceman, Stewart, 168
Diceman, Washington, 195
Diceman, William and Mrs. Frances (née Wells), 196
Diceman family, ix, 195-96
Dick, Albert, 76, 100 (Threshing Machine), illus. opp. 94
Dick, Alexander, 100
Dick, Rev. James, 149, 150, 156, 259
Dick, Robt. and Mrs. (née Graham), 100
Dick, William, 100
Dickinson, Rev. J., 159
Dickout, Henry, 147, 184
Dickout family, 68, 147, 282, 288
Dicks, Mrs. Lawrence (Vera), 247
Dickson, G.P., 249
Dickson, Mrs. John, 50
Dickson, Rev. Wm., 139
Diehl, Rev. C.F., 157
Digby, Jean, 174
Dilworth, John, 112
Dix, Walter, 239
Dixon, Mr., 105
Dixon, Anne, see Irwin, Mrs. William
Dixon, Rev. George, 161
Dixon, Marion, 174
Dobson, William, 128
Dockham, Rev. H., 137
Dodd, Lottie, 169
Dolan, F., 106
Dominion Government Weather Station, 225
Don Head Farm, 113, 114, 198
Donald, Rev. A.G., 147
Donald, Rev. J.F., 148
Donaldson, John, 101
Doner, Miss, 185
Doner, Mrs., 180
Doner, Bishop John Sr., 134, 135
Donneral, James, 181
Donneral, Nicholas, 215
Dooks, Robt., 75, 76, 250
Dorchester, Lord, 16, 17, 18, 51
Dorsey, Mereda, see Troyer, Mrs. Geo. Jr.
Dougherty, Rev. C.J., 152
Douglas, Bert and Mrs. Clara, 247
Dovey, Miss D.E., 181
Downey, Miss, 175
Downing, Mrs. J. (née Georgina Panke), 167, 168

Downs, Johnny, 102
Doyer, Mr., 171
Doyle, Miss, 185
Doyle, Kenneth, 76
Doyle Bros., 123
Drew, Mrs., 247
Drummond, Ann, see McKinnon, Mrs. John Sr.
Drury, Mr., 179, 252
Drury, Mrs. Della, 186
Drury, John, 177
Duck, Mrs. Peter (née Longhouse, Adeline Jane), 206
Dudgeon, Rev. J.H., 149
Dudgeon, Mary, see Bennet, Mrs. Jacob
Duff, Rev. John, 139
Duffield, Ellen, 168
Duggan, Capt., 231
Duncan, Miss, 179
Duncan, Mrs., 171, 245
Duncan, Dr. J.S., 144
Duncan, John, 102, 253
Duncan, Mrs. Marie, 175
Duncan, Rev. T.S., 155
Duncan, Will O., and Mrs., 245, 246, 250, 255
Duncombe, Dr., 152
Duncombe, Christopher, 152
Dundas, Rev. B.B., 151
Dundas, Henry, 51
Dunlop, Rev. Frank, 159
Dunlop, Rev. J.A., 158
Dunlop, J.H., 254
Dunlop, Rev. T., 160
Dunning, C.H., 126, 260
Dunning, Ernest, 183
Dunton, James, 179
Durham, Lord, 231
Dutch Elm disease, see illus. opp. 212
Dyer, Rev. D.A., 153
Dyer, Douglas, 183
Dyer, Edmund, 169
Dygert, Peter, 38

E

Eakins, Rev. C.G., 153
Earler, John, 36
Earll, Wm., 27
East, Francis, 70
East, Fred, 113
East, George, 113
East, Matthew, 113, illus. opp. 111
Easter, John, 36, 40
East's corners, 113
Eberle, Raymond F., 239
Eckhardt family, 52
Eckhart, Phil., 157
Eddy, Rev. Dr., E.B., 134, 155

Eden, A.A., 259

Edey, John, 155, 218, illus. opp. 122

Edey House, 291, illus. opp. 122

Edgar, Robert, 282

Edgeley, 93, 103-5, 133, 138, 166, 176, 206, 214, 215, 220, 237, 257, 291, illus. opp. pages 104, 127, 171, 193, 213

Edgeley Farmers' Club, 104, 220

Edgeley Store, illus. opp. 104

Edgell, John, 23

Education: Chapter 9, see also Schools, adult, 166; Charter 1850, 165; Mechanics' Institute, 166; School histories, 167-86; School Sections & Unions, 166-7; York County Board of Education, 167

Edwards, Ann, see Burr, Mrs. William

Edwards, Ilene, 172

Edwards, J.H., 184

Edwards, T., 143

Edwards, W.E.J., 255

Edwards & Edwards, 127

Edy, Wm., 123

Egan, Rev. J.J., 118, 156

Egan, John and Mrs. Sadie (née Huson), 69, 70, 196

Egan, Johnston, 196, 282

Egan, Richard Jr. and Mrs. Christiana (née Peoples), 196

Egan, Richard Sr. and Mrs. Jane (née Hemphill), 70, 196

Egan family, 196

Elder, David, 105

Elder, George, 105, 139

Elder, Hosie, 139, 169, 174

Elder, James, 105

Elder, Jim, illus. opp. 123

Elder's Mills, 56, 81, 105, 138, 226

Elders, Rev. P., 137

Elections, 67-77

Elgin, Lord, James Bruce, 8th Earl, 82

Elgin Mills, 105, 116, 118, 215

Elibrachy, Mrs. N., 175

Ella, Aubrey, 256

Ella, Bruce, family, 192

Ellerby, Jonathan and Mrs. Mary (née Williams), 74, 226

Ellerby, Jonathan and Mrs. Grace (née Wray), 160, 228

Ellerby, William, 141, 250

Elliot, John Sr., 231

Elliot, Minnie, 245

Elliott, Miss, 177

Elliott, Bessie, see Alford, Mrs. Dick

Elliott, E.H., 178

Elliott, Rev. Fred, 164

Elliott, George and Mrs. Elizabeth (née Gowland), 74, 196

Elliott, James and Mrs. Ada (née Bowman), 128, 197, 245

Elliott, Janet, see Tippin, Mrs. Wm.

Elliott, John Edward Jr. and Mrs. Jane (née Phillips), 196

Elliott, John Edward Sr. and Mrs. Mary (née Campbell), 196

Elliott, Levi and Mrs. Hannah (née Wallace), 126, 160, 224

Elliott, Mina, see McGillwray, Mrs. Gordon

Elliott, Polly, see Currie, Mrs. George

Elliott, Sarah, see McKee

Elliott, Thomas, 196

Elliott family, 196-97

Ellis, Henry, 75

Ellis, Thomas, 70

Ellis, Wm., 179

Ellston, John, 123

Elm Park Pavilion, illus. opp. 126

Elmsley, Chief Justice, 17

Elson, A.S., 184

Emerson, Prof. J.N., 10

Emsley, E.M., 177

Endean Nurseries, 254

Engle, Jacob, 134

English, Rev. Noble, F., 160

Enwright, John, 253

Espby, William H. and Mrs., 106

Etchman, Charles, 110

Etobicoke Historical Museum, 10

Evans, Arthur, 216

Evans, Rev. D.T., 156

Evans, David, 175

Evans, Rev. Dillwyn, 156

Evans, Ernest, 216

Evans, Fred, 239

Evans, John, 29

Evans, Margaret, 177

Evans, Rev. Wm., 161

Everingham, Mrs. Richard (née Longhouse, Elizabeth), 206

Everist, Robert, 177, 183

Evert, Sarah Ellen, 36

Ewers, Chas. F., 176

Eyer family, 134

Ezard, George and Mrs. Mary (née Burton), 191, 255

Ezard, Howard R., 240

Ezard, Marguerite, 168

Ezard, Ruth, see Agar, Mrs. Gilbert

F

Fairs, 124, 247-251, 256

Falconbridge, Mrs. J.K., 152

Family Compact, 229

Faris, Rev. A.L., 148

Farm implements and machinery, 85-97, 117

Farm organizations, 247-53

Farquarson, R.A., 182

Farr, Arthur W. and Mrs. Agnes (née Watson), 75, 128, 160, 197, 250, 258

Farr, Charles E., 162

Farr, Elisha, 36, 40, 71, 159, 277, 282

Farr, Ellerby Gardhouse, 128, 239

Farr, Elma, 185

Farr, Elta, see Snider, Mrs. Joseph

Farr, Floyd W., 163

Farr, George, 128

Farr, Herbert and Mrs. Annie (née Witherspoon), 227, 246

Farr, Mrs. Ila, 163

Farr, James and Mrs. Nancy (née Wilcox), 40, 159, 197, 282

Farr, Louisa, see Cameron, Mrs. Archibald

Farr, Mrs. Marion Estelle, 113

Farr, Mrs. Sam, illus. opp. 110

Farr, William and Mrs. Elizabeth (née Fletcher), and Mrs. Sarah (née Williams), 197, 226

Farr family, 197

Farrand, Mrs. W. Jackson, 245

Fast, M., 110

Fawcett, Rev. Michael, 147

Fawcett, Rev. Thomas, 160

Featherston, Gladys, 172

Feightner, John, 43, 282

Feilders, Mrs. K.J., 186

Fenbroeck, John, 34

Fenner, Mrs., 120

Fenton, Wm., 140

Fenwick, Lizzie, see Snider, Mrs. Wm.

Fenwick, Susannah, see Constable, Mrs. John George William

Fenwick, Susie, 246

Ferguson, Rev. F.A., 160

Ferguson, Hugh, 177

Ferguson, Rev. John J., 160

Ferguson, Rev. Jos. J., 160

Ferguson, Rev. T.A., 151

Ferraro, Peter, 203

Fidler, Isaac, 60

Fieldhouse, Bruce, 258

Fieldhouse, Mrs. Harry, 246

Fierheller, Mrs. Eldon, 245

Finan, Rev. A., 156

Finch, Spencer, 258

Findlater, Rev. J. and Mrs. Sarah (née Jeffery), 142, 149

Findlay, Mrs. S.S. 245

Findlay, Wm. J., 240

Findlay Dairy Farm, 212

Fish, Rev. C., 147, 159

Fish, H.A., 143

Fishburn, Rev. Jeremiah, 157, 158

Fisher, Rev. E.J., 158

Fisher, Eve, see Cober, Mrs. Nicholas

Fisher, Mrs. J., 186

Fisher, Jacob Jr., 31, 32, 43, 59, 122, 215, 279, 282

Fisher, Jacob Sr., 33, 35, 38, 41 42, 43, 44, 106, 156, 157

Fisher, Jim, 103

Fisher, John, 42, 157

Fisher, Mary, 37, 39

Fisher, Michael Sr., 37, 43, 55, 56, 100, illus. opp. 100

Fisher, Rachel, see Oster, Mrs. J.

Fisher, Valentine, 24, 37, 157

Fisherville, 106, 224

Fisher family, ix, 44, 47, 68, 102, 103, 134, 282, 290

Fishley, Mrs. W., 180

Fitzgerald, Miss, 171

Fitzgerald, Mrs. Doris M., xiv, 183

Fitz-Gibbon, Miss M.A., 180

Flannigan, William, 33

Fleck, R., 141

Fleming, Norman, 239

Fleming, Robert, 67

Fleming family, 105, 261, 282

Fletcher, Archie, 257

Fletcher, Rev. Ashton, 160

Fletcher, Dickinson, 40, 72

Fletcher, Elizabeth, see Farr, Mrs. William

Fletcher, Howard and Mrs. Marjorie (née McCourt), 197

Fletcher, Mrs. J.L., 179

Fletcher, Mason, 257

Fletcher, Percy, 197

Fletcher, Pierce and Mrs. Mary (née Nattress), 197

Fletcher, Walter, 197, 282

Fletcher family, 197

Flood, Mrs., 172

Floods and ice storms, 238-39

Fockler, Rev. C.E., 147

Follet, M.E., 185

Follett, Rev. C.W., 160

Ford, Mr., 174

Ford, Rev. O.P., 145

Ford, Rev. Ogden P., 161

Ford, Willa, 174

Foreshew, Sylvia, 168

Forpas, Thos., 35

Forrest, Rev. A.C., 147, 158

Forrest, Alex, 240

Forrester, Marion, 177

Forrester, Rev., 158

Forsythe, Pansy, 169
Fortier, J., 186
Fortner, S.J.T., 143
Fortune, Clara, 177
Foster, Edith, see Witherspoon, Mrs.
    Albert James
Foster, F.J., 123
Fowler, Rev. F.G., 148
Fowlie, Alfred, 174
Fox, Rev., 134
Fox, George, 103
Frame, J.R., 186
Francis, Lieut., 14
Francis, Alan L., 260
Francis, George, 150
Francis, J.E., 123, 249, 260
Francis, J.H., 122, 123
Francis, Samuel, 123
Francklin, Robt., 35
Frank, see also Franks
Frank, Anne, see Velie, Mrs. John
Frank, Catharine, 169
Frank, Elizabeth Ann, 169
Frank, Henry, 124
Frank, John and Mrs. Elizabeth (née
    Walker), 124, 282, 287
Frank, John Jr., 236
Frank, Julia Ann, 169
Frank, Louise, see Graham, Mrs.
    Joseph
Frank, Mandy, 236
Frank, Peter, 64, 69, 90, 147, 184
Franklin, Benjamin, 258
Franks, see also Frank
Franks, Eliza Jane, see Reaman, Mrs.
    Joel, Jr.
Franks, John W., 166
Franks, Nellie, 166, 185
Franks, Peter, 37, 43, 56
Frankum, Ida, 185
Fraser, Mrs., 110
Fraser, D.K., 77
Fraser, David, illus. opp. 73
Fraser, John, 81
Fraser, Joseph and Mrs. Barbara (née
    Raymond), 34, 37, 282, 288
Freak, James, 151
Frederck, Conrad, 35, 36
Frederck, Elizabeth, 35
French, Gertrude, 174
French, W., 143
French, William (II), 106
Frency, Dr. C.H., 118
Frisby, W.G., 182
Frizzell, Richard, 230
Frizzell, S.R., 122
Frogville, 101
Frontenac, Count de, 10

Fry, Arthur, 120
Fry, Rev., E.N., 158
Fry, Gertrude, see Routley, Mrs.
    Frederick William
Fuller, Ray, 128
Fulton, Capt. James (J.P.), 197, 198
Fulton family, 176, 197-98
Fur trade, 7, 8, 10, 11, 13, see also
    North-West Fur trading Co.
Fury, Mr., 152
Fysh, Max, 172

G

Gaffney, Katherine, 99
Gaffney, William, 99
Galbraith, Alexander W., 255
Gale, J.W., 107
Gallagher, Miss Olive, 186
Gallanough, A., 260
Gallanough, Frederick J., 123
Gallaugher, Alma, 181
Galloway, Zachariah, 22
Gallows Hill (Burrlington), 100
Gamble, John and Mrs. Jane (née
    Banyon), 115, 126, 180, 250, 288
Gamble, John W. (J.P.), 61, 67, 68, 72,
    73, 274, 277, 280
Gamble, Moses, 28
Gamble, Richard, 36, 203
Gander Hill, 189
Gapper, Mary, see Mrs. Edward
    O'brien
Gapper, Southby, 155
Gapper family, 59, 229
Garbutt, Mr., 106
Garbutt, George, 141
Gardener, E., 141
Gardhouse, Charles and Mrs. Elizabeth
    (née Wray), 228
Gardhouse, J. Mark, 250
Gardhouse, John, 250
Gardhouse, Wm. J., 128, 250
Gardiner, Mons W., 239
Gardner, Rev., 151
Gardner, George, 112
Gardner, William, 29
Garner, J., 140, 141
Garner, William, 280
Garner family, 121
Garness, J., 106
Garriock, Norn, 128
Garrow, Mrs. Geo., 244
Garton, James, 104
Garvin, Jos. L., 186
Gatchell, Rev. Joseph, 151, 154
Gee, Fraser, 240

Gee, Henry B., 102
General Quarter Sessions of the Peace, 272
George III, King of Great Britain, 21, 232
George V, King of Great Britain, 207
George VI, King of Great Britain, 254
Gerrie, Rev. A.W., 142, 149
Gibbons, Wm., 250
Gibson, Arthur, 174
Gibson, David, 85
Gibson, Rev. John, 152, 153, 155
Gibson, Joseph A., 167
Gibson, Mrs. Minnie (née Cameron), illus. opp. 192
Gibson, Rev. Norman, 151
Gibson, Wm., 282
Gibson family, 107
Gilbert, Rev. Chas., 160
Gilbert, John, 77, illus. opp. 73
Gilbert, Rev. F., 134
Giles, Barbara E., 185
Gilham, William, 252
Gillies, Rev., 142
Gillies, John B., 144
Gilmore, Miss, 169
Gilmore, Gilbert, 260
Gimmerson, Ann, see Train, Mrs. John
Ginn, Thomas, 69, 181
Glass, Raymond, 256
Glass, W.H., 118, 151
Glass, Rev. Wm., 160
Glass family, 107
Glassco, J. Grant, 262
Glassey, Mrs. H., 247
Glassford, Rev. Peter, 139
Glassford, Robt., 174
Glen Lonely, 53
Goesman, John, 37, 56, 132, illus. opp. 135
Goff, Alex, 70
Goff, Rev. E.F., 143, 147, 151
Goggin, Ellen, 181
Gohn, Susan, see Marwood, William Jr.
Golland, William, 102
Gollnitz, Miss, 180
Gomme, Russell F., xiv
Good, Ernest A., 240
Gooderham, Alfred L., 115
Goodfellow, Alice Ann, see Train, Mrs. John Jr.
Goodfellow, James, 287
Gooding, Eldon, 182
Goodman, J., 140
Goodwill, John, 282
Goodwill, Lorne, 163
Gordon, Miss A., 244

Gordon, Rev. Father Edward, 152, 163
Gordon, Fred, 257
Gordon, George, 180
Gordon, Isaac, 39, 282
Gordon, Rev. J.W., 145
Gormley, George, 249
Gough, Alexander, 108, 110
Gould, Fenwick, 179
Gourlie, D. James, 240
Government, 65-77
Government stores, 13
Gowland, Elizabeth, see Elliott, Mrs. George
Gowland, Ella, 139
Grady, John J., 239
Graham, Miss, 180
Graham, C.D., 240
Graham, Charlie, 198
Graham, Clarence and Mrs., 246, 250, 257
Graham, Cora, 177
Graham, Frank, 198
Graham, Fred, 198
Graham, Fred J., 259
Graham, Geo., 177
Graham, Harry, 198
Graham, James R., 167
Graham, John, 118
Graham, Joseph and Mrs. Louise (née Frank), 179, 198, 236
Graham, Louis, 198
Graham, Mary, see Atkinson, Mrs. William
Graham, William, 40, 99, 100, 179, 198
Graham, Wilson, 272
Graham, Wm., 36, 282
Graham family, 101, 198
Grahame, Thomas, 73, 198
Grahame, William, 198
Grahame, William R., 68
Grainger, Mrs. James (née Jessie Burr), 125
Grainger family, 158
Gram, Annie, see Troyer, Mrs. Jacob
Gram, Conrad, 31
Gram, Isaac, 136
Gramm, Peter, 37
Grams, Charles, 279
Granger, F., 106
Grangers, The, 121
Granshaw, John, 68
Grant, Hon. Alex, 35
Grant, Dr. Donald, J., 126, 162
Grant, Rev. J.R., 156
Grant, Rev. James, 150
Grantham, D. and Mrs. Mary (née Topper), 224

Graves, Admiral, 16
Gray, Alexander, 124
Gray, Rev. D. Roy, 159
Gray, Rev. Robt., 140
Gray, Morris, 104
Gray, William, 68, 69
Greaves, Mrs. Biddy, 237
Green, Mr., 169, 175
Green, Flora Josephine, see Reaman,
    Mrs. G.E.
Green, George, 172
Green, John, 249
Green, T.A., 239
Greene, J.A., 120
Gregory, Mr., 117
Grier, Mrs., 185
Griffa, Rev. L., 156
Griffith, A.J., 250
Grigg, Mr., 174
Grimshaw, J., 141
Grogan, Robert, 256
Groskurth, Augustus, 110, 142
Grubb, Andrew, 141
Grubbe, Charles, 257
Gullett, Patricia, see Martin, Mrs.
    Gordon
Gun, Mrs., illus. opp. 105
Gunn, Donald, 67
Gurr, Evangeline E., 168
Guthrie, John, 282
Gwillim, Elizabeth, see Simcoe, Mrs.
    John Graves

H

Haas, Karl, 222
Hadwen, Rev. Thos., 159
Hadwen, Wilbert, 256
Hafenbrack, Isaac, illus. opp. 91
Hagerman, Tonis, 27
Hagerman Bros., 118
Haggart, James, 118, 120
Haggerty, B., 175
Haines, Alfreda, 175
Haines, Miss I., 180
Haines, Philip (Phillip), 32
Haines, Samuel, 32
Haking, Ann, see Troyer, Mrs.
    Jacob
Halbert, Rev. A., 159
Halbert, Isabel, 172
Halbert, Joyce, 180
Hale, Jonathan, 23, 24
Hall, Miss, 180
Hall, Mrs. Andrew, 245
Hall, Joseph, 118
Hall, Norm, 109

Hall, William, 123
Hallawell, William, xi
Hallett, Rev. Alan, 151
Hallett, John C., 127, 128
Hallett, Oda, 185
Halliwell, Rev., 142
Hallowe'en pranks, 237
Halls, 104, 116, 121, 142, 150, 162,
    163, 164, 185, 191, 204, 232, 240,
    245, 259, 260
Halverson, Mrs., 174
Ham, C.T., 112
Hambly, Arthur and Mrs. Myretta (née
    Irwin), 200
Hambly, Edwin, 179
Hambly, Merle, xiv, 143, 200
Hamblyn, Mrs. R., 247
Hamilton, Mr., 105, 215
Hamilton, A., 106
Hamilton, Bertha, 185
Hamilton, Guy, 138
Hamilton, Hannah Owen, 36
Hamilton, Jane, see Hemphill, Mrs.
    William
Hamilton, Jas., 259
Hamilton, John, 35, 68
Hamilton, Maria Livinia, 36
Hamilton, Mary Ann, see McClure,
    Mrs. Andrew
Hamilton, Thomas, 23
Hamilton, William, 141
Hammond, John, 124, 287
Hand, L.E., 254
Hanna, John B., 186
Hanna, Sarah, see King, Mrs.
    William
Hannon, Ed., 181
Hanson, Mr., 175
Hanson, Rev. Thomas J., 145, 161
Hanstock, Robert, 40
Hardy, James, 68
Hare, Evelyn, 258
Harland, Grace, see Wray, Mrs.
    John Jr.
Harman, Miss, 185
Harman, Rev., 151
Harman, Michael, 37
Harmsworth family, 17
Harper, Elizabeth, see Wallace, Mrs.
    George Frazier Jr.
Harper, Phillip, 181
Harrigan, John, 37
Harris, Albert, 260
Harris, Ann, 35
Harris, Mrs. Arthur, 245
Harris, E.B., 253
Harris, H., 141
Harris, John E., 128

Harris, Rev. Samuel and Mrs., 101, 148
Harris, W.W., 112
Harrison, Miss, 177
Harrison, Edward, 282
Harrison, Gertrude, 177
Harrison, Gladys, 168, 257, 258
Harrison, John, 71, 282
Harrison, Mattie, 180
Harrison, Melodye, 180
Harrison, Rev. R.J., 145, 161
Harrison, William and Mrs. Christena (née Whelpten), 116, 118, 120, 151, 198, 199
Harrison, Wm., 182
Harrold, William, 31
Hart, Jessie, 180
Hart, Kenzie, 169
Hart, Mrs. Patricia W., xiv
Hart, Robert, 159, 282
Hart, Rev. Terence V., 160
Hart family, 107
Hartman, Lot, 35, 201
Hartman, Silas and Mrs. Christina (née Johnston), 148, 201
Hartman, William, 73
Harts Corners, 206
Harvesting, 86-7; machinery, 87, 88; methods, 88
Harvey, John, 70
Harvey, Michael, 116
Harvey, Roger, 116
Harvey, Roland O., 166, 167, 168, 180, 185
Harvey, W., 250
Harvie, John, 82
Harvis, S.B., 36
Haughton, Rev. T.R., 145, 153
Hawke, Edward, 55
Hawman, William, 199
Haworth, Miss, 169
Hawthorne Mineral Springs, 123
Hay, Mr., 100
Hay, Rev. Robt., 142, 148, 149
Hay, Rev. W.M., 150
Hayden, James, 110
Hayes, John, 37
Hayhoe, Alan, 115
Hayhoe, Boyce, 115
Hayhoe, Donald, 115
Hayhoe, Edwin, 115, 128
Hayhoe, Harold, xi, 115
Hayhoe, John, 115
Hayhoe, Marjorie, 174
Hayhoe Bros., 115
Hayhurst, Rev. Wm., 160
Hays, Kathaleen, 180
Haystead, John, 68

Haystead, Thomas, 68
Hazard, Thomas, 27
Hazel, William, 180
Heacock, Howard, 257
Head, Sir Francis Bond, 230, 231
Head, Rev. James B., 161
Heathcote, Rev. F.C.C., 145
Heaton, Rev. Henry, 161
Heels, Lorne C., 180
Heffron, Mrs. Kathleen, 181
Heffron, Pat, 186
Hegler, Christian, 168
Heimrich, Rev. E., 158
Heise, Annie, see Reaman, Mrs. George
Heise, Bert, 102
Heise, Christian, 134
Heise, Bishop Henry, 135
Heise, Jacob, 134
Heise family, 47, 134
Helmke family, 52
Hemphill, George, 199
Hemphill, Jane, see Egan, Mrs. Richard
Hemphill, Joseph, 70, 196, 199, 233
Hemphill, Margaret, 199
Hemphill, Thomas, 199
Hemphill, William and Mrs. Jane (née Hamilton), 199
Hemphill family, 199
Henderson, Mr., 142
Henderson, Rev. A.E., 160
Henderson, Grant, 128, 262
Hendry, Annie, 166, 183
Hendry, Gail, see Constable, Mrs. Kenneth
Hendry, Jennie, see Topper (II), Mrs. Robert
Hennessey, Daniel and Mrs., 113
Henry, Mrs. E., 186
Henry, Elmer, 178
Hepburn, Rev. J.N., 150
Herbison, Rev. Robt., 150
Herd, William, 40
Herman, Jack and Mrs. Lorraine, 179
Heron, Samuel, 33, 117
Herrema, Gary, 258
Herrington, J.R., 259
Heslop, Mr., 105
Heslop, Mrs. Jas., xiv
Heslop family, 56, 107
Hesp, Mrs. Charles, illus. opp. 110
Hesp, Gladys, 246
Hewgill, Alma, illus. opp. 123
Hewgill, D.A. and Mrs., illus. opp. 123
Hewgill, John, 154
Hewitt, Rev. G.F., 160
Hewitt, Geo., 143

Hewitt, T.A., 123
Heyland, Rev. Rowly, 160
Heyworth, Jane, see Craddock, Mrs. W.
Hezzelwon, Miss M., 244
Hickly, Elizabeth, 169
Hicks, Albert, 115
Hicks, Charles, 115, 116
Hicks, Fred and Mrs., 115, 116, 245
Hicks, William, 115
Higgins, Rev. A.I., 134, 155
Higgins, James, 121
Higginson, Rev. Chas. A., 151
High, George, 74
High, Miss H., 244
Hill, Rev., 40
Hill, A.S. Hardy and Mrs. Mildred (née Wright), xiv, 228
Hill, Charles, 240
Hill, David, 259
Hill, Rev. Geo. S.J., 145
Hill, Rev. Newton, 159
Hill, P.C., 120
Hill, Thos., 34, 40
Hilts, Jacob, 169
Hilts, Joseph, 36
Hilts family, 134
Hiltz, Rev. J.K., 158
Hiltz, Rev. W., 144
Hincks, John, 182
Hirsch, Miss E., 186
Hirtle, Rev. S.W., 150
Hoag, Russell, 25
Hobson, Marion, 174
Hodginson, Sarah, 35
Hodgkin, Rev. Thomas J., 145, 161
Hodgskin, Rev. T.J., 141, 142, 149
Hodgson, Bill, 256
Hodgson, Colleen, see Barker, Mrs. Brock
Hodgson, Rev. J.A.H., 161, 188
Hodgson, John, 143
Hodgson, Kenneth, 256
Hogg, Mrs. R.C., 167
Hoidge, Thos. B., 166
Hoiles, Bruce, 257
Holderness, John, 253
Holdiway, N., 142
Holland, Lenissa, see Atkinson, Mrs. Thomas
Holland, Robert, 122, 237
Holland, Robert G., 172, 186
Hollingshead, Anthony, 37, 39
Hollingshead, Arthur and Mrs. 206, 245
Hollingshead, Ashsah, see Souls, Mrs. Ashsah
Hollingshead, Isaac, 40
Hollingshead, Robert, 108

Hollingshead, William, 33
Hollingshead, Zelta, 180
Holmes, Betsy Ann, 33
Holmes, Mrs. R., 245
Holtby, C., 101
Holten, Rev. R., 153
Homes, Mr., 185
Homes, Richard, 68
Honey, 87, 91
Honey Pot Farm, 95, illus. opp. 62
Honeywell, Rice, 23
Honnan, Miss C., 186
Hood, Albert, 172
Hood, James, 110
Hood, William, 110, 112, 253
Hoodless, John and Mrs. Adelaide (née Hunter), 243, 244
Hoover, Garnet and Mrs. Florence (née Witherspoon), 227
Hoover, Adam, 41
Hoover, Casper, 41, 42
Hoover, Jacob, 104, 166, 172, 237
Hoover, James, 103
Hoover, John, 42
Hoover family, ix, 47, 134
Hope, 133, 179
Hope, Mrs. Angeline, 172
Hopkins, Mr., 118
Hopkins, G., 141
Hopkins, Mrs. May, 175
Hopper, George, 106
Hopper, Henry F., 118
Hopper, W.J., 124
Horne, Henry, 124
Horner family, 134, 137
Hoshel, Benjamin, 153
Hostrawser, Elizabeth, see McClure, Mrs. Sam Jr.
Hostrawser, John Sr. and Mrs. Ethelene, 76, 247, 250
Hotels & Inns: 37, 100-02, 104, 107-8, 110, 112, 113, 117-21, 123, 127, 141, 193, 218, 221, 223, 230, 232, 237, 244, 253, 259
Houghton, G.R., 239
'House of Concord', 219
Houston, Mrs. Dorland, 186
Howard, Allan, 26
Howard, Geo., 239
Howard, George D., 40
Howarth, Mrs. Madeleine, 180
Howden, Rev. H. Reginald, 155
Howell, John F., 69, 126
Howell, Walter, 123
Howick, Rev. Fred, 139, 162
Howl, Mrs. Arthur, 246
Howland, Ardelia, 142
Howland, Fred, 107

Howland, Henry S., 56, 73, 107-8, 110, 113, 142
Howland, Peleg, 108
Howland, Thomas, 108
Howland, W.P., 107
Howland, William, 108
Howlett, Miss, 180
Howson, Rev. W.G., 151
Huddy, Capt. Joshua, 54
Hudson, Rev. A.G., 160
Hudson, John H., 273
Hudson, John Hampsted, 33
Huenergard, Rev. E., 158
Huff, Mrs., 174
Huff, Peter, 123
Hughes, Miss, 171, 175
Hughes, Mrs., 183
Hughes, George, 110
Hughes, Rev. J., 151
Hughes, Pauline, 168
Hughson, Samuel, 69
Hulse, Clara, 186
Hultse, Mrs. Thomas (née Cherry, Ruth), 140
Humber River, 18, 56, 79, 197, illus. opp. 126
Humber Summit, 149, 162
Humber Valet Cleaners, 111
'Humbercrest', 188
Hume, A.J. and Mrs. Agnes (née Trench), 120, 199, 223, 246, 254
Humphrey, Vincent, 181
Humphreys, Margaret, 171, 174, 258
Hunguski, Arthur, 142
Hunt, Rev. John, 147, 151
Hunter, George, illus. opp. 123
Hunter, Rev. S.J., 151
Hunter, William, 32
Huntington, Ron, 163
Hurlburt, W.H., 186
Hurley, Mrs. P., 175
Hurricane Hazel, 170, 238-9, 250, 262
Huson, Nathaniel, 35
Huson, Rebecca, 35
Huson, Sadie, see Egan, Mrs. John
Hutcheson, Robert, 38
Hutchinson, Frank, 81
Hutchinson, Dr., J.N., 182
Hutchinson, Rev. James, 160
Hutton, Rev. B.L., 137
Hyde, Alfred, 100
Hyland, Henry, 181

I

Ice storms, 238
Imperial Oil Ltd., 109,

Implement factory, 55
Implements, 86, 88, 89
Indian relics, 7, 8, 9, 10
Indian sites, 9, 10
Ingram, Robert, 172
Ingram, William, 97
Innes, Carol, see Proctor, Mrs. Carol
Innes, Leslie and Mrs. Mary (née Ritchie), 199
Irdell, Lt. Abrham, 33
Ireland, Rev. E., 142, 149
Ireland, Elizabeth, see Bryson, Mrs. Norman
Ireland, I., 141
Ireland, Jean, see Murray, Mrs. John
Ireland, Mrs. Jesse (née Jane Cameron), illus. opp. 192
Ireland, John, illus. opp. 95
Irwin, Mrs., 174
Irwin, Mr., 171
Irwin, Rev. David S., 164
Irwin, Doris L., 181
Irwin, Douglas, 200
Irwin, Mrs. G., 246
Irwin, George, 200
Irwin, John and Mrs. Dorothy (née Diceman), 200
Irwin, Murray, 200, 257
Irwin, Myretta, see Hambly, Mrs. Arthur
Irwin, Stanley, 258
Irwin, Rev. W.S., 151
Irwin, William and Mrs. Anne (née Dixon), 142, 199, 200
Irwin family, 199-200

J

Jackes, F.P., 239
Jackman, Frederick, 73, 277
Jackman, H.R., 209
Jackman, N.C., 167
Jackson, Alice, 180
Jackson, Mrs. Ann, 245
Jackson, Bert, 111
Jackson, Charles, 146
Jackson, Earl and Mrs. May (née Stephenson), 200
Jackson, Elizabeth, 170, 179
Jackson, Rev. F.C., 155
Jackson, Frederick and Mrs. Priscilla Jane (née Snider), 200
Jackson, George and Mrs. Ann, 194, 200, 283
Jackson, George C., 240, illus. opp. 97
Jackson, Mrs. Harry, xiv

Jackson, Rev. Henry, 160
Jackson, John and Mrs. Elizabeth (née Taylor), 104, 121, 200
Jackson, Mary, see Jarott, Mrs. William
Jackson, Samuel, 28, 283
Jackson, Walter, 200, 258
Jackson, William, 67, 112
Jackson family, 121, 200-201
James, Cartney, 115
James, Mrs. David, 245
James, Don Carlos, 158
James, E.A., 177, 260
James, Ezekiel, 29
James, Mrs. O., 245
Jamieson, Mr., 181
Jamieson, Andrew, 116, 233
Jamieson, Margaret, see NcNeil, Mrs. Arthur
Jardine, Miss, 171
Jarott, William and Mrs. Mary (née Jackson), 194
Jarrett, Duke, 70
Jarrett, Gibson, 70
Jarrett, Ken, 147
Jarrett, Richard and Mrs. Susannah (née Stump), 124, 220, 246, 288
Jarrett, William, 169
Jarvis, Stephen, 37
Jarvis, William B., 230
Jarvis, Wm. (J.P.), 202, illus. opp. 22, 258
Jarvis, William Monson, 36
Jeanneret, Marsh, xi
Jeffers, Rev. Thos., 160
Jeffers, Rev. Wellington, 151
Jefferson, 107, 179
Jefferson, John, 35, 39
Jefferson family, 107
Jeffery, Alfred, 73, 159, 200
Jeffery, Frances Emma, see Coles, Mrs. Levi, Harry
Jeffery, John (II), 200
Jeffery, John Sr., 159, 200, 283, illus. opp. 197
Jeffery, Richard Jr., and Mrs., 40, 159, 173, 200
Jeffery, Richard Sr., 173, 200
Jeffery, Richard (III), 200
Jeffery, Richard (IV), 200
Jeffery, Richard (V), 200
Jeffery, Sarah, see Findlater, Mrs. J.
Jeffery, William, 69, 173
Jeffery, William and Mrs. Frances Emma (née Standen), 200
Jeffery family, 105
Jeffrey, Alfred, 41, 71
Jeffrey, Pearl E., 185
Jeffrey, Richard, 36, 171

Jeffries, Mabel, 185
Jeffries, Nellie, 185
Jeffs, Eulali, 179
Jenkins, Rev. Wm. and Mrs. Mary H. (née Stockton), 124, 149, 150, 156, 286
Jenkinson, Rev. M.R., 159
Jennings, Rev. Dr. Bruce, 145
Jess, Rev. Marshall, 148
Jewell, Mr., 150
Jewitt, Wm., 178
Johns, Dr. C.P., 183
Johnson, Mr., 180
Johnson, Asa and Mrs. Hannah, 32, 34, 43, 122, 193, 232
Johnson, E.J.A., 171
Johnson, J., 141
Johnson, Sir John, 49
Johnson, Leo, x, xiv
Johnson, Nicholas, 279
Johnson, Robert, 233
Johnson, Sally, see Miller, Mrs. Nicholas
Johnson, Stephen, 28
Johnson, Violet, 174
Johnson, Sir William, 13, 14, 258
Johnson, William Jr., 111
Johnson, Wm. Sr., 75, 111
Johnston, Agnes, see Watson, Mrs. William
Johnston, Alexander, 169
Johnston, Annie, see MacDonald, Mrs. A.
Johnston, Beverley, 185
Johnston, Charles and Mrs., 203, 247
Johnston, Christina, see Hartman, Mrs. Silas
Johnston, David and Mrs. Katherine (née Dalziel), 112, 201, 283
Johnston, Miss E., 175
Johnston, Frances, 186
Johnston, Grace, 201, 255
Johnston, J.K., 181
Johnston, Janet, 201
Johnston, John, 162
Johnston, Mary, 185, 201
Johnston, Maurice, illus. opp. 97
Johnston, Rev. Minton C., 156
Johnston, R.K., 250
Johnston, Robert and Mrs. Margaret (née Anderson), 39, 201
Johnston, Robert and Mrs. Anna (née Orr), 203
Johnston, Robert (II) and Mrs. Tessie (née Norton), 186, 201
Johnston, William, 168, 169
Johnston, Winnifred, illus. opp. 192
Johnston family, 147, 201

Johnstone Bros., 102
Jolliffe, T.W., 140
Jones, Abijah, 31
Jones, Rev. Albert, 144
Jones, Augustus, 36, 39, 51
Jones, Rev. Benjamin, 151, 160
Jones, Evaline, see Kersey, Mrs. Joseph
Jones, George, 135
Jones, Harold, 118
Jones, Rev. Henry, 160
Jones, J., 101
Jones, John, 131, 132
Jones, Rev. P.N., 147
Jones, Rev. Peter, 51, 131, 132
Jones, Rev. Richard, 151, 160
Jones, Rev. S.N., 158
Jones, William, 22
Jordan, Mrs. K., 186
Jordison, I., 141
Joslin, Herbert, 112
Jowson, W.J., 147
Joy Valley Greenhouses, Pine Grove, 115, 254
Joyce, R., 118
Joyce, William, 179
Julian, David and Mrs. Laura (née Watson), 201, 246
Julian, George, 185, 201
Julian, John and Mrs. Susannah (née Murray), 201, 214
Julian, Robert and Mrs. Clara (née Phillips), 201, 257
Julian, Thomas, 201
Julian, Wm., 184
Julian, William and Mrs. (Ann), 201
Julian family, 201
Jull, Rev. K., 161
Junior Farmers & Junior Institute, Vellore, 257-258
Junior Farmers' Centennial Project, illus. opp. 197
Jupp, Rev. Mr., 142, 149

K

Kaiser, ix, 283
Kaiser, Irvine, 174
Kaiser, John, 162
Kaiser, Joshua, 112
Kaiser, Samuel D., 77, 167, 260
Kane, Mary, see Dexter, Mrs. Elisha
Keam, Rev. F.C., 159
Keans, Rev. E., 156
Kearney, Alex E., 260
Keedwell, James, 126
Keefler, Matthias H., 118, 119
Keen, Irwin, 239

Keene, Father E., 152
Keery, J., 175
Keffer, Adam, 42, 157, 158, 167, 283
Keffer, Anna, see Snider, Mrs. Charles Henry
Keffer, Anna Maria (Mary), see Castator, Mrs. Henry
Keffer, Anthony, 170
Keffer, C.H., 260
Keffer, Dorothy, 179
Keffer, Frederick, 252
Keffer, G. Wilfred, 76, 96, 202, 240, illus. opp. 97
Keffer, George and Mrs. Mary (née Murray), 214, 215
Keffer, Henry, 170, 283
Keffer, Herbert, 120
Keffer, Hiram, 111
Keffer, Jacob Jr. and Mrs. Margaret, 42, 67, 120, 156, 157, 202, 283, illus. opp. 22
Keffer, Jacob Sr., 42, 156, 215
Keffer, Jean, see Bryson, Mrs. Jesse
Keffer, Mrs. Jesse, 245
Keffer, Lawrence, 202
Keffer, Lydia, see Oliver Mrs. William
Keffer, Martha, see McKinnon Jr., Mrs. John
Keffer, Mary, 258
Keffer, Michael and Mrs. (Anna Maria), 32, 42, 43, 145, 156, 157, 202, 280, 283
Keffer, Pass, 257
Keffer, Percy, 179, 185
Keffer, Roland, 240
Keffer, Solomon, 170
Keffer, Tom, 103
Keffer, Wilbur, 202
Keffer family, ix, 41-42, 44, 67, 147, 202, 260, 283, 287, 292
Kell, Rev. J.C., 134
Kellam, Everard, 203, 256
Kellam, George, 75, 76, 250
Kellam, George, Jr. and Mrs. Elizabeth (née Tyler), and Mrs. Lucy (née Coanet), 135, 202, 203, 283
Kellam, George Sr. and Mrs. Mary (née Kemp), 202
Kellam, James, 202
Kellam, John and Mrs. Susan (née Cherry), 72, 143, 202, 203, 283
Kellam, John F., 160
Kellam, John H., 250
Kellam, Lorne, 203
Kellam, Lucy Hannah, see Thomas, Mrs. Henry
Kellam, Olivia, 202
Kellam, Robert and Mrs. Jane (née Lawrie), 142, 203

Kellam, Sarah, 202
Kellam, T. Boyle, 128
Kellam, William, 202, 283
Kellam family, 202-3
Kelly, Father, 152, 156
Kelly, Timothy, 40, 283
Kelsey, Miss, 174
Kemp, Rev. Harold, 134
Kendrick Bros., 85
Kennedy, Mr. 183
Kennedy, Arthur, 104
Kennedy, Edgar and Mrs., 104, 245
Kennedy, Ethel, 177
Kennedy, John and Mrs. Hannah (née
    Chapman), 170, 178, 288
Kennedy, Ross, 179, 180, 181
Kennersley, John, 118
Kennie, Henry, 39
Kent, Dr. E.E., 134, 155
Keogh, Rev. T.S., 154
Keown, S., 108
Kerr, Rev. A.S., 147
Kerr, Annie, 203, 246
Kerr, John and Mrs. Susan (née
    Robinson), 203
Kerr, Nelson, 203
Kerr, Robert and Mrs. Elizabeth, 116,
    180, 184, 185, 203
Kerr, William, 181
Kerr family, 203
Kersey, Ann, see Lawrence, Mrs.
    John Rezeau
Kersey, Annie, 204, 246
Kersey, Catharine, see Mitchell, Mrs.
    James
Kersey, Edward, 204, 283
Kersey, Henry, 279
Kersey, Howard G., 186
Kersey, Isobella, see Agar, Mrs. Adam
Kersey, Jonathan and Mrs. Flora (née
    Beaton), 203, 204
Kersey, Joseph and Mrs. Evaline (née
    Jones), 204, 247
Kersey, Mae, 247
Kersey, Margaret, see Burton, Mrs.
    Gideon
Kersey, Mary, see Lawrence, Mrs.
    Isaac Huver
Kersey, May, 204
Kersey, Robert, 256
Kersey, Thomas and Mrs. Margaret
    (née McVean), 203, 204
Kersey, William Jr. and Mrs. Agnes
    (née Lawrie), 202, 203, 205
Kersey, William Sr. and Mrs. Margaret
    (née Beaton), 71, 73, 203, 283
Kersey, William (III), 204
Kersey family, 168, 203-4
Kerswill, Anna, see Mollet, Mrs. Anna

Kerswill, James G., 240
Kerswill family, 107
Ketchum, Jesse, 27
Ketchum, Jesse Jr., 24
Ketola, Miss Dolly, 183
Kettyle, Rev. Harold W., 149
Keys, Henry, 126
Keys, Thomas and Mrs. Etta, 103, 244
Kidd, Rev. James H., 161
Kidd, Wm. L., 186
Kiener, S.D., 34
Kilfedder, James, 169
Kilfedder, Robert, 169
King, Miss, 180
King, Bruce, 204, 258
King, Charles and Mrs. Florence (née
    Mathewson), 204
King, Mrs. Katherin, 172
King, Jesse, 139
King, John, 204
King, Louise, 178
King, Mathew, 261
King, Robert Jr. and Mrs. Susan (née
    Devins), 162, 204
King, Robert Sr. and Mrs. Janet (née
    Turnbull), 36, 40, 204, 283
King, Robert (III), 204
King, Robert (IV) and Mrs. Louise
    (née Usher), 204, 250
King, Susie, 174
King, William and Mrs. Sarah (née
    Hanna), 139, 204
King family, 105, 204
Kingswell, Mr., 236
Kinnear, Thomas, 236
Kinnee, Daniel, 74, 147
Kinnee, Joel, 38, 229, 283
Kinnee, Morley J., 97, 147, 259, 260
Kinsella, Thomas, 123
Kinsley, Wm., 175
Kippen, J.W., 184
Kirby, Geo., 55, 100
Kirby, Hannah, 169
Kirby, Henry, 169
Kirby, Mrs. J., 244
Kirby, J.G., 119
Kirby, James H., 74
Kirby, John, 260
Kirby, Miss M., 183
Kirby, Mary Jane, 169
Kirby family, 141
Kirk, Robert A., 76, 241
Kirkland, S., 106
Kitchen, Mrs. Lena, 172
Kitchen, Wayne, 241
Kitchener, Thomas, 191
Kitching, Rev. Geo., 149, 160
Kitto, Hazel, 180
Klassen, Helen, 181

Kleinburg, 50, 56, 79, 80, 81, 94, 97, 107, 113, 166, 193, 196, 199, 200, 206, 222, 241, 244, 257, 258, 262, illus. opp. 81, 96, 123, 192
Klein, see also Kline
Klein, John N., 56, 107, illus. opp. 105
Klein, Nicholas John, 31, 56-7, 173, 175, 229, 273, 277, 283
Klinck, Elizabeth, see Law, Mrs. Abraham
Klinck, Leonard, 124, illus. opp. 80
Klinck family, 134
Kline, Adam, 283
Kline, Eleanor, 159
Klingerland, Garrett, 35, 39
Knight, J., 110, 112, illus. opp. 110
Knight, Thos., 34, 38
Knight, Wm., 121
Knight family, 141
Knox, Prof. R.G., 240
Knox, Roy L., 180
Kohler, Ernie, 255
Korts, Michael, 33
Kranstz, Nora, 180
Krol, Mr., 184
Kuchun, Peter, 36
Kuhun, Peter, 39
Kulb, Jacob, 202
Kurita, Peter, 175, 183
Kurts, Nicholas, 28
Kurtz, Mrs., 186
Kurtz, Abrahan, 283
Kurtz, Elizabeth, see Atkinson, Mrs. John Jr.
Kurtz, John, 169, 170, 283
Kurtz, Katherine, 170
Kurtz, Michael, 33, 39, 169, 287
Kurtz, Mrs. Tena (née Cameron), illus. opp. 192
Kurtz family, 147, 283, 287
Kyle, Ann Jane, 236
Kyle, H.G., 167
Kyle, Wm., 236

L

Labour Laws, 279
La Force, 18
Lahmer, Miss, see Murray, Mrs. David
Lahmer, Jacob, 64, 74
Lahmer, Jacob & Sons, 90
Laidlaw, Rev. Thomas, 140
Laidlaw, Rev. Wm., 140
Lake, Rev. C.V., 137
Laker, Rev. E.C., 160

Lamb, Garnet, 181
Lambert, Rev. P.J., 147
Lambert, Rev. Robt. K., 147
Lambie, Mrs., 245
Lamon, T.A., 259
Lamont, Rev. G.C., 139, 162
L'Amoureux, Hester, see Burr, Mrs. Rowland
Land grants, 32-43, 51
Lane, John, 260
Lane, William, 67, 154, 283
Lang, Abraham, 30
Langdon, Kenneth, 186
Lange, Rev. Emil, 158
Langford, Hortense, see Witherspoon, Mrs. Elmer
Langstaff, ix, 120, 123-24, 153, 154, 182, 237, illus. opp. 80
Langstaff, Edwin, 64, 90
Langstaff, Dr. George Augustus, 123, 204
Langstaff, Dr. James, 73, 119, 204, 208
Langstaff, Dr. James, II, 205
Langstaff, John and Mrs. Lucy (née Miles), 55, 123, 124, 176, 204, 237
Langstaff, Miss M.L., see McConaghy, Mrs. F.
Langstaff, Dr. Rolph and Dr. Lilliam, 205, 208, 254
Langstaff family, 204-205, 283
Lapping, Mrs. Evelyn, 102
Large, Rev. R.S.E., 151, 159, 160
Larlong, Wm., 35
La Salle, 18
Laskay Emporium, 292
Laver, Estelle, see Barker, Mrs. Roy H.
Law, Abraham (J.P.) and Mrs. Elizabeth (née Klinck), 118, 119, 120, 151, 205, 274, 283, 289
Law, Rev. John, 154, 160
Lawrence, Mrs. 183
Lawrence, Alexander C., 67, 283, 290
Lawrence, Charles, 55, 283
Lawrence, E.W., 128
Lawrence, Elisha, 101
Lawrence, Isaac Huver and Mrs. Mary (née Kersey), 203
Lawrence, James, 37, 68, 72, 277,
Lawrence, John, 72
Lawrence, John Rezeau and Mrs. Ann (née Kersey), 203
Lawrence, Margaret, see Burton, Mrs. Robert
Lawrence, Mary, 33, 283
Lawrence, Peter, 236
Lawrence, Rev. Samuel Albert, 153, 155

Lawrence, W.J., 254
Lawrence & Milligan, barristers, 119
Lawrie, Agnes, see Kersey Jr., Mrs.
  William
Lawrie, Annie, 139
Lawrie, Arthur, 110, illus. opp. 110
Lawrie, Christina, see Dalziel, Mrs.
  John
Lawrie, Gavin and Mrs. Jane (née
  Bennett), 205
Lawrie, Guy, 110, 111, illus. opp. 110
Lawrie, Jane, see Kellam, Mrs. George
Lawrie, Jane, see McGillwray, Mrs.
  William
Lawrie, Jane, see Thomson, Mrs. John
Lawrie, Jean, 139
Lawrie, Jennie, 139
Lawrie, John and Mrs. Isabella (née
  Reid), 71, 73, 204, 205
Lawrie, Margaret, see Agar (II), Mrs.
  Robert, also Nicholson, Mrs.
Lawrie, Mary, 139
Lawrie, Mary Ann, see Natress, Mrs.
  John
Lawrie, Sarah, 148
Lawrie, William Jr. and Mrs. Gwen (née
  Northcott), 139, 205
Lawrie, William Sr. and Mrs. Janet (née
  Bell), 205, 247
Lawrie family, 105, 205
Lawson, Thomas, 143
Lawson, W.J., 226
Lazenby, William C., 120
Leaden, James, 35
Leaden, John, 224
Leaden, Owen, 196, 224
Learoyd, W.H., 143
Leary, Miss, 175, 183
Lebar, Abraham, 30
Lebar, John, 30
Lebugle, Julian, 52
Lee, Erland, 244
Lee, George, illus. opp. 80
Lee, Rev. Herbert, 160
Lee, Miss J.E., 186
Leek, David, 287, 288
Leek, Geo., 249
Lefeuvre, Fred C., 163
Legal Aid, 274
Legg, Alexander, 23
Legg, John, 63
Legge, Ethel, 174
Legge, Geo. F., 107
Legge, James E., 107
Legge, Thos., 107
Legge, W.H., 249, 259
Legge family, 107
Leggott, Rev. T.W., 147

Le Grice, Beryl, 174
Lehman, A.E., 182
Lehman family, 137, 290
Lellyott, Robert, 123
Lellyott, William, 123
Lemon, Maxine, 169
Lendrum, Harry, 239
Lennox, Bessie, see Charles, Mrs. Harry
Leonard, Rev. T., 151
Lerah, Rev. J.E., 158
Lever, Miss G., 120
Lewis, Morgan, 186
Libraries, see Public Libraries
Lichte, Henry, 26
Lichte, Phillip, 27
Lindeman, Rev. H., 158
Lindeman, John Peter, 22
Lindsay, Anne, 180
Lindsay, Arthur, 181
Lindsay, J.T.B., 123
Lindsay, Margaret, 180
Lindsay, Francis & Co., 123
Line, Anne, see Diceman, Mrs. John
Line, Ephriam, 253
Line, Gordon, 206
Line, John, 93, 195, 206, 273, 283
Line, William and Mrs. Susanna (née
  Snider), 206
Line family, ix, 206
Lines, Mr., 49
Lines, Henry, 38
Lines, Mrs. S., 214
Lipincott, Capt. James, 33, 34
Lippincott, Capt. Richard, 43, 45, 54
Liquor regulations and licenses, 275-6
Little, Mrs. C.E., 246
Little, Dora, 175
Little, Joseph, 68
Little, Ollie J., 180
Little, Reginald, 239
Little, Robt. D., vii, 254
Livingston, Mr., 181
Livingston, Bert, 256
Livingston, Carman, 256
Livingston, Gerald and Mrs. Lois (née
  Williams), 227, 258
Livingston, James, 70, 110, 116, 142
Livingston, Roy and Mrs. Viola (née
  Witherspoon), 227
Lloyd, Andy, 104
Lloyd, Forbes, 252
Lloyd, Thomas, 249
Lochead, Rev. Robt., 160
Locke, Mrs. Frank, 245
Locke, Gertrude, see Robb, Mrs. Leslie
Locke, Jas. H., 143
Locke, Rev. John, 160
Locke, Rev. Joseph H., 160

Locke, Louis, 220
Locke, William and Mrs., 104, 237
Lodder, Dr., 261
Lodges: 127, 159, 248, 258-60, 261
Logan, Rev. Clark, 140
Long, Matthew, 171
Longbottom, D.E. & Son, 138
Longhouse, Adeline Jane, see Duck,
    Mrs. Peter
Longhouse, Annie, see Burkholder,
    Mrs. Michael
Longhouse, Daniel and Mrs. Elizabeth
    (née Nattress), 74, 75, 128, 162,
    206, 250
Longhouse, Elizabeth, see Everingham,
    Mrs. Richard
Longhouse, George and Mrs. Mary Jane
    (née Reaman), 88, 170, 171, 205
Longhouse, Gordon and Mrs. Julia (née
    Bridgeman), 128, 206
Longhouse, John, 206
Longhouse, Mary, see Castator, Mrs. Ed.
Longhouse, Mary Ann, see Richardson,
    Mrs. Edward
Longhouse, Myrtle, 206
Longhouse, Rachel, 206
Longhouse, Susanna, see Smith, Mrs.
    John
Longhouse, Wilbert, 206
Longhouse family, 205, 206
Lonsby, Thomas, 123
Lord, Mrs. Amy, xi
Lorne, Marquis of, 119
Lorrance, Richard, 34
Lossee, Joseph J., 38
Lossing, Rev. H.N., 158
Lount, Col., 231
Love, David, 23
Love, James, 23
Love, John, 23
Love, Mrs. Ken (née Devins, Eleanor),
    illus. opp. 192
Love, Richard, 100, 102
Lovering, Rev. H.S., 147
Lower, Corner, 100
Lownsbury, E., 136
Loxton, George, 260
Loyalists, 47, 48
Lucas, John, 142, 149
Ludford, Caleb, 123
Lunau, Rev., 134, 159
Lunau, Jacob, 120, 249
Lunau family, 52
Lund, Mr., 100
Lund, Joseph, 121, 140, 141
Lund, Karl, 115
Lund, Wm., 141
Lund family, 121, 141

Lundy, John, 30
Lymburner, James, 55
Lymburner, Mathew, 67, 283
Lynch, Dorothy, 185
Lynett, D., 182, 249
Lynett, Russell, 118, 120
Lyon, Abigail, see Marwood, Mrs.
    William
Lyon Mills, 122
Lyon, Thomas, 38
Lyons, Barnabas, 55
Lyons, Elizabeth, 154
Lyons, Henry and Mrs. Mary (née
    Cober), 44, 194
Lyons, John, 41, 43, 44, 54, 55, 122,
Lyons family, 176, 290

M

Mabley, Cecil, 259
Maple, xii, 80, 82, 94, 95, 97, 110,
    111, 120, 121, 124, 133, 146, 150,
    173, 179, 184, 191, 195, 204, 206,
    210, 212, 213, 214, 215, 218, 220,
    222, 240, 241, 252, 253, 255, 257,
    258, 259, 260, 273, illus. opp. 97,
    110, 111, 123
Maple Cattle Breeders, 96, 240
McAfie, Ray, 250
McAlister, Rev., 155
McAllister, Annie, 186
McAllister, D.G., 249
McAllister, Florence, 169
McAllister, Thomas, 41, 72
McArthur, Dalton, 77, illus. opp. 73
McArthur, Duncan, 236
McArthur, John, 39
McArthur, Margaret, 236
McArthur, Nancy, 234
McAulay, Wm., 283
Macauley, James B., 35
Macauley, George, 35
McBride, Esther, 174
McBride, George, 34, 38
McBride, Jack, xi
McBride, John and Mrs. Jane (née
    McNeil), 233, 283
McBride, R.P., 185
McBride, William, 69, 112, 233, 283
McCabe, Blanche, 169, 174
McCague, Margaret, see Wright, Mrs.
    Ashford
McCague, John, 124
McCallum, Agnes, 246
McCallum, Annie, 246
McCallum, Barbara, 168, 169

McCallum, Bertha, 181
McCallum, Betty, 179
McCallum, Donald and Mrs. Constance
  (née Ross), 105, 126, 168, 247, 250
McCallum, Dan, 105
McCallum, David, 256, 258
McCallum, Duncan, 250
McCallum, Elmer and Mrs. Vina (née
  Wray), 228
McCallum, Rev. J.W., 147, 151, 160
McCallum, Jean, see Bryson, Mrs.
  James
McCallum, Jack, 186
McCallum, James and Mrs. Sarah (née
  Cameron), 191, 192
McCallum, John, 162, 184, 258
McCallum, John J.P., 110
McCallum, John and Mrs. Lynn (née
  Scarlett), 105
McCallum, M., 186
McCallum, Neil and Mrs. Sarah (née
  Wray), 228
McCann, Violet, 180
McCarthy, Mr., 181
McCauley, James B., 35
McCauly, William, 69, 159
McCleary, Rev. Ray, 140
McCloskey, C., 260
McClung, James A., 143
McClure, Agnes, 185
McClure, Alice, 177
McClure, Andrew Sr. and Mrs. Mary
  Ann (née Hamilton), 208, illus. opp.
  207
McClure, Andrew (II), and Mrs. Verna
  (née Bryson), 178, 208
McClure, Annie, 175, 177, 178, 185
McClure, Bruce, 256
McClure, Cameron, 200, 208
McClure, Elizabeth, see McNeil, Mrs.
  Livingston
McClure, Florence, 172
McClure, John, 127, 128
McClure, Jean, 181
McClure, Kate, 139
McClure, Mary, 139
McClure, Nellie, 181
McClure, Samuel Jr. and Mrs. Elizabeth
  (née Hostrawser), 208, 250, 260
McClure, Samuel Sr. and Mrs. Nancy
  (née Cameron), 208, 236, 250
McClure, Sarah, 185
McClure, William and Mrs. Ellen (née
  Nesbitt),139, 162, 169, 208, 250
McClure, Wm., 177
McClure family, x, 105, 208
McCluskey, Wm., 107
McCluskie, Bertha, 148

McCluskie, Frank and Mrs., 148
McConaghy, Dr. F. and Mrs. M.L. (née
  Langstaff), 181, 185, 208
McConaghy, Francis, 119, 182
McConkey, Ruth, 76
McCormack, Augusta Honoria, 36
McCormack, John, 233, 283
McCormack, Dr. John, 229, 230
McCormack, L., 185
McCormack, Thomas, 171, 174, 181,183
McCort, Susannah, see Beamish, Mrs.
  Henry
McCourt, Marjorie, see Fletcher, Mrs.
  Howard
McCowan, Dougal, 111
McCrae, J.D., 186
MacCrimmon, Rev. J.R., 147
McCubbin, John, 116
McCullough, Rev. Geo., 151
McCuoig, J., 171
McCutcheon, David, 40
McCutcheon, Henry, 209
McCutcheon, Patrick and Mrs. Ann
  (née Parkinson), 70, 209
McCutcheon, William, 69, 209
McCutcheon family, 209
McDavids, James, 55
McDermott, James, 236
McDiarmid, Garnet, 182
McDonagh, Rev. Wm., 160
McDonald, Miss, 167
MacDonald, Mr., 177
McDonald, Alexander, 283
McDonald, Andrew, 283
McDonald, Annie, see Carson, Mrs.
  Ernest
MacDonald, Mrs. Annie (née Johnston),
  201
McDonald, Archibald and Mrs. Mary
  (née White), 38, 209, 233, 283, 284,
  288, 289
McDonald, Bruce, 174
McDonald, Charles, 124, 184, 209
McDonald, Donald, 39, 236, 284
McDonald, Douglas and Mrs., 143, 245
McDonald, Dugald, 185, 210
McDonald, Flora, 236
McDonald, George, 119, 182
MacDonald, Rev. H.R., 134, 155
McDonald, Henry, 174, 179
MacDonald, Rev. J., 134, 145
McDonald, J.W., 185
McDonald, James M., xi, xiv, 73, 123,
  172, 210, 240-1, 260, 271, 277,
  illus. opp. 97
McDonald, Jane, see Burton, Mrs.
  William

McDonald, John, 239
McDonald, John and Mrs. Grace (née Muir), 209, 233
McDonald Sgt. John Sr. and Mrs. Sarah (née MacInnes), 38, 209, 280, 284, 287, 288
McDonald, John (III), 124, 210
McDonald, John G., 172, 179, 181
McDonald, John L., 102
McDonald, Rev. Joseph Wm., 155
McDonald, Louise, see Brownlee, Mrs. James
Macdonald, Mrs. Margaret, 172
McDonald, Mary, 236
McDonald, Milton and Mrs., 210, 246
McDonald, Neil Sr., 146, 233, 273, 284, 289
McDonald, Neil Jr., 233
McDonald, Neil G., 260
McDonald, Ronald, 208, illus. opp. 207
McDonald, Samuel, 209, 236
MacDonald, Thoreau, xi, illus. opp. 188
McDonald, W., 141
McDonald, Wm. O., 75
MacDonald, Sir William, 243
McDonald family, x, 209-10
McDonnell, Alex, 35
McDonnell, John, 34
McDougal, John, 24
McDougall, Catharine, 170
McDougall, Daniel, 39, 68, 104
McDougall, John, 34, 38, 229, 284
MacDougall, William and Mrs., 104 illus. opp. 127
McDougall's Mill Dam, 238
McDowell, Mrs. Wm., 186
McEachern, Donald, 40
McEachern, E.V., 185
MacEachern, Gordon A., 241
McEachern, Neil, 67, 279
MacEachern, Roger, 36, 40
McEachern, Rev. Ronald, 148
McElroy, Henry and Mrs. Ann, 102
McEvoy, W.J., 240
McFadden, Elmer E., 186
McFadden, Rev. Wm., 160
McFarlane, Catherine, see Mackenzie, Mrs. William
McFarlane, M., 102
MacFayden, Mr., 104
McGahoe, D., 102
McGill family, 59, 67, 180, 186, 284
McGillivray, Catherine, 211
McGillivray, Christena, 211
McGillivray, Donald, 71, 211
McGillivray, Flora, 211

McGillivray, Gordon and Mrs. Mina (née Elliott), 139, 211, 247, 260
McGillivray, Jean, 139, 258
McGillivray, Jessie, 210
McGillivray, John Jr. and Mrs. May Susan (née Cairns), 210
McGillivray, John Sr. and Mrs. Nancy, 210
McGillivray, Margaret, 211
McGillivray, Mary, 139, 258
McGillivray, Mary Jane, 211
McGillivray, Maude, see Roberts, Mrs. Maude
McGillivray, Neil, 36, 71, 72, 146, 210, 211
McGillivray, Sarah Catherine, see Peterman, Mrs. Wesley
McGillivray, Simon, 258
McGillivray, William and Mrs. Jane (née Lawrie), 211
McGillivray, Wm. B., 239
McGillivray families. x, 210-11
McGinley, Rev. W.J., 156
McGinn, Andrew, 71
McGinn, Father F.R., 152, 156
McGinn, Mrs. Wilfred, 210
McGown, Jane, see McKinnon, Mrs. Charles
McGregor, Edna, 183
McGregor, Margaret, 180
McGroarty family, 163
McGuire, Alex, 284
McGuire, Charles, 40, 284
McGuire, Rev. David, 153
McGuirl, Chas., xiv, 177
Machinery: farm implements, 91; power, 95
McHugh, Edna, 186
MacInnes, Sarah, see McDonald Sr., Mrs. John
McIntosh, Alex, 110
McIntosh, Rev. J.W., 150, 151
McIntosh, Sandy, 80
McIntyre, Dugald, 234
McIntyre, James (log house), illus. opp. 63
Mack, Rev. W.S., 140
McKane, David, 160
McKarrby, John, 33
McKay, Albert, 212
McKay, Alexander and Mrs. Sally (née McQuiree), 39, 287
McKay, Benjamin, 252
McKay, Caroline, see Watson, Mrs. Joseph
McKay, Rev. Donald, 148
McKay, Eber and Mrs. Elsie (née Castator), 141, 212, illus. opp. 212
McKay, Eleanor, 212, illus. opp. 212

McKay, Elizabeth, see Parsons, Mrs. Matthew
MacKay, Mrs. H., 246
MacKay, Rev. H.J., 134
McKay, Hannah, see Milne, Mrs. Peter
McKay, Jacob, 223
McKay, Jacob and Mrs. Elizabeth (née Wilcox), 211, 284, illus. opp. 212
McKay, Jacob Jr., 212
McKay, Jacob (III), 212
McKay, John and Mrs. Flora (née McKinnon), 26, 290
McKay, Nancy, 211
MacKay, Rev. R.G., 139, 162
McKay, Robert, 110
McKay, William, 223
McKay, William Jr., 212
McKay, William Abbott and Mrs. Elizabeth (née Mattice), 211
McKay, family, 211-12, illus. opp. 212
McKechanie, Alexander, 38, 277
McKechnie, Angus and Mrs. Nellie (née Burton), 191
McKechnie, Donald, 236, 284
McKechnie, Malcolm, 110
McKee, John and Mrs. Sarah (née Elliott), 196
McKeen, Mrs. Evan, 245
McKenzie, Miss, 180
Mackenzie, Major Addison Alexander (Lex), 128, 190, 206, 239, illus. opp. 207
Mackenzie, Annie Matilda, see Dalziel, Mrs. J. William
Mackenzie, Dan, 198
McKenzie, Dave, 106
Mackenzie, Donald and Mrs. Lydia Ann (née Addison), 162, 206
Mackenzie, Donald Ross, 206
McKenzie, Douglas, 181
Mackenzie, Florence, 206
MacKenzie, Rev. John, 139, 162
Mackenzie, Neil, 206
Mackenzie, Paul, 174
Mackenzie, Sarah Ann, 206
Mackenzie, William and Mrs. Catherine (née McFarlane), 206
Mackenzie, William (II), 206
Mackenzie, William Lyon, 66, 229, 230, 231, 259
Mackenzie family, x, 206-207
MacKeracher, Rev. D.A., 161
McKewan, Lorne, 193
MacKinnon, A., 101
McKinnon, Alexander, 171
McKinnon, Angus, 171, 290
McKinnon, Anthony, 233, 284
McKinnon, Arthur, 212

McKinnon, Charles and Mrs. Jane (née McGown), 284, 290
McKinnon, Charles Jr., 38, 284
McKinnon, Donald and Mrs., 69, 212, 222, 246
McKinnon, Duncan, 70, 222
McKinnon, Elmer, 212, 252
McKinnon, Flora, see McKay, Mrs. John
McKinnon, Hugh, 212
McKinnon, John Jr. and Mrs. Martha (née Keffer), 212
McKinnon, John Sr. and Mrs. Ann (née Drummond), 212
McKinnon, John (II), 212
McKinnon, Rev. M., 139, 162
McKinnon, Martin, 71, 212
McKinnon, Neil, 169, 170, 178, 289
McKinnon, Norman, 212
McKinnon, Rev. Warren, 148
McKinnon family, x, 158, 212, 284, 288
McKittrick, Rev. E.J., 145
McLachlan, Rev. Thos., 139, 148
Maclachlan, Wills, 110, 215
MacLaughin, Jos., 167, 220
MacLaughlin, Rev. A., 158, 215
McLaughlin, Herb, 115
McLean, Mr., 176
McLean, Alexander, 284
McLean, Anne, 127
McLean, C.J., 143
McLean, Catherine, 236
McLean, Dr. Charles, 127, illus. opp. 127, 236
McLean, Dan, 204, illus. opp. 95
McLean, Duncan, 253
McLean, Dr. Garnet D. and Mrs. Lillian E. (née Smith), 127, 128, 255, illus. opp. 127
MacLean, Hector, 41, 146, 284
McLean, Hugh, 35, 68
McLean, I., 181
McLean, James, 40, 249, 251, 252, 253
McLean, James B., 72, 111, 259, 277
McLean, Janet, see Dalziel, Mrs. James
McLean, Jean, 127
McLean, John, 39, 69, 128, 233, 236, 284
McLean, Martin, 68, 233
McLean, Mary, 127
McLean, Peter, 127
McLean, Dr. Peter D., 127, 260, illus. opp. 127
McLean, Roderick, 204
McLean, Thomas, 252
McLellan, Dr. Jos., 148
MacLennan, Jean, 186
McLeod family, 105, 106, 222, 249

McLeven, Christine, see Cameron, Mrs. Donald
McMahon. Father Arthur, 163
McMahon, Bernard, 68
McMahon, Rev. Patrick, 152, 156
McMahon, Starr, 212
McMahon, Thomas Franklin and Mrs., 119, 212, 254, 259
McMann family, 158
McMichael, Robert and Mrs. Signe, 262
McMichael Conservation Collection of Art, 217, 262
MacMillan, Grace, 169
McMillan, Mrs. D., 244
McMillan, J., 185
McMillan, Kate, 177
McMullen, Hugh, 68, 284
McMurchy, Archibald and Mrs. Jean (née Cameron), 70, 192
McMurchy, Catherine, see Cameron, Mrs. Archibald
McMurchy, Duncan, 75, 76
McMurchy, James and Mrs. Agnist (née McDougal), 35, 39, 284, 289
McMurchy, Margaret, 181, 185
McMurchy, Marshall, 76, 241
McMurchy, Peter, 181
McMurchy, Ross, 241
MacNab, Sir Allan, 122, 232, 258
MacNabb, Catherine, see Williams, Mrs. Catherine
McNabb, James, 39
McNabb, Sarah, see Peterson, Mrs. Sarah
McNair, Edna, 213
McNair, George, 174
McNair, James, 70, 179, 213, 249
McNair, John, 38
McNair, Leslie, 213
McNair, M., 182
McNair, Robert, 68, 212, 284
McNair, Scott, 75, 213, 241, 254
McNair family, 212-13
McNamara, James, illus. opp. 80
MacNaughton, Alex, 234
McNaughton, Audrey, 171
McNaughton, Miss B., 244
McNaughton, Christina, 236
McNaughton, D., 169
MacNaughton, Donald, 146, 284
McNaughton, J.B., 177
McNaughton, Miss K., 246
McNaughton, Peter, 184, 236, 284, 287
MacNaughton, Rev. Peter, 38, 138, 145, 146
MacNaughton family, 234
McNeil, Rev. A., 134, 151, 153
McNeil, Alex, 69, 213, 236
McNeil, Alex and Mrs. Nan, 213, 256, 257

McNeil, Andrew and Mrs., 185, 246
McNeil, Arthur and Mrs. Margaret (née Jamieson), 38, 68, 146, 213, 233, 236, 277, 284
McNeil, Cameron L., 240, 256
McNeil, Charles, 213, 250
McNeil, Jack and Mrs., 246, 257, illus. opp. 123
McNeil, James, 74, 236
McNeil, Jane, see McBride, Mrs. John
McNeil, John, 250, 284
McNeil, Lillian, 245, 255
McNeil, Livingston and Mrs. Elizabeth (née McClure), 213, 234, 246, 250, illus. opp. 232
McNeil, Margaret, illus. opp. 212
McNeil, R. Alex, 236
McNeil, Stanley, 250
McNeil family, x, 213, illus. opp. 213
McNulty, Rev., 156
McNutt, G., 34, 35, 39
McPhail, Donna, 175
McPhail, M.C., 255
McPherson, Donald and Mrs. Jesse (née Witherspoon), 227
MacPherson, Dr. L.W., 191
McQuarrie, Archibald and Mrs. Emma (née Pickering), 73, 174, 213, 284
McQuarrie, Ethel, 179
McQuarrie, Hector, 284, 287
McQuarrie, John C. (J.P.), 112, 136, 147, 213, 274, 287
McQuarrie, Joseph P., 166, 178
McQuarrie, Lachlan and Mrs., 213
McQuarrie, Matthew, 213
McQuarrie, Mrs. Mervyn, 180
McQuarrie, Miss Olivia, (see Mrs. C.H. Bowman)
McQuarrie family, 213, 288
Macrae & Adamson, 291
McRoberts, Malcolm, 171, 175
McSpadden, Rev. B., 144
MacTaggart, Evelyn, 258
McTavish, Donald, 183
McVean, Margaret, see Kersey, Mrs. Thomas
McVicar, W., 184
McWhirter, Roy, 171, 183
Madden, Leo, 106
Maddock, Miss, 244
Madill, J.J., 260
Madill, John, 283
Madill, Mrs. Verna, 102
Maggs, Leonard, 102
Magrath, Rev. James, 131, 132
Mainland, Margaret, 179
Maitland, A., 68

Maitland, Major-General Sir Peregrine, K.C., 173, 207
Malcolm, Miss, 171
Malloy, Alexander, 74
Malloy, Archibald, 283
Malloy, Barbara, see Cameron, Mrs. Alex
Malloy, Donald, 74, 75
Malloy, Flora, 236
Malloy, Malcolm and Mrs. Agnes (née Cameron), 71, 191, 192, 283
Malloy, Neil, 144, 167, 252, 253, 283
Malloy family, 168, 289, 291
Maltby, Raymond and Mrs. Eleanor (née Wallace), 225
Mann, James, 126
Mann, Sir John, 64
Manning, Mrs. Joshua, 244
Manser, Caroline, see Castator, Mrs. George
Maple Cattle Breeders Association, illus. opp. 97
Maple sugar and syrup, 87, 91
Marchaud, Jacques, 37, 52
Marchaud, James, 33
Markham, Mrs., 146
Markham, Elgin Mills Plank Road Company, 106
Marks, Grace, 236
Marr, Mrs., 180
Marr, Rebecca, see Wray, Mrs. John
Marriage Register, (1819-43) by Rev. Wm. Jenkins, 286-91
Marsh, Henry, 112
Marsh, James and Mrs. Margery (née Atkinson), 187
Marsh, Robert, 249
Marsh, Robt. Sr., 32, 59, 64, 90, 117, 150, 272
Marsh, William, 39
Marshall, Rev. David, 150
Marshall, Miss Ida, illus. opp. 181
Marshall, James, 163
Martin, Rev. D.M., 148
Martin, Duncan S., 172
Martin, Edward, 123, 260
Martin, Mrs. Gordon (née Gullett, Patricia), 172
Martin, John, 123
Martin, John, 175, 179, 183
Martin, Moses, 273, 274
Martin, Nathan, 159
Martin, Thomas, 81
Martin, William B., 172
Martindale, A.F., 183
Marwood, George and Mrs. Hannah (née Nichols), 207
Marwood, William Jr. and Mrs. Susan (née Gohn), 207

Marwood, William Sr. and Mrs. Abigail (née Lyon), 207
Marwood, William (III) and Mrs. Florence (née Nightingale), 207
Mason, Miss Annie, 166, 174
Mason, Charles, 119, 151
Mason & Tisdale, Messrs., 101
Mastin, Gertrude, 179, 185
Mather, Walter, 172
Mathews, 231
Mathews, Mrs. A.T., 247
Mathews, Robert, 68, 283
Mathewson, Emery, 110, illus. opp. 111
Mathewson, Florence, see King, Mrs. Charles
Mathewson, Gilbert, 71, illus. opp. 111
Mathewson, Joseph, 38, 287
Mathewson, Samuel, 70
Mathewson, Susan, see King (III), Mrs. Robert
Mathison, Alexander, 283, 287
Mathison, William, 38
Matson, Mrs. June, 178
Matthews, Abigal, 159
Matthews, Esau C., 70
Matthews, Robert, 159
Mattice, Elizabeth, see McKay, Mrs. William Abbot
Maul, James, 35
Maw & Sons, 113
Maxey, Wilfred R., 240
Maxwell, Rev. F., 134
Maxwell, Wm., 283
Mayerhoffer, Rev. V. Phillip, 39, 40, 145, 157
Mayhew, Sidney W., 260
Maynard, Amos, 126, 260
Maynard, Anne, see Coon, Mrs. Joseph
Maynard, Augustus, illus. opp. 83
Maynard, John, 68, illus. opp. 115
Maynard, Kenneth, 250
Maynard, Amos (Carriage Shops) illus. opp. 83
Mechanics' Institute, 166
Medcalf, Thomas, 35, 37, 38
Medford, Chas., 260
Medon, Frank, 191
Meek, John, 82
Meeker, Miss Blanche, 174
Mellish, William, 100
Melville, A., 283
Melvin, Ansel D., 56, 57
Menzies, Archibald, 162
Mercer, Thomas, 33
Mercer, William, 283
Messmore, Rev., 151
Metcalf, Robert, 68

Metcalf, Thos., 34
Metcalfe, Cora, 186
Metropolitan Railway Station,
    Richmond Hill, illus. opp. 81; see
    also Transportation
Metropolitan Toronto & Region
    Conservation Authority, 114, 262
Michell, Rev. D.C.H., 145
Middlebrook, Miss M., 181
Middleton, Denis, 182
Middleton, Elizabeth, see Topper, Mrs.
    George
Middleton, George, 72
Middleton, Wesley, 249
Middleton family, 101
Milburn, Joseph, 273, 277
Miles, Abner, 33, 116, 117, 118, 119,
    204, 272, 273
Miles, James, 118, 149, 150, 181, 283
Miles, Lucy, see Langstaff, Mrs.
    John
Miles Hill, 110
Milk Delivery, illus. opp. 82
Millar, Solomina, see Pfaff, Mrs.
    Anthony
Millard, Timy (Timothy), 29
Miller, Miss, 174
Miller, Mrs. A., 186
Miller, Charles, xi
Miller, Christian, 42
Miller, Dickson, 174
Miller, Edward, 116, 146, 283
Miller, Elijah, 289
Miller, Frank T., 102
Miller, Fred H., 250
Miller, George, 71, 136, 233, 288
Miller, Gordon and Mrs. Laura, 180,
    246, 247, 250
Miller, Henry Jr., 176, 214, 288
Miller, J.R., 175
Miller, Jacob, 42
Miller, John, 41, 42, 289
Miller, Joseph, 41, 289
Miller, Michael, 41, 42
Miller, Nicholas and Mrs. Sally (née
    Johnson), 43
Miller, Nicholas Sr. and Mrs. Sara (née
    Devins), 38, 41, 42, 43, 44, 50,
    214, 232, 272
Miller, Mrs. Ross, 181
Miller, Ruth, 258
Miller, Sally, 34
Miller, Simon, 231, 232
Miller & Duncan, Barristers, 123
Miller family, ix, 47, 134, 176, 214
Milliard, Reuben, 176
Milligan, Rev., 158

Milligan, Gilbert, 37
Milligan, May, 168
Millikin, Thomas, 186
Mills, H.J., 254
Mills, John, 101-2
Mills, Joseph, 283
Mills, Father Michael P., 163
Mills, Robert, 69
Mills and Bedford Park Greenhouses,
    Richmond Hill, 117
Milne, Mrs. Peter (née McKay,
    Hannah), 211
Milner, Rev. Jonathan, 140
Milton, Robt., 37
Minton, Fred, 103
Misler, Joseph, 38, 287, 289
Mitchell, Agnes, 213
Mitchell, Alexander, 69, 73, 213
Mitchell, Andrew, 138, 213, 214
Mitchell, Audrey, 168
Mitchell, Cecil, 143
Mitchell, Cunningham, 283
Mitchell, David, 213
Mitchell, Rev. E.H., 144
Mitchell, Elizabeth, 213
Mitchell, Irene, 143
Mitchell, James and Mrs. Catharine
    (née Kersey), 203
Mitchell, James (II) and Mrs. Lavina
    (née Devins), 214, 245
Mitchell, James and Mrs. Grisell (née
    Calder), 213, 214
Mitchell, Jean, 213
Mitchell, John, 213
Mitchell, Nellie, 169
Mitchell, Peter, 213
Mitchell, Peter (II), 214
Mitchell, Robert (II) and Mrs. Dorothy
    (née Cousins), 128, 214, 245, 246,
    250, 257
Mitchell, Robert and Mrs. Helen (née
    Bryson), 104, 214
Mitchell, W.J. and Mrs., 128, 245
Mitchell, William, 39, 71, 213, 283
Mitchell family, 101, 213-14
Mizen, Mrs., 245
"Mohawk Dutch", 134
Moir, Rev. John A., 139, 160, 162, 255
Mollet, Mrs. Anna (née Kerswill,
    Anna),153
Monahan, Mrs., 174
Monkhouse, Miss, 178
Monteith, Rev. Robt., 140
Montgomery, John, 37
Montgomery, Jos., 121
Montgomery, Nancy, 236
Moodie, Colonel, 117, 216, 230, 259
Moodie, Alexander, 119, 150

Moody, James, 40
Moore, Miss, 174
Moore, Rev., 159
Moore, Andrew, 30
Moore, Mrs. Bertha, 186
Moore, Cunningham, 181
Moore, Eleanor, 36
Moore, F.A., 260
Moore, George, 186
Moore, J.E., 140
Moore, Mary, see Scott, Mrs. Lorne
Moore, Robert, 259
Moore, Robt., 166
Moore, Mrs. Russell, 178
Moore, Solomon and Mrs. Eleanor
    (née Stephenson), 41
Moore, Mrs. T., 246
Moore, Thomas, 181
Moore, W.F., 174
Moran, Miss, 169
Moran, Miss A., 177
Morby, Jean, 179
More, Rev. J.H., 151
Morgan, Daniel, 28
Morgan, Flo. E., 172
Morgan, Rev. J.W., 147, 160
Morgan, Mrs. Janice, 175
Morgan's Hill, 238
Morgan, John, 252, 253
Morgan, Mary, 177
Morgan family, 107, 287, 290
Morley, John, 67, 221
Morris, Dorothy, see Coles, Mrs. Bonar
Morris, F.T., 124
Morris, Rev. J.T., 151
Morris, Hon. James, 221
Morris, Rev. T.J., 156
Morris, Rev. Wm. D.F., 161
Morrison, Mrs. G., 175
Morrison, Mrs. H., 247
Morrison, Hugh, 69
Morrison, L.B., 186
Morrison, Miss M., 178
Morrow, F.W., 186
Morrow, James, 69, 283
Morrow, John, 116, 181
Mortimer, Rev. George, 155
Mortly, Robert and Mrs. Jane (née
    Atkinson), 187
Morton, Miss I., 177
Mortson, Arnold, 249
Mosgrove, Henry, 70
Mott, Margaret, 175
Mounsey, Alexander, 181
Mounsey, Thomas, 162
Moyle, Miss A., 246
Moyle, Mrs. S.W., 245
Moynihan, Dr. A., 240

Muckle, James, 26
Mudville, (Concord), 166
Muir, Alexander, 124, 185
Muir, Grace, see McDonald Jr., Mrs.
    John
Muldoon, Arthur, 123
Mulholland, David, 67, 154
Mullaney, Harold D., 97
Mullen, G.M., 100
Mullin, Rev. Chas. A., 150
Mulock Cup, 254
Munday, Joseph, 123
Municipal Council of Woodbridge, 97
Munro, Richard L., 171, 261
Munroe, David, 117
Munshaw, Mrs., 60, 263
Munshaw, Balser, 122, 175
Munshaw, Jacob, 67, 279, 283
Munshaw family, 68, 176, 283, 288
Munsie, Wm., 126
Murch, Arthur, 184
Murison, Alex and Mrs. Georgia (née
    Chapman), 193
Murphy, Audrey, 178
Murphy, Bitsy, 39
Murphy, John, 39, 283
Murphy family, 152, 289
Murray, Bruce and Mrs. Glenna (née
    Seed), 215
Murray, Christopher, 214, 283
Murray, David and Mrs. (née
    Lahmer), 214, 215, illus. opp. 170
Murray, Mrs. David C. (née Diceman,
    Ethel), 196
Murray, Donald, 196
Murray, Mrs. Frances, 186, 247
Murray, George, 214
Murray, Gordon, 196
Murray, Isaac Sr., 214
Murray, Isaac and Mrs. Elizabeth (née
    Richards), 167, 214, 215
Murray, John and Mrs. Jean (née
    Ireland), 215
Murray, Leonard, 215
Murray, Mary, see Keffer, Mrs. George
Murray, Susannah, see Julian, Mrs.
    John
Murray, Walter and Mrs., 192, illus.
    opp. 192
Murray, William, 283
Musselman, Mrs., 264
Musselman, Abraham, 283
Musselman, Benjamin, 123
Musselman, I.B., 259
Musselman, Peter, 38, 43, 67, 229,
    230, 283
Myers, Wm., 250

N

Nafe, Jacob, 170
Nafe, Lavina, 170
Nash, Charles, 239
Nash, J., 260
Nashville, 97, 102, 105, 112, 160,
192, 193, 202, 245
Nashville Store, illus. opp. 111
Nattress, Agnes, 174
Nattress, Elizabeth, see Longhouse,
Mrs. Daniel
Nattress, Ethra, 177
Nattress, George, 174
Nattress, Herb, 160
Nattress, Isaac, 40, 74
Nattress, Janey, 139
Nattress, John and Mrs. Mary Ann
(née Lawrie), 162, 173, 177, 205
Nattress, Mary, see Fletcher, Mrs. Pierce
Nattress, Muriel, 174
Nattress, William, 139, 169
Naughton Bros., 105, 119
Naughton family, 105-6, 119, 152
Naylor, John, 258
Naylor, Mary, 258
Neal, Alwyn, 258
Neal, Laura, see Miller, Mrs. Gordon
Neal, Pearson and Mrs. Adeline, 186,
247, 250
Neal, William, 118, 120
Neal family, 107
Neeley, James, 174
Nell, Anne, see Snider, Mrs. Samuel
Nelles, Dr. David A., 123
Nelson, John, 170
Nesbitt, Ellen, see McClure, Mrs.
William
Nesbitt, R.H., 254
Ness, John, 185
Neville, R.W., 119
Newberry, Miss, 180
Newis, Glen, 172
Newman, Robert, 182
Newspapers: 116, 118, 119, 123, 126,
127, 198, 212, 221, 252
Newton, Andrew, 106, 182, 215
Newton, Bertrom, 106
Newton, Miss Elizabeth, 180
Newton, J. Earle and Mrs. Georgia
(née Boyle), 215
Newton, James Jr., 215
Newton, James Sr., 105, 215, 284,
290
Newton, Tom, 106, 259
Newton Bros., 119
Nichol, John, 115
Nichol, Rev. Peter, 139
Nichols, Hannah, see Marwood,
George

Nichols, Hesse A., 153, 167, 180,
259
Nicholson, Mrs. Margaret, formerly
Mrs. Robert Agar (née Lawrie,
Margaret), 205
Nicol, Rev. Peter, 139, 162
Nicol, William and Mrs. Ann (née
Thomson), 222
Nielly, Sam, 142
Nighswander, Grant, 182
Nightingale, Florence, see Marwood,
Mrs. William
Nixon, Gertie, 244
Nixon, Mrs. M., 244
Nixon, Robert, 110
Nixon, William, 140-1
Noble, Arthur, 110
Noble, Herod, illus. opp. 80
Noble, John, 259
Noble, Joseph, 39, 110, 230, 284
Noble, Rev. Norman Henry, 155
Noble, Thomas, 284
Noble, Wm., 121
Noble family, 110, 111, 145
Nobleville (Maple), 110, 259
North, Emma, 174
North-West Fur Trading Co.,
50, 82, see also Fur Trade
Northcott, Gwen, see Lawrie Jr.,
Mrs. William
Norton, David, 26, 128
Norton, John E., 24
Norton, Joseph E., 240
Norton, Tessie, see Johnston (II), Mrs.
Robert
Noseworthy, Miss V., 180
Notter, Miss, 183
Nurse, Rev., 159
Nye, William, 68

O

O'Brien, Mrs., 182
O'Brien, B.T., 184
O'Brien, Edward and Mrs. (née Mary
Gapper), 37, 63, 153, 263, 282
O'Brien, Luke, 169
O'Brien family, 59, 229, 284
O'Connor, James, 236
O'Connor, Patrick, 39
O'Connor, Timothy, 211
Octagonal barn, illus. opp. 91
Octagonal house, illus. opp. 111
O'Donnell, Rev. J.A., 152, 156
Oksanen, Mrs. Helen, 172
Olds, G.D., 186
Oliver, Mr., 174

Oliver, Forrest and Mrs. Nellie (née
　　Thomas), 215
Oliver, Miss J., 244
Oliver, Rev. J.H., 151
Oliver, Mrs. James, 244
Oliver, Joshua and Mrs. Anne (née
　　Wade), 215
Oliver, Laura, 215
Oliver, Thomas and Mrs. Eliza (née
　　Pickering), 215
Oliver, William and Mrs. Lydia (née
　　Keffer), 215
Oliver family, 110, 215
O'Mara, Very Rev. Monsignor John A.
　　(J.C.L.), 163, 164
O'Neil, Rev. James, 153
O'Neill, L.E., 240
Ontario Genealogical Society, xii
Ontario Food Terminal, illus. opp. 193
Oper, Jacob, 42
O'Rourke, Michael, 163
Orr, Allan, 257
Orr, Anna, see Johnston, Mrs. Robt.
Orr, Daniel, 233
Orr, Gordon, 255, 256, 257
Orr, James, 69, 233
Orr, John, 69, 284
Orr, Nora, 180
Orr, Orphie, 258
Orr, Dr. Rowland, 111, 112
Orr, William Andrew, 69, 233
Orser, James and Mrs. Theresa, 116
Ort, Abraham, 24
Ort, Henry, 30
Osburn, Alice, 34
Osler, Rev. Henry Bath, 161
Oster, Aaron, 215
Oster, Alan, 215
Oster, Jacob, 284
Oster, John (Johannes) and Mrs.
　　Rachel (née Fisher), 23, 215, 279,
　　284
Oster, Lorne, 215
Oster, Michael, 67, 215, 290
Oster, Peter, 67, 102, 216, 284, illus.
　　opp. 101
Oster, Samuel, 67, 215
Oster, Thomas, 215
Oster, William, 215
Oster family, ix, 102, 107, 215-16, 290
Oswald, Richard, 20
Outram, John, 179
Overling, Nicholas, 40, 290
Overseers of highways, illus. opp.
　　278-9
Overton, Tom, 174

P

Padget, George, 249
Page, John, 216
Page, John (II), 216
Page, Lewis and Mrs. Rebecca (née
　　Rupert), 33, 37, 216
Page, Lewis Jr., 216
Page, Lucia, 171
Page, Stewart L. and Mrs. Margery
　　(née Wright), 216, 228
Page, Thomas, 121, 216, 274
Page family, 158, 216
Paget family, 59
Painter, D., 183
Palatinate, ix, 15, 47, 48
Palmer, Bertha, 246
Palmer, John, 119
Panke, Georgina, see Downing, Mrs. J.
Park, David, 56
Park, Robert, 71
Parker, Miss, 169
Parker, Benjamin, 136
Parker, John, 136
Parkinson, Ann, see McCutcheon, Mrs.
　　Patrick
Parkinson, Edward, 123
Parr, W., 102
Parsons, Elizabeth, see Wardlaw, Mrs.
　　Peter
Parsons, Mrs. Mathew (née McKay,
　　Elizabeth), 211
Parsons, William, 122, 123, 155
Parsons family, 59, 229
Partridge, Rev. A.M., 147
Pasquale Brothers, 216
Passmore, John, 174
Patentees, 14, 15, 34-43
Paton, Matt., 106
Patrick, Mr., 174
Patrons of Industry, The, 248
Patterson, 55-6, 113, 117, 133, 150,
　　179, 214, illus. opp. 114 and 115
Patterson, Alfred, 113, 114
Patterson, Elizabeth, see Taylor, Mrs.
　　Elizabeth
Patterson, Rev. J. Douglas, 161
Patterson, John D., 114, illus. opp. 111
Patterson, Mabel, 180
Patterson, Margaret, see Burton, Mrs.
　　Henry
Patterson, Peter, 73, 113, 114, 179,
　　249, 260, illus. opp. 114
Patterson, Rev. R.B., 161, 255
Patterson, Robert, 113
Patterson, Sarah, 35
Patterson, Susan, 114
Patterson, Wm., 71, 74, 114, 168, 249
Patterson family, 101

Patterson & Bros., 55, 113, 114, 117,
214, illus. opp. 114, 115
Patton, Miss Francis, 174
Paul, Rev. A.J., 151
Paul, Thomas, 72
Payne, Norman and Mrs. Doris (née
Cook), 174, 194, 258
Payson, Ephraim, 59
Peacock, Rev. Percy, 151
Peacock, Mrs. Roscoe (Gertrude), 247
Peacock, William, 68
Pearce, George, 72, 73, 277
Pearen, Rev. James, 137, 143, 147
Pearse, Elihu, 176
Pearson, Edwin A., 143, 160
Pearson, James Jr., and Mrs. James,
216, 245
Pearson, James Sr., 216
Pearson family, 216
Peck, Mercy M., 159
Peck, Washington, 125, 159, 284,
287
Peckett, Rev. David, 154
Peeler, Florence, see Topper, Mrs.
Alvin
Penn, William, 16, 19
Pennsylvania German folklore society,
x, xi, xii, xiv
Penrose, Isaac, 30
Pentland, Miss H., 246
Percival, Rev. W.W., 119, 150
Peoples, Christiana, see Egan, Mrs.
Richard
Perigo, James, 33, 34
Perkins, Floyd R., and Mrs. Ruth (née
Reaman), 118, 120, 179
Perkins, Lorne, 179
Perry, John W., 76, 109, 241, 289
Petch, Rev. Charles, 158
Peterman, George, 38, 236, 284
Peterman, Henry, 142
Peterman, Jake, 104
Peterman, John, 284, 290
Peterman, Michael, 69, 233
Peterman, Samuel, 70, 116
Peterman, Wesley and Mrs. Sarah
Catherine (née McGillivray), 210
Peters, Henry, 128
Peters, Martha, 186
Peters, Victoria, 180
Peters, Wm. B., 33, 34
Peterson, Rev. John D., 157
Peterson, L.A., 186
Peterson, Mrs. Sarah (née
McNabb), 39
Pettigrew, Rev. R., 162
Petty, Miss, 174

Pfaff, Anthony and Mrs.
Solomina (née Millar), 284,
290
Phelps, Herbert A., 76
Pherrill, E.T., 183
Philip, Rev. S.C., 160
Philips, Jacob, 35
Phillips, Clara, see Julian, Mrs.
Robert
Phillips, Mrs. Ed., 245
Phillips, Jacob, 232
Phillips, Jane, see Elliott, Mrs.
John Edward Jr.
Phillips, John, 37
Phillips, Marion, 258
Phillips, Robt., 167
Phillips, Roscoe, 239
Phillips, Roy, 256
Phillips family, 69, 107, 291
Phillipse, James, 29
Philp, Rev. Samuel, 160
Philp, Rev. Wm., 160
Phenney, Rev. H.H., 144
Phipps, Mrs. A.L., 246, 254
Pickering, Eliza, see Oliver, Mrs.
Thomas
Pickering, Emma, see McQuarrie,
Mrs. Archibald
Pickering, Rev. John, 147, 151
Pickering, Mathew, 284
Pickett, John, 163
Pickett Nurseries, 204,
Pierson, John, 67
Pike, Gen., 54
Pine Grove, 56, 79, 80, 114-6,
125, 141, 160, 161, 163, 178,
180, 195, 227, 238, 249, 254,
262, 280
Pingle family, 52
Pioneer Village, see Black Creek
Pioneer Village
Pipher, Eldon R., 180
Pitt, William, 52
Plaxton, Donald, 118, 120
Playter, Capt. George, 79
Playter, Rev. Geo., 160
Playter, James, 55
Playter, Thomas, 40, 159
Plowing matches, 249, 250-3
Plunkett, B., 141, 250
Plunkett, Chas., 141
Plunkett, Howard, 258
Pollard, Mrs. James, 246
Pollock, Miss Diana, see Taylor,
Mrs. Brian
Poole, Rev. Geo., 160
Population, 58, 64; Population &

assessments (1825-40), 62
Porter, Ann, 159
Porter family, 34, 67, 215, 284, 287-9
Porter, George and Mrs. Dorothy, 38
Porter, Norman, 240
Porter, Thompson, 73, 74
Porter, Wm., 67
Portland, Duke of, 53
Post, Frederick, 37
Post, George W., 21
Post, Mary, see Bowen, Mrs. John
Potter, Miss Eileen, 179
Potts, Rev., 151
Powell, Mr., 118
Powell, Rev. Gideon, 151, 160
Powell, W.D., 33, 35, 36, 40
Powell, William and Mrs. Margaret (née
    Bridgeford); and Mrs. Elizabeth (née
    Chamberlain), 37, 119, 216
Powley, Miss Ada, 171
Prentice, Miss, 172
Prentice, John H., 252
Prentice family, 101, 284, 288
Prest, Beatrice, 186
Preston, Holy Ann, 216-17
Price, Miss Elizabeth, 174
Price, Harry, 256
Price, Harry K., 163
Price, Rev. Percy, 161
Price, Rev. Wm., 160
Price, Wm., 143
Procter, Mrs. Carol (née Innes), 199
Proulx, Father, 155
Pugsley, Mrs. C., 172
Pugsley, Rev. E.E., 154
Pugsley, Wm. H., 119, 120, 249
Pultency settlement, 51
Pumfrey, Mary, see Wray, Mrs.
    John Jr.
Punshon, Morley, 151
Public Libraries:
    Kleinburg, 108, illus. opp. 123
    Maple, 244, illus. opp. 123
    Richmond Hill, 259
    Richvale, illus. opp. 123
Purcell, Miss, 185
Purdy's Mills, 122
Purdy, Wm., 55
Purkis, Josiah, 123, 154
Purpleville, 116,
Purpleville Woods, 210, illus. opp. 63
Puterbaugh, Mr., 233
Puterbaugh, Edgar, 217
Puterbaugh, Isaac, 39, 217
Puterbaugh, Isaac (II), 217
Puterbaugh, John, 70, 184, 217
Puterbaugh, Marion, see Bryson, Mrs.
    Ross

Puterbaugh, Percy, 217, 250
Puterbaugh, Solomon, 67, 284, 290
Puterbaugh family, ix, 34, 39, 217,
    284, 287

Q

Quantz, Daniel, 170
Quantz family, 52, 134
Quarter Session of the Peace, 272,
    274, 275, 276, 277, 279, 280
Quinlon, Father, 155
Quinn, John, 68
Quinté Carrying Place, 49

R

Radcliff, Thomas, 130
Raeside, Robert, 239
Raines family, 101
Rainey, Leonard, 106
Ralph, Bruce M., 76
Ramsay, Margaret, 146
Ramsay, Robert, 110
Ramsey, Dorothy, 171
Rankin, Jim, 154
Rankin, K.S., 175
Ratcliff Chas., 171
Rattelmullar, John Paul, 29
Rattle, Mrs. Evelyn, 172
Rawlings, Mrs., 146
Rawn, Jacob, 25
Ray, Miss Vina, 168
'Raysol', 64
Read, Charles, 174
Read family, 101, 217-18
Reaman, Christle, 88, 170
Reaman, Daniel, 67, 73, 74, 88, 170,
    205, 217, illus. opp. 233
Reaman, Daniel J., 217, 220
Reaman, Daniel S., 169, 217
Reaman, Elaine, xi-xii
Reaman, George and Mrs. Annie (née
    Heise), 205, 217, 284
Reaman, George and Mrs. Martha Ann
    (née White), 119, 136, 261
Reaman, Dr. Geo. Elmore and Mrs.
    Flora (née Green), iv, xi-xii, illus.
    opp. 213, 271
Reaman, Isaac, 136, 217
Reaman, Isaac J., 8, 218
Reaman, Jacob, 217
Reaman, Joel Jr. and Mrs. Eliza Jane
    (née Franks), 126, 128, 177, 236,
    250, 260
Reaman, John and Mrs. Reaman, 8, 43,
    217, 218, 250, 263, 280, 284, 289

Reaman, Josiah, 217
Reaman, Mary, 88, 170
Reaman, Mary, 171
Reaman, Mary Jane, see Longhouse,
    Mrs. George
Reaman, Michael, 64, 70, 90, 284
Reaman, Nicholas, 169
Reaman, Ruth, see Perkins, Mrs. Floyd
Reaman, Walter, 217
Reaman, Warren and Mrs. Hazel (née
    Smith), xiv, 220
Reaman family, ix, 44, 101, 134,
    217-18, 263
Reaman, Godfrey, 42
Rebellion of 1837, 51, 130, 216, 229,
    232, 259
Reddin, Father, 152, 156
Reddit, Mr., 185
Redditt, J.J., 137
Redelmeier, Ernest and Mrs., xi, 114
Redelmeier, Francis, 114, 262
Redelmeier, Willy, illus. opp. 114
Reditt, B., 119
Redman, Mrs., 186
Redman family, 103
Redmond, Joyce, 118
Redpath, Miss, 177
Reed, W., 141
Reeds, Dr. C.R., 240, illus. opp. 97
Reesor, Mr., 104
Reeves, Frank & Son, 254
Reeves, G.J., 141
Reid, Mrs. George, 172
Reid, Isabella, see Lawrie, Mrs.
    John
Reid, Dr. J. and Mrs., 216, 260
Reid, James and Mrs., 76, 192, 241
Reid, John, 154
Reid, Miss Maggie, 154
Reid, Mary, see Evans, Mrs.
    William
Reid, Penny, 175
Reid, Priscilla, 39
Reid, Russell, 186
Reid, Rev. W., 162
Reid, W.H., illus. opp. 96
Reid, William, 104
Reid, Rev. Wm., 143
Reid family, 192
Reimer, Samuel D., 37
Religion, 129-64, illus. opp. 171; see
    also churches
Remembrance Day, 239
Remis, Gwen, 180
Rempel, Mr., 291
Renoux, Francis, 33, 37, 52
Reser, Christian, 26
Rey, Rev. Philbert, 156

Reynolds, Miss, 174
Reynolds, Mr., 176
Reynolds family, 33, 38, 124, 141
Reynolds, Rev. Geo. S., 143
Reynolds, Rev. John, 154
Reynolds, Lulu, 245
Rhodes, Rev. John, 154
Rice, Rose, 175
Richards, Elizabeth, see Murray,
    Mrs. Isaac
Richards, Henry Jr., 124, illus. opp. 80
Richards, Henry Sr., 124, 176, illus.
    opp. 80
Richards, Jesse, 252
Richardson, Miss, 177
Richardson, Mrs. Edward (née
    Longhouse, Mary Ann), 206
Richardson, Jas., 35, 39, 136
Richardson, Leeds, 110, 112
Richardson, Rev. P.W., 145
Richardson, W.G., 177
Richardson, William, 112
Richardson, Rev. Wm., 160
Richeson, Etta, 169
Richie, J., 142
Richmond, 4th Duke of, Lennox,
    Charles Gordon, 116, 119
Richmond Hill Fanning Mill
    Company, 117
Richmond Hill, 64, 80, 81, 82, 94,
    101, 105, 106, 110, 112, 115, 116-
    20, 124, 125, 133, 150, 152 166,
    179, 183, 184, 188, 190, 194, 197,
    198, 199, 204, 205, 208, 209, 211,
    212, 214, 215, 216, 218, 219, 220,
    221, 223, 228, 230, 236, 239, 240,
    241, 245, 249, 250, 251, 252, 253,
    254, 257, 258, 259, 286, illus. opp.
    81, 115, 181
Rickery, Rev. John, 151
Richvale, 94, 120, 133, illus. opp. 123
Riddell, Mrs., 186
Riddell, Andrew, 71, 284
Riddell, George, 169
Riddell family, 158
Riddle, William and Mrs., 123, 245
Rider, Andrew, 36, 40, 284
Rievar, Samuel D., 33
Riley, John, 220
Riley, John Benjamin, 141
Riley, Will, 220
Ring, Audrey, 186
Risebrough, Mrs. Earl (Gladys), 247
Riser, Peter, 26
Risk, Gordon, illus. opp. 73, 77
Ritchie, Mr., 149, 233
Ritchie, Miss I., 180
Ritchie, Mary, see Innes, Mrs. Leslie

Rivalda Farms, 196
Robb, David, 107
Robb, Mrs. James, 245
Robb, Mrs. John, 245
Robb, Mrs. Leslie (née Locke, Gertrude), 245
Robb, Stanley D., 239
Robbins, Benjamin, 124, 287
Roberts, Mrs. Maude (née McGillivray), 210
Roberts, Rev. P.W.A., 145
Roberts, R., 260
Robertson, Miss, 174
Robertson, Bonnie, 180
Robertson, Rev. D.A., 148
Robertson, Harford, 256
Robertson, Isabel, 174
Robertson, Mrs. M.A., 167
Robinson, Austin and Mrs. Mabel (née Bryson), 191
Robinson, Bill, 110
Robinson, Brian, 171
Robinson, C.E., 107
Robinson, Charlotte, 108
Robinson, Ellen, see Devins, Mrs. Peter
Robinson, George, 220
Robinson, Rev. George, 159
Robinson, Dr. Helen, 108
Robinson, Dr. Howard, 108
Robinson, James, 154
Robinson, Luena, see Thomson, Mrs. William John
Robinson, Mary, see Wray, Mrs. George
Robinson, O.D., 249
Robinson, Olga, see Beamish, Mrs. Archie
Robinson, Mrs. Reginald (Violet), 247
Robinson, Rev. S.R., 145
Robinson, Susan, see Kerr, Mrs. John
Robinson, Dr. T.H., 108
Robinson, W.T., 253
Robinson, William, 32
Robinson Cotton Mills Ltd., 127
Robson, Charles, 256
Robson, James H., 75, 181, 250
Robson, Roy, 175, 179
Roden, Mrs. Edward, 246
Rodwell, W., 141
Roe, Frederick A., 126
Roe, Rev. J.S., 139, 162
Roe, Walter, 36, 41
Rogers, Mrs. A.F., 106
Rogers, Rev. J.G., 160
Rogers, R.J., 255
Rolph, Miss Eliza, 132
Rolph, John G., 255

Root, Ernest, 142, 149
Rose, Duard, 177, 182
Rose, James, 68, 159, 284
Rose, Laura, 244
Rose, Rev. Samuel, 151, 160
Rose, Sarah, 159
Ross, Miss, 185
Ross, Alex, illus. opp. 80
Ross, Barbara, 178
Ross, Constance, see McCallum, Mrs. Donald
Ross, Duncan, illus. opp. 63
Ross, Sgt. J., 34
Ross, J.B., 252
Ross, Rev. J.C., 148
Ross, James, 128
Ross, Rev. John A., 139, 162
Ross, Rev. D., 145
Ross, R., 253
Ross, Robert J., 181
Ross family, 147
Routley, Dr. Frederick William and Mrs. Gertrude (née Fry), 97, 111, 112, 147
Routley, J., 259
Rowan, Joseph, 126
Rowat, Arlene, 168
Rowe, Mr., 179
Rowe, Rev. A., 151
Rowe, Cecil, 126
Rowntree, Russell and Mrs. Myrtle, 125, 240
Rowntree, Wm. J., 250
Rowntree, Wm. R., 250
Roy, Mrs. M., 247
Ruggles, James, 33, 36, 40
Rumble, Austin, 257
Rumble, C.L., 142, 149
Rumble, Cliff, 256
Rumble, David, 218
Rumble, Mrs. Frank, xiv, 246
Rumble, Henry, 218
Rumble, Ida, 244
Rumble, Isabel, 172
Rumble, James, 179, 218
Rumble, Jennie, 244
Rumble, John, 218, illus. opp. 62
Rumble, Lizzie, 244
Rumble, Mary (II), 218
Rumble, R., 260
Rumble, Robert, 218
Rumble, Stewart and Mrs., 76, 180, 218, 249
Rumble, Thomas, 179, 218
Rumble, William and Mrs. Mary, 218
Rumble, William Jr., 218
Rumble family, 119, 218
Rumney, Dalton, 249

Rupel, Eliza, 148
Rupel, William, 148
Rupert, Adam, 118, 119, 147, 230,
    284, illus. opp. 111
Rupert, Mrs. J., 195
Rupert, Jacob, 110, 147, 284, illus.
    opp. 111
Rupert, Obediah, 146
Rupert, Dr. Oliver, 111, 147
Rupert, Peter, 120, 121, 178, 284
Rupert, Rebecca, see Page, Mrs. Lewis
Rupert's Chapel, 146
Rupertsville, 110
Russell, Andrew, 74, 79, 170
Russell, Geo., 260
Russell, Peter, 43, 51
Russell, Robert, 179
Rutherford, Albert and Mrs., 76, 77
    186, 250, 256, 257, illus. opp. 73
Rutherford, Charles and Mrs., 234, 245,
    illus. opp. 232, 257
Rutherford, E., 107, 117
Rutherford, James, 171
Rutherford, Stewart, 257
Rutledge, Rev. G.N., 119, 151, 160
Ryan, Austin, 172
Ryckman, Rev. E.B., 151
Ryder, Victor B., 76, 241
Ryerson, Edwy., 132
Ryerson, Egerton, 151, 165
Ryerson, Rev. Geo., 132
Ryerson, John, 151
Ryerson, William, 151
Rymill, Mrs. Nellie, 126

                      S

Sabean, A.H., 292
Saigen, Michael, 33, 37
Saigeon, Harry, 174, 185
Saigeon, John T., 75, 180, 185, 234,
    250
Saigon, Michel, 52
Saint, A.J., 234, illus. opp. 232
St. George, Laurent Quetton, 33, 37,
    52, 53, 117
St. John, Thomas, 101
St. John, Thomas Jr., 102
Sampson, Alfred Sr., 141
Sanders, Henry, 38
Sanders, Rev. J.L., 151
Sanders, Rev. Joseph L., 160
Sanders, Matthias, 122
Sanderson, Rev. A.R., 151
Sanderson, Ed., 249
Sanderson, John, 151, 218
Sanderson, John Jr., 218
Sanderson, John H., 119, 251, 254

Sanderson family, 218
Sanford, Norman, 240
Sappenfield, Rev. J.V., 158
Satterley, Absalom, 29
Saunders, E. and Mrs., illus. opp. 63
Savage, A.G. and Mrs. Susan (née
    Trench), 223
Savage, Milton and Mrs. (née Shand),
    180, 249
Savage, Milton F., 167
Savage, Peter, 117, 120, 151
Savage, Peter G., 259
Sawdon, Herb H., xiv, 172, 186
Sawyer, Joseph, 32
Sayers, Harry W.R., 259
Sayers, Mrs. W., 246
Scarlett, Lynn, see McCallum, Mrs.
    John
Schank, Henry, 25
Schank, Michael, 25
Schell, George, 121
Schell, Jonathan, 88
Schell, Rev. Ralph, 158
Schell family, 134, 158, 285
Schmidt, H.B., 123
Schmidt family, 137
Scholfield, Thomas, 100
Scholfield, William, 169
Schoolcraft, Ann, 169
Schools: 165-186
    Bayview Secondary, Richmond Hill,
        182
    Beverley Acres, Richmond Hill, 182
    Bryson (Upper Sixth) S.S. No. 10,
        167-8
    Burrlington, 100, 168-9
    Carrville, S.S. No. 3, 166, 167
    Chas. Howitt, Thornhill, 183
    Cober, Langstaff, 154, illus. opp.
        171
    Coleraine, 135, 167, 210
    Common Schools, 165
    Concord District, S.S. No. 7, 158,
        170-71
    Crosby Heights, Richmond Hill,
        182
    Don Head Secondary, Richmond
        Hill, 114, 182
    Edgeley, S.S. No. 15, 173-4, 200
    Geo. Bailey, Maple, 178
    Grammar, Richmond Hill, 182
    Hegler (Toronto Gore), 168
    Hope S.S. No. 5, 166, 174, 210
    Jefferson, S.S. No. 21 (Vaughan)
        and S.S. No. 4 (Markham), 167,
        174-5, illus. opp. 180
    Joseph Gibson, Maple, 178
    Kleinburg, S.S. No. 17, 167, 175

Langstaff, 123, 175-7, 183, 232
Langstaff Secondary, 184, 193
Lower Ninth (Vaughan), S.S. No. 13, 177-8
M.L. McConaghy, Richmond Hill, 181, 182, 208
Mackenzie Senior, Kleinburg, 175
Maple, S.S. No. 6, 166, 178-9, 210
Mechanics Institutes, 166, 199
Mount Lebanon, S.S. No. 20, 179
Mudville (Concord), 166
O.M. MacKillop Memorial, Richmond Hill, 182
Our Lady Help of Christians, Richmond Hill, 182
Our Lady of Fatima, Richmond Hill, 182
Patterson, S.S. No. 19, 167, 179-80
Pine Grove, S.S. No. 12, 166, 180-1, 203
Pleasantville, Richmond Hill, 182
Powell Road, Thornhill, 183
Private schools, 182, 184
Purpleville, S.S. No. 11, 166, 181, illus. opp. 181
Richmond Hill High, xi, 184, illus. opp. 181
Richmond Hill Public, 212, 249
Richvale, S.S. No. 24, 153, 182-3
Roselawn, Richvale, 183
Ross Doan, Thornhill, 183
St. Joseph, Richmond Hill, 182
St. Luke's, Thornhill, 155, 183
St. Mary Immaculate, Richmond Hill, 182
Smellies, Vaughan, 67
Stong's, Edgeley, 171
Thornhaven, for Retarded Children, Thornhill, 183, 247
Thornhill, 183-4
Thornhill Secondary, 184
Town Hall, Vellore, 166
Union S.S. No. 1, 183
Union S.S. No. 6, 178
Union S.S. No. 10, 177
Union S.S. No. 23, 177
Union S.S. No. 25, 180
Vellore, S.S. No. 9, 166, 184, 203, illus. opp. 67
Walter Scott, Richmond Hill, 182
Weston High and Vocational, 81, 177, 186, 196
Woodbridge High, 186
Woodbridge, S.S. No. 14, 166, 185-6
Woodbridge Separate, 163
Schooner, Jacob, 232

Schulz, George, 157
Schwalm, Rev. C.J., 152
Scott, Miss, 185
Scott, Alec, 119
Scott, Alfred, 239
Scott, Clayton, 123
Scott, George and Mrs., 141
Scott, J.R., 102
Scott, John, 239
Scott, Rev. John G., 143
Scott, Jonathan, 113
Scott, Mrs. Lorne (née Moore, Mary), 168
Scott, Robert W., 75, 76, 249
Scott, Walter, 182, 186
Scott, Rev. Walter, 150
Scott, Wilfrid, 128
Scott, Rev. Wm., 160
Seager, Albert, 218
Seager, Edmund, 169, 218
Seager, Edward and Mrs. Catherine (née Cain), 67, 155, 218, 284
Seager, Edward (II), 218
Seager, Rev. John, 218
Seager, Julius, 177
Seager, William, 169
Seager family, 218-19
Secrett, Rev. Claude, 153
Seed, Glenna, see Murray, Mrs. Bruce
Seel, Mrs. V., 175
Segsworth, Wm., 154
Seivers, Robt., 119
Semple, Miss M., 175
Seymour, H., 260
Shand, Miss, see Savage, Mrs. Milton
Shank family, 134
Shanklin, Rev. Robert, 152, 153, 155
Sharp, Mr., 177
Sharp, Thomas, 69, 88, 285
Sharpe, Mr., 63
Sharpe, Wm., 110
Shaver, Nicholas, 69, 142, 284
Shaw, Alexander, 34, 39
Shaw, Annie, illus. opp. 105
Shaw, Carl, 76, 109
Shaw, Charles Jr. and Mrs. Enes (née Witherspoon), 109, illus. opp. 105
Shaw, Charles Sr. and Mrs. Jane (née Calhoun), 109, illus. opp. 105
Shaw, Charles (III), 109
Shaw, Earl and Mrs., 109
Shaw, Enes, 179
Shaw, Frank and Mrs., 109, 241
Shaw, Hugh and Mrs., 117
Shaw, John, 109
Shaw, John, 126
Shaw, Rev. John, 160
Shaw, Kathaleen, 242

Shaw, Les, 163
Shaw, Robert, 182
Shaw, William, 109
Shaw family, 241
Shaw's Binder Twine Festival, 241-2
Sheardown, Elizabeth, see Cherry, Mrs.
     James
Sheardown, Samuel, 193
Shepard, Joseph, 136
Shephard, Mr., 55
Sheppard, Mary Eleanor, 146
Sherbourn, S., 141
Sherin, Geo., 9
Sherk, Rev. A.B., 149
Sherman, Miss Mande, 174
Sherwood, x, 82, 93, 120-1, 146,
     156, 195, 292
Sherwood, Samuel, 40
Shier, H.A., 167
Shinck, Jas., 34
Shirk, Rev. A.B., 142, see also, Sherk,
     Rev. A.B.
Shore, Bert, 174
Shore, George W., 186, 255, 260
Shore, Thelma, 186
Short, L., 177
Shortt, Rev. Charles H., 145, 161
Shunk, Amos, 112
Shunk, Miss Carrie, 180
Shunk, Jacob, 38, 43, 104, 221, 279
     285, 289
Shunk, John, 38, 285, 288
Shunk, Mary, see Snider, Mrs. Henry
Shunk, Nathaniel, and Mrs., 112, 244
Shunk, Sarah, see Williams, Mrs. John
Shunk, Simon, 171
Shunk, Simon Jr., 93
Shunk, William, 93
Shunk family, ix, 137, 285
Shur-Gain Research Farm, illus. opp.
     111
Shuter, James, 123
Shuttleworth, Miss, 244
Shuttleworth, Eliza, see Witherspoon
     Mrs. George
Sibley, John, 174
Sibley, W.E., 174
Sillick, Miss, 131
Simcoe, John Graves and Mrs.
     Elizabeth (née Gwillam), xiii, 8, 16,
     44, 47, 50, 51, 122, 165, 232, 248,
     258
Simpson, George, 37
Simpson, Rev. J.M., 119, 151
Simpson, John, 159, 174
Simpson, Napier, 291-2
Simpson, Rev. R.J.D., 159

Sims, Geo. Sr., 106
Sims, T., 140
Sinclair, Mrs. C.J., 245
Sinclair, Samuel, 33, 36, 39
Singing Schools, 104, 236-7
Sisley, Dr. and Mrs., 111, 244
Sisters of St. Joseph, 164
Size, John, 35, 39
Skardon, William, 123
Skeele, A.L., 119, 259
Skeele, Clarence, 106
Skene, Miss A.F., 177, 180
Skinner, Rev. A., 142
Skinner, Rev. G., 149
Slater, J., 249
Slater, Rev. James C., 160
Slater, Rev. S.L., 153
Sleep, Miss, 169
Sliney family, 107, 152
Smale, Miss, 169
Small, Miss, 101
Small family, 35-6, 40
Smart, James, 139
Smellie, David and Mrs. Anne (née
     Dalziel), 67, 73, 219, 285, 289
Smellie, Nelson, 219
Smellie family, 219
Smiley, John, 143
Smith, Miss, 171
Smith, Abraham, 219
Smith, Alfred, 103
Smith, Allan, 138, 219, 291
Smith, Arthur, 81
Smith, Barbara, 236
Smith, Bishop Abram, 137
Smith, Carson, 103, 104, 171, 220
Smith, Chas., 250
Smith, Daniel, 220, 285
Smith, David and Mrs., 103, 104, 138,
     220
Smith, David, 177
Smith, Miss E., 175
Smith, Ebenezer, 250
Smith, Elizabeth, 40
Smith, Frank, 103, 220, 260, illus.
     opp. 193, 213
Smith, Rev. Dr. G.S., 151, 160, 255
Smith, Geo., 112
Smith, Henry, 137
Smith, Henry N. and Mrs., 245, 250,
     255
Smith, J.E., 119, 120, 239
Smith, Rev. J. Lavell, 134, 153
Smith, Jacob Sr., 42, 137, 219, 220,
     285, illus. opp. 63
Smith, James, 240
Smith, James C., 171

Smith, Jerry and Mrs. Effie (née Hollingshead), 219, 246
Smith, Jesse, 104
Smith, John, 34, 35, 38, 43, 56, 67, 137, 139, 162, 171, 219, 220, 280, 285
Smith, John (Schmidt), 114, 195
Smith, Mrs. John (née Longhouse, Susanna), 206
Smith, Joseph, 103
Smith, Lillian E., see McLean, Mrs. Garnet
Smith, Mabel, 172
Smith, Margaret, 120
Smith, Martin, 70
Smith, Menno, 219
Smith, Peter, 38, 285
Smith, Robert, 253, 288
Smith, Rev. Robert, 151
Smith, Samuel, 171, 219, 220
Smith, Samuel and Mrs. Eliz. (née Brown), 56, 69, 125, 171, 190, 285, 287
Smith, Sidney, 103
Smith, Thomas, 40, 71, 285
Smith, Rev. W.G., 151
Smith, Rev. W.W., 142, 149
Smith, Rev. Waldo, 134, 153
Smith, William and Mrs. Mary (née Wray), 228, 253, 290
Smith family, ix, 44, 107, 137, 151, 219
Smithers, Maggie, 185
Smithson, John W., 250
Smithson, W.J., 250
Smyth, Miss Annie, 169
Smyth, Thomas Jr., 168
Smyth, Rev. B.P., 161
Snell, Benjamin, 168
Snell, S.J., 126
Snider, Miss, see Winger, Mrs. Abraham
Snider, Andrew and Mrs., 111, 177
Snider, Bruce and Mrs., 221, 245, 257
Snider, Campbell, 221, illus. opp. 90
Snider, Charles Henry and Mrs. Anna (née Keffer), 221
Snider, D., 260
Snider, Daniel, 104
Snider, David, 220
Snider, Eli, 221
Snider, Elmo, 220
Snider, Esther (Hettie), see Bryson, Mrs. Alexander
Snider, G.E., 181
Snider, Geo. C.H. and Mrs. Dora, iv, xi, xiv, 56, 221
Snider, George, 159, 285

Snider, Henry and Mrs. Mary (née Shunk), 136, 221, 289
Snider, Henry and Mrs. Catherine (née Campbell), 221
Snider, Mrs. J.G., 245, 246
Snider, Jacob, 42, 184, 206, 220, 285
Snider, Jacob Henry, 120
Snider, Jane, 159
Snider, Jesse, 172
Snider, John and Mrs. Mary (née Stump), 43, 170, 220, 285
Snider, Joseph and Mrs. Elta (née Farr), 70, 197
Snider, M.L., 127
Snider, Nelson, 138
Snider, Paul and Mrs., 104, 245
Snider, Percy, 104, illus. opp. 104
Snider, Peter, 142
Snider, Priscilla Jane, see Jackson, Mrs. Frederick
Snider, Samuel Sr. and Mrs. Ann (née Nell), 220, 285, 289
Snider, Bishop Samuel, 103, 135
Snider, Susanna, see Line, Mrs. William
Snider, Vern, 138
Snider, Wm. and Mrs. Lizzie (née Fenwick), 246
Snider families, ix, 137, 220-1
Snow, Rev. Bailey, 161
Snyder, Arthur, 81
Soap making, 235-6
Societies and Organizations, Chapter 12 243-62
Sommerfeldt family, 52
Somerville, Archie, 138, 226
Somerville, Betty Lou, 226
Somerville, Dianne, 226
Somerville, James, 71, 73, 139, 285
Somerville, John, 226
Somerville, Margaret, 226
Somerville, Robert, 139, 205
Somerville family, 105
Sorenson, Dennis E., 180
Soules, Daniel, 32, 36, 59, 250, 279, 285
Soules, David, 122
Souls, Mrs. Ashsah (née Hollingshead), 39
Southern Ontario Research Station, 241
Soverign, Philip, 26
Sparkes, Raymond R., 240
Sparling, Rev. Dr. T.T., 154
Spaulding, Mr., 174
Speer, Rev. J.C., 151
Speers, Mildred, 168

Speight, William, 112
Spencer, Mrs. James, 245
Spregue, Frederick, 28
Spreker, Jacob, 170, 285
Squires, Rev., 151
Stan, Rev. J.H., 151
Standen, Miss Estelle, 246
Standen, Frances Emma, see
    Jeffery, Mrs. William
Stanley, Miss E., 177
Stanley, Eli, 39
Stanton, Greta, 169
Stapley, John, 240
Starr, Rev. J.E., 151
Starr, Rev., J.H., 147
Starr, James, 25
Starr, Rev. John E., 147
Statute labour, 279
Stayner, T.A., 221
Steam engines, 126
Steckley, Christian, 134
Steckley, J.C., 255
Steckley, Bishop Peter, 135
Steckley family, 134
Steele, John, 123, 221
Steele, Thomas, 41, 221
Stegmann, George, 115, 148, 285
Stegmann, John, 22, 148
Stegmann Estate, 249
Stehouwer, Peter, 116
Stephens, Isabel, 168
Stephens, John, 67
Stephenson, Eleanor, see Moore,
    Mrs. Solomon
Stephenson, Francis H., 36, 41
Stephenson, J. Augustus, 36, 41
Stephenson, Dr. James D., 110
Stephenson, Ken, 220
Stephenson, Louisa, 36, 41
Stephenson, May, see Jackson, Mrs.
    Earl
Stevens, Clair, 256
Stevenson, David Townsend, 36, 40
Stevenson, James, 68, 74
Stevenson, John C., 143
Steward, Charles, 29
Stewart, Mrs., 168
Stewart, Alex, 81
Stewart, Rev. Alex, 158
Stewart, Andrew, 250
Stewart, David, 126
Stewart, Mrs. George, 246
Stewart, Rev. J. Wallace, 147
Stewart, John H., 143
Stiles, Evary (Avary), 30
Still, Geoffrey, 142
Stirling, H.E., 254
Stiver, Mr., 176

Stiver, Frank, 252
Stiver, R.L., 249
Stiver family, 52
Stokes, Edward, 33
Stokes, John C., 33, 117
Stoll, Mrs., 174
Stonehouse, John, 141, 285
Stong, Alfred, 220
Stong, Annie, 172
Stong, Mrs. Clarence, 245
Stong, Daniel, ix, 287
Stong, J. Noah, 126
Stong, Magdalena, see White, Mrs.
    Hiram
Stong, Maria Margaret, see Constable,
    Mrs. John William
Stong, Samuel, 220
Stong, Sevald Sr., 37, 170
Stong, Mrs. Wesley, 245
Stong Farm, 291
Stooks (Stokes), John R., 37, 117
Storer, Richard, 196
Storey, Peter, 230, 285
Storey, Wm., 182, 285
Storm, Adam, 179, 285
Stouffer, Abraham, 25
Stover, Jacob, 26
Strachan, Bishop John, 125, 155, 157,
    198, 286
Strachan family, 59, 143
Strangways, Alex, 163
Strangways, Rev. B.R., 154
Street, Joseph, 102
Street, Samuel, 34, 38
Stump, Daniel, 35, 134, 285
Stump, Mrs. Jane, 116
Stump, Mary, see Snider, Mrs. John
Stump, Susannah, see Jarrett, Mrs.
    Richard
Stump family, 134, 285, 287-8
Sturgess, Mr., 185
Sturn, Adam, 230
Suggett, James, 135
Sullivan, Dan, 163
Sullivan, John, 40
Sullivan, Thomas, 163
Summerfeldt, Archibold, 71
"Summerhill," 200, 201
Summers, Daniel, 158
Superior Propane Plant, 112
Sutton, Mrs. George, 245
Swabey, Mrs. H., 245
Swallow, Rev. W.F., 145, 161
Swan, Mr., 100
Swanson, Miss, 186
Sweeney, Mrs., 183
Sweeney, Hugh, 35
Switzer, Mrs. J., 246

Switzer, J.A.E., 182
Switzer, Jean, 175
Syracuse, Eleanor, 255

T

Taber, Mrs. Jessie, 180
Tait, Adeline, 174
Tansley, Mrs. Dora, 181
"Tapawingo," 262
Taxes & tax collecting, 66, 272
Tayles, George, illus. opp. 82
Taylor, Mr., illus. opp. 80
Taylor, Allan, 172
Taylor, Bob, 105
Taylor, Mrs. Brian (née Pollock,
    Diana), 172
Taylor, David, 31, 70
Taylor, Elizabeth, see Jackson, Mrs.
    John
Taylor, Mrs. Elizabeth (née Patterson),
    114
Taylor, Jimmie, 102
Taylor, Ross, 258
Taylor, Sarah, 148
Taylor, W.J., 118, 120, 241
Taylor, William, 105
Taylor family, 151
Teasdale, Frank, 216
Teasdale, Thomas, 216
Tedder, Hannah, 159
Tedder, John, 159
Tedder, William, 135, 142, 202
Tedder family, 147
Teefy, Matthew, 106, 118, 119, 120,
    152, 199, 221-22
Teefy family, 152
Teel, John, 88
Temperance Societies, 260-61
Temple, John, 285
Tenbreck, Priscilla, 34
Tenbroeck, John, 38
Tennyson, Arthur, 169
Tennyson, David, 169
Terry, Benjamin, 30
Terry Eliza, 287
Terry, Mary, 179
Teston, 110, 121, 194, 212, 227,
    illus. opp. 110
Thane, Mr., 121
Thesser, Turcotte, 56
Thomas, Mrs. C., 169
Thomas, Evelyn, 169
Thomas, Miss F., 244
Thomas, Geo., 142
Thomas, George, 222
Thomas, Mrs. H., 244

Thomas, Helen, 258
Thomas, Henry and Mrs. Lucy Hannah
    (née Kellam), 222
Thomas, Henry (II), 222
Thomas, Nellie, see Oliver, Mrs. Forrest
Thomas, Richard, 222
Thomas, William, 72, 75
Thomas, William and Mrs. Elizabeth
    (née Bailey), 222, 244
Thomas family, 141, 168
Thompson, Miss, 178, 180
Thompson, Alfred, 126, 250
Thompson, Andrew, 22
Thompson, Annie, 177
Thompson, Arthur, 176, 260
Thompson, Mrs. C., 245
Thompson, David, 22
Thompson, Eliz., 35, 39
Thompson, Emily, 181
Thompson, George, 38, 285
Thompson, J., 141, 181
Thompson, John, 80, 124
Thompson, Louis, 240
Thompson, Robert and Mrs., 124,
    245, 249, 260
Thompson, Thomas, 68, 230, 285
Thompson, William, 62, 143
Thomson, Ann, see Nicol, Mrs. William
Thomson, Boyle, 222
Thomson, Bruce, 222
Thomson, Christopher, 222
Thomson, David, 35
Thomson, Gordon, 222
Thomson, James, 39, 56, 71, 105, 222
Thomson, James (II) and Mrs. Dorothy
    (née Aitchison), xiv, 222
Thomson, John and Mrs. Jane
    (née Lawrie), 222, 287
Thomson, R.S., 110
Thomson, William and Mrs. Sarah Jane
    (née Bolton), 222
Thomson, William John and Mrs. Luena
    (née Robinson), 222
Thorburn, W., 178
Thomson family, 222-3
Thorne, Benjamin, 37, 59, 89, 122,
    155, 230, 285
Thorne & Parsons, 55
"Thorne Hill," Thornhill, 59, 122
Thornhill, 59, 60, 80, 89, 94, 97, 120,
    122-4, 133, 134, 146, 149, 155, 156,
    161, 182, 190, 194, 199, 204, 207,
    216, 218, 219, 230, 232, 237, 238,
    254, 260, 291
Thornhill Station, 88, 103, 123
Thorpe, Mr. Justice, 248
Thorpe & Halfield's Fanning Mill
    Mfg., 56

Thurston, Rev. A.L., 137
Thurston, Ernest, 256
Tibb, Mr., 141
Tibb family, 168
Tindall, John T., 176
Tinker, Stanley F., 118
Tip family, 134
Tippin, Mrs. Wm. (née Elliott, Janet), 196
Todd, David, 162
Tollgates, 123, 126, 206
   Elgin Mills, 106
   Islington and Steeles, 141
   Langstaff, 123-4, illus. opp. 80
Toll roads, 106
Tolls, 79, 80, 86, 141, illus. opp. 80
Tollgate Corner, 198
Tomlin, Ken, 120
Toole, Mr., 174
Topper, Miss, 185
Topper, Alvin and Mrs. Florence (née Peeler), 224
Topper, Christopher, 224
Topper, Emily, 224
Topper, Fred, 224
Topper, George and Mrs. Elizabeth (née Middleton), 211, 223, 224
Topper, Hannah, see Castator, Mrs. William
Topper, John, 224
Topper, Lily, 179
Topper, Lucinda, 224
Topper, Martha, 224
Topper, Mary, see Grantham, Mrs. D.
Topper, Mary Ann, 223
Topper, Mary L., 186
Topper, Myra, 224
Topper, Robert, 224
Topper, Robert, 141
Topper, Robert (II) and Mrs. Jennie (née Hendry), 224
Topper, Sarah Jane, 223
Topper family, 223-224
Tormore, 99
Toronto & York Road Commission, 82
Toronto Board of Trade, 196
Toronto Carrying Place, 48
Toronto Conference, 154
Toronto Purchase, 45
Torrance, Mrs. 244
Torrance, Clark, 250
Totten, James, 39, 68, 180, 285
Totten, Mary, 180
Town meeting, 66
Townley, Rev. Adam, 160, 161
Towns, 99-128
Township Hall, Vellore, 124, 220, 246, 277, illus. opp. 67

Toye, Rev. H.E., 151
Toye, Reuben, 143
Trails: Humber, 8, 17, 18, 47, 50; Humber-Holland, 9; Indian, 108; packhorse, 9, 79
Train, Arthur and Mrs. Irene (née Devins), 223
Train, Christopher and Mrs. Ann, 70, 223, 285
Train, Jane Frances, see Agar, Mrs. Richard
Train, John Jr. and Mrs. Alice Ann (née Goodfellow), 223
Train, John Sr. and Mrs. Ann (née Gimmerson), 110, 223
Train, Robert, 223
Train family, 147, 223
Transportation, 79-83
Traviss, Miss Flo, 244
Tredell, 45
Tremble, Charles, 36
Trench, Agnes, see Hume, Mrs. A.J.
Trench, Frances, see Atkinson Jr., Mrs. William
Trench, Robert, 285
Trench, Susan, see Savage, Mrs. A.G.
Trench, Thomas, 120, 223, 249, 259
Trench, William Jr., 223
Trench, William Sr., 223
Trench, William (III), 119-20, 151, 223 249
Trench, Rev. William (IV), 151, 223
Trench, Wyck, 223
Trench family, 223
Trevethan, Charles, 119
Troyer, Christian Jr. and Mrs. Magdalena (Cover, Sarey Magdalena) (née Cober), 33, 37, 42, 224, 285, 287
Troyer, Christian Sr. and Mrs. Barbara (née Yoder); and Mrs. Elizabeth (née Becker), 224
Troyer, Emma, 224
Troyer, Frank, 197, 224
Troyer, George Jr. and Mrs. Mereda (née Dorsey), 178, 179, 186, 224, 250
Troyer, George Sr., 197, 224
Troyer, Jacob and Mrs. Ann (née Haking); and Mrs. Annie (née Gram), 224, 226
Troyer, John, 42
Troyer, Martha, 224
Troyer, Michael Jr., 42
Troyer, Michael Sr., 42
Troyer, Samuel and Mrs. Mary Ann (née Baldwin), 224, illus. opp. 91

Troyer family, ix, 44, 137, 224
Trudeau, Rt. Hon. Pierre Elliott, 241
Trueman, Mrs. B., 186
Tucker, Rev. Wm. Guise, 161
Turnbull, Horace, 169
Turnbull, Janet, see King Sr.,
    Mrs. Robert
Turner, Lloyd, 240
Turner, Samuel, 69
Turton, Harvey, 256
Turton, Howard, 256
Tweed, Joseph, 141
Tweedsmuir, Lady (Buchan, Susan
    Grosvenor), 247
Tweedsmuir, Lord, Buchan, John,
    1st Baron Tweedsmuir, 247
Tweedsmuir Histories, xi, xiv,
    143, 246, 247
Tyler, Elizabeth, see Kellam,
    Mrs. George
Tyndall, F.S., 249, 251
Tyndall, Norman, 249, 252
Tyrrell, Wm., 161

U

Underhill, George, 68
Underhill, Thomas, 68
Unger, Miss Hulda, 172
United Breeders Incorporation of
    Guelph, 241
United Empire Loyalists, 48, 72, 116
United Farmers Co-operative, 248
United Farmers of Ontario, 248, 257
Unstead, Rev. E.H., 147
Upper Canada Rebellion (1837),
    51, 130, 216, 259
Upper Corner, 146
Urquhart, Russell, 177, 179, 183
Usher, Louise, see King (IV),
    Mrs. Robert
Usher, Roy, 256

V

Van Loan, Richard, illus. opp. 62
Valliere, Elizabeth, see Constable,
    Mrs. Fred
Vanderburgh, Rev. Fulton, 153
Vanderburgh, Barnabas, 117
Vanderburgh, Goldwin and Mrs.,
    248, 250
Vanderburgh, Peter, 68, 179, 272
Vanderburgh, Richard, 37

Vanderburgh family, 176
VanderPost, Henry, 258
Varden, Miss, 174
Vardon, Miss Muriel, 174
Vaudreuil, de, see de Vaudreuil
Vaughan, Benjamin, 20
Vaughan, 149, 182, 227, 252, 272
Vaughan, xiii, 17, 20, 23, 52, 56, 81,
    101, 117, 122, 124, 150, 152, 182,
    246, 256, 280
    Area Administration Offices, 178
    Area and boundaries, 46-49
    Area and topography, 45-46
    Council, 1970, xi, illus. opp. 73
    Councillors, 1850-1970, 73-7
    Historical Society, xi
    Public School Board, 167
    Township Offices, 273, 277,
        illus. opp. 67, 72, 73, 123,
        and 181
Vaughan Township voters in first
    election (1850), 67-72
Velie, John and Mrs. Anne (née
    Frank), 68, 169, 170, 285, 287
Vellore, 67, 124, 149, 189, 191, 203
    207, 210, 220, 234, 236, 239, 256,
    257, illus. opp. 67, 83, 123, 238
Vellore Junior Farmers & Junior
    Institute, 257
Vent, Miss B., 175
Villages, 99-128
Vincent, Michael Sr. and Mrs.
    Sarah, 135
Von Egmont, Col., 230, 231

W

Wade, Anne, see Oliver, Mrs. Joshua
Wade, Mason, 13
Wagewworth, Joseph, 88
Wagner, Rev. N., 158
Wain, Joe, 255
Wainwright, Lou, 77, illus. opp. 73
Waite, Jas., 143
Waldron, Miss L., 177
Walker, Miss, 169
Walker, Mr., 171, 174, 185
Walker, Abraham, 279
Walker, Elizabeth, see Frank,
    Mrs. John
Walker, Rev. George, 159
Walker, John, 40, 69
Walker, Miss K., 177
Walker, Miss L., 177
Walker, Tom, 111
Walker, Miss V., 177

Walkington, Mrs. Elizabeth (née
   Cameron), illus. opp. 192
Walkington, Janet, 166, 178, 180
Walkington, Robert, 253
Wall, Rev. A., 151
Wall, Allan A., xiv, 255
Wallace, Alex, 33
Wallace, Ann, see Wallace, Mrs.
   Nathaniel
Wallace, Rev. Dr. Archer, 110, 112, 147
Wallace, Bessie, 255
Wallace, Catherine (II), 224
Wallace, Charles, 68, 224
Wallace, Chas. H., 250
Wallace, Chas. Len., 128, 250, 255
Wallace, Doris, 225
Wallace, Eleanor, see Maltby, Mrs.
   Raymond
Wallace, Geo., 126, 128
Wallace, Geo. F., 250
Wallace, George and Mrs. Ellen
   (née Williams), 226
Wallace, George and Mrs. Sarah
   (née Williams), 226
Wallace, George, 225
Wallace, George Frazier Jr. and Mrs.
   Elizabeth (née Harper), 224, 225
Wallace, George Frazier Sr. and Mrs.
   Catherine (née Weir), 71, 224
Wallace, Hannah, see Elliott, Mrs.
   Levi
Wallace, Mrs. Hannah, 126
Wallace, Irene, 245
Wallace, John, 224
Wallace, John Walter and Mrs.
   Muriel (née Chapman), 225
Wallace, Margaret, see Barber, Mrs.
   Ebenezer
Wallace, N. Clarke and Mrs., 74,
   177, 245, 250
Wallace, N. Geo., 160, 250
Wallace, Nathaniel and Mrs. Ann
   (née Wallace), 67, 161, 224, 285
Wallace, Robert T., 126
Wallace, Ruth, 186
Wallace, Thomas and Mrs. Martha, 224
Wallace, Thomas F., 128, 250
Wallace, Rev. Wm., 150
Wallace Bros., 56, 126
Wallace Bros. Mill, illus. opp. 126
Wallace families, 127, 161, 224-5
Wallis, A.W., 148
Wallis, C.S., 141
Wallis, George, 201
Wallis, Joseph T.W. and Mrs., 141
Wallis, W.A., 148
Wallis, William, 141, 151, 161
Walls, J. 171-72
Walter, Isaac, 197

Walwyn, Mrs. B., 175
Wanless, John, 140
Ward, Henry, 171, 183
Ward, Rev. Edward A., 160
Ward, John W., 239
Ward, Russell and Mrs., 191, 245
Ward family, 102
Wardlaw, Effie, 225
Wardlaw, Ella, see Capner, Mrs.
   Albert
Wardlaw, Ella, see Devins, Mrs.
   Albert
Wardlaw, Herbert, 225
Wardlaw, Laura, 225
Wardlaw, Mortimer, 143, 225
Wardlaw, William, 225
Wardlaw family, 225
Wardlaw, Peter (II) and Mrs.
   Elizabeth (née Parsons), 225, 245
Wardlaw, Peter Sr., 40
Warner, Rev. L., 151
Warrell, Stanley, 239
Warren, Mr., 118
Warren, Rev. H.S., 151, 160
Wartsill, Jane, 36
Washington, George, 54, 258
Washington, Rev. Geo., 143
Washington family, 107
Water Resources Commission, 238
Water witching, 237-8
Waterfield, J.S., 176, 177
Waterford, J.S., 172
Waterhouse, Mr., 105
Watson, Mr., 177
Watson, A., 68
Watson, Agnes, see Farr, Mrs. Arthur
Watson, Alex, 177
Watson, Andrew, 181
Watson, Bruce, 225, 250, 257
Watson, Duncan, 258
Watson, Edgar, 160
Watson, Francis, 139
Watson, George, 237
Watson, George Mackenzie, 108
Watson, Gertrude, 168
Watson, Gordon, 240
Watson, J.J., 260
Watson, Jack, 255
Watson, James, 69, 225, 233, 285
Watson, John, 67, 71, 128, 285
Watson, John Archibald, 181
Watson, Joseph and Mrs., 160, 211
Watson, Laura, see Julian, Mrs. David
Watson, Mrs. Leo, 246
Watson, Lloyd, 237
Watson, Margaret, 246
Watson, Marion, 73
Watson, Neil and Mrs. Mary, 102
Watson, Newton, 257

Watson, Rev. R.A., 149
Watson, Robert and Mrs., 74, 225, 245
Watson, Stanley B., 240
Watson, W.J. and Mrs., 102
Watson, W.P., 240, illus. opp. 97
Watson, William, 74, 75, 245, 166, 181
Watson, William and Mrs., 162, 225
Watson, Mrs. William (née Johnston, Agnes), 201
Watson, Wm., 167, 181
Watson family, 225, 236
Watt, John, 141
Watts, Archie, 206
Watts, Thomas, 38, 230, 285
Way, Helen, 181
Way, Rev. W., 142, 149
Weall & Cullen Nurseries, 197
Weatherhead, Norma, 186
Weatherill, Miss, 171
Weatherill, Alma, 246
Weatherill, Mrs. Joseph, 246
Weaver, Jane, 40
Webb, Mrs. Isabella, 183
Webb, Joyce, 174
Webb, Maude, 169
Webster, Rev., 159
Webster, James, 123
Webster, Thomas, 73, 74, 148
Weese, Miss, 169
Weikel, George, 22
Weir, Catherine, see Wallace, Mrs. George Frazier
Weir, Mrs. Hazel, 169
Welbourne, I., 141
Welch, Mr., 168
Weldon, Miss, 175
Weldrick, Annie, 225
Weldrick, Boynton, 76, 239, 249, 250
Weldrick, Burwick, 75, 225, 226, 250
Weldrick, George and Mrs. Hannah (née Boynton), 225
Weldrick, George Jr., 225
Weldrick, John, 225
Weldrick, William, 225
Weldrick family, 225-226
Welfare, 273-4
Welford, Miss, 169
Wellington, Duke of, 124
Wellman family, 198
Wells, E.M., 175, 177, 183
Wells, Frances, see Diceman, Mrs. William
Wells, W.J., 249
Wellwood, Rev. N., 151
Wellwood, Robt. G., 143
Wesley, Miss Geraldine, 177, 183
Wesley, John, 159

Wesley, Dr. W.J., 122
Wesley, Dr. W.R., 123
West, Rev. W.J., 160
Westcott, Miss, 171
Westcott, W.A., 143
Western, W., 141
Westphal, Fred'k Ulr E., 22
Wetchala, Frank, 120
Whelpten, Christena, see Harrison, Mrs. William
White David, 140
White, Edward, 256
White, Florence, 181
White, Henry, 55, 67, 136, 279, 285
White, Hiram Jr., 226
White, Hiram Sr. and Mrs. Magdalena (née Stong), 33, 67, 103, 226
White, Ida, see Ash, Mrs. John
White, Ira, 285
White, Isaac, 59, 67, 103
White, James, 69, 233
White, Martha Ann, see Reaman, Mrs. George
White, Mary, see McDonald, Mrs. Archibald
White, Moses, 59
White, Philip, 54
White, R.E., 255-7
White, Sarah, 226
White, T.R., 143
White, Thomas, 110
White, William, 226
White, Wilmot, 103
White family, 226
Whitehead, Evelyn, 258
Whitehead, John, 101
Whitelaw, Rev. J.M., 140
Whiteman, Henry, 25
Whiteman, Jacob, 28
Whitmore, Aaron, 104
Whitmore, Ella, 104, 138
Whitmore, John, 75
Whitmore, John G., 16, 128, 160
Whitmore, L. Arthur, 104
Whitmore, Lafayette, 104
Whitworth, Ben, 163
Whitworth, Edward, 163
Wice, Ethel, 123
Wice, Russell, 240
Wickets & Pickett, 106
Wideman, Lorne, 171
Wiggins, Joseph, 163
Wilcocks, Col. William, 45
Wilcox, Elizabeth, see McKay, Mrs. Jacob
Wilcox, Nancy, see Farr, Mrs. James
Wiley, Mrs. Norman (Jean), 247
Wilkie, Mr., 190

Wilkie, James, 67, 285
Wilkie, John, 41, 67
Wilkie, Thomas, 285
Wilkinson, Mr., 151
Wilkinson, Brigham, 68
Wilkinson, Dr. J., 126-7
Wilkinson, Rev. H., 151
Wilkinson, John, 285
Wilkinson, Jonathan, 260
Wilkinson, Thomas, 67
Willcocks, Charles, 21
Willcocks, William (J.P.), 21, 22, 23
Willcott, Jonathan, 33
Williams, Mrs. Catharine (née McNabb), 34, 38
Williams, David, 226
Williams, Elias, 34, 38
Williams, Elizabeth, 226
Williams, Ellen, see Wallace, Mrs. George
Williams, Garnet and Mrs. Jean (née Dale), 76, 77, 226, 246, 247, illus. opp. 73
Williams, Mrs. Gordon (Joy), 247
Williams, John and Mrs. Sarah (née Shunk), 159, 224, 226, 285, 288
Williams, Joseph, 35, 39
Williams, Lois, see Livingston, Mrs. Gerald
Williams, Loyremch, 35
Williams, Mary, see Ellerby, Mrs. Jonathan
Williams, Rev. Ralph C., 147
Williams, Richard, 226
Williams, Robert, 226
Williams, Sarah, see Farr, Mrs. William
Williams family, 226-227
Williamson, Norma, see Boddy, Mrs. Jack
Willis, Richard, 115, 161, 250
Willis, Robert, 115
Willison, Rev. Nils, 158
Willoughby, Rev. Wm., 151
Willson, Esther, see Castator, Mrs. Henry
Willson, John, 27
Wilmot, 157
Wilmot, Rev., 142, 149
Wilmot, Col. S., 117
Wilson, Albert, 260
Wilson, Almeda, 181
Wilson, Anthony, 55, 100
Wilson, Rev. F., 151
Wilson, Mrs. Frank, 186
Wilson, George, 121, 174
Wilson, Miss Gertie, 246
Wilson, Rev. J.C., 160

Wilson, Rev. J.E., 147
Wilson, James A., 163
Wilson, John, 181
Wilson, John Sr., 27, 32, 36, 59, 70, 122, 272, 290
Wilson, John R., 253
Wilson, Joseph, 135
Wilson, Jos. J., 121
Wilson, Mrs. Miriam, 172
Wilson, Robert, 250
Wilson, Stilwell, 59, 122
Wilson, Dr. W.J., 119
Wilson family, 70, 107, 121, 158, 199, 290
Winborne, Rowland, 33
Wincup, Benjamin, 136
Windatt, F.M., 76
Winger, Abraham and Mrs. (née Catherine Snider), 103, 104
Winger, Bishop Alvin, 135
Winger, Asa, 103
Winger, Henry, 103, 220
Winger, Jacob, 41
Winger, Jesse, 103
Winger, Peter, 41, 42
Winger, Samuel, 238
Winger family, 101, 134
Winn, Jacob, 24
Winn, Joshua, 24
Winterburne, Rowland, 33
Wintermute, John, 35, 39
Winterton, Fred, 175
Wintjes, John, 110
Wise, Miss Mabel, 245
Wisher, Rev., 142
Wisker, Rev., 149
Wisler family, 137
Wismer, Mr., 176
Wisswasser, Rev., 158
Witherspoon, Albert, 75
Witherspoon, Albert James and Mrs. Edith (née Foster), 128, 227, 250
Witherspoon, Annie, see Farr, Mrs. Herbert
Witherspoon, David and Mrs. Mary Elizabeth (née Blough), 16, 159, 227, 239
Witherspoon, Eliza, see Appleton, Mrs. William
Witherspoon, Elmer and Mrs. Hortense (née Langford), 174, 175, 227
Witherspoon, Enes, see Shaw, Mrs. Charlie
Witherspoon, Florence, see Hoover, Mrs. Garnet
Witherspoon, Frank, 227
Witherspoon, George and Mrs. Eliza (née Shuttleworth), 227

Witherspoon, George Jr., 227
Witherspoon, Jane, 227
Witherspoon, Jessie, see McPherson,
 Mrs. Donald
Witherspoon, Keith, 227
Witherspoon, Nancy, 180
Witherspoon, Peter, 68, 116, 148, 227
Witherspoon, Ross, 227
Witherspoon, Viola, see Livingston,
 Mrs. Roy
Witherspoon, Wilbert, 227
Witherspoon, William (II) and Mrs.
 Annie (née Copeland), 227
Witherspoon families, 227
Withrow, Robert, 163
Withrow, Robt. A., 163
Witty, Bert, 227
Witty, Charles, 227
Witty, John, 227
Witty, Michael, 227
Witty family, 158, 227
Witworth, Mrs. Edward, 247
Women's Institutes, xiv, 105, 243-7
Women's Municipal Jail Farm, 205, 219
Wood, Mrs. Alvin, 246
Wood, Catherine, 175
Wood, Rev. Enoch, 154
Wood, Mrs. Harry, 246
Wood, James, 110, 259
Wood, John, 40, 68, 71, 285
Wood, Mary, 139
Wood, Rev. Scott, 162
Wood, Rev. Shirley Arthur Ralph, 155
Wood, William, 111
Wood, Wm., 160
Wood family, 101
Wood & Etheridge, Messrs., 125
Woodbridge and District Memorial
 Arena, illus. opp. 239
Woodbridge, xiv, 9, 56, 79, 80, 81,
 83, 94, 96, 97, 99, 101, 109, 111,
 116, 124-8, 133, 160, 161, 162,
 166, 185, 192, 201, 203, 206, 207,
 214, 220, 224, 238, 240, 246, 249,
 250, 252, 253, 254, 256, 257, 258,
 260, 262, 291, illus. opp. 82, 83,
 96, 126, 239
Woodbridge Farmer's Company,
 128, 214
Woodbridge, Municipal Council, 97
Woodger, Edward, 182
Woodger, Ruth, 175
Woodruff, Hawkins, 28
Woods, Wm., 112
Wooley, Thomas, 162
Woolley, Lucy, 185
Worrall, Rev. E.W.G., 145

Wragget, George, 135
Wray, Annie, 228
Wray, Elizabeth, see Gardhouse, Mrs.
 Charles
Wray, George and Mrs. Mary (née
 Robinson), 228
Wray, Grace, see Ellerby, Mrs.
 Jonathan
Wray, Harriet, 228
Wray, John and Mrs. Rebecca (née
 Marr), 227
Wray, John Jr. and Mrs. Grace (née
 Harland); and Mrs. Mary (née
 Pumfrey), 228
Wray, John (III), 228
Wray, Lois B., 180
Wray, Martin, 228
Wray, Mary, see Smith, Mrs. William
Wray, Rebecca (II), 228
Wray, Sarah, see McCallum, Mrs. Neil
Wray, Vina, see McCallum, Mrs. Elmer
Wray, William, 228
Wray, William (II) and Mrs. Thelma
 (née Cowan), 228
Wray family, 227-228
Wright, Abraham, 228, 280, 285
Wright, Amos, 205, 228
Wright, Amos (II),228
Wright, Archibald, 223, 228, 285
Wright, Ashford and Mrs. Margaret
 (née McCague), 228
Wright, Bert and Mrs., 186, 250
Wright, David, 162
Wright, Rev. David, 146, 151
Wright, George, 55
Wright, Mrs. Jane, 123
Wright, John, 69
Wright, Joseph, 68, 285, 290
Wright, Miss Laurine, 180
Wright, Dr. Laverne, 228
Wright, Madison, 158
Wright, Margery, see Page, Mrs.
 Stewart L.
Wright, Mildred, see Hill, Mrs. A.S.
 Hardy
Wright, Osmond, 205, 228
Wright, Rev. S.C., 160
Wright, William, 55, 228
Wright, Wm., 151
Wright & Taylor, 228
Wright Bros., 119
Wright families, 119, 226, 289
Wright families, 119, 226
Wrixon, Rev. W.F., 145, 153, 239
Wuerster, Christian, 109, 110
Wyer, Mrs. Helen, 163
Wyllie, George, 81

Y

Yerex, Mrs. G., 246
Yoder, Barbara, see Troyer, Mrs.
    Christian
Yoke Rail fence, illus. opp. 63
Yonge, Sir George, 20, 119
York County Board of Education, 167,
    178
York Central Hospital, 245, 247
York Public Market, 61
"York Region," 271, 272

Yorkville Brick Yards, 200
Youmans, Rev., 151
Young, Arthur, 248
Young, James, 155
Young, Miss Jessie, 180
Young, Joseph, 32
Young, W.H., 128
Younge, Miss, 169

Z

Zeilinskie, J., 260
Zuefelt, Mrs. L., 246